THE PRICE OF GERMAN UNITY

The Price of German Unity

Reunification and the Crisis of the Welfare State

GERHARD A. RITTER

Translated by
RICHARD DEVESON

UNIVERSITY PRESS

OXFORD
UNIVERSITY PRESS

Great Clarendon Street, Oxford OX2 6DP

Oxford University Press is a department of the University of Oxford. It furthers the University's objective of excellence in research, scholarship, and education by publishing worldwide in

Oxford New York

Auckland Cape Town Dar es Salaam Hong Kong Karachi Kuala Lumpur Madrid Melbourne Mexico City Nairobi New Delhi Shanghai Taipei Toronto

With offices in

Argentina Austria Brazil Chile Czech Republic France Greece Guatemala Hungary Italy Japan Poland Portugal Singapore South Korea Switzerland Thailand Turkey Ukraine Vietnam

Oxford is a registered trade mark of Oxford University Press in the UK and in certain other countries

Published in the United States by Oxford University Press Inc., New York

Originally published as *Der Preis der deutschen Einheit: Die Wiedervereinigung und die Krise des Sozialstaats*, by Gerhard A. Ritter

First published 2011

British Library Cataloguing in Publication Data
Data available

Library of Congress Cataloging in Publication Data
Library of Congress Control Number: 2011923746

Typeset by SPI Publisher Services, Pondicherry, India
Printed in Great Britain
on acid-free paper by
MPG Books Group, Bodmin and King's Lynn

ISBN 978–0–19–955682–3

1 3 5 7 9 10 8 6 4 2

Contents

Preface to the English Edition

The events of the years 1989 to 1991—the collapse of the Eastern bloc, the break-up of the Soviet Union, the end of the Cold War, the unification of Germany, and the termination of the division of Europe—constitute one of the great turning-points in European and world history, comparable to the French Revolution of 1789 or the demise of the old Europe at the outbreak of the First World War in 1914. These years also saw a profound change in the history of the German welfare state. A crisis in the welfare state had been brewing for a considerable time. Its underlying causes included the ageing of the German population, an explosion in the costs of healthcare, changes in the world of work resulting from structural changes in the economy, the intensification of competition caused by globalization in export and financial markets, and Germany's struggle to retain its position as a manufacturing centre in the face of competition from low-wage countries. The crisis, in other words, existed before German unification took place. Unification, however, made it significantly more acute.

German unification is the central theme of this book. Although I also deal with the framework of international relations, economic conditions, and the legal system within which unification took place, the book's main focus is the internal process of unification, in particular with regard to social policy, which I discuss in the light of previously unpublished sources. This process involved the extension to the German Democratic Republic—the new *Bundesländer* of the Federal Republic in the east—of the norms, institutions, and actors of the welfare state of the Federal Republic. The book analyses the controversies and problems that arose, and the close connection that existed between the process of unification and the struggle for political power. I argue that in view of the tremendous dynamism of the unification process, and the array of political forces involved, there was essentially no practicable alternative to the transfer of the west German model of social policy to the east. I also show, however, that serious and avoidable mistakes were made, in particular in the financing of unification and in pay policy.

I also wish to emphasize that despite the high financial, economic, and social costs that were entailed by the transformation of east Germany from a dictatorship into a democracy, and from a centrally planned economy into a Social Market economy, the price that the Germans paid for unity and for the freedom of east Germany was not too high, and that the unification of Germany was one of the great moments in German history. Such moments, alas, have been all too infrequent.

This study would not have been possible without the support of many institutions and individuals. It was written in conjunction with work on volume xi of the *Geschichte der Sozialpolitik in Deutschland seit 1945*, entitled *1989–1994. Bundesrepublik Deutschland: Sozialpolitik im Zeichen der Vereinigung* (edited by the present author). I wish to thank the authors of that volume and also, in particular, the members of the scholarly advisory committee for the whole project—Hans Günter

Hockerts, Franz-Xaver Kaufmann, Peter Rosenberg, Hartmut Weber, and Hans F. Zacher—for many useful suggestions. The Bundesministerium für Arbeit und Sozialordnung not only granted access to its own files but also helped me in obtaining permission to use the files of other ministries and of the Bundeskanzleramt. The Bundesarchiv assisted me in exploring their files. The Konrad-Adenauer-Stiftung and the Friedrich-Ebert-Stiftung gave me unrestricted access to the sources in their archives. I am grateful to the politicians, civil servants and experts who granted me interviews. Martin Ammermüller and Werner Tegtmeier helped me by providing documents in their possession. I wish to thank Christiane Reuter-Boysen for her assistance in procuring the source material on which this study is based, and Nils Güttler and Adréana Peitsch for their paperwork and their help in preparing the annotated list of the most important actors in the process of German unification.

I am grateful to the Stiftung Volkswagenwerk for funding the translation of the book and to Oxford University Press for publishing it. My thanks, too, to Richard Deveson for his authoritative translation.

The first German edition of this book was given a very generous reception by reviewers and readers, and after just a year a second edition proved necessary, at which time I took the opportunity to make various minor changes. Some further amendments, taking note of more recent research, have been made for the present English edition.

Gerhard A. Ritter

Berlin,
June 2010

Translator's Note

Several of the German terms that are central to the discussion of social policy and the welfare state are not straightforwardly translatable into British English. The problem is exemplified by the term *Sozialstaat* itself, which cannot be translated as 'social state' and must be translated as 'welfare state', even though German also has the term *Wohlfahrtsstaat*, which is linguistically closer to 'welfare state'. In German, however, *Wohlfahrtsstaat* has connotations of benefits bestowed, of maintenance and relief, whereas *Sozialstaat* implies a constitutionally grounded principle of social solidarity and mutuality. Unfortunately there is no simple way of expressing these, or other similar, philosophical nuances in English.

Problems of translation also arise because the concrete institutions of the welfare state systems of Germany and Britain differ in a number of important respects, so that terms that are linguistically similar do not necessarily describe, say, identical social benefits or forms of organization. Moreover, terminology in Britain itself has regularly changed over the years, as social policy has evolved. The term *Sozialhilfe* illustrates this double difficulty. The British term perhaps closest to it is 'National Assistance', introduced in 1948 (when the Poor Law was abolished), but National Assistance was replaced in 1966 by Supplementary Benefit, which in turn was replaced in 1988 by Income Support. I have used the term 'income support' for *Sozialhilfe* on the grounds that it is the current British term for the roughly analogous German institution. This obscures the fact, however, that the German institution differs significantly from the British one.

One way of dealing with these problems would have been to retain a considerable quantity of German terminology in the main text. I felt, however, that this would have been off-putting to many non-specialist readers. Instead I have for the most part used English terms (though I have also supplied German terms where this has seemed helpful), but have included lists and translations of the most commonly used terms, both German and English, in the glossary of terms and abbreviations at the end. On the other hand, in the notes I have used a greater amount of German terminology, for the benefit of scholars.

Similar quandaries arise over the use of terms describing government ministries and their different departments and sub-departments, and over the terms for the posts of officials within the ministerial structure. In the main text I have used translations for the names of ministerial departments, but kept the German terms for the names of posts. The glossary includes a brief explanation of the relevant terms, together with the translations I have used.

In the notes the subject rubrics of government memoranda and similar documents are given in German, again for the benefit of scholars. Details of senders and recipients, however, are given in English, unless such details themselves form part of a rubric.

I am enormously grateful to Gerhard A. Ritter, who has given me a great amount of help and advice during the preparation of the translation and has answered a very large number of queries. I also want to thank my old friend Paul Davies of Jesus College, Oxford, who has advised me on the translation of many of the legal terms. My warmest thanks, too, to Matthew Cotton of Oxford University Press, for his patience and support.

R.D.

Introduction

On 9 November 1989, after years of debate and controversy, the German Bundestag passed a major reform of the pensions system, which came into force on 1 January 1992. The reform was supported by the parties of the governing coalition—the Christian Democratic Union (CDU) and its sister party in Bavaria, the Christian Social Union (CSU), together with the Free Democratic Party (FDP)—as well as by the main opposition party, the Social Democratic Party of Germany (SPD). Only the Greens voted against it. The law also had the backing of the social partners (trade unions and employers) and of the leading bodies concerned with social policy. There was a general belief, or wish to believe, that this legislation, probably the most important piece of work of the 1987–90 parliamentary term, ensured that pensions would keep pace with demographic developments over the next twenty years. Only an hour later, the astonishing news reached the Bundestag that the border between the German Democratic Republic (GDR) and the Federal Republic had been opened. The sitting was suspended for a short time, and the chief of the Federal Chancellery, Rudolf Seiters, then announced on behalf of the government that the 'wall and the border are becoming more permeable' and expressed the hope that 'this decision by the GDR leadership constitutes a step towards genuine liberalization in the GDR'.[1] At the same time he reiterated an offer that had been made on the previous day in a government statement by the Federal Chancellor, Helmut Kohl, which read: 'To the new GDR leadership I declare my readiness to support a path of change, if the leadership is ready to institute reforms. Cosmetic adjustments are not enough [. . .]. We do not wish to stabilize a state of affairs that has become unsustainable. We are, however, ready to provide wide-ranging help if there is a binding commitment to the fundamental reform of political and economic conditions in the GDR. The SED [Socialist Unity Party of Germany] must give up its monopoly of power, allow independent parties, and make a binding promise of free elections. If these conditions are met, I for my part am ready to talk about providing economic assistance on an entirely new scale.'[2] The spokesmen of other parties also made short statements, and the members of parliament then rose and sang the national anthem.

Two sets of processes were to shape the politics of the period between November 1989 and the autumn of 1990. The first was the collapse of SED rule in the GDR, triggered by the reforms of Mikhail Gorbachev in the Soviet Union and their impact on the Soviet satellite states in eastern Europe, by the mass exodus of GDR citizens via Hungary, Czechoslovakia, and Poland, and by the mass demonstrations on the streets of the GDR. The second was the progression towards German unity. At the outset all those involved underestimated the speed of these processes, and overestimated their ability to manage them. Thus, the Federal Chancellor's 'Ten Point Programme to end the division of Germany and of Europe' of 28 November 1989,[3] which was seen as extraordinarily ambitious when it was published, contained no timetable; Kohl assumed that roughly a decade would be needed before state unification could be achieved. Similarly, even when the State Treaty creating monetary, economic, and social union between the Federal Republic and the GDR was signed on 18 May 1990, there was still an expectation that a year or a year and half would be needed before political union would follow.[4] However, the pressure caused by the great wave of emigration from the GDR to the Federal Republic, the increasingly obvious desire of the citizens of the GDR to adopt the Deutschmark and achieve political union with the Federal Republic, the decline of the economy and the internal disintegration of the GDR, and the struggle among the parties for power within the GDR and then in the reunited Germany in the elections of 1990—in particular in the elections to the Volkskammer (the GDR parliament) of 18 March and the elections to the Bundestag of 2 December—all accelerated the process. There was no 'script' for unification; no 'diary'.[5] Neither the Federal government nor individual government ministries had plans for unification tucked away in a top drawer.[6] Unification was improvised;[7] it was done through crisis management. And owing to the pressures of time, the constant changes of circumstances, and the sheer complexity of the problems involved, it was a process in which the executive arm of government took precedence over the legislature.

The difficulties posed by transforming the GDR economy from a planned to a market system and creating a convergence of living standards between east and west were completely underestimated, as was the length of time it would take to achieve these goals. To a large extent this was because the currency reform of 1948, and the great economic upturn that had followed it, were taken, falsely, as a guiding model. 'A second economic miracle can be achieved on German soil,' it was claimed in the Social Report of the Federal Ministry of Labour published in June 1990.[8] Admittedly, according to an analysis produced by the Federal Ministry of Economics on 7 August 1990, the far-reaching 'process of changeover in all areas of the economy' would not occur 'without some painful temporary frictions' and would not be 'achieved overnight'. There was, however, no cause for panic, the Ministry added. Similar short-term effects had occurred after the currency reform in 1948 and had been quickly overcome, thanks to the Social Market economy and an economic climate favourable to investment.[9]

Both the productivity and the productive assets of the GDR economy were completely overestimated. For example, the State Treaty of 18 May 1990 envisaged that the GDR, after 'priority' had been given to the use of nationally owned assets for the 'structural adjustment of the economy and the reform of the state budget', would, if possible, ensure that savers would be 'granted an attested share of nationally owned assets in exchange for the 2:1 reduction [in the value of their savings] at the changeover' from the east German to the west German currency.[10] In October 1990 it was still expected that the privatization of state-owned enterprises in the east by the *Treuhandanstalt* would generate net proceeds of about 600 thousand million DM.[11] In fact, the *Treuhand*'s balance sheet eventually showed a deficit of 230 thousand million DM,[12] which had to be borne by the taxpayer.

Unification in 1990 created a profound caesura not only in Germany's political history but also in economic and social policy. The colossal transfer payments that were made from west to east gave rise to enormous changes in the economic policy framework. The period between 1982 and 1990 had seen a financial consolidation of the welfare state in the Federal Republic and a slowdown in the rise in public debt.[13] The proportions of gross national product allotted to public expenditure and to expenditure on social policy had both fallen significantly, and annual public budget deficits had been reduced. Job numbers had risen and, after 1986, unemployment—though it remained high—began slowly to fall.[14] Politicians had aimed for 'less state' and 'more market': for greater responsibility on the part of the individual citizen and greater competitiveness in the economy. With unification, these parameters changed. The shares of gross national product devoted to public spending and to spending on social policy rose sharply. Between 1989 and 1995 public debt doubled. In the GDR nearly four million jobs were lost, particularly in industry and agriculture,[15] and in the old *Bundesländer*, too, after an initial boom triggered by a rapid rise in demand for 'western goods', job numbers decreased from 1993 onwards and the level of unemployment increased.

Social policy played a crucial role in the process of unification. Business circles took the view, which was echoed by the Bundesbank, the Finance Ministry, and the Economics Ministry, that a full-fledged extension to east Germany of Federal Republic employment law and the generous benefits of the west German system of social security would frighten off private investors and seriously hinder the necessary reshaping of the east German economy. This assessment, however, failed to prevail against the combined forces of the Labour Ministry (eventually backed by the Federal Chancellor), the Social Democratic opposition, the trade unions, and all the political groupings of the GDR.

The areas of social policy affected by unification were, above all, labour market policy and the social security system. It was hoped that a greatly expanded role for an active labour market policy—which at times involved upwards of two million employees in east Gemany[16]—would help mitigate the effects of economic upheaval and prevent a 'breach in the dyke', a 'catastrophe in employment',[17] that in turn might lead to widespread social breakdown in the new *Bundesländer*.[18] Similarly, it was believed that transferring the relatively generous western system of social security to the east would prevent the population from becoming impoverished and encourage it to accept the new order.

One of the consequences of the massive intervention by the state, with the social security system being used to stave off the effects of economic upheaval, was that the trends that had been gathering pace in the west towards a reduction in the size of the state and a strengthening of subsidiarity and provision by the individual were put into reverse. The state now assumed ultimate responsibility for the living standards of people in the east. This change chimed with attitudes among both politicians and the population in the east, where, through socialization, people had in large measure become used to placing their hopes and expectations on the state. For those who were involved in the planning and implementation of social policy, unification was a stirring experience, as interviews with them make clear. It was a great challenge, which they believed they had met with flying colours, despite the huge workload they had had to bear. They felt, too, that the fact that the transfer to the east of the institutions and standards of the west German welfare state on the whole went well in technical administrative terms[19] served to confirm the efficiency of the existing system. This very fact, though, made it much harder to generate a debate about alternatives, concerning, for example, the dominant role of social insurance within the social security system, the principles governing the financing of social insurance, and the goal of protecting living standards. Likewise, the problems that resulted from the imposition of a heavy and one-sided burden on the people who underpinned the social insurance system (i.e. the insured and employers), instead of on taxpayers, in order to finance the high levels of social payments that were made to the new *Bundesländer* were brushed aside by the government, despite opposition criticism.

Unification damaged the German economy, first and foremost because it gave rise to high levels of public debt and significant increases in labour costs, particularly additional wage costs. The economy had at the same time been coming under growing competitive pressures as a result of the Europeanization of the labour market, the 'globalization' of financial markets, and the growing shift of production to countries with low taxes, wages, and welfare benefits and lighter environmental restrictions. The collapse of the Communist system on Germany's doorstep and the conversion of the countries of eastern Europe, with their low labour costs, into market economies gave further impetus to these trends. Because politicians, officials, and, to a degree, trade union and employers' leaders were almost wholly absorbed by the process of unification, and because of the distraction caused by the unification-led boom of 1990–1, almost three years passed before policy adjusted to the new conditions in the world economy, and when adjustment came, the effects were all the more severe. The same was true of social policy. The necessary restructuring of the German welfare state that had been getting under way was now put on hold, despite the fact that the crisis in labour relations and social security caused by changes in the traditional world of work, mass unemployment, and the ageing of the population was becoming ever more apparent.

The period covered by this book, from late 1989 to the Bundestag elections of 16 October 1994, may be divided into three phases. It goes without saying that the problems posed by unification remained paramount throughout.

The first phase, from the fall of the Berlin Wall on 9 November 1989 to the Bundestag elections of 2 December 1990, was dominated by the dynamics of unification and the political arguments and elections that ensued. A further key feature of this phase was the laying of the legal foundations of German unity. This took place through the State Treaty of 18 May 1990, creating a monetary, economic, and social union; through legislation by the GDR, which, with some differences of emphasis, put the provisions of the Treaty into effect; and through the Unification Treaty of 31 August 1990. Each of these three developments will be discussed in some detail in what follows.

A second phase, from the Bundestag elections of 1990 and the formation of a new government in January 1991 to the autumn of 1992, was largely taken up with the extension of the west German welfare state to the new *Bundesländer*. The crucial features here were the passage of the Pensions Transition Law; the continuation of the build-up of the administrative system for employment (job centres and *Land* employment offices, administering unemployment insurance and employment policy), of state and local government administrative systems for social security and income support, and of the organizations running social insurance, income support and social provision for war victims; and the creation of new jurisdictions in employment law (*Arbeitsrecht*) and social law (*Sozialrecht*) in the east. These changes went hand in hand with the emergence of new socio-political actors in the east, including free trade unions, employers' associations, welfare organizations, and associations representing the interests of the recipients of social benefits—a process that had begun earlier in 1990, largely at the initiative of west German bodies, which continued to dominate it. Despite some strong disagreements on particular issues, the sphere of social policy was largely characterized by cooperation and consensus among the major political forces during the process of unification. This was partly because the government was forced to seek compromises after losing its majority in the Bundesrat (the Federal Council, representing the interests of the German *Länder*) in the first months of 1991.

There was a caesura in the autumn of 1992, signalled by the start of a gradual shift in the orientation of social policy that ushered in a third phase. The costs of unification remained high, public debt was rising rapidly, and unemployment was clearly on the increase—this even before the onset of the sharp recession of 1993. Consolidating public finances and reducing the burdens imposed on the economy by taxes and social security contributions became the central goals of government policy and also an important topic in what was turning into an increasingly heated debate about the future of the German economy. Nevertheless, there were also developments in the opposite direction: benefits for families were increased, various social services were extended, and, in particular, social care insurance was introduced as a fifth pillar of the social insurance system (in addition to the existing insurance provision for old age and disability, illness, accident, and unemployment).[20] Even though changes to the social security network and moves to weaken legal protections for employees exacerbated the differences between the governing coalition and the Social Democratic opposition, several compromises were reached, albeit after lengthy arguments: for example, over the structural reform of the health service at the end of 1992, over the adjustments made to the financing of unification in the Federal Consolidation Programme of March 1993, and, especially, over the introduction of social care insurance in 1994.

The present book is based to a very considerable extent on an assessment of archival sources. I have examined files from the Federal Chancellery, the Finance Ministry, and the government ministries concerned with social policy—in particular, the Federal Ministry of Labour and Social Order; for the period 1989–90 I have also made extensive use of documents of the government of the German Democratic Republic and of the east German ministries responsible for social policy. Files from the Federal Insurance Office and from the Social Insurance Transitional Authority in the east have also been consulted, as have the records of the Federal Insurance

Office for White-Collar Workers. From the Archiv für Christlich-Demokratische Politik I have been able to use the extensive papers of Norbert Blüm and the records of the CDU/CSU parliamentary party, of the executive of the parliamentary party, and of individual working groups of the CDU/CSU in parliament. For my account of the views of the Social Democratic opposition and the trade unions—in particular, the German Trade Union Federation—archival sources in the Archiv der Sozialen Demokratie have been indispensable. Naturally, I have also examined the full range of published sources: records of parliamentary debates and printed parliamentary papers, publications of parties and other organizations, and the scholarly literature.[21] Finally, I have been able to gain a direct insight into the problems that reunification posed for social policy, and the way these were viewed by the people involved, through intensive conversations lasting between two and four hours with fourteen leading politicians and experts in the field from the governments of Helmut Kohl and of the first (and last) freely elected government of the GDR, headed by Lothar de Maizière, from the political parties, and from the senior levels of ministerial bureaucracy.

PART I

GERMAN UNITY

The Framework

1

The Political Framework

1.1 THE DYNAMICS OF THE UNIFICATION PROCESS, AND THE SECURING OF UNITY ON THE INTERNATIONAL FRONT

1.1.1 The Federal Republic and the crisis in the GDR up to the end of the Modrow government

In the elections to the Bundestag of 25 January 1987 the coalition made up of the CDU, the CSU, and the FDP had retained its clear parliamentary majority over the opposition SPD and Greens, winning 269 out of the 497 seats.[1] In the Bundesrat, too, the *Land* governments led by the CDU and CSU had a majority at the end of 1989, though this was a narrower one of 23 out of 41 votes (without the votes of Berlin). Nevertheless, in the spheres of economic and social policy the coalition had become steadily less able to exploit the political position it enjoyed through its control of the legislature. There were growing differences between the liberal business and middle-class wing of the CDU, which was supported by the FDP, and the Christian Social employees' wing of the party, imbued with Catholic social doctrine, which was led by the Federal Minister of Labour Norbert Blüm, who also occupied a powerful position in the CDU as chairman of the party's largest *Land* association, that of North Rhine-Westphalia. The coalition seemed exhausted. After its successes in consolidating the financial situation and introducing laws to reform the health system and pensions, passed in 1988 and 1989 respectively, it appeared to have run out of areas of common ground. True, Helmut Kohl's standing as Federal Chancellor had been strengthened after the failure of the rebellion against his position as party leader in the run-up to the CDU party conference at Bremen in September 1989.[2] It was questionable, however, whether Kohl was the right candidate to lead the CDU to a further electoral victory. By contrast, the SPD, with its new programme 'Progress 90' and its candidate for the chancellorship, the Prime Minister of the Saarland Oskar Lafontaine, had been establishing itself as a modernized force in the eyes of many members of the public. Moreover, its vision of a future 'ecological reorganization of industrial society'[3] seemed to offer a basis for common cause with the Greens. Everything, then, pointed to an opposition victory at the Bundestag elections that were due at the end of 1990, and a consequent change of government. It was at this moment that the exodus of GDR citizens through Hungary, Czechoslovakia, and Poland, the crisis in the GDR, and, above all, the fall of the Berlin Wall on 9 November 1989 transformed the entire political situation.

The dynamics of the process of unification drove Germany's domestic politics into the shadows: the question of Germany's future and its relations with the rest of the world now took centre stage. Chancellor Kohl and the Foreign Minister and Vice-Chancellor, Hans-Dietrich Genscher of the FDP, were propelled to the political forefront. It was the hour of the executive, as the branch of government best able to respond quickly to constantly changing circumstances and to lead the negotiations with the victorious powers of 1945 and with the GDR. The executive's initiatives over unification also enabled it to force the opposition on to the defensive.

While the government, despite various differences over timing and emphasis in unification policy, found itself possessed of a great joint political project, the opposition was highly disconcerted and deeply split. The Greens, who wanted to see the GDR develop into an internally reformed, socialist grass-roots democracy, had pinned all their hopes on the citizens' opposition movement of the earliest days. When the latter were defeated in the Volkskammer elections of 18 March 1990, the Greens lost their partners in the east and were left behind as the move to unification gathered pace.[4]

The Social Democrats, now deprived of their carefully planned electoral strategy, were unable to come up with a clear and agreed position on the future of Germany. The former Chancellor Willy Brandt, probably a majority of the party in the Federal Republic, and the Social Democrats in the GDR all favoured unification. The party's candidate for the chancellorship Lafontaine, however—who regarded the idea of the nation state as outdated—persisted in favouring a policy that was effectively a call for the retention of two Germanys, or at any rate for an application of the brakes to the unification process. He argued that administrative measures should be deployed to stem the flow of people from the GDR into the Federal Republic, warned—not without justification—that unification would have serious financial consequences in west Germany, and insisted that European unification should take priority over German unity.[5] By contrast, Brandt, the party's honorary chairman, declared that he did not want 'the Germans to be left waiting in a siding until such time as a pan-European train reaches the station'.[6] Thus, while the governing coalition was able to present itself as pursuing a policy that was in tune with the tide of history, the opposition, through its disunity and the 'petty' reservations of its shadow chancellor, was perceived as unequipped to shape the process of German unification.

Not only was the political situation transformed, but the cast of political actors had expanded too. Every policy position and initiative on the future of Germany that was proposed within the Federal Republic now had to take close account of developments within the GDR and the political forces in play there. After the failure of the attempt by Egon Krenz, Erich Honecker's successor as general secretary of the SED, to carry out reforms on socialist lines—including a shift to a more market-orientated planned economy, but with the SED continuing to have the sole right to political leadership—the Volkskammer elected the former district secretary of the SED in Dresden, Hans Modrow, as Prime Minister of the GDR on 13 November 1989. Modrow was seen as the most important figure within the reforming wing of the party. Seventeen of the 28 members of his government belonged to the SED, while other ministerial posts were taken by members of the 'bloc parties': four from the Liberal Democratic Party of Germany (LDPD), three from the East German CDU, and two each from the Democratic Farmers' Party of Germany (DBD) and the National Democratic Party of Germany (NDPD). At this stage the government included no representatives of the newly founded parties or of the oppositional citizens' movement groups.

In his inaugural statement of government policy in the Volkskammer on 17 November 1989[7] Modrow announced that an electoral law would be introduced (though he did not specify an election date) and declared his support for constitutional government and economic reform. Socialism, as the foundation of the political and economic order of the state, would be humanized and democratized, though in fact it was not called into question in the discussion that followed, either by him or by the spokesmen of the bloc parties. On the question of the future of Germany, Modrow proposed that relations between the Federal Republic and the GDR should be deepened by the creation of a 'contractual community' (*Vertragsgemeinschaft*), but he said nothing about possible long-term unification. Two weeks later conditions were established for free elections in the GDR, when the Volkskammer removed from the GDR constitution the claim to leadership by the party of Marxism-Leninism (i.e. the SED),[8] although the GDR continued to be described as a 'socialist state of workers and peasants' and as the 'political organization of the working people in town and country'.

At the start of December the 'Central Round Table' was formed,[9] as an organization competing with the Modrow government and the Volkskammer. The Round Table (following the example of the Round Table in Poland) was the product of an initiative by seven political groups and parties—Democratic Awakening (DA), Democracy Now (DJ), the Green Party, the Peace and Human Rights Initiative, New Forum (NF), United Left, and the Social Democratic Party (SDP)—that had come together in resistance to SED rule and that had as their goal a rapid and peaceful transition to democracy in the GDR. The Round Table, which had also been formed with the support of the churches, was composed of equal numbers of representatives of the new parties and groups and of the old bloc parties. The Central Round Table—there were also Round Tables at regional and local levels—played a significant part in the peaceful breaking of the SED's monopoly of power. It saw its role as keeping a check on developments on behalf of the public and exerted a powerful influence over the citizens of the GDR through the media. At its very first meeting, on 7 December 1989, it called for free elections to the Volkskammer to be held on 6 May 1990.

A crucial power struggle arose as a result of the attempt by the Modrow government to preserve the State Security Service (Staatssicherheitsdienst, or 'Stasi'), at least in part, under the new title of 'Office for the Defence of the Constitution' (Verfassungsschutz).[10] This plan foundered in the face of mass pressure, culminating in the spectacular storming of some of the buildings of the

Ministry of State Security in Berlin on 15 January 1990—pressure that had been initiated and supported by the opposition groups on the Round Table. After tough negotiations, a 'government of national responsibility' was formed on 29 January 1990. Modrow succeeded in binding the opposition forces into the governing process, persuading them to commit ministers without portfolio to serve as their representatives in the all-party administration. This enabled Modrow to stabilize the political situation until the Volkskammer elections, which had been brought forward to 18 March 1990. The Central Round Table was an institution of transition to parliamentary democracy. It gradually transformed itself from a mere vetoing body into a steering instrument and a source of legislation competing with the Volkskammer. It suffered from the weakness, however, that it lacked electoral legitimacy and was not underpinned by governmental machinery and personnel. Above all, it failed to articulate a clear conception of the new political, social, and economic order it wished to achieve. In the eyes of the government of the Federal Republic, the Round Table was not acceptable as a partner because the majority of its members were unwilling to agree to the abolition of an independent, reformed GDR or commit themselves unambiguously to a market economy on the western model.[11]

Differences over political goals also caused the Modrow government eventually to fail in its stubborn attempts to persuade the Federal Republic to provide massive economic support for the stabilization of the GDR. Shortly before the fall of the Wall, on 7 November 1989, Kohl, in an address to the CDU/CSU parliamentary party, had come out against advance payments or premature pledges, in view of the dramatic acceleration in the pace of events in the GDR. The critical requirements, he argued, were the ending of party rule by the SED, free elections, and irreversible reforms. The GDR, he said, should follow the model of Hungary and Poland, not of the Soviet Union.[12] After the formation of the Modrow government Kohl emphasized, in a government statement of 16 November 1989, that although immediate help—for example, in the form of an encouragement of travel between the GDR and the Federal Republic—would be possible without reciprocal action by the GDR, extensive economic assistance would be dependent on thoroughgoing reforms of the GDR state and economy.[13] Three weeks later the CSU Finance Minister Theo Waigel stated, in a discussion paper circulated to members of the CDU/CSU parliamentary party,[14] that it was a precondition of the Federal government's offering of support and cooperation that a 'binding decision' should be made in favour of a 'fundamental change in the political and economic systems of the GDR' and that such a change should be 'set irreversibly in motion'. The linking of the offer of assistance from the Federal Republic to the introduction of fundamental reforms met with opposition both from the SPD and—under the influence of the Foreign Minister, Genscher—from the FDP, which demanded economic assistance for the GDR without preconditions.[15] Nevertheless, it remained a key element in the policy of Kohl and the Federal government.

As they differed in their views on the scope and objectives of reforms in the GDR, so Modrow and the Federal Chancellor were in disagreement over their basic conceptions of the future of Germany. Although Kohl, in his famous Ten Point

Programme of 28 November 1989[16]—which he had cleared neither with Genscher nor with the victorious powers—picked up Modrow's idea of a 'contractual community', he regarded it as merely the first step in a process, albeit one without a clear timetable, that would eventually lead, via 'confederative structures', to a federal settlement: in other words, to German unity. Kohl's aim was not only to put German unity onto the international political agenda but also to seize the initiative on the question of Germany's future before the Bundestag elections that were due at the end of 1990. He warned the CDU/CSU parliamentary party on 27 November 1989 that the SPD, at its party conference in Berlin on 18–20 December 1989, would invoke the memory of Kurt Schumacher and its erstwhile strength in the old strongholds of Saxony and Thuringia, in an attempt to 'take over' the German question. This would be the main issue at the Bundestag elections, he said, and the elections in the GDR would have a huge bearing on them. A 'tectonic political shift' was going to affect 'quite new strata' of the German people, and the key factor influencing the chances of the CDU/CSU would be the party's ability to assume the leading role on the question of Germany's future.[17]

At the same time, Kohl wanted to hold out prospects to people in the GDR. His Ten Points badly wrong-footed the Social Democrats. Although the SPD's spokesman on foreign policy, Karsten Voigt, after consulting the chairman of the national and parliamentary parties, Hans-Jochen Vogel, at first voiced agreement with the Chancellor's Ten Points 'on all counts', strong opposition to this approach was soon raised both within the parliamentary party and in the party at large. There was criticism, in particular, that the inviolability of Poland's western border had not been included in Kohl's list. Accordingly, in the vote in the Bundestag on 1 December 1989 only the governing coalition parties supported the programme, while the Social Democrats abstained and the Greens voted against.[18] The Social Democrats' uncertainty about how to proceed left them unable to project a clear image on the question of Germany's future—a crucial source of weakness in the following year.

On the international front, the Allies were firmly committed to German unity, provided that a reunited Germany would have a liberal and democratic constitution like that of the Federal Republic and would be integrated into the European Community in accordance with the 'Bonn/Paris Conventions' (known in Germany as the Deutschlandvertrag) that came into force in October 1954 and were regularly reaffirmed during the ensuing decades.[19] Nevertheless, Kohl's diplomatic offensive initially provoked criticism both in the West and in the Soviet Union. The French President François Mitterrand, with whom Genscher had (according to his memoirs) the 'most important' of his many discussions on 30 November 1989, advised caution regarding the position of the Soviet Union, at the same time demanding that the drive to German unity—which he saw as an historical inevitability—go hand in hand with a move towards further European integration.[20] Mitterrand's public utterances and his conversations with west German politicians were restrained, as he was anxious not to endanger France's close partnership with Germany, particularly within the European Community. We know, however, from notes made by his special adviser Jacques Attali and also from British sources,[21] that he was highly dubious about German unification and at first tried to put a brake on the unification process. His fear was that the equilibrium of Europe would be upset and that there would be a return to the sorts of international tensions that had accumulated in 1913. A reunited Germany, he believed, would stop supporting the further integration of the European Community and would shift its gaze eastwards; and if Germany were to neutralize, then NATO would be weakened. He was also worried that Mikhail Gorbachev's position would be jeopardized were unification to proceed too rapidly. If Gorbachev were ousted, he might be replaced by a military dictatorship that would call a halt to the process of *perestroika*, the programme of reform of the state, economy, and Communist Party in the Soviet Union.[22] In concrete terms, Mitterrand wanted Germany to be even more tightly bound into the European Community through the establishment of a European economic and monetary union. He also wanted German unification to be synchronized with the creation of a Europe-wide security system spanning east and west—a scheme likewise favoured by Gorbachev—and he laid special emphasis on the inviolability of Poland's western frontier.

In a conversation with Gorbachev in Kiev on 6 December 1989[23] Mitterrand criticized the speed with which the German question was unfolding and affirmed the responsibility of the four main victorious powers—the USA, Britain, the Soviet Union, and France—for the protection of Europe. Kohl's Ten Points, he said, had undermined the logical sequence of events; European integration, evolution in eastern Europe, and the creation of a Europe-wide peace framework should take priority over German unification. Mitterrand was clearly disappointed by the Soviet Union's refusal to intervene in the internal affairs of the GDR and pursue a positive policy to head off German unification. Gorbachev also declined Mitterrand's invitation to accompany him on his visit to the GDR. Mitterrand's trip to the GDR of 20–2 December 1989—the first visit to the GDR by a western head of state—was a vain attempt the stabilize the GDR.[24]

In a conversation with the British Prime Minister Margaret Thatcher in Strasbourg on 8 December 1989, on the fringe of a European Community summit, Mitterrand and Thatcher agreed that something had to be done to halt the process towards reunification. Mitterrand conceded that it would be difficult to 'withstand the drive of the people. In history Germany had never found its true frontiers: they were a people in constant movement and flux.' This judgement was confirmed by Mrs Thatcher, who produced from her handbag a map 'showing various configurations of Germany'. Mitterrand thought that they did not have many cards with which to stop the German people. He believed that the Russians would not do very much and that the United States were not to be counted upon. 'All that was left was Britain and France. He was fearful that he and the Prime Minister would find themselves in the situation of their predecessors in the 1930s who had failed to react in the face of constant pressing forward by the Germans.' They agreed on a meeting of the four Allied Powers to reassure Gorbachev and to stop or slow down the process of reunification. In Mitterrand's view, 'it might be a case of Britain, France, the Soviet Union and Italy coming together to contain Germany . . . German reunification depended on many elements, most of them beyond our control. It might happen. It would happen. But if it did so simply as a result of Germa which took no notice of the Allies it would be disastrous.' He 'felt we were threshold of momentous events. We might find ourselves in a position wh had to say no to the Germans. At moments of great danger in the past France had always established special relations with Britain. He felt that such a time had come again. We must draw together and stay in touch.' Mitterrand declared his willingness to come to Britain at any time and continue the discussion.[25]

Talks between Mitterrand and Thatcher were continued at the Elysée palace in Paris on 20 January 1990. It became apparent that in the interval Mitterrand had become more pessimistic about the possibility of influencing the developments in Germany of which he had been so critical. 'The sudden prospect of reunification had delivered a sort of mental shock to the Germans. Its effect had been to turn them once again into the "bad" Germans they used to be. They were behaving with a certain brutality and concentrating on reunification to the exclusion of everything else . . . Of course the Germans had a right to self-determination. But they did not have the right to upset the political realities of Europe. He did not think Europe was yet ready for German reunification and he certainly could not accept that it had to take priority over everything else.' However, 'it would be stupid to say no to reunification. In reality there was no force in Europe which could stop it happening. None of us were going to declare war on Germany. Nor judging by his statements was Mr Gorbachev.' Mitterrand's pessimism, however, was not shared by Mrs Thatcher, who believed that it would be possible at least to slow down the process of reunification. It was agreed that the two countries' Foreign and Defence Ministers would work closely together over policy on Germany and on defence.[26]

Margaret Thatcher had even stronger reservations about German unification. Her hostile view of Germany[27] had been heavily influenced by historical factors—the enmity between Britain and Germany in the First World War, and the reign of terror under the National Socialists—and by her own experiences as a young woman during the Second World War. Her disapproval of unification sprang partly from this perception of Germany and partly from traditional preoccupations of British foreign policy, in particular a fear that the balance of power in Europe might be upset by German hegemony. She also believed that what she saw as Germany's economic dominance within the European Community would be further strengthened. Like the French President, too, she was afraid that Gorbachev's position, and hence the Soviet reform process, might be endangered. And she was particularly anxious that the so-called 'special relationship' between Britain and the United States should not be jeopardized.

In her conversation with Mitterrand in Strasbourg on 8 December 1989 Margaret Thatcher argued that if reunification were to come about simply as a consequence of the total breakdown of the GDR system and the growing demand for unity, then 'all the fixed points in Europe would collapse: the NATO front line; the structure of NATO and the Warsaw Pact; Mr Gorbachev's hopes for reform.' She too placed her hopes on four-power action against unification.[28] In the later talks with Mitterrand on 20 January 1990[29] she clearly did not agree with his pessimistic outlook. She thought, in particular, that 'the need for negotiation on

East Germany's membership of the European Community and the inevitable requirement for a substantial transitional period' could be used to 'slow down reunification . . . We should insist that agreements must be observed and that East Germany must take its place in the queue for membership of the Community.' Both Mitterrand and Thatcher were very disappointed by the attitude of Jacques Delors, who had declared in a speech to the European Parliament on 17 January that there was 'a place for East Germany in the Community should it so wish, provided . . . the German nation regains its unity through self-determination, peacefully and democratically in accordance with the principles of the Helsinki Final Act, in the context of an East–West dialogue and with an eye to European integration. But the form that it will take is, I repeat, a matter for the Germans themselves.'[30]

The attempts by Mitterrand and Thatcher to establish a common policy and revive the *Entente cordiale* of the period before 1914 failed. Despite their common critical attitude towards German unification, they were unable to reach agreement. This was partly a matter of substantive differences of interests. France wanted the process of European integration to deepen and accelerate, while Britain did not. According to Thatcher's memoirs, Mitterrand was reluctant to alter the basic thrust of his foreign policy: 'Essentially, he had a choice between moving ahead faster towards a federal Europe in order to tie down the German giant or to abandon this approach and return to that associated with General de Gaulle—the defence of French sovereignty and the striking of alliances to secure French interests. He made the wrong decision for France.'[31]

Kohl had already made intensive efforts—in a letter to Mitterrand of 5 December 1989 and in a long conversation at the French President's country residence at Latché on 4 January 1990[32]—to allay French anxieties by emphasizing that Germany remained committed to a deepening of the European Community, was opposed to the neutralization of Germany, and did not question the German–Polish border. After some initial hesitation, he gave his consent in principle to Mitterrand's wish for a government conference at the end of 1990 at which European economic and monetary union would be taken further forward.[33] Mitterrand had realized that in the last resort the Soviet Union would not block German unification, and that there was a danger that France would become diplomatically isolated and would damage its traditionally good relations with the Federal Republic. Despite the huge criticisms of the unification process that he made privately and in his discussions with Margaret Thatcher, the French President never came out publicly against German unification, which he believed was inevitable in the long run.

Mrs Thatcher, by contrast, in an interview with the *Wall Street Journal* on 25 January 1990, made a very blunt public statement of opposition to speedy German unification.[34] However, her position began to crumble in the face of unfolding events. After the establishment of the 'Two-Plus-Four' process (dealing with the external aspects of German unity) at a conference of the Foreign Ministers of the four victorious wartime powers and the two German states, the British Foreign Secretary Douglas Hurd advised the Prime Minister on 23 February that 'we must not appear to be a brake on everything. Rather we should come forward with some positive ideas of our own.'[35] A few days later, on 28 February, British representatives overseas were officially informed by the Foreign Secretary that 'the unification of Germany now seems virtually certain', that Britain 'had long supported the principle of German unity', and that 'this is something for the German people to decide, in the first instance'. The statement set out the conditions under which unification could take place, including a united Germany's membership of NATO and German acceptance of its borders with Poland.[36]

In the end British policy, too, was decided by questions of security, in particular the prospect that a united Germany would be anchored within NATO. Moreover, Thatcher's fierce disapproval of Germany was not shared by the British Foreign Office[37] or, specifically, by the British ambassador to Bonn, Sir Christopher Mallaby, who had persistently urged that senior British politicians should make public declarations in favour of German self-determination and unification.[38] By the middle or end of February at the latest the British Prime Minister had ceased to be directly involved in policy towards Germany, and operational control of policy was in the Foreign Office's hands. In the 'Two-Plus-Four' talks Britain played a wholly constructive role. In the view of Patrick Salmon, the main editor of the official British documents on German unification, Britain made a 'distinctive—and, many believed, indispensable—contribution to the final outcome'.[39]

In both Britain and France considerations of relations with the United States played a crucial role in the overcoming of Thatcher's and Mitterrand's initial resistance to speedy German unification. As early as the spring of 1989—that is, well before corresponding moves in the Federal Republic—the USA had already begun to rethink fundamentally its policy towards Europe and thus towards the possible reunification of Germany.[40]

Just one day after Kohl's Bundestag declaration of 28 November 1989 the American Secretary of State James Baker signalled his agreement in principle to German unification, while also enunciating four key principles. First, self-determination was paramount, and no particular version of unity—a federal state, a confederation or 'something else'—could be either ruled in or ruled out. Secondly, unification would have to take place within the framework of Germany's continuing commitment to NATO and to an increasingly integrated European Community, and there could be no 'trading of neutrality for unity'. Thirdly, in the interests of European stability the process of unification should be peaceful, stepwise, and gradual. Fourthly, the inviolability of Europe's borders, above all of the German–Polish border, had to be recognized. Changes to borders—the reference here was plainly to the border between the two Germanys—would be acceptable only if made by peaceful means.[41] These principles were restated by President Bush on 4 December 1989, in a revised version that gave even more emphatic support to German unification.[42] They formed the basis of American policy, which was then developed further in close coordination with the Federal Republic and implemented in a very flexible fashion.

Predictably, the strongest reactions to the Ten Points came from the Soviet Union. Foreign Minister Genscher described his discussions with Gorbachev in

Moscow on 5 December 1989 as the 'most unpleasant' of his meetings with the Soviet Union's leading statesman. 'Never before or after have I seen Gorbachev so agitated and so bitter,' he said.[43] Gorbachev was severely critical of the fact that the Ten Points had been published without prior consultation, objected to what he saw as ultimatum-like demands—by which he meant the linkage between wide-ranging Federal Republic assistance to the GDR and fundamental and irreversible changes to the GDR's political and social system—and deprecated the way the Federal Republic was artificially accelerating the process and showing a lack of respect for existing agreements. If a 'common European house' was to be built, within which relations between the two German states might be developed, then trust was essential. What, though, Gorbachev asked, would be the effect of a confederation, which entailed a unified defence system and a unified foreign policy? 'Where will the Federal Republic end up—in NATO, or in the Warsaw Pact? Or will it become neutral?'[44] At this stage, then, Gorbachev was not envisaging the possibility of Germany becoming unified as a federal republic, but was talking about a confederation. In any case, though, it was a solution that he rejected.

Kohl sought to mollify Gorbachev in a long letter which he sent to him on 14 December 1989. The instability in the GDR, he wrote, was not in the interest of the Federal Republic: it had been caused by the fact that reform had been blocked and delayed, which in turn had prompted the mass exodus from the GDR to the Federal Republic. The Ten Points were designed to provide a stable framework for future developments. They were not a timetable and did not set out a sequence of steps that should be followed: rather, the proposals were interconnected and should be implemented in parallel. He had deliberately not specified an end date. The government of the Federal Republic remained firmly committed to the goal of re-establishing German unity through free self-determination, but would, of course, respect the verdict of the people of the GDR and take heed of the need for security and the feelings of Germany's neighbours. Referring indirectly to Gorbachev's call for the building of a 'common European house', he emphasized that the 'leitmotif' of his Ten Points was the need to 'embed the future architecture of Germany within the future architecture of Europe as a whole'.[45]

The Soviet Foreign Minister Eduard Shevardnadze finally declared, in a speech to the Political Committee of the European Parliament in Brussels on 19 December 1989, that the interest of the Soviet Union lay in the continuing existence of two sovereign German states, and he reiterated the need for priority to be given to the building of the 'European house'. Nevertheless, a certain ambiguity in the Soviet attitude was apparent, inasmuch as Shevardnadze accepted the principle of German self-determination and—going beyond a purely defensive posture—presented a list of seven questions that would have a bearing on the foreign-policy aspects of any hypothetical reunification of Germany. He raised the question of guarantees against a renewed German threat and insisted that Germany recognize existing borders. He also referred to alliance membership, possible German demilitarization, changes regarding the presence of Allied forces in Germany, and the relationship between German unification and the future shape of Europe as a whole. Lastly, he issued a reminder that the interests of other European states needed to be taken into account.[46] His purpose in listing these questions was to make plain Soviet concerns, demonstrate the scale of the obstacles to unification, and delay the unification process. In so doing, however, he also revealed that the Soviet leadership was taking the problem of unification seriously and that the Soviet Union's attitude on the issue had not yet been finally decided.

The Soviet Union's cautious attempt to adapt its policy on Germany to the new situation created by the fall of the Berlin Wall was overtaken by the pace of events within the GDR. A crucial turning-point in the policy of the Federal Republic was Kohl's visit to Dresden on 19 and 20 December 1989. The enthusiastic reception that Kohl was given, by tens of thousands of GDR citizens, as 'Chancellor of the Germans' was, he later wrote, a 'key experience' for him.[47] From that moment onwards he was convinced that the overwhelming majority of people in the GDR were in favour of unification, although the speed of the process, and the way it might be carried through in terms of foreign policy, remained unclear.

In his negotiations with Modrow Kohl agreed to a continuation of economic cooperation on specific matters, but firmly rejected Modrow's demand that the Federal Republic pay 15 thousand million DM in 'burden-sharing' (*Lastenausgleich*) and stressed that it was up to the GDR to create the economic conditions that would encourage investment from western countries.[48] On the other hand, it was agreed that the two sides should embark 'without delay' on negotiations over a treaty of 'cooperation and good neighbourliness', with a view to possible signature in the spring of 1990, before the GDR elections scheduled for 6 May.[49] However, Modrow's attempts, albeit abortive, to preserve the core of the GDR State Security Service, and the overall crisis that had built up within the GDR, caused Kohl from mid-January 1990 at the latest to abandon all closer cooperation with Modrow, whom he increasingly regarded as an obstacle on the path to wider-ranging reforms and to German unity. On 11 January 1990 Modrow reiterated in the Volkskammer that 'a union between the GDR and the Federal Republic [was] not on the agenda and that in the view of many politicians and of public opinion in the states of Europe the separate existence of the GDR [was] essential for the stability of the political situation in Europe'.[50] Distribution to the relevant Federal ministries of the draft of a treaty with the GDR—which had been produced in the Federal Chancellery though not yet given the final seal of approval from on high—was halted,[51] and a GDR draft of 17 January 1990 that was handed over to the chief of the Chancellery, Rudolf Seiters, on 25 January[52] was likewise put on ice. The Kohl government postponed serious negotiations until the Volkskammer elections had been held and a democratically legitimized government formed on the basis of the election results.[53]

The real partner of the Federal Republic government in the period of transition before the elections was not, therefore, the Modrow government, nor even the Round Table and the groups represented on it that had formed the early opposition to SED rule: it was the population of the GDR. Only a minority of the population took part in the large demonstrations for German unity; hundreds of thousands of people left the GDR for the Federal Republic, though they too were only a minority. Behind them, however, stood the majority, comprising many millions, who believed that their chances of a better life—of greater prosperity, but also of guaranteed long-term freedom—lay not in a reformed system of socialism within an independent GDR but in unification with the Federal Republic. It was this belief, together with the collapse of the economy, that prevented the GDR from re-establishing internal stability.

The policy of the Federal government was a risky tightrope act. The government could not afford to radicalize the masses in east Germany, as this might lead to violent clashes and Soviet intervention. On the other hand, it did not want to stabilize the Modrow government prematurely, thereby blocking the way to the Social Market economy and the further dismantlement of SED rule and forfeiting the chance of uniting the two Germanys. Its response to the mass exodus from the GDR was of crucial importance. During 1989 344,000 people had left the GDR for the Federal Republic. The flood did not abate until after the Volkskammer elections of 18 March 1990: between the beginning of 1990 and the elections a further total of 184,000 people[54] moved to the Federal Republic. This was a serious haemorrhage for the GDR, especially since a high proportion of those who left were young, educated, and able to work.[55] For the Federal Republic, likewise, finding accommodation for the new arrivals, bringing them within the social security system, and, above all, integrating them into the labour market posed considerable problems, and they were the subject of intensive discussions within the Labour Ministry and with the relevant authorities in the GDR. The number of unemployed new arrivals rose to 128,000 in December 1989, while the average figure for the months between January and May 1990 was about 135,000. There was also a wave of immigrants of German origin from other countries, in particular Poland, the Soviet Union, and Romania: in December 1989 about 130,000 of these were unemployed. In view of the 'European dimension' of the problem, the Federal Minister of Labour Norbert Blüm called on the responsible commissioner in the European Commission to take a 'Community initiative to support the integration into employment' of the new arrivals from east Germany and the German-origin immigrants from elsewhere.[56] In the event, the integration of the new arrivals from the GDR largely went well, though this was not the case with the other migrants.[57]

Among the west German population, initial enthusiasm at the arrival of fellow Germans from the GDR gave way to a widespread view that the influx should stop. In a representative survey roughly half of those questioned said that the new arrivals were being given 'unjustified preferential treatment' and would deprive the existing population of homes and jobs.[58] These sentiments were picked up and encouraged by Oskar Lafontaine. He demanded that entry of GDR citizens into the Federal Republic should be conditional on the granting of a residence permit involving proof of employment and housing—in effect, that a new wall, built of regulations, should be erected. He wanted the new arrivals to be denied access to the Federal Republic's social security system, and indeed called into question the principle, enshrined in the Basic Law, that citizens of the GDR and Federal Republic had a common nationality, though in this he was opposed by the SPD praesidium.[59] The demand that the undesirable pull factor exerted on GDR citizens by the west German social security system should be eliminated won widespread support, especially among politicians in local government. The Federal government's decision to adhere to existing practice, strongly defended by the Federal Minister of the Interior Wolfgang Schäuble,[60] was highly significant as far as the unfolding unification process was concerned. Together with the demonstrations, the mass departures from the GDR were a visible expression of the lack of legitimacy of the GDR regime and proof of the desire for unity on the part of the GDR's citizens. If the flow of new arrivals had been brought to a standstill, a crucial internal driving force behind the unification process would have been removed, as well as a powerful argument for the inevitability of unification in the negotiations at international level.

A further key push to unification came with the Federal government's announcement on 7 February 1990[61] that it would enter 'without delay' into negotiations with the GDR on the creation of a 'monetary union with economic reform'. The decision to enter negotiations was the outcome of intensive preparatory work in the Federal Finance Ministry that had begun in mid-December 1989, led by Thilo Sarrazin, the director of the national monetary affairs section, with powerful support from Staatssekretär Horst Köhler and subsequently with the backing of the Finance Minister Theo Waigel.[62] By offering union with the Deutschmark the Federal government was seeking to send a signal that people should remain within the GDR. It was, so to speak, echoing the slogan which an increasing number of GDR citizens had begun deploying at demonstrations and on placards in order to voice their displeasure at conditions in the GDR: 'If the Deutschmark doesn't come to us, then we're going to the Deutschmark.' Doubtless the government's principal motives were its wish to stop emigration from eastern to western Germany and its desire to accelerate the pace of German unification, and make unity irreversible, by rejecting the roundabout route of a 'contractual community' and 'confederative structures'. However, party-political motives also played a role in Kohl's decision. As with his declaration of the Ten Points, he wanted to position himself at the head of the movement for German unity, in this instance by ensuring that the 'Alliance for Germany' which had just been formed, at his urging, on 5 February 1990 (with the eastern CDU as its strongest element), had a programme that would exert a wide appeal at the forthcoming Volkskammer elections. The offer of monetary union cut from under the GDR government's feet its demand for a support payment of 15,000 million DM from the Federal Republic: a demand that Modrow raised again when he headed a large delegation on a working visit to Bonn on 13 and 14 February 1990.

Although the government of the GDR had not been given advance notice of the offer of monetary union with economic reform, and made clear, with the backing of the Round Table, that it was not authorized to give the offer its approval,[63] it consented to take part in preparatory discussions on monetary union by committees of experts.[64] However, Modrow had meanwhile been attempting to stabilize conditions within the GDR, gain the initiative with regard to policy on the future of Germany, and put the GDR in a position where it would be able to steer, and put a brake on, the process of unification. Without consulting his own party or the other parties of his governing coalition, he prepared a statement—entitled, after a line in the GDR national anthem, 'Für Deutschland, einig Vaterland' (For Germany, united Fatherland)—which envisaged German unity only as the possible outcome of a long-term step-by-step plan. Modrow's motives were to halt the decline of the SED/PDS, improve the prospects for his party at the forthcoming Volkskammer elections, keep open the possibility of forming a joint government with the SPD after the election, and—if unification proved unpreventable—guide the process along a path that would be acceptable to him and would allow as many as possible of the 'socialist achievements' of the GDR to be preserved.

On 29–30 January 1990 Modrow flew to Moscow, to seek approval of his plan from the Soviet Union. By this time, the Soviet Union's original position of strong opposition to unification had begun to crumble.[65] Gorbachev, who had already come out in favour of the right of self-determination,[66] agreed with Modrow's proposals in general terms. However, he also made clear his considerable misgivings.[67] In particular, he urged Modrow to include in his plan a demand that the Federal Republic leave the NATO alliance and become neutral, and to agree this line with the SED/PDS, the other parties of the governing coalition, and, above all, with the SPD. In his talks with Modrow Gorbachev still assumed that the forthcoming elections in the GDR would yield a majority in favour of the continued existence of the GDR state,[68] in which event the aim should be the formation of a coalition between the SED/PDS and the SPD, the latter party being likely, according to current opinion polls, to emerge as the strongest party in the elections.

Although Modrow accepted the demand for German neutrality, he rejected a further demand that he desist from going things alone, and soon after his return from Moscow, at a press conference in Berlin on 1 February, he presented his programme. This envisaged, first, a 'contractual community', to be followed by a confederation of the two German states, with common organs and institutions of state, and, as a third and final step, the creation of a unified German state in the form of a 'German *Föderation* or a German *Bund* [= federation] through elections in both parts of the confederation'.[69] Coming at the moment when it did, this proposal was tantamount to a call for a brake to be applied to the process of unification.

Modrow's proposal was unacceptable to the Federal government, not only for this reason, but because the military neutrality of the GDR and the Federal Republic that Moscow was demanding as a precondition to federation would have entailed a breach with the Federal Republic's partners in NATO.[70] It would have meant, in particular, that west Germany would lose the support of the United States and become internationally isolated. The plan, however, quickly fell flat, especially after the failure of the Soviet Union to provide the economic support that Modrow had hoped would enable him to stabilize the GDR, which forced the GDR to turn to the Federal Republic for a solution to its economic difficulties.

Even before Modrow's visit to Bonn, a crucial breakthrough on the question of Germany's future took place—following preparatory discussions by the American Secretary of State James Baker in Moscow—at talks between Kohl and Gorbachev in Moscow on 10 February 1990.[71] Gorbachev agreed that the Germans alone could decide the question of unification. A joint statement declared that it was a matter for the governments of the Federal Republic and the GDR 'whether they wish to unite, how they wish to unite, how quickly they wish to unite, and when they wish to unite'.[72] The statement gave a green light to unification, despite the fact that two months later the Soviet Union was to be strongly critical of the decision to proceed to unification via Article 23 of the Basic Law—i.e. through the accession of the GDR to the Federal Republic—rather than through the creation of a new constitution agreed by the people in accordance with Article 146.[73] Even on the question of the Federal Republic's alliance membership and neutrality there was no declaration ruling out continued membership of NATO. On the other hand, the Soviet Union, as one of the four principal victorious powers, retained special rights restricting German sovereignty in Germany and, in particular, in Berlin, and it also held another trump card in the form of its troops in the GDR, the withdrawal of which could take place only with Moscow's consent. The external aspects of German unity would have to be resolved in collaboration with the four powers. The American State Department's answer was to come up with the concept of negotiations within a body composed both of the four powers and of the two German states: these became known as the 'Two-Plus-Four Talks'.[74] Genscher accepted this model, emphasizing that it was a two-plus-four and not a four-plus-two mechanism—in other words, underlining the fact that it was the two German states that would play the leading role on the road to unification.[75]

The confinement of the negotiating body to the two German states and the four powers was very much in the German interest. At a four-power conference Germany's fate would have been the object of political manoeuvrings between the victorious powers, and in the case of other possible alternative procedures—a peace conference attended by all the states that had been at war with Germany, or negotiations involving the 35 members of the Conference on Security and Cooperation in Europe—the outcome would have been difficult to predict and there would have been a danger that discussions would drag on for ever.

The two-plus-four mechanism for negotiations on the external aspects of Germany unity was agreed at a conference of 23 states of NATO and the Warsaw pact in Ottawa on 13 February 1990. The representatives of the Netherlands and Italy argued that they, and all members of NATO, should take part in the negotiations, but Genscher retorted that they were not among the four powers responsible for Germany, nor German states: 'You are,' he said, 'no part of the game.'[76]

The United States' strategy was to delay the negotiations until free elections had been held in the GDR and the process of unification had cleared its first hurdles. The USA also set strict limits on the topics of the negotiations. Accordingly, the question of Germany's alliance membership and any possible restriction on German troop strength was not to be a matter for the negotiations but was to be agreed on a bilateral basis by the powers primarily affected. In addition, it was explicitly stated that German unification was the goal of the negotiations.[77] For the time being, however, all eyes were focused on the forthcoming elections to the Volkskammer in the GDR.

1.1.2 The emergence of a new party system in the GDR and the Volkskammer elections of 18 March 1990

For Kohl and Waigel, the wish to establish a favourable starting position ahead of the Volkskammer elections—party-political considerations, in other words—had played an important role in the decision to offer 'monetary union with economic reform'. The question of Germany's future had become a central issue in the rivalry between the parties, and when the elections were brought forward from 6 May to 18 March competition became intense. It was clear to all the leading politicians that the result of the Volkskammer elections would not only create a new power alignment in the GDR and determine the political landscape during a crucial transitional phase, but would also have a bearing on the outcome of the later Bundestag elections.

The traditional party system in the GDR, made up of the ruling SED and the bloc parties that were wholly dependent on it, had now been expanded by the emergence of new political parties and groupings.[78] The latter had originated out of highly fragmented alternative and oppositional groups that had been formed during the second half of the 1980s, some of them under the aegis of the Protestant church. In the crisis of 1989 they took organized shape and emerged into public view, under names such as New Forum, Democratic Awakening, Democracy Now, the Peace and Human Rights Initiative (the earliest of the groups, founded in 1985), United Left, the Green League, the Green Party, and the Independent Association of Women (UFV). Although they differed as far as their programmes and their social roots were concerned, they all called for an ending of the power monopoly of the SED and for fundamental democratization of the GDR.

The most important of the new political organizations—most of which were members of the Round Table—was the Social Democratic Party (SDP) of the GDR, which had been founded (after lengthy preparations beginning in the summer) on 7 October 1989 in the village of Schwante north of Berlin, following an initiative by two Protestant clergymen, Markus Meckel and Martin Gutzeit. Led principally by theologians and intellectuals, without the involvement of the west German Social Democrats, it was deliberately established as an autonomous party.[79] At first it met with a cool reception, even downright disapproval, from the west Berlin *Land* organization of the SPD and substantial sections of the SPD in west Germany, which wanted to adhere to the policy of promoting dialogue with, and the internal reform of, the ruling SED. However, in the wake of the mass demonstrations and the SED's clear loss of power after the fall of the Wall, the west German SPD changed tack. At a party conference in Berlin on 18 December 1989 it officially recognized the east German SDP as its 'sister party' and agreed to give it its full backing. At a delegates' conference in Berlin on 12–14 January 1990 the east German SDP agreed to rename itself as the Social Democratic Party of Germany (SPD). It also came out unambiguously for a joint monetary and economic system with the Federal Republic and the speedy political unification of Germany.[80] Leading politicians in the SPD hoped that the party, some of whose strongholds before 1933 had been in what later became the GDR, would form by some margin the strongest party in the Volkskammer and that the SPD would go on to achieve 'the capacity to achieve a structural majority' in a later united Germany.[81]

This put the CDU in a tight spot. The east German CDU, led by Lothar de Maizière—who replaced Gerald Götting, generally seen as Honecker's puppet, on 10 November 1989—had begun to free itself from loyalty to the SED and, indeed, to socialism and to speak out in support of the market economy, albeit with strong social protections, and German unity. From the outset de Maizière favoured close cooperation with the west German CDU. Kohl, however, had considerable reservations, as did the general secretary of the party, Volker Rühe.[82] These doubts sprang partly from distaste for a link with a party of so-called 'Blockflöten',* discredited after decades of subjection to the SED, and partly from the view that de Maizière and the new leadership were unworldly political 'novices'. There was also some unhappiness that de Maizière and his party were still members of the Modrow government.[83] However, it was gradually felt that because the east German CDU had a relatively well-developed organization, a party bureaucracy (admittedly deeply implicated in the old system), and, above all, a sizeable membership—many of whom had joined the CDU so as to distance themselves from the SED—it was in practice the only partner with which a convincing election campaign could be fought in the GDR. At Kohl's urging, therefore, on 5 February 1990 the east German CDU came together with the German Social Union (DSU)—which had been founded on 20 January 1990 and had the backing, in particular, of the CSU—and with the earlier opposition grouping Democratic Awakening (DA), to form an electoral alliance, the 'Alliance for Germany'.

A week later the liberals followed suit. At west German FDP urging, the 'Association of Free Democrats' (BFD) was formed from a merger of the bloc party the LDPD (now re-named as the LDP) with the German Forum Party (a splinter group from New Forum) and a new east German FDP, founded on 4 February 1990 in east Berlin on the western model.[84]

The SED managed to stave off complete collapse. No major internal reforms of the party took place, but the old party leadership was removed and replaced by a new group, headed by Gregor Gysi, new party rules were adopted, and the party's name was changed to 'Party of Democratic Socialism' (PDS). (At first the initials 'SED' were added, but they were dropped before the Volkskammer elections were held.) The aim was to retain at least some of the party's large financial resources as well as sections of the bureaucracy of full-time staff and the elaborate membership organization that went with it. This aim was met, although party membership rapidly declined.[85]

The losers in this reshaping of the parties in the run-up to the elections were the original opposition groups. They were faced with a choice: whether to reconstitute themselves as political parties, without help from outside and without extensive organization and bureaucratic structures, or to remain as open grass-roots movements. Attempts by the majority of the groups on the Round Table to

* *Blockflöte* is the German word for the musical instrument, the recorder. The term was also applied as a nickname to the east German bloc parties. (Transl.)

persuade the west German parties and their leading figures to remain at arm's length from the Volkskammer elections, in order to give equal opportunities to all groups,[86] failed. Increasingly, the involvement of the western parties in the elections turned the poll into a kind of dress rehearsal for the Bundestag elections in the east.

The election campaign fought by the CDU, in which the party deliberately went on to 'the offensive',[87] was largely devoted to the issue of German unity, and in particular the question of the speed and form of the process of unification. The parties making up the 'Alliance for Germany' and the 'Association of Free Democrats' campaigned for as rapid an introduction of the Deutschmark as possible and for GDR accession to the Federal Republic in accordance with Article 23 of the Basic Law, which allowed accession to the Basic Law itself. Kohl was given great prominence by the 'Alliance' as the driving force behind the unification process, and Foreign Minister Genscher, who was very popular in the east, played a starring role for the liberals. In their election manifesto 'Yes to German unity—an opportunity for Europe', adopted at a party conference in Leipzig on 22–5 February 1990, the east German Social Democrats came out firmly for German unity, but the party also emphasized the need for the east to be actively involved in influencing the shape of unity and for social protections to be guaranteed.[88] There were differences among the Social Democrats on the question of the path that should be followed to unification. Some members of the party's executive, including the party leader and top candidate Ibrahim Böhme—who was later exposed as an 'unofficial collaborator' of the State Security Service—argued for unification on the basis of a new constitution, to be drawn up jointly by the GDR and the Federal Republic and presented to the people in a vote in accordance with Article 146 of the Basic Law. A clear majority in the party, however, and the rank and file in particular, favoured the quicker and simpler route laid down in Article 23.[89] The PDS,[90] and also most of the smaller organizations with their origins in the oppositional citizens' movement, such as Alliance 90 (B90), United Left, and the alliance of the Green Party and the Independent Association of Women, warned against over-hasty monetary union and the unthinking surrender of sovereignty and the 'social achievements' of the GDR.

The election was held on the basis of a strict system of proportional representation without thresholds,[91] and turn-out was high, at 93.4 per cent. It was in effect a plebiscite on the question of rapid German unification. More than three-quarters of the votes cast went to parties that had come out firmly in favour of rapid unification and that were closely allied to parties in the Federal Republic. The 'Alliance for Germany' was the clear winner. The SPD, which had been well ahead in all the opinion polls up to the beginning of March[92] and had already planned the structure of the government it hoped to lead, down to junior ministerial posts,[93] fell well short of its own expectations. The PDS, however, secured one-sixth of the vote. The results were especially disappointing for the parties and groups that had emerged from the oppositional citizens' movement: together they won less than 6 per cent of the vote, with 2.9 per cent going to Alliance 90 (the amalgamation of New Forum, Democracy Now, and the Peace and Human Rights Initiative).

Table 1 Results of elections to the Volkskammer of the GDR, 18 March 1990

Turn-out	Those entitled to vote (as a percentage of the population)	Invalid ballots
93.4%	75.7%	0.5%

	Share of vote (%)	Number of seats (total)
Alliance for Germany, comprising:	48.0	192
CDU	40.8	163
DSU	6.3	25
DA	0.9	4
SPD	21.9	88
PDS	16.4	66
BFD	5.3	21
B90	2.9	12
DBD	2.2	9
Grüne-UFV	2.0	8
NDPD	0.4	2
DFD	0.3	1
AVL	0.2	1
Others	0.4	—
Total		400

Note: For full names of parties, see Glossary.

Source: Based on Ritter and Niehuss, *Wahlen 1946–1991*, p. 191.

Significantly, surveys conducted after the election showed that the CDU and DSU did best not only among the self-employed and members of religious communities, but also among blue-collar workers. The PDS, though obtaining the leading share—31 per cent—of the vote among the 'intelligentsia', which included many functionaries of the old regime, gained only 11.9 per cent of the blue-collar vote, well below its overall figure.[94]

1.1.3 The effect of unification and the approaching Bundestag elections on German politics and international relations

The elections strengthened the position of the governing coalition in Bonn and its policy of a rapid move towards unification. In east Berlin, after difficult negotiations and, at first, strong resistance from within the Social Democratic Party, a government was formed on 12 April 1990, consisting of the CDU, the SPD, the DSU, the DA, and the Liberals. A detailed coalition agreement was concluded, containing sections on social policy (largely formulated by the Social Democrats) that later served as part of the basis of the negotiations over the State Treaty on monetary union. In the preamble to the document[95] the parties agreed to 'accomplish German unity for the whole of the GDR in a speedy and responsible manner, following negotiations with the Federal Republic on the basis of Article 23 of the Basic Law, and, in doing so, to make a contribution to a peaceful order in Europe'. The inaugural government statement of 19 April 1990 by the new Prime Minister de Maizière[96] highlighted, as aims of the coalition, the conversion of a 'state-led command economy into an ecologically orientated social market economy', the provision of social protection under unification, and the conversion of wages, salaries, pensions and savings accounts at the ratio 1:1; in the case of wages and pensions an allowance was to be paid, before the currency changeover. The government also called on the Federal Republic to show solidarity and act in the common interest: 'Die Teilung kann tatsächlich nur durch Teilen aufgehoben werden.'*[97]

On the whole, the statement by the new government was well received in the Federal Chancellery.[98] The clear commitment to Europe and the unconditional Yes to German unity were particularly welcome. Note was taken of the dignity and self-confidence with which de Maizière demanded 'the GDR's right to a say regarding the path to German unity'. There was approval of the fact that, in the part of the statement detailing the government's programme, policy positions were formulated in a more binding way than in the coalition agreement[99] and that contentious issues, such as time-limited abortion on demand, were not mentioned. The most important feature of the statement, as the Federal Chancellery saw it, was its remarks on the switch from dirigiste state planning to a social market economy, which had to proceed 'at a high tempo, and yet in well-ordered steps'. The 'goal and key reference point' was 'throughout, the legal and economic system in the Federal Republic and the European Community, together with the verdict in favour of large-scale transitional arrangements'. It was also noted, however, that de Maizière had stressed 'the protection of property rights resulting from land reform and from purchases made in good faith'.

The Federal Chancellery was unhappy that the statement did not censure the previous system and made no mention of the difficult economic and financial situation. In its view, the much briefer section on foreign policy was pallid in comparison with the declarations on domestic issues.[100] The Chancellery welcomed the fact that although the statement—unlike the coalition agreement—called for Poland's western frontier to be recognized, nothing was said about '*Procedere*' and, in particular, there was no demand for the initialling of a frontier treaty with Poland, or for the complete withdrawal of nuclear weapons from German soil. In addition, there was no equation of American and Soviet forces. On the other hand, some concern was felt that the statement made no mention whatever of NATO or of a united Germany's membership of NATO, whereas it did emphasize the GDR's loyalty to the Warsaw Pact and its wish to strengthen political cooperation with the Warsaw Pact states. Moreover, there was no clear 'rejection of demilitarization and German neutralization', which would have been desirable.

The government statement, then, indicated that although the new GDR coalition shared the Federal Republic's goal of a united Germany, it would exert strong

* 'The reality is that division (*Teilung*) can only be overcome by sharing (*Teilen*).'

pressure on behalf of the interests of the people of the GDR. Clearly, too, in some respects the new government's ideas concerning international backing for the unification process and for the shaping of a future European and international order were significantly different from those of the Federal Republic.

De Maizière held the view that unity should come about in a well-ordered manner, secured by treaties between the GDR and the Federal Republic which took the interests of the east Germans into account, and that it should not be finalized until negotiations with the victorious powers on the international aspects of unification had been concluded. He was against premature unification through an unconditional GDR declaration of accession, as was proposed by the DSU in the Volkskammer on 17 June 1990. In this he had the support, in particular, of Richard Schröder, the leader of the Social Democrats in the Volkskammer.[101]

The western Social Democrats faced the difficulty that they had to try to reconcile the politics of opposition in Bonn with the politics of coalition government in east Berlin. In view of the forthcoming Bundestag elections it might have seemed natural, on grounds of party-political tactics, to adopt a clear policy of confrontation with the Federal government. The potential benefits of a polarizing strategy of this sort, which the SPD's candidate for the chancellorship, Lafontaine, was pursuing, were significantly improved by the Social Democrats' victory in the elections to the *Land* parliament in Lower Saxony on 13 May 1990—a few days before the signing of the State Treaty on 18 May 1990[102]—when a CDU/FDP coalition was replaced by a 'Red–Green' one. In addition, in June 1990 the Allies abandoned their objections to the possession of full voting rights by the four Berlin members of the Bundesrat, so that the SPD-led *Länder* governments now had a clear majority in that chamber, with 27 out of 45 votes. On the other hand, there were also two arguments against these confrontation tactics. First, there was a danger that the party would be seen by the electorate as hostile to German unity. Secondly, account had to be taken of the Social Democrats in the east, who, working closely with western Social Democrats, had been very successful in their efforts to protect the social interests of the population in east Germany.

For the east German Social Democrats, however, working constructively as the junior partner to the CDU and as the coalition's social conscience was not paying off in political terms. At the local elections on 6 May 1990 they actually did a little less well than in their already poor showing at the Volkskammer elections.[103] Powerful voices among the east German Social Democrats, supported by a section of Social Democrats in the west, accordingly began calling for the party to leave the east Berlin coalition in order to strengthen its political profile and establish clearer battle lines before the Bundestag elections. Nevertheless, for the moment the split in the coalition was averted. The east German Social Democrats accepted, by a large majority, the State Treaty, and played an important part, through their representatives in the government, in the negotiations over the Unification Treaty until just under two weeks before the latter was signed.

In July 1990 the DSU ceased to be represented on the GDR Council of Ministers, when the party withdrew its two ministers, and the liberals also left the east Berlin coalition. On 15 August 1990 the Minister of Agriculture Peter Pollack—who had no party affiliation but had been nominated by the Social Democrats—and the Social Democrat Finance Minister Walter Romberg were dismissed by de Maizière, and at this point the SPD finally withdrew from the coalition too. De Maizière defended Romberg's dismissal—which had been preceded by deep-seated differences over the terms of financial questions proposed in the Unification Treaty[104]—on the grounds that the minister had not followed a clear line and had refused to recognize the Prime Minister's ultimate authority over policy.[105] The Social Democrats regarded the dismissal of the ministers, which had taken place without the involvement of the Volkskammer, as unconstitutional. The party leadership, the parliamentary party leadership, and then, on 19 August, the parliamentary party as a whole decided—albeit in the face of opposition from Schröder, the head of the parliamentary party—to leave the government. Schröder had prepared an address to the parliamentary party, but the party decided to take a vote without discussion and he was unable to deliver it. He had intended to argue that the party should invite de Maizière to discuss the issues at stake and should propose that the vacant ministerial posts be filled by widely respected non-party experts, agreed by the government and Social Democrat opposition in Bonn, until a new united German government was formed. It was 'absurd', he would have said, 'to go into opposition eight weeks, at most, before this state comes to an end'. The only way to strengthen the party's image and standing was to make constructive proposals that would clarify the issues for the voters, who did not understand the dispute over financial burden-sharing by the *Länder*. Breaking up the coalition would only weaken the position of the GDR in the ongoing negotiations over the Unification Treaty and hence damage both the country and the party.[106] Despite the collapse of the coalition, which led to Schröder's resignation as parliamentary party leader and his replacement by the party leader Wolfgang Thierse, the SPD party in the Volkskammer—like the party in the Bundestag—eventually endorsed the Unification Treaty. Before the Treaty was signed on 31 August 1990 there was an emotion-filled overnight sitting of the Volkskammer on 22–3 August at which the GDR's accession to the Federal Republic on 3 October 1990 was agreed by 294 votes to 62, with 7 abstentions.[107]

In the meantime decisive moves had also been made to secure German unity on the international front. At the first of the Two-Plus-Four meetings of Foreign Ministers in Bonn on 5 May 1990 the Soviet Foreign Minister made the surprising proposal that the internal and external unification processes, which until then had been, as it were, running on twin parallel tracks, should be decoupled.[108] The effect of the proposal would have been to speed up the move to unity on the domestic level but postpone to some unspecified date Germany's attainment of sovereignty, as well as decisions about the alliance membership of a united Germany and the withdrawal of Soviet troops. Foreign Minister Genscher at first clearly had some sympathy for this suggestion. He was anxious to circumvent any possible obstacles to internal unity and to protect the position of Gorbachev, who might have been weakened by a brusque rejection of the Soviet initiative.[109] In the end, however, after the idea of decoupling had been firmly rejected by Kohl, the CDU/CSU parliamentary party, and the western powers, Genscher yielded and announced in the Bundestag on 10 May 1990 that German unity should not be burdened with unresolved questions.[110]

However, during the following weeks the Soviet Union's firm opposition to NATO membership of a united Germany began to soften. In discussions at the summit meetings between the American President and Gorbachev in Washington and Camp David on 30 May to 3 June 1990 Gorbachev gave his assent to Bush's statement that in keeping with the CSCE Final Act, every country—and hence also a united Germany—was entitled to choose freely the alliances to which it wished to belong and that such choices should be tolerated, not contested.[111]

This was an about-turn by the Soviet Union, and it was an important step on the road to German unity. Gorbachev's concession—which was included, with his consent, in the American statement at the closing press conference—astonished all those involved and had evidently not been cleared with the Soviet leadership. In the weeks that followed, a significant hardening of the Soviet position became apparent again, probably as an attempt to take the wind out of the sails of the criticism that was likely to be voiced at the conference of the CPSU in Moscow on 2–14 July. This hardening was particularly noticeable at the second Two-Plus-Four meeting of Foreign Ministers that was held in east Berlin on 22 June 1990 (the 49th anniversary of the German attack on the Soviet Union). The Soviet Foreign Minister Shevardnadze proposed that after a long and highly complex procedure involving two treaties, the GDR's existing international agreements and treaties—and specifically, GDR membership of the Warsaw Pact—should remain in force for a transitional period of at least five years and the troops of the four powers should continue to be stationed in their current status, though at lower levels. Germany, he said, should become a zone free of nuclear weapons. The Bundeswehr and the National People's Army (NVA) should remain as parallel forces, confined to the territory of the Federal Republic and the GDR respectively. Only after the transitional period had elapsed should a united Germany be granted the freedom to decide on any future alliance membership.[112] This proposal was totally unacceptable both to the Federal Republic and to the western powers.

The representatives of the GDR, however, disagreed with the common western position on key points. The GDR's Social Democrat Foreign Minister Markus Meckel, a clergyman, and his closest foreign-policy colleagues—the east German clergyman and Social Democrat Volkskammer member Hans-Jürgen Misselwitz, the peace researcher and teacher at the Freie Universität in Berlin Ulrich Albert, and the psychotherapist Carlchristian von Braunmühl, also from the west—were close to the peace movement. They took the view—at odds with that of the Federal government—that a border agreement with Poland should be signed, or at least initialled, *before* reunification. In addition, they were in favour of expanding the CSCE into a Europe-wide peace framework, were anxious for the pace to be forced on disarmament, and saw the ultimate goal as the elimination of the two alliance blocs altogether. In the meantime, they argued, the character of the two blocs should be fundamentally altered, with an expansion of their political roles and a contraction of their military ones, and certain basic elements of current NATO strategy should be abandoned. The possibility of German dual membership of both military blocs was not to be ruled out. All nuclear weapons belonging to the victorious powers stationed on German soil should be removed. The NVA should be retained in addition to the Bundeswehr, as a territorial army, at least for an extended transitional period. In addition, Meckel and his advisers urged that the European Community should be extended to include the GDR and the reform states of eastern Europe. At the heart of Meckel's foreign policy was the notion that the GDR could act as a mediator between the blocs and between east and west.[113]

There was little coordination of foreign policy between the Federal Republic and the GDR, mainly because Meckel flatly refused to hold consultations with diplomats in the Bonn Foreign Ministry. The GDR tried to translate its key policy ideas into reality and establish an independent policy identity by pursuing various concrete initiatives. It first sought, with Poland and Czechoslovakia, to promote the expansion of the CSCE into an instrument of Europe-wide security policy and institutionalize it much more solidly than before through the creation of a 'council for security and cooperation' and an independent CSCE headquarters.[114] A further proposal of Foreign Minister Meckel's was the creation of a special security zone in central Europe. The aim of these suggestions was to undercut the disagreement between the western powers and the Soviet Union over the alliance membership of a united Germany by interlocking the two alliances.[115] The propositions, however, were badly prepared and came to naught, thereby discrediting the GDR's new foreign policy, which most diplomats in the Federal Republic and among the western powers regarded as the work of dilettantes.

At the ministerial meeting on 22 June Meckel stated—to the dismay of the representatives of the Federal Republic and the western powers—that the GDR would refuse to 'get up from the Two-Plus-Four table' until an 'understanding over [the] principles and timetable' of a European security organization had been reached. He proposed, *inter alia*, the denuclearization of Germany, a unilateral declaration by Germany to halve the troop numbers of the NVA and the Bundeswehr, special security provisions regarding the territory of the GDR, and a declaration by the member states of NATO and the Warsaw Pact, the terms of which he did not, however, spell out.[116] In the view of Chancellor Kohl's foreign-policy adviser Horst Teltschik, the effect of accepting these demands would have been the 'singularization' of Germany, a weakening of the NATO alliance, and a stiffening of the position of the Soviet Union, which otherwise feared becoming isolated. The GDR's proposals—which were ignored by the western powers—also posed the risk of 'delaying the completion of German unity' by 'subordinating the unification process to the construction of a European security organization', without specified preconditions or a timescale.[117] Moreover, they were inconsistent with the strategy of the governments of the USA and the Federal Republic, which was to avoid overloading the Two-Plus-Four process and to seek to resolve disputes with the Soviet Union by means of bilateral negotiations and agreements.

The path towards this goal was smoothed by Gorbachev's victory over his opponents at the conference of the CPSU on 2–14 July 1990. After dramatic clashes over Gorbachev's *perestroika* reform project and his plan for a shift to a market economy—though questions of foreign policy and the future of Germany were also the subject of heated discussion—Gorbachev was re-elected as general secretary of the party by 2,411 to 1,116 votes. At the same time, his chief opponent Ligachev was heavily defeated in a vote for the newly created post of deputy general secretary.[118] Gorbachev's position was therefore safe, for the coming months at least, and he had gained greater room for manoeuvre on foreign policy.

During Kohl's visit to Moscow and Gorbachev's native Caucasus on 14–16 July 1990[119] the final steps in the securing of German unification on the international level were taken. Gorbachev now accepted, in direct talks with the Federal Republic, that a united Germany could be a member of NATO, and he also agreed the terms on which the remaining unsettled questions would be resolved. Soviet troops would remain on former GDR soil on a transitional basis, and no NATO units would be allowed to move in, although German territorial troops not integrated into NATO would be able to do so. Moscow agreed to the surrender of the rights of the four powers, enabling the united Germany to attain full sovereignty. The continuing presence of the Soviet troops on former GDR soil, which was set to last for between three and four years, would be dealt with in a separate treaty. On this latter point, it became clear in the talks that the length of time that Soviet forces would stay in place would depend, essentially, on the scale of German payments to cover their withdrawal and the accommodation of the soldiers and their dependants after their return to the Soviet Union. The call for the simultaneous withdrawal of western forces from the Federal Republic, which the Soviet union had previously demanded as a *quid pro quo* for the withdrawal of its own troops, was dropped. The upper limit of German troop numbers was set at 370,000.

The reasons why Gorbachev made his concessions, and the relative weightings that the different reasons had for him, are not entirely clear. Undoubtedly a crucial consideration was his fear that German unification would take place without Soviet participation and that his country would become isolated internationally. In addition, Kohl and the western powers had made concessions of their own on certain points that were vital to the Soviet leader. The Federal Republic, which in January had already complied with the Soviet request for a subsidy for its purchase of foodstuffs from the west,[120] had stood surety for a credit of 5,000 million DM to improve the Soviet Union's economic position.[121] Kohl had also promised his strong backing for a big international programme to provide economic assistance to the Soviet Union, though the promise proved to be of little avail.

At a meeting of NATO Foreign Ministers at Turnberry in Scotland on 7–8 June 1990 and, more particularly, at the summit of heads of state and government in London on 5–6 July the signal had deliberately been given that NATO was ready to move from confrontation to cooperation between the alliances. It had been stressed that NATO was a defensive alliance and that its political components would be enhanced. The Warsaw Pact states had been told that they could establish permanent diplomatic relations with NATO, and military contacts would also be strengthened. NATO strategy would be re-examined, with a view to making nuclear armaments weapons of last resort. In addition, the CSCE would be strengthened and institutionalized, in line with the Soviet Union's long-expressed wish.[122] The London Declaration marked, in a sense, the end of the Cold War and the acceptance by the West of the Soviet Union and the other members of the Warsaw Pact as partners instead of adversaries. NATO's signal immediately met with a very positive reception in Moscow.

In this new atmosphere of political cooperation, the Federal Republic's offer to put relations with the Soviet Union on a new footing through a treaty on 'partnership and cooperation' perhaps also played a part in influencing the Soviet leader's attitude.[123] Gorbachev's priorities also have to be taken into account. His key goals were to continue the policy of *perestroika* and prevent the collapse of the Soviet empire, the possibility of which was already looming with the growing desire for independence in the Baltic states. Under such circumstances, the chance to shed burdens was welcome.

A further obstacle on the way to the international securing of German unity was removed with the resolution of German–Polish disagreements over a border treaty.[124] The Polish government had consistently demanded that such a treaty be signed, or at least initialled, *before* German unification took place. Kohl, on the other hand, maintained that only a united Germany could sign such a treaty. Kohl's manoeuvrings on this question generated some international mistrust, particularly on the part of France and Britain. Domestically, too, his attempt to link the solution of the border question to Polish abandonment of the demand for reparations and to the issue of the rights of the German minorities in Poland aroused considerable criticism, attracting fire not only from the Social Democrats and the Greens but also from the Chancellor's coalition partner, the FDP. Kohl's rejection of the initialling of a border treaty before unification was, in fact, constitutionally debatable, since if the GDR acceded on the basis of Article 23 of the Basic Law, then the Federal Republic's treaties would remain valid. His position sprang in part from his anxiety to overcome resistance from within his own party and among the expellees' associations. In his view it was essential to link the question of German unity to the issue of the Oder–Neiße line: people in Germany needed to be given the choice either to accept that the claim to the German territories in the east had to be abandoned or to let unification fail.[125] In the end, Poland, which on security grounds was primarily interested in the withdrawal of Soviet forces from GDR territory, shifted its position and agreed that the border treaty should not be signed and ratified until after reunification and the establishment of full German sovereignty, though it emphasized that signature should follow as soon as possible thereafter.

A new problem arose from the Soviet Union's demand that the Federal Republic should make significant financial payments to cover the costs of provisionally retaining its forces stationed in the GDR and then transporting them and their dependants back to the Soviet Union for re-housing and re-training. The issue had to be resolved by the intervention of Kohl, who went much further than the Federal Republic's original offer and promised the Soviet Union assistance of 12,000 million DM, together with an interest-free credit of 3,000 million DM for a five-year period.[126] A further question, finally, was the military status of the territories of the former GDR. The Soviet Union eventually secured an undertaking that after the withdrawal of Soviet forces the German troops stationed on former GDR soil would continue to be forbidden from being armed with nuclear weapon carriers and that foreign forces would not be allowed to be either stationed or moved there.[127]

On 12 September 1990, at a solemn ceremony in Moscow, the 'Treaty on the final settlement with respect to Germany'[128] was signed, and Germany regained sovereignty over its internal and external affairs. The borders of the united Germany were defined, and it was agreed that Germany would make no territorial claims against other states in the future. Even before the treaty was ratified—in Moscow this did not take place until 4 March 1991, after considerable argument[129]—the four powers suspended their rights and responsibilities on 1 October 1990,[130] so that when unification took place on 3 October 1990 the united Germany was a sovereign state from the outset.

Let us now return to the domestic problems. After the Volkskammer's decision on accession to the Federal Republic, taken on 23 August, there were lengthy party-political arguments over the timing of the common elections to the Bundestag, with a date of 2 December finally being agreed. There were similar arguments about a new electoral law, which was finally adopted by the united German Bundestag, meanwhile enlarged by the addition of 144 members from the east.[131] Under the new legislation, separate electoral regions in west and east Germany were designated. As originally passed, the electoral law specified that the usual threshold of 5 per cent that had applied in the old Federal Republic should apply to the electorate as a whole. The Federal Constitutional Court, however, declared this provision unconstitutional, on the grounds that it contravened equality of electoral opportunity and put the young parties in the new *Bundesländer* at a disadvantage.[132] The amended electoral law specified that parties would be eligible for the allotment of seats on the basis of second votes provided that they achieved more than the threshold figure of 5 per cent of the vote in only *one* of the two electoral regions, or if they captured at least three direct seats. In addition, parties based in the eastern electoral region would be allowed to form combined lists. The effect was to improve significantly the chances of those parties that had candidates only, or predominantly, in the east.

The new rules specifying separate electoral regions in the east and west were intended as a kind of 'revolution dividend' for the civil rights movement in the GDR. In practice, however, it mainly benefited the PDS. The latter succeeded in returning 17 members to the Bundestag, on the basis of 11.9 per cent of the vote in the new *Länder* and in east Berlin, though it won only 2.4 per cent of the votes across Germany as a whole. The electoral combination of Alliance 90 and the Greens in the new *Länder*, with its origins in the civil rights movement, also profited from the new arrangements, gaining 8 Bundestag seats on the basis of 6.1 per cent of the vote in the eastern electoral region; the only part of the western region in which it put up candidates was west Berlin.

Before the Bundestag elections were held, the Volkskammer on 22 July 1990 passed a constitutional amendment[133] setting in train the establishment of five new *Länder* in east Germany, and on 14 October Landtag elections were held in Brandenburg, Mecklenburg-West Pomerania, Saxony-Anhalt, Saxony, and Thuringia.[134] Although the collapse of enterprises and markets, the problem of redundancies and short-time working, unresolved questions about property ownership, and revelations about Stasi activities were central issues in these elections, there was little polarization and—in contrast with the earlier Volkskammer elections—very few leading west German politicians were involved in campaigning.

The Landtag elections saw the parties of the Bonn governing coalition consolidate their position in the east.[135] On a significantly lower turn-out, the CDU was returned as the largest party in four of the *Länder*. In Saxony it actually secured an absolute majority, and in Thuringia it fell short by a single seat. Only in Brandenburg did the SPD finish ahead of the CDU, to form a governing coalition under Manfred Stolpe with Alliance 90 and the FDP. In the other *Länder* the new *Land* governments were headed by the CDU, either on its own (in Saxony) or in coalition with the FDP. In Mecklenburg-West Pomerania this happened despite a stalemate, as an SPD member left his party in anger and, as an independent, gave his support to the CDU/FDP government. As a further consequence of the elections, the Bonn coalition won a majority in the Bundesrat, with 35 out of the new total of 68 seats. The Social Democrats had made gains everywhere, but with an average of about 25 per cent across the five *Länder* they remained weaker than they had expected, even though their hopes had been much scaled back since the Volkskammer elections. While the various oppositional groups, campaigning under different labels, made gains in all five *Länder*, the DSU and the PDS fell back to well below their results in the Volkskammer vote.

As the political forces shaped up, first, for the Landtag elections and then, particularly, for the Bundestag elections on 2 December 1990, the processes of consolidation of the party system in the east and fusion between the eastern and western parties continued. The Association of Free Democrats and the bloc party the NDPD merged into the FDP. The CDU parties in the GDR and the Federal Republic amalgamated into a single party and also absorbed the DA and the DBD, likewise an earlier bloc party. The DSU clung on to a separate existence but secured only 1 per cent of the votes at the Bundestag elections and sank into insignificance. The east and west German Social Democrats, which had previously held separate party conferences, held a joint conference in Berlin on 27 and 28 September to seal their own unification. In the east, Alliance 90 and the Greens came together to form a single party, though the merger of this party with the west German Greens took place only after long and difficult negotiations during the subsequent parliamentary term.

As expected, the central issue of the Bundestag elections was German unity. The CDU's campaign was strongly focused on Kohl as the 'Unity Chancellor'. Its manifesto, 'Yes to Germany—Yes to the Future', emphasized that unity had been made possible only through the unwavering resolve of the Kohl government

Table 2 Results of Landtag elections in the five new *Bundesländer*, 14 October 1990

	Brandenburg	Mecklenburg-West Pomerania	Saxony-Anhalt	Thuringia	Saxony
Those entitled to vote (as a percentage of the population)	74.0	72.9	75.4	74.9	75.7
Turn-out (%)	67.1	64.7	65.1	71.7	72.8
Invalid ballots (%)	2.9	3.3	3.0	2.6	2.5
Votes (%)					
CDU	29.4	38.3	39.0	45.4	53.8
SPD	38.2	27.0	26.0	22.8	19.1
PDS-LL	13.4	15.7	12.0	9.7	10.2
FDP	6.6	5.5	13.5	9.3	5.3
B90	6.4	2.2	—	—	—
Grüne	2.8	4.2	—	—	—
Grüne/NF	—	—	5.3	—	—
Grüne/NF/DJ	—	—	—	6.5	—
Forum	—	2.9	—	—	5.6
DSU	1.0	0.8	1.7	3.3	3.6
Rep	1.2	0.9	0.6	0.8	—
DFD	—	—	1.1	0.8	—
CSU	—	1.1	—	—	—
Others	1.0	1.5	0.8	1.5	2.4
Number of seats					
CDU	27	29	48	44	92
SPD	36	21	27	21	32
PDS-LL	13	12	12	9	17
FDP	6	4	14	9	9
B90	6	—	—	—	—
Grüne/NF	—	—	5	—	—
Grüne/NF/DJ	—	—	—	6	—
Forum	—	—	—	—	10
Total	88	66	106	89	160

Note: For full names of parties, see Glossary.

Source: Based on Ritter and Niehuss, *Wahlen 1946–1991*, p. 181.

and promised that if Germans stood solidly together throughout the country, then a thriving economy would be created and a high level of social and environmental protection would be guaranteed. The party highlighted an improvement in financial support for families, protection for those needing social care, and improved housing provision, especially in the east, as the main tasks in social policy during the forthcoming parliamentary term.[136]

The CSU, while emphasizing the part that the Finance Minister Theo Waigel had played during the process of reunification, made Bavarian autonomy the centrepiece of its manifesto.[137] Characteristically, it also launched fierce attacks on the Social Democrats, accusing them—on the strength of the SPD's own description of itself in December 1989 as the 'party of democratic socialism'—of being close to the PDS and of having missed the bus on German unity: under their leading candidate Lafontaine, it claimed, the Social Democrats had confined themselves to 'doom-saying, scare-mongering, and stoking up envy and fear of the future'. The CSU's concrete messages included a rejection of tax increases. As the 'social conscience' of the Bonn coalition, it argued for more home-building, insurance arrangements to cover the costs of social care, and increases in family benefits.

The FPD gave particular prominence in the campaign to Hans-Dietrich Genscher—the 'man from Halle'—who was especially popular in the east, and emphasized his key role in the unification process. On social policy, it stressed the importance of individual responsibility, as against the role of the state. The party's subsequent disagreements with the CDU/CSU were foreshadowed by its firm rejection of a general scheme of social care insurance 'on grounds of economic principle and financial policy'.[138]

The electoral slogans of the Social Democrats made virtually no reference to unification.[139] Their leading candidate Oskar Lafontaine had fiercely and repeatedly criticized the government's recent policy on the future of Germany as overhasty and not based on solid economic and financial foundations, and during the campaign he conveyed the impression that he was dubious about, if not privately hostile to, unity and highly sceptical about its repercussions. As an electoral tactic, this was ill judged. The party's political blueprint for a modern Germany, drawn up by a working group under Lafontaine that had been set up on 17 October 1988[140] and published as the document 'Progress 90', contained no answers to the specific challenges posed by German unification. The party's election manifesto, 'The new path: ecologically, socially and economically strong',[141] identified the 'ecological reorganization of industrial society' and the 'ecological reorientation of the social market economy' as the outstanding tasks of the 'next decade'. It emphasized the Social Democrats' credentials on social issues and put forward a detailed programme for expanding social security, for example through the provision of basic age and invalidity protection and the introduction of separate statutory social care insurance. The SPD accused the coalition of concealing the fact, for electoral reasons, that taxes would need to rise in order to finance German unification. It argued instead for a temporary solidarity contribution in the form of a supplementary tax for higher earners.

The main items in the Greens' manifesto were calls for the ecological and social reorganization of industrial society, unilateral disarmament, emancipation and self-determination for women, and radical grass-roots democracy. On social policy, they stressed the dangers of rising social tensions in Germany as a whole in the aftermath of unification with the GDR. Their concrete proposals included a shortening of the working week to 35 and eventually 30 hours a week, with wages to be fully adjusted to compensate; the introduction of quotas in education and employment, with at least 50 per cent of places to be offered to and filled by women; and a system of needs-based basic social protection, with an indexed initial basic allowance of 1200 DM in all social protection systems.[142]

Table 3 Results of elections to the 12th German Bundestag, 2 December 1990

	Electoral region West	Electoral region East	Federal Republic
Those entitled to vote (as a percentage of the population)	77.7	74.9	77.2
Turn-out (%)	78.6	74.5	77.8
Invalid ballots (%)	1.1	1.5	1.1
Votes (%)			
CDU	35.5	41.8	36.7
CSU[a]	8.8	—	7.1
SPD	35.7	24.3	33.5
FDP	10.6	12.9	11.0
Grüne	4.8	0.1	3.8
B90/Grüne	0.0	6.1	1.2
PDS	0.3	11.1	2.4
DSU	0.0	1.0	0.2
Rep	2.3	1.3	2.1
Graue	0.8	0.8	0.8
ÖDP	0.5	0.2	0.4
NPD	0.3	0.2	0.3
Others	0.3	0.2	0.3

Number of seats	10 old *Bundesländer*	5 new *Bundesländer*	Berlin	Federal Republic
CDU	195	61[b]	12	268
CSU	51	—	—	51
SPD	200	30	9	239
FDP	60	16	3	79
B90/Grüne	—	7	1	8
PDS	1	13	3	17
Total	507	127	28	662

a. The CSU traditionally fields candidates only in Bavaria.

b. Including 6 'Überhangmandate' (additional seats). Under the electoral law for Bundestag elections, each voter has two votes: a first vote, for a candidate in a constituency, and a second vote, for a party list. The number of seats allotted to each party is determined by its share of the votes for the party lists in each *Land*. However, if in a particular *Land* the constituency candidates of a party win more seats than they would be allotted on the basis of the party list vote, they are given them as additional seats. In 1990 all 6 additional seats were won in the new *Länder* and went to the CDU.

Note: for full names of parties, see Glossary.

Source: Based on Ritter and Niehuss, *Wahlen 1946–1991*, p. 104.

The Bundestag elections of 2 December 1990 returned the governing Bonn coalition to office with 398 out of 662 seats and thus a clear parliamentary majority. The CDU was the strongest party in all of the five new *Länder*, Brandenburg included.[143] With 319 seats, the CDU/CSU came close to achieving an absolute majority on its own. The FDP also did well, obtaining one of its best results since the founding of the Federal Republic.

The Social Democrats lost a little ground in the old *Bundesländer* in comparison with the elections of 1987. In the eastern electoral region, where they had not yet managed to build up a wide-scale organization, particularly in the rural areas, their showing of 24.3 per cent was a slight improvement on their position at the Volkskammer elections but less good than their results at the October Landtag elections in the east. The west German Greens, with 4.8 per cent of the votes in the western electoral region, just failed to reach the electoral threshold and enter the Bundestag. On the other hand, the PDS, despite losing one-third of the share of the votes it had obtained at the Volkskammer elections, succeeded in returning members to parliament, as did the combination between Alliance 90 and the eastern Greens.

1.1.4 German unity within the framework of international relations and domestic politics

German unification took place at a time when the international situation was unusually favourable. The watchwords were détente, disarmament, and the ending of the Cold War. In the Soviet Union, at Gorbachev's instigation, comprehensive reform of the Communist system through *perestroika* and *glasnost* was under way. On the international plane, the decisive event was the abandonment by the Soviet Union and its Warsaw Pact allies of the Brezhnev Doctrine, which had sanctioned the prevention, by force if necessary, of systemic change in the Communist states within the Soviet sphere of influence. Each of these countries now had, at least in principle, a free hand to choose the political path it wished to follow.

Gorbachev's first thought had been that in the GDR, too, the rigid dictatorship of the Honecker era could be replaced by a new, reformed Communist system: the GDR would remain a separate and independent German state, still committed to socialism. This vision, however, was overtaken by events. The crucial factor here was the attitude of the population of the GDR, which, through mass exodus and mass demonstrations, brought the already ramshackle political, social, and economic GDR system to the point of collapse, and which from mid-December 1989 onwards demanded not only freedom and democracy but also, by a large majority, unification with the Federal Republic. The Volkskammer elections of 18 March 1990 were an unequivocal vote for German unity by the people of the GDR.

Since the Soviet Union had ruled out the option of the use of military force to suppress the movement for freedom and unification, and had recognized, in principle, the right of every nation to self-determination, in the last analysis it had no way of blocking these developments. Nevertheless, as we have seen, lengthy and difficult negotiations were necessary before the Soviet Union agreed to surrender its rights in Germany as one of the four victorious powers, accept a united Germany's membership of NATO, and withdraw its troops from GDR territory without the simultaneous withdrawal of the forces of the western powers from the Federal Republic. There were various reasons why the Soviet Union gave way. First, the western alliance stood united, after some initial disagreements. Secondly, the Soviet Union was deserted by its allies in the Warsaw Pact. The most important states in eastern Europe—Poland, Hungary, Czechoslovakia, and Romania—had already accepted German unification by January 1990, and by July 1990 they had decided, on grounds of their own security, that they preferred a united Germany to be a member of NATO than to be neutralized.[144] A third factor was the Soviet Union's economic weakness and its consequent wish for financial support from the Federal Republic and the western industrial countries. A fourth was that Gorbachev hoped to reduce the political pressures he faced at home. In his view, the German question was less important than the need to continue the policy of economic and party reform, and to avert the danger that the Soviet Union might break up if the Baltic republics were to split away and other nationalist conflicts within the Soviet empire were then to become more acute. In the fifth place, the looming break-up of the Warsaw Pact meant that it would simply be impossible in the long run to maintain a military outpost, with Soviet troops, on the territory of the former GDR. A sixth factor was the Soviet Union's fear of international isolation, which might jeopardize the processes of disarmament and the ending of the Cold War. Here the Soviet Union set particular store by good relations, not just with the United States as the leading world power, but also with the Federal Republic, which was a vital trading partner and, in Soviet eyes, the most important power in Europe. Finally, good personal relations between Gorbachev and President Bush and Helmut Kohl, to whom Gorbachev made crucial concessions in February and July 1990, also played a key role.

Soviet policy suffered from the further disadvantage that it contained no clear vision of a future shape of Germany and Europe. The idea of a 'common European house' remained vague and was not translated into operational terms. On the question of alliances, the Soviet Union wavered between advocating the neutralization of a united Germany, German membership of both military blocs, and the minimal demand that NATO be prevented from extending its reach into eastern Germany. Overall, Soviet policy gave the impression of being at the mercy of events; it did not seem to constitute a serious or consistent attempt to direct them.

The opposite was true of the United States. The USA adhered with astonishing consistency to a policy of seeking the unification of Germany and the liberation of eastern Europe from Soviet domination, while at the same time ensuring that Gorbachev's position remained secure and that the goals of carefully calibrated disarmament, NATO reform, and the ending of the Cold War were not jeopardized. From November 1989 onwards, American policy, in which both President Bush and the Secretary of State James Baker were intimately involved, was worked out and conducted in close coordination with the Federal Republic. The United States fully achieved its objective as far as Germany was concerned: namely, a united Germany allied to the west. As the unambiguous leader of the western alliance, the USA also succeeded in persuading the United Kingdom and France, after initial hesitations, to commit themselves to the basic principles of its policy. The mechanism of the Two-Plus-Four talks played an essential role here.

Britain and France were at first uneasy about German unification, as they were afraid that the international order would be destabilized and that a united Germany would dominate Europe. They were also fearful that rapid German unification would put Gorbachev's position at risk and jeopardize the domestic reform process in the Soviet Union. They did not, however, pursue any concrete policy of fending off German unification. Wary of international isolation, they shrank back from acting alone. Nor did any form of joint action, in which the Soviet Union might also have become involved, materialize, since there were basic conflicts of interest between Britain and France. In the British case, interests of security policy were ultimately paramount. Britain was opposed, in particular, to Gorbachev's idea that the alliance blocs might be replaced by a common European peace framework—a notion that France's President Mitterrand also temporarily toyed with—and was also anxious not to endanger its close relations with the United States. France's central aim, on the other hand, was to strengthen European integration by laying the foundations for a European economic and monetary union—to which Britain was hostile—and to tie Germany more closely into the European Community. In the final analysis, each country recognized that the internal process of German unification could not be halted, since the Soviet Union would not exercise a veto, and that its own security-policy interests would accordingly best be met by the integration of a united Germany into the NATO alliance.

German unification was a catalyst for European integration.[145] At the start of 1990 the French president of the European Commission, Jacques Delors, came out firmly in favour of German unification and the absorption of the territory of the GDR into the European Community. In an interview in early January 1990 he said that east Germany should be given its place in the Community as soon as 'it becomes a pluralistic democracy with an open market economy'.[146] A little later, in a speech to the European Parliament, he described east Germany as a 'special case'.[147] This signalled a change from previous policy, which had been that the deepening and further integration of the Community should, for the time being, take priority over expansion and that no new members should be admitted before the end of 1992. Concurrently, Delors—with the support of the German commissioner Martin Bangemann—sought to dispel the anxieties within the Commission and the member states of the Community about German hegemony in Europe. A trade and cooperation agreement between the European Community and the GDR was initialled as early as 13 March 1990, before the Volkskammer elections, and signed on 8 May. By this time, however—a few days before the signing on 18 May of the State Treaty between the Federal Republic and the GDR creating a monetary, economic, and social union from 1 July 1990—the agreement had already been overtaken by events. Since the European Community, like the Federal Republic, favoured GDR accession via Article 23, it was assumed in Brussels that there would not be any formal accession negotiations and that the territory of the GDR would be incorporated into the Community by dint of its becoming part of a reunited Germany. Certainly, unification on the basis of Article 146 might well have necessitated extremely difficult and long-drawn-out new negotiations with a united Germany, and it was in the interests of both the Federal Republic and the GDR that such negotiations should be avoided. As it was, though, accession via Article 23 also required numerous transitional arrangements. The task of working out these arrangements—in close cooperation with the ministries in Bonn and the government in east Berlin—was assigned to the European Commission, which thereby gained an opportunity to enhance its profile, and to the European Council.[148]

A final document agreed at a special summit meeting of European Community heads of state and government in Dublin on 28 April 1990 'warmly' welcomed the unification of Germany and expressed confidence that unification would be a 'positive factor in the development of Europe as a whole and of the community in particular'. At the same time, the Community declared that it expected to be informed about all important measures taken by the two German governments concerning the alignment of policies and legislation and to be 'fully involved with these discussions'.[149]

The same summit meeting gave its blessing to a German–French initiative to convene, concurrently with the planned governmental conference on European monetary union, a further governmental conference on the creation of a political union in Europe. This decision reinforced the linkage that Kohl had always emphasized between German unity and European unification. The initiative was a compromise between the French government, which was primarily concerned to see the rapid implementation of European economic and monetary union, and the Germans, who wanted to give priority to strengthening the Community's democratic legitimacy through an extension of the powers of the European Parliament and working towards the goal of a common foreign and security policy. The view, often advanced, that Kohl agreed to European monetary and economic union as the price, so to speak, for Mitterrand's acceptance of German unification, does not square with the facts, since Kohl had already voiced his support in principle for monetary union in 1988 and merely confirmed it in 1990.[150] What is true is that the timetable had shifted. The original German position had been that monetary union would, as it were, crown the prior achievement of political integration. It now became increasingly clear that political union—which was bound to meet with considerable opposition from the British—would not be implemented before monetary union and that it would not be possible, for example, to tie the former, as a kind of precondition, to the latter.

The incorporation of the GDR gave rise to a string of fundamental problems over and beyond the question of the transitional arrangements. If the GDR were to be incorporated into the European Community customs area through German–German monetary union on 1 July 1990, how would it be possible, on the one hand, to ensure that it would continue to adhere to its trade agreements with the COMECON states—as Bonn and east Berlin wished, both in the interests of maintaining east–west trade and as a concession to the countries of central and eastern Europe and to the Soviet Union—but also, on the other hand, to prevent the European Community from being inundated with goods from the east? Again, how were the various forms of aid that the Federal Republic was providing on a large scale to the east German agricultural sector and other areas of the economy, in order to support the transformation of a planned economy into a market economy, to be reconciled with European Community competition law? These and other questions were resolved in close cooperation with the European Commission, which became involved in the negotiations over the State Treaty shortly before these were concluded and took part in the negotiations over the Unification Treaty from the outset.[151]

A particularly knotty problem arose as a result of the European Commission's wish that the GDR should receive financial support from the European Community, first before its accession to the Federal Republic and then in the form of a special structural fund for the new *Bundesländer*. Kohl vigorously opposed this proposal, as he was very anxious, on grounds of foreign policy, to avoid giving the impression that German unity was taking place at the expense of the weaker member states. He was also concerned, for domestic reasons—in particular, because of the constant sniping within the Federal Republic at the scale of German net payments to the European Community—to block any increase in contributions by the Community member states, and by the Federal Republic in particular. In the end, however, he accepted an arrangement whereby the new *Bundesländer* would receive an annual payment of a thousand million ECUs from EC funds in each of the years 1991, 1992, and 1993, without the need for an increase in EC funding or a reduction in payments for regional development.[152]

The main international actors, however, in the process towards German unity were the Soviet Union, the United States, and the Federal Republic itself. The role that the GDR played in the internal unification process has in many ways been underestimated, and in the State Treaty and the Unification Treaty it was able to secure at least some of its objectives. Nevertheless, apart from bringing its interests to bear during the negotiations with the EC over transitional arrangements, it had little real influence over the shaping of the external conditions of German unity, owing to its lack of professionalism and the isolation of its representatives at the Two-Plus-Four talks. The United Kingdom and France played a part in working out the concrete details of the Final Settlement of 12 September, following the lead of the United States, but they had not been involved in the crucial decisions. The European Community, and in particular the European Commission, provided extremely constructive support for the unification process from January 1990 onwards, and thereby also tied the smaller EC member states into the process to a certain extent.

Within Germany the principal actor was the population of the GDR. In casting aside SED rule the east Germans were greatly inspired by the reform movement in Poland, where Solidarity had, since its foundation in 1980, become the bearer of popular hopes for freedom and democracy not only among Poles but throughout the Soviet Union's sphere of influence in Europe. In 1989 further encouragement came with the establishment of 'Round Tables' in Poland, the semi-free elections of 26 June, and the formation of the first non-Communist government, under Tadeusz Mazowiecki. The east Germans were also strongly influenced by Charter 77 in Czechoslovakia, which had become a manifesto for the opposition movement, and by events in Hungary, which opened its borders to the West even before the fall of the Berlin Wall. As far as opposition in the GDR was concerned, the key role at the start was played by various groups within the civil rights movement, some of which made considerable use of the protective umbrella provided for dissidents by parts of the Protestant church. The aims of the civil rights movement were freedom and democratic reform and not—except for a few participants—the abolition of the GDR, which at first seemed out of reach. However, the emergence of an elemental mood among the wider population, and of the demand for the elimination of the GDR and for German unification, pushed the original participants in the civil rights movement to the sidelines. The Federal government and the newly formed parties within the GDR, some of which were heavily supported by the parties in the Federal Republic, seized the opportunity to steer the movement into political channels.

It was of crucial significance that the process of unification took place in the year 1990, with elections to the Bundestag due at the year's end. It was soon clear that the question of Germany's future would be the key issue in the election campaign. That had already been the case with the elections to the Volkskammer, the results of which had rightly been seen as a referendum on unification.

The ways in which the parties presented themselves to the electorate was thus inevitably bound up with issues of unification policy. As a consequence, neither the parties in the governing coalition nor the opposition wanted an all-party coalition, or a Grand Coalition of CDU/CSU and SPD, on unification policy, not only because they differed in their emphases concerning the content and timing of policy but because they made different assumptions about the effects of unification policy on their electoral chances. These considerations, admittedly, did not prevent the Social Democrats from eventually agreeing to the State Treaty and supporting the Unification Treaty. In the last analysis it was the government that held the levers of the process in its hand. Kohl exploited this fact with great skill, in particular when he issued his Ten Points at the end of November 1989 and offered monetary union at the start of February 1990. Kohl also became the dominant German political figure with regard to the securing of German unity at the international level. In this he was supported, very effectively and loyally, by the Federal Chancellery and, in particular, by his closest foreign-policy adviser, Horst Teltschik. Within the government Kohl's most significant collaborator—and opponent—in the external aspects of unification was the Foreign Minister Hans-Dietrich Genscher, together with the Foreign Office.[153] Although Kohl and Genscher shared the goal that German unification should be achieved without any impairment of the Federal Republic's allegiance to the west, there were differences of emphasis between the two men. Genscher, for example, was readier than Kohl to make a clear and rapid accommodation with the Poles over their wish for a final confirmation of Poland's western border. He was also initially prepared—like his American opposite number, James Baker—to grant more firmly defined special military status to the former territory of the GDR than eventually happened in the treaty of 12 September 1990 and to accept a greater reduction in German forces after unification. In addition, he paid more heed than Kohl to the proposals from Moscow, in an attempt to fathom the Soviet position. Nor was their rivalry confined to differences on policy: as the leading figure in the FDP, Genscher was also happy to boost his party-political standing through the good publicity he garnered from playing a key role in the unification process.[154]

The hallmark of Kohl's political style was to build confidence with foreign heads of state and government through countless telephone conversations, semi-personal letters, and face-to-face discussions. He deliberately used ostensibly private 'man-to-man' contacts as a way of achieving important political breakthroughs. A characteristic example of his technique was his relationship with Gorbachev, in which he succeeded in repairing the damage that had been done in 1986 by his inappropriate comparison of the Soviet leader to the Nazi Propaganda Minister Joseph Goebbels.[155] The personal nature of the Kohl–Gorbachev relationship became vividly apparent when the two men had their walk beside the River Rhine during Gorbachev's visit to Bonn in June 1989, in the course of which they exchanged memories of their youth. Kohl invoked the Rhine to voice his conviction that Germany would eventually be reunited. The waters of the river, he said, flowed to the sea: 'And if you dam the river, it will go over the bank and destroy it, but the waters will still go to the sea—and it's the same with German unity.'[156] There was a similar personal touch about Gorbachev's invitation to Kohl to his dacha in Archys, a village in the Caucasus, in mid-July 1990, after the former's agreement in Moscow that a united Germany could be a member of NATO. Kohl also built up a close personal relationship of trust with the American President George Bush, whom he visited regularly in Washington and at Camp David and with whom he became on first-name terms. The initial tensions between Germany and France over the question of unification were likewise eased through letters and meetings between Kohl and Mitterrand, similarly conducted with first names. Only with Margaret Thatcher were relations lukewarm, owing to the British Prime Minister's mistrust of the German Chancellor.

Genscher, too, pursued his own highly personal style of diplomacy. He built up a particularly close relationship of trust with his Soviet opposite number Eduard Shevardnadze. Their meeting on 11 June 1990 in Brest, where Shevardnadze's elder brother had been killed in the first days of Germany's invasion of the Soviet Union in 1941, was a particularly emotional one. The visit of the two men to the cemetery where Shevardnadze's brother was buried was the expression of a close friendship that was also politically significant.[157]

It is also important to note, finally, that the time factor played a part in German unification. In a conversation with Bush in Washington on 17 May Kohl compared his situation with that of a farmer 'who wants to get the hay crop in as a precaution, because there may be a thunderstorm'.[158] Genscher, too, believed that 'a silken-threaded sword of Damocles' was hanging over everyone's heads and that unforeseen circumstances could put a stop to the process of unification or even send it into reverse.[159] The idea that there was only a narrow window of opportunity for unification sprang mainly from the fear that Gorbachev might be assassinated, or that he might be deposed by his political opponents within the Soviet Union, and that this might lead to a military dictatorship which would reject all forms of concession to the West and even attempt to suppress by force the democratization movement in eastern Europe and the movement towards unification in Germany. Worries about Gorbachev's position ran in two conflicting directions. For Thatcher and Mitterrand they provided an argument for putting a brake on, if not blocking, the unification process. The precariousness of Gorbachev's position, however, could also be taken as a sign that it was vital to complete unification as quickly as possible and ensure that it could not be put into reverse.

Teltschik has posed the question: what would have happened if Iraq's invasion of Kuwait, and the subsequent Gulf War, had taken place, not at the beginning of August 1990, but two months earlier?[160] The war occupied all of the USA's attention during the months that followed, and it also caused America to take greater account of the views of the Soviet Union. The internal process of German unification would probably still have been unstoppable at the beginning of June, but it is highly debatable whether the parallel process of negotiations over the external aspects of unification, the Allies' surrender of their rights in Germany, and the withdrawal of Soviet troops from the GDR would have come to a successful conclusion. Exploiting the window of opportunity to achieve German unification was undoubtedly a work of statesmanship. On the German side it was done, not by planned management of the process from above, but in flexible and instinctive reaction to constantly changing events—events that were primarily driven, as far as the internal process of unification was concerned, by the people of the German Democratic Republic.

1.2 GOVERNMENT AND OPPOSITION, 1991–1994

1.2.1 The coalition agreement and the announcement of the government's programme

The elections to the Bundestag of 2 December 1990 were the final stage in the formation of the newly unified Federal Republic after the dramatic events of the preceding year. In east Germany a start had been made in establishing a new system of administration at *Land* level, reforming the structure and administration of local government, recasting the legal system, adapting the system of social security, and creating an autonomous system of industrial relations. On the labour market a reduction in employment was already in train, as the centrally planned economy began to be replaced by the Social Market economy. It was clear that the central task in domestic policy during the coming years would be to steer the huge process of transformation in the new *Bundesländer* in a way that would be socially acceptable and would foster unity.

The adoption of the Basic Law of the Federal Republic as the constitution of the new united German state had little effect on the legal framework of the political system. The size of the Bundestag had increased, from 497 seats at the elections of 1987[161] to 662 at those of 1990; the Bundesrat had also expanded. In the latter, the four *Länder* with more than 7 million inhabitants—namely, North Rhine-Westphalia, Bavaria, Baden-Württemberg, and Lower Saxony—each received an extra sixth vote under the terms of the Unification Treaty.[162] Nineteen additional votes—four each for Saxony, Saxony-Anhalt, Thuringia, and Brandenburg, and three for Mecklenburg-West Pomerania—were allotted to the five new *Länder*, making a total of 68 votes in the Bundesrat. In the enlarged Bundestag the parties of the old Federal Republic enjoyed a clear dominance. Their total of 637 members so heavily outweighed the small minority of members belonging to 'eastern parties'—17 members of the PDS and 8 of Alliance 90 and the eastern Greens—that the latter were thought to have little political future. It was also notable that although representatives of the new *Länder* were included on the leadership committees of the united parties, the processes of policy- and decision-making within the parties at national level continued to be dominated by the old leadership groups from the west.

The elections put the CDU/CSU in a very strong strategic position within Federal politics. In contrast with the situation in the previous parliamentary term, there was no majority in the Bundestag for a possible 'traffic light' (red, yellow, and green) coalition of the SPD, FDP, and Greens, owing to the poor showing of the Greens in the west. Since a coalition involving the PDS was out of the question, a Grand Coalition of the CDU/CSU and the SPD would have been the only alternative to a continuation of the previous government. The powerful position of the CDU/CSU—though the FDP had made considerable gains in votes and seats—was reflected in the detailed coalition agreement between the CDU, CSU, and FDP that was signed, after lengthy negotiations, on 16 January 1991.[163] The agreement's general statements on economic policy, which emphasized competition, deregulation, privatization, the freeing-up of markets, financial consolidation, and further reductions in the role of the state, were in line with the policies that the government had pursued during the preceding eight years. The reality, however, was that there was a need for massive state intervention in order to meet the new calls for an improvement in infrastructure and the provision of regional assistance in the east. There had been fierce arguments about the FDP's demand—which was eventually defeated by resistance from the Finance Ministry and the CSU in particular[164]—that a low-tax region be created in the new *Bundesländer* to encourage investment from western Germany and abroad and to help new businesses to become established.[165] Although it was already quite clear that the financial costs of German unity were going to impose a heavy burden, tax increases were expressly ruled out as inimical to investment. Instead, the coalition pledged itself to abolish the local capital tax on business and the wealth tax in order to safeguard the position of the German economy when the European Single Market came into effect on 1 January 1993.[166]

With regard to social policy, three sub-commissions were set up to negotiate the coalition agreement, one on general social-policy issues, another on social care, and a working group on women and the family headed by Rita Süssmuth for the CDU/CSU. As Blüm, the Federal Minister of Labour, saw it, the CDU/CSU faced two key tasks in social policy: first, to even out the differences between the old and new

Bundesländer and create a unified German welfare state, and, secondly, to enhance the CDU/CSU's social-policy image in its arguments with the FDP over family policy and, especially, over the introduction of social care insurance. The FDP, Blüm said, 'is pushing us over tax policy, so we should push them over family and social policy'.[167] Social policy, he warned his party's members of parliament, would determine the outcome of the next Bundestag elections.[168] Blüm's powerful intervention in favour of social care insurance won Kohl's backing, though Kohl also thought it necessary that the party conduct a wide-ranging discussion about the form that such insurance should take.[169]

The question of social care insurance had been a highly contentious item in the coalition negotiations. Blüm's call for a commitment to statutory social care insurance was rejected by the FDP, which favoured private insurance schemes. The agreement to 'bring before the German Bundestag by 1 June 1992 a draft law on insurance for social care'[170] did not resolve the differences between the parties on the issue but merely papered over them, postponing the moment when they would have to be settled.

As far as other areas of social policy were concerned, the parties agreed, among other things, to continue an active labour market policy, with special arrangements for the east, to seek to achieve further flexibility in working hours, to combat the abuse of existing unemployment benefit and unemployment assistance, and to extend financial support for families and children. They also agreed to reform the organization and financial structure of statutory health insurance by extending freedom of choice among health insurance companies and reducing structurally determined differences in contribution rates.

In a move that was highly significant both for the future financing of German unity and for social policy, it was decided to raise sharply the contribution rate for unemployment insurance from 1 April 1991 by 2.5 percentage points, to a total of 6.8 per cent of employee wages and salaries borne jointly by employers and employees.[171] At the same time, contribution rates for pensions insurance were lowered by one percentage point. Even more important in the long term, however, was the decision to combine pensions insurance for blue- and white-collar workers in the new *Bundesländer* with pensions insurance in the west, within a single all-German system of financing, starting from 1 January 1992. A similar financing system already existed for unemployment insurance. What this meant in practice was that the cost of the high levels of transfer payments to the east that would plainly be needed to finance pensions and unemployment benefit, and to stave off mass unemployment through a rapidly expanded and active labour market policy, would have to be met, not by the taxpayer, but solely by insurance contributors. As the German Trade Union Federation and the Social Democrat opposition complained, the effect would be to impose greater burdens on employers through additional wage costs and a hidden tax increase on employees.[172]

By contrast, the Federal Finance Ministry's plan to incorporate the miners' guilds' pensions insurance scheme, for which the Federal government had deficit liability, into the blue- and white-collar workers' pensions insurance finance system—a plan that would have removed a burden of 5,300 million DM from the Federal budget—was abandoned after opposition from the Federal Ministry of Labour.

One notable feature of the new cabinet was the appointment of Jürgen Möllemann of the FDP as Economics Minister. Another was the division of the Ministry for Young People, the Family, Women, and Health into three separate ministries, each headed by a woman. Hannelore Rönsch (CDU) became Minister for the Family and Senior Citizens, Angela Merkel (CDU) from the east took charge of the Ministry for Women and Young People, and Gerda Hasselfeldt (CSU) was made head of the Ministry of Health, with the ministry taking over the important department of health and health insurance from the Labour Ministry. At the same time, the Labour Ministry, headed by Blüm, was given responsibility for setting up the new system of social care insurance, the most important new reform project in social policy for the forthcoming parliamentary term.

In his statement of 30 January 1991 announcing the government's new policies[173] the Federal Chancellor Helmut Kohl declared that the aim of bringing about 'equal living conditions for people throughout Germany' was an 'absolute priority'. His comments on financial policy were explosive. He promised a new system of financial relations between the Federal government and the *Länder* and a reversal of the sharply increased borrowing requirements in public budgets, and—flying in the face of the governing parties' election promises and the terms of the coalition agreement—announced increases in revenues through tax rises. The latter, he said, were necessitated, not by the costs of unity, but by expenditure on the Gulf War, in which Germany was obliged to support its partners and allies. The passages in the statement devoted to social policy largely adhered to the terms of the coalition agreement. There was strong emphasis on the need for unions and employers to exercise joint responsibility in maintaining employment levels and supporting structural change in the east, and an appeal for a broad political consensus on the question of social care insurance. Although it was already clear that sizeable burdens were going to be placed on the German economy, owing to the wide-scale collapse of many sections of industry in the new *Bundesländer* and the intensification of international competition as the former Communist states of central and eastern Europe established themselves as market economies, this problem was not specifically referred to in the statement—in part because unification had triggered a short-term boom in west Germany.

In the debate on the following day, Hans-Jochen Vogel, for the Social Democrats, accused Kohl of breaking his election pledge not to raise taxes. He also criticized the government for lacking a coherent vision for forging social unity in Germany and presented an eight-point plan of the Social Democrats.[174] Kohl, he said, had 'glossed over' the scale of the task in the new *Bundesländer*, when he should have appealed to the 'forces of solidarity' within the population; this was a 'cardinal error'. Vogel directed particularly fierce criticism at the sharp rise in unemployment insurance contributions, the effect of which would be to require employers and employees alone, and not the self-employed, civil servants, or the wealthy, to finance the alleviation and elimination of unemployment in the east. That task, he said, ought to be the responsibility of the community as a whole.

Vogel accepted the invitation to take part in discussions on the question of social care.

The government statement's proposals in that field were strongly attacked by the SPD's spokesman on social policy, Rudolf Dreßler. Despite Blüm's election pledges, Dreßler said, the coalition had not reached agreement over the question of social care insurance. The Health Service Reform Law of 1988 had been a failure, and the increase in unemployment insurance contributions was a breach of a key election promise that building up the system of social security in the east was a task for the state as a whole and should not be borne solely by contribution payers in west Germany. The coalition was guilty of carrying out upward redistribution, in violation of the supreme principle of any welfare state, the 'commandment of solidarity on the part of society as a whole'. Furthermore, by passively accepting the consequences of an incoherent economic and financial policy, the coalition had failed to offer its own vision in social policy.

Government and opposition, then, laid out the lines of a clash over social policy that would persist during the coming years. The differences of opinion that were present within the coalition, on the other hand, were visible only in part. However, Hermann Otto Solms, the leader of the FDP parliamentary party, emphasized that the FDP, despite the 'agreement that had been forced through in the Unification Treaty', was not prepared 'to accept as lawful the expropriations carried out in the years before 1949' and argued for the idea, rejected by the CDU/CSU, of a low-tax region. Similarly, the liberals' spokesman on social policy, Dieter-Julius Cronenberg,[175] criticized the extension to the new *Bundesländer* of the Federal Republic's highly specialized system of employment law, in particular its regulations concerning payments to be made in the event of large-scale redundancies, and rejected as irresponsible the imposition of extra compulsory contributions to statutory social insurance to cover the cost of possible social care.

1.2.2 The struggle for control of the Bundesrat

Just a few weeks after the Bundestag elections the government lost its majority in the Bundesrat. Its room for manoeuvre was therefore reduced, and the position of the Social Democrats was correspondingly strengthened, although the latter now also had to accept a greater share of political responsibility. Following Landtag elections in Hesse on 20 January 1991, the CDU/FDP coalition there was replaced by a government of the SPD and the Greens. There was an even more dramatic shift of power in Rhineland-Palatinate, where the CDU had dominated *Land* politics and regularly provided the *Land* Prime Minister since the first Landtag elections of 1947. After a hard-fought campaign centred on the Federal government's proposals for tax increases, branded as a 'tax lie', the election on 21 April 1991 saw the SPD increase its share of the vote by six percentage points, enabling it to form a new government with the FDP, under Rudolf Scharping as *Land* Prime Minister.[176] The *Länder* led by the SPD, including three in which it shared power with the FDP, now had 37 of the 68 votes in the Bundesrat.

The SPD's position was further strengthened when Landtag elections in Hamburg on 2 June 1991 replaced the joint SPD and FDP governing coalition with a government comprising the SPD alone. Nevertheless, despite these electoral successes the SPD was able only to block the formation of majorities in the Bundesrat: it could not exert majority control. It now had 29 votes, on its own and in combination with the Greens. However, in Rhineland-Palatinate and Brandenburg, with 8 votes together, the FDP—which had to pay heed to the wishes of its coalition partners in Bonn—was a partner of the SPD in *Land* government and could not be simply outvoted when *Land* voting in the Bundesrat was being determined. Conversely, though, the CDU-led senate in Berlin, with its 4 votes, likewise had to take account of the attitude of its SPD coalition partner in Bundesrat votes.

Accordingly, coalition agreements in the *Länder*, whether their governments included parties in the Bonn coalition or in the Bonn opposition, generally made provision for abstention on controversial Federal policy questions, or allowed decisions to be taken on a case-by-case basis in the light of the *Land*'s interest. In the case of 'consent' bills (bills requiring the consent of the Bundesrat)[177] abstention was tantamount to rejection, since their passage required an absolute majority vote of at least 35 in the Bundesrat. This meant that important reforms might be blocked. The government attempted to circumvent possible opposition in the Bundesrat by splitting off 'non-consent' parts of bills into separate items of legislation. There were strict limits to this tactic, however. In the end compromises had to be sought with the opposition over almost all important proposals. That said, the opposition could not indefinitely sustain a purely negative posture either, for fear of incurring criticism in the media, alienating voters, and jeopardizing the interests of the *Land* governments they themselves led. In practice, consensus solutions with the opposition were usually found, often via the Mediation Committee of the Bundestag and Bundesrat,[178] or, especially, through direct negotiations between leading party representatives. This put a strain on the Federal coalition, since on the central areas of social policy, such as the introduction of social care insurance and structural reform of the health service, the positions of the CDU/CSU were closer to those of the SPD than they were to those of the FDP. The FDP therefore came under considerable pressure, though in the end it had to be involved in every compromise solution for the sake of the preservation of the coalition.

The stance of the Bundesrat, however, was not determined solely by the party-political composition of the *Land* governments. On financial questions, in particular, the *Länder* had common interests *vis-à-vis* the Federal government. There were also differences between eastern and western *Länder*, city and non-city *Länder*, and rich and poor *Länder*, all of which could influence decisions by the Bundesrat. Thus in February 1992 the Federal government succeeded, against SPD resistance, in getting Bundesrat approval for an increase in VAT from 14 to 15 per cent when the SPD-led government in Brandenburg,[179] which urgently needed extra financial resources for reconstruction, broke ranks with the other Social Democratic *Länder*. After taking note of Brandenburg's position, the governing Grand Coalition of SPD and CDU in Berlin also accepted the proposal.[180]

Some of the subsequent Landtag elections also affected the distribution of power in the Bundesrat. At the Bremen parliamentary elections on 29 September 1991 the SPD lost its absolute majority and had to form a 'traffic light' coalition with the FDP and the Greens. In Baden-Württemberg the CDU suffered a heavy defeat on 5 April 1992 and, unable to continue governing on its own, went into a Grand Coalition with the SPD. In this instance, significantly, and also after elections held at the same time in Schleswig-Holstein, the SPD was unable to profit from the CDU's losses, and far-right parties—the German People's Union (DVU) in Bremen and Schleswig-Holstein and the Republicans in Baden-Württemberg—won seats in the *Land* legislatures.[181]

1.2.3 Changes in the party system and the Bundestag elections of 16 October 1994

In the eyes of many contemporary observers—political scientists, sociologists, and journalists—the declining cohesiveness of the two major political parties, the CDU and the SPD, and the steep fall in turn-out by voters at Landtag elections from 1991 onwards were symptoms of a general crisis in the German party system. These phenomena were seen as harbingers of the collapse of the two big parties and an expression of disenchantment with politics on the part of the people.[182]

The governing coalition seemed politically weak and worn out. It was depleted in personal terms, too, following the voluntary resignation of Hans-Dietrich Genscher and the fall of the ministers Gerhard Stoltenberg (CDU), Jürgen Möllemann (FDP), and Günther Krause (CDU) in the wake of political scandals. On the other hand, the coalition benefited from the fact that the SPD was unable to come up with a convincing candidate for Federal Chancellor. Björn Engholm, Oskar Lafontaine's successor, was forced by his involvement in a political intrigue to give up his position as Prime Minister of Schleswig-Holstein and withdraw from his candidacy for the chancellorship. In a primary election of party members the Prime Minister of Rhineland-Palatinate, Rudolf Scharping, was chosen as leader in preference to Gerhard Schröder and Heidemarie Wieczorek-Zeul, but he did not have a united party behind him, lacked personal charisma, and seemed to be no match for Kohl as an electoral campaigner. The Social Democrats' organization in the five new *Bundesländer*, comprising only about 27,000 members—fewer than in the Weser-Ems region of the party—was quite undeveloped. Moreover, when the party, after its collapse in local elections in Hesse on 7 March 1993, stepped up its propaganda against what it saw as the Kohl government's icy indifference on issues of social welfare, it scared off middle-class voters, as indeed it did by its one-sided stress on social issues generally.[183]

Opinion polls initially predicted that the government would be convincingly defeated at the Bundestag elections on 16 October 1994, following the sharp recession of 1993.[184] However, although unemployment remained high, the first signs of economic recovery in the spring of 1994[185] enabled the CDU/CSU to make up the ground it had lost to the SPD, and it went into the lead from June 1994 onwards. Likewise, Chancellor Kohl, whose personal rating had at first been well behind that of the Social Democrats' candidate, Scharping, overtook his rival in the electorate's affections at the beginning of June 1994.[186] In the European elections of 12 June 1994 the CDU once again came out well ahead of the Social Democrats. On the other hand, since the Greens, with over 10 per cent of the votes, did far better than the FDP, which failed to cross the 5 per cent threshold,[187] and the PDS made strong gains in the east, it was by no means clear that the coalition was going to be able to maintain its governing majority in the Bundestag.

Economic and social issues played a much greater part in the 1994 Bundestag election campaign than had been the case in 1990. The CDU and CSU, in their joint manifesto entitled 'We will safeguard Germany's future',[188] presented themselves as the parties which had surmounted the recession of 1993 and carried out policies that would protect the country's economic position during the years ahead. They emphasized, as their main achievements, the consolidation of the nation's finances, the introduction of social care insurance, the implementation of reforms strengthening the welfare state, and, most of all, the successful establishment of effective infrastructure in the east. The SPD was accused of espousing tax policies inimical to investment and efficiency and of rejecting new technology, and much was also made of the fact that after the Landtag elections in Saxony-Anhalt on 26 June 1994 a minority government of Social Democrats and Greens was being kept in power by the PDS. The CDU/CSU sought to stir up the electorate by attacking 'red socks' (a reference to loyal SED supporters in the old GDR) and highlighting the CSU's slogan 'Freedom, not Popular Front'.[189]

The SPD portrayed itself as the alternative to a government that had run into the sands and, with its slogan 'Looking forward to change—Germany/SPD',[190] tried to create the impression that the removal of the government was assured. Its manifesto, 'Reforms for Germany',[191] put 'work for all', 'social justice', and 'protection of nature and the environment' at the forefront. At the same time the party stressed its seriousness by pledging that all of the specific measures in its programme, including the first moves towards the 'introduction of basic social protection appropriate to need', would be subject to strict 'conditions of financial viability'.

For the FDP, the campaign was a matter of life or death. At the most recent Landtag elections in 1993–4, in Hamburg, Lower Saxony, Saxony-Anhalt, Brandenburg, Saxony, and Bavaria, it had failed (as in the European elections) to clear the 5 per cent threshold[192] and was therefore no longer represented in the legislatures of these *Länder* or in the European Parliament. Campaigning under the slogan 'This time everything's at stake—FDP/The Liberals',[193] it tried not only to mobilize its own voters but to persuade supporters of the CDU/CSU to give it their second votes in order to ensure that the party would continue to be represented in the Bundestag and that the governing coalition would survive. On the other hand, the FDP's detailed manifesto, entitled 'Think liberal—vote for results',[194] upheld the party's traditional image as a party of business. In particular, its statements on health and social security policy and on social issues generally went much further than its previous positions on reform of the welfare state via a reduction in the role of the state and an increase in private provision by the individual.

By contrast, the manifesto of the PDS, 'Opposing the dismantling of the welfare state and the shift to the right',[195] not only highlighted the interests of the east Germans but portrayed itself as the only party truly committed to the welfare state. It proposed reforms in employment and social policy which it estimated would cost 300,000 million DM per annum.

The manifesto of Alliance 90/The Greens[196] called for a strengthening of democracy and minority rights within a multi-cultural and tolerant society, the reform of world society based on ecological and mutualist principles, and, in particular, a 'feminist policy for an emancipated society'. Their demands with regard to social policy were more specific and less ambitious than those in their 1990 manifesto. Although 'large strides towards shorter working hours' were proposed, wage adjustments were to be 'socially graduated' rather than comprehensive, and no figures were specified for the Federally financed scheme of 'basic social protection orientated to need' that they advocated as a supplement to inadequate benefits under unemployment and pensions insurance. Nor was there a reiteration of the 1990 demand that at least 50 per cent of all jobs and education and training places should be allocated to women. By dispensing with some of their most radical demands, Alliance 90/The Greens clearly hoped to improve their chances of being able to form a governing alliance with the Social Democrats.

The Bundestag elections gave the governing coalition a narrow majority: it won 341 out of the 672 seats, including 12 of the 16 additional seats. The losses incurred by the CDU/CSU (–2.4 per cent) were relatively small, as were the gains made by the SPD (+2.9 per cent). The real loser was the FDP, which obtained only 6.9 per cent of the vote. Although it comfortably cleared the 5 per cent threshold, and plainly received second votes from supporters of the CDU and CSU, it lost a good quarter of its 1990 share of the vote in the west[197] and almost three-quarters of its 1990 share in the east. In the Landtag elections in the Saarland, Mecklenburg-West Pomerania, and Thuringia, held at the same time as the Bundestag elections, the FDP's share of the vote remained well below 5 per cent. The gainers were Alliance 90/The Greens and, especially, the PDS, which almost doubled its share of the vote in comparison with December 1990 and, by winning 4 direct seats in east Berlin, was able to surmount the 5 per cent threshold, now applicable to the whole of the Federal Republic, and enter the Bundestag with 30 seats. The small parties, with a total of 3.5 per cent of second votes, remained insignificant. The overall result showed that fears that German politics was in a state of crisis, that support for the large parties (the CDU, CSU, and SPD) was being eroded, and that the party system was on the point of fragmentation were unfounded. Moreover, the proportion of those not voting at all, roughly 20 per cent, was if anything on the low side in comparison with other democratic states.

The most significant feature of the election was a confirmation of the trend towards the formation of different party systems in eastern and western Germany, which had already become apparent in Landtag and local elections in the new *Bundesländer* from late 1993 onwards. In the east the PDS won roughly 20 per cent of the vote, while the FDP and Alliance 90/The Greens registered percentages well below their shares in the west, failing to reach the 5 per cent threshold in any of the

Table 4 Bundestag elections in the old and new *Bundesländer*, 16 October 1994

	Old *Bundesländer* including west Berlin		New *Bundesländer* including east Berlin		Federal Republic as a whole	
	Second votes (for party lists)	First votes (for constituency candidates)	Second votes (for party lists)	First votes (for constituency candidates)	Second votes (for party lists)	First votes (for constituency candidates)
Those entitled to vote (as a percentage of the population)	74.6	74.6	76.5	76.5	75.0	—
Turn-out (%)	80.5	80.5	72.6	72.6	79.0	—
Invalid ballots (%)	1.3	1.6	1.4	1.7	1.3	—
Votes (%)						
CDU/CSU	33.2/8.9	36.6/9.5	38.5	40.9	41.5	45.0
SPD	37.5	39.7	31.5	31.8	36.4	38.3
FDP	7.7	3.4	3.5	2.9	6.9	3.3
B90/Grüne	7.9	7.1	4.3	3.8	7.3	6.5
PDS	1.0	0.4	19.8	20.5	4.4	4.1
Rep	2.0	1.9	1.3	0.5	1.9	1.7
Graue	0.5	0.4	0.5	0.3	0.5	0.4
Others	1.4	0.8	0.5	0.1	1.1	0.7

Number of seats	10 old *Bundesländer*	5 new *Bundesländer*	Berlin	Federal Republic
CDU	179[a]	56[c]	9	244
CSU	50	—	—	50
SPD	205[b]	38[d]	9	252
FDP	40	5	2	47
B90/Grüne	42	4	3	49
PDS	5	21	4	30
Total	521	124	27	672

[a] Including 2 additional seats (cf. Table 3, note[b]).
[b] Including 1 additional seat.
[c] Including 10 additional seats.
[d] Including 3 additional seats.

Note: For full names of parties, see Glossary.

five new *Bundesländer*. In the Landtag elections in the east in 1993–4, similarly, only Alliance 90/The Greens had retained a presence in a *Land* legislature, with just 5.1 per cent of the vote in Saxony-Anhalt, but they dropped out again at the next Landtag election in 1998. In all the other eastern legislatures they, like the FDP, lost all their seats. Whereas the party system in the west was made up of two large parties (CDU/CSU and SPD) and two smaller ones (Alliance 90/The Greens and FDP), with the latter—the FDP especially—constantly in danger of losing representation at *Land* level, in the east there were three large parties, of which one, the PDS, was a distinctly regional party.

However, it was not only the party system in the east that differed from that in the west: the character of the parties differed too.[198] The eastern parties had their origins either in the regime parties of the old GDR—as in the case of the PDS and of significant sections of the CDU and the FDP—or in the citizens' movement, as in the case of the SPD and Alliance 90/The Greens. In addition, apart from the PDS all of the eastern parties—and especially those originating in the citizens' movement—had many fewer members relative to their numbers of voters than did the parties in the west, with the consequence that they were often unable to field candidates in local elections. Elements of direct democracy played a larger role in the eastern parties, while the link between the social structure and the party system was less pronounced than in the west. Thus at the Bundestag elections in 1994 (as earlier at the Volkskammer elections on 18 March 1990) more blue-collar workers voted for the CDU than for the SPD, and disproportionally few voted for the PDS.[199] Voters' identification with a party was less deeply rooted, so vote-switching between parties was more common. That said, a trend away from a system of class- and denomination-based parties with large electoral support, membership, and organization, and towards looser, broader-based parties heavily influenced by the media, popular individual politicians, and pressing current issues, has also been visible in the west, if on a lesser scale. These trends are connected to the decline in importance of large political and social organizations, especially the trade unions and the churches.

In the new *Bundesländer* the PDS,[200] which many observers at the end of 1990 had predicted would soon completely collapse, emerged as a third major party, though at the 1994 Bundestag elections it still came some way behind the CDU and SPD. Its survival and growth in the east was due in part to its relatively strong organization, but above all to the fact that it was able to project itself as a party of protest against the influence of the 'Wessis'—the westerners—and as the representative of the particular interests, especially the social interests, of people in the east. It had firm roots at local level, particularly in the big cities. One of its strengths was that it helped people to exercise their rights within the new social protection system, for example in completing applications for pensions, welfare benefits, and housing benefits.

The PDS, however, was unable to build much support in the west at the 1994 Bundestag elections, at subsequent Landtag elections up to 2005, or at the Bundestag elections of 1998 and 2002. Clearly, the party's political stance and leadership, and the social make-up of its members and voters, were too heterogeneous, and the party was too heavily identified as the successor party to the SED, for it to be seen in the west as anything other than a party based on small groups of Communists and left-wing socialists; it failed to win acceptance as a party of social justice and the welfare state. It continued, however, to try to make inroads into political territory where it could compete, from the left, with the SPD—which necessarily had to keep to the middle ground in order to win an electoral majority—and with the Greens. In the Bundestag elections of 18 September 2005 the PDS's successor party, The Left/PDS, in alliance with the Electoral Alternative for Labour and Social Justice (WASG) from the west, and with support from individual trade unionists and former members of the SPD (notably, the former SPD leader Lafontaine), won a *succès d'estime* in the old *Bundesländer*. Subsequently the PDS and WASG merged under the single label 'Die Linke' (The Left). In the 2005 Bundestag elections the party's forerunners won more than 5 per cent of second votes in Berlin and six of the ten old *Bundesländer*. The party has continued to strive hard to establish itself as a fifth party in *Land* politics in the west, and has been successful in this ambition in all *Land* elections in the west, with the exception of Bavaria, from 2007 onwards. It is now represented in all German *Land* parliaments apart from those of Bavaria, Baden-Württemberg, and Rhineland-Palatinate.

In the five new *Bundesländer* the PDS had already transformed the political landscape by 1994. Although the SPD in Brandenburg, and the CDU in Saxony, won absolute majorities at the Landtag elections, not least thanks to the popularity of their Prime Ministers Manfred Stolpe and Kurt Biedenkopf, in the other new *Bundesländer* the PDS held the balance of power. Grand Coalitions between the two major parties, which were formed in Thuringia and Mecklenburg-West Pomerania, were the only realistic alternative to collaboration with the PDS and the ending of that party's political isolation. This latter option—which in practice was available, at least in the short and medium term, only to the Social Democrats—was first followed in 1994 in Saxony-Anhalt, with the formation of a minority government of Social Democrats and Greens with PDS support, and some years later SPD/PDS *Land* governments were formed in Mecklenburg-West Pomerania and Berlin. The Social Democrats thereby strengthened considerably their strategic position *vis-à-vis* the CDU in eastern Germany and thus also in the Federal Republic as a whole.

The new political pattern in the east was also reflected in the make-up of the Bundesrat. After the eight Landtag elections of 1994 the CDU and CSU had only ten votes in the Bundesrat, by virtue of their governments in Saxony and Bavaria. There were no longer any CDU/FDP governing coalitions in the *Länder*. The SPD, on its own and in combination with the Greens (or with the STATT-Party in Hamburg), controlled 34—i.e. half—of the 68 votes in the Bundesrat. In four of the CDU-led governments (in Berlin, Baden-Württemberg, Mecklenburg-West Pomerania, and Thuringia), with 17 Bundesrat votes, the Social Democrats were represented as junior partners. The remaining 7 votes went to governments led by the SPD in coalition either with the FDP alone (in Rhineland-Palatinate) or with the FDP and the Greens (in Bremen).

The political framework of the German federal system, then, placed considerable constraints on the freedom of manoeuvre of the Federal government, and not least with regard to social policy. Even more plainly than in the parliamentary term 1990–4, the choice facing the SPD during the following four years lay between a policy of confrontation, which in practice would be bound to block further projected reforms, and one of cooperation, which would be tantamount to the formation of a quasi-'grand coalition' with regard to all legislation affecting the interests of the *Länder* and hence requiring *Länder* approval. Which path would be taken, however, would depend not only on whether or not the two parties would be able to reach agreement on matters of substance—agreement in which the FDP would likewise have to be involved—but also on considerations of political tactics, as these were weighed both by the government and, especially, by the opposition in the struggle for power. In the event, the SPD adopted a confrontational approach and won the Federal elections of 1998, forming a coalition with the Greens with Gerhard Schröder at its head. The coalition continued after the 2002 Federal elections. In the Federal elections of September 2005, however, it lost its majority when the SPD came second to the CDU/CSU by a margin of four seats, and a Grand Coalition of the CDU, CSU and SPD was formed, with Angela Merkel of the CDU as Federal Chancellor. After the Federal elections of 2009 Merkel remained Chancellor, heading a coalition with the FDP, while the SPD went into opposition.

2

German Unity and Social Policy

The Legal Framework

The injunction to strive for German reunification had been enshrined as a goal of state policy in the preamble to the Basic Law, and had also been indissolubly linked to the right of self-determination under international law. It followed that a decision to reject reunification, if freely taken, would also be accepted as binding. The Federal Constitutional Court held firmly to the reunification doctrine, despite efforts to contest it both by the GDR before 1990 and by significant political forces and currents of public opinion and intellectual discourse within the Federal Republic, which argued that the state should abandon the goal of reunification as a 'sham' and recognize the division of Germany as permanent. The Federal Constitutional Court also declared that the 'constitutional organs of the Federal Republic [were] under an obligation' to work towards the 'restoration of the unity of the state', to 'keep the aspiration for reunification alive within the country, support it unwaveringly outside the country, and refrain from doing anything [that might] prevent reunification'.[1] This obligation included the retention of the principle of unified German citizenship, under which people coming to the Federal Republic from the GDR were entitled to full citizens' rights, including rights of social protection.

Two paths to unification were available: via Article 146, under which a new common constitution could be drawn up, to be confirmed by the people; or via Article 23, allowing accession to the Basic Law. The freely elected representatives of the GDR finally decided to follow the path via Article 23. This avoided the delays and uncertainties that would inevitably have been involved if a new constitution had had to be created and that might, under the circumstances, have endangered the whole project: negotiations about the conditions of entry of the new German state into the European Community would have been necessary, for example. Moreover, drawing up a new constitution would have meant reaching agreement over the composition of a constituent assembly, either on the basis of each state's share of the overall population or according to a principle of parity between the two German states, and there would also have had to be agreement on procedures as well as on content: for example, concerning participation by the *Länder*. Agreement would have been necessary, too, about the method whereby acceptance of the draft constitution would be sought—whether by a referendum of the population of the new state as a whole or by separate referendums in the two existing states. Over and beyond these considerations, however, it is also clear that the decision to proceed via Article 23 reflected the fact that the Basic Law had widespread acceptance not only within the old Federal Republic but also among crucial sections of the new political elites in the GDR.

Under Article 4 of the Unification Treaty, amendments to the Basic Law were confined to a minimum.[2] The call for reunification in the preamble was deleted, as was Article 23, in recognition of the fact that the reunited Germany had acquired its conclusive and definitive borders and was making no claim for recovery of the eastern territories lost in 1945. As already mentioned, the make-up of the Bundesrat was altered. In a new Article 143 the law of the new *Bundesländer* was allowed to differ from the Basic Law, in certain respects, for a transition period extending either till 31 December 1992 or till 31 December 1995, and the ruling out of the restitution of property expropriated under occupation law and occupation sovereignty between 1945 and 1949 was certified as constitutionally safe. The obligations of the GDR and its legal successors were set out in a new paragraph to Article 135a of the Basic Law. Under Article 6 of the Unification Treaty, Article 131 of the Basic Law, on civil service law, was suspended for an indefinite period;[3] this also enabled the new *Bundesländer* to deploy civil servants on a much smaller scale than in the old *Bundesländer* for the performance of public tasks.

The new Article 146 kept the question of the creation of a new constitution open in principle. In practice, however, it was clear that as a consequence of unification there would be only small-scale constitutional changes. The areas in which these might occur were outlined in Article 5 of the Unification Treaty.

Among the terms of the Basic Law underpinning social policy is the 'social state' (*Sozialstaat*) principle (Article 20, paragraph 1 and Article 28, paragraph 1), which is closely linked to the protection of human liberties and human dignity. By guaranteeing the individual a decent minimum living income, the 'social state' principle ensures that the economic conditions of human liberty are fulfilled.[4] The primary way in which the needs of the individual and of the family are to be met is through participation in the economy by means of gainful employment. Assistance for those who through need or frailty are unable, either temporarily or in the long term, to make adequate provision for themselves is to be provided only on a subsidiary basis, by larger bodies founded on the principle of mutual solidarity or, in the last analysis, by the state.

The Basic Law thus gives legislators considerable leeway when translating social goals of state (*Staatsziele*)—the guaranteed minimum income, social protection, and greater equality for the weak—into practical policies. In particular, its statements about the form of economic system that is to serve to realize these goals have deliberately been left open. It was not until the State Treaty of 18 May 1990 between the Federal Republic and the GDR, creating a monetary, economic, and social union, that the principles of the Social Market economy—private property, competition, free determination of prices, and, in principle, the free mobility of labour, capital, goods, and services—were set out as a new common economic order.[5] Nevertheless, what constitutes a just social order remained undefined. After reunification this fact was often a cause of puzzlement, particularly in the new *Bundesländer*. The famous statement by the civil rights campaigner Bärbel Bohley,

'We expected justice and we got the *Rechtsstaat* [a state under the rule of law]', is a clear expression of the view that there is a notion of justice that is recognized by, and can be made binding on, all fair-minded people and that a law-governed welfare state, with its apparatus of institutions, procedures, and norms, is not sufficient as a foundation for the organization of society. People who had grown up within the authoritarian and, to a degree, totalitarian system of the GDR had been instilled with a belief in a just social order—an order that had meanwhile been exposed as profoundly unjust. They perhaps now expected that this 'just' order would come to pass in the new democracy instead.[6] Slowly and reluctantly, however, they had to recognize that in an open, pluralist society there are many competing visions of a just society, no single one of which is acceptable to everyone.

It was no accident, therefore, that there were strenuous efforts on the part of the GDR and the new *Bundesländer* to give more precise definition in the constitution to the social goals of the state and to flesh out the concept of a just social order. These efforts found expression in the draft of a constitution for the GDR that was produced by a working party of the Round Table, (envisaged as the contribution by the GDR's citizens to the discussion and development of a new joint constitution of the unified German state), in the *Land* constitutions of the five new *Bundesländer* in the east, and in attempts to expand the Basic Law by the inclusion of new basic social rights such as the rights to work, housing, and social protection.

In the event, however, unification did not bring about far-reaching changes in the legal framework of social policy. This was, of course, first and foremost a consequence of the decision by both states to proceed to unification, not via Article 146 of the Basic Law and the creation of a new constitution decided on by the people, but via Article 23 and the accession to the Federal Republic of the new GDR *Länder* that had been established in the interim.[7] It was also a consequence of the concomitant decision to wait until the period after unification before examining further amendments or additions to the Basic Law over and beyond those amendments (mentioned above) that were made necessary by accession.

The changes to the legal framework of social policy that took place between 1989/90 and 1994 reflected conflicting tendencies. On the one hand, there was a continuation of the trend, evident since the late 1970s, to reduce the extent to which the state was broadly responsible for promoting people's welfare and 'quality of life', and to place greater emphasis on the importance of other objectives, such as the protection of internal and external security and, especially, the protection of the 'natural foundations of life' (enshrined in Article 20a of the Basic Law in 1994). On the other hand, with the social union between the two states, the extension to the GDR of the social order of the Federal Republic through treaties, legislation, and the establishment of new systems of administration became a key part of unification. In addition, the extent to which society as a whole should undertake responsibility for matters of social protection expanded and became more precisely defined, through the introduction of social care insurance and guaranteed nursery school places and as a result of decisions by the courts, notably the Federal Constitutional Court.

Important areas of Federal German social legislation had been brought together in the Social Statute Book (*Sozialgesetzbuch*) from the 1970s onwards. At the time of German unification, however, work on codifying the law on social policy was still unfinished. Although the 'general parts' of the code had been completed, in Books I (1975), IV (1976), and X (1980, 1982), by 1990 the only 'particular parts' that had been systematically compiled were Book V, dealing with health insurance law (following the Health Service Reform Law of 1988), Book VI on pensions insurance law (following the pensions reform of late 1989), and Book VIII on the law governing services for children and young people (following a law of June 1990). Nevertheless, despite the gaps in the project, and its huge size, many sub-divisions, and complexity, the fact that the Social Statute Book existed was a significant asset during the process of unification. This is apparent, especially, if we compare the position as regards employment law. Although the codification of employment law had also been planned and some preliminary work on it had been done, the scheme had ultimately fallen victim to opposition from the interest groups involved, employers and trade unions alike. Furthermore, Federal German employment law is not only enshrined in a range of different pieces of legislation, but is in many respects determined by judicial decisions. Whereas the GDR's Labour Statute Book (*Arbeitsgesetzbuch*) of 1977 had been an integrated codification of both employment and social legislation, citizens' access to the employment law of the Federal Republic was an extremely complicated business. Many in the former GDR found this difficult to understand and saw it as a denial of legal rights.[8] In addition, the stipulation in Article 30, paragraph 1 of the Unification Treaty that there would a 'new integrated codification' of employment contract law, of the public law on working hours, and of legislation protecting women workers, together with an 'up-to-date revision' of health and safety legislation generally,[9] was only partly met and was insufficient to make up for the lack of a full codification of employment law, which would have included, for example, the law governing industrial disputes.

The Federal Republic's social legislation, which was extended to the new *Bundesländer* by the Unification Treaty, was similarly far more complex than the corresponding legislation of the GDR. The GDR's pensions law, for example, contained roughly 120 paragraphs, whereas Book VI of the Social Statute Book, dealing with pensions insurance law, runs to about 320 paragraphs. On the other hand, in the GDR many of the relevant regulations that had the force of law were contained in executive provisions and decrees, a system that not only was irreconcilable with the Federal Republic's principles of legality but made access to the law difficult for the citizen since a whole range of different legal sources had to be taken into account.[10]

The Unification Treaty and, especially, the Pensions Transition Law of 25 July 1991[11] involved significant changes to the law on social benefits, but there was no explicit general clarification of the extent to which these new regulations affected the Social Statute Book.[12]

At first, the process of unification fully preoccupied everyone involved in politics, administration, and the drafting of legislation, so that further work on the Social

Statute Book came to a halt. Further progress, however, was made during the parliamentary term 1990–4, with the creation of the new social care insurance system, the regulations governing which were laid down in Book XI of the Social Statute Book.

2.1 THE END OF THE SOCIALIST CONSTITUTION OF THE GDR

After the Berlin Wall came down and the process of internal reforms began, there were in theory a number of different possible ways in which the GDR could make a constitutional transition from a socialist dictatorship based on the SED's monopoly of power to a democracy based on freedom and the rule of law. The speediest route was immediate accession to the Federal Republic and the adoption of the Basic Law as the new constitutional order. At first, however, the external political preconditions for this option were lacking: they did not come about until the Two-Plus-Four talks had reached a successful conclusion and the conversations between the Federal Republic and the Soviet Union had taken place. Moreover, if this course had been taken, the GDR and its citizens, whose own interests were subsequently brought to bear in the State Treaty of 18 May 1990 and the Unification Treaty of 31 August 1990, would have been mere passive spectators of the unification process and mere objects of Federal Republic legislation. A second route would have been to reinstate the 1949 constitution of the GDR, which was partly based on the Weimar constitution of 1919 and which, though in practice it had been ignored by the SED, did provide for a federal system of parliamentary democracy and the rule of law. This option, however, would have entailed making important modifications to the GDR's existing political and legal institutions—for example, through the creation of a chamber of the *Länder*—and, although a few such proposals were put forward,[13] they were not pursued with any vigour. A third route was to create a new GDR constitution, and the Round Table began work on this task immediately after its inaugural meeting on 7 December 1989. There were a number of ways in which such a constitution might be envisaged: as a fundamental settlement for a democratic GDR that would be independent in the long term, as a settlement forming the basis for a relatively lengthy transition period, culminating in unification, or as an essential element in a new constitutional settlement, in accordance with Article 146 of the Basic Law, that would cover the united Federal Republic as a whole. In all such cases, however, a crucial problem remained: how could the reforms of the state, the economy, and society that were necessary for the transition to democracy, a market economy, and the rule of law be implemented on a constitutional basis before the process of drawing up this GDR constitution and confirming it in a referendum had been completed?

The Modrow and de Maizière governments and the GDR Volkskammer opted for a fourth route: namely, to change the existing GDR constitution of 1968/74, through individual amendments and then by a Law on Constitutional Principles. The period of the Modrow government already saw some first constitutional amendments, which ended the SED's monopoly of leadership, made it possible to introduce private ownership into areas of the economy where previously only 'property of the people' had been allowed, and established the constitutional preconditions for free elections.[14] In addition, laws were passed protecting freedom of assembly, opinion, information, and the media, which did not entail amendments to the wording of the constitution but were in clear contradiction of previous GDR practice.[15]

The next decisions regarding constitutional matters were taken when the de Maizière government was formed after the Volkskammer elections of 18 March 1990. The 'New Constitution' working party, set up by the Round Table, had been unable to complete its work on the constitution by the time of the Round Table's final meeting on 12 March 1990. As well as the document entitled 'Viewpoints for a new constitution', 'materials' produced by four sub-groups had been submitted to the Round Table that still had to be completed, revised, and consolidated into a single overall draft.[16] The Round Table decided—with opposition from the CDU, SPD, and DA (the LDP abstaining)—that the 'New Constitution' working party should produce a final document from those parts of the draft that had been submitted and those that were still incomplete, and should make the document available for public discussion; the working party should also take part in the business of the constitutional committee of the Volkskammer. The Volkskammer, it said, should announce a referendum on the GDR constitution for 17 June 1990, as well as a law establishing *Länder*, and the Round Table working party's draft constitution should be included in the debate about the creation of a new German constitution in accordance with Article 146 of the Basic Law.[17]

The draft constitution was approved by the working party on 4 April and submitted to the Volkskammer.[18] It was referred to in the coalition agreement of 12 April 1990, which stated that the coalition, 'with regard to the further development of the constitution, supports transitional arrangements . . . that take into account both the constitution of 1949 and the draft constitution of the Round Table'.[19] The programme announced by the de Maizière government on 19 April 1990 did not refer to constitutional questions. The working party's draft constitution, however, was proposed separately by Gerd Poppe of Alliance 90/The Greens (a minister in Modrow's previous 'government of national responsibility' and the most important advocate on behalf of the 'New Constitution' working party), and was discussed in a question-time period.[20] Here it became clear that the constitution was opposed by the CDU, DSU, and DA—which believed it would impede rapid progress towards German unity—that the liberals had reservations, and that the Social Democrats wanted to take issue with the draft.[21] Finally, on 26 April a majority in the Volkskammer rejected the motion by the Alliance 90/Green members that the draft should be proposed as a new constitution for the GDR and put to a referendum; even an attempt to refer the draft to the relevant committees for further discussion was defeated by 179 votes to 167, with four abstentions. A draft constitution produced by a commission convened by de Maizière's GDR Justice Minister Kurt Wünsche also came to nothing: it was not debated in the parliament, and remained unpublished.[22]

The remaining key changes that were made to the GDR constitution were based, primarily, on the Law on Constitutional Principles, which, after contentious debates, was passed on 17 June 1990 by the two-thirds majority required for constitutional amendments.[23] In it the GDR declared itself to be a state governed by the rule of law, dedicated to freedom, democracy, federalism, social welfare, and ecological responsibility. These 'principles' provided guarantees of private property, free economic activity, free collective wage bargaining, access to legal redress in the event of infringements of the law by public authorities, and the independent administration of justice. The law, which was to remain valid until a Basic Law had been enacted, also stated that any constitutional principles that conflicted with it were henceforth invalid and that both the old GDR constitution and the entire GDR legal apparatus were to be interpreted and applied in accordance with it. A particularly important stipulation was that in contradistinction from previous arrangements, the constitution could also be amended by 'constitutional laws' passed by a two-thirds majority, without the need for express amendment of the text of the constitution itself.[24] Among constitutional laws later passed in this way, the Law Establishing *Länder* of 22 July 1990,[25] which paved the way to the creation of the new *Länder* of Mecklenburg-West Pomerania, Brandenburg, Saxony-Anhalt, Saxony, and Thuringia, was especially important.

2.2 THE DEBATE OVER THE ENSHRINING OF BASIC SOCIAL RIGHTS IN THE CONSTITUTION

The Law on Constitutional Principles, by enshrining the protection of the natural environment and the protection of labour as tasks of the state, went further than the Basic Law of the old Federal Republic. In particular, Article 7, which laid down that the state should protect the workforce, foster the individual's right to 'lead, through work, a life of human dignity in social justice and economic freedom', and 'create the necessary conditions for these', was an attempt to carry over into the new dispensation the basic social rights that had been contained in the GDR constitution—in particular, the 'right to work' that was highly valued by the GDR population.[26]

The draft constitution prepared by the Round Table working party differed from the Basic Law by being more a constitution for a society than one simply for a state. In addition to its pacifist and ecological features and its calls for grass-roots democracy and referendums, it gave particular prominence to social objectives. These included an obligation by the state to work towards ensuring equal rights for women; state financing and support for nursery schools and crèches; citizens' rights to adequate housing; the rights to work and to the promotion of employment; and greatly strengthened protection against dismissal for the disabled, pregnant women, and single parents. In some respects, such as the restriction on levels of compensation to owners in the event of nationalization of productive assets, and the prohibition of private ownership of agricultural enterprises larger than 100 hectares, the constitution also reflected socialist ideas.[27] The 'social achievements' of the GDR, which had of course been closely linked to the economic system based on planning, were thus to be preserved in the new democracy. In a similar way, the coalition agreement of 12 April 1990 declared that in the event that no new GDR constitution were to materialize, 'social security rights', including in particular the 'rights to work, housing and education', should be included in an amended Basic Law, albeit not as legally enforceable individual rights but as stipulated goals of state.[28]

These aspirations, which were supported by the west German Social Democrats, found their way, in part, into Article 5 of the Unification Treaty. This article also referred to possible future constitutional changes which 'the legislative bodies of the united Germany' would address, on the basis of the recommendations of the governments of the Federal Republic and the GDR, and listed some rather vague 'reflections concerning the inclusion of goals of state in the Basic Law'.[29] However, despite intensive discussions in a Joint Constitutional Commission of the Bundesrat and Bundestag,[30] the two-thirds majorities that would have been necessary for the adoption of rights to work, housing, and social security were not achieved. On the other hand, some new principles were added to the Basic Law by means of constitutional amendments passed on 27 October 1994. These included the establishment as a goal of state of 'protection of the natural foundations of life within the framework of the constitutional order' (Article 20a), a ban on discrimination on the basis of 'disability' (Article 3, paragraph 3, clause 2),[31] and the requirement that the state promote the 'actual realization of equality of rights between women and men' and work towards 'the removal of existing disadvantages' (Article 3, paragraph 2, clause 2).[32] In addition to the adoption of some new basic rights, an 'asylum compromise' between the CDU/CSU and the SPD paved the way for a constitutional change passed on 28 June 1993 that introduced significant restrictions on the right to political asylum, in order to reduce the sharply rising number of asylum seekers.[33] The unwillingness to incorporate into the Basic Law certain ambitious social goals which, though desirable, could not be guaranteed by the state was due in part to a fear that proclaiming them would arouse expectations among the population that could not be fulfilled. It was felt that the basic rights enshrined in the Basic Law would lose their unconditional legal validity—which they possessed in the Federal Republic—and would become mere 'constitutional poetry', as had happened with the extensive catalogue of rights in the Weimar constitution, which in practice had been unenforceable.

By contrast, social rights assumed a prominent role in the constitutions of the new *Bundesländer*.[34] In these constitutions a clear distinction was not always drawn between programmatic goals of state, which did not allow the individual to make any unconditional legal claims, and basic rights enforceable through the courts.[35] In the constitution of Brandenburg, for example, the *Land* is obliged, 'to the extent that its powers permit, to ensure the realization of the right to work through a policy of full employment and job creation' (Article 48, paragraph 1). The *Land* is also tasked with ensuring, 'to the extent that its powers permit, the realization of the right to adequate housing, in particular through the promotion of housing ownership, through measures of social housing construction, and through rent control and rent subsidies' (Article 47, paragraph 1). The constitution of Saxony-Anhalt states that the *Land* shall 'strive, to the extent that its competence allows, to ensure that meaningful and permanent work is created for all' (Article 39, paragraph 2). In addition, the *Land* and the local authorities shall 'ensure the provision for all, under appropriate circumstances, of adequate living accommodation fit for human habitation, through support for housing construction, the maintenance of existing housing, and other suitable measures' (Article 40, paragraph 1). The constitution of Mecklenburg-West Pomerania declares that the *Land* shall contribute to 'the creation and maintenance of jobs'. It shall ensure, 'to the extent that general economic equilibrium allows, a high level of employment' and shall work with district and local authorities to ensure that 'appropriate housing meeting socially acceptable standards is available to each individual' (Article 17, paragraphs 1 and 3). According to the constitution of Thuringia it is the 'constant task of the Free State to create the opportunity for each individual to earn his living through freely chosen and permanent work' (Article 36), and to ensure that a 'sufficient quantity of suitable housing is available' (Article 15). According to the constitution of Saxony the *Land* recognizes, as 'a goal of state, the right of each person to a life of human dignity, in particular the right to work, to adequate housing, to an adequate living, to social security, and to education' (Article 7, paragraph 1).

However, the rights to work and to housing, although unambiguously enshrined in the separate constitutions of the east German *Länder*, have failed to gain recognition as subjective individual rights enforceable under the law.[36] Likewise, the obligations placed on the legislatures and governments of the *Länder* to ensure a high level of employment and adequate housing have been of only limited significance, as they are not binding on those to whom they were really addressed, namely the legislatures of the Federal Republic and the Federal government.

2.3 SOCIAL POLICY AND PROBLEMS ARISING FROM UNITY: DECISIONS BY THE FEDERAL CONSTITUTIONAL COURT AND THE EMPLOYMENT AND SOCIAL COURTS

By contrast, the interpretations of basic rights that resulted from the judgements on social law by the Federal Constitutional Court, and the concrete obligations that these judgements imposed on legislators, were of great significance for Federal Republic social policy.[37] For example, decisions by the Federal Constitutional Court on 28 February 1980 and 1 July 1981[38] had laid down that the guarantee on property in Article 14 of the Basic Law also extended to the pensions of the insured and to expectancies from statutory pensions insurance. These judgements, however, did not amount to a constitutional guarantee that the existing pensions system would continue in its current form: rather, according to a judgement by the Federal Constitutional Court of 28 April 1999, the system can be 'placed on a different basis by legislation'.[39] In practice, though, the scope for change via legislation is constrained by the fact that acquired rights have to be taken into account and that long transition periods have to be provided before new regulations can come into effect. Both the social courts and the Federal Constitutional Court have paid considerable attention to the terms in the State Treaty, the Unification Treaty, and the Pensions Transition Law of 1991 dealing with the conversion of the GDR's existing systems of supplementary and special provision for particular groups into the Federal Republic system of statutory pensions insurance, and (as required by those documents) have closely reviewed the questions of 'unwarranted' and 'excessive' payments; various of their decisions have led to amendments of the Pensions Transition Law. The long-drawn-out arguments that have ensued over these decisions, which have been viewed, by those adversely affected, as 'criminal law on pensions', cannot be discussed in detail here.[40] In four judgements on 28 April 1999[41] the Federal Constitutional Court finally approved the fundamental decision that the GDR supplementary and special provision systems for particular groups should be converted into the statutory pensions insurance system, and that payments and entitlements should accordingly be limited on the basis of the contributions ceiling. (In the German statutory social insurance system, contributions, as a percentage of wages and salaries, are paid only up to a certain ceiling, or *Beitragsbemessungsgrenze*, higher for pensions insurance than for health insurance. People with a high income from wages or salaries thus pay only a limited contribution, but also receive a limited pension.) The Court also made clear, however, that the expectancies acquired under these supplementary and special provision systems were subject to the protection of the guarantee on property, that the existing restriction of payments to a maximum of 2,700 marks per month should be lifted, and that pensions entitlements already in existence on 3 October 1990 should be indexed to earnings. For many of those concerned[42]—including most of the GDR academics who had already been entitled to pensions at the time of unification—this meant a significant increase in their pensions, although these remained well below those of comparable people in the west, who were receiving civil-service pensions under different systems of old-age insurance.

A judgement of the Federal Constitutional Court of 24 April 1991 was directly connected with reunification. The Court ruled that the provision in the Unification Treaty that employment relationships of employees in public facilities that were being wound up could be terminated was compatible in principle with the Basic Law. The Court complained, however, that dismissal regulations under the law protecting expectant and nursing mothers had been breached, and demanded that the 'special position of the severely disabled, of older employees, of single parents, and of others similarly affected' should be taken into consideration 'in the filling of posts in the public services'.[43]

There were many other areas in which the Federal Constitutional Court expressed its view on problems that arose from unification. During the period between September 1990 and May 1994 alone, it made 63 judgements and decisions on internal constitutional questions.[44] These included judgements on matters affecting the justice system, such as the admission of GDR judges into the judicial service and the possible revocation of the right of GDR jurists to work as lawyers within the legal system. In the criminal law the general ban on retrospective legislation was lifted in cases of extremely serious criminal acts (for example, those committed by border guards and their superiors) which, though not subject to prosecution under GDR law, were punishable as contraventions of generally recognized human rights. On the other hand, the Court ruled that crimes of espionage committed by the GDR against the Federal Republic should not be prosecuted under the criminal law. It also took the important decision to confirm the decision made at unification that no reversal of the expropriations that had been carried out by the occupying Soviet power between 1945 and 1949 was possible in practice.[45] Repeatedly, in its judgements on problems arising from unification, the Court had recourse to the formulae 'the unique historical nature of the tasks needing to be dealt with' and 'the unique legal situation'.[46]

Already back in 1980 the Federal Constitutional Court had criticized discrepancies in the ways in which retirement pension incomes were taxed, and had called for changes. Legislation had not followed, however, and a second complaint in 1992 likewise had no immediate effect. Not until the new millennium did reform take place.[47] A key factor affecting the practice of early retirement at the age of 60 after preceding unemployment was a judgement by the Federal Constitutional Court of 23 January 1990[48] on §128 of the Employment Promotion Law, laying down the conditions governing the obligations of employers to reimburse the pensions insurance and unemployment insurance systems in the case of the early retirement of older employees. Although the Court upheld the principle that unemployment benefits should be reimbursed, it also ruled that it was a violation of the Basic Law (Article 12, paragraph 1) to require such reimbursement if an employee met the conditions for other social benefits—for instance, from health, accident, or pensions insurance—that caused a claim to unemployment benefit and/or unemployment assistance to be suspended or lapse either wholly or in part. Furthermore, reimbursement, and with it the placing of the onus of the social consequences of unemployment on to the employer, was not justified if the latter had no specific responsibility for the onset of unemployment. Hence there was, as a rule, a significant ground for dismissal without notice, and thus no obligation to reimburse, if the employee was no longer able, on grounds of health, to perform in the long term the work that he had contractually undertaken. This judgement amounted to such a comprehensive undermining of the principle of the reimbursement obligation that §128 was repealed.[49] In a law of 18 December 1992 amending the Employment Promotion Law and other legislation[50] the obligation by employers to reimburse unemployment benefit in the case of early retirement by older employees was reintroduced in principle. The law also stated that severance payments made in cases of employees giving up work without good reason could be partly set against unemployment benefit. However, the new law was hedged around with so many exceptions—for instance, small businesses with no more than 20 employees were excluded—that it was an ineffective tool for stemming the tide of early retirements and reducing the burden that these were placing on the social insurance system.

A decision by the Federal Constitutional Court that had explosive political consequences was that of 4 July 1995,[51] on the constitutionality of Article 116, paragraph 3 of the Employment Promotion Law, which had come into force on 15 May 1986 after bitter arguments both inside and outside parliament. The new judgement laid down that a claim to unemployment benefit lapsed if an employee who had been made unemployed as the result of a labour dispute had last been employed by a business which fell within the scope of the disputed collective agreement by virtue of its spatial or substantive sphere of operation, or, where that was not the case, if he had an interest in the outcome of the dispute in (approximately) the same way as the striking employees.[52] This widening of the full risk of loss of earnings to include employees indirectly affected by a labour dispute undermined the trade unions' tactic of concentrating on strikes at key individual firms and thereby limiting the costs they incurred by taking industrial action. The trade unions saw the new ruling as a threat to their ability to conduct disputes and thus to the principle of free collective bargaining. The Court, however, rejected a claim by the Metal Workers' Union that the ruling was unconstitutional and also denied applications for judicial review made by various SPD-governed *Länder*. The new ruling, it declared, posed no threat (for the present) to the rough parity in strength between unions and employers' organizations or to free collective bargaining. The key significance of the judgement was that it seemed to place upon the state the responsibility for ensuring structural balance between the two sides of industry and hence implied that if one side became more powerful than the other, then the state would be obliged to take counter-measures, either through legislation or through the courts.[53]

The effects of decisions by the Federal Constitutional Court with regard to financial support for families, based on Article 6, paragraph 1 of the Basic Law dealing with the special protection of marriage and the family, were particularly wide-ranging. In a judgement of 29 May 1990[54] the Court held that 'when a family is taxed, the minimum living income of all of the family members must remain free of tax'.[55] This underlined the duty of the state to take account of people's reduced ability to pay tax as a result of bringing up children. In addition, in a judgement of 7 July 1992 the Court issued statements of principle on inadequacies in family support in the Federal Republic and called in particular for a reform of pensions insurance, since parents were now at a serious disadvantage.[56] As possible means whereby support for families might be built into old-age insurance it mentioned extending the existing allowance made under pensions law for the time involved in bringing up children, and, in the case of widows' and widowers' pensions, taking into account the duration of marriage and the provision of care within the family by the surviving partner. 'The protection of pension expectancies under §14, paragraph 1 of the Basic Law does not preclude a moderate degree of redistribution within the statutory pensions insurance system, payable by those without children or with few children.... At any rate, irrespective of the means whereby the adjustment is made, there needs to be a guarantee that any such reform in fact serves to lessen discrimination against the family. Legislators charged with this constitutional task must be seen to take account of this requirement.'[57] In its calls for improvements in support for families, which became increasingly vocal, the Federal Constitutional Court was openly pointing up the implications of its view that policy-making in this area had been a failure, and that in the light of the demographic changes of the preceding decades there would be a crisis in the economy and society, and in particular in the social security system, if fundamental reforms were not carried through.

Consistently with its decisions on family support, rulings of the Federal Constitutional Court on 10 November 1998[58] laid down that child benefit should correspond at the minimum to the sum arising as tax relief at the top rate of income tax on the basis of tax exemption for minimum living income for a child. In addition, the costs of child care up to a certain level above the minimum should be deductible from taxable income for all parents. The Court's rulings on family support were typified by the close linkage it made between income tax law, social protection law, and pensions law. The spectacular judgements issued by the Court in this area in the 1990s coincided with a rapidly growing awareness of the economic and social problems that were arising as a result of the ageing of the population, and also of the mounting significance that family policy had been assuming in elections during this period. Despite the general effort to stem the growth of public spending, these trends were generating a considerable increase in state benefits, including tax concessions, for families with children—a rise between 1992 and 1999 of about 30 per cent, from 224 to 292 thousand million DM. This represented an increase from 7.1 per cent of gross national product to 7.6 per cent.[59]

Of course, the legal framework for social policy was also shaped in important ways by decisions of the employment courts—which deal with wide areas of employment law not regulated either by the constitution or by legislation (such as the law on industrial disputes)—and the social courts. In particular, the Federal Social Court played a key role in amending the original regulations dealing with the conversion of the GDR systems of supplementary and special provision for particular groups into statutory pensions insurance, mainly prior to the decisions of the Federal Constitutional Court of 28 April 1999 mentioned above.[60] The judgement of the Federal Social Court of 29 January 1998 was also of great importance. It had been alleged that the substantial contribution made by the insured in the west to the financing of pensions in the east was unconstitutional, on the grounds that benefits unrelated to insurance—such as the establishment of German unity—had been conferred. The Court rejected this complaint.[61]

2.4 THE EUROPEAN DIMENSION OF SOCIAL POLICY, AND JUDGEMENTS BY THE EUROPEAN COURT OF JUSTICE

The European Community and decisions of the European Court of Justice came to have an increasingly important bearing on the social policy of the Federal Republic. Although the original treaty establishing the European Economic Community—the most important precursor of the European Union—had already expressly included among its objectives the 'improvement of the living and working conditions of labour' and 'raising the standard of living', and had specified the creation of a European Social Fund to further these aims,[62] European social policy at first concentrated mainly on establishing the principle that domestic social protection regulations should apply to workers who wished to exercise the basic right of free mobility of labour and move from one country of the community to another in search of work.[63] Until now there has been no attempt to go further by harmonizing European social protection and employment law, owing to the considerable differences that exist in the economic capacity of the member states and in the national systems of social security that have been built up over the years. At the same time, however, there has been growing coordination of legislation on social policy, and there have been attempts to reduce welfare discrepancies by the use of structural funds and—for instance, in the area of labour market policy—to encourage a degree of convergence through the adoption of common procedures for dealing with similar problems.[64] Most importantly, the Single European Act of 1986–7, the 'Community Charter of Fundamental Social Rights of Workers' of 1989, the Maastricht treaty of 1992–3, which created the European Union as a legal entity, and the Amsterdam treaty of 1997 expanded considerably the ability of the European Community (and later Union) to play an active role in social policy. The Maastricht treaty was a confirmation of the German position, which sought to establish a community-wide set of binding minimum standards as a goal of European social policy.[65] At present these standards apply, in particular, to the area of health and safety protection and to the issues of equality of opportunity between men and women in the labour market and equal treatment in the workplace.

The development of common standards within European social-policy law was driven forward by the European Court of Justice, which applied itself particularly to combating discrimination against women and proscribed discrepancies in social entitlements on the basis of an individual's nationality.[66] The court's ruling on the export of social benefits, which was criticized by many as entailing excessive costs, was also path-breaking.[67] According to this ruling, financial benefits from contributory systems of social security—including the continued payment of wages in the event of sickness—were exportable to other countries, with the exception of unemployment benefit. (In the latter case, employees wishing to claim benefit had to be available for work in the labour market of the last state in which they were employed.[68]) This was one of the reasons why the German Minister of Labour Blüm was opposed to pensions-based minimum protection against poverty based on a few years of contributions to pensions insurance.[69] In the meantime, as a consequence of the free movement of goods and services within the European Single Market, foreign suppliers have been able to provide social benefits, such as health services, inside Germany, while social insurance benefits in kind—such as dental treatment, purchase of spectacles, and nursing care—may be claimed abroad in addition to services occasioned by acute illness. The free movement of workers within the European Union has become the free movement of citizens. According to a more recent judgement by the European Court of Justice, even the migration of European Union citizens from the income support system of one country to that of another may become permissible in future.[70]

Although German policy-makers were critical of what they saw as the unjustifiable extension of the powers of the European Union in the wake of the European

Court of Justice's decisions on the export of social benefits, they supported the extension of the right to co-determination on the part of employees, and after long negotiations succeeded in establishing the principle that European works councils could be set up in multinational enterprises.

There has, then, been a significant broadening of the European dimension of social policy as a result of the extension of the powers of the European Community and the decisions of the European Court of Justice, while the role of national social policy has been correspondingly narrowed. There are many indications that this process will continue. Nevertheless, social policy, unlike economic and financial policy, remains firmly within the competence of the individual member states of the European Union. A 'European welfare state' is still very unlikely to come into being, nor would it be desirable unless it had much stronger democratic foundations. These, however, will probably not be laid until such time as a 'political union' is created.[71]

3

The German Economy and the Process of Unification

3.1 CHANGES IN THE ECONOMIC SYSTEM AND IN THE LEGISLATION AND INSTITUTIONS GOVERNING SOCIAL POLICY

The foundations of the Federal Republic's economic system and of the legislation and institutions governing social policy—the Social Market economy, and 'social partnership' between the management and unions—remained essentially unchanged after 1989. With unification, these principles were extended to the territory of the former German Democratic Republic. As we have seen, the State Treaty of 18 May 1990 provided a definition of the Social Market economy and declared that its essential elements included a system of employment law based on freedom of association, free collective bargaining, co-determination, and protection against unfair dismissal, and a universal system of social security.[1] Free trade unions and employers' associations were set up in the new *Bundesländer*, independent welfare associations and economic and social-policy interest groups were created, and systems of administration of economic and social affairs were established to implement economic and social policies. For many observers, the fact that the norms, institutions, actors, and benefits of the Social Market economy and the west German welfare state were so swiftly and successfully extended to the former GDR was proof of the vitality and efficiency of the Federal Republic system.

There were also growing numbers of pessimistic voices, however. The collapse of large sections of east German industry, and the rapid rise in unemployment in both parts of Germany from the autumn of 1992 onwards, were seen as grounds for querying the 'German model'.[2] The latter may be taken to mean the transformation, through consent, of an industrial society into a modern information- and service-based society in which the state and the two sides of industry work closely together and the social costs of the transformation are borne by generous social benefits. For some critics, this model needed to be radically re-thought.

Unification had led to a shift in the balance of the German economy. The role of the state had increased significantly. The state not only was responsible for building up the infrastructure of the old GDR, which had been completely neglected, but was playing a vital part in the transformation of the GDR economy through the *Treuhandanstalt*, which was both 'an auction house and a ministry of industry'.[3]

Political priorities oscillated between rapid privatization, with the modernization of enterprises that were thought to be viable in the medium term, and the attempt to preserve on a long-term basis particular key concerns in the traditional industrial centres of eastern Germany and thereby prevent entire regions from falling victim to economic devastation. The active labour market policy of the Federal Institute of Labour was strengthened to a degree that would previously have been almost unthinkable, and its character was transformed by the creation of new policy instruments. The expanded role of the state was symbolized, above all, by the huge transfer payments that were made to the east and by a dramatic increase in the level of public debt, although the debt in turn placed constraints on the state's very ability to act.

There were also important changes in the system of labour relations. Free trade unions and employers' associations were quickly set up in the east and wage settlements concluded, although problems were caused by the fact that these new bodies were overwhelmingly dominated by west German organizations and officials. A proposal that was rejected was the creation of a low-wage region in the east. Like all economic special areas, a low-wage region would have given rise to numerous problems. It would have necessitated wide-ranging controls in order to prevent abuses, and massive limitations on collective bargaining. Although such a region might have been in the interests of east German enterprises,[4] it would have put west German businesses under greater competitive pressure and might also have caused greater numbers of skilled workers to move from the east to the west.

Taxpayers and contributors to social insurance were additional, invisible participants in wage negotiations.[5] The state had to help out either directly, by financing redundancy schemes for workers laid off by *Treuhand* enterprises and providing subsidies to the Federal Institute of Labour, or indirectly, through losses of tax revenue and the provision of income support (*Sozialhilfe*) and housing benefit. Insurance contributors had to cover the cost of early retirement schemes and the rationalization (i.e. elimination) of jobs consequent on excessive pay settlements, by making higher contributions for unemployment and pensions insurance. The effect on the industrial relations system was an erosion of the influence of union and management organizations, particularly of the employers' associations, and growing non-adherence to negotiated collective agreements.[6] Regional collective agreements covering whole sections of industry, which had been typical of the German system, were now increasingly replaced or supplemented by agreements confined to individual firms. The new watchwords were greater flexibility and deregulation, as private recruitment agencies, for example, were allowed to operate alongside the Federal Institute of Labour.

A fundamental question was also being asked, however. Was it right to extend the west German model of a Social Market economy—based on high wages, high productivity, stable industrial relations at both regional and enterprise level, and high social benefits—to the ailing east German economy, which was poorly equipped to cope with the conditions prevailing in the world economy, suffered from far lower productivity, and was in the throes of a process of transformation?[7] Were the Federal Republic's rigid regulations in employment law, the elaborate rules on environmental protection, and the high taxes—admittedly partly offset by the numerous deductions that were available to encourage economic activity—not bound to put a brake on the transformation process and make the crisis in the east German economy even more acute? Yet what was the alternative? If the extension of Federal Republic law to the east had taken place in a slower, step-by-step fashion, a wealth of transitional arrangements would have been necessary, and as soon as one exception had been granted, another would have had to follow. The resultant lack of legal clarity would also have made investment more difficult. This was certainly the case with questions to do with property, where many issues remained unresolved.

Basic questions were also being asked about the paramount role of social insurance within the German social security system and about its structure and financing. The relative importance of social insurance continued to grow in the early 1990s. In addition to the introduction of social care insurance as a fifth pillar of the insurance system, and the large-scale financing of early retirement to relieve the pressure on the labour market, social insurance was being required to bear a considerable share of the cost of German unification by providing social protection during the transformation process through pensions and unemployment insurance.[8] At the same time, however, the social foundations of the insurance system, which was reliant primarily on long-term full employment on the part of the workers dependent upon it, had become increasingly fragile as a result of changes in the world of work.[9] There were mounting worries that the 'social insurance state' had become over-burdened and that the rise in social insurance contributions, which was forcing up labour costs, might be one of the causes of the low number of jobs and the high level of unemployment.

The economic system and the legislation and institutions governing social policy, then, were undergoing conflicting pressures. On the one hand, the Social Market economy was being extended to the new *Bundesländer*; on the other hand, it was also being increasingly called into question as an effective instrument for dealing with economic change. State intervention was on the rise, in particular in order to guide the process of transformation in eastern Germany; at the same time, however, market forces were being strengthened, for example through the privatization of state enterprises. The process of work procurement was being liberalized, and employment law was being changed by deregulation. The west German system of industrial relations was being introduced in the new *Bundesländer*; and yet the system was becoming less efficient, as people tried to find new ways of resolving conflicts of interest and to develop a wage policy consistent with economic imperatives. The scale and tasks of social insurance were being expanded, on the basis of its traditional institutions and principles; but there were also considerable efforts to limit the size of the social insurance state, to make its financing less dependent on gainful employment, and to encourage individuals to make provision for themselves.

In the old Federal Republic there was a continuity of existing norms, institutions, and economic and social actors, though they were coming under challenge. In the new *Bundesländer*, on the other hand, the arrival of the western system meant extreme discontinuity—a complete break with the economic and social conditions of the past. The wrong turnings that were taken, the new burdens that were assumed, and people's differing responses to these changes all left their imprint on the new, common state that had been created. At the same time, the new state was facing changes in the demographic structure, in the world of work, in the European Union, and in the world economy. This combination of factors posed problems of an unprecedented kind.

3.2 THE EUROPEANIZATION OF ECONOMIC AND FINANCIAL POLICY, AND THE EFFECTS OF GROWING GLOBALIZATION

West European societies in the late twentieth century had certain common features that distinguished them from, for example, the United States, Japan, the former Soviet Union, and countries of the Third World.[10] These included the relatively large role of industry within the structure of employment, and a less pronounced gap between rich and poor. West European countries also possessed highly developed welfare states, in which, despite specific national differences, working conditions were more strongly regulated by employment law and in which the public systems of social security, longer established, accounted for a significantly higher share of gross domestic product.[11] Moreover, as we have seen,[12] the social policies of the member states of the European Community were becoming increasingly closely coordinated. Admittedly, the principal role in shaping social policy remained in the hands of the individual nation state. However, more significant than any concrete interventions made into German social policy by the institutions and norms of the European Community were, first, the growing removal of economic and financial policy from the separate jurisdictions of the nations of Europe, particularly after the creation of the European Single Market and the establishment of monetary union in many of the states, including Germany; and, secondly, changes in the economic framework resulting from the Europeanization of markets, including labour markets, which were placing constraints on the scope of each nation's social policy.

More significant still, as far as changes in the framework surrounding national social policy are concerned, was the process of globalization, the management of which has so far remained beyond the effective reach of institutions and regulations. Of course, international competition is nothing new, particularly in goods markets. The decades immediately after the Second World War were characterized by the expansion of free trade. This process went hand in hand with a huge extension of the welfare state, a trend that continued until the economic crisis of 1973–4. Programmes to stabilize incomes by means of social benefits eased the move away from economic protectionism and lessened people's resistance to the transformation of economic structures.[13]

During the 1980s there were powerful counter-movements to this civilizing of capitalist economics through a strongly welfarist social market economy. The governments of Ronald Reagan in the United States and Margaret Thatcher in the United Kingdom led the way, inscribing a pure form of market economics on their banner.[14] In particular, they favoured greater flexibility in labour markets, which they sought to achieve by restraining trade unions, deregulating working conditions, and reducing the levels of social benefits.

These attempts to scale back the welfare state and give freer rein to market forces, as an alternative to resolving economic and social conflicts of interest through forms of social partnership between the two sides of industry, have to be seen against the backdrop of the changes that were happening in the world economy.[15] There were fears that the taxation of capital receipts or the lowering of interest rates by national central banks in order to encourage employment might drive away mobile international capital. Barriers to free international exchange on goods markets were being removed. Labour costs, and hence the welfare state, were coming under pressure as a result both of the increasing Europeanization of the labour market and of the influx of workers from low-wage regions outside the European Community. Even more important, there was mounting competition over the location of production. An increasing number of businesses were switching larger proportions of their production to countries where taxes and labour costs were lower, the procedures for obtaining permission to build and run industrial plants were less protracted, and there were few if any regulations on environmental protection.

Transfers of production abroad might, of course, also be necessary if access to markets was to be created or improved; they were by no means an effect of the cost of labour alone. Naturally, too, workers' skills, prospects for cooperative labour relations, standards of public infrastructure, the degree of access to high-quality services, and the level of political and social stability in the potential new locations of production were also important factors.

Trends towards globalization were significantly reinforced by the increasing role being played by multinational enterprises, the growing strength of the newly emergent economies in Asia, and the collapse of the Communist bloc in eastern Europe. In particular, the states of eastern central Europe, with their large numbers of skilled workers, favourable exchange rates, and low labour costs, posed a stiff challenge to the German economy in the competition for capital investment, industrial relocation, and market outlets once they had made the transition from planned to market economies and entered the international economy.

Taken together, these developments all made for a weakening of labour as a factor of production, and a strengthening of capital. They also strengthened the roles of management and of knowledge skills, which were becoming of mounting importance in the development of new research-based technologies and the provision of high-quality advisory and financial services for businesses. Increasingly, too, capital was shirking its share of responsibility for meeting the home community's costs, by migrating to other countries or threatening to do so. Labour, on the other hand, was steadily becoming the 'pack mule',[16] laden with an ever heavier burden as far as the financing of social security was concerned.

3.3 BURDENS IMPOSED ON THE WELFARE STATE BY THE TRANSFORMATION OF THE EAST GERMAN ECONOMY

3.3.1 The weaknesses of the GDR economy

In the early 1990s the greatest challenges to the economy and the welfare state in Germany came from the crisis caused by the transformation of the east German economy.

The collapse of the German Democratic Republic in 1989–90 was, to a significant degree, the result of its economic weakness,[17] particularly in comparison with the Federal Republic. (The comparison was constantly made by both politicians and population.) The GDR economy started from a worse position at the end of the Second World War, since much industrial plant had been dismantled and reparations to the USSR had been set at a high level.[18] The relocation of firms outside the GDR and, especially, the loss of skilled and, mainly, young workers as a result of mass migration to the Federal Republic before the building of the Wall[19] further magnified the gap between the economies of east and west. Although there was a far larger proportion of women in the GDR workforce,[20] the higher numbers were not sufficient to compensate.

In the medium and long term, however, the principal weakness of the GDR economy was the fact that it was insulated from the market and run by a centralized, inflexible planning bureaucracy that was subject to political imperatives. The absence of competition meant that enterprises were under little or no pressure to reduce costs and increase productivity. In addition, there was great wastage of economic resources, thanks to the high subsidies of basic foodstuffs, rents, public transport, children's clothing, and energy. These subsidies benefited rich and poor alike and by 1989 accounted for almost a quarter of planned public expenditure,[21] at the expense of necessary investment. Nor did subvention apply only to articles of mass consumption. Energy and raw materials were also subsidized, through irrational pricing policies. There were even subsidies for bungalows, prefabricated houses, cement, roof tiles, floor and wall tiles, windows, doors, building timber, sailing, rowing, and folding boats, upright and grand pianos, flowers, ornamental plants, mushrooms, game, and much else besides. Prices were completely distorted. A breeder of rabbits received 60 marks for every animal he produced; if he wished to buy back the slaughtered creature, in the form of rabbit meat, he had to pay only 15 marks, despite the labour that had been expended.[22] This absurd example of pricing policy illustrates the failure of the direct control mechanisms that operated in the absence of the controls provided by the market. The extreme levelling-out of wages and salaries that was characteristic of the GDR also reduced incentives to improve performance.

In addition, basic errors of policy decision-making steered the economy in the wrong direction. These errors included the enforced drive, after 1945, to build up primary and heavy industries on GDR soil, where they had largely been lacking, and the neglect of consumer-goods industries, the service sector, and the precision-engineering and optical industries, which previously had been highly developed. A sectoral economic structure based on misconceived and outdated models was retained in the years that followed.[23] This was in part due to the fact that the GDR economy was badly isolated from the international division of labour and instead geared to the interests of the other socialist countries that made up COMECON, in particular the Soviet Union.

While the service sector was neglected, agriculture and, within the industrial sector, industries that were in decline in the industrial states in the west—metal production, shipbuilding, and textiles and clothing—continued to employ far too many people. Typically, the GDR's economic and social protection system put a brake on inter-sectoral structural change[24] and on the movement of workers between enterprises. The right to work made it virtually impossible to dismiss an employee against his will. More important, employees in the larger enterprises received a 'general provision'[25] covering everything from outpatient services to pensioner care, from kindergartens to housing allocation to holidays, and since the system of allocating these benefits was based entirely on the workplace, most workers were loath to take the risk of changing jobs. Thus, whereas in 1986 the proportion of workers in the Federal Republic who changed jobs was 20.5 per cent, the comparable figure in the GDR was only 7.4 per cent.[26] Because enterprises, constantly under pressure to increase production, could generally pass on their wage costs through prices, they tended to hoard their workers, in order to protect themselves against losses of working hours caused by illness, pregnancy, or the pressure of child care. Over-staffing and a high level of concealed unemployment[27] were the product of behaviour that was entirely rational in terms of the interests of enterprises and their managers but that would have been disastrous in a competition-based market economy.

As with structural economic change, so there was a widespread failure to keep up with international research and modern technological developments. For example, although there was a drive to build up microelectronics in the 1970s and 1980s, the results did not come close to matching world standards. The first 256-kilobyte chips to be manufactured in the GDR cost 536 marks each to produce: the cost on the world market was about 8 marks.[28]

The extent to which labour productivity in the GDR lagged behind that in the Federal Republic was at first seriously underestimated, in part because the GDR's official statistics deliberately disguised the real situation. The GDR planning commission claimed in 1989 that the gap was in the order of 30 per cent, while the most detailed western study undertaken before the fall of the Berlin Wall, by the German Institute for Economic Research, calculated that GDR industry's shortfall in 1987 was about 50 per cent.[29] In fact, average productivity in the GDR at the end of the 1980s remained at below 30 per cent of the level in the Federal Republic.[30]

In addition to the lack of innovation, the GDR economy was characterized by an ageing capital stock, heavy pollution of the environment, and a severe dearth of investment in the maintenance and improvement of the infrastructure. Postal and telephone services were completely undeveloped: only 17 out of every 100 households had a telephone.[31] There was no modern system of information communication. The lack of coordination within the centralized planning bureaucracy meant that the large economic combines, which in 1982 accounted for over 90 per cent of industrial production in the GDR,[32] tried to solve the problem of inadequate supplies and construction facilities by manufacturing their own input products and doing their own building work. Instead of profiting from specialization and the division of labour, they became vertical producers with marked tendencies towards autarky. The hope had been that these large enterprises would promote innovation in products and production methods by undertaking their own research and development. By and large, this did not happen, partly because enterprises did not have sufficient modern research equipment, but also, and more importantly, because they were not subject to any pressures of competition and innovation, as it was always easy for them to sell their products. High-cost and high-risk innovations would also have had to compete for priority with the imperative of meeting planning targets through increases in the mass of manufactured goods. A hallmark of the GDR was the 'tonnage ideology': a concentration on quantity, rather than the quality, of products. It was only natural, in these conditions, that there was an almost complete failure to produce goods that could compete on world markets. Marketing, too, was very poor.

Because western foreign exchange was urgently needed in order to pay for imports, the GDR's own products had to be sold by dumping. In due course the huge deficit in trade with non-socialist countries led to a high level of debt.[33] According to what was probably an over-pessimistic analysis, presented on 30 October 1989 by the head of the state planning commission of the Politburo of the SED, Gerhard Schürer,[34] the GDR was on the brink of insolvency. In his view, the halting of further indebtedness would have caused a fall in living standards of between 25 and 30 per cent in 1990 and deprived the state of all legitimacy in the eyes of the population. Ultimately, if the weaknesses of the GDR economy were to be overcome, there was no alternative to replacing the planned economy with a market economy orientated to the world economy as a whole. An independent GDR would probably have made this transition in a less abrupt manner, but it would not have been able to stave off economic and social hardship and mass unemployment.

3.3.2 The GDR's advantages and disadvantages in the transformation process: a comparison with the states of eastern central Europe

If we compare the GDR with the other former Communist countries in eastern central Europe that also underwent economic transformation,[35] the particular nature of the GDR's situation becomes clear.

1. The GDR enjoyed the advantage that the legal, economic, and social protection system of the Federal Republic was a sophisticated model that had evolved and been tested over decades: a new system did not have to be developed in the midst of

a lengthy and, inevitably, controversial political process. The GDR suffered from the disadvantage that it was not able to make adjustments to the new order to suit its particular needs.

2. Monetary union served as a shock therapy. The adoption of the Deutschmark and the conversion of wages and salaries at the ratio of 1:1 was—given the GDR's secret exchange rate of 4.4 to 1 on the proceeds of exports—tantamount to a sudden revaluation of about 340 per cent.[36] The GDR was thus forced to make a 'cold start'[37] and was unable, unlike the economies of eastern central Europe, to improve its international competitiveness by means of low exchange rates and low wages. Its transition into the international economy and a situation of acute competition with suppliers in the old *Bundesländer* and abroad was much more abrupt than was the case with the other ex-Communist states, which were able to use trade policy to extend the process of adjustment over a longer period.

3. Whereas the eastern central European states had only limited support from outside, the new *Bundesländer* had the advantage of receiving considerable financial and administrative help from the old Federal Republic. This help included improvements to the infrastructure, the reorganization of the administrative apparatus in the east German *Länder*, and changes in local government to cope with new tasks.[38] It also took the form of support for the economy and, not least, social policies to protect people during the upheaval, with a greatly expanded active labour market policy and generous benefits within a sophisticated system of social security. At the same time, however, this support—particularly the dispatch of west German executives into leading administrative roles—had the effect of making east Germans feel that their lives had been taken over by outsiders.

4. While the eastern central European states were able, at least to some degree, to insulate their internal markets by their national economic policies, the disappearance of the internal German border created a single German market in which it was difficult to preserve the sharp differences in levels of wages, salaries, and social benefits that had existed between east and west. The hope of west German economic experts that wages and salaries in the east would rise only in tandem with increasing productivity proved illusory. Trade unions, and initially also employers, had no vested interest in the emergence of a low-wage region in the east, which would have posed a competitive threat to the west German economy and put pressure on western working conditions and wages.[39] In the event, some convergence of wages and salaries took place fairly quickly. Average basic negotiated wages in the east rose from roughly 35 per cent of western levels at the time of monetary union on 1 July 1990 to 60 per cent by the end of 1991—though with wide differences between different sectors of the economy—and, after a flattening-out of increases after 1993, to 84 per cent by the end of 1994.[40] Real wages, however, were significantly lower, as there were no binding pay agreements in many enterprises in the east and, in contrast with the west, only a few employees were paid above agreed rates; moreover, additional payments that were customary in the west, such as holiday pay, a thirteenth-month salary payment, or employers' contributions to tax-deductible savings, were seldom available in the east. On average, real wages across the whole of the economy of the new *Bundesländer*

stood at 46.7 per cent of the west German level in 1991 and at 70.5 per cent in 1994, while productivity rose from 31 per cent to 56 per cent in the same period. Unit wage costs, i.e. the wage costs of producing a product, were on average about 50.6 per cent higher in the east in 1991 than in the west, and were still roughly 26 per cent higher in 1994,[41] so that the economy in the east German *Länder* remained at a significant disadvantage. Even in 2000 productivity in eastern Germany had barely reached 70 per cent of the west German level, while real wage costs per employee were at 80 per cent, putting employers under huge pressure to reduce employment numbers.[42] Since then, the position of the economy in the east relative to that in the west has significantly improved, and, because of lower wages, east German industry now even has a slight advantage in terms of lower unit wage costs. On the other hand, unemployment in the east has remained much higher than in the west.

5. A key difference between the new German *Länder* and the states of eastern central Europe lay in the attitudes of the population to the changes in their material situation. People in eastern Germany expected, in the main, that living standards would soon be on a par with those in the west: accordingly, they bemoaned the fact that they continued to fall short, even though most incomes had risen substantially. By contrast, the comparison that the citizens of the post-Communist states in eastern central Europe made was with their position as it had been before the collapse of the old regimes: they were therefore prepared to regard even modest improvements as a success story.[43]

3.3.3 The collapse of trade with eastern Europe and the Soviet Union; problems of investment arising from the resolution of property questions

The position of the east German economy was exacerbated by the collapse of its markets in eastern Europe. During the German–Soviet negotiations in the spring and summer of 1990 there was much discussion of the question of the maintenance of the GDR's payment and delivery commitments to the Soviet Union, and of Soviet exports to the GDR, on the basis of the existing treaties between the two countries. Trade with the GDR accounted for between 10 and 12 per cent of the Soviet Union's foreign trade. A large part of this trade was in relatively high-value GDR industrial products, through which the Soviet Union also obtained indirect access to western technology and hence important assistance in modernizing its dilapidated economy. In return, the Soviet Union was a significant supplier of raw materials and energy to the GDR. The Soviet Union accounted for between 36 and 39 per cent of the GDR's foreign trade, and almost half a million jobs in the GDR[44] were dependent, directly or indirectly, on these exports.

Even before monetary union was implemented, many enterprises in the GDR were encountering problems over payments and deliveries owing to losses of production, strikes, and disruptions in supplies. In addition, trade and industry in the GDR were now viewing west Germany as their main trading partner—a partner that would pay with the coveted Deutschmark. Simultaneously, western products were ousting many goods produced within the GDR, as well as products from the Soviet Union and from other eastern bloc countries. To make matters worse, the USSR was failing to honour its delivery commitments, especially with regard to oil.

The USSR was worried that after the establishment of monetary union on 1 July 1990 the entire GDR market would break away, with devastating consequences for the Soviet economy and for Gorbachev's reforms. In particular, products of the Soviet armaments industry, which hitherto had formed an important part of the GDR's imports, were now of absolutely no interest to the GDR. Already on 19 April 1990, before the start of the negotiations between the Federal Republic and the GDR on monetary union, the Soviet Union had demanded that the GDR ensure that it fulfilled its economic commitments to the Soviet Union, if necessary with the help of the Federal Republic.[45] This demand, of course, raised the question whether the Soviet Union in turn would be in a position to provide the necessary western hard currency in exchange. In the Soviet view, the foreign trade of the GDR, and later the new *Bundesländer*, needed to be underpinned by billions in annual subsidies.[46] On the question of the 'foreign trade relations that [had] evolved' between the GDR and its trading partners in eastern Europe, which were to be developed and expanded, the State Treaty on monetary union pledged to ensure the 'protection of confidence' after 1 July 1990, while also referring explicitly to market economy principles.[47] However, the 'protection of confidence', which was not precisely defined, was ultimately no more than a non-binding assurance and a gesture of good will: it did not constitute a guarantee that the existing trade pattern would continue.

During new negotiations with the Soviet Union in August 1990 it emerged that as a result of the increase in GDR exports to the Soviet Union, largely supported by the state, and a simultaneous decline in imports from the Soviet Union, the latter had built up a huge mountain of debt. The Soviet Union demanded, in vain, that the debt be written off.[48] This difficult situation was inevitably made worse by the GDR's departure from COMECON and its integration into the European Community, which brought further impediments to trade with the Soviet Union. Instead of the expansion of trade with a united Germany that Gorbachev had hoped for, trade contracted.

In point of fact, the Federal Republic had a strong interest in the continuation of trade between the territory of the former GDR and the Soviet Union and other eastern bloc countries, on grounds not only of foreign policy but of economic policy. It realized that there were opportunities here for winning new markets in eastern Europe, and it also hoped that maintaining and expanding trade with eastern Europe would keep many enterprises in eastern Germany alive and thus help stave off the mass unemployment that was widely feared. The Federal Republic could not, however, force enterprises in the GDR to preserve their old trading relationships, nor was it prepared to provide thousands of millions of marks to subsidize trade on a long-term basis and thereby delay indirectly the transition from a planned to a market economy in the new *Bundesländer*.

Nevertheless, the Federal Republic did support GDR enterprises with about 5,000 million DM in export subsidies during the second six months of 1990 alone.[49] In addition, in the German–Soviet 'Treaty to develop comprehensive cooperation in the areas of economics, industry, science and technology' of November 1990[50] it committed itself, albeit in non-binding terms, to develop German–Soviet trade, to support the implementation, through 'appropriate measures', of previously concluded agreements on deliveries of goods and the provision of services, and to support, within the European Community, transitional arrangements taking the interests of the USSR into account. Trade subsidies on a limited scale were also to be continued. Even so, the sharp fall in trade, and with it the loss of jobs in eastern Germany dependent on trade, could not be prevented.

Another of the reasons that have been seen as particularly responsible for the serious economic crisis in the new *Bundesländer*, apart from the collapse in trade with the eastern bloc, is that inadequate private investment was made in the aftermath of unification, particularly by west German companies, though also by western industrial countries generally. This unwillingness to invest in eastern Germany on a large scale was caused partly by the poor state of the east German infrastructure and partly by the fact that in many branches of the economy west German firms were able to supply the east German market from their production centres in the west. The lack of clarity as far as questions concerning property in the east were concerned was also a factor.

Securing agreement to deal with the so-called 'outstanding property questions' in the GDR was one of the most complicated and controversial tasks that had to be dealt with in the negotiations that took place among the different Federal ministries, among the political parties in the Federal Republic, and between the Federal government and the government of the GDR—the latter negotiations also involving constant interventions by the Soviet Union.

The Modrow government had maintained, in a declaration of 1 March 1990 on property questions in the GDR,[51] that the existing situation, which was the result partly of the expropriations of agricultural estates and commercial and industrial enterprises that had been made by the occupying Soviet power between 1945 and 1949, and partly of expropriations made by the GDR itself, should remain essentially unchanged. As far as the period after 1949 was concerned, the property mainly involved land and blocks of flats that had been acquired for minimal compensation, assets of people who had 'fled the Republic' (i.e. crossed the border illegally), and property belonging to citizens of the Federal Republic, which for the most part had not been expropriated, though it had been placed under state control and in many instances sold. A further category was small and medium-sized expropriated private or semi-public businesses, which, following a decision by the GDR Council of Ministers of 9 February 1972, were transferred to 'public ownership' in return for a minimal financial settlement. These latter firms, at most, would be returnable if applications were made.[52] Altogether, somewhere between 40 and 50 per cent of commercial enterprises and between 50 and 60 per cent of the agricultural land area,[53] as well as many houses and other pieces of land, came under the rubric of 'outstanding property questions'. The position of the Modrow government was shared by the Soviet Union. The latter emphasized, in particular, that the measures carried out by the Soviet military administration between 1945 and 1949 had been lawful.[54] For the Federal Republic, which had to take account both of the interests of the many people who had fled the GDR and of the property guarantee enshrined in Article 14 of the Basic Law,[55] the Modrow government's attitude was unacceptable. On the other hand, it also saw clearly that resistance on the part of the GDR population to claims by west Germans meant that the property situation '[could] not be reversed automatically' and that 'socially acceptable compromises' would have to be found.[56]

The de Maizière government at first took only a slightly different line from the Modrow regime. In a discussion between de Maizière and the Federal Justice Minister Klaus Kinkel on 3 May 1990, the GDR Prime Minister said that his government had no scope whatever for reversing the expropriations that had been carried out under Soviet occupation law before 1949. He gave a very cautious indication that it would be prepared to return property acquired by later expropriations where that was feasible. In many cases, however, it would not be possible, either because changes of use had occurred—such as the conversion of land and housing for public purposes—or because GDR citizens had 'honestly' acquired rights of use or ownership of expropriated property under GDR law.[57] The Soviet Union's position was repeated in a memorandum of 28 April 1990, presented to the German embassy in Moscow, which contained an unmistakable warning: 'Nothing in the draft treaty between the Federal Republic of Germany and the German Democratic Republic shall provide a justification for calling into question the legality of the measures and decrees that were taken by the Four Powers, either jointly or, within their former zones of occupation, separately, on the matters of denazification, demilitarization, and democratization. The legality of these decisions, especially with regard to matters of land and property, shall not be subject to any subsequent examination or revision by German courts or other organs of state.'[58] After very arduous negotiations a joint declaration by the Federal Republic and the GDR was finally issued on 15 June 1990, stating that the expropriations that had been made on the basis of occupation law could 'not be reversed' and that this view, held by the governments of the Soviet Union and the GDR, was being 'noted' by the Federal Republic 'in the light of historical events'.[59] The future all-German parliament, however, would retain the right to make such 'public settlement payments' (*staatliche Ausgleichsleistungen*) to previous property owners as it might think fit. The word *Entschädigung* (compensation) was thus deliberately avoided, in order to exclude the possibility of higher payments in excess of those made under the system of settlement payments for war losses that had applied in the old Federal Republic.[60]

As far as the expropriations made after 1949 were concerned, it was agreed in principle that property should be returned to the original owners. Where this was not actually possible, because land or buildings had been 'devoted to communal use, converted into complex apartment buildings or housing estates, utilized for commercial purposes, or incorporated into new enterprise units', compensation would be paid. In cases where GDR citizens had 'acquired, in an honest manner, possession or material rights of use of returnable property . . . a socially acceptable settlement should be reached with the former owners, through exchange of land of comparable value'—which in practice was scarcely ever feasible—or through financial compensation.

The issue of the explicit recognition of expropriations carried out under occupation law was raised once again by the Soviet Union in the final phase of the negotiations on the 'Two-Plus-Four' treaty. Only after the two German Foreign Ministers, Genscher and de Maizière (who had meanwhile taken over from Meckel), had stated, in a 'joint letter' to the four Foreign Ministers of the victorious powers referring to the declaration of 15 June 1990, that they were prepared to acknowledge the legality of the Soviet measures did Moscow cease to insist that it would handle this matter itself in the 'Two-Plus-Four' treaty.[61]

The decision to exclude restitution of expropriations carried out between 1945 and 1949 was accepted only with great misgivings by the FDP and sections of the CDU/CSU, particularly on grounds of constitutional law,[62] and later also met with strong criticism from the public at large, from those directly affected, and from scholars.[63] Critics also cited a statement that Gorbachev had made to the British historian Lawrence Stone on 5 July 1994 that the question had not been discussed at his level, as President of the USSR, and that there had been no question of a choice between, 'on the one hand, a ban on restitution and, on the other, no big treaty [with Germany]'. However, Gorbachev took a different line when talking to *Der Spiegel* on 5 September 1994, saying that the statement in the joint declaration by the two German governments of 15 June 1990 that 'the expropriations carried out on the basis of occupation law or through occupation authority (between 1945 and 1949) could not be reversed' had taken account of the Soviet position.[64] However one judges the response of the Federal government to the dilemma in which it found itself *vis-à-vis* the Soviet Union, which returned to this issue several times in the course of the negotiations, it is clear that if restitution of expropriations made before 1949 had not been ruled out, there would have been no certainty of a two-thirds majority in favour of the first State Treaty or the Unification Treaty in the Volkskammer of the GDR.

The position of the Federal government was later supported by the Federal Constitutional Court in judgements issued on 23 April 1991 and 18 April 1996.[65] The Federal Republic might, however, have given more generous compensation to those affected. The Law on Compensation and Settlement Payments of 27 September 1994, which was passed only after the parliamentary Mediation Committee had twice become involved,[66] provided for fairly low compensation payments for financial losses incurred after 1949 and settlement payments for losses incurred before 1949. For medium-sized claims, payments amounted to about 25 per cent of the restitution value; for higher claims the figures were much smaller.[67]

As far as the economy of the GDR was concerned, the decision of principle that 'return [of property should come] before compensation' was far more significant than the ruling out of restitution of expropriations carried out between 1945 and

1949. During the final phase of the negotiations on the Unification Treaty the west German Social Democrats and, at their urging, the SPD-led *Bundesländer*[68] pressed hard for this principle to be reversed. In particular, the leader of the SPD Hans-Jochen Vogel argued that that was the only way of ensuring social harmony and guaranteeing legal security for investment.[69] The demand that compensation should take priority over return of property was then also taken up by the GDR government. The two German governments finally agreed in the Unification Treaty that there should be no 'reassignment of property rights over land or buildings' if 'the land or building in question is needed for urgent . . . specifiable investment purposes: in particular, if it enables a place of business to be established and if carrying out this investment decision merits support on economic grounds, in particular because it will create or safeguard jobs'.[70]

These terms were enshrined in a separate law, though since the legislation dealt only with land and buildings but not businesses, it was of no wider significance. Later the principle of 'return before compensation' was relaxed further by a law of 22 March 1991 on removal of impediments[71] and a law of July 1992 on priority of investment. Whether or not the doctrine in fact constituted a real impediment to investment in the early years after unification has been a matter of dispute among scholars.[72] Opponents of the priority of restitution have maintained that the fear of restitution claims delayed the processes of privatization and reform and scared off potential investors. Defenders of the principle have argued that redressing the wrong of expropriation and upholding the right of private ownership of the means of production were essential preconditions for the establishment of a market economy and that restitution allowed former property owners to participate in the rebuilding of the economy. They also claim that it was not restitution as such that deterred investment, but the dilatoriness of the authorities in clarifying ownership rights. In the present author's view, it is evident that while delays in sorting out ownership rights played a part, investors were also deterred from making a greater commitment in eastern Germany because they were reluctant to take over enterprises with large workforces. There is no doubt, however, that the government's policy of directing very high subsidies to the real-estate sector, which led to a building boom that soon collapsed, together with the fact that an excessive share of state transfer payments went to consumption instead of investment, also contributed to the decline of the GDR economy.

3.3.4 The crisis in the east German economy and the development of the labour market

One of the consequences of the dramatic change from a planned to a market economy, and of the shock therapy of monetary union, was a huge decline in production in the east and the loss of approximately three and a half million jobs, particularly in industry and agriculture.[73] In part, these job losses were absorbed by an easing of the conditions under which people could take early retirement: roughly 800,000 east Germans aged 55 or over availed themselves of this opportunity. In addition, hundreds of thousands became commuters, continuing to live in the east but taking up jobs in west Germany or west Berlin, while others moved permanently to the old *Bundesländer*.[74] Most importantly of all, an active labour market policy was initiated, which at its height involved upwards of two million employees.[75] Yet despite these adjustments, the number of those officially registered as unemployed in the new *Bundesländer* rose above 800,000 by the first quarter of 1991 and stood at more than 1.2 million a year later.[76] The average rate of unemployment in the east during 1992 was 14.8 per cent, more than twice as high as the rate in the west (6.6 per cent). Having reached a provisional record level of 18.3 per cent in February 1994, it fell below the previous year's rate after August 1994 but still stood at an average of 16 per cent for the year as a whole.

Table 5 gives a breakdown of labour market statistics in eastern Germany.[77] It demonstrates graphically the extent of the crisis in employment and of the shortage of regular jobs. The figures show that the rate of under-employment—in other words, of both overt and concealed unemployment—was more than twice the official unemployment rate, with over one-third of the potential workforce affected at certain times.

Unemployment among women was particularly high, in 1994 reaching an annual average of 21.5 per cent, almost twice as high as the rate among men (10.9 per cent). There were several reasons for this. Women in the GDR had been employed in disproportionately high numbers in agriculture and in sectors of industry—such as textiles and clothing, food production, chemicals, and light industry—that suffered particularly severe falls in production; by contrast, the building industry, which at first underwent a boom, was a predominantly male domain. In addition, women workers made up a relatively high proportion of the lesser skilled, whose jobs were particularly at risk as restructuring of the economy took place and jobs were lost through rationalization.[78] Women were also frequently less mobile than men because of family ties. The ending of the special provision that had been granted in the GDR to single mothers and married women with small children meant that it was now more difficult to combine work and family life, and firms were less willing, in view of the surplus of labour, to take the particular circumstances of women with small children into account. As a result of these structural problems, the proportion of women among the long-term unemployed, i.e. those unemployed for a year or more, was particularly high: 68.9 per cent at the end of September 1992 and as much as 76.7 per cent three years later.[79] Although a large proportion of women over 55 ceased employment permanently—between 1989 and 1991 the proportion of women aged between 55 and 59 who were in employment shrank from 77.8 to 36.6 per cent, and of those aged between 60 and 64 from 29.7 to 8.1 per cent[80]—willingness to work remained very high among women in eastern Germany overall.[81]

The scale of the economic upheaval that workers in eastern Germany had to cope with is reflected not only in the high levels of unemployment and the massive increases in early retirement but also in the disappearance of the very close

Table 5 The labour market in eastern Germany, 1990–1995 (in 1,000s)

	1990	1991	1992	1993	1994	1995
Supply of jobs						
Persons capable of gainful employment	9,060	8,234	7,556	7,354	7,445	7,453
Persons in employment[a]	8,820	7,321	6,386	6,205	6,303	6,406
• Registered unemployed	240	913	1,170	1,149	1,142	1,047
• Hidden reserve[b]	0	727	1,272	1,336	1,085	933
Potential number of persons capable of gainful employment	9,060	8,961	8,828	8,690	8,530	8,386
Unemployment						
Registered unemployed	240	913	1,170	1,149	1,142	1,047
Persons employed in labour market policy schemes[c]	543	1,881	1,984	1,672	1,335	1,105
• Job creation schemes[d]	5	257	543	365	379	419
Short-time working[e]	341	900	197	97	52	51
Training and re-training[f]	7	170	432	356	252	254
Early retirement[g]	190	554	812	854	652	381
Hidden reserve	0	0	20	113	155	266
Under-employment	783	2,794	3,174	2,934	2,632	2,418
Unemployment rate (per cent)[h]	2.7	11.1	15.6	15.6	15.3	14.0
Under-employment rate (per cent)[i]	8.6	31.2	36.0	33.8	30.9	28.8
Employment promotion rate under Employment Promotion Law (per cent)[j]	6.0	22.8	26.3	22.7	17.9	14.8

[a] Including those employed in short-time work and job creation schemes.

[b] Including persons not gainfully employed but involved in labour market policy schemes (training, re-training, early retirement).

[c] i.e. equivalents of employed persons. The number of those in e.g. short-time work (more than half of whom had losses of working hours of more than 50 per cent in 1991–2) was considerably higher.

[d] Job creation schemes, employment promotion under §249h of the Employment Promotion Law.

[e] Including bad-weather pay.

[f] Including professional re-training and language courses.

[g] Including persons on pre-pension transitional benefit and the older unemployed under §105c of the Employment Promotion Law.

[h] Registered unemployed as a percentage of persons capable of gainful employment.

[i] Under-employment as a percentage of the potential number of persons capable of gainful employment.

[j] Persons employed in labour market policy and other schemes as a percentage of persons capable of gainful employment.

Source: Simplified table based on data in Kurt Vogler-Ludwig, 'Arbeitsmarkt Ost', in *Wiedervereinigung*, p. 235.

links that had previously existed in the GDR between the employee and his or her original place of work. By the end of 1993 only 29 per cent of those who had been employed in November 1989 were still working in the same enterprise.[82] Between November 1989 and November 1994 57 per cent of east Germans of employable age had taken part in labour market policy schemes, some of them in several.[83]

3.3.5 Economic development and economic structures

At first, the economies of eastern and western Germany developed in diametrically opposed directions. The gross domestic product of the new *Bundesländer* fell from 336,000 million GDR marks in 1989 to 234,000 million DM in 1991, a contraction of about 30 per cent;[84] growth resumed only after this latter date. By contrast, the west German economy enjoyed a marked unification boom, as opportunities for sales opened up in the east. Gross domestic product in the west rose sharply in real terms, by 5.7 per cent in 1990 and 5 per cent in 1991.[85] The number of those in employment in the west rose during the two years after 1989 by 1.2 million to just on 29 million, and the unemployment rate fell significantly, from 7.9 to 6.3 per cent.[86]

In 1992/3, however, west Germany was seriously affected by the recession in the world economy. Gross domestic product, though still showing a small increase of 1.8 per cent in 1992, fell by 2 per cent in real terms in 1993. This was the largest drop in the history of the Federal Republic before 2009; only in 1967, 1975, and 1982 had there been negative economic growth.[87] Although economic expansion got under way again from the spring of 1994 onwards—just in time for the Bundestag elections—and gross domestic product in the west rose by 2.1 per cent in 1994 overall, growth was not sufficient to reverse the fall in the number of those in employment, in Germany as a whole, by almost 1.6 million to just on 35 million.[88] The rate of unemployment in the old Federal Republic increased sharply between 1991 and 1994, from an annual average of 6.3 per cent to one of 9.2 per cent.[89]

In eastern Germany—again contrary to the trends in west Germany—gross domestic product rose strongly in the years 1992, 1993, 1994, and 1995 (admittedly from a very low base in 1991), with nominal increases of 27.6, 22.4, 14.8, and 6.6 per cent respectively. The upturn, however, was not self-sustaining. Having begun to catch up with the west, growth in the east then began to falter again as the construction boom came to an end, and subsequent rises in gross domestic product came into line with those in the west, even falling somewhat behind in most years from 1997 onwards. Unemployment rates in east Germany also rose sharply, from 14.9 per cent in 1995 to 19.5 per cent in 1997.[90]

It is clear, therefore, that the steep collapse in employment in east Germany between 1990 and 1992 was not reversed. Unemployment in the east persisted at a stubbornly high level, and productivity remained well behind that of west Germany, at 56 per cent in 1994 and 60.4 per cent in 1997.[91] We should also note the weakness of east German industry in export markets: with 18.8 per cent of the population of Germany, and a 9.3 per cent share of German gross domestic product, east German enterprises were responsible for only 5.4 per cent of the country's exports.[92]

Was the structure of the economy in the east successfully modernized, and to what extent did it come into line with the economy in the west? It should be borne in mind, first, that the west German economy too had been undergoing difficult structural change over the decades.[93] Agriculture had been in decline since the

1950s, and jobs had also been lost in the industrial sector, notably in mining, shipbuilding, textiles, wood processing, chemicals, and iron and steel. The success stories had been electrical engineering, especially the production of data processing equipment, synthetic materials manufacture, the motor vehicle industry, and mechanical engineering. The west German economy was notable for breadth of specialization and a strong emphasis on exports in high-quality, price-sensitive segments of the market.[94] On the other hand, there were fields where Germany undoubtedly lagged behind other countries, such as microelectronics, information and communications technology, and biotechnology and genetic engineering: in other words, cutting-edge technologies[95] characterized by high spending on research and development. Overall, from the economic crisis of 1973–4 onwards, industry declined in terms of its share of value creation and employment (though there were considerable variations from one branch of activity to another) while the tertiary sector expanded,[96] particularly as far as services in the narrower sense were concerned.

Compared with other modern western societies, however, the Federal Republic had advanced less far along the road towards a services society. In 1987 the share of the industrial sector in the national economy was higher, at 40.5 per cent, than in any other OECD country, and the proportion of those employed in the tertiary sector, namely 54.3 per cent of all those in civilian employment, was well below the corresponding proportion in the United States (69.9 per cent).[97] Admittedly, this difference is partly explained by differences in the way the statistics are recorded, with some business-related services in Germany being included within the industrial sector. Nevertheless, retail trades in Germany had lower staffing levels than in the USA, doubtless mainly owing to the substantially higher wages and wage costs that prevailed in Germany.[98]

In the east, the change of system accelerated the process of structural change in the economy.

As Table 6 shows, agriculture in the east was hit particularly hard by the collapse in jobs: between 1990 and 1993 its share of those in employment went from 10.8 to 4.2 per cent,[99] a fall of over 60 per cent. The same was true of manufacturing industry. In certain areas of employment, such as textiles, the clothing industry, and leather production and processing, 90 per cent of jobs were lost; the figure in mechanical engineering was 75 per cent.[100] On the other hand, building and construction, banking and insurance, and personal services—the latter including, in particular, the hotel and restaurant trade, which had been under-developed in east Germany—saw a significant rise in the number of those employed.[101] In the construction industry, however, there was only a short-lived boom, brought about primarily by public investment to develop the infrastructure and repair the fabric of buildings in towns and cities, and over-staffing rose. The retrenchment that followed in the mid-1990s was one of the main causes of the later weak rate of growth in the east German economy.

There were, however, other significant differences from the west German economic structure. Agriculture in the west was dominated by family businesses, whereas in the east it consisted mainly of large-scale enterprises. In the east, in

Table 6 Changes in employment in the GDR (or new *Bundesländer*), 1989–1993, by area of the economy

Area of the economy	1990	1991	1992	1993
Agriculture and forestry	80.2	46.5	30.0	24.8
Manufacturing, energy, mining	88.2	60.7	40.1	34.0
Building and construction	100.00	108.0	123.6	138.4
Commerce	91.2	82.6	79.3	80.1
Transport and communications	95.0	81.4	72.6	67.8
Banking and insurance	119.3	141.9	159.0	165.8
Education and science	89.0	82.7	78.5	67.6
Health	98.9	98.9	96.9	93.9
Regional administration, social insurance	94.8	92.8	102.0	108.3
Personal services	112.4	130.3	140.0	150.1
Other services	80.8	67.8	73.8	80.5

Note: Annual averages (1989 = 100), including employment supported by labour market policy measures.
Source: Lutz *et al.* (eds), *Arbeit, Arbeitsmarkt und Betriebe*, p. 71.

1995, 93.5 per cent of productive land was cultivated by farms of over 100 hectares; in the west, the figure was 15.4 per cent.[102] More than half of all agricultural land in the east was cultivated by successor enterprises to the earlier collective farms and was run by managers and staffed exclusively by waged employees. These enterprises—unlike the individual farms and farming partnerships run by owners or tenants, usually family members—at first proved to be fairly inefficient.[103] Likewise, east German industry cannot be said to have become very streamlined. It is true that already by 1994 there were firms that had equipped themselves with modern plant and had nothing to fear from competition with west German companies, in terms either of price or of product quality. This was not the case, though, as far as the great majority of enterprises were concerned. Most of them lagged far behind western businesses both in productivity and, despite high levels of public and private investment,[104] in capital equipment, and often had great difficulty in adapting to modern market-orientated forms of management.[105] It is also significant that only a few of the large German companies operating on a global scale decided, as Jenoptik AG did, to locate their headquarters in the new *Bundesländer*.

In commerce and transport the number of those employed fell from 1.5 to 1.1 million between 1989 and 1994; in the public service it fell from 2.3 to 1.5 million.[106] Even so, staffing levels in the public service in east Germany remained higher than in the west. For example, in 1994 east German local authorities, despite having shed nearly 200,000 posts, still employed on average roughly 50 per cent more people than did their west German counterparts: 30.7 employees per 1,000 inhabitants, as opposed to 20.2.[107]

By contrast, the number of those employed in the service sector almost doubled between 1989 and 1994, rising from 619,000 to 1.22 million.[108] Nevertheless, the growth in services did not make up for the collapse of large sections of industry, as the total number of those working in manufacturing industries fell from 4.39 to 2.19 million during the same period.[109] Moreover, except for some newly flourishing recreation areas and the service centres in large cities, the service sector was dependent on industry for its survival and growth.[110]

Changes in the different sectors of the east German economy between 1991 (or 1989) and 1996, and the structural differences and similarities between the economies of east and west Germany, are shown in Tables 7 and 8 respectively.

Among the striking statistics are the very high proportion of gross value creation accounted for by the construction industry in the east, the sharp decline in which since 1996[111] has exacerbated unemployment in the new *Bundesländer*, and the significantly lower figures, compared with the west, in manufacturing industries and in services. A comparison of the proportions of those in employment in individual types of manufacturing industry[112] similarly shows that although the structure of the east German economy became closer to that of the west, important differences still existed in 1996.

Table 7 Gross value creation in east Germany, 1991–1996, by sector of the economy (in 1991 prices, thousand million DM)

	1991	1992	1993	1994	1995	1996
Total	208.41	224.35	242.83	265.60	279.60	286.07
Agriculture and forestry	6.95	6.70	7.46	7.30	7.50	8.00
Production industries						
• total	75.17	81.64	90.56	104.06	110.00	111.50
• manufacturing	34.98	36.79	41.10	47.45	50.61	53.50
• construction	24.28	31.79	35.72	44.48	48.21	47.00
Commerce and transport[a]	29.37	30.70	34.41	36.92	38.47	39.00
Services[b]	45.62	54.34	57.87	62.87	67.60	71.50
State, private households[c]	51.30	50.97	52.53	54.43	55.97	57.00

Proportion (%)[d]	1991	1992	1993	1994	1995	1996	1996[e]
Total	100	100	100	100	100	100	100
Agriculture and forestry	3.3	3.0	3.1	2.7	2.7	2.7	1.3
Production industries							
• total	36.1	36.4	37.3	39.2	39.3	38.9	34.1
• manufacturing	16.8	16.4	16.9	17.9	18.1	18.6	26.5
• construction	11.7	14.1	14.7	16.7	17.2	16.4	4.7
Commerce and transport[a]	14.1	13.7	14.2	13.9	13.8	13.7	15.0
Services[b]	21.9	24.2	23.8	23.7	24.2	25.0	36.4
State, private households[c]	24.6	22.7	21.6	20.5	20.0	19.8	13.2

[a] Including communications.
[b] Banking, insurance, housing rental (including use by owners), other services.
[c] Including private non-profit organizations.
[d] Proportion of unadjusted gross value creation.
[e] Former Federal Republic.

Source: Jahresgutachten 1996/1997 des Sachverständigenrates zur Begutachtung der gesamtwirtschaftlichen Entwicklung, *Reformen voran bringen*, BTDrs 13/6200, 18 November 1996, p. 72.

Table 8 Numbers of people in employment (within Germany), 1989–1996, by sector of the economy (in 1,000s)

Former Federal Republic

Numbers in employment	1989	1990	1991	1992	1993	1994	1995	1996
Total[a]	27,658	28,479	29,189	29,457	29,002	28,656	28,464	28,156
°agriculture, forestry, fisheries	1,028	995	970	930	882	840	801	751
°production industries	10,997	11,309	11,450	11,306	10,766	10,341	10,135	9,784
°commerce, transport, communications	5,158	5,314	5,547	5,658	5,611	5,534	5,446	5,367
°services	4,992	5,294	5,592	5,853	6,022	6,200	6,366	6,536
°state, other areas[a]	5,483	5,567	5,630	5,710	5,721	5,741	5,716	5,718

Proportion (%)	1989	1990	1991	1992	1993	1994	1995	1996
Total in employment	100	100	100	100	100	100	100	100
°agriculture, forestry, fisheries	3.7	3.5	3.3	3.2	3.0	2.9	2.8	2.7
°production industries	39.8	39.7	39.2	38.4	37.1	36.1	35.6	34.7
°commerce, transport, communications	18.6	18.7	19.0	19.2	19.3	19.3	19.1	19.1
°services	18.0	18.6	19.1	19.9	20.8	21.6	22.4	23.2
°state, other areas	19.8	19.5	19.3	19.4	19.7	20.0	20.1	20.3

New* Bundesländer *and east Berlin

Numbers in employment	1989	1990	1991	1992	1993	1994	1995	1996
Total[a]	9,747	8,820	7,321	6,387	6,219	6,330	6,396	6,259
°agriculture, forestry, fisheries	976	781	454	282	233	227	224	213
°production industries	4,386	3,944	2,987	2,282	2,171	2,207	2,235	2,143
°commerce, transport, communications	1,513	1,405	1,241	1,146	1,129	1,135	1,121	1,096
°services	619	684	932	1,011	1,111	1,223	1,306	1,338
°state, other areas[a]	2,225	2,007	1,707	1,666	1,575	1,538	1,510	1,469

Proportion (%)	1989	1990	1991	1992	1993	1994	1995	1996
Total in employment	100	100	100	100	100	100	100	100
°agriculture, forestry, fisheries	10.0	8.9	6.2	4.4	3.7	3.6	3.5	3.4
°production industries	45.0	44.7	40.8	35.7	34.9	34.9	34.9	34.2
°commerce, transport, communications	15.5	15.9	17.0	17.9	18.2	17.9	17.5	17.5
°services	6.4	7.8	12.7	15.8	17.9	19.3	20.4	21.4
°state, other areas	23.1	22.8	23.3	26.1	25.3	27.3	23.6	23.5

[a] Including soldiers.

Sources: For 1989 and 1990, Statistisches Bundesamt, *Tabellensammlung*, 3/97, pp. 13–18; for 1991–6, *Statistische Übersichten*, West volume, table 80. Employment numbers are calculated according to place of work.

The same applies to the job structure of those in employment.[113] The proportion of self-employed in the east rose from about 2.2 per cent in 1989 to 7 per cent in 1994, closer to the figure in the west (9.6 per cent). On the other hand, even in 1994 there was scarcely any incidence of family members assisting the self-employed in the east: the rate was 0.2 per cent, compared with 1.6 per cent in the west. In 1994 the proportion of white-collar workers in the new *Bundesländer* was 49 per cent and of blue-collar workers 41.5 per cent, together making 90.5 per cent. This constituted a significantly higher proportion of those in employment than in the west, where the figures were 46.2 per cent for white-collar workers and 34.7 per cent for blue-collar workers, giving a total of 80.9 per cent. On the other hand, since there was slow progress in creating civil-service appointments in the *Länder* and local authorities in the east after 1989 (there had been no *Beamte*, or civil servant, category in the GDR), the proportion of civil servants in the east in 1994, 2.3 per cent, remained well below that in the west, 7.9 per cent.

3.3.6 Transfer payments to east Germany and their consequences

In eastern Germany demand for goods and services in 1991, at 358,000 million DM, was more than 50 per cent higher than the gross domestic product of 234,000 million DM. In 1995, when gross domestic product had risen to 442,000 million DM, demand stood at 610,000 million DM. In other words, there was still a yawning gap of 40 per cent between production and consumption[114] that had to be bridged from outside, by both private and public funds.

The major source of this funding was public transfer payments, which between 1991 and 1995 amounted in total to 615,000 million DM net, or 4.25 per cent of west Germany's average annual gross national product (see Table 9). According to recent calculations, €1,200 thousand million net (i.e. after deduction of east German tax revenues and social insurance contributions) were transferred from west to east Germany between 1991 and 2006.[115] The president of the German Bundesbank, Axel A. Weber, said in September 2005 that roughly two-thirds of Germany's under-performance in the decade after 1995 was attributable to the costs of unification.[116] From an economic point of view it was, and remains, a matter of particular concern that a large proportion of the transfer payments was directed, not to investment, but to general financial purposes, to subsidies, and, above all, to social benefits. The high level of social benefits shows just how significant the attempt to cushion the effects of unification was. Table 10, which does not include all social benefits, indicates the ways in which the financial transfers were allocated within the social insurance system.

It should be noted that a considerable proportion of the expenditure—140,000 million DM between 1991 and 1995, or 23 per cent—was borne by transfers by west German contributors from within the pensions and unemployment insurance system. The high level of social expenditure in the east, together with the recession of 1993, caused a sharp rise in the social expenditure rate, i.e. in the share of gross domestic product taken by the social security budget.

Table 9 Public payments to the new *Bundesländer*, 1991–1995 (excluding transactions by the *Treuhandanstalt*) (in thousand million DM)

Gross payments	1991	1992	1993	1994	1995	Total
°Federal government	75	88	114	114	135	526
°West German *Länder* and local authorities	5	5	10	14	10	44
°'German Unity' fund	31	24	15	5	—	75
°European Community budget	4	5	5	6	7	27
°Federal Institute of Labour	24	25	15	17	16	97
°Statutory pensions insurance	—	5	9	12	17	43
Total, comprising:	139	152	168	168	185	812
°°social benefits	56	69	78	73	79	355
°°subsidies	8	10	11	17	18	64
°°investment	22	23	26	26	34	131
°°general financial purposes (not specified)	53	50	53	52	54	262
Federal revenues in east Germany						
°tax revenues	−31	−35	−37	−41	−43	−187
°administrative revenues	−2	−2	−2	−2	−2	−10
Total	−33	−37	−39	−43	−45	−197
Total net payments	106	115	129	125	140	615

Source: Deutsche Bundesbank, *Monatsbericht Oktober 1996*, vol. 48, p. 19. The figures for transfer payments do not include tax losses arising from special tax deductions for private investment in the east, nor assistance given by the *Treuhand* to its firms.

Table 10 Financial transfers within the social security system, 1991–1994 (in thousand million DM)

Financial transfers	1991	1992	1993	1994	Total
1 **Old-age protection**					
Total, comprising:	8.2	14.7	19.9	27.5	70.3
°pensions insurance[a]	—	4.5	8.8	12.5	25.8
°Federal Labour Ministry budget (Federal subsidy etc.)	8.2	10.2	11.1	15.0	44.5
2 **Labour market policy schemes and unemployment insurance**					
Total, comprising:	31.5	45.1	48.7	40.7	166.0
°Federal Institute of Labour[b]	23.6	24.6	15.1	17.4	80.7
°Federal Labour Ministry budget (Federal subsidy, early retirement etc.)	7.9	20.5	33.6	23.3	85.3
3 **War victims (Federal Labour Ministry)**	0.3	0.9	1.7	1.4	4.3
4 **Total, comprising:**	40.0	60.7	70.3	69.6	240.6
°social insurance	23.6	29.1	23.9	29.9	106.5
°Federal Labour Ministry budget	16.4	31.6	46.4	39.7	134.1

[a] According to *Rentenversicherungsbericht 1994*.

[b] Omitting Federal subsidy.

Source: Based on *Unterrichtung durch die Bundesregierung*, BTDrs 13/2280, 8 September 1995, p. 116.

The social expenditure rate in the Federal Republic had fallen significantly between 1982 and 1990, from 30 per cent to 26.9 per cent, partly as a result of the policy of financial consolidation and partly because of economic expansion. It then rose to 31.4 per cent in 1996, primarily owing to the very high level of social benefits, relative to gross domestic product, in the east.

The enormous scale of the transfer payments and the sharp rise in the social expenditure rate signalled, of course, the end of the policy of financial consolidation. The state expenditure rate (state expenditure as a percentage of gross domestic product in current prices), which had fallen from 50.1 per cent in 1982 to 45.8 per cent in 1989, rose again to 50.0 per cent in 1993.[117] The increase in public debt, from 929,000 million DM in 1989 to more than twice that amount—1,996,000 million DM—in 1995, was even more dramatic.[118] A surplus of 107,000 million DM in the foreign trade balance under the old Federal Republic in 1989 was replaced by a deficit totalling 125,000 million DM in the years 1991 to 1994.[119] The Federal Republic's net foreign assets of nearly 460,000 million DM at the end of 1989 proved to be invaluable in helping cushion the impact of unification on the country's trading position.

Rising social expenditure sent additional wage costs soaring. In the old *Bundesländer* employers' and employees' social insurance contributions alone (exclusive of accident insurance) rose from 35.5 per cent of employee gross earnings in 1990 to 39.1 per cent in 1994 and 42.1 per cent in 1997.[120] That said, critics of the high level of additional wage costs often overlook the fact that only the minority of these costs (roughly 45 per cent) arise out of social insurance contributions and other statutory social benefits paid by employers (paid holidays, continued payment of wages in case of sickness), while the majority (roughly 55 per cent) are accounted

Table 11 The social security budget of the Federal Republic of Germany, 1991–1996
Federal Republic

Year	Total social benefits					Gross domestic product	
	Thousand million €	Direct benefits in thousand million €	Change (%)[a]	Social expenditure rate (%)[b]	€ per inhabitant	Thousand million €	Change (%)[a]
1991	427.0	399.7	—	27.8	5,338	1534.6	—
1992	484.2	453.4	13.4	29.4	6,008	1646.6	7.3
1993	508.9	476.6	5.1	30.0	6,269	1694.4	2.9
1994	531.2	497.7	4.4	29.8	6,524	1780.8	5.1
1995	562.5	525.6	5.9	30.4	6,889	1848.5	3.8
1996	588.5	532.9	4.6	31.4	7,186	1876.2	1.5

Note: Key social security budget statistics (in current prices).
Source for these and subsequent statistics: *Sozialbericht 2005*, pp. 192f. The figures for the social expenditure rate contained in earlier *Sozialberichte* were revised significantly downwards in the revised data on national income and expenditure published by the Federal Statistical Office on 28 April 2005. This was due to the rise in the nominal gross domestic product.

West Germany

Year	Total social benefits					Gross domestic product	
	Thousand million €	Direct benefits in thousand million €	Change (%)[a]	Social expenditure rate (%)[b]	€ per inhabitant	Thousand million €	Change (%)[a]
1991	370.5	344.9	—	26.2	5,781	1416.3	—
1992	402.3	374.0	8.6	26.9	6,202	1495.7	5.6
1993	419.0	389.6	4.2	27.8	6,394	1509.6	0.9
1994	437.0	406.7	4.3	27.9	6,636	1588.7	3.9
1995	461.5	428.6	5.6	28.4	6,975	1622.4	3.4
1996	481.9	433.4	4.4	29.3	7,252	1642.5	1.2

Note: Key social security budget statistics (in current prices).

East Germany

Year	Total social benefits					Gross domestic product	
	Thousand million €	Direct benefits in thousand million €	Change (%)[a]	Social expenditure rate (%)[b]	€ per inhabitant	Thousand million €	Change (%)[a]
1991	56.5	54.9	—	47.8	3,553	118.3	—
1992	81.9	79.4	45.0	54.3	5,207	150.9	27.6
1993	89.9	87.1	9.8	48.7	5,746	184.7	22.4
1994	94.1	91.0	4.7	44.4	6,049	212.1	14.8
1995	101.1	97.0	7.4	44.7	6,520	226.0	6.6
1996	106.6	99.4	5.5	45.6	6,904	233.7	3.4

[a] Changes from previous year, per cent.
[b] Social expenditure relative to gross domestic product, per cent.

Note: Key social security budget statistics (in current prices).

for by negotiated and firm-based additional employment costs.[121] In Germany, typically, public allocations constituted only a relatively small proportion of total expenditure in the social security budget: indeed, they fell from 38.0 per cent in 1960 to 29.1 per cent in 1990, though they rose again, to 32 per cent, in 1994.[122]

Given the level of social benefits, and the fact that they were financed predominantly by contributions by the insured (28.8 per cent in 1990; 30.0 per cent in 1994) and by employers (38.7 per cent in 1990; 35.6 per cent in 1994),[123] the question arises whether there is a direct connection in the Federal Republic between, on the one hand, the high, and rising, levels of social expenditure and, on the other, the decline in job numbers and the emergence of mass unemployment. This thesis would seem to be borne out if a comparison is made with the 'employment miracle' in the United States, where 20.3 million jobs were created between 1990 and 1999, predominantly in the services sector, and the unemployment rate fell from 7.5 to 4.3 per cent.[124] Fritz W. Scharpf, in particular, has studied this issue closely, making detailed comparative studies of the connections between the welfare state and levels of employment, and of the viability of welfare states in an age of increasing globalization.[125] He has drawn a distinction between those parts of an economy that are particularly exposed to international competition—notably, export industries, agriculture, trans-national transport, and management services—and those that are protected from it by being centred on local markets, such as retail trades, hotels and restaurants, private households, education and health services, and the social services. In the Federal Republic the proportion of employees working in the areas of the economy exposed to international competition is especially high.[126] As the rising export statistics show, the principal way in which the Federal Republic has been able to maintain its internationally competitive position, despite high labour costs, is through increases in productivity (though its share of world exports has admittedly been falling noticeably).[127] For employees, on the other hand, the need to adapt to rapid changes in international markets has made for a less stable employment environment. Workers have had to come to terms with frequent alterations in the qualifications required by new technologies and systems of communication, and, if their qualifications are inadequate, have run the risk of losing their jobs.

By and large, however, the importance for employment of this sector, very highly developed in Germany, has been declining in modern western societies. Conversely, while in most countries there has been a substantial growth in employment in areas of the economy that are protected from international competition, in the Federal Republic the proportion of employment in these areas has been very low in international terms.[128] Germany has differed from the Scandinavian countries, for example, where employment-generating public-sector social services financed by the state play a much larger role, but also from the United States, where in the past decades many millions of low-paid jobs providing basic social services have been created in the private sector. In the Federal Republic tight limits have been set on the expansion of the public service sector, for financial reasons: the high level of public debt, and the threat to the international competitiveness of German businesses posed by higher taxes. On the other hand, the shortfall in privately provided personal services, where it is more or less impossible to increase labour productivity, is closely bound up with the character, costs, and mode of financing of the German welfare state.

Jobs liable for social insurance are not attractive to employees in Germany when the net wages are not significantly higher than rates of unemployment benefit (long-term or otherwise) or of means-tested income support. Conversely, if wages are higher, then such jobs are generally too expensive for the private employer seeking personal services. There have been proposals to resolve this dilemma by providing forms of extra state-financed income—perhaps through negative income tax or a 'citizen's income'—or by reducing social insurance contributions for employees in low-paid employment.[129] As yet, however, such proposals have not found favour, for economic and financial reasons. The commission of enquiry into demographic change set up by the Bundestag at the end of 1992 estimated that in comparison both with the USA and with other states in the European Community, there was still an untapped potential for between five and seven million service sector jobs, mainly simple jobs involving minimal qualifications.[130]

The shortfall in jobs was caused partly by the high rates of social insurance contributions and partly by the relatively generous scale of transfer payments for social security. At the same time, the fact that a high proportion of the population was not in gainful employment was driving the costs of the welfare state, especially the financing of unemployment and early retirement, ever higher. The vicious circle whereby high social expenditure led to rising unemployment, which in turn imposed greater burdens on the welfare state, was a result of the link, particularly close in the German system in comparison with other countries, between social insurance and employment. However, it was also significantly exacerbated by the 'unification crisis', which placed heavy new burdens on social insurance, and by the erosion of the organizational structures on the two sides of industry, which undermined the system of labour relations in east Germany.[131] The so-called 'German model', promoted by the Social Democrats in the elections of 1976, had once been internationally recognized as a relatively frictionless solution to the problems of structural economic change, achieved by binding trade unions and employers' associations into a neo-corporatist system of negotiation and mediation of interests. The model had begun to come under pressure even before 1990, owing to structural unemployment, the ageing of the population, and the increasing globalization of markets, among other factors. The severe crisis that afflicted it from the early 1990s onwards, however, was primarily an effect of German unification.

3.4 COMPARATIVE LIVING STANDARDS IN EAST AND WEST GERMANY

The high transfer payments that were made in the first years after unification—averaging between 7,000 and 8,000 DM per inhabitant annually in east Germany in the years 1991–4—played a substantial part in improving living standards in the new *Bundesländer*. Although standards in the east remained significantly below those in the west in 1994 (as is still the case at the time of writing), average net total annual income per worker in employment in east Germany rose from 16,728 DM in 1991 to 25,182 DM in 1994, or from 55.7 to 78 per cent of the corresponding income of a worker in west Germany.[132] Average disposable income per private household in the east grew more rapidly still, moving from 1,765 DM to 3,196 DM per month over the same period, or from 47.7 to 78 per cent of disposable household income in the west.[133]

It is significant that although the range of incomes in the east increased between 1990 and 1994, it remained considerably less wide than that in the west. In 1990 only 3.4 per cent of all east Germans had an income of less than 50 per cent of average income, and only 1.1 per cent had an income in excess of 200 per cent of the average. By 1994 these figures had shifted to 8.5 and 2.2 per cent respectively, but they still contrasted with corresponding figures of 11.4 and 5.1 per cent in west Germany in the same year.[134] Negotiated weekly blue-collar working hours in the east fell by 0.6 hours to 39.6 hours between 1990 and 1994, but remained about two hours longer than those in the west.[135] Annual holidays were, on average, five days shorter than in the west in 1990 and two and a half days shorter in 1994.[136]

In 1993 the size of an average home in the east, at 64.4 square metres, was considerably smaller than the western figure (86.8 square metres), and homes were also less well equipped. Only 87.8 per cent of homes had an indoor WC (as against 98.6 per cent in the west), and only 57.3 per cent a modern heating system (compared with 91.1 per cent in the west).[137] On the other hand, rents in the east were also significantly lower. In 1994 pensioners in the east spent 15.4 per cent of their disposable income on rent, and persons in employment 11 per cent; the corresponding figures in the west were 23.9 and 17.7 per cent.[138]

There was pronounced inequality between east and west with regard to wealth. In 1993 average net monetary wealth per private household in west Germany was 53,800 DM: more than three times the level of private-household wealth in the east, which stood at only 15,300 DM.[139] Moreover, in 1993 only 27.7 per cent of eastern households were owner-occupied, compared with 50.5 per cent in the west.[140] In the case of productive assets the distribution between east and west has been even more unequal. A considerable proportion of the approximately 14,000 eastern enterprises, formerly in public ownership, that were sold by the *Treuhand* passed into the hands of west German or foreign firms and owners, owing to the dearth of available capital in eastern Germany. Often east Germans got a look-in only when an enterprise was taken over by managerial staff or other parts of the workforce. Many of these enterprises were small or medium-sized businesses in the tertiary sector. Overall, east Germany was, in significant measure, 'capitalized by west Germany'.[141]

Both within east German society, and in comparison with west Germany, unification has led to an especially marked improvement in the financial position of older people. In the German Democratic Republic average pensions in 1988, at 37.7 per cent of gross earned income, were extremely low by west German standards.[142] With the large increase that was implemented at the start of monetary union on 1 July 1990, and then with the several increases that followed at fairly short intervals until 1994, the 'benchmark pension' (the old-age pension of an average wage-earner with 45 years of insurance) more than doubled, reaching a level of 75.2 per cent of the benchmark pension in the west.[143] By 1994 *average* pensions of insured persons stood at 88.5 per cent of western pensions in the case of men, while for women, most of whom had been employed for much longer than women in the west, the corresponding figure was actually 128 per cent.[144] However, when interpreting these statistics one must also bear in mind that in east Germany, average pensions from statutory insurance include the pensions of doctors, pharmacists, judges, university teachers, and others on higher incomes, whereas their opposite numbers in the west mainly have either civil servants' pensions or pensions based on occupational insurance systems. It should be remembered, too, that in the east retired people are dependent almost exclusively on income from statutory pensions insurance, while in the west many more pensioners receive additional income from supplementary provision for public servants, company pensions, private life insurance, or personal wealth; many also own their own house or flat. Even though statutory insurance pensions were roughly equal between east and west by 1995, net household incomes of people aged 65 and over in the east were significantly lower in all types of households—married couples, men living alone, widows, divorced and single women—than corresponding household incomes in the west.[145] Even in 1999 married couples aged 65 and over in the west derived only 56 per cent of their gross income from statutory pensions insurance, as against 91 per cent in the east. Average incomes of elderly married couples in the west, at €1,997 per month, were accordingly well above those of couples in the east (€1,783).[146] On the other hand, as far as statutory pensions insurance on its own is concerned, in 2002 average pensions for men in the east, at €1,085 per month, were considerably higher than those for men in the west (€997), and the same was true for women (€654 versus €466).[147]

The position of those over the age of 60 in the east has improved markedly in comparison with other social groups. In 1990 46.3 per cent of those over 60 had an income below 75 per cent of average income, and only 25.3 per cent had an income above 100 per cent. By 1994 only 11.9 per cent of this group had an income below 75 per cent of average income, while 54.4 per cent now had an income in excess of 100 per cent.[148] This group clearly gained significantly from unification. The biggest losers from unification were single mothers with young children. They were particularly severely exposed to the risk of unemployment and, if they lost their jobs, also forfeited the social benefits that were typically associated with the workplace in the GDR. Many of the advantages that they had enjoyed in the GDR, such as preference in the allocation of housing, or extended exemption from work in the event of children's illness, either ceased to be relevant or were discontinued.

Young families also lost out as a result of unification. The GDR's policy of encouraging a high birth rate had led many young people to live together, supported by high subsidies from the state. Under the new dispensation they found themselves disadvantaged by a combination of factors. Young women of child-bearing age and women with (several) children were particularly affected by unemployment, as well as by cutbacks in the provision of non-school children's services such as crèches, day-care centres, and kindergartens or by the rising costs of such services, which in the GDR had been free of charge. At the same time, rises in housing rents, and the abolition of the subsidies on food, energy costs, and children's clothing which such families had previously received, led to a disproportionate increase in living costs. In addition, the rise in incomes of larger households was significantly smaller than that of two-person households.[149]

Relative income poverty, defined as income of less than 50 per cent of average income in east and west Germany respectively, affected 3.4 per cent of the population of east Germany in 1990 and 8.5 per cent in 1994, but even in 1994 it was considerably less widespread than in west Germany, where the figures changed very little during the same period (10.9 per cent in 1990, and 11.4 per cent in 1994).[150] Similarly, although the proportion of those receiving regular assistance with living costs in east Germany rose after 1990, the figures for 1996—1.9 per cent of Germans and 5.7 per cent of foreigners—were well below those in the west, where 3 per cent of Germans and 8.6 per cent of foreigners were in receipt of this form of income support.[151]

The statistics on changing social conditions outlined here show that east German society was becoming more like west German society, with its greater range of living standards, but that the differences between rich and poor nevertheless continued to be less pronounced, by and large, than in the west, owing to the considerable levelling-out of incomes and wealth that had taken place in the GDR. Furthermore, in 1994 there was still a substantial disparity in living standards between the old and the new *Bundesländer*, even though some of the ground had been made up by the east.

3.5 CHANGES IN THE WORLD OF WORK

As well as unification, changes in the world of work posed a serious challenge to the German welfare state and, in particular, to the traditional system of social insurance. In comparison with social security systems in other countries, the German model is based very heavily on contributions by employees and employers, and therefore on gainful employment. To ensure an adequate level of social protection, especially in old age and in the case of disability, an employee typically needs to have been in long-term full-time employment in a normal employer–employee relationship that is liable for social insurance and protected under employment law (regarding unfair dismissal, for instance). This normal employment relationship, which had gradually become the established pattern during the course of industrialization in western countries, entered a state of crisis in the 1970s and has since been at growing risk of being eroded away.[152]

There are a number of reasons why this happened. Structural changes in the economy caused traditional skilled qualifications to decline in significance and forced the under-skilled, and the insufficiently adaptable, out of the labour market. Structural unemployment emerged, creating a hard core of long-term unemployed who were unable to find jobs, even in periods of economic expansion. In addition, the secondary labour market based on active and passive state employment schemes became increasingly important; government policies and economic pressures encouraged people to take early retirement on grounds of age or disability, so depleting the potential labour force; and a 'hidden reserve' of people who would have been in employment under other labour market conditions was generated.

At the same time, the growing tendency for women to seek employment served to increase the supply of workers, while also prompting a desire for more individualized forms of employment that would provide a better balance between work and family life. Men, too, were moving in a similar direction, wishing to devote more time to the family, consumption, and leisure. Primarily, however, the trend towards more individualized working relations was driven by technological developments, and by the endeavour of many employers to circumvent the legal regulations surrounding the normal employment relationship. Various forms of spurious freelance employment sprang up, allowing employers to avoid paying social insurance contributions. The lack of absorptive capacity in the normal labour market, however, also reinforced people's willingness to adopt self-employed status. In addition, short-term employment contracts, part-time work (preferred by many women), subcontracted work, home working, 'small-scale employment' (*geringfügige Beschäftigung*)—for which employees do not have to pay taxes or insurance contributions, while employers pay at greatly reduced rates—and even illicit work became more significant. All of these forms of work—to which should be added work in call centres and 'portfolio careers' made up of several part-time jobs—had the effect of loosening the previously close link between the employee, a particular firm, and a job provided by the latter.

According to an analysis by the 'Commission for Questions about the Future' set up by Bavaria and Saxony, the proportion of people in a normal employment relationship in the old *Bundesländer*, relative to all employees, fell from 80 per cent in 1985 to 68 per cent in 1995.[153] Statistics of forms of employment in Berlin show that the proportion of full-time white- and blue-collar workers in a 'normal employment relationship', relative to the residential population able to work, fell from 44.7 per cent in 1991 to 32.3 per cent in 1998.[154] According to an inquiry by the German Bundesbank in 2005[155] the number of workers employed on a full-time basis fell by one-fifth between 1991 and 2004, from 29.5 to 23.75 million. This decline particularly affected employees liable for social insurance, who now numbered just under 27 million, of whom 4.25 million were working for limited hours. The number of full-time employees liable for social insurance fell by 3.25 million between 1993 and 2004, whereas the number of those working part-time, many of them women, rose by one million. In the new *Bundesländer* part-time working increased by as much as 60 per cent, although the proportion of part-time women workers, relative to all women workers liable for social insurance, remained significantly lower, at one-quarter, than in the old *Bundesländer*, where the proportion was nearly one-third. The majority of women in the east undertook part-time work only because they were unable to find full-time work, whereas 93.5 per cent of part-time women workers in the west made a deliberate choice to limit their working hours. In mid-2004 4.75 million persons in employment were working on a 'small scale': this was almost twice as many as in 1991 (nearly 2.5 million). Roughly 2.5 million of those in employment in 2004 were working on short-term contracts, while around 400,000 people were engaged in subcontracted work. The number of self-employed, including family members assisting the self-employed, rose by one-fifth between 1991 and 2004, to 4.25 million. The decline in full-time jobs liable for social insurance represented by these figures indicates that a growing number of employees now had insufficient protection via statutory pensions insurance.

The old categories enshrined in employment and social law, which are based on the model of the normal employment relationship between employee and employer, no longer reflect the diversified and increasingly informal nature of employment. There is growing public awareness, too, of the roles of unpaid family work[156] and voluntary work. It is becoming increasingly clear that the traditionally clear-cut distinction between the normal employee–employer relationship and other forms of employment—and indeed the distinction between employment and non-employment—is an outdated one.

The creeping erosion of the normal employment relationship, evidenced by demands for deregulation and increased flexibility in employment law, has been given added impetus by the increase in competition over the location of production, itself a result of globalization. Competition over location has weakened the position of labour as a factor of production, and strengthened that of capital and knowledge. This change is reflected in the decline in the power of the trade unions, which so far have had little success in attracting workers involved in the new forms of employment or including them in negotiated wage agreements.

Changes in the world of work and the crisis in employment—in particular, the existence of both overt and concealed mass unemployment—pose the question whether the close connection in Germany between the social insurance system and employment, primarily within the framework of a normal employment relationship, may not have to be abolished, or at least loosened, in the not too distant future. If adjustments of some sort are not made, it may be impossible to prevent the social insurance system from collapsing, as ever smaller numbers of people in long-term employment find themselves shouldering an ever greater financial burden.

4

The Social Structure and Expectations from Social Policy

4.1 DEMOGRAPHIC CHANGE AND ITS CONSEQUENCES

For a long time, politicians and policy-makers in the Federal Republic ignored the great problems that the dramatic fall in the birth rate and the steady ageing of the population were going to cause to society, to the economy, to the labour market, and, especially, to the various systems of social insurance. Attitudes began to shift in the early 1990s. In the autumn of 1992 the German Bundestag set up a commission of enquiry, composed of members of parliament and non-political experts, into demographic change. The commission was charged with compiling 'general social data relevant to demographic change'. It was also asked to assess the 'social, economic and social protection effects that demographic change [would have] on later generations', to establish what 'steps [would] need to be taken', and to recommend what 'policy decisions [would] be necessary'; in the meantime, any such decisions would be deferred.[1] The commission produced two interim reports, in June 1994 and in October 1998, and a final report in May 2002. These reports, together with the population forecast produced by the Federal Statistical Office in June 2003,[2] form the principal basis for the discussion that follows.

The fundamental problem was the ageing of German society, caused by the combination of increasing life expectancy and a constantly low birth rate. In 1990 the proportion of the population aged 60 or over was 21 per cent; forecasts predicted that by 2030 the proportion would rise to more than 30 per cent.[3] In the old Federal Republic the net reproduction rate, which is based on the number of female births and indicates the extent to which the age-specific fertility rate for a given time-period is sufficient to ensure the continuance of a population over the long term, had already fallen below 1 in 1970, and since the mid-1970s had stood at between 0.60 and 0.69.[4] In other words, for every 100 women, only between 60 and 69 girls who would themselves reach child-bearing age were being born. The fall in the number of births was the result not only of the shift towards two- and one-child families but of an increase in childlessness: the proportion of childless women in the old Federal Republic had risen from 9.2 per cent of those born in 1935 to a projected 23 per cent of those born in 1960.[5] Since then the proportion of both women and men remaining childless throughout their lives has risen by a further one-third, and is the highest in the world.[6]

In the German Democratic Republic, too, there was a sharp fall in the birth rate from the late 1960s onwards and a fall in the net reproduction rate.[7] Nevertheless, probably as a result of the state's wide-ranging measures in demographic, social, and family policy, from the late 1970s onwards the birth rate was significantly higher in east Germany than in the west.[8] With unification, however, a dramatic change took place in the east. The number of births fell steeply, from almost 200,000 in 1989 to 108,000 in 1991 and to nearly 79,000 in 1994. Even in 1997, although there was a renewed rise, to 98,500, the number was still well below half the figure for the 1980s.[9] Plainly, some people were postponing the moment when they would have children. Others, though, were perhaps deciding not to have children at all, in view of mass unemployment and the general upheaval in the economy. Women with small children, in particular, were fearful that there would be fewer opportunities for them in the labour market, which in any case was shrinking. Furthermore, the family policy measures that the GDR had promoted—for example, preferential treatment in the allocation of housing—were now being phased out, and the closure of many child care facilities made it more difficult for women to combine employment with bringing up children.[10]

The ageing of the population has significant consequences for the labour market, for economic innovation, and for the system of social protection. In addition, all west European countries are seeing the 'dis-employment' of the elderly,[11] even in the expanding service sector, at the very time when levels of life expectancy are high and rising. In the old *Bundesländer* the labour-force participation rate (the ratio of the labour force to the working-age population) for men aged between 55 and 60 fell from 94 to 81 per cent between 1960 and 1990, and that for men aged between 60 and 65 from 67 to as low as 35 per cent. By 1996 the labour-force participation rate of these two age-groups in Germany as a whole had fallen further, to 76 and 30 per cent respectively.[12] In comparison with other countries of the European Union, the labour-force participation rate in Germany for all workers aged between 55 and 65, at 37.8 per cent in 1999, was admittedly in the middle range: certainly much higher than the comparable rates in France, Italy and Belgium, but well below the figures for Denmark, Sweden, and the United Kingdom.[13] All the same, the average age at which men began to draw a pension fell from 61.5 to 59.5 years in the two decades up to 1993.[14] Early retirement became the rule. In effect, the interest of firms, which was to obtain a socially acceptable reduction in the number of older employees, prevailed over the interests of society as a whole, and of those bearing the cost of social insurance in particular, in retaining a high level of employment, including of older people. In most cases, early retirement was effected through a redundancy agreement guaranteeing the individual in question a net income of about 90 per cent via a combination of a redundancy payment and unemployment benefit, followed at the age of 60 by a pension on grounds of unemployment. The costs that firms were thereby able to pass on, at the expense of the unemployment and pensions insurance systems, were enormous. Roughly speaking, 100,000 receivers of unemployment benefit cost the Federal Institute of Labour about 2.4 thousand million DM per year, while a complete year-group of people taking early retirement generated about 12,000 million DM in additional payments.[15] About three-quarters of those beginning to draw a pension in 1996—roughly 70 per cent in the west and 95 per cent in the east—were employees who were leaving employment before the age of 65.[16] Among single women aged between 60 and 65 the labour-force participation rate in the old Federal Republic almost halved between 1960 and 1990, falling from 39 to 21 per cent, and in Germany as a whole it fell to 14 per cent by 1992. In the east the falls in labour-force participation rates for older people in 1992, reinforced by early-retirement regulations and the provision of transitional pre-pension payments, were particularly sharp: to 44 per cent for men aged 55 to 60 and to 16 per cent for those aged 60 to 65, and to 26 and 3 per cent for the corresponding age-groups of women.[17] The actual level of employment of older people was considerably lower still, since the labour-force participation rate includes the unemployed and, in particular, the long-term unemployed, many of them older workers.[18] Recent legislation has sought to raise the labour-force participation rate, by making early retirement more difficult to obtain and imposing substantial reductions from the statutory pension. The Grand Coalition formed in November 2005 announced that in the long term the statutory pensionable age would be raised from 65 to 67.[19] These government measures have halted the trend towards early retirement, and have even led to a slight rise both in the age at which people are drawing their pension and in the labour-force participation rate for employees over 55. So far, however, attempts at radical change have failed, as there have been insufficient numbers of jobs suitable for older employees.[20]

In its first interim report in 1994 the commission of enquiry predicted that the size of the potential workforce would at first remain static, or show only a slight increase, but would then decrease considerably until about 2010; it also forecast that the workforce's age profile would become higher, for demographic reasons.[21] Government policy would therefore have to provide solutions to different sets of problems: high, albeit slowly declining, unemployment up to 2010, and a probable labour shortage thereafter. Preparations would have to be made for after 2010, when the lowering in the age profile of the workforce would need to be reversed and the labour-force participation rate for women considerably increased.[22]

The second report, produced in 1998, was less definite in its predictions about changes in the labour market. It did say that there would be an improvement on the supply side as a result of the changing age structure of the population, and that this would outweigh the effects of the rise in women's employment. However, the commission's studies concluded that unemployment would continue at a high level, or even increase, until 2010. The strain on the labour market would probably not relax until after that date: indeed, according to most forecasts a more substantial fall in unemployment would not take place until after 2015, and even then unemployment would be far from eliminated.[23] The commission's final report of 2002 stated merely that a 'clear improvement on the supply side of the labour market . . . as a result of the decline in the size of the workforce is foreseeable in the long term'.[24] It should be noted, of course, that all of these predictions were based on models containing variables whose values are very difficult to determine. Crucial factors, such as the effects of business cycles, changes in productivity, policies on working hours, legislation on pensionable age, women's levels of employment, the extent of immigration, economic demand at home and abroad, and the willingness of firms to recruit older workers, cannot be known for certain or are liable to substantial error.

As far as the financing of the systems of social security is concerned, changes in the youth and age quotients are particularly important. The youth quotient denotes the proportion of those aged between 0 and 20 relative to that of the central generation of 21- to 59-year-olds, i.e. most of those of working age; the age quotient denotes the proportion of those aged 60 and above. The two figures taken together indicate the size of the burden carried by the generation of working age. Between 1950 and 1990 the youth quotient in the Federal Republic fell from 59.3 to 39.0 per cent, while the age quotient rose from 26.0 to 36.5 per cent.[25] In the GDR the youth quotient also fell, though less sharply, from 60.2 to 48.6 per cent, while the age quotient rose from 30.9 to only 34.5 per cent. In both parts of Germany, in other words, the overall burden on the central generation fell considerably as a result of the fall in the number of births, especially after 1970. After 1990 the age quotient in the united Germany rose further, to 43.9 per cent in 2001. According to forecasts by the Federal Statistical Office based on middle-range assumptions about average life expectancy and immigration, the age quotient is expected to reach 54.8 per cent in 2020 and 77.8 per cent in 2050.[26]

The increase in the proportion of elderly people in the population, particularly of the very old (those aged 80 and over),[27] will have powerful effects on the labour market, consumption, services for the elderly, the health service, the health insurance system, social care and social care insurance, and, of course, pensions insurance. In the public debate on the question, a number of ways of compensating for the reduction in the potential workforce and of reforming social insurance have been proposed. These include continuing to increase labour productivity, raising the retirement age, increasing the female labour-force participation rate—which in Germany is well below that in the Scandinavian countries and in the United Kingdom[28]—and introducing a selective immigration policy designed to encourage integration.[29] As far as the latter is concerned, however, no increase in immigration to Germany that is feasible is likely to have much impact. Even if there were an annual average net inflow of 200,000 people—which would require a very much larger gross inflow, given the high number of those who leave the country—the number of 20- to 65-year-olds in the population is still likely to shrink by about 10.3 million between 2001 and 2050, from 51.1 to 40.8 million, while the number of those aged 65 and over is likely to rise from 14.1 to 22.2 million, an increase of about 8.1 million.[30]

Discussion has also centred on the medium- and long-term impact of the ageing of the population on provision for the elderly. Competing objectives and interests are involved here. For some, the chief priority has been the preservation in old age of living standards enjoyed by the individual during his or her working life; for others, it has been the prevention of poverty in old age within the population generally. In addition, there have been heated debates about the extent to which the generation of working age will be able to bear the burden of supporting the elderly;

about whether or not objectives of family policy should be relevant (for instance, whether the period spent bringing up children should be taken into account for pensions insurance); about the reduction of the burden on labour markets through early retirement; and about calls to increase the competitiveness of the economy by lowering, or at least halting any further rises in, social insurance contributions. Feelings have run high because these various aims are not all compatible with one another. A few of the reforms that have been suggested may be mentioned here. One, which began with the so-called 'Riester pension' (proposed in 2000–1 by the Minister of Labour Walter Riester) and was reaffirmed under the terms of the coalition agreement of 11 November 2005, has been that provision for the elderly through statutory pensions insurance should be supplemented by employees' firms and by private financial arrangements, supported by the state.[31] A reform of 2004 took account of demographic change by linking the size of pensions to the ratio of pensioners to insurance contributors. Other reforms include switching partially or completely from the system of pensions financing based on current contributions (*Umlageverfahren*) to a system based on accumulated capital (*Kapitaldeckungsverfahren*); introducing a system of basic protection for all citizens, financed through taxation, but allowing for supplementation by company pensions and private individual provision; guaranteeing minimum protection within the framework of statutory pensions insurance; introducing a system of 'citizen's insurance' or of a per capita flat rate within the health insurance system, supplemented by state benefits for those on low incomes and for children's insurance;[32] extending contributions liability to all employment income, or to all adults, employed or otherwise; raising the pensionable age; requiring firms to pay a value-creation tax; reducing provision for surviving dependants; establishing a separate system of old-age protection, including for non-employed women; or creating a parent's pension, or a graduated system of contribution rates depending on a person's number of children.[33] Almost all of these suggestions have had the aim of removing, or at any rate loosening, the link between statutory pensions insurance and employment, tying pensions policy more closely to old age protection policy, and taking account of the changes that have occurred in the world of work and the age structure of the population.

The ageing of the population has, of course, also affected both statutory and private health insurance inasmuch as older people are, on average, more susceptible to illness. Similarly, social care insurance has been affected by the rapidly mounting demand for such care, particularly by the very old.[34] The extent to which increased immigration into Germany may be able to ease the strain on the systems of social protection will depend crucially on the absorptive capacity of the labour market, the qualifications and the age and family structures of new immigrants, the point in time at which immigrants cease employment on grounds either of disability or age, and their life expectancy.[35] Even under favourable assumptions, immigration will at best mitigate the problems of the social protection systems: it will not solve them.

Like the ageing of the population, alterations in family structure have been a key feature of demographic change in Germany in recent decades. Although in the early 1990s families with married parents were still the predominant family type, constituting 83 per cent of all families with children,[36] conventional marriage and family have been losing their hold as life-patterns, particularly among the younger generation. Non-marital partnerships, with or without children, single-parent families, and one-person households have become increasingly common, and marriage rates have fallen sharply. An individual's likelihood of contracting at least one marriage in his or her lifetime—the first-marriage rate—fell equally for both men and women in both parts of Germany between 1960 and 1990, from almost 100 per cent to approximately 60 per cent.[37]

In east Germany the number of new marriages abruptly dropped to below half after unification. At the same time, the number of divorces, which had been particularly high in the GDR, fell to less than one-fifth.[38] This was probably a result, not only of the new marriage law, but of the rising need for family security, as a counterbalance to the drastic changes that were taking place in society, the state, and, particularly, working life. Even in 1996 divorces in the east stood at only two-fifths of the average figure for the late 1980s.[39]

In both west and east Germany the number of non-marital partnerships has increased sharply, especially among the younger generation. According to estimates by the Federal Statistical Office, the proportion of people living in such partnerships, relative to the overall population, rose from 0.4 per cent in 1972 to 3.5 per cent in 1992.[40] The true figure, however, was probably much higher, as the calculations did not include partners who, though maintaining formally separate households, were in fact predominantly living together in a single household. In the new *Bundesländer* 4.3 per cent of the population were living in non-marital partnerships. A very striking difference between east and west Germany is that in 1991 in the west only 18.5 per cent of these partnership households also included children, whereas the figure in the east was 55 per cent.[41] In other words, a non-marital partnership in the west would appear much more commonly to constitute a stage preliminary to marriage than has been the case in the east. A significant difference between the Federal Republic and the GDR before unification lay in the proportion of births outside marriage, where the figure was 10.5 per cent in the west but 33.6 per cent in the east. By 1998 these rates had risen to 15.9 per cent in the old *Bundesländer* and 47.1 per cent in the new.[42] The high proportion of births outside marriage in the GDR was a consequence, albeit unintended, of the state's social policies. Under these policies unmarried mothers were granted paid leave from work for up to three years after the birth of a first child. In the case of illness of the first child, they were allowed an extended break from employment, with wages continuing to be paid at a level equivalent to sickness benefit; they were also given priority in the allocation of places at crèches and kindergartens. Similarly, the prospects for unmarried persons and couples of getting a flat were always better if they had a child. Those who had a second child often got married, as the relative advantages that flowed from being unmarried then lapsed.[43]

The number of single parents—in 1991, in the old *Bundesländer*, 83.5 per cent of them women; in the new *Bundesländer*, 87 per cent—has risen sharply in all age-groups, but especially so among the younger. In 1997 there were 2.8 million single-parent households, encompassing 3.8 million children.[44] Single parents constitute a group with particularly pronounced problems, in both parts of Germany. In the GDR—unlike the position in the Federal Republic—the great majority of single parents were in employment. In 1995 73 per cent aspired to work full-time, despite the multiple demands imposed by household tasks, bringing up children, and holding down a job; 15 per cent wanted part-time work. Only 29 per cent, however, were actually employed.[45] The ambition of single parents in the east to provide for themselves and not be dependent on income support is also evident from the fact that while at the end of 1995 29.7 per cent of single parents in west Germany, a much less employment-orientated group, were obtaining income support (in the form of assistance with living expenses), the figure for east Germany was only 12.5 per cent.[46] It is significant, too, that the great majority of single parents in the new *Bundesländer*, unlike many of their opposite numbers in the west, do not subscribe to a 'singles' lifestyle but are looking for a partner.[47]

Those with large numbers of children in Germany have become increasingly at risk of poverty. Whereas the proportion of older people receiving income support was falling, children and young people were steadily becoming one of the main recipient groups. At the end of 1996 over a million children and young people below the age of 18 were in receipt of income support—that is, 38 per cent of all recipients. Almost half of these were children of single mothers.[48] The chances of a child under the age of 7 becoming a recipient of income support almost quadrupled between 1980 and 1996.[49]

A final key element in the long-term change in the social structure is the increase in the number of one-person households. Only part of the total is made up of people who have deliberately chosen to live alone. Many are widows and widowers, students and trainees, young employed people who have not yet embarked on family life, or people who have separated and are seeking a new partner. The important point, however, is that rising levels of prosperity have enabled them to establish their own households: they have not needed to lodge with relatives or strangers.

In the old *Bundesländer* the proportion, relative to all households, of private households consisting of only one person rose from 19.4 per cent in 1950 to 36.3 per cent in 1997: in other words, almost doubled. The corresponding figure for the new *Bundesländer* and east Berlin in 1997 was somewhat lower, at 31.2 per cent. By 1996 the proportion of one-person households in large cities (of 100,000 people or more), where the trend towards a more individualistic lifestyle has been especially pronounced, had risen to 44.3 per cent of all households; indeed, in some cities, such as Munich, they formed an absolute majority of households.[50] The proportions both of two-person households and of people living in two-person households also increased considerably. Correspondingly, the proportion of larger households fell sharply: in 1950, in the old Federal Republic, 16.1 per cent of households comprised five or more members; in 1997 the figure was 4.9 per cent, and in the east it was only 3.3 per cent.[51]

The effect of the decrease in births and the rising numbers of single parents, childless marriages, and families and partnerships with only one child has, of course, been that many people now live without a spouse or partner, without children or grandchildren, and without siblings. Kinship networks are becoming smaller. Rising life expectancy has similarly increased the proportion of people living on their own, particularly in the case of older women. As ageing increases, and especially as the number of people in their eighties grows, demands for social care will inevitably follow suit. The likelihood, however, that those needing such care will be able to avail themselves of the support of a spouse, children, or siblings will steadily diminish, not only because of the decline in kinship networks, but also because more women, who in the past mainly took on the tasks of caring, are now in employment. People are much more commonly having to construct their own social networks outside the family in order to avoid becoming lonely, especially in old age. This has been happening at a time when the demand for social services is rising across the board. The introduction of social care insurance in 1995 was a response to needs that were becoming ever more significant in society as a result of the ageing of the population, changes in family structure, a growing pluralism and individualism of lifestyles, and the mounting level of female employment.

4.2 SOCIAL STRATIFICATION IN WEST AND EAST GERMANY

By and large, the old Federal Republic saw itself as an 'open and middle-class society' with a high level of social mobility, and this perception has persisted in the old *Bundesländer* after unification. In fact, however, there is great variation in west Germany as far as the social status, social situation, and lifestyles of individuals and families are concerned. Social status is determined, first and foremost, by a person's profession and his or her position within that profession. Doctors and academics, for example, have considerable social prestige. This indicates that an important factor governing a person's status, in addition to wealth and household income (where the number of income-earners within the household is of great relevance), is the individual's level of education. In general, people with a university education are ranked above graduates of higher secondary schools (*Gymnasium* or *Realschule*), while the latter in turn take precedence, in the common estimation, over people who have attended 'merely' a general secondary school (*Hauptschule*), either obtaining or failing to obtain a *Hauptschulabschluss* or school-leaving qualification. Similarly, white- and blue-collar workers who have completed vocational training are accorded a higher position than unskilled workers. In addition to these factors, social status depends on one's housing conditions, on the security associated with one's job (particularly high in the case of posts in the civil and other public services), and on one's state of health.

Similar criteria apply in east Germany. The radical political and economic changes that have taken place, and the replacement of some of the elites who had been particularly closely associated with the old regime,[52] have given rise to a far greater amount of both upward and downward social mobility than previously existed, and job security has assumed even more significance. In the east, too, a person's level of education and possession of qualifications obtained before unification play an important role. At the same time, the individual's chances of finding a job, or of becoming unemployed or losing status or skills, have been heavily dependent on the area of the economy in which his or her last job before unification belonged. Formal qualifications, and a job linked to them, or technical knowledge and professional skills and experience have proved to be precious resources in the new situation.[53] Other factors from the GDR era have also continued to have an effect: the high number of women seeking employment; the fact that leading executives, with their focus on technology and the particular enterprise, have often found it hard to realize the importance of rapid market integration; the belief that the enterprise and its management should fulfil their social responsibilities to their employees; and the strong identification of employees with 'their' enterprise.[54]

In both west and east Germany there are similar problem groups. In addition to single mothers and families with large numbers of children, whom we have already mentioned, these include the long-term unemployed, workers without professional training qualifications, immigrants—disproportionately represented among those receiving income support[55]—the disabled, and those in need of social care. Frequently problems overlap: unemployment and a lack of qualifications, for example.

The demand for social protection in Germany is considerable. Society is called upon to preserve people's social status in the event of unemployment, illness, disability, need of social care, and old age, and to prevent the groups exposed to these problems from becoming impoverished and marginalized. At the same time, certain groups are inadequately integrated into society and scarcely reached by social policy measures: these include, in the west, the homeless and, in the east, a sizeable body of young people whose frustration at the circumstances in which they find themselves has found expression in violence and hostility to foreigners, on a much greater scale than among young people in the west.[56]

As we have already seen,[57] although the social structure in the east has become closer to that in the west since unification, considerable differences remain: in job structure, in household incomes, in housing conditions, and, above all, in wealth. Social inequality in the east has increased, but remains much less pronounced than in the west. It is very instructive to see how differently people in east and west Germany respond when asked to place themselves within a scheme of social stratification. In 1993, 29 per cent of west Germans, when questioned, described themselves as belonging to the lower or working class, 14 per cent to the upper-middle or upper class, and 58 per cent, a clear majority, to the middle class. In the east, by contrast, 59 per cent of people regarded themselves as belonging to the lower or working class, 40 per cent to the middle class, and only 2 per cent to the upper-middle or upper class.[58] A pyramid-shaped class structure with a wide base, of the sort exemplified by east Germany, is a defining feature of a working-class society. An onion-shaped structure with a broad 'waist', on the other hand, is typical of a society, like that of west Germany, that regards itself as middle-class. The markedly lower self-valuation found in east Germany overstates the real differences between the social classes and is clearly one of the surviving effects of the prestige accorded to the working class in the official ideology of the GDR.

Nevertheless, it is a symptom of the widespread feeling among east Germans that they are under-privileged in comparison with the population of west Germany.

4.3 *ZEITGEIST* AND SOCIAL POLICY IN WEST AND EAST GERMANY, AS REFLECTED IN OPINION SURVEYS

What was the socio-cultural framework surrounding social policy in the early 1990s? What were people's main concerns? What shaped their ideas and hence influenced, if only indirectly, their political behaviour? These are difficult questions to answer, particularly in quantitative terms. The best indications come from representative surveys of public opinion that have been conducted by a number of different institutions, and these are the principal source for the discussion that follows.[59] I shall try, in particular, to establish whether there were significant differences between east and west Germany. How did people in the east cope with the establishment of a completely new political, economic, and social-policy system—one that seemed to devalue their previous experience and understanding of the world, called their qualifications into question, and in very many cases deprived them of one of the central reference-points in their lives in the GDR, the factory or enterprise where they worked? What expectations did they have of the new system, and to what extent were these expectations fulfilled or disappointed?

Probably the most important difference between east and west Germany lies in attitudes to the importance of work. The GDR was a working-class society, and people were integrated into society primarily through work and the enterprise where they were employed. Losing one's job, therefore, not only was feared because of the loss of income involved but could also lead to a severe collapse of self-esteem and cause damage to social relationships. According to a survey conducted in November 1990, east Germans, by a wide margin, saw unemployment as the greatest problem facing society, and it remained their greatest source of anxiety in 1993.[60] By contrast, for west Germans in late 1990 the problems of unification—in particular, the question how it was going to be financed—were at the forefront of their minds; unemployment scarcely featured. Although this had changed by 1993, as a result of the economic recession, anxiety about unemployment remained considerably less significant than in the east and ranked only a little higher than anxieties about crime, the influx of asylum seekers, the maintenance of peace, and the costs of unification. Understandably, individuals' fears that they themselves might become unemployed were much stronger in the east than in the west.[61] Similarly, 58 per cent of those questioned in the east regarded financial protection against unemployment as inadequate, as against only 24 per cent in the west.[62]

The different weightings that were given to work as a sphere of life were highly significant. In the west, work was viewed as 'very important' by only 37 per cent of those questioned—well below the protection of the environment (57 per cent) and only just ahead of leisure (32 per cent). In the east, by contrast, 58 per cent of people saw work as 'very important', as compared with figures of 41 and 24 per cent with regard to the environment and leisure respectively.[63] 30 per cent of people in the west, but only 11 per cent in the east, regarded leisure as more important than one's job or profession.[64] Hedonistic values, which were widespread in the west, particularly among young people, found little echo in the east.[65] In the late 1970s and the 1980s there had been a marked upsurge in post-materialistic ideas in the Federal Republic. (This was seen as one of the reasons for the electoral success of the Green party.[66]) Particularly among the young and in schools and universities, values such as leisure, individual self-realization, and protection of the environment came to take precedence over those of work, material well-being, social order and stability, and other notions of obligation and social acceptability. In the east, although there were many post-materialists among the opposition groups in the early days before unification, such attitudes were less common in the community generally. Environmental protection was also a less prominent consideration.[67] There was a change after the economic crisis of 1992–3, when post-materialist values lost ground in the west too, and went on to the defensive.[68] Reunified Germany is a more materialistic society than the old Federal Republic. During the same period individualistic lifestyles also increasingly caught on in the east. Nevertheless, solidarity and a sense of obligation towards the community have continued to be more strongly emphasized in the east than in the west.

In the east, women were particularly affected by mass unemployment and the radical changes that occurred in the economy. Admittedly, even under the GDR, emancipation and equal rights for women were a matter more of lip service than of reality: leading positions in the party, the government, and the economy were almost entirely the preserve of men, while women were assigned the tasks of looking after children and the home, in line with the traditional division of gender roles.[69] All the same, by contrast with the situation in west Germany, almost all women had full-time jobs, including women with small children.[70] The trajectory of women's lives was accordingly also different. In west Germany, women's lives generally consisted of a traditional sequence of discrete phases: a job before marriage or the birth of the first child, domestic work until the youngest child was ready for school, and then a return to employment, albeit often part-time, as home commitments became fewer again. In east Germany, on the other hand, employment and work in the home were synchronized, the system being made possible by an extensive array of child care facilities.[71] Although many in the west assumed that the 'excessive' level of female employment in the east would decline and return to the 'normal' level prevalent in the west,[72] this assumption proved false. Even though women were hit particularly hard by unemployment and found it very much more difficult to combine work and family than before, their desire to work remained high, partly for economic reasons but also because they were fearful of losing the social contacts and stimulation that went with a job. Thus in 1993, among non-employed women aged between 18 and 63, 76 per cent in east Germany wanted to have a job, while the figure in west Germany was only 23 per cent.[73]

Attitudes formed under the GDR, then, continued to be influential in the unified Federal Republic; and they generated corresponding expectations from the state. For example, a working paper of 8 February 1991 produced by the

Ministry of Labour, Social Affairs, Health, and Women in Brandenburg declared that it was discriminatory and patronizing for mothers attending employment centres to be required—unlike fathers—to prove that their children would be cared for while they were working. The paper called for a continuation of children's day-care provision, further education and training, and special employment programmes for women over 45, partly in order to prevent women from losing a sense of self-esteem when unemployed.[74]

Such demands were directed in the first instance at the government and at state job centres. In the GDR the state had been the main agency for dealing with social problems. In west Germany, on the other hand—and particularly among the economic and some of the political elites—there was a view, backed by the Kohl government from 1982 onwards, that the state should give ground to the market, the world of work should be deregulated, and the role of private individual provision with regard to social protection should be extended.[75] After 1992 this view was central to the debate about Germany's economic standing and about programmes and legislation to restrain social expenditure and encourage competitiveness and employment.

Among the general population, however, even though self-help bodies in the field of social provision were seen in a very positive light and were becoming increasingly important, there was no evidence of any real desire that the role of the state should be reduced. According to a survey conducted in 1990, dealing with nine areas of provision, most of them social, respondents were almost unanimous, in both east and west Germany, that the state should be responsible for health care and the protection of the elderly. In addition, majorities of between 70 and 80 per cent in the west, and in some cases well over 90 per cent in the east, believed that the state should also provide suitable housing for those in a weaker financial position, guarantee employment, ensure an appropriate standard of living for the unemployed, and regulate prices. Sixty-four per cent of people in the west saw it as the task of the state to reduce differences of income, and 52 per cent that it should safeguard growth; in the east the corresponding figures were 84 and 80 per cent.[76] In both parts of Germany, in other words, there was a firm belief that the state was responsible for the provision of social benefits and for the country's economic condition. This belief was further reinforced by unification. In October 1991, for example, 66 per cent of people in east Germany took the view that the state should provide credits to businesses, and 39 per cent thought that the state should guarantee the purchase of businesses' products.[77] After unification, too, not only the general population but also the new elites in the east strongly agreed with the view that the state should be responsible for solving economic problems (though this was not the case in the west).[78] The fact that people in the east have been such strong supporters of the role of the state is, of course, not only a reflection of socialization under the GDR but is also an effect of the severe crisis through which east Germany has passed.

There is also widespread appreciation in both west and east Germany of the dominant role played by the state with regard to social policy. A study of statutory health insurance conducted in 1994[79] showed that there was a high degree of satisfaction with the benefits provided by health insurance and that people were critical, not so much of the high contribution rates—the lowering of which was the central aim of all health reforms from the mid-1970s onwards—as of cuts in benefits. This reflected not only the very high value that people placed on their own health and sense of security, but also their approval of the principle of interpersonal redistribution, between the healthy and the sick, the young and the old, and individuals and families, within the framework of mutual support provided by the statutory health insurance system.

A study of the period from the mid-1970s to the end of the 1980s has shown that the notion of the 'social state' (*Sozialstaat*), as a constitutional principle, was viewed positively in the Federal Republic.[80] (The notion of the *Wohlfahrtsstaat*, or 'welfare state', has tended to be seen as denoting simply a wide range of benefit payments and the dominance of the principles of maintenance and relief.) The protection of income in old age and in the event of disability, illness, and unemployment was regarded as a particularly important social achievement. Few of those surveyed said that too many benefits were available, while problems were perceived mainly with regard to financing and inadequate benefit provision in individual areas. In other words, while a section of the west German elites was critical of the wide scope of social provision, the mass of the population did not share this view and, if anything, wanted state activity to be increased and benefits expanded.[81]

Similarly, there was considerable criticism of the cuts in social benefits which took place after 1993 and which—together with the extension to east Germany of the west German systems of employment law and social security and the expansion of social insurance through the introduction of social care insurance—dominated the debate on social policy in the early 1990s. According to a survey conducted in 1994, 60 per cent of people in west Germany took the view that social benefits should remain at their previous level, 28 per cent believed that they should be extended, and only 12 per cent favoured cutbacks. In east Gemany only 28 per cent were in favour of continuing at previous levels, while 71 per cent wanted benefits to be extended and a mere 1 per cent supported cuts.[82]

Behind these differences lay different ideas of what a proper social policy should be. Germans in the new *Bundesländer* are more strongly influenced by the socialist model, in which the state has total responsibility and the goal is equality of outcome, while west Germans tend to favour the *Sozialstaat* culture of the Social Market economy, in which, although the state has a primary responsibility, provision made by the individual and by other social institutions also plays a role and the goal is equality of opportunity. (There is majority support in both east and west, however, for the view that the 'performance principle', or *Leistungsprinzip*—the principle that reward should be determined by the readiness to work hard and efficiently—has priority over the 'need principle', or *Bedürfnisprinzip*, though such support declined between 1991 and 1995, especially in the east.[83]) East Germans expected significantly more from social policy, in terms both of scope and content, and were dissatisfied with actual outcomes. Whereas in west Germany the views on social policy of those questioned were strongly influenced by their own economic situation, this was of only marginal significance in the east. Plainly, socialization under the GDR—or, more precisely, the legacy of socialist social policy[84]—had had an important effect, while the shortcomings of that system, such as the low level of pensions, were rarely seen any longer as a central feature. In a representative survey conducted in 1994, 60 per cent of east Germans regarded social protection in the Federal Republic as inferior to that under the GDR, as against only 21 per cent who regarded it as better.[85] A more recent study of changes in political attitudes in east and west Germany has shown that the view that social protection was better in the GDR has even gained ground.[86] That said, it is clearly difficult to separate the effects of socialization from subjective responses to the consequences of unification,[87] in particular the economic crisis and mass unemployment.

An important feature of east German attitudes is the split between, on the one hand, the view of the overwhelming majority of people that their own personal living standards have improved since 1990 and, on the other, the belief—likewise overwhelmingly supported—that the changes in society at large have been for the worse. This latter belief is held even by most of those who have not lost their jobs, have been able to improve their professional situation, and have seen their incomes rise by more than the average.[88]

In east Germany, to a much greater extent than in west Germany, social security is seen as an essential part of democracy. On the other hand, although the 'social-policy achievements' of the GDR are viewed positively,[89] the loss of them has not been a central criterion in people's assessment of the realities of democracy in the Federal Republic. Judgements concerning the political and economic system of the unified Federal Republic are complex and varied. Commitment to the basic values of democracy—a division between government and opposition, a multi-party system, freedom of expression, and the right to demonstrate—is very high in both east and west Germany, at 90 per cent.[90] The proportion of those in the east who believed that it was right to adopt a political system on the western model rose from 68 to 77 per cent between May 1992 and October 1995, while the proportion of those who thought it was wrong fell from 31 to 17 per cent.[91] However, east Germans are much less satisfied with the reality of democracy in the Federal Republic and its mode of functioning than are west Germans.[92] In east Germany political institutions are judged much more by their results than they are in the west. Many Germans in the new *Bundesländer* take a fairly critical view of democratic procedures and the effects of the rule of law.[93]

East Germans have been especially disappointed by the market economy. In February and March 1990, at the time of the elections to the Volkskammer, 77 per cent of them had a favourable view of the economic system of the Federal Republic; by August 1994 the figure had fallen to 38 per cent. During the same period the proportion of those who were critical of it rose from 5 to 33 per cent, and of the undecided from 18 to 29 per cent.[94] People complained, in particular, about deficiencies in equality of opportunity, social justice, equal rights, protection from crime, and social security.[95] Significantly, a clear, and growing, majority believed that socialism was a good idea that had simply been badly implemented. The proportion of those who took this view rose between 1991 and 1994 from 69 to 78 per cent, as against fewer than 40 per cent in the west during the same period.[96]

The proportion of those in the east who thought that socialism was basically a good idea fell by only a small amount between 1994 and 2002, and the stark difference between east and west on this point persists.[97] On the other hand, although the idea of socialism is viewed positively in the east, and many people are critical of the realities of the political, economic, and social-policy system of the Federal Republic, this does not mean that they are mourning the death of the GDR, let alone that they would like to undo the fact of unification. The deficiencies of the GDR system—the lack of political freedom and of freedom to travel, the spying that was conducted on citizens, and the shortages of high-quality consumer goods—are only too obvious to them.

Within the unified Federal Republic, however, a specific east German identity and mentality have taken shape,[98] and these are reflected in a distinctive attitude towards social policy. In part this is because there is stronger support altogether for the role of the state in managing the economy and providing social protection, and because ideas of equality and social justice are more pronounced. There is also greater scepticism—though this has been growing in the west too—about large organizations such as churches, trade unions, employers' associations, and political parties. This different attitude towards social policy is undoubtedly, therefore, a symptom of the continuing influence of attitudes formed during the GDR era. Primarily, however, it is a product of deep-seated anxieties about the continuing economic crisis and the persistence of mass unemployment, and of a feeling among east Germans—engendered, despite the significant rise in average incomes since unification, by the disparity in living standards between east and west, as well as by the influence of west German elites in east Germany—that they are in a less privileged position than west Germans within the newly unified German state.[99]

This mind-set has had its influence on concrete issues. Economists, for example, are agreed that it was a mistake to allow wages in the east to rise rapidly, bringing them closer to, though not fully on a par with, wages in the west before a corresponding increase in productivity had been achieved. This was a key factor in the decline in competitiveness and contributed to the collapse of large sections of east German industry. A majority of east Germans, however, saw the wage rises not as a question of economic rationality but as a matter of justice, and did so in increasing numbers. In July and August 1990 55 per cent of those questioned accepted the link between wage levels and productivity, and only 36 per cent wanted to see a rapid move towards wage parity. By October 1991 only 22 per cent were prepared to wait for productivity rises as a precondition for alignment: 64 per cent believed that the principle of equal pay for equal work meant that wages should be raised to western levels as quickly as possible.[100] This is not to say that the wage policy pursued by the trade unions and the employers' organizations between 1990 and 1992 was correct. It is clear, however, that any other wage policy would have been at odds with the spirit that prevailed in east Germany at the time.

PART II

THE CREATION OF THE SOCIAL UNION

5

The Central Features of the Social Union: The Legislation and Institutions Governing Social Policy in the Federal Republic and the GDR Compared

The fall of the Berlin Wall and the unification of Germany led to a change of priorities in social policy in the Federal Republic. The Social Report of the Federal Labour Ministry for 1990, listing ten principles and objectives of welfare reform, portrayed the legislative term 1987–90 as a success story in social policy.[1] It cited improvements in the financial situation of the pensions and health insurance systems, financial consolidation within social insurance generally, and an increased level of employment as evidence that the German welfare state had met the challenges of the day and that it was adaptable and capable of development. It identified the 'strengthening of self-help' and the 'expansion of social security systems based on mutual solidarity, through neighbourly support, small networks and self-help groups', as important tasks for the future.

However, in referring to the 'great challenge' that would be involved in shaping a common welfare state for the whole of a reunited Germany, the report also made plain that after the period of consolidation the central task that would face social policy in the coming years was a new and entirely different one.

The governing coalition's social policy was based on two fundamental principles.

1. Social equilibrium and social protection were central elements of the Social Market economy. Economic and monetary union with the German Democratic Republic accordingly had to be accompanied by a union in social policy. This view was shared by the government, by political and social forces in the GDR, and by the Social Democratic opposition and the trade unions in the Federal Republic. It won through against the view—widespread in economic and financial circles, and supported by sections of the Federal government—that it would be essential, in order to ease the transition from a planned to a market economy and improve the competitiveness of the east Germany economy, to make substantial cuts in the social benefits and regulations governing working conditions in east Germany. Those arguments were outweighed by a recognition that social policy was necessary

in order to prevent mass migration from east to west Germany and to cushion the impact of the transformation in the east and make it acceptable to the population, as well as by a fear that cuts would create a precedent for dismantling the welfare state in Germany as a whole.

2. The west German welfare state and its specific norms, institutions, and actors were to be extended to east Germany as fully and rapidly as possible, except in so far as transitional regulations would be necessary.[2] This principle was a clear rejection of any notion that the two systems might be combined in some way, or that particular features of the east German social security system—viewed positively by many people—might be carried over into the new common welfare state. The decision was directed, in part, at the GDR government, which wanted to preserve and extend the 'social achievements' of the GDR state. It was also aimed, however, against elements among the west German Social Democrats and in the trade unions who hoped that unification with the GDR would create the opportunity of reforming the whole German welfare state in ways that they favoured, or at least of retaining certain features of the east German system that could then serve as models for subsequent reform in the west. The main counter-arguments to these ambitions were that the process of unification was a highly dynamic one which left no time for the legislation that would be required, and that a Pandora's box of political controversy and social conflict might be opened if such a course were pursued. In addition, the overwhelming majority of actors within social policy believed that the Federal Republic's system of social security had, on the whole, proved its worth and that any attempt to combine the two systems was doomed to failure, since the systems were basically incompatible. The sheer inertia of the west German institutions and traditions was a further factor, as was a concern that the process of adaptation to free market conditions by the east German economy ought not to be made any more difficult. The benefits provided by the west German welfare state were already considerable; saddling the system with the 'social achievements' of the GDR would overburden state and society in Germany as a whole.

All the same, the enormous problems that would be entailed by extending to east Germany the west German economic system and the legislation and institutions governing social policy were clearly underestimated. At first, too, there was little conception of what it would mean for people in the east to have to get to grips, virtually overnight, with the change from a relatively simple system to an unusually complex one—a system, indeed, that left many west Germans themselves confused about their rights in matters of taxation, benefits, and protection against dismissal. The social-policy system in the east, by contrast, had made do with approximately 10 per cent of the regulations laid down in the old Federal Republic[3] and also employed fewer and less well-qualified staff.

The negotiations on the legal foundations of the social union, the extension of the norms, institutions, benefits, and actors of the west German welfare state to the GDR and the new *Bundesländer*, and the attempt to stem mass unemployment and mitigate its effects through social protection were the central and overriding features of social policy in the early 1990s.

The Social Report for 1993, while expressly describing the German system of social security as one of the 'most efficient in the world',[4] also made clear that the financial burdens of German unity necessitated a 'redirection of all public services'[5] and that social policy could not be exempt from this process. The effort to make savings in social expenditure in order to foster employment and economic growth, the intense arguments over adjustments to the Federal financing system in the Federal Consolidation Programme, and the debates about ways in which the parameters of the German economy might be improved were all ultimately consequences of the changes in the financial and economic framework. Questions about the financial limits of the welfare state and the appropriate balance between competitiveness and social protection once again took centre stage, as they had done in the 1980s.

At the same time, new ways of solving social problems were sought, and found, within the existing institutions. The Health Service Structure Law of 21 December 1992, for example, was an attempt to restrain the influence of the providers of health benefits, in favour of benefit recipients, and to improve the flexibility and efficiency of the health care system by enhancing competition. When social care insurance was introduced the government stuck firmly to the principle of statutory social insurance for the great majority of the population, despite fierce criticism from the FDP and business interests. On the other hand, by abolishing a public holiday in compensation for the employer's contribution to social care insurance, the government effectively departed from the principle of parity between employer and employee in the financing of social insurance. And, much more clearly than in the case of health, the budgetary principle of linking expenditure to revenue constituted an abandonment of the traditional principle of basing contributions on the meeting of need.

The key fact about the debates and decisions concerning social policy in the 1990s, however, was that proposals which posited fundamental alterations to the German welfare state and its institutions—in particular, the principle of social insurance—had no real chance of being implemented. For all the flexibility over details, the only reforms that were feasible were ones that retained continuity with the existing system. Within this reform process, the influence of political and social actors and wielders of veto power was heavily dependent on the particular area of social policy in question, on the extent to which their active involvement in the implementation of legislation and regulations was essential, and of course on the overall political, legal, economic, and social-policy frameworks that have been described in Part I.

In 1990, the year of German unification, the Federal government was the dominant actor in the west, in view of the dynamic nature of the unification process, the government's role as negotiator with the GDR and the victorious Allied powers, and the sheer complexity of the problems involved. During 1991–4, on the other hand, the opposition had to be brought into the central decision-making processes in social policy, particularly with regard to legislation, owing to its powerful position in the Bundesrat. Until unification was achieved, in the autumn of 1990, the government of the GDR and the political forces that stood behind it played an important part in laying the legal foundations for, and helping implement, the social union between the two parts of Germany. Subsequently, however, their influence waned, as a result of the internal collapse of the GDR and the lack of any realistic alternative to unification. In order properly to understand the positions of the actors, we need to consider briefly the main differences between the social-policy systems of the GDR[6] and the Federal Republic and some of the problems that arose as a result of them.

In the GDR the Socialist Unity Party of Germany (SED) had originally had a defensive attitude towards social policy, which it regarded as a sort of capitalist 'field hospital', with only marginal, and steadily dwindling, importance in a socialist state. In the mid-1960s, however, it abandoned this view and allotted a substantial role to a specifically socialist social policy, partly for purposes of competition with the Federal Republic and partly as a way of legitimizing the state itself.[7] The 'unity of economic and social policy' that was proclaimed at the ninth party congress of the SED in 1976 was intended as a fusion of economic efficiency and social security within a political strategy directed from above; increases in living standards were seen as conditional on improvements in productivity. This change of tack took place at a time when the welfare states that had been so rapidly developed in the western industrial countries during the first decades after the Second World War were coming under severe strain as a result of the economic crisis of 1973–4 and when both the crisis and the need to reshape the welfare state had become topics of intensive debate among politicians and economists. However, the GDR's hope that improvements in social benefits would induce the population to be more willing to work, and to work harder, and that they would enhance the country's economic strength was not fulfilled. In particular, the high subsidies on basic consumer goods and the state's guarantee of employment, which led to over-staffing in enterprises and administrative organizations—to say nothing of planning errors, overblown bureaucracy, and the cost of the comprehensive machinery of repression—overstretched the economy and prevented necessary investment.

The overburdening of the GDR economy was especially evident in the industrial and other enterprises, which played a central role in social policy. In the capitalist market economy of the Federal Republic, the social obligation associated with work within the firm consists primarily in the exchange of labour for wages, while the social additional and consequential costs associated with work—resulting, for example, from ill-health, disability, age, unemployment, and motherhood—are largely handled by general systems of social security separate from the workplace: in the language of social protection law, they are 'externalized'. In the GDR, by contrast, such costs were transferred back into the workplace, or 'internalized'.[8] The result was that industrial and other enterprises had the main responsibility for maintaining employment, and in practice, even if not in law, they were commonly unable, for social reasons, to make employees redundant. Enterprises were also required to bear sizeable additional burdens by setting up workplace-based health services, financing health cures, maintaining child care facilities (crèches, kindergartens, and day-care centres for school-age children), providing and maintaining housing, holiday accommodation, cultural centres and sports facilities for employees, and providing care for retired workers. This meant that enterprises and work brigades—which also functioned as centres of communication and community activity—were carrying out tasks on behalf of society that were bound to impair their profitability and prevent managers from basing their decision-making on criteria of economic rationality. When these workplace-centred services and institutions were systematically dismantled, after the switch to a market economy, there was considerable unhappiness, and many people felt that their quality of life and sense of security had been severely damaged.

Social policy in the GDR, like wages and prices, was controlled exclusively by the centralized state, which in turn was dominated by the SED. In west Germany, on the other hand, important roles were played, not only by actors within the Federal political system, but by the market, the two autonomous sides of industry, the self-governing providers of social insurance, the social-policy associations (representing the interests of recipients of benefits), churches, and independent welfare associations, with the governments of the *Länder* and local government also playing an important part within the framework of national social policy. In the GDR social policy was far less adaptable, and dissatisfaction with policy or with the allocation of resources—from which the political system was, to some extent, protected in west Germany—was accordingly liable to be aimed directly against state and party leaders and thus to threaten the system as a whole.[9] In addition, the welfare state was far less solidly enshrined in law than was the case in the Federal Republic. There were no separate independent employment or social courts, and there was no constitutional court to prescribe specific goals for social policy.

Let us consider the most important areas of GDR social policy in turn. Its centrepiece was the right to work. This was the 'social achievement' of the state that was viewed in particularly positive terms by the population, especially after the fall of the Wall and the collapse of the Communist system.[10] It was, however, a key factor contributing to the overburdening of industrial enterprises and the inefficiency of the economy. It is true that the GDR was successful in staving off overt unemployment—unlike the Federal Republic, where from the crisis of 1973–4 onwards there were only moderate declines in unemployment even during phases of expansion—and unemployment insurance, which had become meaningless, was therefore formally abolished in 1978. The right to work, however, was complemented by the obligation to work, and by 'socialist work discipline', which in turn went hand in hand with the state's system of repression, and particularly the persecution of the so-called 'asocial'.[11] Full employment was achieved only through economically absurd levels of over-manning in many enterprises and administrative organizations: a serious misallocation of human capital. Moreover, the fact that workers could not, in practice, be made redundant weakened the motivation to work and placed almost insurmountable obstacles in the way of enterprises' adjusting to changes in production and market conditions.

The implementation of the right to work also gave rise to a host of practical problems.[12] To the annoyance of the SED leadership, the right to work was regarded as the right to a particular job, to a form of employment commensurate with one's qualifications, and to protection against any requirement to change one's place of work. This led to fossilization of the labour market and made it far harder to bring about necessary changes in the structure of the economy. As a result there were many job vacancies, particularly for the highly qualified, though also for the semi- and unskilled.

Employment law was simpler and clearer than in the Federal Republic. It was, however, highly politicized and, where conflict with the central interests of the SED was involved, was not enforceable through the courts. Following a preliminary codification in the Statute Book of Labour of 12 April 1961,[13] a Labour Statute Book of 1977 provided a codification both of the entire body of employment law and of social law.[14] In the Federal Republic, by contrast (as has already been mentioned),[15] only social law had been formally codified in the successive volumes of the Social Statute Book; employment law was split up among a great variety of different statutes and judicial decisions, retained the anachronistic distinction between '(waged) workers' (*Arbeiter*) and '(salaried) employees' (*Angestellte*), and was in any case full of gaps. Nevertheless, although the GDR attempted to ensure that the Labour Statute Book would be retained in purified form after unification—with the replacement of dirigiste regulations by a freer conception of employment relations, and the dropping of references to a socialist planned economy[16]—the effort came to nothing.

The role of employees in influencing wages and salaries and shaping employment relations was considerably less significant in the GDR than in the Federal Republic. This was primarily because there were no free trade unions or independently negotiated wage agreements. Nor was there any equivalent in the GDR of the elected works council (*Betriebsrat*) as the representative organ of workers in the system of workplace co-determination (*Mitbestimmung*), particularly with reference to social-policy questions. Although GDR 'plant trade union leaderships' were able to take up social problems on behalf of workers, they were first and foremost instruments for implementing the prescriptions of the state and the SED. The direct concerns of workers in the workplace were most likely to be dealt with, if at all, by the work brigades.[17] 'Griping' in the workplace was standard practice, and was less risky than after unification, since there was no sanction of dismissal.

After the fall of the Wall there was a general welcome in east Germany for the new, enhanced role of trade unions, now no longer compelled to follow the instructions of a governing party with a monopoly of power. There was disagreement, however, as to whether the Free German Trade Union Federation (FDGB, the umbrella body in the GDR) and the existing trade unions in the east should be converted into free trade unions or replaced by new organizations, and whether works councils or reformed 'plant trade union leaderships' should play the principal role in representing workers in the co-determination process within the workplace. At first, too, there was a failure to understand that free collective bargaining presupposed strong employers' organizations capable of entering into binding agreements and a degree of equilibrium between the two sides involved in wage negotiations, and that a 'trade union state' was not a desirable alternative to SED dictatorship.

As in the Federal Republic, the core element of social security in the GDR was social insurance. There were, however, many differences of detail. Since there were no 'civil servants' (*Beamten*) in the GDR, there were no civil servants' pensions. Despite the major role played by industrial enterprises in social policy, all existing enterprise-based pensions in the GDR had been abolished and no new ones had been granted.[18] Income support, which continued to be the important bottom level of social protection in the Federal Republic, had remained significant in the first decades of the GDR, in the form of social welfare,[19] but was seen as a relic of capitalism and eventually completely marginalized: by 1989 only 5,553 people were still in regular receipt of it.[20] In the case of accident insurance there was no subdivision into different branches, and professional cooperative associations did not run the system.[21]

The German system of social insurance, subdivided on the basis of risks and occupational groups, had been replaced—in line with ideas earlier promoted by the German labour movement—by a unified form of insurance for workers of all types, which in 1956 was put under FDGB control as an administrative system run exclusively by the insured, without the participation of employers, though it was subject to directives from the SED.[22] Members of the coexisting system of State Insurance for members of cooperatives and the few self-employed accounted for just 9 per cent of the resident population by 1989.[23]

The insurance elements that had originated from the traditional German system were steadily downgraded, while welfare and maintenance provision were expanded. At the same time, the authorities shied away from raising the income ceiling on contributions, which had been fixed at 600 marks a month but was well below later average wage and salary levels. As a result state subsidies had to be repeatedly extended, until by 1989 they stood at over 48 per cent of total social insurance expenditure.[24]

The Achilles heel of GDR social policy was the inadequate level of protection in the case of old age and in the event of invalidity, together with the poor degree of support for surviving dependants. This was because the SED's system was based so one-sidedly on production. While the rate of employment of women rose, the social security system marginalized those people who were no longer relevant to the employment process: the elderly, war victims, and those with physical and mental disabilities. Insurance-based pensions for the elderly and the disabled provided only a very undifferentiated form of low-level basic support. People in these categories were saved from impoverishment only by the high subsidies on goods required for basic needs.

The average value of pensions within the unified system of insurance for workers of all types was only 26.7 per cent of gross incomes in 1971 and 37.3 per cent in 1988. (Incomes were, in any case, very low by west German standards.[25]) In 1970 65 per cent of pensioner households were on or below the poverty line, and even in 1988 the figure was as high as 45 per cent. The number of female pensioners living on their own who were in poverty was especially high.[26] Unlike pensions in the west, pensions were not indexed to earnings, so pensioners did not automatically benefit from economic growth and rising productivity, and were not regularly adjusted to keep up with rises in living costs. Pensions were increased only when the state and the party leadership decided, from time to time, that this was appropriate.

A substantial increase in pensions was introduced on 1 December 1989,[27] and minimum pension levels, graded according to the length of the insurance contribution period, were raised to between 330 and 470 marks per month. The highest pension, in the case of a contribution period of 50 years with regular maximum contributions, was still only 510 marks per month. The west German system, by contrast, despite certain redistributive elements, was essentially based on contributions according to income, and, for the individual who had been in long-term full-time employment liable to insurance, it provided at least an approximation, during old age or in the event of invalidity, to the standard of living that he or she had achieved while working.

The weaknesses of the GDR system led to the establishment in 1971 (after preliminary changes in 1968) of a Voluntary Supplementary Pensions Insurance scheme, which was also designed to mop up purchasing power and so stem inflationary pressures. Under the scheme additional voluntary contributions, matched by payments by enterprises, could be made in order to raise pension levels. Although between 70 and 80 per cent of employed people eventually took up the offer, which was given massive publicity,[28] the scheme involved long expectancies before pensions could be drawn, and at the time of unification the effect on average pension levels was accordingly not great. In 1989 men received, on average, pensions of 106 marks per month from the supplementary scheme and women 36 marks.[29] In 1983 average net household incomes of pensioners in east Germany stood, nominally, at only a quarter of west German levels, though they were closer to one-third of those levels when differences in purchasing power were taken into account.[30]

The creation of Voluntary Supplementary Pensions Insurance, which made for a more individualized system and gave more scope to the criterion that contributions and pensions should be graduated according to *Leistung* (work performance), was significant in representing a dilution of the principle of unified insurance. The principle, however, had been breached much earlier, in 1950, when a web of supplementary and special systems of provision was set up that steadily grew more extensive until it became almost too complex to understand.[31] These systems were designed to ensure the loyalty of the professional elites and of the groups that were particularly closely associated with the political and economic system. At the time of German unification there were sixty-one supplementary schemes. With some of them, contributions had to be paid; with others—such as the scheme for teachers—they did not. There were great differences in the benefits paid. In addition to these schemes there were four special schemes for the employees of the Ministry of State Security, the People's Police, the National People's Army, and the administration of customs. Employees had to pay 10 per cent of their salary and could receive, in the case of a full pension after long service, 90 per cent of their final salary. At the end of June 1990, immediately before monetary union came into force, about 230,000 people were in receipt of benefits from supplementary schemes and 120,000 in receipt of benefits from special schemes, while 1.6 million people—about 10 per cent of the population—had expectancies under these schemes.[32]

At unification the task as far as pensions insurance was concerned was to convert the GDR's system of minimum protection into the performance-based insurance system of the Federal Republic while at the same time giving everyone a guarantee that they would receive, at the least, a pension in Deutschmarks that they had previously received in GDR marks.[33] The strong points of the west German pensions system—the fact that pensions were higher and were indexed to rises in earnings, as well as the closer connection between benefits and income and contribution levels—were, basically, accepted as an improvement on the GDR system. Beyond that, however, the GDR had various desiderata. These were that a system of minimum pensions should be preserved, that compensation should be made for the ending of subsidies, that the pensions system should retain the GDR's more extensive use of added pensionable years (for example, with regard to the care of dependants and the bringing up of children), that its much more comprehensive system of social insurance liability should continue, and that contribution rates, much lower in the GDR, should be raised only gradually. Extremely difficult problems were also thrown up by the incorporation of the supplementary and special provision systems for particular groups into general statutory pensions insurance.

Even before unification, it had been necessary to introduce a form of unemployment insurance. This had been done to protect from impoverishment employees who had lost their jobs as a result of the upheaval in the economy, and to build up an effective administrative system for employment to manage insurance, provide careers advice, vocational training and re-training, and initiate and finance job creation measures. The change had been effected in close cooperation with the Federal Republic and was not controversial.

Probably the most important feature of the employment-centred character of GDR social policy was the systematic, and successful, encouragement of female employment. This was primarily a consequence of the labour shortage, though it also sprang from the regime's insistence that everyone in society—in this instance women—should be included in the employment process. Female employment was promoted partly negatively, through the withholding of long-term support from widows who were able to work and a policy of ensuring that a single pension would be insufficient to provide upkeep for a retired married couple, and partly positively, through the wide-scale provision of child care facilities and improved job training for women. Closely linked to the employment policy was the state's family policy, which was significantly strengthened from the 1970s onwards, mainly to counteract the decline in the birth rate (in which aim it was partially successful). A paid 'baby year' was introduced, enabling mothers to leave work for a full year following the birth of a child. At first the 'baby year' was available only to mothers with two or more children, but in 1986 it was granted upon the birth of a first child, while paid maternity leave for mothers giving birth to a third child was extended to eighteen months.[34] The pensions insurance system also offered special rewards to working women. To compensate for the fact that the retirement age of 60 for women was five years lower than that of men, women were granted up to five years extra pensionable years on entering pensions insurance. This recognition as pensionable of a period devoted to bringing up children occurred fifteen years before similar recognition took place in the Federal Republic, and was more generously framed.[35] For example, mothers of three or more children were granted three years per child, in comparison with one year per child after 1986 in the Federal Republic. On average, these extra pensionable years worked out at seven for women in the GDR. On the other hand, in view of the important role played by elements of minimum protection in the GDR, the increase in pensionable years meant much less than it would have done in the Federal Republic: one added pensionable year, for example, raised the value of a pension only by six marks per month at the most.

The effect of the promotion of female employment was to near-double the rate of employment among women of working age, from 44 per cent in 1950 to 81 per cent in 1989: a rate far higher than that in the Federal Republic. The difference between east and west was particularly great as far as married women were concerned. In the GDR in 1988 74 per cent of married women with two children aged under 18 and still living at home were in full-time employment, and a further 17.5 per cent were employed part-time; in the Federal Republic the comparable figures for women in this group were 16 and 24 per cent respectively.[36]

We should not ignore the downsides of the GDR's policies for women and families. Since there was actually little change as far as traditional perceptions of gender roles and the division of household tasks were concerned, women had to carry the double burden of family and job responsibilities. Again, average incomes of women in the GDR were well below male earnings, at 76 per cent.[37] This was partly because typically female forms of employment—in education, health and social work, and the textiles and clothing industries—were considerably less well paid, and partly because women had fewer opportunities for promotion than men and were more often employed at levels below those for which they were qualified.[38]

There were fundamental differences between the two parts of Germany with regard to health services. In the Federal Republic the highly complex and differentiated health system is largely financed publicly, in particular through statutory health insurance. Health care, on the other hand, is dominated by private providers of health services. Outpatient care is in the hands of independently practising doctors, pharmacies are privately owned, and in recent decades specialisms provided by self-employed professionals, such as opticians, audiologists, physiotherapists, and masseurs, have expanded. Even in inpatient care an important role is played by private clinics and church-funded hospitals, in addition to local public hospitals.

The health system in the GDR was based on ideas that had been propounded by the socialist labour movement during the Weimar Republic.[39] Although a small private sector was retained,[40] the system was, essentially, a fully nationalized one. Nationalization was also a corollary of the struggle against the 'bourgeois' foundations of the health professions. The individual citizen was entitled to medical services on the basis of his or her contribution to social insurance, which guaranteed basic care for the population. However, as with old-age protection, further health provision systems grew up alongside the general territorial and enterprise-based system, amounting to fourteen in all.[41] These additional systems offered a mostly higher level of medical care for particular population groups.

In outpatient care, polyclinics and ambulatories (outpatient medical centres) played a central role alongside health services provided in the workplace. The system had several advantages, which were acknowledged in the west: the close interlinking of in- and outpatient services, the emphasis on prevention and early identification of disease, and, for conditions such as pregnancy, the so-called 'Dispensaire' principle, i.e. the integration of pre-treatment care, treatment, and aftercare.[42] Moreover, costs were kept much lower than in the Federal Republic.

The main shortcoming of the system, which was again heavily employment-orientated, was that older people who had ceased to be involved in the production process were relatively neglected with regard to health cures, the allocation of scarce drugs and other medical supplies, and the prevention of age-related illnesses.[43] In addition, many hospitals and other buildings were antiquated, shabbily furnished, and in need of repair, provision of modern medical equipment was poor, and there were shortages of medication.[44] Doctors, nurses, and other medical personnel were unhappy with their low levels of pay. As in the years before the building of the Wall, when about 7,500 doctors left for the west—more than half of all the doctors in the GDR in 1960[45]—so in 1989 there was a mass exodus of doctors into the Federal Republic.[46] In 1990 life expectancy in the GDR was 69.8 years for men and 75.9 years for women: significantly lower than in the Federal Republic, where the figures were 72.6 and 79 years respectively.[47] The reasons for these differences were, of course, complex and not a function solely of the health system. Factors such as environmental damage, behaviour-related health risks, and the emigration of mainly healthy elements of the population before 1961 also played a part.

Despite the weaknesses of the GDR system, it was by no means a foregone conclusion that after unification east Germany would adopt the west German model, assigning outpatient care to doctors in individual practices and establishing a 'fragmented' system of fiercely competing statutory health insurance companies. That this did happen, at a time when there was an intense debate about reform of the west German health care system,[48] was due in part to the fact that the FDP, with its commitment to independent doctors and a wide range of insurance providers, occupied a key position in the governing coalition. In addition, the leading institutions within the Federal German health sector were powerful organizations, skilled at publicity, and they firmly rejected as detrimental to their interests even a partial preservation of the GDR system, as well as any far-reaching changes to the Federal system, in consequence of unification.

GDR society, in which incomes and differences in wealth were largely levelled out, displayed far less economic inequality than society in the Federal Republic, let alone the United States. Political power, however, which in the Federal Republic was widely dispersed, was centred on a small 'caste-like power elite at the apex of the bureaucratic apparatus'.[49] This elite also enjoyed social privileges in the form of western goods, villas and hunting trips, high-quality services, and superior health care and provision for old age. The existence of these privileges, which were not based on economic performance and were at odds with the Marxist principle of equality, caused great offence and was an important reason why the leadership cadres, and with them the whole political system, lost their legitimacy in the crisis of 1989–90. Social privileges were also granted to the middling and lower ranks of the *nomenklatura*.[50] It was a key feature of this system of social differentiation, however, that privileges were not legally enforceable but were dispensed arbitrarily and could be equally arbitrarily withdrawn.

With unification, the GDR adopted not only the Federal Republic's political and economic system but also, albeit with some transitional arrangements, the immensely complex web of institutions and regulatory standards and the overall high levels of material benefits that made up the Federal system of social policy. This cushioned the social impact of the transformation of the GDR from an economically inefficient socialist planned economy, closely regulated from the centre and based largely on state enterprises and enforced cooperatives, to a capitalist market economy founded on private property. Despite the mass unemployment that followed the change, the rights and the material circumstances of those affected were, with the exception of some small groups, significantly improved, as a comparison with the former Communist-ruled countries of eastern central and eastern Europe—and with their problems in social policy—makes plain.[51] The cushioning effect of social policy also helped ensure that the transition from a planned to a market economy and from dictatorship to democracy took place without real political or social upheaval. At the same time, however, the adoption of the Federal Republic's regulations and standards imposed a heavy and indeed excessive burden on east Germany's economic capacity. Moreover, the high levels of transfer payments, and the drastic increases in public debt and additional wage costs to which these payments gave rise, placed a huge strain on the Federal budget and on the economy of Germany as a whole. The abrupt transformation also provoked a deep-seated sense of insecurity among the population in eastern Germany, a feeling that persists to the present day.

In view of the fact that a fierce debate had already been under way among academics and politicians since the mid-1970s concerning the 'crisis' in, and the need for 'reconstruction' of, the welfare state in Germany, and bearing in mind too that at least some of the institutions and social achievements of the GDR had been seen by west German policy-makers and experts as possible models for social-policy reform, the question arises whether an alternative way of extending the west German system of social policy to the east might have been feasible. That question is at the centre of the chapters that follow. These discuss and analyse in detail the consequences for social policy, first, of the reform efforts that took place under the Modrow government after the opening of the internal German borders on 9 November 1989 and, next, of the intensive negotiations between the Federal Republic and the GDR that concluded with the signature and ratification of the State Treaty on monetary, economic, and social union of 18 May 1990 and of the Unification Treaty of 31 August 1990—treaties which laid down the legal basis for the extension to the east of the west German constitutional framework in the social field.

6

The Social Policy of the Modrow Government

The social policy of the Modrow government was not based on new fundamental principles. The Prime Minister's inaugural policy statement of 17 November 1989, which included announcements on the extension of cooperation with the Federal Republic in a 'contractual community' (*Vertragsgemeinschaft*), on economic reform, on democratization, and on guarantees of constitutionality, touched only marginally on questions of social policy.[1] The substantial increase in pensions that took place on 1 December 1989 had already been approved in late November 1988 and the decision had been announced publicly on 24 October 1989, a few days after the fall of Honecker but before the formation of the Modrow government.[2] A reduction in subsidies in order to consolidate the public finances, which had at first been planned,[3] was abandoned, for fear of popular disapproval.

Modrow's original intention had been to retain the socialist economic and social-policy framework, albeit in a democratized form and with the introduction of market elements, and to preserve the GDR as a separate state. When he was forced to abandon these goals, in the light of the collapse of state authority, the crisis in the economy, and the pressure by the GDR population for unification with the Federal Republic, he made it his main aim to introduce an extensive social-policy programme (mainly devised by the Round Table) for the new common German state, within the framework of a social union. On this scheme the high levels of social benefits provided in the Federal Republic would be combined with the social rights guaranteed to citizens of the GDR, and employees would also be granted wide-ranging further rights of co-determination. As far as concrete social policies were concerned, however, the government's actions were largely a response to problems that had arisen as a result of the critical state of the country's economy and system of social protection.

6.1 THE CRISIS IN THE HEALTH SYSTEM

In the health system, centralized management collapsed and was replaced by increasingly autonomous health services. Many heads of regional and district health departments and many medical directors of health services were forced to resign their posts, in response to pressure either from the grass-roots or from colleagues who insisted in having a say in new arrangements.[4]

Dissatisfied with wages and salaries that were far lower than those paid to their opposite numbers in the Federal Republic, and unhappy at their often poor working conditions, about 10,000 health and social service workers, including about 4,000 doctors and dentists and 4,000 nurses, left the GDR in 1989, and this exodus made yet more acute a situation that was already at crisis point. A notable expression of the widespread anger that doctors felt at the 'utterly impoverished public health system' in the GDR was a letter sent to Modrow and Gysi on 10 January 1990 by Professor Helga Günther, chief physician in the X-ray department of the city hospital in Friedrichshain and occupant of the chair in radiography at the Academy of Medical Education in the GDR. As a child of anti-fascists and victims of the Nazis, Professor Günther said, she had until now stayed faithful to the ideals of the SED, which she had joined at the age of 17. Almost all 'comrade senior consultants and professors' had left the party after 7 October. 'The catastrophic situation into which the Stalinist methods of our leadership comrades have led us is not so much being dismantled too slowly by those comrades who have been in positions of responsibility since the change [*Wende*], but is being restored.' She criticized, in particular, the preferential treatment given to doctors in the government hospitals and the hospitals of the Ministry of State Security (the Stasi). She could not remain a member of the party, she said, 'if real change does not take place at once'.[5] The crisis in the health system had already been discussed before the mass exodus of doctors and care personnel had begun, in an analysis of the state of national medical and social care which the SED had produced on 11 August 1989.[6] There was a shortage of staff per bed in hospitals, the analysis said. About 160,000 applications for places in retirement and nursing homes—including 20,000 urgent applications—were having to be turned down. The 'functional capacity' of hospitals, cure facilities, and medical research institutes was being curtailed, if not jeopardized, by 'damaged roofs, faulty heating systems, and worn-out laundries, kitchens and sanitation facilities'. Shortfalls in supplies of medication would impede the treatment of patients. The disparity in standards of medical technology and equipment, compared with other countries, had widened and was continuing to grow. The GDR was becoming increasingly dependent on imports of modern medical technology and was making greater use of medical goods provided by non-socialist economies. A detailed study completed by a tripartite working group on the 'renovation of health and social services facilities' in April 1990 concluded that in the period between 1991 and 1995 alone, investment of the order of 21,000 million marks would be necessary in order to maintain functional capacity in a part of health and social services and bring them into line with standards in the Federal Republic. The resources that would be required by the year 2000 to make up lost ground and raise standards further would be significantly greater still. Special attention would need to be paid to areas that had been particularly badly neglected: psychiatric services, rehabilitation, the majority of hospitals that had ageing buildings, nursing homes, and many of the facilities in university clinics and medical schools.[7]

The severe crisis in the health system was also the subject of a number of dramatic letters sent to leading figures in the state and the SED by Professor

Klaus Thielmann, GDR Minister for Health and Social Services in the Modrow government during the transition period until April 1990.[8] In a letter of 7 November 1989 to the general secretary of the SED, Egon Krenz,[9] Thielmann referred to the much higher rates of salaries and wages in the Federal Republic and called for a substantial rise in the salaries of doctors (who were looking for a 100 per cent increase), dentists, and other health service employees, and for a significant injection of new resources and finance into the health care system. He noted that expenditure on health, at 5 per cent of national income, was far too low in comparison both with developed countries and with the Soviet Union. He received no reply. On 20 November 1989 he wrote to Modrow describing the very poor state of important areas of the GDR's health and social services systems and the low level of life expectancy of GDR citizens by international standards, and reiterating the demand that Modrow 'take action, publicly and by seizing the political initiative, to redistribute expenditure away from national defence and state security and towards the economy and social services. I am talking about financial resources and a redistribution both of national income and of manpower.'[10] Thielmann hoped that a decision on these lines would create confidence and stabilize the situation.

Two months later, in a five-page letter to Modrow,[11] he emphasized the potentially explosive political effects of the desperate state of the health and social services systems. It 'may force our government to give up the struggle. Failure in the areas of health and social services, however, would mean forfeiting the credibility of a political system that is supposed to serve people and protect them from destitution. We are talking about a vital nerve here.' He warned of personal consequences—in other words, his resignation—if his renewed demands for substantial rises in salaries and wages for employees in the health and social services systems were not met. In fact, after a decision by the Council of Ministers and in the wake of wage negotiations, significant pay increases in the health system came into effect on 1 March 1990.[12] Thielmann believed that further expenditure on health was also necessary if, with the establishment of a contractual community and 'closer cooperation and coalescence between the two German states, we are to bring to bear basic ideas in the fields of health and social services policy to which we have been dedicated during the history of the GDR and which should not be lost. It is in these areas especially that we have the opportunity of introducing our own independent viewpoint. The social principles of our health and social services systems are not in dispute. Excluding commercialization from these fields has been a historical achievement.'[13]

The Modrow government kept firmly to the principle of a state-dominated health service. On 14 February 1990 Thielmann had written to regional medical officers[14] that with regard to decisions on applications by doctors for permission to set up their own practices, it was now to be assumed that 'by and large, there is a proven need in all areas of outpatient care in the districts in question' and that each doctor or dentist should be free to decide 'whether he wishes to work as an independent medical practitioner in his own practice'. If practitioners possessed the professional skills, then regional medical officers should issue permits to practise. This concession, however, was partially withdrawn, after criticism from, *inter alia*, the GDR Health and Social Services Trade Union. An 'explanatory' and 'more detailed' letter of 26 February 1990 and a Ministry statement of the same day[15] emphasized that decisions about independent practices at local level were the responsibility of regional medical officers, who had to take account of the concrete health care situation in their particular districts. In addition, consultation with the social insurance administration would have to be carried out in the case of each such decision, and there should be the 'greatest possible openness and democratic involvement, including working groups of the local "Round Tables"'. It was expressly emphasized that a state health service was the fundamental principle of health care in the GDR. Furthermore, in the forthcoming process of coalescence between the two German states 'the dominant role played by the state health and social services system in the GDR' would remain 'an element unconditionally worth preserving'.[16] Thielmann also criticized the growing trend for 'calling workplace health facilities into question and terminating their use'.[17] In line with this thinking, Thielmann wanted the statements on the health system in the Social Charter to include express pledges of a 'strong state and local government sector, using and expanding efficient polyclinics and ambulatories', and of 'guaranteed health care in the workplace'.[18]

6.2 EMPLOYMENT POLICY AND THE ADMINISTRATIVE SYSTEM FOR EMPLOYMENT

The other main area of social policy, besides health, in which action was required was employment policy. According to the Directorate-General for Research of the European Parliament, the opening of the borders had caused the GDR, by the first week in May 1990, to lose roughly 5 per cent of all people in employment,[19] including a considerable number of younger people with good qualifications, who were in short supply in the health system as well as in other branches of the economy such as the craft trades and transport.

More alarming in the longer run, however, was the growth in unemployment resulting from reductions in the numbers of jobs in industry and commerce, the bloc parties, and the trade unions, and from redundancies among state employees—for example, through the dismantling of parts of the extensive system of repression and surveillance. On 21 December 1989 a press statement was issued announcing the formation of a working group to deal with the provision of jobs for the unemployed and to guarantee the right to work.[20] The specific aim was to organize training and re-training and the allocation of appropriate work through committees run by labour offices (which existed at district level in the GDR).

The GDR had no institutions capable of operating an effective labour market policy. The labour offices, which were closely linked to local organs of the state, served primarily to allocate workers to enterprises, functioning as instruments for directing labour and enforcing the de facto obligation to work and cooperating closely with district planning committees in the 'preparation and implementation of the national economic plans for developing and making full use of the labour capacity of society'.[21] They were not equipped to offer employment advice (which was the responsibility of departments for professional training and advice run by regional and district councils under the general management of the Ministry of Education), organize further education and re-training, or provide any effective form of job-finding in the event of unemployment.

The problems that arose in the wake of the opening of the internal German border were the subject of conversations in east Berlin and Bonn in January and February 1990 between senior officials of the Federal Ministry of Labour and representatives of the GDR Ministry of Labour and Wages. The questions discussed included the employment of people who were commuting from the GDR into west Berlin and the Federal Republic, and west German support in the rebuilding and development of an administrative system for employment that would operate a system of unemployment insurance and an active labour market policy in the GDR.[22]

The GDR, however, was plainly worried that it was going to become heavily dependent on the Federal Republic. It sent a delegation from the Ministry of Labour and Wages to Austria between 9 and 12 January 1990, tasked with making a close study of Austria's employment policy: in particular, the way in which the Austrian Ministry of Employment and Social Affairs cooperated with employers' associations and trade unions in the development and implementation of employment policy, the role and structure of job centres and the qualifications of their staffs, methods of job-finding and other measures for reducing unemployment, and the provision of unemployment benefit and unemployment assistance. The delegation's terms of reference—which also referred to the agreements on principles concerning further cooperation between Austria and the GDR that had been reached at a meeting of Modrow and the Austrian Federal Chancellor of 24 November 1989—explicitly emphasized that 'all attempts at interference in the internal affairs of the GDR' would be rejected.[23]

As unemployment mounted, the Council of Ministers of the GDR issued three decrees at the beginning of February 1990 'regarding the provision of state and enterprise financial support to citizens during the period of arrangement of employment',[24] the introduction of early retirement benefit, and the 're-training of citizens to ensure employment'. Although the first of these decrees studiously avoided any reference to unemployment, and attempted to suggest that the current phase was purely transitional and that there was no basic infringement of the right to work, at the same time preparations for a system of unemployment insurance were put in hand.[25] Support payments were relatively generous: the previous net average monthly wage of those affected was paid in full out of funds from the state budget, up to a limit of 500 marks. The difference between this support payment and 70 per cent of the previous net wage, up to a further 500 mark limit, had to be borne by the enterprises.

The aim of the early retirement regulation[26] was to give enterprises and administrative management the opportunity to reduce their cost burdens by shedding older staff in a socially acceptable way. Early retirement benefit, payable before a person became entitled to an invalidity or old-age pension, could be claimed from the fifth year before pensionable age onwards—i.e. after the age of 60 in the case of men and 55 in the case of women—and amounted to 70 per cent of preceding net earnings, with a minimum of 500 marks per month if the previous net wage was not lower than this. Enterprises making application could claim reimbursement from the state budget of half the early retirement benefit paid. The re-training measures[27] were intended to deal with the changes in the labour market and stave off unemployment by enabling people to obtain new skills and qualifications.

In parallel with these decrees, the Council of Ministers passed a resolution on 8 February 1990 concerning 'measures to reorganize the tasks of the labour offices and assign them the task of guaranteeing the right to work under the conditions of the transition to a social market economy in the GDR'.[28] The measures involved detaching the labour and wages offices in the regions, and the labour offices in the districts, from local organs of state and began the process of transforming them from instruments of a centrally planned economy into providers of services to citizens, with a focus on careers and employment advice, job-finding, the organization and coordination of training and re-training schemes, the protection of living standards 'during the period of arrangement of employment', and support for 'citizens with impaired health'. A decree of 8 March 1990 then established a central administrative system for employment.[29]

The GDR's administrative system for employment was finally built up on the west German model, in close cooperation with the Federal Institute of Labour. On 18 February 1990 a working group was formed at the head office of the Federal Institute of Labour, with responsibility for coordinating activity during the reorganization and development of the GDR's employment administration system. On 22 and 23 February, in talks in east Berlin, Staatssekretär Bernhard Jagoda from the Federal Labour Ministry and Heinrich Franke, president of the Federal Institute of Labour, agreed to set up five model local job centres in east Germany, to advise the remaining job centres about how to carry out their new tasks, and to provide technical support.[30] At the beginning of May 1990 the Federal Institute of Labour board decided—after discussions in which the new Minister of Labour and Social Affairs in the GDR, Regine Hildebrandt, was also partly involved—to develop a self-governing labour market organization, financed through contributions by employers and the employed, and to establish properly functioning job centres in the GDR with roles and structure based on the west German model,[31] in advance of an eventual unified German administrative system for employment. Hildebrandt pointed out that the GDR population was psychologically unprepared for unemployment and that the level of unemployment had 'at all costs' to be 'kept as low as possible' in order to prevent the Social Market economy from being viewed as unacceptable.[32] With huge Federal Republic support in terms of staff, beginning even before the May meeting, and then with equally substantial financial backing, an organizational plan drawn up by the Federal Institute of Labour was put into effect, replacing within months the GDR's 227 local labour offices and 15 regional offices with 38 main employment offices and 161 local job centres.[33] To help in the process, *Land* employment offices in the Federal Republic were paired with particular regions of the GDR to support the process.[34] The establishment of the employment administration system—which was also strengthened by the appointment of the SPD member of the Bundestag and former Federal Minister of Labour Herbert Ehrenberg as an adviser to the GDR government—provided the institutional framework not only for guaranteeing benefit payments to the unemployed in lieu of wages but, especially, for the implementation of an active labour market policy that would play a crucial part in cushioning the effects of the transformation of the economy and reducing the level of unemployment.

As well as responding to the new problem of unemployment, in which it increasingly took its cue from the Federal Republic, the Modrow government also reformed the right to social welfare as a 'minimum protection for citizens not entitled to unemployment benefit',[35] in a decree of 8 March 1990.[36] GDR citizens now received for the first time the legal entitlement, under specified conditions, to income support and other assistance that had existed in the Federal Republic since 1961.

6.3 CO-DETERMINATION IN ENTERPRISES AND FIRMS

The Modrow government's cautious attempts to follow its own path on the question of co-determination for employees led merely to some preliminary proposals, which will be discussed briefly here, but—with one exception—not to any specific new laws or decrees. The exception was a decree of 1 March 1990 on 'the conversion of nationally owned combines, enterprises and facilities into joint-stock companies', which proposed, for the new businesses, a form of co-determination similar to that operating in the coal and steel industry in the Federal Republic, with employees and capital on an equal footing.[37] According to a position paper prepared for the chairman of the German Trade Union Federation, Ernst Breit, by the Federation's department for social questions, the 'introduction of Coal and Steel Co-Determination in all sectors and large firms' constituted a recognition of a long-standing and unanimous demand by the west German trade unions and was a 'milestone in the ongoing development of the right to co-determination in the Federal Republic, in a future united Germany, in the European Community, and, potentially, in the states of eastern Europe'. The Federation was unhappy, however, that co-determination had been defined as applying only to the workforce of an enterprise and 'not to employees in general' and that the representation of the interests of employees by external organizations (i.e. trade unions) was therefore 'initially [being] cut out of the scheme'; it also objected to the separate representation of a managerial employee, as this jeopardized the Federation's commitment to a unified form of representation of employees. On the other hand, it welcomed the fact that the presence of employees' representatives would ensure a linkage with the representation of employees' interests within the enterprise, that the resolution of deadlocks would be in accordance with the form of co-determination operative in the coal and steel industry, and that the sale of parts of an enterprise would have to be agreed with the supervisory board (made up of equal numbers of representatives of employees and shareholders, together with a 'neutral' member)—the latter a provision that went further than the Federation's demands. The Federation also emphasized the 'immense problem of training, coordination, and advice' that would face the representatives of enterprise workforces—who would turn in growing numbers to the trade unions in the Federal Republic—as a result of the new tasks posed by the conversion of 5,000 state-owned businesses and combines.[38]

At the government's request, the employment law group at the Humboldt-Universität in Berlin drafted a decree on works councils. This specified that the employees of an enterprise should decide by majority vote whether their interests ought to be represented through the enterprise's trade union organization or by a works council.[39] If the decision were in favour of a works council—which would then exercise all of the participatory rights of employees that were reserved for enterprise trade union leaderships under the Labour Statute Book of 1977 and other legal provisions—then the trade unions' monopoly role in representing workers' interests at enterprise level would be broken. In a parallel process, a working group set up by the Economics Ministry and headed by the GDR expert in economic law Professor Rudolph Streich prepared a 'proposal on norms' for a GDR-specific system of co-determination involving 'social supervisory boards' in business enterprises.[40] The notable feature of this proposal was that it envisaged that boards would be made up of equal numbers of three groups: members of the workforce, representatives of owners of funds and capital, and members of elected bodies. The latter bodies would consist of the Volkskammer of the GDR, regional, or *Land*, parliaments, and 'representatives of the people' at local level. Representatives of elected bodies might include not only expert elected members and members of committees and of local government administration, but also independent specialists in the enterprise's field of operations, representatives of citizens' movements, interest groups, and consumer associations, and representatives of the relevant trade unions. The supervisory board would not only be an organ of co-determination but would have wide-ranging powers of decision-making, although on questions of 'social strategy' the works council would possess a right of veto. Plainly, by seeking the incorporation of social groups into the running of enterprises, the Economics Ministry working group was hoping to create a new form of socialist industrial democracy.

In addition to these different proposals regarding works councils and co-determination at enterprise level, a further group of experts set up by the Economics Ministry, consisting of GDR specialists in employment and economic law, judges, and trade union officials, and with participation for a time by experts from the German Trade Union Federation,[41] drafted a 'law on the representation of the interests of employees in enterprises and concerns'[42] that was an attempt to codify the right of co-determination generally. Although the draft was based on west German provisions, it envisaged wider rights for trade unions within the enterprise and for works councils on business and economic questions, refrained from creating a special position for managerial employees, and omitted the wide-ranging regulations specified under Federal Republic law for protecting minorities in the election and composition of works councils. Like the other proposals mentioned, this draft, which might have served as a basis for discussions on the extension to east Germany, 'in adapted form', of the west German Works Constitution Law (*Betriebsverfassungsgesetz*), as envisaged in the coalition agreement of the de Maizière government, proved to be a dead-letter.

6.4 THE FDGB AND THE TRADE UNION LAW

By contrast, the attempts by the GDR's Free German Trade Union Federation (FDGB) and individual GDR trade unions to preserve their organizations within enterprises against competition from works councils, and to maintain a central power role in the new state, led to constitutional changes and a new law governing trade union rights in the GDR, which was enacted on 6 March 1990. After the Volkskammer elections of 18 March 1990, however, the new law was ignored and in the State Treaty of 18 May it was formally annulled.[43]

Although the SED, through its successor party, the PDS, managed to retain at least the core of its organization and a part of its financial assets after the establishment of the unified German state, neither the FDGB leadership organization nor the individual trade unions of the GDR achieved a similar outcome. The key reasons for this were that they had lost the confidence of the trade union rank and file and that their attempts at reform after the fall of the Wall never advanced beyond some first wary steps. At meetings of employees of enterprises and trade union representatives the old leadership cadres were frequently defeated in votes of confidence, and in many enterprises 'unofficial' works councils were elected or spontaneously established.[44] Many managers, who were struggling to keep their enterprises in being, also distanced themselves from the trade unions. Within the trade union movement severe tensions arose between the central FDGB organization and individual unions, which wanted to adopt the west German model and transform the FDGB from a body with an extensive bureaucratic apparatus, dominating the whole trade union movement, into a mere umbrella organization coordinating the operations of the individual unions, which would undertake free collective bargaining and achieve financial independence. Were such a change to take place, the FDGB bureaucracy would be drastically reduced in size and would lose control over membership contributions.[45] The central executive of the FDGB resigned on 9 December 1989, following pressure both from rank and file members and from the executive committees of the industrial unions, and a thirty-three-strong committee, taking over effective leadership of the FDGB, was formed to make preparations for an extraordinary general conference of the unions.[46]

The most important result of the seven-week work of the committee was a draft of a trade union law and related constitutional amendments, which were discussed at the general conference between 31 January and 1 February 1990 and adopted as the unions' reform proposal.[47] The purport of the draft law was to guarantee the continuing existence of the unions and their apparatus of officials and to protect their monopoly role as representatives of workers' interests. It was clear that the unions were seeking, before the new democratic Volkskammer elections on 18 March 1990, to lay the foundations of a socialist trade union state in which they would have a dominant position. The unions would be independent of both the state and the political parties—as they had not been under the GDR—and would represent the interests not only of their members but of all 'working people'. The unions' grass-roots organizations in enterprises would be involved, through local leaders, in all decision-making on personnel matters in enterprises. The organizations would also be included from the outset in all discussions of 'questions concerning the reproduction process in the enterprise'. In addition, every decision to change the 'production profile, to reduce or cease production, to change forms of ownership or use of resources, or to close an enterprise or a department of an enterprise' would be conditional on their agreement. The draft law also gave the trade unions the 'right of co-determination, joint decision-making and oversight regarding the use of all enterprise-held funds for working and living conditions derived from expenses and profits', and made them responsible for concluding collective industrial and other agreements.[48] The right to strike was guaranteed, as was the right to call for a general strike as a 'measure of last resort'; lockouts were expressly forbidden.

Trade union representatives in enterprises would be exempted from their normal jobs without loss of earnings, and enterprises would also be obliged to guarantee the pay of these employees by making monthly contributions to the funds of the relevant trade unions and to create the conditions required for trade union work by providing typists, technical assistants, printing and computer technology, office space, and transport.[49] The right of union officials to continue in employment in enterprises would thus be protected. There were particularly wide-ranging provisions giving the unions—which would also have access to all media—the right to initiate legislation and requiring all laws and legal regulations 'concerning the working and living conditions of working people, such as pay, social security and pension rights, prices and taxation, health and safety at work, and environmental protection' to be conditional on union agreement.[50] The effect of this draft law, if it had been passed, would have been to erode significantly the legislative powers of parliament and make the trade unions a fourth dominant constitutional power alongside the executive, the legislature and the courts.

After a general strike had been threatened, the Volkskammer accepted the law and the accompanying constitutional amendments, subject to some alterations, deletions, and additions. The constitutional amendments were passed with 14 votes against and 35 abstentions; the Trade Union Law itself was approved with 6 votes against and 53 abstentions.[51] The law as passed strengthened the trade union conference's draft by effectively ruling out claims for damages against trade unions arising out of industrial disputes and specifying that in the case of disruptions to production caused indirectly by an industrial dispute the workers affected would be guaranteed continued payment of their wages. The draft was watered down by the removal of the right to veto—though not the right to initiate—legislation and of the right to call for a general strike. Strikes would be permissible only if a conciliation procedure had failed, and could be suspended by the government if they were damaging to the public interest.

Even in its watered-down version, the law—which failed to stem the trade unions' loss of legitimacy and the decline in their power—was subjected to fierce criticism, on the grounds that it embodied the unions' anti-pluralist bid to be the sole representatives of workers, was tantamount to a usurpation of the functions of parliament, ignored the role of works councils, and sought to shore up the bureaucratic apparatus of the GDR unions. Employers and the Federal Labour Ministry, in particular, condemned it for offering a life-support mechanism to the socialist planned economy. It would, they argued, be an 'impediment to investment of the first order', would restrain entrepreneurial freedom during the process of adjustment to a market economy, and would completely overturn the balance between the two sides of industry in favour of the unions.[52]

6.5 THE SOCIAL CHARTER

The Social Charter was also roundly condemned in the Federal Republic. It was hammered out in lengthy discussions of the Round Table, accepted by the GDR government, and adopted on 7 March 1990 by the old Volkskammer, with three votes against and eleven abstentions, in the last sitting of the chamber before the elections of 18 March.[53] The purpose of the Charter, in line with the recommendations of the Round Table and the decision of the Volkskammer, was to embody the position of the GDR in the negotiations over monetary, economic, and social union with the Federal Republic and in the discussions about the shape of the future constitution. The Charter's target audience, therefore, was not the Modrow government but the new coalition that would be formed after the elections. The Charter would, it was hoped, induce the new government to commit itself to a comprehensive programme of basic social rights and to the retention and expansion of the 'social assets' of the GDR's citizens. The Charter was accordingly also targeted, indirectly, at the Federal Republic, with the intention that the latter would adopt the programme as the basis for the new common welfare state that was to be created and, in the final analysis, finance it.

Modrow had already asserted strongly, in a government statement of 20 February 1990[54] on the negotiations that had been held in Bonn on 13 and 14 February, that the 'principle of social justice' had to be upheld by both sides during the unification process and that economic union, monetary union, and social security were inseparably connected. It would therefore be 'the binding obligation of any future government' to 'defend the right to work under the conditions of a social market economy' and to 'strive for social protection for young and old, as well as for families'. The Federal government's proposal to back up monetary union with unemployment insurance and an alignment of the pensions system did not go far enough, he said. 'Does a future Germany not also need a social charter, to uphold inalienable values and secure them for the future? It is important, not least, to preserve the social assets of the citizen, especially the right to his own adequate living space, and to protect savings deposits and other products of his labour.' (This was a reference to the conversion of the entire monetary assets of the GDR at the exchange rate of 1:1.) Modrow also stressed that land reform should not be called into question, that the question of state-owned property had to be handled carefully, that day-to-day developments in the economy should be democratically regulated by trade unions and works councils, and that where subsidies were reduced, compensation should be paid 'in every case'.

The social ideals of the Round Table and the GDR government were given more precise expression in two further documents: the 'Baselines for a social charter' that were presented to the Volkskammer by the ministers Tatjana Böhm of the Independent Association of Women and Gerd Poppe of the Peace and Human Rights Initiative, and the 'Positions of the government of the GDR with regard to basic rights in the social compact'[55] with the Federal Republic. According to these documents, the move towards unity by the two German states had to include a social compact that would lead to improvements in living standards and working conditions and guarantee the maintenance of current standards of social security. Unity had to be achieved 'through a reciprocal process of reform of the two German systems of social security', and these should be raised to a higher level. The social assets of the citizens of the GDR should be preserved and their personal property should be protected by law.

Specifically, the documents called for the retention of the rights to work, to housing with effective rent control, and to free education, training, and health care. Free collective bargaining and the right to strike should be secured, lockouts should be forbidden, and industrial and other enterprises should be responsible for making available and financing workplace-based meals, medical care, the continuation and growth of enterprise-based provision of holidays and convalescence periods, and workplace-based child care. Further demands included the democratization and humanization of working life, guarantees of equality between the sexes in both the workplace and the family, protection of the socially disadvantaged, and the maintenance and expansion of an integrated state-guaranteed system of social insurance, incorporating unemployment insurance, the linking of pensions to employment earnings and prices, and the retention of minimum pensions and state subsidies on at least the existing scale.

The Social Charter sought to 'provide the cornerstones in terms of social welfare legislation' that would make possible the 'introduction of a truly *social* market economy'.[56] Its weakness was that it said nothing about how the programme was to be financed and took no account of the serious economic and financial crisis that the GDR was facing. In practice, the Charter's authors were looking to the Federal Republic to finance the programme, but this would have made the reform and modernization of the GDR economy more difficult and massively more expensive. Not surprisingly, reaction in the west was vehement. There was much talk of a lack of a sense of reality. In an article headlined 'Rotten Egg of a Round Table',[57] Horst Seehofer, Parlamentarischer Staatssekretär at the Federal Labour Ministry, wrote that the Social Charter was still operating 'in large part, with the thought-patterns of socialist castles in the air', that it postulated an oversized role for the state, and that it showed no understanding of the 'freedom of autonomous entrepreneurs', of the notion of a social partnership between the two sides of industry, or of the primacy of the 'performance principle' in the social insurance system. The guarantee of the right to work and the ban on lockouts were subjected to particularly fierce attack.

For some of the most prominent supporters of a social charter, on the other hand, the demand for a charter went hand in hand with firm ideas on the questions of the path to German unity and the speed of the unification process. Poppe, for example, expressly rejected the view of the *Frankfurter Allgemeine Zeitung*, in its discussion of the Social Charter, that unification should take place under the 'umbrella of the Basic Law', and argued that supporters of an 'Anschluss' of the GDR with the Federal Republic via Article 23 of the Basic Law should, if they were consistent and honest, refuse to assent to the Social Charter. The demands contained in the Social Charter should be included in a new GDR constitution, which should be drawn up before the framing of a new common German constitution by a constituent assembly of representatives of the two German states. This was the only practicable route, Poppe argued, whereby the 'social security and social identity' of the GDR and the 'dignity of [its] citizens' could be ensured.[58]

The coalition government that was formed after the Volkskammer elections opted for the quicker and simpler route to unification via Article 23, rather than by the creation of a new joint constitution via Article 146. At the same time, however, in the negotiations over the State Treaty on monetary union and the Unification Treaty, it tried to secure the broadest possible system of protection of the social interests of the citizens of the GDR within the new state. Although it was forced to abandon some of the maximalist demands contained in the Social Charter, it was, to a considerable degree, successful in this ambition.

7

The State Treaty on Monetary, Economic, and Social Union

7.1 FIRST CONTACTS BETWEEN THE LABOUR MINISTRIES OF THE FEDERAL REPUBLIC AND THE GDR AFTER THE FALL OF THE BERLIN WALL

During the first months after the fall of the Berlin Wall very concrete problems took centre stage. The GDR had to deal with the destabilization of its economy caused by the mass migration of workers into west Germany and the upsurge in commuting by east Germans into west Berlin and the border areas of the Federal Republic. For its part, the Federal Republic was especially worried by the increase in illicit work, the excessive strain on the labour market, the rise in social benefits, and the possible misuse of benefits by new arrivals and commuters from the GDR. The public debate had been instigated, in particular, by Oskar Lafontaine, the Prime Minister of the Saarland and later the SPD's candidate for the chancellorship.[1] Specific proposals focused on ending the regulated admissions procedure for those who had come from the east and cutting back the benefits they were being paid.[2] The aim of such proposals was to reduce the burden that was being carried by cities and rural communities, which were responsible for finding accommodation for the new arrivals, and to send a signal that the movement of population would be halted. The proposals at first also won widespread support among members and supporters of the CDU. They were rejected, however, by the government and CDU/CSU members of the Bundestag, after pressure from the Federal minister Wolfgang Schäuble. Schäuble later revealed, when presenting a book by the Green politician Antje Vollmer, that he would have resigned as Interior Minister if the government had ended the established process for admitting GDR citizens and had restricted freedom of movement.[3]

The new problems that arose after the opening of the Wall, in particular the unwelcome pull effect of the Federal Republic's social benefits, were first discussed internally within the Labour Ministry, by a project group on 'social policy aspects of the change in German–German relations', and, after interdepartmental groundwork, at a conference of political Ministry heads and departmental heads on 9/10 December 1989;[4] contacts were then made with the GDR authorities. Following the drafting of a preliminary text on 22 December 1989, and of other documents,[5] the first conversations took place in east Berlin on 3 January 1990.[6] It became clear that while there was a common interest in solving the problems that had arisen from the lifting of travel restrictions and the collision of the two systems of social security, there were also differences in approach. The GDR was primarily concerned to stem the outflow of workers, cream off currency from GDR workers who were commuting to the west, and build up an effective administrative system for employment on the west German model to operate unemployment insurance and an active labour market policy. The Federal Republic was anxious first and foremost to prevent the abuse of social benefits. The two sides' different attitudes on the question of citizenship were also a recurring theme during the talks—GDR citizens being regarded as Federal nationals within the Federal Republic, but Federal Republic nationals being treated as foreigners within the GDR. It was agreed, as a first step, to set up a pilot project for exchanging information, in particular about commuting to west Berlin and areas near the border.

These talks between the two ministries on 'cross-border employment' were continued in Bonn on 30 and 31 January and in east Berlin on 12 and 13 February 1990. The Federal Republic side also proposed further topics for discussion: namely, regulations regarding working conditions and social insurance arrangements for west German employees working in the joint-venture enterprises that were envisaged by the Modrow government, questions of social insurance law arising out of cross-border employment, cooperation with regard to health and safety at work, and outline arrangements for cooperation between providers of social benefits.[7] A Federal Labour Ministry note on the programme for the negotiations[8] shows that the Federal government was prepared to offer the GDR concrete assistance in building up a system of unemployment insurance and developing a productive labour market policy, help with improving the GDR's facilities for professional and medical rehabilitation, emergency aid in the form of materials and equipment for the health service, and comprehensive advice for reshaping the GDR's system of protection for the elderly. These social policy measures would, it was hoped, induce people to remain in the GDR.

In the talks held on 12 and 13 February[9]—by which time the offer of monetary union had been made—the GDR representatives launched the idea of a 'social compact'. Plainly, they were now prepared to incorporate individual areas of Federal Republic law into GDR law. They continued to insist, however, that Federal Republic citizens were foreign nationals and refused to agree that west German workers should have entirely free access to the GDR labour market.

However, their insistence on the sovereignty of the GDR was overtaken by events. Although the Federal Chancellor Helmut Kohl, in his Ten Point Programme of 28 November 1989, had seen the creation of a unified federal state as the ultimate stage in a lengthy process initially involving 'confederative structures', in the course of only a few weeks that final objective had come on to the agenda, mainly as a result of pressure by the people of the GDR, who, in large demonstrations, had been demanding rapid unification and, above all, the adoption of the Deutschmark.

One question concerned the role that social policy should play in the process. On 12 December 1989 the Federal Labour Minister, Norbert Blüm, had written to the Chancellor[10] drawing his attention to the problems caused by the new freedom of mobility, given the gulf in living standards between the two German states. In his ministry's view, Blüm said, the main aim should be to 'bring forward the reforms in the GDR, so that people there can live in freedom and in socially acceptable conditions'. The reforms in the GDR would create opportunities to 'end the division of Europe and thereby the division of Germany', and social policy had a part to play in bringing the two Germanys together.

On 9 January 1990, in a letter to Rudolf Seiters, the chief of the Federal Chancellery, Wolfgang Vogt, Parlamentarischer Staatssekretär in the Federal Labour Ministry, proposed that to support the 'coalescence of the two German states', a 'joint commission on employment and social security' should be set up, under Blüm's chairmanship, to complement the joint commissions on other policy areas that had been established after a meeting between Kohl and Modrow on 19 December 1989; this additional commission should also address the question of health services.[11] Seiters did not endorse this suggestion until 31 January, noting that the way in which health policy might be included would need to be clarified.[12]

Independently of this proposal, which was to be overtaken by events, an inter-ministerial and coalition working group on 'benefits legislation' had been set up on 23 January 1990 under the chairmanship of Horst Seehofer, Parlamentarischer Staatssekretär in the Federal Labour Ministry. Its members included the chief of the Federal Chancellery, representatives of other Federal ministries, a representative of the *Land* Baden-Württemberg, and a number of coalition party members of the Bundestag with a special interest in social policy and the German question. The group conducted a thorough review of the ways in which it might be possible to restrict benefits to new arrivals from east Germany (*Übersiedler*), across the whole area of social policy. (In the view of the coalition party members, migrants of German extraction from other parts of eastern Europe, or *Aussiedler*, ought to be treated on the same basis.[13])

With the offer of a 'monetary union with economic reform', made on 7 February 1990, the concrete problems caused by the opening of the internal German border became overshadowed by the fundamental question of the unification of the two German states. The offer to east Germany to adopt the Deutschmark was undoubtedly the riskiest decision that Kohl and the governing coalition took on the road to internal German unity. Essentially, the decision was made on political grounds. It flew in the face of the views of the Bundesbank, whose president, Karl-Otto Pöhl, was not consulted or even informed beforehand, though he subsequently accepted the decision as a political one. It also ran counter to the collective judgement of economists, who believed that monetary union would be economically justifiable only if it came as the crowning stage of a lengthy process of convergence between the economies of the Federal Republic and the GDR and of gradual transition to full convertibility of the GDR mark.[14] The view that a low exchange rate for the GDR mark would be significantly better for the survival chances of the GDR economy, especially its industry, was irrefutable on economic grounds, all the more so since the assumption made by the government's experts that it would be possible to insist that low wage levels in the east (at about one-third of western levels) should be increased only in line with rising productivity[15] was plainly a delusion.

The fierce criticisms of the Federal government's decision by Pöhl and leading west German economists[16] did not, however, take account of the political situation faced by the government, which wanted to send a signal that east German citizens should stay at home, or of the dynamics of the unification process. The proposed alternative—stemming the flood of internal migrants by imposing restrictions on access and employment, and planning the step-by-step economic convergence of the two states over a period of years (possibly extending beyond the foreseeable future)—would have been interpreted by east Germans as tantamount to rejection by the west. Moreover, given the enormous difficulties that the east Germans would have had in building up a competitive economy, there would only have been a deepening of west German doubts whether unity was desirable at all. In practice there would have been no speedy move to German unity, and a policy of waiting for a European solution, which might never come about—Lafontaine's policy—would have prevailed.[17]

7.2 THE DRAFTING OF THE STATE TREATY

The Federal Republic's original offer to the GDR of a 'monetary union with economic reform' did not include the proposal of a social union. However, the cabinet committee on 'German unity' that was set up on the same day decided to establish a working group on 'alignment of the systems of employment and social order and of education and training', and during the following weeks this group, with the Federal Labour Ministry playing the lead role, would work out what specific offers would be made to the GDR in the area of social policy.

Hans Tietmeyer, for many years Staatssekretär in the Federal Finance Ministry and from 1 January 1990 a member of the board of directors of the Bundesbank and leader of the Federal Republic's delegation in the treaty negotiations with the GDR, later voiced his regret that the idea that the social union should be deferred—or at least that 'some parts of the Federal Republic's highly developed systems of employment and social law [should] not be applied for a transition period'—in order to ease the process of economic transformation, had not been followed, for political reasons.[18] One factor was the pressure from the GDR, which from the outset maintained that monetary, economic, and social union were inseparable. According to Tietmeyer, however, the primary responsibility lay with resistance and interference on the western side. And it is certainly true that not only the Social Democrat opposition and the western trade unions but also the Federal Labour Ministry repeatedly stressed the need for generous social initiatives in order to cushion the effects of the reconstruction of the GDR economy.

The breadth of the scope of a 'social union' also needs to be borne in mind. In the GDR the system of social security was codified in the Labour Statute Book, so that employment and social law were much more closely interconnected than was the case in the Federal Republic. Furthermore, industrial enterprises were responsible for providing the bulk of social benefits specified by statute. A social union would therefore necessarily encompass employment law as well as social law.

From the start Blüm came out in favour of a social union giving 'social shape and backing' to the 'profound economic changes' that would accompany monetary union, and of wide-ranging Federal support for the GDR.[19] His position is very clear from the set of questions that he forwarded to Kohl on 9 February 1990, for the Chancellor to put to Prime Minister Modrow at the negotiations with the GDR delegation in Bonn on 13 and 14 February. Developing and aligning the systems of social security, Blüm argued, should essentially proceed according to a single set of principles, which in practice would be the west German ones. These included the principles that financing should be contributory, with contributions by both employers and employees; that benefits for the elderly should be financed on a redistributive basis through contributions by the working population; that pension benefits should be based on the length of the period over which, and the level at which, contributions were made; and that social insurance should be removed from the GDR national budget, with the shaping of the social insurance budget becoming, to a large degree, the responsibility of the social partners. In addition, Blüm wanted to know whether Modrow would agree to the principle of a multipartite system of social security rather than a unitary social insurance scheme. He also emphasized that pensioners should be guaranteed a reasonable livelihood. On the question of the GDR's readiness to develop, with Federal support, a system of social security to cover unemployment and job training and re-training, he urged that Modrow be asked whether he would be willing to adopt the structure and benefits of the west German system of employment administration.

In order to resolve the policy questions posed by a social union, Blüm proposed that a joint committee should be formed, chaired by the Ministers of Labour of the two states. To ensure rapid implementation, working groups should be created, in particular to build up an employment administration system, establish an active labour market policy, and construct a form of pensions insurance matching that of the Federal Republic. Importantly, Blüm urged that Modrow also be promised discussions with the Federal Finance Minister about finance to support social security, industrial training and re-training, and the protection of the purchasing power of pensions.

Blüm made public his conception of a 'welfare state Germany' (*Sozialstaat Deutschland*) before Modrow's visit, in an interview with the *Handelsblatt*.[20] He said that the Federal Republic's models of unemployment and pensions insurance and its employment promotion machinery should be extended to the GDR and that if this were done, then 'the whole debate about the level of social benefits for new arrivals would be settled at a stroke'. He reckoned on an average level of unemployment benefit of 750 DM per month and an average pension level of 840 DM: i.e. respectively, 63 and 70 per cent of average net earnings of 1,200 marks in the GDR. 'As living standards there rise, and wages soar, so social benefits will increase. On Day X they will be identical in the Federal Republic and the GDR.' At first, though, contribution levels would have to differ, and for a transitional period the Federal Republic would have to provide start-up funds from government coffers.

Before making his statement Blüm had seen a specific proposal on the alignment of the two pensions insurance systems by the chief executive of the Association of German Pensions Insurance Providers, Rudolf Kolb, and his deputy, Franz Ruland;

this paper was also later released as a basis for public discussion.[21] The paper suggested that the way to bring the two systems into alignment was for west German pensions law to be adopted in the GDR and the administration of pensions to be reorganized, with the FDGB ceasing to be involved; individual earnings points would be calculated according to employment income during a person's working life, and earnings-related indexation would be established. Pensions expectancies and pensions in east Germany would thus be based on wage growth, as in west Germany, with the goal the protection of living standards. This would give pensioners 'sufficient prospects to induce them to remain where they are living'.[22] Pensions reform, however—which would, of course, require the guarantee that existing pensions and pensions expectancies would be at least maintained—would oblige the GDR to turn to the Federal Republic for financial help over and beyond some 'narrowly defined compensation to the GDR for migration',[23] entailing the significant use of Federal Republic tax funds. 'Unification of the two German states will not be "free of charge".'[24] This proposal was important because for the first time the difficult technical problems that would be thrown up by the reorganization of the GDR's pensions system (apart from the GDR's systems of supplementary and special provision for particular groups within the population) were being addressed in detail.

Following the GDR delegation's visit to Bonn in February 1990, a commission of experts of the two states was formed, to prepare for a monetary union and a joint economic community. The commission in turn set up a working group on social security under the chairmanship of Bernhard Jagoda, Staatssekretär in the Federal Labour Ministry and later the president of the Federal Institute of Labour, and the deputy to the GDR Minister for Labour and Wages, Ingolf Noack.[25] Within the Federal Labour Ministry an 'ad hoc planning staff for alignment of the systems of employment and social order in Germany' was established, led by the Regierungsdirektor Werner Sasdrich, to analyse and assess the consequences for social policy of developments in the GDR and, with the relevant sections of the Ministry, prepare proposals for bringing the two systems of employment and social security into line with one another.[26] On 2 March Blüm gave an interview to *Die Welt* in which he spelled out in greater detail, on the basis of the work of the commission of experts and the analysis conducted in the Labour Ministry, his ideas about the 'social backing' for monetary union. The principles of wage- and contribution-related benefits, earnings indexation, and the 'protection of living standards' would be extended to the GDR, he said, and pensions would be converted on the same terms as wages. 'Any start-up financing by the Federal government' would be time-limited and degressively structured from the outset. Contribution levels in the GDR, which were very much lower than in the Federal Republic, would 'gradually' be raised to Federal levels.[27]

The interim report by the commission of experts, which was delivered on 13 March, a few days before the Volkskammer elections[28] (no further report was produced), gave an overview of the GDR system and recorded broad agreement in favour of the introduction of a multipartite contributions-financed system of social insurance, independently administered by employees and employers and subject to legal regulation by the state. There should be separate budgets, independent of the state budget, for pensions, health, accident and unemployment insurance. In place of the current system of statutory old-age insurance in the GDR, which essentially offered a very low level of basic public provision with small increments, based on previous contributions, the west German system of insurance should be adopted, allowing for a considerable degree of variation in benefits according to the level of contributions and the length of time over which contributions were made. The report argued that it appeared feasible to convert GDR pensions over a short time-period, using Federal Republic pensions law as a model, with a resultant old-age pension for an average GDR wage-earner with 45 insurance years of approximately 70 per cent of the average net employment income of a GDR worker—for most people, a significant increase. The GDR side, however, maintained that the existing system of minimum pensions, which were not provided for under Federal Republic pensions law, should be retained.

The documents of the discussions[29] show that minimum pensions had 'the function of a guideline value of a minimum living standard', particularly as a new system of income support would have to be set up in place of the GDR's entirely marginalized system of social welfare.[30] The GDR also planned to make payments of 150 marks per month to every inhabitant of the GDR as compensation for the cessation of subsidies on food, thereby retaining a disastrous flaw in its economic policy. As far as other questions were concerned—such as the adoption of Federal Republic employment law (with its pillars of freedom of association, free collective bargaining, works constitution regulations, and co-determination), the interconnections between economic, monetary and social policy, and the new separation of competences and financial liability in the areas of health care and social security—the commission proposed to go into these more deeply in subsequent discussions.

It is clear, then, that as early as the period of the Modrow government the GDR was prepared to adopt the basic principles of the Federal Republic's social security system, particularly with regard to unemployment and pensions insurance, even though many details, as well as the extent of the assistance that was expected from the west, remained unresolved.

The crucial issue, however, was what offer would be forthcoming on the part of the Federal Republic. Discussions on this matter in the working group on 'alignment of the systems of employment and social order' established by the 'German unity' cabinet committee began, after careful preparation within the Labour Ministry's departments, on 14 February and concluded with the submission of a report to the cabinet committee on 6 March 1990.[31] The report revealed important differences among the relevant ministries. As far as employment law was concerned, the Federal Ministries of Economics and Finance disagreed with the position of the Labour Ministry, arguing that the law on protection against dismissal and the coal and steel industry system of co-determination should not be adopted immediately, so as not to impede the necessary process of structural change. In addition, these ministries believed that the implementation of costly employment promotion measures should be deferred until the more urgent task of creating a system of unemployment insurance had been carried out; at any rate, the GDR should not be allowed to assume that the whole range of instruments for boosting employment that was available in the Federal Republic under the latter's Employment Promotion Law should be at their disposal too. In particular, the Finance Ministry objected to the payment of benefits for short-time workers during the initial year, in view of the 'great danger' that 'a resolution of the adjustment problems of individual branches of the economy [would be] postponed and the structure preserved'.[32]

On pensions insurance, the working group agreed only to a gradual increase of the GDR's net pension level to about 70 per cent of the net employment income of people with 45 years of insurance. The Labour Ministry's proposal that there should be a rise in pensions, backed up by Federal start-up finance, to compensate for the abolition of price subsidies was not adopted. The Finance Ministry warned against an excessively rapid and large increase in pensions and against the retention of the 'social achievements' of the GDR (a minimum pension, and the inclusion of all people in employment within a unitary insurance system), and rejected the granting of a Federal subsidy to support pensions insurance in the east.[33] The Economics Ministry, too, wanted an assurance that 'the adjustment of social benefits [would] not set in train a pensions, wages and prices spiral'.[34]

There was a fundamental divergence between the Labour and Interior Ministries, which could not be resolved at the level of the 'German unity' cabinet committee, on the question of equal treatment, under pensions law, of new arrivals from the GDR and German-national immigrants from eastern and south-eastern Europe. Under the law, new arrivals from the GDR and German-national immigrants from eastern Europe had hitherto received, by dint of employment in their countries of origin, pensions based on the much higher levels applicable in the Federal Republic. This integrationist principle—like that of common citizenship for Germans of both east and west, to which the Federal Republic had always adhered, and which the GDR had strongly opposed—had been a key material element of German unity. It was now agreed that the integrationist principle, which was operating as an unwelcome pull factor on GDR pensioners and inducing them to move to the Federal Republic, would have to be replaced at some future date by the 'export principle': in other words, pensions would have to be calculated according to the criteria applicable in the pensioner's place of origin.

In the Labour Ministry's view, such a ruling, entailing much less favourable terms for pensioners as a sub-group among future arrivals from the GDR, ought also to apply to German nationals migrating from eastern Europe and the Soviet Union, who likewise should not be given an incentive to come to the Federal Republic. The Interior Ministry, however, opposed treating immigrants from outside Germany on the same terms. (This would also have entailed rescinding or amending the social insurance treaty with Poland, which was based on the integrationist principle.[35]) The Interior Ministry's position eventually prevailed.

With regard to health insurance, the main topic of controversy was the extension to the GDR of the Federal Republic principle of continued payment of wages by firms in the event of illness, in place of the GDR system of continued payment of only 90 per cent of net wages out of health insurance. The Economics Ministry took the view, in opposition to the Labour and Finance Ministries, that the current GDR law should remain in force, so as not to put at risk the viability of the GDR's industrial and other enterprises. The Labour Ministry favoured a gradual raising of contributions, while the Finance Ministry argued for the immediate adoption of the statutory health insurance contribution rate at the level of 12.6 per cent of wages and salaries up to a fixed ceiling and rejected obligatory initial support from the Federal budget.[36]

The report also emphasized that in view of the completely different structures that existed in the GDR in the areas of health care and health insurance, it would be possible to bring structures and benefits into alignment only gradually. Certain particular elements of a free health care system should be introduced at once—freedom for doctors to set up their own practices, a diversity of hospital providers, permission for private pharmacies to conduct business, and private provision of medicines and medical aids—but the vital need was to ensure that health care provision continued to function effectively.

While the Finance Ministry was prepared to agree to start-up financing only for unemployment insurance (though it eventually also agreed, with reluctance, to such financing for pensions insurance—a position that was later enshrined in the State Treaty), the report proposed similar Federal financial support for accident and health insurance.

In the cases of social provision for war victims, which in the GDR was provided at a very low level within the overall framework of general social insurance, and of support for families, the working group saw no immediate need for action. The Finance Ministry, clearly fearful of the cost of extending the relatively generous provision available to war victims in the Federal Republic, stressed the 'need for a very lengthy process of adjustment', opposed the Labour Ministry's proposal that benefits should be raised during the transition period, and, on the basis of a comparison of the extent of support for families in the Federal Republic and the GDR, argued that 'with family benefits it would be impossible to achieve the highest levels in every case'.[37]

One of the thorniest and most contentious problems was the conversion rate at which the currency changeover should take place. In the campaign for the Volkskammer elections all the GDR parties had called for a rate of 1:1 for monetary holdings and wages. The Bundesbank, the Federal Finance Minister and the Federal Economics Ministry, on the other hand, supported a conversion rate of 2:1 for debts, savings accounts, and cash holdings in excess of 2,000 marks (with a rate of 1:1 up to that amount), as well as for wages and pensions, though it was accepted that compensation should be paid for the raising of social insurance contributions and the dismantling of subsidies.[38] The Federal Union of German Employers' Associations favoured a conversion rate of 1:1 for pensions, along with gradual alignment with the Federal pensions system. They argued that for employee incomes a conversion rate should be found 'at which, taking into account the likely compensation payments, the purchasing power of incomes [would be] protected'.[39] This view was broadly the same as the Bundesbank's proposal for wages conversion, which became public knowledge as the result of an indiscretion.[40] The chairman of the FDP, Count Lambsdorff, speaking on the party's behalf, cited the low level of pensions in the GDR and maintained that confining the 1:1 conversion to savings accounts up to 2,000 marks would not meet with popular assent. The trade unions were in favour of the conversion of wages, pensions, and a portion of savings at the rate of 1:1. The western SPD also broadly took this view. Opinions in the western CDU/CSU were divided, with the employees' organizations and almost all specialists in social policy favouring a conversion rate of 1:1 for wages and pensions. The CDU/CSU parliamentary party supported a 1:1 rate for the accounts of small savers but did not commit itself to a rate for wages and pensions.

In this situation the unambiguous plea by Blüm, the Federal Minister of Labour, for a conversion rate of 1:1 for employment incomes and pensions, which he voiced in a letter to the Federal Chancellor of 27 March 1990,[41] took on great significance as far as the eventual decision by the Federal government was concerned. In Blüm's view, any other conversion rate would 'open up profound social fault lines and have destabilizing political consequences'. If the rate were 2:1, people in the GDR would be faced with 'glaring losses relative to their previous, already lower, living standards'; this would apply 'particularly to pensioners, families, and the unemployed. Millions of people would fall below the income support threshold.' In addition, the aim of 'persuading people to stay at home' might not be fulfilled. In a later interview Blüm emphasized that he had told the supporters of a 2:1 conversion rate that 'reunification would then inevitably take place in the west and the Wall would have to be rebuilt'.[42] An attachment to the letter to Chancellor Kohl strongly criticized the Finance Ministry's model, which called for a halving of gross GDR incomes through the conversion ratio and 'compensation for part of the reduction' through 'partly appropriate and partly arbitrary allowances', and which, while nominally lowering average net wages by 18 per cent, would in fact reduce them even more sharply by virtue of the abolition of price subsidies. Net wage levels of this kind would jeopardize social union, Blüm said. By contrast, the Labour Ministry's guiding principle was to ensure a 'combination of monetary union, economic community and social union, so that neither 'employees, nor pensioners, nor large families . . . [would] become socially marginalized'.[43]

The Labour Ministry's objective tallied with the expectations of people in the GDR, who were mounting massive demonstrations against a conversion ratio of 2:1.[44] Even before the Federal government embarked on the official negotiations, it was accepted that it would be politically impossible to convert wages and salaries at a rate other than 1:1. Blüm plainly had Kohl's support on the point,[45] and the leaders of the coalition parties also gave it their endorsement. On the question of the conversion of monetary holdings, the two governments eventually reached a compromise on 2 May, whereby monetary holdings and claims would essentially be converted at the rate of 2:1 but GDR citizens would be able to exchange cash and money in savings accounts at the rate of 1:1 for amounts between 2,000 and 6,000 marks, the exact quantity being determined by the individual's age.[46] On the question of the debts of the GDR's enterprises the position of the president of the Bundesbank, Otto Pöhl, prevailed. Pöhl had pointed out to Kohl that at a rate of 1:1 the GDR's debt burden, standing at 34,000 million marks, would also have to be paid off to foreign creditors in Deutschmarks and that the debts of enterprises and combines owed to the GDR national bank, at 260,000 million marks, would result in annual interest payments of 20,000 million DM. Many east German enterprises would therefore go bankrupt.[47] In fact, even the ratio of 2:1 for debts proved too high, encumbering GDR enterprises with debts that endangered their survival. In the end most of the debts had to be paid off by the *Treuhand*.

Work on a draft of the State Treaty continued in parallel with the discussions on the currency conversion. On 26 March 1990, after a meeting with the Labour Ministry's Staatssekretäre, Otfried Wlotzke, the head of the Ministry's Department III (dealing with employment law and health and safety regulation), presented a wide-ranging position paper on 'Requirement[s] for a position on a system of social security in the GDR to be determined in a state treaty/law on basic principles'. The paper expressly stated that there should be a clear undertaking that those provisions in the GDR constitution and employment law that differed from these requirements—particularly the GDR's trade union law—would be rescinded. Amplifying the text of the 6 March report by the 'German unity' cabinet committee, the paper said that the treaty should create the conditions whereby citizens of the Federal Republic should be 'permitted, without administrative obstacles, to take up employment in the GDR'. In addition, the GDR should ensure that 'in particular, provisions are removed from its employment law that involve the leading role of the SED, democratic centralism, and a centrally planned and controlled economy'.[48] In a position paper of 29 March the Finance Ministry, using calculations based on a model of the financial effects of alignment of the employment and social security systems, argued that pensions should initially be set at a lower level, that wages and pensions in the GDR should be fixed at roughly one-third the level of west German wages and pensions, and that a large-scale active labour market policy, with high consequential costs, should not be adopted. At the same time the Finance Ministry raised the question whether the west German pensions insurance system might not contribute to 'settling the deficits' in the east German pensions insurance system.[49]

A 'first sketch of a proposal to the GDR' on the creation of a 'monetary union, economic community, and social community'[50] was ready on 4 April 1990. An official 'working paper for the discussions' was passed to the GDR on 24 April.[51] During work on the draft by the Bonn ministries the conflicting positions of the Labour Ministry on the one hand, and the Economics and Finance Ministries on the other, emerged yet more clearly than had been evident in the earlier discussions in the working group of the 'German unity' cabinet committee. An 'information note' of 3 April produced by the Labour Ministry's planning staff on alignment of the employment and social security systems in Germany not only listed ten contentious points but also drew attention to the fact that the Finance Ministry, backed by the Economics Ministry and the Chancellery, had even 'called into question' the entire projected 'chapter on the social community in its current form'. According to the note, 'The Ministry of Labour's view that the basic structures of our employment law and social security system should be extended to the GDR in conjunction with monetary union came under attack. It was said that this would be damaging to investment and the economy, and would ultimately also do a disservice to the people of the GDR. In particular, social protection against dismissal and the extension of employment promotion measures were rejected. Extending our social insurance law to the GDR would be unreasonable, in view of the heavy cost burden, and protection against dismissal would interfere with layoffs and have an adverse effect on private investment.'[52] The Finance Ministry, for its part, believed that a 'comprehensive programme of re-training backed only by the promise of Federal financial support [was] unacceptable', since the promotion of skills was primarily the responsibility of enterprises and would not prevent or end unemployment. Furthermore, the Ministry argued, there was not the infrastructure necessary for providing employment training and re-training. It would not be sensible to extend west German job creation schemes, since 'roughly 60 per cent of participants remain unemployed after the completion of schemes—and in the GDR the figure would probably be even higher', and there was a 'danger of taking government money and refinancing work, resulting in a quasi-subsidizing of wages'. With regard to pensions insurance, the Finance Ministry, as well as favouring only a gradual and non-immediate raising of the pension level, insisted particularly, against massive resistance from the Labour Ministry, that the GDR's systems of special provision for particular groups of the population should be incorporated into social insurance. It rejected a public subsidy of 18.8 per cent, as existed in the west German pensions insurance system, and called instead for the creation of a financial combine of the western and eastern insurance systems, which would have the effect that pensioners in the west would pay for the deficits in the east. The Labour Ministry's proposal that the current level of pensions should be guaranteed, provided that no increase took place, was rejected, on the grounds that there would then be a risk that the minimum pension system, which was incompatible with the basic principles of Federal pensions insurance, would be preserved. The Finance Ministry was prepared to agree to start-up financing from the Federal budget in the case of unemployment insurance but not, as the Labour Ministry favoured, for health, pensions, and accident insurance.[53]

The main concrete points of disagreement which discussions between Staatssekretäre and Ministers had still failed to resolve by 19–20 April were as follows:[54]

1. There was disagreement whether the continued payment of wages in the event of sickness should be the responsibility of the employer or of health insurance. In the end the Labour Ministry's position, that the employer should be responsible (as in the Federal Republic), prevailed over the view of the Economics Ministry.

2. On the controversial questions of the raising of the net pension level to 70 per cent of the average earned income of a wage-earner with 45 insurance years, and the guarantee of continued payment of existing pensions at least at current levels after conversion to the Deutschmark, the decision went in favour of the Labour Ministry, and against the Finance Ministry, after an intervention by Kohl.[55] The Federal Chancellor, plainly for reasons of electoral tactics, wanted pensioners in the GDR to start benefiting from the advantages of the west German system as soon as possible.

3. There was fierce dispute whether the GDR's four existing systems of special provision for members of the National People's Army, the police, customs, and state security, and the systems of supplementary provision for specific groups, some of them closely associated with the state, such as the technological and scientific intelligentsia, teachers, party and social functionaries, and employees of the railways, postal service, public administration, and major state-owned enterprises, should be incorporated into general pensions insurance or should continue to be treated separately. The Labour Ministry, partly out of fear of overstraining the pensions insurance system, wanted to transfer old-age protection for these groups to the state budget, but came up against the combined opposition of the Finance, Interior, and Defence Ministries. In the draft treaty of 24 April 1990 the problem was bracketed for future resolution. A Finance Ministry paper of 9 May on points still under dispute with the Labour Ministry devoted particular attention to this issue. Subsequently the Labour Ministry accepted a compromise whereby people receiving pensions through the supplementary provision system for particular groups should be transferred to general pensions insurance but that the consequent additional costs, which the GDR estimated would amount to 1,300 million DM per annum, should be borne by the GDR's state budget, and hence later by the Federal budget. People receiving payments from the special provision systems—with the exception of members of the armed services (the National People's Army, the Stasi, and border troops)—would, contrary to the Labour Ministry's position and in accordance with the view of the Finance Ministry, also be incorporated into statutory pensions insurance, since during the transition period there would 'of necessity' be no terms and conditions of employment under public law for people in public service, and since otherwise there would be a danger that the Federal budget would ultimately have to bear the costs of provision. In addition, it would be easier to implement payments cuts in a unitary old-age protection system.[56] The settlement that was finally agreed in the State Treaty ruled that all special and supplementary provision systems for particular groups, including those for the armed services, would be closed and incorporated into statutory pensions insurance, which would be reimbursed from the state budget for the resultant additional expenditures. The transfer of these systems was to prove one of the thorniest problems in the new pensions system in the east, particularly as the treaty enunciated the principle that unjustified payments should be abolished and excessive ones reduced.[57] Calls for so-called 'criminal law on pensions' to be abolished were to keep the Federal Republic's courts busy.[58] It would certainly have been more logical if these systems, which in some ways resembled the Federal Republic's systems of provision for civil servants (*Beamten*) and supplementary provision for the public service (*öffentlicher Dienst*), had been dealt with separately outside statutory pensions insurance.

4. The Finance Ministry's demand that pensions insurance in the GDR should not receive a start-up subsidy—in contrast with the position in the Federal Republic, where pensions insurance of white- and blue-collar employees received a Federal subsidy (at that time, 18.8 per cent of pensions expenditure)—was a sweeping one. It might have encouraged the attitude that the state should withdraw

from the financing of pensions insurance in the Federal Republic too. After the relevant provision in the 'first sketch' had been bracketed as controversial, the draft treaty of 24 April 1990 and the State Treaty itself expressly laid down that the state should be involved in spending on pension insurance through a subsidy, at a level not specified. The Finance Ministry's view that start-up financing should not be provided for accident and health insurance carried the day against the Labour Ministry and, later, the GDR's delegation at the negotiations. However, the Finance Ministry had to accept such financing not only for unemployment insurance but also for pensions insurance.

5. Although the Finance and Economics Ministries had originally hoped that Federal employment law should be extended to east Germany in strictly limited terms, only the employer's duty to notify in the event of mass redundancies and the regulations regarding redundancy schemes were actually omitted in the draft.[59]

The statement, in the draft's general principles, that 'so long as, and in so far as, trade unions able to conduct collective bargaining do not exist . . . agreements between the employer and the works council regarding wages and other terms and conditions of employment are permissible' was heavily criticized by the leadership of the German Trade Union Federation and was eventually deleted during the concluding negotiations on the treaty, following submissions to the Federal Chancellery and the Labour Ministry; the leader of the GDR delegation, Günther Krause, also expressed his strong disapproval. Tietmeyer later complained, not without reason, that the process of structural adaptation in the GDR was made more difficult as a result.[60]

7.3 THE NEGOTIATIONS WITH THE GDR

By the time of the final negotiations between government ministries on the Federal Republic side, the coalition agreement of 12 April 1990[61] reached by the newly formed government in the GDR had been published. The detailed statements contained in the agreement were highly significant indications of the stance that the GDR was likely to adopt in the discussions on the State Treaty, not least on matters of social policy. Many of the relevant passages bore the stamp of the eastern SPD, one of the parties in the new coalition, which had been closely advised by social policy experts in the western SPD.

The preamble to the coalition agreement declared that the aims of the GDR Grand Coalition were to bring about the unification of Germany through the accession of the GDR to the Federal Republic according to Article 23 of the Basic Law and to secure not only freedom and the rule of law but also prosperity and social justice for all of the GDR's citizens. If there were not to be a new constitution for the GDR, the preamble stated, then rights to social security, in particular rights to work, housing, and education, should be incorporated in an amended Basic Law as 'individual rights not enforceable through the courts' and guaranteed in the form of goals of state. In the event, however, the basic social rights contained in the GDR constitution of 1974[62] were not incorporated into the Basic Law, either through the State Treaty of 18 May or through the Unification Treaty, nor was this done through the constitutional amendment of 27 October 1994. Although these rights were enshrined in the constitutions of the new *Länder* that were formed in east Germany in October 1990, they largely took the form of wish-lists.[63]

A central demand of the GDR with regard to the social union was for 'start-up finance and forms of internal German financial compensation' in order to 'compensate for the differences in economic power' between the two German states. Great emphasis was placed on the role of an employment promotion law in shaping an active labour market policy and, especially, meeting the interests of women.

The GDR was particularly anxious to achieve an independent system of employment law, more favourable to its own workers than that of the Federal Republic: for example, by including more extensive protection against dismissal, not only for the severely disabled, but for women, single parents, and members of large families. Department III of the Federal Ministry of Labour, which dealt with these matters, advised strongly against this line, on the grounds that it might have negative effects on the willingness of west German employers to invest in the east and that positive resistance to the removal of these 'more favourable' regulations in the GDR might make later unification of the two German states more difficult to achieve. Moreover, the department argued, west German employees, who would also need to play their part in reunification, would be very unsympathetic to such an approach.[64]

On the question of co-determination, likewise, the coalition agreement specified that the Federal Republic's regulations were to be adopted only in 'modified form'. The GDR government plainly proposed to extend to all larger enterprises the Federal model of parity representation that operated in the coal and steel industry,[65] thereby significantly strengthening the rights of employees. These plans, which were also rejected by the Federal Labour Ministry, had no chance of being put into practice.

With respect to pensions insurance, as the Federal Finance Ministry at once noted,[66] the GDR side, with its formula of a 'gradual', rather than immediate, raising of the net pensions level to 70 per cent of employment income for a wage-earner with 45 insurance years, did not go so far as the more generous position taken by the Labour Ministry. Central GDR demands that conflicted with west German pensions law were for the retention of minimum pensions, the 'retention or introduction of a general system of statutory pensions insurance' for all, and the raising of employment incomes and pensions, even before the currency conversion at the ratio 1:1, through a 'per capita supplement' arising 'out of the re-apportionment of current product and services subsidies'. The effect of these measures would have been to continue to place excessive strain on the GDR economy and state.

As far as the organization of social insurance was concerned, the GDR coalition was prepared to adopt the Federal Republic model of self-administration and a separation of the individual branches of insurance. Because of differences among the coalition parties, however, nothing was said on the question whether in the case of pensions insurance there should be a unitary system of providers or a division between provision for blue- and for white-collar workers (*Arbeiter* and *Angestellte*).[67] The very natural idea that the organization of pensions insurance for blue-and white-collar workers should be merged—compensatory financing had existed on a significant scale since 1969—was also strongly backed by the Federal Audit Office in a letter of 24 April to the Labour Minister, Blüm,[68] and had widespread support among experts on social insurance and interested sections of the public. The call for amalgamation reflected, moreover, the growing alignment between the roles of blue- and white-collar workers both in the employment process and in terms of legal status, an alignment marked by the replacement of the older terms by the more general category of 'employee' (*Arbeitnehmer*). Employment and social law in the GDR had not distinguished between blue- and white-collar workers, and the process of assigning individual groups of employees from the former GDR to either the Federal Insurance Office for White-Collar Workers (BfA) or the *Land* insurance offices (for blue-collar workers) later proved to be fraught with difficulties. One of the problems concerned the form that the organizational unification should take. The state of Bavaria favoured a federalist solution, whereby BfA pensioners would be taken on by the *Land* insurance offices; the Federal Audit Office preferred a centralized solution, in which the 21 white- and blue-collar insurance providers would be brought together to form a single national insurance provider.[69] In the end it took fifteen years, until 1 October 2005, before the problem was resolved and the 26 existing pensions insurance providers (consisting of the BfA, the 22 regional *Land* insurance offices, the Federal Miners' Insurance Institute, the Seafarers' Office, and the Railwaymen's Insurance Office) were consolidated into two national providers—the 'German Pensions Insurance Alliance' (bringing together the BfA and the Association of German Pensions Insurance Providers) and the 'German Pensions Insurance Office for Miners, Railwaymen and Seafarers'—and, from early 2006, the 'German Regional Pensions Insurance Office', comprising 16 *Land* insurance offices.[70]

Like the organization of pensions insurance, health insurance was also a contentious issue for the coalition parties in the GDR. The SPD wanted a regionally structured but unitary health insurance system for the whole area of the GDR, while the CDU and DSU took the view that it would not be feasible to stand in the way of a multipartite system. Eventually a compromise was reached, whereby a regionally structured non-profit health insurance system based on uniform contributions would be created, but with the possibility that this might later be replaced (assuming freedom of choice and the obligation to accept members) by a non-unitary health insurance system.[71] The intention was that by contrast with Federal Republic social law, all people in work—that is, including the self-employed—would be liable to statutory health insurance.

As far as the system of health care was concerned, the coalition proposed substantial divergences from the Federal Republic model. It was agreed to move away from an entirely state-run health care system and adopt some important elements of the west German system: in particular, to build up a system of public professional councils (*Kammern*) for doctors, dentists, and pharmacists and to allow medical professionals, pharmacists, scientists working in medical fields, psychologists, and providers of other therapeutic services to set up their own practices (albeit with preference being given to GDR citizens in the short and medium term).

However, it was also expressly stated that 'polyclinics comprising a variety of legal entities' should be preserved, as 'an essential foundation of outpatient care directly available to the citizen'. Likewise, effective elements of the GDR's highly developed workplace-based health service should be retained, as should the close connection between in- and outpatient care.

As was also apparent from its objectives regarding policy for young people, women, and families, the GDR coalition government was willing to adopt the principles of Federal Republic legislation on employment and social security that were part and parcel of the Social Market economy and to make significant improvements to social benefits, again on the Federal Republic model. At the same time, however, its aim was to preserve those GDR social benefits and rights for employees that went further than provision in the Federal Republic—in particular, benefits for women and families, and in the provision of health services and child care, where east Germans regarded the Federal Republic as lagging well behind.

On 18 April 1990 the Federal Finance Ministry's influential cross-departmental working group on 'internal German relations', headed by Thilo Sarrazin, presented a 'summary and assessment of the coalition agreement of the governing parties of the GDR'. This noted that the basic purport of the coalition agreement, with its declaration in favour of establishing German unity via Article 23 of the Basic Law, and its clear views on the structure of a new monetary and economic system for the GDR, 'essentially [accorded with] the objectives in our draft of the State Treaty'. Nevertheless, the working group said, the coalition agreement called for a series of cost-heavy measures—notably start-up finance, forms of internal German financial compensation for unemployment, pensions, and health insurance, and support for agriculture and environmental protection—that went 'well beyond the financial support envisaged in the draft of the State Treaty'. The conversion of savings accounts at the ratio of 1:1, the conversion of wages, salaries, and pensions at the ratio of 1:1 with a prior monthly increase by 280 marks for each employee and pensioner, and the 'forgiveness or revaluation of the debts of publicly owned enterprises' would lead to 'claims for state compensation of the order of 140,000 million DM'. Moreover, the proposed increases in wages, salaries, and pensions before monetary conversion would give rise to wage costs that would 'put the competitiveness of many enterprises at risk and lead to high unemployment . . . In the interests of preserving as many jobs as possible, a nominal wage level should be arrived at that will enable enterprises which make substantial productivity gains to offer speedy wage increases and that will not place at risk those enterprises which are greatly in need of structural adaptation.' The proposed involvement of GDR citizens in modernizing and clearing the debts of publicly owned enterprises that were to be privatized, 'through the issue of share certificates by the *Treuhand* company with a price reduction of up to 80 per cent', would reduce the financial resources available for restructuring and modernizing the publicly owned enterprises and increase 'the risk of over-burdening the Federal budget'. As far as social security was concerned, the working group was particularly critical of the fact that a level of benefits was being proposed that was 'not matched by the capacity of the

GDR economy'. Overall, the GDR government's readiness to adopt the basic principles of the Federal Republic's economic and social-policy framework was welcomed, but the group also warned that extraordinarily heavy financial burdens would arise if the GDR were to achieve its goals with regard to economic reconstruction, to the sharing by GDR citizens in the proceeds that were currently expected from the privatization of the publicly owned enterprises, and to the creation of a generous system of social security.[72]

The west German Social Democrats saw the treaty negotiations with the GDR, which began at the end of April 1990, as an opportunity for promoting their own goals in social policy. The party hoped that the introduction of new regulations in the GDR would also create a favourable climate for social reform in the Federal Republic. The strategic and tactical thinking of the west German Social Democrats emerges from a highly instructive note[73] by the member of the Bundestag and former governing mayor of Berlin, Dietrich Stobbe, who was appointed as the representative in Berlin of the party chairman, Hans-Jochen Vogel, after the Volkskammer elections of 18 March.[74] Stobbe emphasized the urgent need for the eastern and western Social Democratic parties to work closely together and establish common policies: this was essential, he argued, if a 'unified and tight-knit German Social Democracy' was to go forward into the forthcoming all-German elections. On the question of the difficult balancing act between being in government in the east and in opposition in the west, he proposed that the coalition agreement, once it had been scrutinized, should be used as a 'yardstick for government behaviour in Bonn and an instrument for debate in the German Bundestag'. The government of the GDR would seek to 'demonstrate independence' in the economic and social spheres. 'In this situation,' Stobbe said, the SPD would have the 'opportunity to couple government activity in the GDR and opposition activity in the Bundestag in a way that will force the Federal government into making concessions and enhance the SPD's profile in both German states'. In the event, it is clear that the close coordination that Stobbe called for between the eastern and western Social Democrats in the State Treaty negotiations above the technical expert level mainly occurred during the preparatory and early phases of the talks. During the final phase, pressures of time, but also the unresolved disunity within the west German Social Democratic Party, forestalled closer cooperation.[75]

Arguments among the Social Democrats about the repercussions for social policy posed by the fall of the Berlin Wall, and about the question of alignment between the social security systems of the two German states, had begun long before the negotiations on the treaty. On 21 December 1989 Rudolf Dreßler, at the time the leading Social Democrat expert on social policy and a deputy chairman of the parliamentary party, wrote a long memorandum in which he discussed the problems that had arisen in the wake of the opening of the border, suggested that the regulatory systems governing social policy in the two states might be harmonized within the framework of a confederation, and argued that social-policy measures should be used to accompany and encourage freedom of movement in both directions. The memorandum went into considerable detail with regard to income support, pensions insurance, health care, problems of employment law, and other social benefits such as support for children and housing; two appendices analysed the GDR's system of protection for the elderly and its health service.[76] On 20 February 1990, after the Federal government's proposal of monetary union, Dreßler produced a discussion paper on the 'standardization of pensions insurance'[77] in which he argued for a blend of what he regarded as the best features of the two systems. The Federal Republic's insurance principle should be retained, he said, along with the quantitative level of benefits and earnings indexation, while 'minimum protection within the pensions system, the inclusion within statutory insurance of all people in employment, and a unitary organization of providers for blue- and white-collar workers' should be adopted from the GDR side. He also outlined for the parliamentary party a programme for social union, with proposals regarding employment promotion measures, unemployment insurance, the organization of social insurance, and health services.[78]

On 26 April, just days after the Federal government had presented the draft treaty to the GDR government, Dreßler sent detailed, concrete suggestions for amendments, in the form of an 'advisory paper', to the GDR Minister of Labour and Social Affairs, Regine Hildebrandt.[79] One of the most important points in this document was the recommendation that the GDR should abandon the commitments it had made in the coalition agreement regarding a system of social insurance divided on a risk basis in line with the Federal Republic model, a multipartite system of health insurance, and a separation between blue- and white-collar workers within pensions insurance. In addition, the draft treaty's proposal for organizations for support of the elderly in certain professions—which was strongly supported by the FDP, in particular, within the Bonn coalition[80]—should be rejected, as it was 'in conflict with the basic social insurance principle of statutory insurance for all people in employment'. Dreßler's paper was particularly critical of the fact that the Federal government's draft made no mention of preserving minimum pensions permanently and including them in standard pensions indexation, and that it failed to refer to transitional payments to all pensioners to compensate for the ending of subsidies. Dreßler also urged that a guarantee should be given that the GDR's existing levels of social benefits for the disabled and those in need of social care would be maintained, as well as benefits allowing people to combine employment with bringing up children.

In further suggestions for amendments to the draft, Dreßler argued that contribution rates in the GDR's social insurance system should be increased gradually and not immediately, that health insurance should be included in start-up financing, and that the Federal government should provide support for investment to expand and modernize the GDR's in- and outpatient health services. He also highlighted the respects in which the proposed treaty diverged from Federal social and economic law, to the disadvantage of employees in the GDR. On these latter points, the Federal government eventually accepted that the draft treaty should be adjusted. It dropped the original proposal that employees should be responsible for half of the costs of accident insurance, replacing it with the Federal Republic regulation that employers should bear the cost alone, agreed to incorporate the duty of employers to notify in the event of mass redundancies, and accepted that regulations governing redundancy schemes should also be valid in the east.

In other ways, too, a comparison of the draft—the 'whole thrust' of which was strongly criticized as 'problematical' by the GDR in an undated 'note'[81]—with the final treaty shows that the GDR, which submitted detailed counter-proposals,[82] succeeded in obtaining significant concessions, particularly in the field of social policy. Some of the changes to the Federal Republic's original draft went back to a move made on 2 May 1990 by the east German Social Democratic ministers in coordination with the Social Democrats in the west.[83] While accepting, albeit with some misgivings, the terms of the currency changeover,[84] the ministers submitted an extensive catalogue of proposed amendments, which were inserted into the text of the Federal working paper.[85] A Federal Labour Ministry report on the situation following the talks of 3 and 4 May in east Berlin even speaks of the GDR's 'own draft', which, 'on the questions not yet resolved, contained positions that went back to the situation at the start of the talks in Bonn on 30 April and 1 May'.[86] There was clearly also a political purpose behind the SPD ministers' move: namely, to promote the image of the SPD, ahead of the GDR local elections on 6 May 1990, as the 'social conscience of unity' and as a better representative of the interests of the GDR's citizens than the eastern CDU.[87]

This ploy, however, did not come off. In the local elections the eastern SPD, with 21 per cent of the votes, only just managed to retain the disappointing level of electoral support it had received in the Volkskammer elections,[88] and it abandoned its course of confrontation within the government, especially as the Prime Minister, Lothar de Maizère, who also wanted to obtain maximum social protection for GDR citizens, adopted some of the demands for improvements. In any case, the eastern SPD could ultimately not afford to take the risk of rejecting the treaty, and with it the currency changeover, in view of the mood among the population of the GDR.

After further difficult negotiations by the experts,[89] a conversation between Kohl and de Maizière on 14 May 1990, discussions between the Finance Ministers and between the Federal Chancellor and the Prime Ministers of the *Länder* about the financial package and its funding, the State Treaty between the Federal Republic and the GDR 'on the creation of a monetary, economic and social union' was finally signed at the Schaumburg Palace on 18 May. The treaty retained the core of the original draft treaty proposed by the Federal Republic. It extended, in large measure, the legal, economic, and social-policy framework of the Federal Republic, with its institutions and norms, to the GDR. Significantly, the introduction of the Social Market economy, which was referred to in the preamble to the treaty and the principles of which were defined in Article 1, paragraph 3[90]—thereby acquiring the status of legal norms for the first time—had never been a matter of controversy during the negotiations.

The Federal Republic, however, had accommodated the wishes of the GDR on many points of detail, including in the area of social policy. In particular, the Federal Finance and Economics Ministries failed in their attempts to whittle away some of the rights of employees—for example, over dismissal and redundancy schemes—and, in the area of collective bargaining, to make employment law more flexible by involving enterprises in negotiations on wages and working conditions.

Importantly, too, the Federal government abandoned its aim of including, under a general statement on 'industrial action', the right to impose a defensive lockout alongside the right to strike. The German Trade Union Federation was opposed in principle to a right to defensive lockout—which is governed, not by the constitution or by legislation, but solely through decisions of the courts—and protested fiercely against any such move.[91] On labour market policy, too, the GDR was successful in ensuring, in Article 19, that 'active labour market measures, such as job training and re-training' were to be of 'particular importance' and that the 'interests of women and the disabled' should be taken into account.

The GDR's commitment to align its pensions insurance and health insurance law to that of the Federal Republic required that after a transition period the organization of social insurance would have to be altered, with multipartite systems for pensions and health insurance, even though this had been strongly criticized, and not without reason, by the GDR, the western SPD, the trade unions, and many experts in social policy. The FDP[92] and the insurance providers, however, had been insistent on the point. The existing east German system of comprehensive statutory insurance, covering both pensions and health, for all people in employment was allowed to continue for the transition period. Nevertheless, the GDR, against its wishes, had to allow organizations for support of the elderly in certain professions to be set up,[93] to agree to release independent professionals and the self-employed from statutory social insurance on condition of furnishing proof of sufficient protection from another source, and to accept income ceilings on statutory insurance and contributions in pensions and health insurance.[94]

The GDR's demand that a per capita supplement equivalent to the average cut in subsidies be granted ahead of the conversion of employment incomes and pensions at the ratio of 1:1 and of the removal of price controls—a demand that was subsequently scaled back to apply only to lower income groups and, above all, to pensioners[95]—was not accepted. In overall terms, however, the settlement was fairly reasonable for the GDR's pensioners, apart from the downgrading, in some cases considerable, of the position of members of the special and supplementary provision systems for particular groups.[96] The decision to set existing pensions immediately, rather than gradually, at a net pension level of 70 per cent of average net earnings of wage-earners with 45 insurance years, along with the introduction of earnings indexation of pensions, constituted a significant improvement in old-age protection, especially for the mass of older pensioners.[97]

On the particularly controversial question whether the GDR's existing system of minimum pensions should be retained permanently and be indexed to earnings, a compromise was reached that took significant account of the concrete interests of GDR pensioners. In the State Treaty itself the question was left unmentioned, though a guarantee was given that all pensions from statutory pensions insurance would continue to be paid at least at current levels. The GDR was, however, allowed[98] to provide compensation, through its own legal regulations, for social hardship suffered by pensioners. Subsequently, in its Pensions Alignment Law of 28 June 1990, the GDR, with the agreement of the Federal government, introduced a social allowance that raised low pensions to a minimum level of 495 DM per month (as compared with the earlier GDR minimum pension, which had been set at 330 marks).[99] This social allowance was not cut back when pensions were next increased, but it was also not indexed to earnings. For those receiving pensions, however, the distinction between a pension entitlement based on contribution payments and a tax-financed non-indexed social allowance was academic. In the view of the Federal Republic, these minimum pensions were a temporary substitute for a system of income support, which still had to be built up in the GDR.[100] Unlike income support in the Federal Republic, however, the minimum pension was not conditional on a means test on the pensioner's part: until the start of 1992 it was paid even in cases where the pensioner had significant additional sources of income or the pensioner's spouse was earning a good income.[101]

The GDR failed in its attempt to delay raising its low insurance contributions to the level of those in the Federal Republic for a transitional period until 1 January 1992. (In the GDR the employee paid 10 per cent up to the ceiling of 600 marks; this level, far too low, had stayed fixed for many decades.) However, so-called 'production workers', who paid a much lower rate of tax than other employees in the GDR, were granted subsidies of between 10 and 30 DM per month on their pensions insurance contributions if their monthly wages were lower than 800 DM.[102] This provision was later extended to all employees.

In the article of the treaty dealing with health insurance the GDR obtained agreement that investment for reforming and modernizing in- and outpatient health services would be financed out of the state budget. However, its hope that start-up finance for health insurance would be provided from Federal funds was not realized.

Finally, on the initiative of the GDR Minister of Health, Professor Jürgen Kleditzsch of the CDU,[103] an Article 22 on health services was included, which pointed the way towards further changes. Although existing structures of health care would remain in place for the time being, to ensure that medical services continued to be provided, the GDR would 'gradually undertake changes in the direction of the system of health care provision in the Federal Republic, using private service providers: in particular, through the introduction of privately practising doctors, dentists, and pharmacists and independent providers of medical supplies, and through the authorization of both private and free non-profit hospital providers'.

7.4 THE RATIFICATION OF THE STATE TREATY

Ratification of the State Treaty in the Federal Republic was by no means a foregone conclusion, since it required the agreement of the Bundesrat. After the Landtag elections in Lower Saxony on 13 May 1990 the CDU/FDP *Land* government was replaced by an SPD/Green coalition, with the result that the SPD-led *Länder* now had a majority in the Bundesrat. The election result reflected a shift, even if only a temporary one, in the national mood. Chancellor Kohl commented on this when he spoke to the CDU and CSU members of parliament on 15 May. It was, he said, a great 'time for demagogues'—for those who were trying incite social envy. He accused the Social Democrats of playing a sophisticated double game: stirring up the population in eastern Germany by telling them that their social benefits were too small, while at the same time seeking to provoke popular anger in the west at the many demands being made by the east. 'The Social Democrats are gambling on a bear market,' he said. He also told his party colleagues not to assume that time was on their side, warning them that the SPD wanted the all-German elections to take place at a moment when problems in the GDR would be particularly severe.[104] This analysis was correct as far as the central tactics of the SPD's candidate for the chancellorship, Oskar Lafontaine, was concerned, although Lafontaine had not succeeded in carrying all of his own party with him. However, the mere fact that the west German Social Democratic Party was vacillating and internally divided meant that the process of ratification of the State Treaty by the legislative bodies of the GDR and the Federal Republic had become a complicated matter and posed political risks.

A majority of SPD *Land* Prime Ministers were inclined to accept the treaty, especially since the likely consequence of rejection was that the GDR would accede via Article 23 without a treaty. That would probably cause the east German *Länder* to become immediately involved in the process of distribution of finances between the Federal government and the *Länder* (the *Länderfinanzausgleich*) and hence entail the imposition of a considerably higher financial burden on the west German *Länder*. Essentially, however, the SPD's decision turned, not on the content of the treaty, but on fundamental attitudes towards monetary union and on tactical considerations with regard to the forthcoming Bundestag elections. Lafontaine, the Prime Minister of the Saarland, who had been nominated unanimously as Social Democratic candidate for the chancellorship by the party's executive on 19 March 1990, had originally tried to foil monetary union, which he regarded as premature. Even on 22 April he had declared, at a meeting of the leadership groups of the west and east German Social Democratic parties, that his objective was not the re-establishment of the German nation state but social unity, which would take years to achieve.[105] After the treaty had been signed, he realized that monetary union was inevitable. Nevertheless, he took the line that the Social Democrats should vote against the treaty in the Bundestag in order to register the party's opposition, ineffective though this would be in view of its minority position. In the Bundesrat, too, he argued, the *Länder* led by the Social Democrats (either on their own or in coalition with the Greens) should reject the treaty, despite the fact that the treaty would not be defeated there either, since the Hamburg senate, led by an SPD/FDP coalition, was expected to approve it.[106]

Though this tactic was scarcely likely to appeal to the voters, Lafontaine insisted that it was a condition of his continuing to stand as candidate for the chancellorship. His attitude aroused fierce opposition among the Social Democrats in the east, who had, after all, taken part in the negotiations on the treaty. Their parliamentary leader, Richard Schröder, appealed to Lafontaine to stop treating the question in terms of Federal party politics and see it 'from the point of view of Germany as a whole'.[107] In a letter of 30 April to Hans-Jochen Vogel, the party chairman and leader of the parliamentary party, and Gerhard Jahn, one of the parliamentary party's whips, Dietrich Stobbe had spelled out clearly the different situations of the eastern and western Social Democrats: 'Unlike the SPD in Bonn, the SPD in the GDR cannot defer its decision on the State Treaty until the parliamentary debate on ratification, but has to synchronize it with the decision of the GDR government [to sign the Treaty]. The reason, obviously, is that the decisions of the SPD ministers in the cabinet and of the parliamentary party cannot afford to diverge. The decision by the SPD in the GDR therefore has to precede the decision by the SPD in Bonn.'[108] Many of the leading west German Social Democrats were opposed to Lafontaine's position. However, in order to maintain unity within the western SPD and, at the same time, keep the candidate for the chancellorship within the fold, a decision was taken by the party executive on 21 May 1990, and endorsed by the Social Democratic *Land* heads present at the meeting (Lafontaine himself was absent), to make approval conditional on the Federal government's attitude to concrete demands by the SPD for improvements to the treaty.[109] These demands related to temporary measures to prevent the collapse of enterprises that were capable of modernization, an environmental union equal in status to the economic union, appropriation for general and social purposes of the financial resources of the SED, the Stasi, the bloc parties, and the GDR's mass organizations, and an agreement that the path to German unity could be 'undertaken only with consent at all levels of state and among the leading political forces within the Federal Republic and the GDR'. The Social Democratic Party in the Bundestag also endorsed this decision, with eight votes against and six abstentions.[110]

Lafontaine had at first agreed by telephone to the party executive's decision, but he then declared in an interview with *Der Spiegel* on 28 May 1990 that he did not approve of the State Treaty, which had been 'cobbled together', and that there was no necessity for the SPD in the Bundestag to 'back a decision that [would] lead to mass unemployment'. After protests against his attitude by leading Social Democrats in both east and west, Lafontaine told the party leadership on 5 June that he would write a letter announcing his resignation from the position of candidate for the chancellorship. Vogel and Willy Brandt, however, persuaded him to refrain.[111]

In the meantime conversations at the highest level, involving Federal Chancellor Kohl and the SPD party chairman Vogel, had begun in Bonn on 29 May.[112] Since the text of the State Treaty itself could not be altered, the most that these talks were likely to achieve was to add some commitments and amendments to the law implementing the treaty. With regard to its central demands, such as complete forgiveness of the debts of the GDR's enterprises, the SPD failed to persuade the Federal government to make any concessions: the assessment and use of the resources of the Stasi and the GDR parties were deemed to be the business of the GDR. However, the Social Democrat-led majority on the Bundesrat did succeed in adding an article to the law enacting the treaty which required the Federal government, when implementing the economic union, also to take into consideration the protection of competition, the social obligations of property owners, freedom of association including free collective bargaining, consumer protection, social housing provision, and an active labour market policy.[113] The enunciation of these principles—which were to a large extent enshrined in the State Treaty already—and the granting of some further concessions enabled the leaderships of the Social Democratic Party and parliamentary party to save the SPD's face and, on 14 June, to endorse the State Treaty, while at the same time proclaiming the improvements that the party had secured.[114] The party was unable, however, to present a united front in the legislative chambers. Although the Social Democrats in the GDR Volkskammer were unanimously in favour of the treaty, in the Bundestag a minority group of 25 SPD members and one independent member voted against, along with a majority (34) of the Greens.[115] The treaty was passed in the Bundestag with 444 members in favour and 60 against. In the Volkskammer 302 members voted in favour, 82 against, and one member abstained.[116] In the Bundesrat on 22 June two *Länder*, the Saarland and Lower Saxony, each headed by a leading Social Democratic politician—the former by Lafontaine, the *Land* Prime Minister and candidate for the Federal chancellorship, the latter by Gerhard Schröder, the later Chancellor—also voted against the treaty.

These divisions among the Social Democrats put the party in a very difficult position in the two sets of elections that took place a few months later: the Landtag elections held in the five new *Bundesländer* on 14 October 1990, and the Bundestag elections held on 2 December.[117] In eastern Germany, in particular, the party was accused of not being sufficiently firmly committed to German unity. The SPD's share of the east German vote at the Bundestag elections, 24.3 per cent, was well below the party's expectations. For that matter, the Greens failed even to reach the 5 per cent threshold in the west.

The scale of the disappointment felt by eastern Social Democrats at the line taken by Lafontaine is evident from a letter of 26 June 1990 addressed to Lafontaine on behalf of the Social Democrats in the Volkskammer by Gunter Weißgerber, a member of the Volkskammer and the chairman of the Kurt-Schumacher-Gesellschaft in the GDR. 'Many Social Democrats in eastern Germany,' Weißgerber said, 'regard themselves as belonging to the patriotic tradition of August Bebel,[118] Kurt Schumacher,[119] Willy Brandt and Helmut Schmidt. . . . People here accuse you especially of having failed to show a sense of solidarity: certainly, you were unable to communicate one. A majority of working people assume that you are completely lacking in such a sense. This, too, is a reason why only 30 per cent of workers voted for the SPD. They are saying that though Lafontaine, the party's leading politician, talked about a GDR nationality and other visionary things, he does not understand what the national question means here, or the people's needs.' Weißgerber proposed that Lafontaine should arrange to stay for a week or two (without his personal chef) in a part of the GDR 'where things stink the worst ("stink" in both the literal and the figurative sense)', in order to appreciate those 'needs'. If he did not understand this, 'the SPD [would] no longer be able to count on the workers in "post-communist eastern Germany"'.[120]

8

The Social Legislation of the de Maizière Government

The State Treaty required the GDR to adapt its legislation, including its legislation in the areas of employment and social security, to the parameters of the Social Market economy. In many cases the GDR did so by taking over Federal laws word for word. In other instances, however, it added elements of its own, in the interests of its citizens.

In this it had support from officials of the Federal Ministry of Labour.[1] A particularly important figure, as far as the areas of the labour market and unemployment insurance were concerned, was the head of the sub-department for social provision for war victims and care medicine, Ministerialdirigent Dr Klaus Leven. Leven played a key role in drafting the GDR's Employment Promotion Law and shaping the new labour market policy, and continued to exert considerable influence on the latter, after finishing his activity in the GDR, in his subsequent role as vice-president of the Federal Institute of Labour. Ministerialrat Dr Martin Ammermüller, head of Section IV b 1 in the Labour Ministry, dealing with issues of basic principles and benefits law in statutory pensions insurance, was sent to east Berlin as an adviser in the field of social insurance, in particular pensions insurance. Ammermüller was centrally involved in drafting the GDR's Social Insurance Law and Pensions Alignment Law. Many people in the new *Bundesländer* still remember him today, because he made regular broadcasts on GDR radio explaining to the population the changes that were being introduced, particularly those affecting pensions. After his work in the GDR he rose rapidly. In December 1990 he became chief executive of the Social Insurance Transitional Authority and, when this was wound up, president of the Federal Insurance Office; from 1993, as Ministerialdirektor, he was head of Department II in the Labour Ministry, dealing with labour market policy and unemployment insurance, before becoming a member of the board of directors of the Deutsche Angestellten-Krankenkasse on 1 March 1997. The head of Section III a 5, dealing with the employment law jurisdiction, Ministerialrat Dr Rolf Schwedes, was appointed as an adviser in the area of employment law, including works constitution regulations (*Betriebsverfassung*). Gerd Fischwasser, retired Ministerialdirektor from the Federal Ministry of Labour, was chosen to deal with questions of rehabilitation in the GDR Ministry of Labour and Social Affairs.

At first there were misgivings that these advisers would act as 'minders', keeping tabs on the Ministry of Labour and Social Affairs (headed by the east German Social

Democrat Dr Regine Hildebrandt) to make sure that it did not deviate too far from the social policies of the governing coalition in Bonn. As work got under way, however, doubts were quickly replaced by a recognition of the great expertise and energy shown by the advisers, and also of the loyalty that they displayed towards their new superiors. Hildebrandt and her then Staatssekretär Alwin Ziel have both acknowledged that Blüm sent them some of his best people.[2] Other advisers from the Federal Republic who helped in setting up the new administrative system for employment in the GDR were the president of the *Land* employment office for North Rhine-Westphalia, Olaf Sund, and—as mentioned earlier—the SPD former Federal Minister of Labour, Herbert Ehrenberg. The head of Department V of the Federal Labour Ministry, Ministerialdirektor Karl Jung, who was appointed by the GDR Health Minister Kleditzsch in September 1990 to 'establish a multipartite system of health insurance in the GDR',[3] played an important part in coordinating the development of health insurance. In the area of accident insurance, the legal adviser to the General Union of Commercial Trade Associations, Dr Albrecht Valentini, worked in east Germany as adviser, first, to the Joint Social Insurance Provider and later to its successor organization, the Social Insurance Transitional Authority.

The de Maizière government was responsible for an extraordinarily wide range of social legislation. Only a few of the areas that were of particular importance can be discussed here.

8.1 EMPLOYMENT LAW AND HEALTH AND SAFETY LEGISLATION

In accordance with the provisions laid down in the State Treaty, the General Outline Law of 21 June 1990[4] brought into force in the GDR the basic principles of the collective employment law of the Federal Republic: the Collective Agreement Law, the Works Constitution Law, including regulations governing the adoption of redundancy schemes but omitting special representative committees of managerial employees and with transitional regulations applicable until the first elections of works councils, as well as regulations governing co-determination in firms. The Federal law on protection against dismissal was also put into effect. The Trade Union Law enacted by the Modrow government had already been rescinded by the State Treaty.

In the case of individual employment law and of health and safety legislation, the GDR essentially retained its Labour Statute Book of 1977. The Statute Book was, however, altered by a law of 22 June 1990[5] which removed dirigiste regulations and administrative state intervention based on the principles of a planned socialist economy and, through a total of 173 amendments, some of them fundamental, introduced freedom of contract and the free establishment of industrial relations. In certain important respects the law continued to diverge from Federal Republic employment law. In particular, the GDR's lack of a distinction between blue- and white-collar workers (*Arbeiter* and *Angestellte*) was retained, as this was in keeping with modern employment relationships. On the other hand, §613a of the Federal

Republic's Civil Code was adopted as a new §59a, allowing for the prohibition of dismissal by reason of a transfer of the undertaking and requiring the continued payment of 100 per cent (as opposed to a previous 90 per cent) of net wages by the company, rather than through health insurance, for the first six weeks in the case of sickness.

In a number of instances the GDR's regulations with regard to employees were more generous than those of the Federal Republic.[6] These included special protection against dismissal for people carrying out military service, pregnant women, mothers and fathers of children less than a year old, and single-parent employees with children up to the age of three. In addition, women in full employment and with their own household were granted, under specified but very widely drawn conditions,[7] one day of paid home working per month, paid for by the enterprise in which they were employed. Mothers were entitled to maternity leave of twenty weeks—compared with eight weeks in the Federal Republic—after the birth of a child, and they had wide-ranging rights to time off work until the end of the child's first year or, if a place in a crèche was not available, until the child was three. Regulations governing time off work to care for sick children were also generous. On the other hand, the existing obligation on the employer to offer an employee, before dismissal, a reasonable alternative job was discontinued. Some prohibitions on dismissal—for example, during illness or holidays, and for pensioners and for those about to draw a pension or take early retirement—were watered down. Nevertheless, the generous regulations on early retirement brought in by the Modrow government remained in place.[8]

In certain respects the GDR's regulations regarding employees were less favourable. The notice period for white-collar workers was shorter, reimbursement of employees for health cures applied only to cures approved by the social insurance system and, for periods of convalescence, only if the individual was unable to work. In the Federal Republic continued payment of salaries existed for white- (though not for blue-) collar workers, as well as in the case of privately financed preventive, healing and convalescence cures and for all periods of convalescence prescribed by physicians. In the GDR the admissibility of Sunday and holiday working was subject to less strict exemptions.

Despite the fact that many of the GDR's 'social achievements' were preserved, the new law came under fire in the Volkskammer, principally from the PDS but also from Alliance 90/The Greens, because, *inter alia*, it made it easier to dismiss employees.[9] The SPD's spokeswoman, Heidrun Dräger, argued that the social policy rights guaranteed in the amended Labour Statute Book should be included in the discussions between the two Germanys,[10] thereby touching on an issue that was to play a major role in the negotiations over the Unification Treaty.

In the Federal Republic there was criticism that the terms of the legislation were more generous with regard to employees. Employers, and also the FPD's spokesman on social policy, Dieter-Julius Cronenberg, complained in particular about the adoption of §613a of the Federal Civil Code, arguing that it would make the privatization and modernization of enterprises more difficult.[11] Within the Federal Labour Ministry there were fears, voiced in a note of 11 June 1990, that it would be politically controversial in the Federal Republic whether the GDR, in view of its miserable economic position and the high costs of the process of unification, would be able to 'afford the regulations, which are more generous than those in the Federal Republic. In addition, efforts to introduce these regulations here as well will probably be given an impetus. It has to be remembered that all of these provisions entail considerable cost burdens for companies.'[12] The Federal Republic, however, had no legal leverage *vis-à-vis* the GDR, in consequence of the State Treaty, which according to Blüm restricted the changes that were to be made by the GDR in the area of individual employment law to what was 'absolutely necessary', in order to avoid giving the impression that it was a 'treaty of conquest'.[13]

8.2 THE GDR EMPLOYMENT PROMOTION LAW

Adoption of the Federal Republic's active labour market policy, in order to mitigate the social hardship caused by the transformation of the economy, was a central aim of the GDR in the negotiations on the State Treaty, and despite the misgivings of the Federal Finance Ministry the GDR succeeded—with the support of the Federal Labour Ministry—in achieving its objective. The requisite machinery and norms were established through the GDR's Employment Promotion Law of 22 June 1990.[14] Although the law was closely modelled on the Federal Republic's law of the same name,[15] it differed from it in important respects. Some of the differences were the result of the particular circumstances of the GDR and had the broad agreement of the Federal Republic. Others, however, reflected political differences, in particular a desire that the regulations affecting employees in the GDR should be more generous than those in the Federal Republic.

In the first category was a difference in organization, prompted by the fact that there was no institution in the east corresponding to the Federal Institute of Labour in the west. Although labour market administration in the GDR had in the meantime been separated from general state administration, for a transition period in the second half of 1990 it was directly run by the GDR Ministry of Labour and Social Affairs,[16] which was responsible, in particular, for all questions of finance. Whereas the tripartite self-governing organizations of the Federal Republic's administrative system for employment were composed of equal numbers of representatives of employers, employees, and public bodies, in the east so-called advisory councils were to advise the head of the central employment administration system and the directors of the job centres until organizations corresponding to those in the west had been set up.[17]

More significant still were differences in benefits law, agreed with the Federal Republic, that were made necessary by mass unemployment.[18] A crucial element here was short-time working benefit, which provided 68 per cent of net wages for cancelled working time in the case of workers bringing up a child and 63 per cent in other cases. In contrast with the Federal Republic, the benefit could also be paid if a job was not expected to survive or, in the case of 'zero short time', if no work could be done at all. Under particular circumstances the employment administration system could reimburse the employer in full for contributions to pensions and health insurance. In addition, those receiving short-time working benefit could take part in re-training measures and gain qualifications with payment of a maintenance benefit at a level above that of short-time working benefit. People on short-time work could be concentrated in an 'independent enterprise-organized unit'.[19] The main aims of these regulations were to give employers a period of reflection, without cost to themselves, before deciding whether to make an employee redundant, to relieve the strain on the job centres that were just coming into existence, to get the human-resources departments of the combines that were about to be disbanded involved in dealing on a temporary basis with the administrative challenge of structural unemployment, and to stave off the politically undesirable sight of long queues building up outside job centres.[20] At the end of each of the four quarters after the start of monetary union on 1 July 1990, between 1.7 and 2 million employees received short-time working benefit,[21] making this the first significant instrument for mitigating the damaging social consequences of the transformation of the east German economy.

A further regulation that differed from the Federal Employment Promotion Law enabled applicants for training places who were at a disadvantage as a result of market conditions, rather than through lack of education or on social grounds, to receive extensive assistance in supra-enterprise facilities.[22] In addition, graduate employees could receive support on training and re-training schemes at universities and technical higher education colleges. Under specified circumstances up to 100 per cent of wage costs could be reimbursed for job creation schemes, and local authorities were able to operate as the key providers of such schemes. By contrast with the Federal Republic, unemployment benefit could be paid at once if the employment relationship was ended by a contract of termination (*Aufhebungsvertrag*). Finally, employers were not obliged to reimburse unemployment benefit paid, after dismissal, to older employees who had been employed for many years.[23]

The trade unions in the Federal Republic approved of the easier conditions attached to the receipt of short-time working benefit and the generous support given to job training and re-training. They particularly applauded the provision regarding a minimum protection of 495 DM per month in the event of unemployment, which—analogously to pensions insurance—could trigger payment of a social allowance additional to unemployment benefit and unemployment assistance, and they also approved of the omission of what they saw as the preferential treatment given to employers in employment disputes by the provision in §116, paragraph 3 of the Federal Republic's Employment Promotion Law prohibiting the payment of unemployment benefit to employees indirectly affected by an employment dispute.[24] The trade unions were critical of the fact, however, that the regulations supporting year-round employment in the construction industry, and with it the payment of bad-weather money, had not been adopted, although it appeared that the GDR seemed to want to add a provision of this sort before the winter break.[25]

The Federal Ministry of Labour regarded non-means-tested minimum protection, which—unlike the social allowance in the case of pensions insurance—had not been agreed with the Federal Republic, as at odds with the income replacement principle in unemployment insurance. It also believed that minimum protection would remove all incentive for those on low wages to seek employment.[26] The Ministry accordingly opposed this regulation outright, citing the availability of income support instead. Its view, however, did not prevail, nor did its wholesale opposition to the removal of the prohibition on payment of unemployment benefit to employees indirectly affected by an employment dispute.[27] A motion to that effect was introduced suddenly and unexpectedly by the east German Social Democrats in the Volkskammer shortly before the final vote on the law and was accepted by 105 votes to 87, with 10 abstentions. In the negotiations on the Unification Treaty the western trade unions sought vainly to preserve this pro-union regulation, making strong representations to the Prime Minister de Maizière, the Labour and Social Affairs Minister Hildebrandt, the GDR's lead negotiator on the State and Unification Treaties Günther Krause, and the parliamentary leaders of the GDR governing coalition.[28] In a letter to the GDR's chief negotiator on social policy, the Social Democrat Alwin Ziel, Krause complained that in §119 of the law the term 'annulment [*Lösung*] of the employment relationship' had been replaced by the formulation 'notice of termination [*Kündigung*] of the employment relationship' and that this opened up the possibility of mutually agreed cancellations of contracts with the cost to be borne by unemployment insurance, and hence of benefit abuse. In addition, he criticized the regulation that employees indirectly affected by an employment dispute should also receive short-time working benefit and unemployment benefit, on the grounds that, like the alteration to §119, it was a clear deviation 'from the statutory regulation in the Federal Republic' and an 'unambiguous violation of the State Treaty'.[29]

However, despite the Federal Labour Ministry's fundamental opposition to minimum protection for the unemployed and the alterations to §116 in the Employment Promotion Law in the GDR, Blüm, in correspondence with Cronenberg of the FDP, vigorously defended the special provisions on employment promotion, in particular the provision regarding short-time workers, which 'the employers' side [had] also consistently supported'. 'The shift from a planned economy to a Social Market economy with virtually no transition period' was, he said, 'a unique economic and socio-political event', and so the special regulations in the GDR Employment Promotion Law would not give rise to 'prejudicial effects'. In view of the great opportunities, as well as the many risks, presented by monetary, economic, and social union, it was the job of policy-makers to 'minimize the risks wherever possible, in the interests of those people affected in the GDR'.[30] In particular, job training and re-training should be supported, and to that end a pluralistic system of education and training provision should be built up in the GDR, in cooperation with providers in the Federal Republic.[31]

Labour market policy was one of the few policy areas in which there was an attempt to do justice to the critical economic situation faced by the new *Bundesländer* by building on the existing institutions and norms and at the same time looking for new ways of mitigating the impact of mass unemployment.[32]

In order for the new machinery created by the GDR Employment Promotion Law to be applied, however, it was necessary to set up an effective system of labour market administration, creating institutions out of virtually nothing in as short a time as possible.[33] For political reasons it was not appropriate to continue to employ all 3,600 members of staff of the old labour offices. By 1 July 1990, when the law came into force, 4,000 new people had been taken on. By the end of 1991 over 25,000 people were working in the job centres in the new *Bundesländer*, familiarizing themselves with completely new tasks and legal regulations while operating in often cramped conditions and with inadequate technical support. In 1991 alone, a flood of 2.7 million applications for income replacement benefits had to be processed, an average of three times as many per job centre as in the west. The eastern job centres were so overstretched that they had to follow a rule of 'speed before accuracy' and came close to the limits of what was 'legally defensible' in attempting to 'alleviate the tensions, not expressly resolved in the legislation, between western norms and eastern realities, by interpreting the law in a sensible way'.[34] Although a massive reduction in job numbers was necessary across the GDR (except in the construction industry and some parts of the service sector) in order to increase economic competitiveness and reduce the costs of state and local government administration, in the employment administrative system—as in social insurance—the profusion of new tasks and the complexity of the new regulations generated a heavy demand for extra workers who could be quickly trained.

8.3 THE NEW SOCIAL SECURITY SYSTEM

Even more unequivocally than was the case in the Federal Republic, the main foundation of social security in the GDR was the social insurance system. The basis on which the system was to be reformed was spelled out in the State Treaty of 18 May 1990, although the treaty left the GDR considerable scope for deciding the concrete ways in which the new system would be shaped. A 'first step towards alignment'[35] was taken in the GDR Social Insurance Law of 28 June 1990, which was drafted in four weeks by a five-member working group, assisted in significant ways by Martin Ammermüller.[36] In this legislation the GDR deliberately decided against simply adopting the corresponding Federal Republic legislation wholesale, both because 'radical, comprehensive alignment with the Social Insurance Law of the Federal Republic' would have jeopardized the 'provision of benefits in an area that [was] a very sensitive one for citizens', and because in practice the implementation of Federal Republic law would not have been feasible without a lengthy period of preparation, not least so that insurance staff could be trained.[37]

The step-by-step adjustment of the east German organizational structure of social insurance to that of the Federal Republic involved combining the GDR's previous systems of social insurance for blue- and white-collar workers and of social insurance for the self-employed and members of cooperatives administered under State Insurance into a unitary system of health, pensions, and accident insurance provision. Managerial authority over social insurance for blue- and white-collar workers had previously been exercised by the Free German Trade Union

Federation, individual trade unions, and the enterprise trade union organizations; this was now ended. Income and expenditure accounts would be split according to branches of insurance, unlike previous practice.[38] Certain benefits went beyond those provided in the social insurance systems in the Federal Republic: for example, in health insurance, features of the support provided for the care of sick children, support totalling 200 DM a month for the care of severely injured children, prolonged payment of weekly benefits after the birth of a child, and support for mothers during the so-called 'baby year'; in pensions insurance, the pension for war victims, attendance allowance, blindness benefit, and special nursing care benefit. Claims for these benefits were to be reimbursed through the state budget.[39]

Until 1 January 1991, when independent insurance providers for the individual self-administered branches of insurance were due to be established—though the law as yet said nothing about the election of these, or of their specific responsibilities—the Minister of Labour and Social Affairs would be responsible for social insurance in general and the Minister of Health for health insurance.[40]

The financing of social insurance was removed from the state budget. Expenditure was to be financed, primarily, through contributions by the insured and employers in the case of pensions and health insurance and through an accident levy on employers[41] in the case of accident insurance. For pensions insurance, where a fixed sum had been designated in the state budget in the second half of 1990 to cover the shortfall between income and expenditure, a state subsidy of 18.8 per cent was earmarked for 1991. Contributions to pensions insurance were set at 18.7 per cent of wages and at 17.7 per cent from 1 April 1991, as in the Federal Republic. By contrast, health insurance contributions—which in the Federal Republic varied in amount among the different providers within statutory health insurance—were set at a uniform rate of 12.8 per cent of wages, equivalent to an average of the contribution rates in the Federal Republic. Although it was likely that there would be a financial deficit, no state subsidy was expressly earmarked, a fact which drew strong criticism from the GDR Health Minister, Kleditzsch.[42]

The significant features of the new system were that existing benefits were retained unaltered, patients were exempted from a share of payment in respect of benefits in kind under health insurance (unlike the system in the Federal Republic), insurance contributions were to be raised sharply by the raising of the previous contributions ceiling of 600 DM to 2,700 DM in pensions insurance and 2,025 DM in health insurance—with a possible consequential reduction in net wages—and there was a far more comprehensive liability to social insurance than in the Federal Republic. The possibility of opting out of statutory social insurance in statutory health and pensions insurance was granted only to the self-employed—though not to farmers, nor, in the case of pensions insurance, to craftsmen or freelance artists—who made the relevant application to the insurance provider within five years of first undertaking self-employment and who could prove that they had an entitlement to benefits of equal value from another insurance scheme for themselves and their dependants.[43] Health Minister Kleditzsch, who complained to his ministerial colleague Hildebrandt about the drastic restrictions on options for private health insurance, was told by her that allowing greater scope for opting out would be disastrous in view of the scale of the likely financial shortfall, and that in any case it would always be possible to take out supplementary private insurance.[44]

The Federal Labour Ministry, which was also unhappy about the limited scope for opting out of statutory social insurance, was primarily concerned that the closure of the systems of supplementary and special provision for particular groups, called for in the State Treaty, had not been implemented and that 'rules, indispensable in respect of pensions insurance', for the reimbursement by the state of expenditure on transferred claims and expectancies from these systems had not been specified. It was also critical of the fact that provision had been made for medical, but not for professional, rehabilitation in the new pensions insurance benefits.[45]

For those affected, even more important than the Social Insurance Law, which dealt with the overarching aspects of the new social insurance system, was the GDR Pensions Alignment Law of 28 June 1990.[46] In addition to regulating the export of pensions, the principles of which had already been laid down in the State Treaty, this measure brought the level of pensions into line with that of the Federal Republic and regulated the closure of the systems of supplementary provision and their eventual transfer into the general statutory pensions insurance system. The GDR's specifications regarding the granting of pensions and the recognition of insurance years remained in place, with only a few exceptions. Pensions themselves were, by and large, increased substantially, with indexation to earnings. A so-called 'benchmark pensioner' with 45 years of employment and average earnings over that time-period now received 70 per cent of net average earnings of 960 DM per month, in other words 672 DM.[47] For pensioners who had begun drawing their pensions in 1970 or earlier—that is, before the introduction in the GDR of voluntary supplementary pensions insurance—this meant an increase of 202 DM on the previous pension of 470 marks. Since documentation for the period before 1970 was lacking, the level of pensions in statutory insurance was dependent solely on the number of allowed years of employment, not on the individual's varying levels of income during his or her working life. For those who had reached pensionable age in 1971 or later, there were, additionally, for the majority of pensioners, variations in the level of the pension dependent on individual average earnings over the preceding twenty years, based on pensions under the voluntary supplementary pensions insurance system, with its different contributions and benefits.[48] One of the weaknesses of the GDR pensions system had been that a pension first awarded ten or twenty years earlier was not on a par with a pension awarded on the basis of earnings from more recent years, so that older pensioners—unless they were able to obtain a further pension from the supplementary provision system—had had to have recourse to minimum pensions. The updating of comparative values provided by the new law meant that pensioners who had reached pensionable age earlier and had been insured for a long time saw their pensions rise particularly sharply. For a benchmark pensioner who had reached pensionable age in 1970 or earlier, the increase amounted to 42.98 per cent, while for someone starting to draw a pension in 1990 it was only 11.63 per cent.[49] For people who had reached pensionable age in 1970 but had accumulated fewer than 24 insurance years, there were no increases; likewise for a date of 1990 and a total of 37 insurance years. A guarantee was given, however, that existing pensions would continue to be paid at least at the same level.

Relatively generous provision was made in the case of pensions of surviving dependants. The widow's or widower's pension, paid as a second benefit additional to a person's own, higher pension, was raised from 50 marks to 90 DM, while the surviving dependant's pension, based on the aligned pension of the deceased, was taken to begin from the year at which the dependant's pension began and was based on 45 working years by the deceased, unless an earlier date of death or a higher number of working years could be proved.[50] This provision, made because of the lack of relevant documentation, was particularly favourable to widows whose husbands had died young.

Disabled ex-servicemen, a group that had been badly treated by the GDR, also saw their material circumstances improve significantly, and civilians suffering from disabilities directly caused by war were now included in the same group for the first time. Previously, a disabled ex-serviceman with an injury of at least 66.66 per cent had received a pension of 470 marks per month. Since there was no documentation for the period up to 1970, the level of pensions under statutory insurance had been dependent solely on the number of allowed years of employment, not on the individual's varying levels of income during his working life. The level was now raised to 672 DM across the board. Additional income was set against the war disability pension by up to half, but the latter had to amount to 150 DM at a minimum. This benefit, which resembled the basic benefit under the Federal Social Provision Law,[51] was also payable in the case of a higher old-age or invalidity pension, rather than the war disability pension.

The law also laid down that old-age and invalidity pensioners, those receiving accident benefits, and the recipients of a full widow's or widower's pension were to receive a social allowance if their monthly pension was lower than 495 DM. This social allowance, which could amount at a maximum to 165 DM (based on the lowest GDR minimum pension of 330 marks), was payable irrespective of any other income received by the pensioner and of income or pensions received by the pensioner's spouse and had to be funded from the public purse. In the calculation of the level of the social allowance, however, the widow's or widower's pension of 90 DM, paid as a second benefit, also had to be taken into account.[52] The social allowance, which effectively established a minimum pension, was not watered down, but neither was it indexed to earnings, as the GDR had wished. On the other hand, the law called for regular adjustments of pensions to be made in line with changes in net wages and salaries in the GDR. In fact, pensions were raised sharply on 1 January 1991 and 1 July 1991, in both cases by 15 per cent.

In the case of accident insurance, existing pensions were calculated by reference to gross average employment earnings, which were 1,140 DM per month in 1990, giving a person with an injury of 100 per cent a pension of two-thirds, i.e. 760 DM. In addition there was an allowance of 10 per cent for a child and—a regulation criticized by the Federal Labour Ministry because it diverged from Federal benefits law[53]—an allowance at a fixed level of 200 DM for a married person. The pension inclusive of allowances, however, was not to exceed 85 per cent of the gross employment earnings norm.[54] As against these standardized existing pensions, the new pensions coming into effect under accident insurance were to be based on average earnings of the preceding year, with a contributions ceiling of 2,700 marks, including for the period before 1 July 1990.[55] New pensions might accordingly be higher or lower than existing ones.

Probably the most difficult task that had to be dealt with in the pensions alignment process was closing the supplementary and special provision systems for particular groups, as called for in the State Treaty, and transferring into statutory pensions insurance the claims and expectancies arising from them. During the preparation of the law the Ministry of Labour and Social Affairs in the GDR carried out extensive research to work out how many claimants would be involved and what the scale of the benefits payable to them would be.[56] In fact, however, the new GDR law closed only the existing supplementary provision systems for particular groups, with effect from 30 June 1990. Pensions from supplementary provision were to continue to be paid unchanged until they were transferred into the pensions insurance system. It was specified, however, that supplementary-system pensions for people who had been employed full-time in, for example, party head offices, public organizations, or the state bureaucracy, or as chief executives of centrally directed combines or similarly high-level heads of central economic organs, would be limited to a maximum of 1,500 DM per month.[57] Nevertheless, at the same time such people remained entitled to a pension from the normal statutory insurance system. The limit of 1,500 DM also applied to members of the special provision systems for the army, the police, and the customs service, though these individuals did not receive any supplementary social insurance pension as they had not belonged to the statutory insurance system.[58] These special provision systems remained in force for the time being.

As far as full-time employees of the Ministry of State Security were concerned, whose provision system was closed from 30 June 1990, a separate law[59] reduced their old-age and invalidity pensions by half of the amount in excess of 495 DM and limited them to 990 DM. (The government had initially proposed a 1200 DM limit.[60]) All additional expenditure arising as a result of the transfer of the supplementary and special provision systems had to be reimbursed to the pensions insurance system from the state budget.

Honorary pensions for 'fighters against fascism', at 1,700 DM per month, and for 'victims of fascist persecution', at 1,400 DM, as well as benefits to their surviving dependants, continued to be paid at the existing levels. The payment of allowances to former members of militias—which had mainly been granted, at the rate of 100 DM per month, to those who had served for 25 years as members of enterprise-based militias—was ended, while in the case of the roughly 1,200 honorary pensions of the Council of Ministers, pension increases were halved through the pensions alignment and later pensions adjustments, and thus effectively phased out.[61]

Staatssekretär Ziel calculated that as a result of the pensions alignment there would be additional costs of 3,200 million DM in the second half of 1990 and—without taking further pensions adjustments into account—double that amount for the year 1991.[62] For pensioners, the alignment meant that about 2.24 million insured persons' pensions, or 78 per cent of the total of 2.89 million, were raised by an average of 141 DM per month. Widows' pensions were raised, on average by 101 DM.[63] About 674,000 pensioners—640,000 women and only 34,000 men—received a social allowance of 87 DM, on average, in addition to their pension. Overall, pensions were raised by an average of 30 per cent.[64]

Finally, social security in the GDR was amplified by the Income Support Law of 21 June 1990,[65] which established a system of basic protection conditional on a means test. An extension of the fourth social welfare decree issued by the Modrow government on 8 March 1990, the law created a clear statutory right to state aid under circumstances of proven need. Borrowing a formulation from the Federal Income Support Law of 1961, such aid was to enable the recipient to 'lead a life consonant with human dignity'.[66] In the GDR, where the same motive fuelled the insistence on minimum protection under pensions and unemployment insurance, recipients of welfare benefits had commonly been stigmatized as beneficiaries of alms, and so the notion of income support had to overcome a considerable amount of prejudice. Although the GDR law was closely modelled on the Federal Income Support Law of 1961, unlike that measure it covered fewer forms of support and involved fewer regulations regarding support providers; Independent Welfare Associations were specified among the latter in addition to state and local government institutions. The level of standard payments was to be determined 'by the Ministry for the Family and Women in agreement with the Ministry of Finance, taking actual living costs into account' (§20). In an implementation regulation attached to the law, the standard payment to the head of household was set at 400 DM per month.[67] Benefits for other adult family members were set at 80 per cent of benefits to the head of household, and at between 50 and 90 per cent for children in accordance with age.[68] As against the Federal Republic model, the law also dealt with support for the sick and for care in institutions—principally, homes for the elderly and nursing homes—under the heading of 'support in special life-circumstances'. On the other hand, as in the Federal Republic, next of kin were obliged to pay maintenance, while recipients of income support were required to disclose details of their own and their family's income and wealth and to accept offers of reasonable work.

In the GDR, and then the new *Bundesländer*, income support at first played a significantly smaller role than in the Federal Republic. This was due partly to the high rate of employment in the GDR and the fact that pension rights were based on employment, but also to the fact that it took some time before a comprehensive organizational structure could be set up. The staffs of local social security offices and higher-level providers of income support, and the organizations of the Independent Welfare Associations—which could latch on to existing GDR organizations only in the case of church bodies and the Volkssolidarität (People's Solidarity)—also had to familiarize themselves with the complexities of the Income Support Law, geared as it was to individual cases.[69]

8.4 THE START OF THE REORGANIZATION OF THE HEALTH SERVICE AND OF THE ESTABLISHMENT OF A MULTIPARTITE SYSTEM OF HEALTH INSURANCE

The State Treaty of 18 May 1990 prescribed a 'step-by-step change in health provision in the GDR', bringing the system closer to that of the Federal Republic, the alignment of the GDR's system of health insurance with that of west Germany, and legislation to establish contractual relations, involving rights of reimbursement, between the health insurance organizations and the providers of benefits. In a letter to Dr Hans-Jürgen Thomas, the head of the Hartmann Alliance (the influential association of doctors), Blüm wrote that although the 'need for a fundamental reform of the health service in the GDR [was] incontestable', in view of the 'basic differences . . . between the health systems of the two German states' adjustment could proceed only 'in a step-by-step fashion'. He did not, however, share the Hartmann Alliance's fear that the 'temporary retention of particular health care institutions in the GDR would continue in the long term'. In his view, the necessary alignments should be carried out 'as speedily as possible', in the interests of creating a unified social order in Germany.[70]

Nevertheless, it was at first assumed that there would be a fairly lengthy transitional period, during which the GDR's system of outpatient care, delivered through polyclinics, ambulatories, and enterprise-based health care services, would be retained so as to ensure a continuity of medical services. The Social Democratic opposition, in addition, not only wanted to preserve the central 'social achievements' of the GDR health system but hoped that these would serve as a model for a reform of the system in the Federal Republic. It called, *inter alia*, for the distinctions between white- and blue-collar workers in statutory health insurance to be eliminated, for civil servants in the GDR (a category not yet created) to be included in statutory insurance, for cover for outpatient services to be 'compulsorily' transferred to the health insurance companies, and for the insurance companies to assume responsibility for planning the demand for doctors. It also said that an approved list of drugs[71] and the regulation requiring doctors to limit prescriptions to specified drugs should remain in place. The Federal Association of the General Local Health Insurance Providers (AOK-Bundesverband) likewise declared that the polyclinics and ambulatories were a 'basis for future development' and said that allowing doctors to set up their own individual practices should be only a 'third stage' of re-alignment.'[72]

Soon afterwards the Federal Ministry of Labour, in conjunction with the GDR Ministry of Health, produced the draft of a decree laying down that the task of ensuring the continuation of medical services should be divided between doctors in their own practices and polyclinic facilities and that the establishment of individual practices should be refused if suitable medical care was guaranteed. With regard to the planning of the demand for health services, the continued existence of local, state, and enterprise-based facilities should be protected, and they would be promised a system of flat-rate reimbursement. In addition, authorization to treat members of health insurance schemes should be granted only to doctors with permanent residence in the GDR. Finally, in order to bear down on costs, a list of free prescription drugs should be compiled, while fixed prices for drugs could be specified in certain cases.[73] The draft decree was rejected by most of the specialists in health policy in the CDU/CSU and aroused a storm of angry protest in the FDP, which numbered many doctors among its supporters and was a passionate advocate of the interests of doctors in west Germany. The Federal Medical Council, the Federal Union of Health Insurance Physicians, the Association of White-Collar Health Insurance Companies and the associations of the pharmacists and the pharmaceutical industry also all fiercely opposed the draft, which eventually had to be withdrawn.[74]

In fact, the crucial decisions setting the course of a fundamental reorganization of the health service of the GDR were taken by the de Maizière government. On 12/13 May 1990, at a conference in Bad Honnef,[75] a joint health commission of the Federal Republic and the GDR was formed, under the co-chairmanship of Dr Horst Schönfelder, Staatssekretär in the GDR Ministry of Health, and Werner Chory, Staatssekretär in the Federal Ministry for Young People, the Family, Women, and Health. The commission and its eleven working groups, to which representatives of the *Bundesländer* and of the GDR's regions were also to be invited, were tasked with creating a unified health care system.[76] In addition, the Federal Labour Ministry and the GDR Health Ministry set up eight working groups to deal with 'statutory health insurance/health care',[77] and the leading groups in statutory health insurance, the Federal Insurance Office, and the Private Health Insurance Association were invited to give intensive support to the GDR, within the framework of the 'working group on social union with the GDR',[78] over legislation in the health field and the development of a multipartite system of health insurance.

As far as the development of the health insurance system was concerned, there was controversy whether a basic health insurance provision system, organized by regions, should be created first, and replaced only later—after reforms to the structure of health insurance had been carried out and a system of risk compensation among the insurance schemes introduced—by a multipartite system of health insurance modelled on the Federal Republic system. This was the view of the Federal Association of the General Local Health Insurance Providers, backed by the Social Democrats and trade unions,[79] but the Association was unable to overcome the combined opposition of the employers, the other insurance providers, the FDP, and sections of the CDU/CSU.[80] The GDR Health Insurance Companies Establishment Law of 13 September 1990[81] provided for the establishment of a General Local Health Insurance Provider in each region of the GDR and retained, for the time being, the single contribution level of 12.8 per cent of monthly wages for all members of health insurance schemes, as laid down in the Social Insurance Law. However, it also allowed other insurance companies to be set up, and these, fiercely competing among themselves, spread across the new *Bundesländer* in the east.

With regard to the organization of health care provision, a GDR Health Insurance Companies Contracts Law of 13 September 1990[82] refrained from prescribing the planning of demand for outpatient services that the Federal Labour Ministry had initially wanted and enshrined the principle of support for doctors setting up their own practices. A time limit of 31 December 1995 for the licensing of polyclinics and ambulatories, taken over from the Unification Treaty of 31 August 1990, was, effectively, a death sentence for these clinics, even though the limit was later lifted. Although the Federal Labour Ministry at first opposed the closure of the outpatient facilities and the wholesale dismissal of the doctors, dentists, nurses, and other staff employed in them,[83] and argued that the polyclinics and ambulatories should receive part payments at the level of the share of the costs falling on statutory health insurance,[84] it was not possible to prevent their demise. Already by April 1991 the number of doctors in individual practices exceeded that of doctors in polyclinics; by the end of 1994 the latter constituted only 3 per cent of all doctors in outpatient work.[85] The reorganization of the GDR's health service was completed by a Hospital Financing Law of 30 August 1990[86] and the establishment of public health departments[87] and of medical councils and associations of health insurance physicians[88] as self-governing bodies for the medical profession.

A key feature of the health policies and health legislation of the de Maizière government was the powerful influence of the FDP and the huge pressure that was exerted by the doctors' professional organizations, most of the leading statutory health insurance bodies, and the associations representing the interest groups involved.[89] The influence of these organizations was so considerable that the idea—supported by other powerful political and social forces as well as by many experts—that unification might be combined with reforms of the German health care system and the structure of the health insurance system, and that individual elements of the GDR health care system (such as the linkage between in- and outpatient care and the stronger emphasis on preventive medicine) might be extended throughout Germany, never had a realistic chance of being fulfilled.

Preparation of the legislation to reorganize the GDR health care system partly intersected with the parallel negotiations over the Unification Treaty. Kleditzsch believed that the treaty ought to contain a separate chapter on the health care system and health insurance, but his views were only partially adopted.[90]

9

The Unification Treaty

9.1 THE COURSE OF THE NEGOTIATIONS AND THE PRINCIPAL PROBLEMS

Preparatory work on the Unification Treaty had begun in the Federal Ministry of the Interior in February 1990[1] and had become more intensive before the State Treaty was ratified. In the view of the Federal Minister of the Interior, Wolfgang Schäuble, who led the Federal negotiating delegation with a firm hand, it was the job of the GDR, which wanted unification, to resolve its own ideas about the modalities of GDR accession to the Federal Republic. For this reason, but also because it was essential to mobilize all the political forces within the Federal Republic, particularly those in the *Länder*, if the two-thirds majority required for passage of the treaty was to be secured, Schäuble deliberately adopted a different procedure from that which had been followed with the State Treaty and refrained from attempting first to 'build up a fully agreed negotiating position within the Federal Republic'.[2] Besides, until the negotiations had been concluded it was possible that the GDR would unilaterally announce its accession and that the necessary provisional arrangements would be set out, not in a treaty, but through transitional legislation passed by the all-German legislature formed after unification. This path to unity, however, was favoured neither by the de Maizière government nor by Schäuble, who foresaw that it would give rise to unnecessary delays and complications.

After preliminary discussions, the leader of the GDR delegation, Günther Krause, presented Schäuble on 29 May 1990 with a working paper addressing what he saw as the central questions for the GDR.[3] On the same day Schäuble gave Krause a note on 'basic structures of a state treaty establishing German unity'.[4] These proposals were further developed in a Federal Interior Ministry 'discussion paper' containing 'elements for obtaining a settlement to establish German unity',[5] which was presented to Krause on 23 June 1990 and to the Federal Republic *Länder* and the Bundestag parties two days later; in turn, the GDR produced a list of topics.[6] The first round of negotiations then began in east Berlin on 6 July 1990.[7] Further rounds followed on 1–3 August, 20–4 August and 30 August, and the Unification Treaty was signed on 31 August 1990. A series of outstanding problems was dealt with in a supplementary agreement signed on 18 September 1990.[8]

One of the most difficult problems, which was resolved at the end of July, before the second round of negotiations started, was whether GDR law should remain broadly valid, with Federal Republic law applying only on an exceptional basis, or whether Federal Republic law should become the norm and GDR law the exception. Schäuble strongly favoured the first alternative—which had been followed when the Saarland had acceded to the Federal Republic on 1 January 1957—because he feared that adopting the complex details of perfectionist Federal Republic legislation in the east would create a top-heavy bureaucracy, make it difficult to exercise a flexible approach to new problems arising during the reconstruction process, and impose too much strain on people in the new *Bundesländer*. The Federal Ministry of Justice, which wanted legal unity to be established quickly, on the basis of Federal Republic law, supported the second alternative.[9] It had the backing of the other ministries, and also of the employers, the latter maintaining that the current legal uncertainty had, 'unfortunately, too often been a deterrent to urgently needed investment and hence to the employment of new staff'.[10]

Blüm, the Minister of Labour, in a note to Schäuble of 28 June 1990, passionately supported the position of the Justice Ministry.[11] Following that course, he argued, would ensure that the principle of legal unity was taken into account from the start and that there would be greater clarity about the legal situation. Moreover, the legislative time and energy that would be required to establish 'interim law' for the territory of the GDR would be excessive as far as employment and social insurance law were concerned. Further considerations were that extending Federal Republic law would send the right signal regarding the task, already begun, of building up the organizational structures of an efficient multipartite system of social insurance in cooperation with the insurance providers and their associations in the Federal Republic, and that it would ease the GDR's process of adjustment to European Community law. In Schäuble's view—which was correct enough—Blüm had perceived that this would be a way of 'extending the social achievements of the west to the accession territory much more quickly and less contentiously, even though it would cost the Federal finances dear'. To Schäuble's astonishment, the Finance Minister did not pick a fight with Blüm over the issue, since he plainly wanted, as Schäuble saw it, to seize the opportunity to plant 'his wide-ranging tax laws and other regulations on the new part of the joint state without the risk of tedious future arguments'.[12] Since Schäuble also failed to secure the hoped-for support of the *Länder*, and the GDR did not maintain its opposition to the general principle of the extension of Federal Republic law, agreement was reached, in the second round of negotiations on 1–3 August 1990, that Federal Republic law should essentially prevail unless other provisions were expressly stipulated.[13]

Schäuble did, however, succeed in his insistence that unification was not the moment for attempting to solve problems that were a matter of controversy within the Federal Republic, for extending social protection rights and benefits, or for introducing legal reforms.[14]

9.2 SOCIAL POLICY IN THE UNIFICATION TREATY

The most important discussions on arrangements for bringing together the systems of social security and employment law of the Federal Republic and the GDR had been taken in the State Treaty of 18 May 1990. However, a number of fundamental questions concerning the alignment of the systems remained unresolved, and both the Federal Ministry of Labour and the GDR Ministry of Labour and Social Affairs believed that they needed to be addressed in the Unification Treaty.[15] Negotiations on these questions took place within Working Group 3 on 'employment and social security/family and health'.[16] The leading members of this working group were, as in the negotiations on social policy questions for the State Treaty, Staatsssekretär Jagoda of the Federal Labour Ministry and Staatssekretär Ziel of the GDR Ministry of Labour and Social Affairs. Other participants in the negotiations were Parlamentarischer Staatssekretär Dr Hans Geisler from the GDR Ministry for the Family and Women, Staatssekretär Schönfelder and Professor Hicke from the GDR Ministry of Health, Dr Noack from the Ministry of Labour and Social Affairs, one representative each from the office of Staatssekretär Krause and the Federal Interior Ministry, and one representative each of Bavaria and the Berlin Senate.[17]

Discussions between the different government ministries on the details of the treaty and its extensive appendices, which contained specific determinations concerning the extension of Federal Republic law and the continuing application of GDR law with regard to the areas of responsibility of individual ministries, began after the first round of negotiations on 10 July 1990 and continued until the second half of August. It would take up too much space here to describe in detail the separate stages of the negotiations on matters of social policy; instead, the most important areas of controversy will be outlined. Not all of the disagreements were between the GDR and the Federal Republic: in the final phase of the negotiations the most important differences over social policy arose between, on the one side, the Federal Ministries of Labour and for Young People, the Family, Women, and Health and, on the other, the Federal Ministry of Finance, which was primarily anxious to lower the costs of unification.

9.2.1 Employment law and health and safety regulation

One of the central social policy demands of the GDR in the negotiations over the Unification Treaty was that the GDR Labour Statute Book, as amended on 22 June 1990,[18] should be retained until new Germany-wide laws on employment contracts and working time had been drawn up.[19] At a time of 'profound economic and social change', the GDR said, it was 'not reasonable, as far as either employers or employees [were] concerned', that a 'unified, comprehensible set of regulations' should be replaced by regulations that were 'fragmented and full of gaps'.[20] Moreover, Federal Republic employment law was outdated: for instance, in its anachronistic distinction between blue- and white-collar workers (*Arbeiter* and *Angestellte*). And the GDR's more favourable regulations for employees, especially women, should remain in place for as long as possible, to ensure that the new legal framework would be found acceptable to the population. The representatives of the Federal Labour Ministry, however, were insistent that a single system of employment law should be established.[21]

The differences between the negotiators—which also involved points of detail—are apparent from several documents: a Federal Labour Ministry note on the first round of talks between its representatives and representatives of the GDR Labour Ministry on 11 July 1990,[22] an interim report of 20 July 1990 on the results of the discussions of experts,[23] and detailed argument papers on the points under dispute prepared by Department III of the Labour Ministry (responsible for employment law and heath and safety regulation) and dated 27 July 1990.[24] Only a few key issues can be mentioned here. The GDR opposed the adoption of the distinction, still retained in parts of Federal Republic employment law, between blue- and white-collar workers, for example with regard to notice periods and continued remuneration in the event of illness. On the other hand, it agreed to the removal of home workers and apprentices from the category of employee through the adoption of the Federal Republic's laws on home workers and professional training. The GDR was against the adoption of the Employment Promotion Law of 1985, demanded by the Federal Labour Ministry, inasmuch as it made it easier for temporary contracts to be introduced. It wanted to retain, while the Federal government wanted to remove, the chapter of the Labour Statute Book on professional re-training (§§145–59), which contained regulations supporting re-training via employment contracts and thus imposed duties on the employer. The GDR argued that its very generous, but costly, regulations granting paid time off work for employees needing to care for sick children should be maintained, whereas the Federal Labour Ministry was prepared to accept these provisions only for a transitional period. The GDR's negotiators also set great store by retaining the chapter of the Labour Statute Book on 'social care' (*soziale Betreuung*) (§§227–39), according to which, *inter alia*, the employer was obliged to help with the provision of accommodation for employees and, together with local representative bodies, ensure that employees were easily able to travel to work. In addition, former employees should, where possible, be eligible for 'social care'. These were not, however, legally enforceable rights. In the Federal Labour Ministry's view, they belonged 'for the most part . . . to a system with a centrally directed (state-owned) economy'. Moreover, after the introduction of free collective bargaining in the GDR it was the 'responsibility of the relevant bargaining parties to create concrete regulations . . . beneficial to employees'. Adoption of these parts of the Statute Book, even for a transitional period, was therefore firmly rejected, especially as the provisions were all 'mere empty formulae or, at most, statements of intent'. The GDR Ministry of Labour and Social Affairs also wished, in opposition to the Federal Labour Ministry, to retain the limitations on employee liability existing in the GDR. On the other hand, there was agreement that for a transitional period, until an independent jurisdiction for employment law had been established—which the GDR accepted in principle—the existing employment chambers and senates of the local and district courts in the GDR should remain in place. The GDR's Supreme Court, however, should cease to be the court of third instance in employment matters and this role should be transferred to the Federal Employment Court.

The position of the Federal Labour Ministry hardened in the course of the negotiations. Whereas the note of 11 July 1990 still maintained that it might be possible for the Labour Statute Book to be preserved for a transitional period, albeit with many amendments, the 27 July argument paper on the Labour Statute Book stated clearly that it was 'indispensable' that 'in future a single unified system of employment law [should] apply in both parts of the state as a whole. Employment law and economic law make up a unified whole; no barriers can, therefore, continue to exist.' Moreover, the retention of different and, especially, more generous employment law provisions in the territory of the GDR would 'be met with incomprehension in the rest of the Federal Republic, and would be rejected'.[25] It would also, as the interim report of 20 July 1990 had already emphasized, constitute an obstacle to investment by employers.[26]

The Unification Treaty finally reached a compromise: Federal Republic employment law would, essentially, be extended to the former GDR, but the unified German legislative authority was charged with providing, 'as speedily as possible, a new codification of the contents of' employment contract law, the law on working time for employees, and the law specifically dealing with the protection of women employees.[27] The GDR's existing unitary system of regulation of notice periods and continued remuneration in the event of illness for white- and blue-collar employees, which the Federal Constitutional Court had already advised should be adopted in the Federal Republic,[28] remained in place. The Federal Republic's Employment Promotion Law of 1985 was adopted for the former GDR. The provisions in the GDR Labour Statute Book concerning professional retraining and 'social care' ceased to be applicable. On economic grounds and for reasons of employment policy, the ban on night work for female workers was not extended to the east, and the same applied to the ban on the employment of women on construction sites; the extension of restrictions on working time on Sundays and holidays was withheld for a transition period until the end of 1992. As far as technical health and safety legislation was concerned, which in the Federal Republic itself still had to be adapted to conform to EU guidelines in many respects, transitional arrangements ensured that existing facilities at GDR enterprises could continue in operation.

With regard to worker protection measures, many of the GDR's more generous regulations were retained, albeit only for a transitional period in most cases. The statutory minimum holiday entitlement of twenty working days remained. (In the Federal Republic, wage agreements usually provided for substantially longer holiday entitlements.) The generous existing provisions for time off work to care for sick children, which the GDR had wanted to preserve for at least two years, were to continue only until 30 June 1991. The GDR's 'housework day' was to remain until 31 December 1991. The dismissal (without fault of the employee) of fighters against fascism and victims of fascism continued to be unlawful. Special protection against dismissal for pregnant women remained valid until 31 December 1990; for mothers and fathers of children aged up to one year it remained in force if their children were born before 31 December 1990, while for single-parent employees with children aged up to three it continued to apply if the children were born before 1 January 1992. For births before 1 January 1991 the GDR's regulations allowing maternity leave of twenty weeks (as against eight weeks in the Federal Republic) after the birth of the child continued in force, as did the easier conditions regarding paid time off work after the ending of maternity leave, for a period extending up to three years if a place in a crèche was not available. The limitations on employee liability, which had been significantly more restricted in the GDR than in the Federal Republic, remained in place in the new *Bundesländer* until 31 December 1991.

As far as the improvement of health protection within industrial and other enterprises was concerned, the GDR's Central Institute for Industrial Medicine became the basis of the new Federal Institute for Industrial Medicine in Berlin, despite opposition from the Federal Medical Council. As Blüm wrote to the Minister for Research and Technology, Heinz Riesenhuber, there could be no question of 'withholding from every institution in the former GDR the right to make a contribution to the social protection system of the Federal Republic of Germany'.[29] Blüm did, however, assure the president of the Federal Medical Council, who was afraid that 'a whole area of medicine and a whole branch of medical training [would be] politicized', that the new Federal Institute would not 'perpetuate the centralized, dirigiste tradition of the Central Institute for Industrial Medicine' and that it would not be granted any authority over regulations governing the training and career development of enterprise-based doctors'.[30] The real role of the Federal Institute, he said, would be to support the Federal Labour Ministry in its departmental responsibility for workplace health and safety. In this, as he wrote to the board of the General Union of Commercial Trade Associations,[31] the 'qualifications and practical experience of the former Central Institute [ought also to] be made use of'.

9.2.2 Agreements on protection measures against rationalization

A serious problem arose as a result of the agreements on protection measures against rationalization that had been concluded, in particular, during the period of the Modrow government and confirmed and registered by the Ministry of Labour and Wages in accordance with the regulations of the GDR Labour Statute Book. According to documents of the GDR Ministry of Labour and Social Affairs, a total of 41 agreements on protection measures against rationalization had been registered from 11 December 1989 onwards: of these, 3 contained regulations akin to redundancy schemes, 11 dealt with the public service, and 22 related to social organizations, associations, and parties. The 5 agreements relating to commerce[32] involved 1.4 million employees, out of a total of 8.2 million. In part, these agreements provided for significant interim financial aid for people obtaining more badly paid jobs, compensation payments for people taking early retirement, disturbance allowances (for removal and furnishings) for those changing jobs, extensions to notice periods for long-serving members of staff at enterprises, and more besides.

Writing to the chairman of the German Trade Union Federation, Heinz-Werner Meyer, the Minister for Labour and Social Affairs, Regine Hildebrandt,[33] said that such agreements, which were designed to protect the vested rights of employees in the event of structural changes and rationalization measures, imposed additional burdens on the enterprises concerned and were a threat to their survival: 'The obligations have become millstones round the enterprises' necks. They are an obstacle to their efforts to make the changes that are needed in order to increase competitiveness, a precondition of job security.' Moreover, they would 'significantly interfere with, or even [make] impossible', negotiations over freely agreed contracts. Of the two alternative ways of dealing with the problem that were possible in principle—nullifying the agreements through legislation, or 'reaching consensus between the negotiating partners'—she expressed her preference for the latter, noting the opportunities for the financing of adaptation and orientation periods that would become available after 1 July 1990 as a result of the GDR Employment Promotion Law. She said that the employers' and employees' central organizations and the trade unions and employers' associations of the branches of the economy concerned—apart from the public service sector, which would have to be included later, on grounds of practicability—should cooperate on reaching a compromise. According to Meyer, the German Trade Union Federation was also in favour of the replacement of the existing agreements on protection measures against rationalization by new negotiated agreements that would take account of the opportunities created by the Employment Promotion Law. Money for short-time working and maintenance payments during re-training should be built up, he argued, and employers should be obliged to make use of these new opportunities. Until then, however, the existing agreements should remain in force. He opposed the holding of tripartite or multilateral talks, since these were matters for unions and management alone and not for government, unless the latter was a party to negotiations; moreover, the Trade Union Federation was 'absolutely not a participant in concrete wage negotiations'.[34] The GDR Public Services Trade Union took a much stronger view. It said that the arguments in favour of cancelling the agreements on protection measures against rationalization were, 'without exception, a reflection of the completely one-sided views of employers and [were] dubious both factually and legally'. Cancellation would make the 'introduction of a market economy more brutal, not more social'.[35]

The Federal Economics Ministry, on the other hand, argued that there was a pressing need for the agreements on protection measures against rationalization to be ended, either by legislation or by notice of cancellation, as they were a great disincentive to investment and would make it more difficult to modernize enterprises. They imposed a sizeable burden on the public finances, which had to provide the relevant resources, and hence ultimately on the Federal budget, while the commercial justification for them had disappeared. In addition, they would hinder forthcoming wage negotiations. The Ministry noted, moreover, that the Federal Employment Court had ruled that collective agreements could, exceptionally, be cancelled if there were sufficiently serious grounds for doing so.[36] In a position paper for Krause[37] the Federal Economics Ministry's urgent recommendation was rejected on both legal and political grounds: according to the GDR General Outline Law of 21 June 1990 existing valid and registered agreements were to continue to be applicable, while instant notice of cancellation would also lead to 'significant unrest among employees and the trade unions representing them' and would make wage negotiations 'more difficult, not easier'. The paper pressed for new collective agreements to be reached 'as quickly as possible'.

This initially unsuccessful initiative by the Federal Economics Ministry had been supported by Blüm, who believed that the agreements were additionally objectionable because they led to the 'unjustified financial betterment of particular groups of employees'.[38] The Unification Treaty finally laid down that those agreements on protection measures against rationalization that had been concluded up to 30 June 1990 would cease to be valid on 31 December 1990, although until new regulations on wage negotiations had been agreed, employees who had acquired rights and entitlements under these agreements up till that date would be protected as far as those rights and entitlements were concerned.[39]

9.2.3 Early retirement, pre-pension transitional benefit, and labour market policy

There were sharp differences between the Federal Ministry of Labour and the GDR Ministry of Labour and Social Affairs with regard to the continuation of the relatively generous provisions on early retirement that had been introduced by the Modrow government. The GDR believed that these provisions were imperative on grounds of labour market policy. The Federal Republic, on the other hand, objected that they put GDR citizens at a financial advantage over its own citizens, and was also critical of the additional financial burden that they imposed.[40] The GDR argued that the level at which early retirement benefit was calculated, at 70 per cent of net employment income, should also apply to pre-pension benefit; the Federal Labour Ministry described this as 'unemployment benefit de luxe'.[41] In the Unification Treaty it was finally agreed[42] that the GDR's provisions on early retirement should continue to apply only to existing cases and therefore be gradually phased out. In addition, early retirement benefit of 70 per cent would in future be paid only on the basis of the contributions ceiling in unemployment insurance and would be reduced to 65 per cent, with indexation to rises in earnings, when the next increases were implemented. According to Klaus Leven, the capping of early retirement benefit by means of the ceiling had not been part of the nearly finalized draft of the Unification Treaty. Its omission would have meant that the large earners in the big combines, loyal to the GDR regime, would have received 'fantastic early retirement benefits'; Noack, of the GDR Labour and Social Affairs Ministry, argued strongly in favour of the arrangement. After an 'absolutely indignant' Leven drew Blüm's attention to the question, Blüm intervened and the capping was then included in the treaty.[43]

For new cases of early departure from employment, application could be made to the Federal Labour Ministry, and the Ministry would be able to reject an application if there was a clear shortage of labour, in the relevant region, in respect of the kind of work that the applicant had previously done; otherwise, pre-pension benefit was introduced for men from the age of 57, and for women from the age of 55 until the end of 1990 and from the age of 57 thereafter. Benefits were set at 65 per cent of the person's last average net remuneration from employment and, for employees whose entitlement originated before 1 April 1991, were raised by five percentage points for the first 312 days. These benefits, which were significantly higher than unemployment assistance (*Arbeitslosenhilfe*), were available to men for three years at a maximum and to women, initially, for five years (though from 1991 onwards they would likewise be available only for three years) until the earliest point at which a pension could be drawn. The provisions were to apply until 31 December 1991 in the first instance, but with the possibility of extension for a further year. In fact, the poor state of the labour market was such that on 1 July 1991 the minimum age for receipt of pre-pension benefit was lowered to 55 all round and the period for which it could be paid was extended to a maximum of five years.[44] On the question of the encouragement of early transition to retirement, therefore, the GDR's wishes largely prevailed, except that benefits which the Federal Republic regarded as particularly over-generous were capped.

Other regulations that were not controversial remained in place, albeit with various time limits. These were the special regulations in the GDR's Employment Promotion Law making it easier for people to receive short-time working benefit, support for job creation schemes in job centre regions with good employment conditions, the possible takeover of the full cost of gross wages in the case of job creation schemes, individual support for job training, further training, and re-training at higher education institutions, and support for those taking part in educational schemes, including cases where applicants were not directly at risk of unemployment. The provisions omitted from the Employment Promotion Law on the productive promotion of winter construction did not come into force until 1 April 1991, but those on bad-weather payment became applicable when the GDR acceded to the Federal Republic.[45]

9.2.4 Pensions insurance

As far as pensions insurance was concerned, the main decisions of principle had already been made in the State Treaty and subsequent GDR legislation. It had also been agreed that the Federal Republic's pensions law would not be extended, by specific legislation, to the new *Bundesländer* until the major pensions reform that had been passed in November 1989 came into force on 1 January 1992. In addition, consensus had been reached on the essential principles whereby existing rights and entitlements were to be protected. Thus it was agreed that the pensions of people who would reach pensionable age before 30 June 1995 would have to be paid at at least the level that would have been applicable on 30 June 1990 under the GDR's pensions law, and that entitlement to a pension under the law continued to hold good. Protection of pension rights, however, did not extend to benefits under the supplementary and special provision systems for particular groups.[46] The remaining special provision systems would terminate on 31 December 1991, with regulations governing the terms of their conversion.[47] In fact, conversion took place earlier, the day after the Pensions Transition Law came into force on 1 August 1991. However, a decision about the supplementary provision systems for the parties was at first deferred; these were not converted until 30 June 1993, under supplementary legislation to the Pensions Transition Law, enacted on 24 June 1993.[48]

Under the new pensions arrangements, Federal-wide pensions insurance providers would extend their coverage to the new *Bundesländer*, and *Land* insurance providers for workers' pensions insurance would be established in each of the new *Länder*; the provider for Berlin was extended to east Berlin. The work of the pensions insurance providers, and also of accident insurance providers, would be carried out by a Social Insurance Transitional Authority from 1 January 1991 until the insurance providers were up and running; the latter would be required to take over by 31 December 1991 at the latest. The right to rehabilitation, which had also been made subject to new regulations under the pensions reform of 1989/92, with effect from 1 January 1992, would come into force in the east a year earlier, on 1 January 1991, with certain restrictions.

There was considerable disagreement between the GDR and the Federal Republic, however, on the question of the GDR's social allowance that had been paid, under pensions, accident, and unemployment insurance, in the case of low pensions. The representatives of the GDR Ministry of Labour and Social Affairs wanted the social allowance to be retained and indexed to earnings, in the same way as with the pensions alignment. The Federal Ministry of Labour was firmly opposed to indexation, and also argued that if the social allowance were retained at its current level and in its existing form, it should be time-limited.[49] The eventual solution was that new applications for the social allowance under pensions, accident, and unemployment insurance would be accepted only until 31 December 1991 and that payments would be made only until 30 June 1995 at the latest. Indexation to earnings would not be provided. Blüm viewed this as an 'acceptable compromise' and specifically asked the chairman of the CDU/CSU Bundestag working group on labour and social affairs, Horst Günther, who succeeded Wolfgang Vogt as one of the two Parlamentarische Staatssekretäre at the Federal Labour Ministry in January 1991, to assist in the implementation of the new arrangements.[50]

The differences between the Federal Labour and Finance Ministries with regard to the financing of pensions insurance were even more serious. The Finance Ministry was concerned to reduce the burden on the Federal budget created by the social policy costs of German unification, while the Labour Ministry was anxious, above all, to prevent excessive demands from being made on the pensions insurance providers. The Finance Ministry did not share the Labour Ministry's view that the Federal government should bear the cost of dealing with the inherited burden on the pensions insurance system and with the loss of contributions that would be caused by the assignment of civil-servant status to employees in the former territory of the GDR.[51] More challenging still was Waigel's demand that the eastern and western pensions insurance providers should form a financial combine, in order to save the Federal government from having to take on the probable deficits of the east German insurers.[52] This would mean, as the Federal Labour Ministry correctly noted, that 'the west German contribution payers [would be] called on to provide finance through a social insurance contribution procedure inappropriate for purposes of modernizing structural shortcomings'. The result, it argued, would be to jeopardize the reforms that had been successfully carried out in the Federal Republic, hamper the 'controlled adaptation of the social insurance system in the former territory of the GDR to that of the Federal Republic', and undermine the strategy of 'clearly assigning financial responsibilities in the two territories through separate budgeting'.[53] The Federal pensions insurance system would also have to assume responsibility for repaying the capital loans taken out to cover the deficits in the GDR pensions insurance system up to 1991.[54] Furthermore, setting up a financial combine would lead to serious arguments with the SPD and provoke 'the fiercest resistance' on the part of the self-governing insurers, whose cooperation was going to be of particular importance in the future. A financial combine, the Labour Ministry maintained, should therefore not be established until such time as 'wages and pensions have become similar in the two parts of Germany'.[55] Despite this opposition, however, the Finance Ministry's position prevailed: not in the Unification Treaty but, following the election of 2 December 1990, in the coalition agreement announced on 16 January 1991, whereby a combined system of financing would come into effect from 1 January 1992.[56] The mutual system of pensions insurance—like the unemployment insurance system—was accordingly compelled to bear a significant part of the financial burden of German unity.

9.2.5 Social provision for war victims

There were also disagreements within the Federal government on the question of social provision for war victims. The Labour Ministry wanted the Federal Social Provision Law and the relatively generous benefits provided under it to be extended to the new *Bundesländer* on 1 January 1991—albeit at a lower level[57]—while the Finance Ministry maintained that an extension was, 'at best, conceivable only from 1992 onwards, and then on a gradual basis'.[58] The Labour Ministry calculated that the cost in 1991 of taking over provision for war victims would amount to 1,650 million DM.[59] On that reckoning, the 'doubts regarding finance' could be overcome 'in good time'.[60] The Labour Ministry's point of view was backed by Chancellor Kohl, who had plainly been influenced by representations from the Association of War Victims, the Disabled, and Social Pensioners,[61] and it won out. Blüm at once pressed hard for a functioning administrative apparatus to be set up as quickly as possible to deal with claims.[62] In the GDR, at the start of 1990, only about 5,000 people had been in receipt of a modest war disability pension; by 1 January 1994 the number of people in the new *Bundesländer* obtaining benefits under the Federal Social Provision Law stood at 212,425.[63]

9.2.6 Health insurance and health care

The creation, on 1 January 1991, of a multipartite system of health insurance based on the Federal Republic model was not controversial, following earlier legislation by the de Maizière government. On the other hand, the GDR was opposed to any dismantling of the financial advantages that GDR citizens enjoyed over citizens of the Federal Republic with regard to statutory benefits. These advantages comprised exemption from supplementary charges for orthodontic treatment, the purchase of drugs, hospital treatment, inpatient check-ups and recuperation, and the obtaining of medical aids, and also the provision of benefits by health insurance schemes: for example, compensation for a significant proportion of loss of earnings when someone was caring for a sick child over a four- to ten-week period. Other benefits not provided under Federal Republic statutory health insurance were inpatient treatment for up to twenty-six weeks for people in need of nursing care and subsequent accommodation in a residential home at a cost of 125 DM per month.[64] The existence of these advantages—also opposed by the Federal Labour Ministry—strengthened the unwillingness of the Federal Finance Ministry to provide the Federal subsidies to the health insurance providers in the east that the Labour Ministry, as well as the GDR, believed were absolutely necessary. With a deficit estimated to be approaching 4,000 million DM in the second half of 1990, the subsidies would be 'inevitable on a temporary basis', though it would also be 'vitally necessary' to bear down on costs.[65] The Labour Ministry argued that since health care in the GDR had been organized as a national health service, the service's deficits were the product of government actions and should therefore not be inflicted as a burden solely on mutualist health insurance financed by employers and the employed. A financial settlement made internally within the GDR would result in a completely unacceptable contribution rate of 18 per cent, instead of the 12.8 per cent that had been envisaged.[66]

The Finance Ministry was firmly opposed to the settlement of the deficits by the Federal government, as this would release the 'health insurers in the territory of the GDR from all pressure to act in an economical way' and would impose an 'entirely unjustifiable extra burden on the Federal budget'. Waigel accordingly proposed that as with pensions insurance, all the German statutory health insurers should form a financial combine, which would allow the deficits to be borne by all insured persons on a mutual basis.[67] His proposal, though, was not adopted. Unlike the unemployment, accident, and pensions insurers, the health insurance schemes retained separate budgeting systems for the new *Bundesländer* and the territory of the old Federal Republic.[68] (Not until 1999 were the resources for a Germany-wide system of risk equalization for the new *Bundesländer* made available through statutory health insurance.) On the other hand, the opposition of the Finance Ministry, and also of the FDP, was strong enough to defeat all efforts by the Labour Ministry, the Federal Ministry for Young People, the Family, Women, and Health, the *Bundesländer*, and the GDR to secure a state subsidy for health insurance.[69] Instead, the health insurers were given loans to cover their deficits. In fact, however, the loans, amounting to 3,000 million DM, that were made to the health insurers in the second half of 1990 were never repaid.[70]

In view of the financial situation, the Unification Treaty sought not only to reduce the extra benefits (with varied transitional periods)[71] but also to bear down on costs, principally through a reduction in fees to doctors and dentists in line with the low basic wage level in the new *Länder* and a lowering of prices for drugs to 45 per cent of the west German level.[72] Fees and prices would be increased once wages and salaries in the east began to rise. These attempts to keep a firm lid on costs led to bitter arguments with the interested parties and could not be sustained over the longer term. In complex negotiations with the Federal Union of Health Insurance Physicians and, later, the Federal Union of Health Insurance Dentists, the health insurers' national associations succeeded in agreeing amendments to the existing national outline contracts for the new *Bundesländer* that represented a compromise between the interests of the providers and funders of health insurance benefits.[73] The price reduction for drugs was fiercely opposed by the pharmaceutical industry, which for a while threatened to boycott the delivery of medication (apart from insulin) to the east. In a letter of 27 December 1990 to the National Pharmaceutical Industry Board and the National Union of German Pharmacists' Associations Blüm drew attention to the 'socio-political dimensions' of such a boycott. 'As has already become clear in the media,' he wrote, 'people will find it hard to understand how there can be deliveries to countries inside and outside Europe, with considerable price reductions, but there is a reluctance to accept similar, or indeed, smaller, reductions in the new *Bundesländer*.'[74] The Federal Labour Ministry believed that the reductions were necessary and would relieve the financial burden on the insurance providers in the east by roughly 3,000 million DM. The pharmaceutical industry regarded the measures as ill-conceived and impracticable, as a split system of prices would lead to market manipulation—for example, to the re-import into the west of cut-price drugs from the east.[75] It was also concerned that large parts of the east German pharmaceutical industry would collapse, because they were not competitive with the west. With the FDP threatening to make the issue a make-or-break one as far as the continuation of the coalition was concerned, the Labour Ministry eventually had to give way. The compromise that was reached, after difficult negotiations, abandoned the price reductions and instead required the pharmaceutical industry, the pharmaceutical wholesalers, and the pharmacies to play a limited role in covering the health insurers' financial deficit by supplying medication until 31 December 1991.[76]

Finally, the Federal Ministry of Labour and the Ministry for Young People, the Family, Women, and Health, with GDR support, attempted to add to the Unification Treaty an article on the health system committing the legislators of a united Germany to 'create the conditions whereby the standard of inpatient care' for the population in the east would be 'speedily and permanently improved and brought into line with the situation in the rest of the territory of the Federal Republic. The shortfall in investment in hospitals, preventive and recuperative facilities, and nursing homes'—and, in the view of the Ministry for Young People, the Family, Women, and Health, also of old-age homes—'particularly with regard to buildings and technical equipment, [should be] dealt with through the framework of a "joint Federal and *Land* programme" of investment aid in the health and social security systems; the joint programme [should] make available the necessary financial support for a period of 10 years.'[77] This ambitious proposal was not accepted, as the Federal Finance Ministry stood firm against any form of mixed funding to meet the costs of investment in hospitals.[78] Although—contrary to the Finance Ministry's wishes—the treaty charged the legislators of a united Germany with the task of improving the standard of inpatient care, the detailed specifications concerning the financing of investment in hospitals and preventive and recuperative facilities that were included in the annexes to the treaty were based on the assumption that the *Länder* alone would be responsible.[79] It was only in December

1992, in the Health Service Structure Law, that the Federal government undertook to assume a share in the financing of investment aid for the modernization of hospitals in the new *Bundesländer*, at a level of 7,000 million DM overall for the period 1995–2004.[80]

The structural changes to the provision of outpatient care, through the wide-scale phasing-out of ambulatories, polyclinics, and workplace-based health care facilities, which initially were licensed to provide outpatient care only until 31 December 1995,[81] and their replacement by doctors in individual practices, have already been described.[82] The GDR made no great efforts during the negotiations over the Unification Treaty to preserve these institutions on a long-term basis.[83]

9.2.7 Policy on the family and women

The GDR strove very hard to preserve its 'social achievements' in the areas of family policy and policy for women and to win agreement in the Unification Treaty for further steps to be taken to promote equality between men and women. The outline here of the GDR's efforts in these areas does not include an account of the bitter political struggles that took place to retain the GDR law on abortion, which nearly caused the treaty to fail.[84]

The differences in benefits for women and families, and in the corresponding legal provisions, between the GDR and the Federal Republic were set out in detailed synopses by the SPD group in the Volkskammer, the SPD in the Federal Republic, and the Federal Ministry of Labour.[85] In addition, the GDR Ministry for the Family and Women drew up for the GDR' s coordination staff on German unity a 24-page catalogue on these issues for the use of the negotiators. This document demanded, in particular, that the legislators of a united Germany should develop the law 'so as to make work more compatible with family life'; should examine the level of child benefit, 'taking into account the judgement of the Federal Constitutional Court of 29 May 1990'; should extend 'parental leave and the granting of child-raising allowance to two years generally'; should extend job protection after the birth of a child; and should improve the 'inadequate terms of the [Federal Republic's] Maintenance Advance Law' (on alimony).[86] A further central demand was that since a law of 20 July 1990[87] had now tidied up the ideological content of the GDR's Family Statute Book of 20 December 1965,[88] the statute book should be retained in the *Länder* of the former GDR. The amended legislation, the GDR Ministry argued, had created a modern system of family law on the 'basis of strict equality between men and women, comprehensive equality of legal status' of children born within and outside marriage, 'strict respect for parents' personal responsibility for their children', and contractual agreements regarding property.[89] In some areas, adopting Federal Republic law would mean 'also adopting outdated regulations that would need to be amended' and would hinder the development of a future joint system of family law.

The Ministry set considerable store by the maintenance of child care facilities, arguing that these would continue to play an 'important role alongside the family . . . especially for single parents':[90] the Federal government, in addition to local authorities, should undertake part of the responsibility for financing them. In view of the high rate of female employment, the Ministry also regarded as unacceptable any cutting back of the existing high level of benefits paid in the event of children's illness. In general, the 'establishment of German unity should not be overburdened by significant and perceptible retrograde steps with regard to family-policy benefits for particular groups in the population'.[91] A further important demand was that aid should be given to central organizations of the Independent Welfare Associations to back up the Income Support Law and other pieces of social security legislation: 1,500 million DM should be placed at these bodies' disposal from the Federal budget for 1991.[92]

Within the Federal government the Minister for Young People, the Family, Women, and Health, Ursula Lehr, pressed particularly hard for more account to be taken of the interests of families and women in the unification process. The Federal Republic's institutional arrangements should not, she said, simply be extended to the GDR: for example, the Federal Republic lagged behind the GDR with regard to child care facilities and the granting of paid time off work to parents of sick children.[93] The Ministry supported the proposals, introduced by the GDR Ministry for the Family and Women in the third round of the negotiations on the Unification Treaty, that the maintenance of child care facilities should be guaranteed and that aid should be provided for building up a pluralist structure for the Independent Welfare Associations.[94]

The relevant committees of the eastern and western Social Democrats, the German White-Collar Workers' Trade Union, and the German Trade Union Federation called for greater heed to be paid to the interests of women in the unification process.[95] However, the statements on family policy in the Unification Treaty remained fairly general, partly because of the opposition of the Federal Interior and Finance Ministries[96] to wide-ranging demands in this area. The role of the Federal government in helping meet the costs of maintaining day-care facilities for children in the east was confined to the period up to 30 June 1991. As mentioned earlier, the special protections afforded under GDR employment law to pregnant women, mothers of very young children, and single parents were phased out on differing time-scales. The same applied to extended paid time off work, supported through health insurance benefits, for people caring for sick children. Certain exceptions were allowed, and transition periods were laid down—for example, regarding the securing of alimony payments[97]—but by and large the new *Bundesländer* were obliged to adopt Federal Republic family law. In the case of abortion, after fierce controversy between east and west, between the CDU/CSU and the SPD, and, within the coalition, between the CDU/CSU and the FDP, a compromise was reached, whereby until new regulations covering the whole of Germany came into force by 31 December 1992, the GDR's regulation allowing terminations in the first three months of pregnancy remained valid. This enabled women from west Germany, too, to seek terminations in the new *Bundesländer*, where west German law (which did not allow them) did not apply.

In addition, Article 31 of the Unification Treaty charged the legislators of a united Germany with the tasks of 'developing legislation to secure equality of rights between men and women' and, 'in view of differences in the initial legal and institutional situations with regard to the employment of mothers and fathers, of framing the legal position so as to ensure the compatibility of family and work'. On 27 October 1994, in one of the relatively few constitutional changes that was triggered by unification, a rider was added to Article 3, paragraph 2 of the Basic Law, on equality between men and women, declaring that the 'state . . . promotes the actual realization of equality of rights between women and men' and works towards 'the removal of existing disadvantages'.[98]

9.3 THE RATIFICATION OF THE UNIFICATION TREATY

Because the Unification Treaty—unlike the State Treaty of 18 May 1990—contained constitutional amendments, ratification required two-thirds majorities in the Bundestag, the Bundesrat, and the Volkskammer. Also in contrast with events surrounding the State Treaty, the Social Democrat opposition in the Federal Republic was closely involved in the negotiations. In the GDR, members of parties besides the governing parties took part in the negotiations, as representatives of the future *Länder*, nominated by the Volkskammer, and de Maizière kept the chairmen of the parties in the Volkskammer regularly briefed about the progress of the discussions.[99] Kohl, similarly, gave leading Social Democrats the opportunity to voice their central demands and assist in finding compromise solutions, particularly during the final phase of the negotiations. The parliaments, too, through the two 'German unity' committees, were kept relatively well informed from an early stage.

Although the Federal government and the *Länder*, and government and opposition, at first cooperated well, a crisis blew up shortly before the negotiations were concluded. Following the dismissal of a GDR Social Democrat minister and a SPD-sympathizing minister on 16 August, the Social Democrats resigned from the de Maizière coalition on 19 August. On the same day the heads of government in the Social Democrat-led *Länder* issued a statement[100] fiercely criticizing the Federal government for its refusal to make an immediate assessment of the financial position and carry out necessary tax increases. They also called for changes to a number of central points in the draft treaty. Their principal demands were that compensation should take priority over restitution of property, in order to give legal security to investment; that the GDR *Länder* and local authorities should be given greater financial backing; that the assets of the SED/PDS, the other bloc parties, and the 'mass organizations' of the GDR should go towards the economic restructuring of the GDR; and that the cost of dismantling the GDR's over-staffed public service should not be imposed on the new *Bundesländer*. In the area of social protection the Social Democrats demanded that it should be made more difficult to issue tenants with notices to quit and that pre-pension regulations and hospital financing should be improved. Agriculture, they also argued, should be better assimilated to conditions within the European Community. On abortion, counselling and support should be provided, not punishment. Finally, there should be a new constitution, founded on the Basic Law and subject to a referendum, in which protection of the environment and the implemention of a 'social state' (*Sozialstaat*) should be made goals of state. The chairman of the SPD, Hans-Jochen Vogel, the candidate for the chancellorship, Oskar Lafontaine, the Prime Minister of North Rhine-Westphalia, Johannes Rau, and the deputy leader of the parliamentary party, Herta Däubler-Gmelin, raised a number of these demands in a letter to Kohl of 24 August 1990,[101] emphasizing that in view of the political make-up of the Bundesrat, and the fact that constitutional amendments were planned, the Unification Treaty would need to be acceptable to the Social Democrats.

In the end, a number of clarifications were made and compromises reached—in particular, at a meeting in the Chancellery on 26 August 1990 involving Kohl, Seiters, Schäuble, Genscher, and Waigel, and leading figures from the coalition parties and the Social Democrats,[102] as well as in a series of working groups. These changes were sufficient to allow the Social Democrats to vote for the treaty. A note of 3 September 1990 prepared for Gerhard Jahn,[103] one of the SPD's parliamentary whips (who in the debate on 20 September 1990 was to set out the reasons why his party had agreed to support the treaty),[104] claimed that the negotiations with the coalition had led to a number of further important improvements on the draft of 26 August. These included regulations regarding terminations of pregnancy, the possibility of holding a referendum on a new constitution, more precise statements regarding the issue of dropping the insistence on restitution of land and buildings so as to promote investment, and the transfer of GDR state financial assets to local government. The raising of pre-pension benefit from 65 to 70 per cent for 312 days in the case of employees whose entitlements pre-dated 1 April 1991 was also cited as a victory for the SPD.

After the treaty had been signed, Vogel singled out for particular approval the regulations concerning the opening of the Stasi files (on which the Volkskammer had insisted), the partial adoption of the GDR Rehabilitation Law of 6 September 1990 in the supplementary agreement of 18 September 1990, and the fact that the GDR's agricultural interests would be given more consideration. In a message to the chairman and parliamentary leader of the east German SPD, Wolfgang Thierse, he urged that the Unification Treaty be given united backing.[105]

The Social Democrats in the Bundestag voted unanimously (apart from one abstention) in favour of the Unification Treaty, although Peter Conradi and a number of other SPD members of parliament declared that they were supporting the treaty with reservations, because it had not been subjected to adequate parliamentary debate.[106] A total of 13 CDU/CSU members voted against the treaty, some citing the retention of the abortion regulations in the GDR, some the recognition of the Oder–Neiße line, which Herbert Czaja and other members had in vain called on the Federal Constitutional Court to block through an interim order.[107] Other CDU/CSU members also supported the treaty with considerable misgivings. Altogether, 68 CDU/CSU members of parliament who voted for the treaty put on record their opposition to the acceptance of post-1945 land reform.[108] In the FDP, 32 of the 46 members of the parliamentary party stated that they supported the treaty in spite of the fact that the party refused to accept the expropriations that had been carried out between 1945 and 1949 on the basis of occupation law or occupation sovereignty.[109] Three Green members voted for the treaty and 33 against. The treaty was approved by the Bundestag on 20 September 1990 by 440 votes to 47, with three abstentions.[110] On the following day the Bundesrat voted unanimously in favour.

In the Volkskammer de Maizière defended the treaty as preferable to a mere transitional law and hailed as especially welcome the provisions on pre-pension benefit, the transitional regulations on health and pensions insurance, on maternity and child-raising allowance and paid time off work in the event of a child's illness, and the retention of the social allowance until 30 June 1995.[111] Wolfgang Thierse, speaking for the Social Democrats, particularly stressed the contribution his party had made in securing improvements to the original draft treaty.[112] Fourteen SPD members of the Volkskammer—including Walter Romberg, who had been dismissed as Finance Minister on 16 August 1990—said that they were supporting the treaty only with considerable qualms of conscience, on the grounds that financial provision to the *Länder* and local government was insufficient, the prospects for farmers were uncertain, the instruments for aiding the economy were inadequate, and the social entitlements of GDR citizens would be further eroded.[113] The PDS and a majority of Alliance 90/The Greens voted against the treaty.[114] The treaty was approved by the Volkskammer on 20 September 1990 by 299 votes to 80, with one abstention.[115]

10

The Social Policy Actors and the Unification Process

10.1 THE DOMINANT ROLE OF THE EXECUTIVE

The negotiations on the legal foundations of German unity were the hour of the executive. Although the dynamic forces behind unification were the exodus of hundreds of thousands of Germans who arrived in the west, the wish for unity on the part of the overwhelming majority of people in the east, and the internal disintegration of the German Democratic Republic, it was the governments of the two states that had to translate these dynamic processes into a concrete unification policy, secure the policy on the international front, and obtain agreement on the norms, institutions, and transitional arrangements in accordance with which unification would be carried out.

It was in the Federal Chancellery that the key decisions were taken: above, all, by the Chancellor himself, in collaboration with a small group of close advisers. This was the case with the Ten Point Programme for reunification announced by Kohl on 28 November 1989, the breaking-off of the negotiations on a 'contractual community' with the GDR in mid-January 1990, the offer of monetary union of 7 February 1990 (though here preparatory work by the Federal Finance Ministry played a very significant part), and the setting of objectives and establishment of a rough timetable for negotiations over the State Treaty on monetary union and the Unification Treaty. The process of negotiations was coordinated by the cabinet committee on 'German unity', formed on 7 February 1990, and its working groups on particular areas, and by the leader of the Federal delegation at the State Treaty negotiations, Hans Tietmeyer, and the chief Federal negotiator at the Unification Treaty negotiations, Wolfgang Schäuble. The detailed implementation of the government's strategic and political objectives, however, was essentially the work of the ministerial bureaucracy, which was much more closely involved—down to the level of heads of sections (*Referate*)—in shaping the outcome of important issues than was usually the case in the preparation of legislation. In normal times the system of government in the Federal Republic is typified by extraordinarily complex processes of consultation and negotiation, in which parties and interest groups exercise a central influence and the *Länder* also play an important part. In the case of the State Treaty these processes were almost completely bypassed; with the Unification Treaty, where the interests of the *Länder* and, through them, of the opposition carried more weight, they played a greater role, but still a smaller one than usual.

There were several reasons why the processes of policy- and decision-making were simplified and personalized, and also largely centralized and bureaucratized.

1. A key constitutional reason why the position of the executive was so powerful was that in accordance with Article 59, paragraph 2 of the Basic Law, the negotiated treaties could be ratified, or rejected, by the parliamentary bodies only in their entirety: they could not be amended in detail. At most, additional points could be introduced in the laws that were passed adopting the treaties.

2. There was huge pressure to prepare the unusually complex treaties as rapidly as possible. This was partly because it was feared that the favourable situation on the international front—in particular, the readiness of the Soviet Union to make concessions—might change and that with any procrastination the opportunity of reuniting Germany might be forfeited. At the same time, the internal break-up of the GDR—which could, of course, unilaterally declare its accession to the Federal Republic without any treaties—and, in particular, the tremendous pressure for speedy unification that was coming from the people of the GDR and from the Volkskammer ruled out all delay.

3. As is customary with negotiations between states, the central executives first had to make contact with one another. It was largely up to them to decide the extent to which they would choose to bring in other political and social actors and institutions, or accept that they would have to do so in order to secure their actions politically.

4. Unification necessarily entailed a great deal of improvisation: there were no ready-made plans for unification in the drawers of the ministries' desks. Nor, however, did the political parties have their own strategies for managing the process of transformation to democracy and a market economy in east Germany, for bringing together the differing elements of the two states, and for deciding what the character of a unified German state should be. In this situation, reliance on the experience and expertise of the Federal ministerial bureaucracy constituted the lesser risk. The consequence, however, was that the GDR, whose political and economic systems had, after all, collapsed, and whose bureaucratic experts not only possessed little negotiating experience but also had to assimilate quite unfamiliar ideas and methods, found itself at a disadvantage. The dominance of the west German ministerial bureaucracy strengthened the hand of those who wanted to extend the Federal Republic's system as comprehensively as possible to the east.

5. The battle of the parties to achieve political majorities in the Volkskammer, in local government in the GDR, in the east German *Länder*, and, above all, at the Bundestag elections that were due at the end of 1990 had a powerful influence over the initiation of the negotiations, their time-scale, and their character. It strengthened the position of the existing governing coalition in the Federal Republic, which was able to determine the issues on which the elections would be fought and outmanoeuvre the opposition by portraying criticisms of specific features of the way the government was proceeding—for example, over the financing of unification or

detailed aspects of the treaties—as evidence of hostility to German unity as such. At the same time, the divisions within the Social Democratic Party over central questions of the future of Germany, and the obvious reservations of its candidate for chancellor, Oskar Lafontaine, about the re-establishment of a German nation state, were grist to the mill of the government camp.

10.2 THE FEDERAL MINISTRY OF LABOUR AND SOCIAL ORDER

Social policy played a central role in the negotiations over unification, and the range of questions that were at issue in this area was considerable. The goal of the negotiations as far as social policy was concerned was to combine the creation of a market economy with the norms, institutions, and benefits of the Federal Republic welfare state: free collective wage bargaining, co-determination, an active labour market policy, a multipartite system of social insurance, and systems of social protection and support. If this could be achieved, then the effects of the economic upheaval would be mitigated and social harmony would be ensured.

The key role on the Federal Republic side in shaping social policy under unification was played by the Ministry of Labour under Norbert Blüm. The second ministry with responsibility for social policy, the Ministry for Young People, the Family, Women, and Health, was less influential. The minister, Ursula Lehr, had no power base within the CDU, whereas Blüm was head of the CDU *Land* association with the largest membership, in North Rhine-Westphalia, and had a good relationship with the Chancellor, Helmut Kohl. Moreover, until the new government was formed in January 1991, statutory health insurance was also the province of the Labour Ministry.

Blüm was closely involved in the government's decision to offer a social union as well as a monetary and economic union. In this, he had the support of all the political forces in the GDR, the Social Democratic opposition, and the trade unions. He and his ministry, over which he had firm control, were advocates of the view that the west German welfare state and its pattern of rules and benefits should be extended to east Germany in as full a form as possible. With his colleagues he fought strongly, and successfully, against the efforts of those who hoped to use unification with the GDR as a roundabout way of undermining the welfare state legislation of the Federal Republic.[1] Despite considerable resistance from other government ministries, the views of Blüm and his ministry prevailed on a number of significant issues: a conversion ratio of 1:1 for salaries, wages, and pensions; an immediate, rather than gradual, raising of the level of a 'benchmark pension' to 70 per cent of net employment income; a generous active labour market policy to reduce mass unemployment in the east; and the extension to the new eastern *Bundesländer* of west German law on social provision for war victims. As an advocate of the Christian Social tradition of social committees and employees' interest groups within the CDU, and as a popular and effective electoral campaigner, Blüm in a sense represented the left wing of the party. In addition, on many issues he had the backing of Chancellor Kohl:[2] for example, in his support for the east German pensioners, where Kohl well understood the importance of the pensioner vote. Overall, Blüm and his advisers regarded the extension of the Federal Republic's systems of employment law and social security to the east as first and foremost a matter of economic principle and of social justice. However, by counting on a second 'economic miracle', similar to the one that followed the currency reform of 1948, they seriously underestimated the scale of the economic problems that would be caused by the sudden conversion of the currency and the introduction of the complex regulations of Federal employment law and the full range of benefits available under the Federal social security system.[3] Writing to a concerned citizen on 28 March 1990, Blüm promised that 'no pensioner, no ill person, no unemployed person, no war victim and no recipient of income support [need] fear reductions in benefits as a result of the process of German unification.. . . On the contrary: a united Germany will develop great economic strength, with prosperity for all and new opportunities of employment.'[4] And on 11 June 1990 he wrote to his 'Dortmund friends' that an increase in taxes to pay for unification—the favourite theme of the Social Democrats—would not be necessary.[5] By the start of 1991 this hope had proved to be illusory.

Opposing the Labour Ministry's position were the Federal Ministries of Economics and Finance, the latter backed by the Bundesbank. Their primary concern was that Federal Republic employment law should be made more flexible and streamlined when it was extended to the east, in order that private investment would be attracted and economic reorganization made easier. They also wanted social benefits to be aligned more gradually, so that the competitiveness of east German enterprises could be strengthened and the costs of unity reduced. Although the Economics Ministry, under Helmut Haussmann of the FDP, was relatively weak, the Finance Ministry—responsible for the Federal budget and headed by Theodor Waigel, a key figure in the governing coalition as leader of the CSU—brought the whole of its considerable weight into play. The Finance Ministry's views were determined primarily by financial, rather than economic, considerations. The Ministry was initially able to block the use of Federal funds for the wholesale modernization of the east German health system, succeeded in enforcing the establishment on 1 January 1992 of a Germany-wide financial combine in pensions insurance (similar to a previously established combine in unemployment insurance), thereby imposing a substantial share of the burden of the costs of unification on employers and employees, and insisted that the time-periods for dismantling the financial advantages which people in the east enjoyed in terms of employment, social security, and family law should be as short as possible. Konrad Weiß, of Alliance 90, who had taken part in the negotiations over the Unification Treaty as a representative of the future *Bundesländer* in the east, said in the final debate on the treaty in the Volkskammer: 'The shadow of the Federal Finance Minister was ever-present at the negotiating table.'[6]

The leader of the negotiations on questions of social policy on the Federal side was Bernhard Jagoda of the CDU, who had been a member of the Bundestag between 1980 and 1987 through the *Land* list for Hesse and had been his party's parliamentary spokesman on social policy from 1985. After narrowly failing to be re-elected to the Bundestag in January 1987, he had been appointed by Blüm—partly owing to the excessive workload that the latter was carrying as head of the CDU in North Rhine-Westphalia—to the newly created post of second permanent Staatsssekretär in the Federal Labour Ministry. He not only had Blüm's backing but also enjoyed high regard in the CDU/CSU in the Bundestag. He was supported, on the different topics of the negotiations, by the relevant senior officials in the Labour Ministry and other ministries. On the day of German unification, 3 October 1990, the Labour Ministry (following a decree issued by Staatssekretär Tegtmeier on 25 September 1990) established a branch in east Berlin headed by Ministerialdirektor Jung, who also retained his existing post as head of the Ministry's Department V (for health and health insurance).[7] This branch was initially housed in the GDR Labour Ministry in Karlhorst, but later relocated to the offices of the former Prime Minister of the GDR in the Klosterstraße in Berlin-Mitte. The branch reported directly to Staatssekretär Jagoda, and its specialist sections came under the supervision of the corresponding departments of the Federal Labour Ministry. Jung and his permanent deputy Martin Ammermüller exercised a general supervisory role and were responsible for coordination within the branch and for the branch's press and publicity activities.[8]

The branch came to employ between 90 and 100 officials, some 20 to 30 of them coming from Bonn. Eleven sections were set up in addition to the senior management. The existing senior posts in the GDR Ministry of Labour and Social Affairs—permanent Staatssekretäre and heads of departments and sub-departments—were dissolved, with effect from 3 October 1990. After that date the terms and conditions of employment of the occupants of these posts ceased to be valid, unless the posts were assigned to Federal Labour Ministry staff. As far as the other parts of the GDR Ministry were concerned, decisions whether to retain or dismiss personnel were deferred until 31 December 1990. Employees were assigned to the branch in Berlin and placed, where possible, in one of its sections irrespective of whether they were likely to be retained or not. In the long run, of the 203 members of staff of the Ministry of Labour and Social Affairs and the approximately 50 employed in the health insurance area of the GDR Ministry of Health, between 60 and 70 were retained. The other employees were to be offered employment opportunities in the field of social insurance within the new *Länder* until the end of 1990.[9]

10.3 THE GDR'S DELEGATION TO THE NEGOTIATIONS

Jagoda's chief negotiating partner on the GDR side was Alwin Ziel, Parlamentarischer Staatssekretär in the Ministry of Labour and Social Affairs headed by Regine Hildebrandt. Ziel had come to Mecklenburg from West Prussia as a refugee at the age of four. He trained at a college of education and became a teacher but, as a professed Christian, encountered difficulties and gave up his job, first working as a speech therapist and then qualifying in law through a distance-learning course with Humboldt University. In 1988 he went to west Germany to visit relatives and did not return, hoping that his family would be allowed to join him. They were prevented from doing so, however, and when his wife, a pharmacist, came under massive pressure from the Stasi and fell seriously ill, he went back to the GDR, where he spent a spell in prison and suffered discrimination as a 'traitor' or potential spy. In the autumn of 1989 he was active in the citizens' movements 'New Forum' and 'Democracy Now' and in December 1989 he joined the SDP, soon to become the SPD. There he soon reached a prominent position, partly thanks to his legal expertise. After the elections to the Volkskammer of 18 March 1990 he played an important role, as a party whip, in the formation of the governing coalition before being nominated as Parlamentarischer Staatssekretär. Within the east German SPD, Ziel was a supporter of the maintenance of the coalition and blamed the eventual collapse of the coalition in August 1990 on plotting at the SPD's Bonn headquarters and 'Lafontaine's stupid manoeuvring'.[10] In the negotiations with the Federal Republic he was a key figure, a sort of 'junior Krause'. He was, effectively, the SPD's leading agent within the GDR delegation. He had the backing of the SPD's parliamentary leader Richard Schröder, who was in close regular contact with de Maizière and often asked Ziel to accompany him to his discussions with the Prime Minister when problems between the SPD and the CDU—in particular, tensions between Krause and the Finance Minister, Romberg—needed to be resolved. Ziel's relations with Krause and, especially, with de Maizière were good. Schröder, the parliamentary leader, was more important to him than his minister, Hildebrandt, who regularly had to be told that her plans were not feasible, primarily on financial grounds.[11] Blüm and Hildebrandt, whose position in the eastern SPD was particularly powerful by virtue of her unusually great popularity, on the whole got on well together, since both were convinced that a social union was desirable and each recognized that the other was motivated by genuine social commitment. According to Blüm, Regine Hildebrandt—'the only woman who can speak without drawing breath'—was a rare example of a truly good person who stood up for the weak. He also believed, however, that she was 'swamped' by her good intentions and failed to see clearly what was politically achievable.[12]

In the GDR three ministries in particular were responsible for social policy: the Ministry of Labour and Social Affairs, the successor to the Modrow government's Ministry of Labour and Wages; the Ministry of Health, which was also responsible for health insurance,[13] with Jürgen Kleditzsch of the CDU at its head and Staatssekretär Dr Horst Schönfelder and Professor Hicke as its chief negotiators; and the Ministry for the Family and Women, headed by Christa Schmidt of the CDU, in which the Parlamentarische Staatssekretär Hans Geisler of the CDU was primarily responsible for the negotiations. In the Ministry of Labour and Social Affairs Ziel was supported, above all, by Ingolf Noack, who had been one of the deputies to the Minister of Labour and Wages, and the GDR's 'pensions Pope', Heinz Weiße. The officials who had been assigned to the Ministry by the Federal Labour Ministry did not themselves take part in the negotiations, nor were they informed by Bonn about the relevant bargaining positions being adopted by the Federal government.[14] Despite their conflicting interests and some initial wariness, Jagoda and Ziel soon developed a relationship based on mutual trust[15] and together had a significant share in deciding the details of the social union of the two Germanys.

Ziel and Hildebrandt were in very close contact with the west German Social Democrats. In particular, their contact man in Berlin, Dietrich Stobbe, advised them—in Ziel's words—'intensively, day and night', and, in a genuine partnership, showed great understanding for his east German colleagues who had grown up in such a different society.[16] Other contacts were Gerhard Jahn, a west German SPD parliamentary whip, and, on questions of social policy, Rudolf Dreßler and his staff.[17]

The GDR government's coalition agreement of 12 April 1990, which underlay the GDR's conduct of the negotiations on the State and Unification Treaties, was heavily influenced in its passages on social policy by advisers from the west. Dreßler drew Hildebrandt's attention to those points in the draft state treaty that were particularly debatable from both the SPD's and the GDR's point of view. The GDR's position was agreed in intensive discussions with western Social Democrats ahead of each of the negotiating rounds on social policy, the Social Democrats also making clear to Ziel which proposals they believed would be acceptable to Jagoda and which would come up against a brick wall.[18]

On many points the GDR delegation agreed with the leading figures in social policy in the Federal Republic: for example, on the adoption of freedom of association, free collective bargaining, and—apart from a few divergences over details—works constitution regulations and co-determination within enterprises, as well as on the principle of an earnings-indexed pension, the introduction of unemployment insurance, and a wide-ranging, flexible and active labour market policy. It was common ground, too, that there should be no reductions in social benefits and rights as the western welfare state was extended to the east. However, the GDR delegation was unsuccessful in its attempt to secure the permanent retention of other 'social achievements' of the GDR, though it did have important partial successes on the questions of the guaranteed maintenance of rights and entitlements and the granting of a social allowance in pensions insurance, as well as on the law on dismissal and on pre-pension benefit.

The GDR did not achieve its objective of a unified rather than multipartite health insurance system, nor did it manage to preserve ambulatories, polyclinics, and enterprise-based health care as central pillars of outpatient medical care alongside individual doctors' practices. The minister responsible, Jürgen Kleditzsch, who was under heavy pressure from the benefit providers' associations and health insurers in the Federal Republic, by and large accepted—unlike Regine Hildebrandt—the west German system of health care and the multipartite system of insurance as the model for the GDR. Any hopes that western Social Democratic ideas on the reform of the west German welfare state could first be implemented in the GDR, and then serve as precedents and inspirations for new regulations covering Germany as a whole, were unrealistic.

Although the leaders of the parliamentary parties in the GDR—Schröder especially—were regularly kept informed about the negotiations by de Maizière,[19] the Volkskammer was given little information in advance of the debate on ratification of the State Treaty and had little influence on the course of the negotiations. The government's secretiveness provoked a debate, initiated by the PDS, on 10 May 1990 on the 'state and contents' of the negotiations on the State Treaty. In the debate the CDU's Günther Krause was sharply criticized for his conduct of the negotiations, not only by the PDS but also by Alliance 90/The Greens and the SPD-backed Finance Minister Walter Romberg.[20] He defended himself on the grounds that so far there had been discussions only at the level of experts and Staatssekretäre and the government had not yet entered into political negotiations.[21] Alliance 90's motion of no confidence in Krause's conduct of the negotiations, in particular in the area of social policy,[22] was not put to a vote, as de Maizière argued that such a motion could be directed only against the Prime Minister, not against an individual whom the Prime Minister had appointed as Staatssekretär.[23]

As far as the Unification Treaty was concerned, the procedure the GDR would follow at the negotiations was decided, in accordance with de Maizière's recommendation, at the GDR Council of Ministers. The different government ministries would conduct negotiations exclusively in their respective areas of responsibility. Questions of fundamental principle would be dealt with by Günther Krause and the working group on 'German unity', which would also coordinate negotiations on matters transcending ministerial boundaries. It was important, de Maizière said, to ensure that conflicting positions on the Federal Republic side were not imported into the GDR and that forty-year-old battles between different political forces in the west were not fought out in the Unification Treaty. The basis of the negotiations should be the coalition agreement. The negotiations should be conducted, 'not by parties, but by the government': there should be no 'party-political declarations *within the negotiations*' or public declarations of divergent opinions by members of the government. The negotiators should be ready to compromise and should ignore the interests of party activists, for the sake of achieving the necessary two-thirds majority in parliament. The Prime Minister also emphasized strongly that he had ultimate overall authority (*Richtlinienkompetenz*) over general matters of policy regarding the future of Germany.[24]

In addition to Krause and his staff and the representatives of government ministries, members of the Volkskammer also took part in the negotiations on the Unification Treaty on the GDR side, as 'representatives of the future *Länder*'.[25] Naturally, they were unable to exert nearly as much influence over the negotiations as the representatives of the west German *Bundesländer*, which could consult their staffs of experts, their many long-standing contacts in the political parties, and, in particular, the Bundesrat, which had to agree to the treaty.

De Maizière's hope that the GDR would be able to sort out its problems on its own before going on to forge unity with the Federal Republic as an equal partner[26] was illusory. The weaknesses of the GDR's position were that it had no alternative other than accession to the Federal Republic, given the pressure of expectations on the part of its citizens, that its process of internal break-up could not be halted, and that the GDR was becoming ever more dependent on the Federal Republic in terms both of finance and of personnel—for example, in the building-up of an administrative system for employment to introduce unemployment insurance and an active labour market policy, and of other branches of social insurance. The collapse of the coalition following the dismissal and resignation of the SPD ministers in the middle of August 1990, shortly before the negotiations were concluded, further weakened the government's position. On the other hand, we should not understate the degree of freedom of action that the GDR had, and the influence it was able to bring to bear, especially in the negotiations over the State Treaty on monetary union. In an election year the interests of the east Germans, as potential voters who might decisively affect the make-up of the parties in the Bundestag and Bundesrat, could not be ignored. Clearly, too, German unification would be a success in the long run only if the east Germans were to become emotionally committed to the new state.

The lack of experts on the east German side was mitigated in part by the contribution of specialists from west Germany. Although the GDR experts had inside knowledge of the particular circumstances in the east, too little use was made of them.[27] The fact that there was a partial overlap of interests with political and administrative forces in the west, particularly with the Social Democrats but also with the Federal Ministry of Labour, did something to bolster the GDR's position.

The GDR, then, played an important part in ensuring that no large-scale dismantling of social benefits and social protection for employees occurred and that the specific social interests of the GDR's citizens were taken into account in a series of transitional regulations. Whatever one's judgement concerning the economic consequences of these negotiating successes of the GDR, Alwin Ziel was correct to say that the delegation that negotiated the State Treaty 'did its utmost to represent the interests of the citizens of the GDR' and, overall, secured an improvement of their social position.[28] The same was true of the Unification Treaty.

10.4 THE ROLES OF THE BUNDESTAG, THE COALITION PARTIES, AND THE SOCIAL DEMOCRATIC OPPOSITION

The roles of the Bundestag and the western parties in the creation of the social union were, like the role of the Volkskammer, marginal, although particular committees of the Bundestag were kept broadly informed about the state of the negotiations from time to time. The first, and only, actual debate in the Bundestag on the preparation of the State Treaty, the ratification of which was naturally a matter of thoroughgoing deliberation in parliament, took place on 27 April 1990. Rudolf Seiters, the Chancellery Minister, defended the Federal government against the charge that the *Länder* had been insufficiently involved, and detailed some of the key features of the Federal Republic's proposals, in particular the conversion of wages and salaries at the ratio of 1:1, the raising of the level of pensions to 70 per cent of net employment income, the offer of start-up funding for pensions and unemployment insurance, and support for the GDR in the implementation of an active labour market policy in which the main emphasis would be on professional qualifications and job creation schemes.[29] Count Lambsdorff, speaking for the FDP, maintained that the Federal government's proposals had gone 'to the limit of what [was] economically possible and economically defensible'. He warned against collective agreements that took no account of the specific situations of the different branches of the GDR economy and GDR regions and enterprises, and argued, against de Maizière, that subsidies on energy and housing should be dismantled and that west Germans and foreigners should be allowed to acquire land and property in the east.[30]

For the Social Democratic opposition, the deputy parliamentary leader Herta Däubler-Gmelin—standing in for Oskar Lafontaine, who had been severely injured in an assassination attempt—complained that the costs of unification had not been spelled out clearly, that the proposed social union was not properly underpinned, and that there was a danger that a socially divided Germany would be created. Unity, moreover, was being treated too much as the private business of the Chancellor and the CDU/CSU and not as the business of the German people as a whole. She reiterated the offer of close cooperation with the government that had been made by the leader of the SPD, Hans-Jochen Vogel, in the autumn of 1989[31] and restated the party's proposal, made on 14 February 1990 and repeated on 23 April, that a joint advisory committee should be formed consisting of eleven members each of the Bundestag and the Bundesrat 'to ensure the participation of parliament in the process of German unification'.[32] Rudolf Dreßler, the SPD's spokesman on social policy, maintained that the proposed dismantling of subsidies, without compensatory funding, and the raising of social insurance contributions would lead to a lowering of average net incomes by a quarter, from 960 to 720 GDR marks per month. He argued for the retention of minimum pensions in the GDR, the initial development of a unified, rather than multipartite, system of health insurance, and a reorganized common health service covering the whole of Germany in which the failings and shortcomings of the Federal Republic's system would be rectified. He warned against the danger that the 'GDR [might] be misused as a lever for continuing the policy of dismantling the welfare state in the Federal Republic'.[33] His fear that insurance contributors in the Federal Republic would be called on to provide financial support to pensions insurance in the GDR was countered by Blüm, who stated categorically that 'German unity should not be financed out of the pension fund.... While wage differentials remain as they are at present, we cannot have a unified pension fund.... No pensioner here need fear that a single mark of their pension is under threat from German unity.'[34] In the event, Blüm was not able to deliver on these promises.

A proposal that a joint Bundestag and Bundesrat committee should be set up, giving the opposition a considerably stronger role, was rejected by the coalition.[35] Instead, a 'German unity committee' of the Bundestag, comprising 39 members, was formed on 11 May 1990, a few days before negotiations on the State Treaty were concluded. This committee, in a total of twenty sittings up to 19 September 1990, coordinated the deliberations of the different committees on ratification of the State and Unification Treaties and discussed questions concerning relations between the two Germanys, partly in joint sessions with a parallel committee of the Volkskammer.[36] The committee did not take part in the negotiations themselves, and it exerted no influence on the State Treaty and only an indirect and marginal influence on the Unification Treaty.

The CDU/CSU parliamentary party was likewise not included in the decision-making process and was not kept closely informed about the negotiations. At a meeting of the parliamentary leadership on 5 February a question about the possible involvement of the party in the decision-making process received the answer that the Federal government had to take the lead in the negotiations.[37] Admittedly, a week later, Seiters, the Chancellery Minister, stated that representatives of the CDU/CSU—as well as other politicians with relevant expertise—should participate in the working groups of the 'German unity' cabinet committee and that the parliamentary party should be consulted over the selection of members.[38] In practice, however, the negotiations bypassed both the CDU/CSU parliamentary party and its parliamentary leadership, prompting the party's chairman, Alfred Dregger, to call on 26 March for better cooperation between the government 'German unity' committee and the parliamentarians. In particular, Dregger said, the government's working groups should work together with the CDU/CSU parliamentary experts, and the parliamentary leadership should be kept informed.[39] A day later, at the CDU/CSU working group on labour and social affairs, Blüm reported on preparations for the negotiations with the GDR and stressed that although a social union was being offered to the GDR by the Federal Republic, the main legislative measures necessary for its implementation would have to be decided by the GDR itself. A meeting of the employees' group of the CDU/CSU, held on the same day, concluded that a conversion rate of 1:1 for wages and pensions and an increase in net benchmark pensions to 70 per cent of net employment income—in line with the Labour Ministry's policy—were necessary.[40] On 23 April the Finance Minister, Waigel, gave the CDU/CSU parliamentary leadership[41] a detailed explanation of the draft treaty that would be put to the GDR, and on 24 April he gave a similar account to the parliamentary party as a whole. He asked the members to appreciate, however, that it had 'naturally not been possible in recent days and weeks to deal with each draft of a treaty of this sort in, as it were, a parliamentary-party or a parliamentary way', since issues had to be resolved within the government. Ratification would be 'parliament's great moment', but the preliminary work 'really [had] to be the ministries' job'.[42] The CDU/CSU members of the Bundestag subsequently received detailed information about the state of the negotiations on 8 May, with reports by the Chancellery Minister, Seiters, and the leader of the negotiations for the Federal government, Hans Tietmeyer. The text of Tietmeyer's address, however, which referred to the questions that were still a matter of disagreement with the GDR, was deliberately not published, and the parliamentarians were warned not to reach any kind of firm position, as the negotiations were not yet at an end.[43]

A week later, on 15 May 1990, Seiters reported on the negotiations of the preceding days. At the meeting the CDU/CSU whip Friedrich Bohl referred to the fact that in coalition circles once again 'the question has been discussed. . . whether everything has to be put into this State Treaty, including whatever amendments of Federal laws will have to be made, or whether these will be separated out: in other words, whether one part will be the State Treaty and the other the amendments of Federal laws'. It had been decided to take the first route, 'because a separation would naturally have meant that there was a quite normal legislative procedure, with the possibility of holding hearings and, of course, making changes in the course of the legislative process. That way we would certainly never have been able to keep to the timetable. *Everything will therefore be in a single law, and all that will be left to do is to say Yes or No.*'[44] Finally, at a special meeting on 18 May, a few hours before the solemn signing of the treaty, the CDU/CSU parliamentary party gave the document its unanimous support (save for the abstention of Herbert Czaja).[45] The CDU/CSU parliamentary party also played no significant role in the subsequent ratification process.

The CDU/CSU members of the Bundestag were similarly kept out of the negotiations over the Unification Treaty. Debate centred on the protection of the life of the unborn child, on the final confirmation that the territories east of the Oder–Neiße line had been lost, and on the question whether to accept that the expropriations carried out under occupation law between 1945 and 1949 would not be reversed; there was no real discussion of the treaty's main contents.[46] Czaja objected to the fact that assent to the treaty was being linked to assent to several constitutional amendments. At a meeting of the parliamentary leadership on 3 September 1990 Schäuble, the chief negotiator on the Federal Republic side, countered by pointing out that the majority had accepted the 'inseparable character of the arrangements' and hence also the principle of a single vote.[47] Members were accordingly deprived of the opportunity of rejecting detailed aspects of the treaty without calling the treaty *per se* into question.

Leading figures in the coalition parties—particularly the chairmen of the parliamentary parties and of the parties at large—were kept much more fully informed and were also consulted ahead of some, though not all, crucial decisions.[48] Experts on particular areas of policy within the coalition parties were also given information concerning their fields. However, apart from the inter-ministerial and coalition working group formed on 23 January 1990, under Horst Seehofer, to review policy on benefits to Germans arriving in the Federal Republic from east Germany or elsewhere,[49] no coalition working group shadowed the treaty negotiations with the GDR. The coalition parties had agreed in principle not to indulge in 'cherry-picking', i.e. fastening on issues that were in their own particular interest.[50] Those points regarding the State Treaty that were of special importance for the FDP, such as the rapid introduction of multipartite systems of social and health insurance and the exclusion of compulsory social insurance for the self-employed, were communicated for consideration to both Tietmeyer and Jagoda by Dieter-Julius Cronenberg, the FDP spokesman on social policy, 'at the Chancellor's request'.[51]

Essentially, however, the heads of the coalition and the coalition parties merely gave their blessing to conclusions that had been reached at executive level. Likewise, the cabinet—as against the cabinet committee on 'German unity', and its working groups, which took part in the preparations for the negotiations—in effect exercised only a notarial function, formally confirming decisions that had been taken elsewhere. This, admittedly, was consistent with Helmut Kohl's governing style generally.[52]

The Social Democratic opposition was not included in the government's decision-making over policy on the future of Germany, nor in the negotiations with the GDR. Vogel's proposal that there should be broad cooperation among the various political and social forces during the forging of German unity—contrary to Lafontaine's tactic of polarization—was not taken up by the government. It is true that Blüm, who had placed Social Democrats in leading positions in his ministry—notably the permanent Staatssekretär Werner Tegtmeier and the sub-departmental heads Ministerialdirigent Peter Rosenberg and Ministerialdirigent Klaus Achenbach—was in favour of seeking broad-based political and social support for unification policy. In his note to the Federal Chancellor of 12 December 1989, for example, he suggested that the coalition should discuss 'whether and how—as was done with the reform of statutory pensions insurance—consensus with the opposition and the main social groups can be found'.[53] Similarly, a working paper of the Federal Labour Ministry of 9 January 1990 argued that since it was going to be 'very difficult to find solutions for the great problems that lie ahead' and, 'given the attitudes of citizens and interest groups, to implement them and win acceptance for them', it would be reasonable to 'strive to achieve consensus among all the main political and social groups'.[54] On the other hand, the proposals by Blüm and the Labour Ministry that the Social Democrats should be brought in early on during the shaping of the unification process were not adopted.

Nevertheless, although the west German Social Democrats did not take part directly in the decision-making that preceded the signing of the State Treaty, they did exert considerable indirect influence on the discussions, particularly as regards questions of social policy, through their sister party in the GDR. Their hope was that they would be able to use regulations affecting the east as a means of winning support for their own social policy objectives in the west. In this, they had the backing of the German Trade Union Federation and individual trade unions in the Federal Republic. Although the social policy objectives of the west and east German Social Democrats were largely identical, there was an important difference (as has been mentioned earlier)[55] in the two parties' tactics, since the east German Social Democrats, as members of the governing coalition, had to reach their decision whether to accept or reject the State Treaty *before* it was signed, whereas the west German SPD did not need to do so until the time of ratification.

In the negotiations on the Unification Treaty, the ideas of the west German Social Democrats came into play not only through their sister party in the east but also, and more significantly, through the Social Democrat-led *Länder* in the west. The problem the Social Democrats faced here was clearly outlined in a document on the draft of the Unification Treaty prepared by the party's working group on social policy. It was understandable from the GDR's point of view, the document said, that the GDR was trying to retain its 'superior' legislation in some fields, 'at least on a transitional basis, as special legislation for the territory of the GDR after unification', while 'at the same time adopting Federal law, where it is superior in material terms. . . immediately after unification'. It was not the SPD's job to 'call for a deterioration in social security in the GDR', but there would be a significant threat to the party's legitimacy—'particularly among financially less well-off population groups in the Federal Republic'—if it were to support demands, essentially, for an improvement in the position of GDR citizens, instead of calling for the same legislation for both parts of the country where circumstances were the same.[56] The party, however, judged—correctly—that the Federal government was not fundamentally willing to work out new common positions with the GDR.[57] The Social Democrat *Bundesländer*, likewise, were primarily concerned to protect their specific *Land* interests and were not prepared to share in the costs of securing improvements in the situation of the citizens of the GDR. Vogel's claim, in the debate on the ratification of the State Treaty, that it was only through the joint efforts of the west and east German Social Democrats that the monetary union also became a social union[58] is not sustainable, in view of the early and massive commitment shown by Blüm and the Labour Ministry. It is true, however, that the attitude of the SPD, the trade unions, and the GDR strengthened the Labour Ministry's hand *vis-à-vis* the Finance and Economics Ministries and was an important factor in ensuring that attempts to extend only a watered-down version of the west German welfare state to the GDR had no chance of succeeding. On the other hand, the SPD's influence was not powerful enough to translate the party's own ideas on social policy into reality through the indirect GDR route.

Politically speaking, the SPD was hampered by its internal differences over the question of the future of Germany, which left it unable to adopt a unified strategy that could be clearly communicated to the people. Underlying these differences was a fundamental disagreement whether the party should follow a cooperative or a confrontational policy of opposition: the party's candidate for the chancellorship, Lafontaine, favoured a policy of confrontation, while the honorary chairman, Willy Brandt, and (with some differences of nuance) the chairman of the party in the country and the Bundestag, Hans-Jochen Vogel, were committed to a cooperative approach. The divergence over strategy also sprang, particularly during the period up to the ratification of the State Treaty on monetary union, from a division over policy about the future of Germany as such. Whereas Brandt, along with a majority of the parliamentary party, believed that the rapid establishment of German unity would be the realization of a historic objective of the Social Democrats, Lafontaine was more concerned about social unity and attacked the Federal government's decision to accelerate the process of unification on the grounds that it put social unity at risk. On the other hand, after the forging of monetary union had signalled that unification was inevitable and that a confrontational approach no longer had any purpose, Lafontaine then gave the impression, through his gloomy prognoses of the economic and social consequences of unification, that German unity itself was not close to his heart and should not be a priority, either, for the party that he would be representing as candidate for the chancellorship in the Bundestag elections.

By and large, the strategy of cooperation was supported by the older and middle generations in the Social Democratic Party, and by the party's right wing and centre. Younger Social Democrats, whose attitudes had been shaped by the unrest of 1968 and the following years, were more inclined to favour confrontation. Differences also manifested themselves among the party's politicians. Whereas an overwhelming majority of members of the parliamentary party backed a cooperative strategy, the Social Democrat Prime Ministers in the *Bundesländer*, whose states made up a majority in the Bundesrat between May and October 1990, were (apart from Schröder, of Lower Saxony, and Lafontaine, of the Saarland, who opposed the State Treaty) concerned first and foremost to defend the *Länder's* interests, while accepting the State Treaty in broad terms. The eastern SPD, as a junior partner to the CDU in the de Maizière government until the break-up of the coalition on 19 August 1990, pursued a largely cooperative strategy, tempered by occasional disagreements with the policy of the Federal government, though at the same time it exerted massive pressure on behalf of the social interests of the citizens of the GDR.

The executive of the SPD in west Germany adopted an intermediate position. Vogel, the party chairman, who was inclined to favour a cooperative strategy, nevertheless tried to stop Lafontaine from standing down as candidate for chancellor. Lafontaine, though he prevented the party from committing itself unequivocally to a cooperative strategy, was unable, as candidate for chancellor, to establish his authority within the party over matters of general policy. The result was that the Social Democratic Party was in a state of internal stalemate on a crucial question in German politics and presented a confused, and confusing, image to the German public.[59] This undoubtedly contributed significantly to its defeat in the Bundestag elections in December 1990.

10.5 THE *BUNDESLÄNDER*

The *Länder* of the Federal Republic came under heavy pressure during the weeks and months after the Wall was opened and large numbers of people flooded into the country from the east, and it was inevitable that they would be severely affected by the financial repercussions of any process of unification. All the same, they did not take part in the decision-making that led to the offer of monetary union, the preparation of the draft of the State Treaty, or the negotiations on the State Treaty with the GDR, nor were they kept well informed about any of these developments.

Just two days after the meeting between Modrow and Kohl in Dresden on 21 December 1989, the conference of *Bundesländer* Prime Ministers demanded that the *Länder* should participate 'fully' in the process by virtue of 'their constitutional rights'.[60] The *Länder* based this demand on a written agreement of 17 December 1987 between the Federal government and the *Länder* 'on the participation of the *Länder* in agreements between the Federal Republic of

Germany and the German Democratic Republic'. This document had laid down that the *Länder* should be kept fully informed, from the earliest possible stage, about all negotiations that might affect their interests, that their interests should be taken into account, and that their consent should be obtained with regard to all questions that touched on the exclusive jurisdiction of the *Länder* and that imposed obligations on either the Federal government or the *Länder*.[61]

The *Land* that took the lead in the attempts that were made to translate this agreement into practice and enable the *Länder* to play a significant role in the unification process through an enhancement of their rights of participation was North Rhine-Westphalia, governed by the Social Democrats, which currently chaired the conference of *Land* Prime Ministers. The chief of the state chancellery of North Rhine-Westphalia, Staatssekretär Wolfgang Clement (who became a minister in June 1990), was selected as spokesman for the interests of the *Länder*, and of those led by the Social Democrats in particular.

On 25 January 1990 Clement informed the chief of the Federal Chancellery, Seiters, of the outcome of a preliminary discussion by the *Länder*, at which the latter, going beyond the terms of the agreement of 17 December 1987, had demanded that they should take part, with four representatives, in any forthcoming treaty negotiations with the GDR. In addition, the heads of the state and senate chancelleries in the *Länder* would be at the Federal government's disposal as a permanent committee for discussing questions concerning the 'contractual community' envisaged by the talks between Modrow and Kohl in December 1989. Clement also gave notice that the *Länder* should be sent all documents relating to treaties with the GDR, as well as treaty drafts themselves.[62]

The Federal government, however, rejected this call for close collaboration. At a meeting between Seiters and the chiefs of the state and senate chancelleries on 30 January 1990, all that was agreed was that the *Länder* should participate on committees dealing with matters in which their interests were affected. They should also be informed and consulted at the monthly meetings between the head of the Federal Chancellery and the heads of the state and senate chancelleries; these meetings should also serve to coordinate the activities of the Federal government and the *Länder vis-à-vis* the GDR. Whether or not the *Länder* should take part in talks with the GDR should be decided flexibly on a case-to-case basis.[63] The Federal government was not prepared to accept, though, that the *Länder* had the right to a say over the conduct of the negotiations or that decisions should be conditional on their agreement. In a memorandum, the Federal Ministry for Internal German Relations rejected the constitutional argument of the *Länder* that the establishment of a 'contractual community' with the GDR would affect the federal structure of the Federal Republic and therefore require the agreement of the *Länder*. The Ministry maintained that the representation of the Federal Republic in its external relations was a matter solely for the Federal government, and it opposed the demand that the rights of the *Länder* under the terms of the agreement of 17 December 1987 should be enhanced.[64] Accordingly, when Clement, in a letter of 6 February 1990, repeated the call that the *Länder* be allowed to participate in work on the 'contractual community' with the GDR,[65] the Federal government again gave a guarded response, ruling out any alteration to the 1987 agreement, though it did state that it was willing to treat flexibly the question of participation by representatives of the *Länder* within the negotiating delegation.[66] An arrangement on these lines regarding the participation of the *Länder* in the discussions and negotiations with the GDR was finally reached at a meeting between the Federal Chancellor and the heads of government of the *Länder* on 15 February 1990.[67] Afterwards Seiters said specifically that the *Länder* would 'not be involved in the negotiations that had now begun with the GDR over a monetary union. . . That did not affect the constitutional position. They would, however, be brought in if their financial sovereignty was involved.'[68]

The proposal that a joint committee of the Bundesrat and the Bundestag should be formed to enable parliament to take part in the unification process was unequivocally rejected, as was a wider proposal that a joint committee and the conference of *Länder* Prime Ministers should become interlocutors with the GDR for developing suggestions regarding the future structure of Germany.[69] Repeated subsequent efforts by the *Länder*[70] to be included in the ongoing negotiations with the GDR also failed, since in the Federal government's view no matters affecting their spheres of competence were at stake.[71] The assurance that was eventually given, namely that two representatives of the *Länder* would be brought into the negotiations once discussions were being conducted on a political level,[72] was effectively meaningless—except with reference to financial questions—since the negotiations by the experts were not concluded until 13 May and the draft based on them was not made known to the *Länder* until 14 May, four days before the State Treaty was signed. In the event, the representatives of the *Länder* did not play a real part in the discussions on monetary, economic, and social union at any stage.[73]

The financial interests of the *Länder* were, however, taken very fully into account in the talks between the Federal Chancellor and the *Länder* Prime Ministers on the creation of the 'German Unity Fund' on 16 May 1990,[74] and this helped secure the support of the *Länder* for the State Treaty in the Bundesrat.

The weakness of the *Länder* during the negotiations on the State Treaty was due in part to the fact that not even the SPD-led *Länder* were able to work out an agreed approach to the contents of the treaty. This is very clear in respect of social policy. Statements such as that by the Social Democrat Berlin deputy mayor and senator for health and social protection, Ingrid Stahmer, that 'something [could] be learned' from the GDR in the field of social policy, were few and far between. Stahmer had in mind a system of basic protection with regard to care of the elderly, the amalgamation of pensions insurance for blue- and white-collar workers, organizational reform to rectify the shortcomings in the existing multipartite system of health insurance, a strengthening of preventive medicine, closer coordination of in- and outpatient medical care, and improved protection for citizens in need of nursing care. Her plan to develop a social policy lobby led by the *Länder* came to nothing, however.[75]

When the *Land* ministers and senators for employment and social security were finally informed by Jagoda, at the Federal Labour Ministry on 2 May, about the state of the talks on the social union, they complained unanimously that the *Länder* had been insufficiently involved in both the preparation of the draft and the negotiations, and warned against the push towards centralization. It was also evident from the discussion that some of those present hoped that 'changes within the Federal Republic (notably, organizational reforms of health and pensions insurance) could be initiated through the GDR route'. The representatives of the Labour Ministry, however, emphasized that it was not politically practicable to 'overburden the process of German unification, which was difficult enough in any case, with a bid to alter [the] prevailing legal order' in the Federal Republic 'through the GDR route'.[76]

Unhappiness at the exclusion of the *Länder* from the negotiations over the State Treaty on monetary union and the wider problems concerning the future of Germany was not confined to the SPD-led *Länder*. On 10 April 1990 the Prime Minister of Bavaria, Max Streibl, wrote to Kohl that he was very worried that 'in view of the pressing material problems in economic and social policy, the basic need to create a federal state structure [was] being ignored'. He urged that the five original *Länder* in the GDR be re-established as soon as possible—in part, in order to remove officials in the existing GDR regions who did not have democratic legitimacy—and that the optimal re-drawing of the boundaries of the eastern *Länder* be deferred till later.[77]

In the case of the Unification Treaty the position of the *Länder* was very much stronger. It was clear from the start that the structure of the future German federal state would be a crucial question, as would the new state's financial constitution. The *Länder* led by the Social Democrats had meanwhile acquired a majority in the Bundesrat, which, along with the Bundestag, was required to assent to the treaty by a two-thirds majority in view of the constitutional amendments involved. In addition, at the meeting of 16 May 1990 Kohl had promised the *Länder* (which, when they later supported the State Treaty in the Bundesrat on 22 June 1990, were nevertheless sharply critical of the fact that they had not been included in the treaty negotiations)[78] that with the Unification Treaty negotiations they would be participants.[79] In the event the *Länder* were included in the Federal negotiating delegation in the form of six representatives, from North Rhine-Westphalia, Hamburg, Lower Saxony, Bavaria, Baden-Württemberg, and Berlin, each of whom was also able to nominate a colleague in support. The other *Bundesländer* were each to have one civil servant with observer status. The specialist talks between the different government ministries would be attended by at least two *Länder* representatives, who would also take part in the negotiations if matters affecting the interests of individual *Länder* were under discussion.[80] Leadership of the negotiations was unambiguously in the hands of Schäuble, the Interior Minister, on the Federal side and Günther Krause on the GDR side. Wolfgang Clement acted as spokesman for the *Bundesländer* and mainly voiced the interests of the SPD-led *Länder* in the negotiations. A further key role was played by Reinhold Kopp, the chief of the state chancellery of the Saarland, as the representative of the Social Democratic candidate for Federal chancellor, Oskar Lafontaine.[81] The negotiations were effectively three-way, between the *Länder*—through which route the Social Democrat opposition was also brought in—the Federal government, and the GDR, the position of the latter being significantly weakened after the departure of the Social Democrats from the governing coalition in August 1990.

The role of the *Länder* in the negotiations need not be described in detail here,[82] particularly since questions of social policy were only a subsidiary part of their contribution. The *Länder* were primarily concerned to block any centralization of the federal order in a united Germany, and unanimously adopted 'benchmark points' to this effect on 5 July 1990.[83] The main issues in which they were interested were financial structure, the allocation of votes in the Bundesrat, the location of the seat of government, the re-federalization of legislation, the possibility of re-drawing the boundaries of the eastern *Länder*, the scope of the constitutional amendments, and the question whether there should be a referendum on a possible new joint constitution founded on the Basic Law. The SPD-led *Länder* did try to take up the GDR's demand that some of the latter's 'social achievements' should be preserved, but they did so without any great energy, and the GDR policies were in any case somewhat at odds with 'sober budgetary considerations' which, in the judgement of Konrad Weiß of Alliance 90, 'always took priority over the ideas of unity', including for the *Länder*.[84] As has already been mentioned,[85] in the final phase of the negotiations the Social Democrats pressed their views and interests directly in talks between their leaders and the Federal Chancellor on 26 August 1990 and in the cross-party working groups set up on the basis of these talks. Wolfgang Clement was again in charge of coordinating the SPD side, while the parliamentary party was now represented directly in the working groups.[86]

Wolfgang Jäger, in his book on 'the ending of the division of Germany', characterized the genesis of the Unification Treaty as a 'paradigm case of the process of the negotiation of democratic consent that dominated the sphere of domestic politics in the Federal Republic of Germany, particularly during the 1980s and after reunification'. 'The parties of the governing coalition, the government ministries, the opposition in the Bundestag, and the *Länder* governments—which differ among themselves in terms not only of parties but of regional interests—reach consensus through a tough process of bargaining.'[87] This description is certainly accurate in the case of the Unification Treaty, inasmuch as the political institutions, and the political forces underlying them, were more heavily involved than they were either during the first phases of inter-German relations after the fall of the Wall or during work on the State Treaty on monetary, economic, and social union, when the government and administration played the dominant role. It understates, however, the part that was played by the GDR, which was a serious partner in the negotiations, at least until the middle of August 1990, and, above all, that played by the Federal government and the ministerial bureaucracy on the western side.

The coalition parties and the Bundestag had no substantial influence on the negotiations. The large organizations of the social interest groups were, as we shall see, more or less ignored in the decision-making process, though they did play an important role in the extension of the west German health care system to the GDR. The Social Democratic opposition, through the *Länder*, had only a limited influence on the treaties; certainly, it would have been impossible in an election year to persuade the population in either the west or the east that the treaties should be rejected. The *Länder* successfully protected their own immediate interests, particularly on matters of finance, by ensuring that the costs of unity were borne overwhelmingly by the Federal government while at the same time resisting tendencies towards centralization. On other questions, however, they remained in the background.

The position is particularly clear with regard to all questions of social policy, where the differing views of the Federal Ministries of Finance and Labour and of the GDR—which latter, in turn, were largely shaped by the east German Social Democrats—had to be reconciled. In this process it was the experts within the ministerial bureaucracy who, in the final analysis, determined what measures and deadlines were required, so that a great mass of Federal laws and regulations could be extended to the former GDR, and what parts of GDR legislation should remain, at least temporarily, in force. Their role, thanks to their matchless skill in these specialist fields, was crucial. The part played by the executive was not as great with the Unification Treaty as it had been with the State Treaty, but it was still the dominant one.

10.6 THE ROLE OF THE MAJOR SOCIAL FORCES AND THEIR ORGANIZATIONS

The big organizations of the social partners—the trade unions and the employers' organizations—were not included in the central processes of decision-making on relations between the two Germanys, in the activities of the inter-German working groups that were set up from late 1989 and early 1990 onwards, or in the preparations for the State and Unification Treaties, the treaty negotiations, and the processes of ratification. Exceptionally, however, a working group made up of representatives of the National Union of German Employers' Associations, the German Trade Union Federation, the German White-Collar Workers' Trade Union, and the Federal Ministry of Labour was set up on 18 January 1990. This group, and its sub-groups, met on several occasions and, in addition to exchanging information, it discussed, in particular, the problems that were being caused by the large number of new arrivals in west Germany from the east. The trade unions were at first mainly concerned to ensure that the new arrivals' lack of awareness about their rights was not exploited by employers seeking to circumvent collective agreements. Later, questions of employment law, social insurance, the implementation of the State Treaty, and preparatory work on the Unification Treaty came under the group's purview, and there were exchanges of information about the development of trade unions and employers' organizations and the state of collective negotiations in the GDR.

With regard to the Unification Treaty, the National Union of German Employers' Associations and the German White-Collar Workers' Trade Union favoured the wide-scale extension of Federal Republic law to the GDR, while the German Trade Union Federation was looking for a detailed study that would spell out 'which useful provisions of both old and new GDR law and of Federal Republic law would need to underlie the transitional legislation'.[88]

There was a wide divergence in the trade unions' initial responses to the Federal government's offer of monetary union. The economics department at the headquarters of the Metal Workers' Union was fiercely critical of the offer, describing it as 'dangerous actionism' and 'a scenario for economic and social destabilization devised by radical believers in the miracle powers of market forces'; they urged mass resistance to the government's policy.[89] An analysis by the social policy department of the German Trade Union Federation, on the other hand, concluded that monetary reform was inevitable and imminent and that the DGB should now call for 'massive accompanying employment and social protection measures'.[90]

On 20 February an 'information exchange' took place at the Federal Chancellery between Kohl and leading representatives of business and the trade unions, at which both latter groups signalled their basic support for the government's unification policy. Tyll Necker, the president of the Federal Association of German Industry, voiced opposition to project-linked emergency aid, large-scale financial support to consumers, and tax increases, and called, in particular, for the establishment of a market-based framework and support for private investment to build up the GDR economy.[91] The head of the Trade Union Federation, Ernst Breit, explicitly backed a rapid move to German unity and welcomed the offer of monetary union and an economic community, but also warned against the danger of mass unemployment, at least in the short term, and the serious social problems that would follow in its train. His call for 15,000 million DM in emergency aid for the GDR echoed that of Modrow but was rejected by Kohl and the business representatives. Nor was there support for Breit's suggestion that an 'All-German Table' (obviously modelled on the 'Round Tables' in the GDR) should be established to facilitate regular discussions.[92]

The first official statement by the German Trade Union Federation's national committee on German unity, issued on 7 March, emphasized the importance of ensuring that the German unification process was incorporated within the wider process of European unification, and also called for unconditional recognition of the western border of Poland. The ending of the division of Germany, the statement said, would create the opportunity to 'bring into line, in the light of altered circumstances, the basic principles of the economic and social policy structures that had evolved historically in the two German states'. The Federation had in mind, in particular, a ban on lockouts and the establishment of comprehensive rights of co-determination. The statement proposed a conversion ratio of 1:1 for GDR wage and salary earners and pensioners and compensation for the dismantling of price subsidies 'through state income transfers such as housing and child benefit'.[93]

Two days later, in a joint statement, the German Trade Union Federation and the National Union of German Employers' Associations welcomed the offer of economic unity and monetary union between the two German states as an important step towards political unity. The new economic order in the GDR, the statement said, would have to be backed up by measures of social protection, although 'alignment with the social protection standards of the Federal Republic would be reached only in stages' and the disparities in wage levels would be evened out only through projected economic growth and improvements in productivity. The statement called for financial support from the Federal government and the *Länder* to improve infrastructure and the environment, Federal start-up finance for unemployment insurance, extensive provision of labour market services and support facilities, the creation of a unified system of social insurance based on contributions and earnings, a gradual improvement in the living standards of pensioners, the introduction of co-determination in firms and enterprises, and private and public investment to create new jobs. The unions and employers concluded by appealing to the people of the GDR to stay in their country, especially as 'the capacity of the Federal Republic to receive new arrivals is virtually exhausted'.[94]

It is possible that part of the reason why the position of the Trade Union Federation became closer to that of the employers was that the unions were fearful that a 'cut-price' social policy would be introduced in the GDR. The unions obviously had accurate information that the Federal Finance and Economics Ministries wanted, in opposition to the Labour Ministry, to extend an attenuated version of the social-policy order of the Federal Republic to the GDR. The files of the Trade Union Federation include a note that 'great effort [had been] needed within the Federal government. . . to secure the idea of the *social union* as a further goal of policy on the future of Germany' and that the Federal Chancellor had played a 'good role' in the process. At the instigation of a senior official in the Federal Chancellery[95] the head of the Trade Union Federation's liaison office in Bonn, Günther Horzetzky (later Staatssekretär in the Federal Labour Ministry during the Grand Coalition of 2005–9), put forward the proposal that there should be confidential talks between the Federation's chairman, Breit, and other trade union leaders and the Federal Chancellor. The unions should provide urgently needed public support for the 'internal government negotiating position' that was committed to social policy—a clear reference to the position of the Labour Ministry—and seek to prevent low wages from being used as the main incentive for the transfer of private capital, which would cause unification to work to the disadvantage of 'ordinary people'. This initiative was described, by analogy with the alliance between Chancellor Adenauer and the trade union leader Hans Böckler in the early years of the Federal Republic,[96] as presenting a 'historic opportunity'.[97] However, although the trade unions nominated their representatives on 17 March—Ernst Breit, Monika Wulff-Matthies, Franz Steinkühler, Hermann Rappe, Heinz-Werner Meyer, and Gerd Muhr[98]—the projected meeting did not take place, probably owing to the change in the political situation that followed the Volkskammer elections of 18 March and the wage negotiations that were taking place.

The trade unions' hopes that they would be able to exert greater influence over the Chancellor and play a significant role in the unification process were not fulfilled. This was partly due, also, to the discrediting and disintegration of the Free German Trade Union Federation in east Germany—which had been closely allied to the old regime and with which the west German Federation, after several months of wavering, finally severed relations at the beginning of May 1990[99]—and the collapse of individual trade unions in the GDR. This meant that the west German unions no longer had partners in the GDR that were accepted as legitimate by workers.

On 18 April 1990 the national board of the German Trade Union Federation agreed a set of 'principles regarding the employment and social-security order in a united Germany'. These called, *inter alia*, for a right to work, to be enshrined as a 'basic social right with constitutional status' and implemented by means of 'a rigorous policy of full employment'; equality between men and women, recognized as a goal of government, again with constitutional status; a ban on lockouts; the right of trade unions to operate freely in firms; and the right of workers to a share in firms' productive assets.[100] This was followed, on 30 April, by a 'First assessment of the Federal government's draft of the State Treaty with the GDR'.[101] Like the Social Democrats, the unions were critical of the draft's watering-down of social rights and benefits under their extension to the GDR, and called again for reform of the welfare state in Germany as a whole.

On 15 May 1990 the German Trade Union Federation and the newly formed Representative Council of the GDR trade unions produced a joint response to the treaty in the draft version of 12 May (a version broadly identical with the later treaty proper).[102] The response was presented to Federal Chancellor Kohl by the head of the Trade Union Federation, Ernst Breit, and the head of the Public Services and Transport Union, Monika Wulff-Matthies, and submitted to the east German government by the chairman of the Representative Council, Peter Rothe. This position paper conceded that the amended draft had responded to the unions' criticisms on certain important points—for example, the extension of redundancy scheme regulations to the east—and took substantial account of the unions' principal concern, which was that 'the process of German unification should not lead to any deterioration in the social position of workers in the two German states'. On the other hand, Breit said, it was regrettable that 'the historic opportunity created by a German economic, monetary, and social union was not also being used to make improvements to the German economic and social security systems that were long overdue'.[103] So balanced a statement—like the unions' detailed criticisms of the State Treaty, which will not be discussed here—was not calculated to mobilize union members into wresting major alterations from the government.[104]

The German Trade Union Federation also spoke out at various stages of the negotiations over the Unification Treaty, in particular in joint statements with the head of the Representative Council of the industrial and other trade unions in the GDR issued on 27 July and 17 August 1990.[105] As far as social policy was concerned, the unions called in particular for the constitutional enshrinement of goals of state with regard to social security; the reform of the Federal Republic's organizational structure of social insurance, especially of statutory health insurance; the retention of the GDR's system of polyclinics, ambulatories, and enterprise-based health services; the development and adoption of a comprehensive scheme to protect those in need of nursing care; the further development and earnings-indexation of the social allowance to provide needs-based minimum protection within pensions and unemployment insurance; the maintenance of the GDR's regulations on pre-pension benefits and extension of these benefits to the Federal Republic; the adoption in the Federal Republic of the GDR's regulations providing a better balance between work and family life; and the retention of the more employee-friendly provisions of GDR employment law, with a view to the establishment of a unified employment law code by the legislators of a united Germany.

Overall, the trade unions in the Federal Republic and the GDR did not play a significant independent role in the unification process.[106] The central ambition of the west German trade unions was to extend their organizations to the east.[107] Their other main focus was on wage negotiations, where they wanted to achieve a rapid alignment of east German wages with those in the west in order to prevent the east from becoming a low-wage region. They also hoped that they would be able to acquire a part, at least, of the east German trade unions' assets, to help fund future union activity.[108]

The employers were even more clearly lacking in legitimized partners in the GDR than the trade unions, and their own organizations in the east had to be built up from scratch. A paper on the draft of the Unification Treaty produced by the National Union of German Employers' Associations in mid-August 1990[109] welcomed the fact that the draft provided for a more thoroughgoing extension of Federal Republic law to the east than had been specified in the State Treaty. On the other hand, it was critical of the preservation, either temporary or open-ended, of special regulations for the GDR such as the special protection against dismissal for 'fighters against fascism', pregnant women, nursing mothers, and parents of very young children, the retention for one year of the paid housework day, the continuation of paid time off work for parents of sick children, and the payment of a social allowance in pensions and unemployment insurance. These, it argued, placed an added burden on firms, limited the freedom of enterprises to run their own affairs, and posed a threat to jobs; they also gave GDR workers preferential treatment over their west German opposite numbers. By and large, however, the employers' demands were not taken into account either.

It should be added that as a new system of industrial relations developed in the GDR, and then the new *Bundesländer*, after the spring of 1990, the interests both of the trade unions and of the employers were defined, particularly in the early years, entirely by the west, and the specific problems affecting the economy in the east were to a large extent ignored.

Only brief reference can be made to the roles of other social forces and organizations in the unification process. As has already been mentioned,[110] the Association of German Pensions Insurance Providers provided an important stimulus to pensions reform in the GDR through its detailed analysis of the technical problems arising from the conversion of the GDR's pensions system into the Federal Republic system. The pensions insurers, however, had little influence on the basic decisions concerning organizational structure and the level of benefits under pensions insurance in the GDR. On the other hand, they did play a vital part in the building-up of new pensions insurance organizations in the east.

The various providers of statutory health insurance, which rapidly embarked on a race to stake out territory in the east, had an important influence on the decision to create a multipartite system of health insurance, rather than the unitary system that was favoured, at least as a temporary measure, by the General Local Health Insurance Providers. The service providers' organizations, especially those of the doctors, were important in helping shape the legislation of the de Maizière government,[111] so that instead of a pluralist system of outpatient care—with doctors in individual practices existing alongside the local, national and enterprise-based health care facilities that had dominated the GDR health care system—the west German system was replicated in the east, with a near-monopoly of doctors in individual practices.

The Association of War Victims, the Disabled, and Social Pensioners undoubtedly exerted some influence over Chancellor Kohl with regard to the extension to the new *Bundesländer* of the Federal Social Provision Law, which was agreed, contrary to the wishes of the Federal Finance Ministry, at the same time as the Unification Treaty and came into force on 1 January 1991.[112]

In certain specific areas, then—particularly with regard to health care—interest groups succeeded in exerting a degree of influence on individual decision-makers or political parties. Overall, however, it is clear that the shaping of the unification policy of the Federal Republic, and the detailed implementation of the policy in the treaties with the GDR, were dominated by the executive.

German Unification and Social Policy: Conclusions

In conclusion, let us ask two questions. First, were there any politically feasible alternatives, as far as central areas of social policy were concerned, to the near-total adoption of the west German system of employment law and social security by the GDR? And secondly, did reunification with the GDR provide an impetus for further changes to the German welfare state?

As our analysis of the negotiations has shown, the adoption of west German norms and institutions was the lowest common denominator on which the political and social forces in the Federal Republic and the GDR were able to achieve consensus. There was agreement that perpetuating two different parallel sets of institutions and norms would be a deterrent to investment, and would fairly soon become unworkable. The option of simultaneously reforming the west German welfare state and fusing the systems of employment law and social security of the two states would take a considerable amount of time—time that was lacking, partly because there was a risk that the international situation might cease to be propitious and partly because there was such intense pressure for rapid unification from the population of the GDR. Besides, there was no majority political support in the west for any significant changes to the Federal system. And in any case, there were no coordinated plans for reorganization in existence, ready to be immediately introduced. It was clear that at an early stage the governing parties had reached agreement on the basic principle that 'in the event of accession by the GDR, there should be no attempt to resolve old disputes by means of transitional legislation'.[1] Staatssekretär Bernhard Jagoda, who exerted a major influence on the Federal Republic's conduct of the negotiations on questions of social policy, pressed this view particularly strongly.[2] All proposals for changes, he said, should be a matter for the all-German legislative bodies that would come into being after unification.

There was never any chance that the Social Democratic opposition and the trade unions would be able to preserve those institutions and arrangements in the GDR that they regarded as progressive and use them as precedents for reforming the united German welfare state. Under the circumstances, it was a significant achievement that the SPD, the unions, and, above all, the Federal Ministry of Labour were able to block the efforts of those within the Federal government and in business and financial circles who wanted to see a dismantling of social protection for workers and a reduction in welfare-state benefits in the GDR.[3] In the end, the GDR confined itself to ensuring that certain social rights and entitlements were retained, at any rate for a transitional period.

Similarly, if we consider specific areas of social policy, it is clear that there was no real likelihood of major reforms. The shortcomings of the health care system had long been the subject of intense debate in the Federal Republic, and the Public Services and Transport Union, for example, proposed reforms in 1990 that took their inspiration from the health care system of the GDR. Nevertheless, the GDR Health Minister, Jürgen Kleditzsch, himself set out the course for adoption of the west German system.[4] The polyclinics and ambulatories, the licensing of which was originally planned, under the Unification Treaty, to end on 31 December 1995, were among the few innovative features to be imported into the German welfare state from the GDR system, the time limit being removed by the Health Service Structure Law of December 1992. Even so, pressure from the bodies representing doctors was such that few of these facilities survived very long after unification, and they came to play only a minor role in the new *Bundesländer*, alongside doctors in individual practices. As a result, the close link between in- and outpatient medical services and the special emphasis on preventive medicine that had been regarded as superior elements of the GDR system also largely disappeared.

With regard to pensions insurance, it should be noted that during the preparatory work and negotiations on the State Treaty the discussions, apart from dealing with the question of the level of pensions in the east, focused only on the amalgamation of the separate insurance systems for blue- and white-collar workers and the problem of basic protection in pensions law. Issues that are at the forefront of discussion today—such as the lowering of contributions in order to reduce additional wage costs, the expansion of statutory insurance through the encouragement of company and private pensions, and the problem of enhancing the pensions formula (for example, by taking higher life expectancy, unemployment, and the smaller number of children into account)—were not central themes in 1990.

It is also very significant that there was no proposal that the system of financing pensions based on current contributions might be either partly or wholly replaced by a system in which pensions were paid from an accumulated capital fund within statutory pensions insurance. If a capital cover scheme based on pensions insurance had been in existence in west Germany, it would have been quite impossible to bring the east German pensioners into the mutualist system of pensions insurance, and their pensions would have had to be paid by the state alone for a long transition period until a sufficient capital stock had been built up.

It is not surprising, therefore, that when Vasso Papandreou, the European Community commissioner for social policy, education, and employment, asked Staatssekretär Jagoda what elements of social policy the Federal Republic had adopted from the GDR, Jagoda was unable to offer her any examples.[5] The wider question, however, as to the effects that unification had on the German welfare state in the medium and longer term requires a more complicated answer. Equal treatment of blue- and white-collar workers under the law governing continued payment of wages in the event of illness and under the law of dismissal, which were conceded to the GDR, came about primarily as the result of judgements by the Federal Constitutional Court[6] and were later extended to the west. A unified definition of employee status and a unitary pensions insurance organization for employees were finally implemented in 1 October 2005.[7] The anachronistic bans, under health and safety law, on night work for women and on the employment of women on building sites were not extended to the GDR, in order to obviate even higher unemployment, and were then lifted in the west in 1994; here, too, rulings by the Federal Constitutional Court,[8] as well as by the European Commission, played a significant role. Although the Unification Treaty's stipulation of reform of the regulations governing health and safety under public-employee law, in conformity with European Community law and also with the corresponding regulations within GDR health and safety law, was not followed by comprehensive codification in health and safety legislation, the fragmentation in German health and safety law was nevertheless reduced by a law passed on 7 August 1996.[9]

The active labour market policy was considerably expanded in quantitative terms when it was extended to the east and its existing machinery was modified and enlarged. Then, on 1 January 1993, a new §248h of the Employment Promotion Law made it possible, in the areas of the environment, social services, and youth services, to provide productive employment for the previously unemployed, for employees on short-time work, and for people working on job creation schemes, with employers receiving subsidies for wage costs at the levels of the various forms of unemployment benefit that would otherwise have been paid.[10] Following positive results in eastern Germany, a similar mechanism was introduced in west Germany in 1994, with §242s of the Employment Promotion Law, albeit only for those among the unemployed whom it was particularly hard to place in jobs.[11]

In the area of industrial relations, the precarious position of many enterprises in east Germany led to some loosening of the terms of regional collective agreements and the introduction of more flexible regulations and agreements taking greater account of the particular circumstances of individual enterprises.

In statutory health insurance, as a result of pressure from the interested parties, the west German multipartite system of different insurance providers was introduced in the east, despite widespread criticism from the GDR and from the political and social groups associated with the SPD in the Federal Republic. Nevertheless, proposals for a system of risk equalization across health insurance funds, such as already existed for pensioners, and for freedom of choice between insurers gained impetus as a result of unification with the GDR, where, unlike the Federal Republic, a standardized health insurance contribution had previously existed, and these ideas were incorporated into the Health Service Structure Law of December 1992. Moreover, the long-standing debate in the Federal Republic about the introduction of social care insurance took on new vigour as a result of the situation in the GDR, where care homes had been funded from the public purse—albeit at an inadequate level, so that for a long time there had not been enough places for those in need of care—and where about 500,000 people had received care benefits from social insurance in 1989.[12]

Article 31 of the Unification Treaty laid down that the legislative bodies of the united Germany should develop further the legislation on equal rights of men and women and improve the balance between work and family life. The amendment to Article 3, paragraph 2 of the Basic Law that was passed on 27 October 1994, whereby the state was obliged to promote the 'actual realization of equality of rights between women and men' and work towards 'the removal of existing disadvantages',[13] should be seen against the background of German unification, and the same applies to the implementation of a legal right to a kindergarten place and the eventual changes that were made to the legal regulations governing termination of pregnancy.[14] That said, the wide range of opinions on policy towards women and the family prevalent in different groups in politics and society meant that no truly significant new legislation to promote equal rights between the sexes and improve the balance between work and family life was introduced for many years after unification. In recent years, however, the position of families with small children has been considerably improved, following the introduction of a very generous parental allowance (particularly generous in the case of persons with high earnings), paid to cover 12 months' leave in the case of care of a new-born child or 14 months if the father is involved, as well as of a programme to expand the number of crèches for children below the age of three.

Altogether, it is clear that in these as in other areas the changes which were brought about by unification were limited in scope and that reforms were successful mainly in cases where there was already an impetus for change by virtue of prior debates in the Federal Republic and, often, also of prior initiatives by the Federal Constitutional Court or institutions of the European Community. In many instances, too, the particular circumstances of the GDR—such as mass unemployment, or the pattern of female employment, which was much less restricted to 'typical' women's jobs than was the case in the Federal Republic—had made new regulations necessary on economic or social grounds.

The underpinning of German unity through social policy needed to be, and was, a remarkable feat of organization. The task was analogous to jumping on to a moving train and steering it in a new direction without putting the passengers at risk—the passengers being the Germans in the east, who trusted that their pensions would continue to be paid, that they would receive support if they became unemployed, and that they would still have access to medical care. For all this to happen, it was not necessary merely that the new norms should be quickly adopted by functioning administrative machinery: new institutions also had to be created, such as a system of income support, an effective administrative system for employment, and independent social and employment courts, and new actors in the realm of social policy had either to be built up or extended into east Germany from the west, including free trade unions, employers' associations, professional associations, pensions and health insurers, medical councils and health providers' organizations, and Independent Welfare Associations. All of this was achieved in an unparalleled effort by administrators and the relevant political and social institutions and forces. The trauma of the shift from a planned to a market economy was mitigated, and the large-scale social conflict that would otherwise have been likely did not materialize.

Unification did not alter the essential character of the German welfare state. Indeed, the successful extension to east Germany of the institutions, norms, benefits, and actors of the welfare state was seen by many as proof of the system's efficiency and effectiveness in the face of new challenges. That success, together with the fact that the political, social, and administrative forces in Germany were fully taken up with the task of bringing about the social union of the Federal Republic and the GDR, served to drive into the background the debate that had been in train before 1990 about ways in which the German welfare state might be reformed to cope with the new challenges it faced—the ageing of the population, the explosion in the costs of health care, shifts in family structure, changes in the character of the world of work, and growing international competition for capital, markets, and the location of production. And yet the postponement of the debate, and the high financial costs of unification, merely served to exacerbate the structural problems of the German welfare state in the medium and longer term. There was less justification than ever, therefore, for evading these problems, even though any solutions would be bound to deprive many people of some of their claims and rights to social protection.

PART III

CHANGES TO THE GERMAN WELFARE STATE AFTER GERMAN UNIFICATION, 1990–1994

11

The Build-up of Welfare-State Institutions and Providers in the New *Bundesländer*

The extension of the Federal German welfare state to the new *Bundesländer* was of central importance in persuading people in the east to accept the new order, even though there were widespread complaints that some of the 'social achievements' of the GDR—in particular, the right to work—were being lost. In an opinion survey conducted in east Germany in November 1996, those interviewed were asked what had promoted unity: 81 per cent of the answers referred to the massive financial support that had been provided by the west, but an almost equal number, 80 per cent, cited the rapid alignment of pensions.[1] According to a survey conducted in November 1993, of the forms of assistance that were viewed as especially urgently needed, job creation measures for the unemployed took pride of place, ahead even of improvements to roads and the modernization of housing. At the same time, 78 per cent of those questioned confirmed that such measures were already under way.[2]

After the legal foundations of the social union had been laid, the principal objective was to complete the build-up of the administrative systems for employment and social security that had been started in 1990[3] and to create a modern system of employment relations based on free collective bargaining. This required close collaboration among the social policy bureaucracies of the Federal Republic, the *Länder* and local government, the providers of social insurance, the Independent Welfare Associations, the social partners (trade unions and employers' organizations), and the other actors in the field of social policy. The key tasks at the outset were to take on staff and train them for their new roles, to acquire and equip the necessary office space, and to provide finance for developing the administrative machinery and funding the social benefits that the machinery would deliver. In this process, east Germany was massively dependent on the west, both for financial support and, initially, for personnel. The work that was done in the individual areas of social policy, and the changes in policy that took place during the years 1990–4, can be described only in broad outline here. The emphasis will be on the general character of the problems that arose and on the significance they had for east Germany.

11.1 THE ADMINISTRATIVE SYSTEM FOR EMPLOYMENT, AND EMPLOYMENT PROMOTION POLICY

The basic structure of the administrative system for employment in the east, with 38 employment offices at regional level and 161 job centres at local level, had been established during the period of the de Maizière government.[4] At unification on 3 October 1990, the Federal Institute of Labour became responsible for their management; in 1991 two further *Land* employment offices were formed, one for Saxony and a joint one for Saxony-Anhalt and Thuringia. Mecklenburg-West Pomerania was assigned to the North office in Kiel, and Brandenburg and east Berlin to the Berlin-Brandenburg office.[5] In the Federal Institute of Labour's original plan, only two *Land* employment offices were to have been created: a North office, covering the *Länder* Mecklenburg-West Pomerania, Brandenburg, and Berlin and responsible for 18 regional employment offices, and a South office, covering the *Länder* Saxony-Anhalt, Saxony, and Thuringia and responsible for 25 regional employment offices.[6] A hundred and sixty-five million DM were made available from Federal government funds to set up the new offices, and in the course of 1992 about 2,000 members of staff were brought in from the west.[7] At the beginning there were problems concerning the vetting of personnel who had remained in post from the days of the GDR. A group of personnel experts from the Federal Institute of Labour screened staff for professional capacity and political suitability, especially at senior level, where many old SED cliques had stayed on. By 6 March 1991, as a result of the vetting, 12 directors, 30 departmental heads, and 40 managers of local job centres had been relieved of their responsibilities, and 3 directors, 4 departmental heads, and 3 local managers remained under review. In addition, 83 people who had worked for the GDR's Ministry of State Security and Office for National Security ceased employment.[8] The effectiveness of the employment administrative system was further impaired by a shortage of staff, and by the fact that at first the new members of staff from the east were inadequately qualified to administer the new legislation. According to a statement made by Norbert Blüm, the Federal Minister of Labour, to CDU/CSU parliamentarians on 2 March 1993, 12,000 out of the 15,000 members of staff employed in the east were not familiar with the Employment Promotion Law.[9] Delays in building up the new administrative system and increasing the number of providers of training were also caused by a lack of office space. The Labour Ministry accordingly asked the Federal Ministry of Defence for permission to use barracks of the National People's Army as homes for the new job centres (and also for the social insurance providers), and the request met with considerable success.[10] Job creation schemes were initially slow to get under way, owing to a shortage of providers: by the end of September 1990 the offer of a combination of short-time working and training schemes had been taken up by only a few employees—23,700, or 1.4 per cent of those on short-time work—primarily because in many cases short-time working benefit had been increased, from either 63 or 68 per cent to 90 per cent of net wages based on collective agreements. In addition, women were at first heavily under-represented on job creation schemes.[11]

By 1993 staffing numbers at job centres had been built up, office space had been bought or rented, and local authorities had become the most important providers of job creation schemes. In addition, commercial employment agencies, either split off from GDR industrial enterprises or newly formed, had also come to play an important role.[12] A key factor here was that from 1 April 1991 a new instrument of labour market policy meant that companies that had successfully applied for licences to provide job creation schemes within the framework of a special programme could now also receive grants to cover part of their non-personnel costs.[13] Overall, there was a shift within the active labour market policy away from short-time working towards training and re-training (though this was later partly reversed by the amendment to the Employment Promotion Law passed on 18 December 1992) and towards job creation schemes.[14] The early retirement regulation, which remained in force until the autumn of 1995, and pre-pension transitional benefit, which eventually was made payable until 31 December 1997 at the latest, were also vitally important as tools for reducing unemployment during the period 1990–4.[15] The number of people receiving early retirement or pre-pension benefit rose from 554,000 to 852,000 between 1991 and 1993, before falling to 619,000 in 1994. Because of the very poor state of the labour market, and despite the high costs entailed, the age limit for receiving pre-pension benefit was lowered from 57 to 55, mainly as a result of pressure from the employers, and the length of the period of entitlement to the benefit was extended to a maximum of five years, so as to create a smooth transition into pensions insurance.[16] Altogether, the effect of the active labour market policy in the new *Bundesländer* was to take nearly 2 million people out of the labour market in 1991 and 1992, 1.6 million in 1993, and 1.3 million in 1994.[17] Expenditure on the policy in the east at first rose sharply, from 29,500 million DM in 1991 to 40,700 million DM in 1992; in 1993 it rose less steeply, reaching 41,900 million DM. In the same year total expenditure for the east by the Federal Institute of Labour was 50,500 million DM, or 18 per cent of east German gross domestic product.[18] In 1994 expenditure on the active labour market policy in the east fell to 34,800 million DM, and by 1997 it had declined significantly, to 18,600 million DM.[19]

Behind these figures lay a sharp change of direction in labour market policy. The primary purpose of the shift was to reduce the level of Federal subsidy to the Federal Institute of Labour, but there were also mounting doubts about the effectiveness of the active labour market policy as a bridge towards employment in the normal labour market. In addition, the Federal government was responding to the criticism that commercial employment agencies, in particular, might become competitors with local crafts businesses[20] and that the *Länder* and local authorities in east Germany were making extensive use of job creation staff, instead of their own paid public service officials, to fulfil their statutory public obligations, particularly with regard to decisions on applications for housing benefit.[21] In the face of strong opposition from the Social Democrats, who wanted to replace the Employment Promotion Law with an employment and structural promotion law to combat structural unemployment,[22] the 10th amendment to the Employment Promotion Law, passed in December 1992, generated initial savings of 5,800 million DM a year. These savings were obtained in a number of ways: through a reduction in support measures for the integration of unemployed immigrants of German extraction from eastern central and eastern Europe, new regulations limiting access to training and re-training schemes, restrictions on training grants for employment of the long-term unemployed, a partial adjustment of the conditions attaching to support for job creation schemes in the east so as to bring them into line with those in the west, restrictions on benefits for professional rehabilitation, and a tightening of conditions on early retirement at the expense of unemployment insurance.[23] At the same time, the new paragraph 249h of the Employment Promotion Law made it possible for wage cost subsidies at the level either of average unemployment benefit or of average unemployment assistance to be provided to enable the unemployed, people on short-time working, and participants in job creation schemes to be employed on projects of environmental improvement or social and youth services in the east. The law also gave the Federal government the authority to set the Federal Institute of Labour's budget, even in the face of opposition from the Institute's own self-governing leadership—a situation that in fact arose in January 1993.[24] The Federal government eventually succeeded in breaking up the initially united front of opposition to the law in the new *Bundesländer* and persuading those eastern *Länder* in which the CDU was a participant in government to come round in its support. This meant that a two-thirds majority vote against the draft law in the Bundesrat could not be achieved, and that registration of an objection to the legislation by a simple majority vote in the Bundesrat could be overridden by an absolute majority vote in the Bundestag.[25]

The shift in direction in labour market policy deepened the differences between the government and the Social Democratic opposition, the latter backed by the trade unions, and marked the 'break-up of the consensus on bringing about German unification in a socially acceptable way'.[26] Within the governing coalition, it went hand in hand with a decline in the influence of the Christian Democratic Association of Employees in the CDU/CSU and a rise in the influence of the FDP's ideas on labour market policy.[27]

Overall, the implementation of an ambitious active labour market policy, especially in the first years after unification, had the effect of staving off social upheaval in the east. As a bridge to a normal labour market, however, it was only a limited success. It sharply reduced overt unemployment, but it also postponed, rather than accelerated, the structural transformation of the economy that was needed. It did not rectify the low level of productivity in the east, which was the Achilles heel of the east German economy and was also a partial cause of the problems involved in the extension to the east of west German employment law and the new system of industrial relations.

11.2 PROBLEMS IN THE EXTENSION OF FEDERAL GERMAN EMPLOYMENT LAW TO THE EAST

Under the Unification Treaty, Federal German employment law was to be extended to the new *Bundesländer*, with some exceptions and some transitional regulations. In the event, however, serious problems arose.[28] The main difficulties were twofold. The first was how the Federal legal order, which had 'grown over the course of forty years' and been constantly adjusted to changing circumstances through decisions of the courts, could be applied 'overnight' to the very different conditions that had been created by the collapse of the Communist system, when 'the institutions and individuals that would have to apply it (courts, personnel managers and works councils) and the people who would be affected by it (in particular, employees) did not have the preparation to enable them to do so'. The second difficulty sprang from the fact that the employment system of the GDR had been regulated 'in a perspicuous and easily understood way' by the Labour Statute Book, so that the 'lack of a comprehensive codification of Federal German employment law, and the extensive role of judge-made law in employment relations', made it very difficult for either employees or employers to get their bearings. People repeatedly asked: 'Where does the law say this? And they constantly wanted the Ministry to give a *definitive* opinion, or (falsely) regarded the Ministry's legal opinion as a definitive interpretation or decision.'

Only a few of the specific problems can be outlined here. For example, there was uncertainty whether, and under what circumstances, terms and conditions of employment would remain in force after 3 October 1990. In the aftermath of the 'large-scale collapse of enterprises', or of 'proposed restructuring', employees were unilaterally assigned work tasks that had not been previously agreed, and working hours were altered and pay scales changed. There were objections to the new, less generous regulations governing the granting of time off work in order to care for sick children, 'especially as at the same time a large number of child care facilities were closed and the situation of working parents was made even more difficult'. Problems were also caused by the move from the 43¾- or 42-hour week to the 40-hour week, by the effects on earnings of the unilateral introduction of part-time working by employers, and by the extension to part-time employees of reductions in working time for full-time employees, implemented without notice of the change or an offer of the introduction of short-time working.

The biggest problems, naturally, arose with regard to abrupt endings of the employment relationship and, linked to this, the regulations governing severance payments. Notice of dismissal, as a legal institution, had existed in the GDR, but little use had been made of it, particularly as enterprises had been obliged to offer employees subject to dismissal either a contract of variation (*Änderungsvertrag*) of terms and conditions of employment, involving acceptance of a suitable new job within the enterprise, or a contract of transition (*Überleitungsvertrag*) into another enterprise. Dismissal as such was seen as a stigma, so a mutually agreed contract of termination (*Aufhebungsvertrag*) was commonly used in order to end the employment relationship. Because employees had little comprehension of the new law, many of them continued to enter into such contracts after unification without considering, or even realizing, the fatal consequences. In such cases a job centre would impose a waiting period before unemployment benefit could be paid, and the regulations governing dismissal—for example, the requirement that the main welfare office give its consent in the case of the dismissal of the disabled, or the involvement of the works council in dismissal cases—ceased to be applicable. Frequently, employees who wanted to contest their dismissal missed the deadline for contacting the enterprise's employment arbitration panel or the employment court and instead took their requests for clarification of their circumstances to the Labour Ministry, which of course was unable to provide a legal decision. Commonly, people failed to understand the grounds for dismissal, protesting that they 'had not done anything wrong'. It also came as a great surprise that one could even be dismissed while one was ill—something that had not been the case in the GDR.

In a sense the collaboration between works councils and employers enabled the old GDR ideology to persist. On the other hand, the rights of the works councils were often completely ignored. In the GDR, dismissals could not come into effect unless they had the consent of the trade union leadership within the enterprise. This led many dismissed employees to believe, after unification, that they had been dismissed by the works council, or that the works council had co-signed their dismissal notice, or that the notice contained a rider that the works council had expressly agreed to their dismissal. In other cases, contrary to the new legal situation, the works council either failed to obtain a satisfactory hearing before the issuing of a dismissal notice or was not heard at all. It was also difficult to communicate to those affected that although the works council had the right to lodge an objection to a dismissal, in the last resort it could not block it. For their part, employers were unaware of the criteria that the Federal Employment Court had ruled as applicable in the case of dismissals necessitated by the situation of the firm, so that employees were incorrectly given notice on grounds of 'social' or 'structural change'. In some instances the reference to social factors that was mandatory in the selection of employees for dismissals was not undertaken; in many instances it was faulty. Often, however, 'social selection' could not be undertaken, because departments were closed down wholesale. In addition, it was not clear from the law whether or not 'social selection' could be dispensed with in cases of dismissal 'on grounds of inadequate demand'.

There were frequent complaints that employers were hanging on to the 'old cliques' while getting rid of employees who voiced uncomfortable criticisms. The concept of a notice of variation (*Änderungskündigung*) involving a continuation of the employment relationship but with altered terms and conditions had not existed in GDR law. As a result, notices of variation were widely misinterpreted as endings of the employment relationship. In addition, many enterprises unilaterally altered work tasks, working hours, or shift systems without issuing notices of variation.

In the GDR, judicial settlement of disputes over claims under employment law had been frowned on, and such disputes had mainly been settled in other ways. This attitude meant that many dismissed employees let the three-week deadline for making a complaint against dismissal elapse and confined themselves to lodging an objection with the works council. Many others simply assumed that the state authorities would intervene, in the way with which they were familiar. Repeatedly, therefore, people turned to the Labour Ministry, asking it to 'cancel or examine the dismissal notice, to induce the employer to reinstate them, to assess the prospects of success of a complaint', or, 'if arbitration or employment court proceedings had been started, to exert its influence on the courts'. In some instances employers fell foul of the special regulations regarding the dismissal of disabled employees, by failing to obtain the agreement of the main welfare offices, or ignored the regulations, which remained valid for a transition period after unification, giving special protection to mothers and fathers of children up to one year of age and to single parents of children up to the age of three.

There were very considerable difficulties with regard to severance payments attendant on the cancellation of a contract of employment, which were not recognized under GDR employment law. There was a widespread impression among employees in the new *Bundesländer* that a severance payment was a 'reward for long and loyal service to the enterprise' and that claims to severance pay were therefore always valid. Differences in the regulations governing severance payments, whether between different sectors of the economy or on the basis of some other form of social protection, accordingly 'came in for fierce criticism, as being unjust'. It was also hard to explain that there was 'no automatic connection, in law, between the ending of an employment relationship and some form of severance payment', and that claims needed to be based on pay contracts, company agreements, or, less usually, individual contractual arrangements. In addition there were cases in which 'self-appointed' managing directors—because they failed to understand their role as employers, and in some instances also because they themselves were among those with rightful claims—drew up 'generous redundancy schemes' which took no account of the financial and economic situation of their enterprises and their prospects of survival but which benefited their originators.

Finally (as will be discussed below[29]), a general set of regulations governing redundancy schemes was passed, with the cooperation of the trade unions. People failed to understand, however, that these regulations applied only to the enterprises that were being administered by the *Treuhand*. There was also disbelief, and bitterness, when it was realized that severance payment claims regulated by pay agreements were valid only if collective agreements concluded before 30 June 1990 (agreements on protection measures against rationalization) had also been registered.

Older employees who had been induced, either by moral pressure or by the threat of dismissal, to leave their enterprises and opt for early retirement under GDR regulations or for payment of pre-pension transitional benefit on the basis of the Unification Treaty felt duped when they became aware that, by contrast with the situation under the GDR, they no longer belonged to their enterprise once their employment relationship had ceased.

As far as collective employment law was concerned, the parties to collective agreements encountered significant difficulties with the clause of the law requiring that in order to secure a declaration of the extension of an agreement to all employees in an industry, 50 per cent of the affected employees within the industry concerned should be covered by that agreement. Problems arose because there was a lack of adequate statistical data, owing to the premature closure of the joint Statistical Office in the new *Bundesländer*, and because employers in the east were often disinclined to join employers' organizations. In practice, there was accord, albeit temporary, between the Labour Ministry, the new *Bundesländer*, the National Union of German Employers' Associations, the German Trade Union Federation, and the parties to collective agreements that 'the yardstick should be generously applied in respect of the 50 per cent clause'. A second problem was that GDR enterprises were over-manned with managerial personnel who 'could not be used or redeployed in the course of the restructuring of enterprises in accordance with their predominantly academic education'. This situation was dealt with by notices of variation.

Altogether, then, the extension of Federal Republic employment law to the east created considerable problems of adjustment for the employers and employees affected. It provoked a huge rise in the number of cases heard by the employment courts, increased people's reluctance to accept the new order, and played a part in fostering subsequent nostalgia for the days of the GDR.

11.3 THE DEVELOPMENT OF A NEW SYSTEM OF INDUSTRIAL RELATIONS

Trade unions and employers' organizations were united in the view that the west German system of industrial relations, with co-determination by freely elected works councils and independently negotiated regional collective agreements, should be extended to the GDR and, later, to the new *Bundesländer*. In their joint statement of 9 March 1990 they deliberately avoided giving a potential boost to company-level regulation within the pay negotiations system—for example, through company-level wage settlements.[30] The State Treaty of 18 May 1990, however, sanctioned a dual structure of representation of interests. Through the treaty the GDR system, in which the unions, themselves dependent on the SED and the state, had had a monopoly role in representing employees' interests through the plant trade union leaderships they installed and controlled, was complemented by the introduction of freely elected independent works councils. Soon after the fall of the Wall, the first works councils had been spontaneously elected, often at the instigation of higher-qualified white-collar employees.[31] The GDR's 'General Outline Law' of 21 June 1990 then laid down[32] that works councils elected on democratic principles by a majority of the workforce in a secret ballot could remain provisionally in office. The Unification Treaty specified that new elections of works councils under the Works Constitution Law should be held by 30 June 1991 at the latest.[33]

The works councils, which underwent a variety of training sessions in preparation for their tasks,[34] played an important role in the restructuring of the east German economy.[35] Since the managements of the GDR's enterprises lacked legitimacy, and the works councils had the confidence of workforces, works councils often had a considerable influence over what had previously been managerial decisions. At the same time, however, the works councils were forced to share responsibility for the huge reductions in staffing that went hand in hand with rapid privatization and restructuring and to try to make the process as socially acceptable as possible, particularly through negotiations on redundancy schemes with severance payments. The distinctive feature of the east German works councils, in addition to the often substantial influence that they had on company policy during the early phase of the transformation process, was their ability to respond flexibly to critical developments and—springing from the east German tradition in social policy that had evolved over the preceding decades—their strong orientation to the enterprise and their commitment to the specific interests of the enterprise's workforce. Not infrequently, this latter attitude led the works councils to form alliances with management and brought them into conflict with the trade unions.[36]

The west German trade unions and employers' associations extended their respective organizations into east Germany and opposed the emergence of separate organizations in the east, with their own distinctive approach to representing their members' interests. Although the German Trade Union Federation and most of the individual unions at first hoped that they would be able to cooperate with the existing GDR trade unions, transforming them into democratic institutions from within, in the course of the spring and summer of 1990 they were forced to acknowledge that the GDR unions had become completely discredited in the eyes of their members and were not capable of being reformed. On 9 May 1990 the east German Trade Union Federation surrendered its powers to a 'Representative Council' of the various industrial and other trade unions of the GDR, and on 30 September 1990 it was formally dissolved.[37]

In building up their organizations in the GDR, and later the new *Bundesländer*, the trade unions of the Federal Republic worked to varying degrees with old GDR unions and, for a transitional period, with new unions formed under their influence. In some cases the members of these unions were taken over wholesale, while in others there was an attempt to recruit new members in the east on an individual basis. There were differences, too, in the readiness of western unions to retain east German union officials in post.[38] The union that went furthest in an exclusionist direction was the Metal Workers' Union, which took over almost no officials from its parallel organization in the GDR and insisted that all new members in the east go through an individual application procedure.[39] With the exception of Saxony, which became the union's new Dresden district, east Berlin and the other new *Bundesländer* were annexed to west German regions. Apart from one case, officials from the west were appointed as heads of the 35 administrative districts of the Metal Workers' Union in the east.[40] In other unions, by contrast, east Germans preserved more of a presence.

The German Trade Union Federation established regional organizations in each of the five new *Bundesländer*.[41] At first, because of the mass redundancies, the main activity of the Federation was to provide legal protection: in mid-1991, 230 out of 290 Federation officials at secretary level were working on issues of legal protection and only 60 were dealing with organizational questions in the 33 newly created administrative offices. For unions not affiliated to the Federation, the task of organizing in the east was even more difficult. The German White-Collar Workers' Trade Union (the DAG) had no access to the old union structures in the east and had to build up its organization from nothing.[42] This brought it into competition with the German Trade Union Federation and its affiliated unions, which were unwilling to hand over the organization of white-collar workers to the DAG without a fight.[43] Neither the DAG, however, nor the Christian trade unions were as successful in recruiting members as the Federation's affiliates. In 1991 nearly 4.2 million members of the German Trade Union Federation, or 35 per cent, were from the east. Within the DAG, the 111,000 members from the east represented only 19 per cent of the union's total membership, while the 8,000 eastern members of the Christian trade unions constituted a tiny minority of about 3 per cent.[44]

In the years that followed, a central problem for the trade unions in the east was the massive decline in their newly acquired membership. Between 1991 and 1994 the number of members of trade unions in the east shrank by nearly 1.6 million, or over 37 per cent (compared with a fall of about 6 per cent in the west); all unions were affected, apart from the police trade union and the Christian unions.[45] As a result, the high levels of organization that the affiliates of the German Trade Union Federation had enjoyed in the east—initially, 53 per cent (compared with 32 per cent in the west)[46]—also disappeared. The Metal Workers' Union alone lost over half of its more than a million members in the east between 1991 and 1995.[47]

The collapse in union membership was caused in part by the sharp fall in the number of people in employment, but also by the thwarting of initial hopes that the unions would be able to exert a strong influence on the process of transformation of the east German economy and on the protection of jobs. There were problems, too, resulting from the make-up of union membership in the east. A substantial proportion of union members in the new *Bundesländer*—almost half in the case of the Metal Workers' Union[48]—were pensioners or unemployed and paid only a symbolic membership fee. In addition, the actual payment of fees was at first very sluggish, and the incomes of members in employment, and hence their fees, were in any case lower in the east than in the west, so that a significant financial shortfall arose. Incoming revenues were not sufficient to match the high expenditures entailed by the work on building up union organization, the huge demand from members for intensive personal advice on matters of employment and social law,[49] and the representation of members before the employment and social courts. On the other hand, if the unions had not tried rapidly to strengthen their presence in the east, they would have risked becoming ineffective and made themselves less attractive to members. The unions in the east were therefore forced to seek financial help from headquarters, but many of these were chronically short of cash themselves.

There were also difficulties over the demarcation of spheres of organization, not just between the German Trade Union Federation and the German White-Collar Workers' Trade Union (and the German Civil Service Association), but between different unions within the Federation. The organizational areas that had been operated by the old GDR trade unions often did not tally with those used by the Federation's unions, and this gave rise to fierce inter-union conflicts over the organization of particular groups of workers.[50] Although the Federation tried to arbitrate, many of these disputes could not be resolved. There were especially bitter disagreements between the Mining and Energy Trade Union and the Public Services and Transport Trade Union. The west German Mining and Energy Union at first tried to capture all the members of the east German Mining, Energy, and Water Supply Trade Union and the Bismuth Trade Union, the latter representing uranium mining workers of the Soviet–German company Wismut AG in the Erzgebirge. In this, it was fiercely resisted by the Public Services Union, which had traditionally represented many workers in the energy field in the west, particularly those employed by public works departments and city administrations. At the beginning of February 1991 the German Trade Union Federation finally ruled that the organizational demarcations between different unions that had prevailed in the Federal Republic before unification should serve as an obligatory pattern for Germany as a whole. In the dispute in question this meant that the Mining and Energy Union had to surrender about two-thirds of the membership under contention—roughly 70,000 workers in the east German energy and water supply industries—and the two unions were told to reach an agreement over the remaining one-third of members, who largely consisted of the workers in brown coal power stations and in industrial and mining power stations for coal refining. The prospect of further conflict appalled many east German union members, weakened their commitment to their unions, and was an important factor in the decline in membership numbers.[51]

Before unification, discussions had begun in the west on ways in which the trade unions might modernize their policies: for example, whether there should be a move towards more differentials in pay agreements, or whether more attention should be paid to environmental issues. These debates contrasted sharply with the preoccupations of employees in the east, which were overwhelmingly about job security and improvements in living standards. After unification, although the discussions on differentials and the environment stagnated or were even stifled,[52] the growing disparity in union members' concerns, particularly between the employed and the unemployed, and between western supporters of 'post-materialist values' and easterners anxious about traditional social problems, made it difficult for the unions to resolve policy issues and take decisions, and militated against internal union solidarity.

The employers' associations had no opposite numbers in the east with whom they could forge links. In addition,[53] because the state had been virtually the only employer in the east, with the exception of a handful of small businesses, genuine entrepreneurs did not emerge until the large combines began to be broken up and the industrial enterprises were privatized. Some specific employers' associations were set up in the east—for example, a 'Registered Association of the Berlin and Brandenburg Metal-Working and Electrical Industries' was founded on 11 April 1990[54]—in which the directors of the publicly owned enterprises assumed leading positions, but they did not get beyond the initial stage and were later swallowed up by the west German employers' associations. Generally, the west German associations played the main role in the development of entrepreneurs' associations. A joint 'GDR information office' of the National Union of German Employers' Associations and the Federal Association of German Industry began work in west

Berlin as early as 1 March 1990.[55] Its aims were to establish contacts with state-run offices and public institutions, establish links with entrepreneurs and entrepreneurs' organizations in the GDR, and encourage the creation of entrepreneurs' and employers' associations. More important in the development of the east German employers' associations was the backing provided by west German trade associations of particular industries through partnerships and sponsorships; this work was largely completed by the end of 1990. The *Treuhand* agency gave support, on the employers' side, to the establishment of these associations by effectively requiring firms to join the relevant employers' association.[56] However, although west German organizational structures were carried over into the east, such as the division into trade associations and non-trade-based *Land*-level associations in the National Union of German Employers' Associations, the separation that was prevalent in the old *Bundesländer* between business and employers' associations at local level and at *Land* level was not extended to the new *Bundesländer*, except in Saxony, where separate regional organizations were formed.[57]

The main problems that faced the employers' organizations concerned policy on pay agreements. The dilemma was that while, on the one hand, low wages were an incentive to private investors and would help improve the competitiveness of the east German economy, on the other hand higher wages in the old *Bundesländer* would inevitably encourage particularly capable skilled workers to migrate westwards. The hope that the west German side had entertained, when offering monetary union to the east, that wages and salaries would rise only in line with increases in productivity turned out to be delusory. Even before monetary union, in the second quarter of 1990, there was a huge rise in wages of about 20 per cent, despite a decline in productivity, as a result of flat-rate increases designed to cushion the rise in living costs expected after the removal of subsidies and to improve the starting-point for employees when wages were converted at the ratio of 1:1 on 1 July 1990. In the subsequent 15 months, collective agreements led to wage rises averaging about 50 per cent.[58] These were 'political wage rounds' which were not based on the productiveness of the east German enterprises, and the effect of them was to accelerate the fall in the number of jobs.

The trade unions had two main motives in pressing for these wage increases not backed by increases in productivity. They were opposed to the idea of a low-wage region in the east, which, by inducing workers to migrate to the west, would inevitably also put pressure on western wages. They also hoped that high wage settlements would win them favour among new members in the east, partly by helping the unemployed through income replacement benefits. On the entrepreneurs' side, the main factors in the first wage rounds were that east German managers lacked legitimacy, had little experience of wage negotiations, and indeed in many cases regarded themselves as representatives of the interests of the workforce. Later, after west German employers' associations had taken charge of wage negotiations, the interests of west German companies assumed the dominant role, one central consideration being that an increase in the purchasing power of employees in the east would boost the sales of the companies' products. In addition, many entrepreneurs were worried about the emergence of competition in the east, based on low wage levels: for western entrepreneurs, the east was first and foremost a market in which to sell, not a location in which to produce. On top of this, both sides of industry, unions and employers alike, had a vested interest in the creation of a unified economy, within which there would be no differences in wage structures over the longer term, and in the allaying of eastern workers' fears through rapid rises in wages. At the same time, this would satisfy eastern workers' expectations that equal work should be rewarded with equal pay.

As has already been mentioned,[59] the state—and hence taxpayers, who in the last analysis had to bear the economic costs of excessive wage settlements in the form of income replacement benefits, income support and housing benefit—was the third party in wage negotiations. This was especially clear with regard to redundancy schemes, which, though they had originally been opposed by the Federal Ministries of Finance and Economics, were enshrined in the State Treaty of 18 May 1990. However, the problem with actually implementing the right to redundancy schemes in the GDR, and then the new *Bundesländer*, under conditions of mass dismissals was that most enterprises lacked the financial resources to make severance payments of any size. At the same time, payments imposed an extra burden on the processes of privatization and modernization of businesses.

In the initial phase, during the second half of 1990, a number of quite excessive redundancy payment schemes were agreed, the cost of which was borne by the *Treuhand* agency.[60] Then, at the instigation of the Federal Ministry of Labour,[61] and following lengthy negotiations, a 'Joint Declaration' was issued on 13 April 1991 by the *Treuhand*, the German Trade Union Federation, and the German White-Collar Workers' Trade Union.[62] This recommended that for economically viable enterprises a severance payment equivalent to four months of gross earnings should be regarded as 'appropriate in most cases'. For non-viable enterprises, so-called discretionary sums would be made available by the *Treuhand* in the case of mass redundancies, with the total amount of redundancy payment not to exceed a sum of 5,000 DM per employee affected; the sum would be reduced for employees who were making longer-term claims for benefits under training or job creation schemes or who would reach pensionable age within a year. The task of dividing up the total amount of the redundancy payments into different severance sums corresponding to each individual's particular social needs was left to workers' representatives and management within the enterprise. The finance for the scheme was provided, in this instance, by the Federal government: following Blüm's urging, 10,000 million DM were made available.[63] This was a departure from the earlier principle that redundancy schemes should not be implemented if an enterprise lacked sufficient resources of its own; at the same time, though, a cap was placed on the level of claims. The *Treuhand*'s guidelines were subsequently amplified in agreements with individual trade unions: by mid-1992 such agreements had been reached with the German White-Collar Workers' Trade Union, the industrial unions in chemicals, textiles, construction, metal-working, wood-processing and synthetic materials, the media, and leather-working, and with employees of restaurants. Industry-specific problems and the changing age structure within enterprises were to be addressed under these agreements. Discretionary sums for redundancy at the standard allocation of 5,000 DM were increased by 30 per cent in the first quarter of 1992 and by 25 and 10 per cent in the two following quarters respectively,[64] though they remained substantially below average severance payments in the old *Bundesländer*, which had already stood on average at 13,360 DM in the mid-1980s.[65] In the first year after the 'Joint Declaration', 1.2 million employees who had been made redundant received severance payments, and by mid-1992 7,500 million out of the 10,000 million DM that had been allocated to finance the scheme had already been used up.

After 1991, two different strategies were pursued in pay negotiations. In some cases short-term agreements were made, which could be quickly revised; in others, collective agreements covering several years were negotiated, spelling out a gradual transition towards complete alignment with western pay levels. The agreement reached in March 1991 on behalf of 1.1 million employees in the eastern metal-working and electrical industries was a particularly significant one. It specified a series of annual pay increases on 1 April of each year until 1 April 1994, when eastern wages under pay agreements would come fully into line with those in the west.[66] However, since productivity in the east rose only slowly and remained well below the levels that had been forecast, and since there was a change in the general economic situation with the onset of a sharp recession in the autumn of 1992, on 18 February 1993 the employers' association United Metals took the extraordinary step—an unprecedented one by employers in the history of pay bargaining in Germany—of announcing that it was terminating the agreement.[67] The purpose of this move was to send a signal that current wages policy, based on a consensus about reconstruction, should be changed, not only in the east but also in the west. Heated arguments were followed by abortive attempts at conciliation, and the result was a large strike in the metal-working industry in Saxony between 3 and 14 May 1993. Eventually an agreement was reached, postponing the alignment of eastern with western wage levels under pay agreements until the middle of 1996. In addition, a hardship clause stated that with the consent of both parties, represented on the basis of parity on arbitration panels or commissions within individual enterprises, payments below agreed rates would be allowable, 'in order to avert the threat of insolvency, to protect jobs or, especially, to prevent threatened redundancies' and 'to improve the prospects of modernization on the basis of a proposed modernization plan'.[68]

More important in practice than this hardship clause, which was invoked relatively rarely,[69] were clauses on revision, 'opening' (permitting derogations by works agreements), and relaxations for small and medium-sized enterprises which increasingly became included in collective agreements after 1992[70] and which led to a loosening of region-wide agreements and a growth in company-based agreements on wages and working conditions, particularly in eastern Germany.

The employers' associations were faced with a dilemma. On the one hand, the shift away from region-wide collective agreements—which were central to the German system of industrial relations, as the Labour Minister Blüm strongly emphasized[71]—was likely to call their *raison d'être* into question. On the other hand, they also had to take account of the interests of members who were aware that their businesses were at risk. The process of reforming regional agreements and making them more flexible, so that individual businesses had more room for manoeuvre,[72] was a piecemeal one, as was the postponement of the alignment of eastern with western wages, despite the fact that economists were virtually unanimous that the delay was necessary.

One way out of the dilemma, for which the heads of small and medium-sized enterprises, in particular, increasingly opted, was to withdraw from their employers' associations and abandon regional collective agreements. This was happening in the old *Bundesländer* too, but it happened on an especially big scale in the east. According to a study by the German Institute for Economic Research, in the winter of 1993/4 64 per cent of the enterprises in manufacturing industry in the east (which admittedly employed only 26 per cent of all employees) did not belong to an employers' association with the capacity to enter into regional collective agreements.[73] With the winding-up of the *Treuhand*, the trend towards smaller-sized firms, and the growth of 'outsourcing'—i.e. the transfer of areas of activity previously undertaken by large enterprises to new independent businesses[74]—that proportion became greater still. The same applied to the withdrawal from regional agreements—often tacitly approved by works councils—the result of which was the payment of wages at lower than negotiated levels. A survey of 700 entrepreneurs conducted by the Ifo Institute at the end of 1996 revealed that 47 per cent of those questioned no longer felt bound by the terms on working time laid down in negotiated agreements, 43 per cent did not pay a full Christmas bonus or full holiday pay, 37 per cent did not pay a full wage in the event of illness, and 30 per cent did not pay agreed salaries and wages.[75]

The erosion of the position of both trade-union and employers' organizations was a symptom of a lack of commitment towards them on the part of their members, particularly on the employers' side. Underlying the failure of commitment by employers was the fact that prospering and ailing enterprises had different vested interests, and that the interests specific to east German businesses were not adequately represented at the senior levels of the employers' associations. Like the continuing shortfall in competitiveness of many east German enterprises, the decline in the effectiveness of the social partners served to prevent the process of alignment in living standards between east and west from advancing beyond certain limits, and it also caused the differences in the social circumstances of employees in the east to become significantly more marked.

11.4 SOCIAL INSURANCE

11.4.1 The development and further alignment of pensions insurance in the east

Statutory pensions insurance, a central element of the system of social protection in the Federal Republic, was extended to east Germany in a series of steps. The State Treaty of 18 May 1990, and the GDR's Pensions Alignment Law of 28 June 1990 that was based on the treaty, introduced the principle of the indexation of pensions to increases in earnings and brought in the west German law on contributions. Under the Unification Treaty, guarantees of pension security for pensioners and those approaching pensionable age were given. Finally, with the Pensions Transition Law of 25 July 1991[76] west German benefits law was extended to the east from 1 January 1992 onwards, and existing pensions were simultaneously revalued.

On 1 January 1991 the law on rehabilitation was extended to the new *Bundesländer*. Here there proved to be a serious problem about preserving the former GDR's arrangements for health cures, as there was a sharp fall in applications for cures after unification, owing to the general difficulty of the economic situation and widespread anxiety about jobs. The representatives of the new *Länder* were told that as the successor authorities, they were now responsible for state-run cure facilities and had to ensure that they did not collapse. For their part, the pensions insurance providers sought to encourage an increase in applications for health cures, particularly for children's cures, in order to help the cure facilities get through this barren period.[77]

The first task was to build up a new organization for pensions insurance in the GDR, and later the new *Bundesländer*. The pensions insurance providers played a crucial constructive role in this process. Along with the other leading social insurance bodies in the Federal Republic, they had met leading figures from the corresponding bodies in the GDR on 10/11 May 1990 at the Linowsee near Berlin and set up working groups to deal with the problems of transforming the GDR's social insurance system.[78] On 31 May 1990 the GDR Labour Minister Regine Hildebrandt thanked the president of the Federal Insurance Office for White-Collar Workers, Helmut Kaltenbach, for the 'extensive help that [had] already been provided' and accepted his offer to make available the head of the Office's general department, Fritz Rauschenbach, as an 'experienced adviser'.[79] She also obtained the services of Rudolf Kolb, the influential managing director of the Association of German Pensions Insurance Providers, to advise, in particular, on the development of *Land* insurance authorities from 1 August 1990 onwards.[80] Initially, 'information offices' were set up in the fourteen regions of the GDR, in which specialists from the west German pensions insurance providers gave advice to GDR district social insurance administrators, especially with regard to rehabilitation and the monitoring of contributions. In addition, five *Land* insurance authorities from the old *Bundesländer* were designated as so-called corresponding authorities, each of which was to provide advice and support for one of the new *Bundesländer*.[81]

At first it was difficult to ensure a steady flow of contributions. Often, due social insurance contributions were not collected from wages or paid by employers, or they were forwarded, as in GDR days, to the state budget rather than to the social insurance providers by the tax offices; it was not until 1 January 1991 that the latter passed on the role of collecting contributions to the health insurers on behalf of *all* social insurance providers. To close the growing gap in finances and make sure that pensions were paid on time in August 1990, an advance of about 2,400 million DM had to be provided from the Federal budget.[82] Inspectors from the social insurance providers were deployed, and at times the entire contributions collection personnel of the western pensions insurance providers were also used. By the end of the year the weak points in the system had been more or less ironed out and the east German social insurance deficit reduced.[83]

An especially difficult challenge, as pensions insurance in the east was developed, was the recruitment of staff. On 7 August 1990 the east German minister Hildebrandt appealed to GDR social insurance personnel to remain in their jobs, holding out the promise that they would be given guarantees of continued employment.[84] Pensions insurance was particularly seriously affected,[85] because many members of staff were leaving to work for the health insurers, which had been established earlier than the *Land* insurance authorities and could offer employment in the same location.

The *Land* insurance authorities had at their disposal about 2,000 employees from the pensions insurance department of the former social insurance system of the GDR, and a further 4,000 people were taken on. By the summer of 1992 the Federal Insurance Office for White-Collar Workers had installed more than 4,000 new members of staff, about 90 per cent of whom came from east Berlin and the new *Bundesländer*. A further 600 people were recruited by the Federal Miners' Insurance Institute for their work in the east.[86]

To ensure that there would be sufficient office space to cope with the building-up of the west German welfare state in the east, Blüm, adopting the principle of 'swords into ploughshares', had obtained an agreement with the GDR Minister for Disarmament and Defence, Rainer Eppelmann, whereby barracks and other property of the National People's Army would be made over to the Federal Institute of Labour and the social insurance providers.[87] In a presentation in November 1992 the deputy managing director of the Association of German Pensions Insurance Providers, Eberhard Schaub, described how he had made two helicopter flights over the entire territory of the GDR, inspecting possible locations for what were later selected as the administrative centres for the *Land* insurance authorities of Brandenburg, Saxony-Anhalt, Saxony, and Thuringia.[88] At first, however, there were difficulties in actually taking over some of the properties, as the Bundeswehr officers who were now in charge of the barracks either refused to acknowledge the agreement made by Blüm and Eppelmann or claimed not to have heard of it. In October 1990 the then deputy managing director of the Association of German Insurance Providers, Franz Ruland, had to appeal to Blüm to tell the Federal Defence Ministry to adhere to the terms of the agreement so that the *Land* insurance authorities could begin their work on time.[89] There were also complications in clarifying the ownership status of buildings that had come under *Treuhand* administration. Blüm's request that the pensions insurance providers, and not just the *Länder* and local authorities, should be allowed to acquire Federally owned properties at reduced prices was flatly turned down by Waigel, the Federal Finance Minister,[90] and the providers were eventually obliged to pay about 80 million DM for buildings that were originally to have been made over to them free of charge.[91]

The Unification Treaty had stated that for a transition period, lasting until 31 December 1991 at the latest, the responsibility for handling pensions and accident insurance in the east—though not for health insurance, which it was believed would be ready to function by 1 January 1991—should rest with a 'Social Insurance Transitional Authority', in succession to the 'Joint Social Insurance Provider' set up by the State Treaty. However, by the late autumn of 1990 the Joint Provider was in a state of total breakdown, as most of the roughly 8,000 members of staff, including almost everyone in the general departments of organization, personnel, and administration and a large proportion of those responsible for pensions insurance, had accepted appointments with the health insurance companies, especially the General Local Health Insurance Providers, from 1 January 1991 onwards.[92]

The new head of the Social Insurance Transitional Authority, Martin Ammermüller, accordingly wrote to Blüm on 14 November 1990, just two days after taking up his post,[93] that in his view the Transitional Authority should not be fully built up only to be dismantled after a short transition period, and that most of its tasks should be taken over by the *Land* insurance authorities from 1 January 1991. However, he said, this would necessitate massive support from the west German pensions insurance providers: Blüm should brief them and appeal to them to undertake the responsibility. After discussions with the self-governing pensions insurance providers on 22 November and a special conference of managing directors on 29 November 1990, the providers said that they would be prepared to take over the functions of the Transitional Authority as early as the coming year. At the same time, through the Association of German Pensions Insurance Providers, the *Land* insurance authorities, which took over about 20 per cent of GDR social insurance personnel available at local and regional level, were given responsibility for paying out all pensions and social care benefits for blue- and white-collar workers and miners. The Federal Insurance Office for White-Collar Workers took on those members of staff in the central administration of the Joint Provider who had not gone over to the health insurance companies, together with the personnel of the supplementary provision systems. It was given the job of dealing with all the work arising in connection with the supplementary provision systems, centrally administering the Transitional Authority's financial resources, and releasing people from compulsory insurance, which had to be done centrally; it was also to support the Transitional Authority in terms of personnel and material resources.[94]

'At the last moment', then, the pensions insurance providers stepped in to ensure that pension benefits in the east could continue to be paid.[95] The Transitional Authority, employing between 30 and 40 members of staff in three departments,[96] retained a general role regarding matters of principle and coordination, in particular the calculation of pensions, which was done by the computer centre in Leipzig, whose staff of about 150 were also allocated to them. It also remained responsible for the continued running, for a limited period, of the medical assessment service, for which about 700 new employment contracts, including 260 for doctors, were created,[97] winding up the assets of the GDR's social insurance,[98] and sorting out legal squabbles resulting from actions by the GDR Joint Social Insurance Provider.

For several months during 1991 the debate on social policy in the Federal Republic was dominated by the drafting and passage of the Pensions Transition Law of 25 July 1991. The debate, and the contents of this complex piece of legislation, can be discussed only briefly here.[99] By 25 February 1991 a draft bill, prepared by the experts in the Ministry of Labour, was ready; the document, running to more than 500 typed pages, adhered closely to the principles laid out in the Unification Treaty. After hearings with the relevant associations on 13 March 1991,[100] the coalition parties and the Federal government introduced identical drafts in April and these were given a first reading in the Bundestag on 26 April 1991.

The draft bill was fiercely criticized by the SPD,[101] and on 17 May 1991 also came under fire from the Social Democratic majority in the Bundesrat.[102] In both cases the Social Democrats' main objection was that because the legislation was one-sidedly based on west German pensions law, west German preconceptions were being 'foisted' on the east and the opportunity for carrying out a major reform of pensions in Germany as a whole was going begging. More specifically, critics attacked, as detrimental to women, the removal of minimum pensions and of the GDR's generous regulations on added pensionable years for those bringing up children or caring for dependants and for women taking their pension at 60. There was criticism too—also voiced by the advisory committee on social policy, in a statement issued on 28 May 1991[103]—of the incorporation of eastern pensions insurance into a unified Germany-wide pensions system, because by making contribution payers in the west finance the deficit in the east, it would force them to carry an unfair share of the burden of the costs of German unity.[104]

The difficult tactical situation that faced the Social Democrats was outlined by Rudolf Dreßler on 7 May 1991, ahead of the sitting of the Bundesrat, in a letter to the Social Affairs Ministers of the SPD-led *Länder*.[105] In principle, he said, the SPD would not be able to vote for the Pensions Transition Law, because to do so would 'wipe out all the progressive elements in earlier GDR legislation'. It was also clear, however, that the party could not, 'in the final analysis, allow the Pensions Transition Law to fail completely', since it would not be right to withhold from the new *Bundesländer* the partial improvements it included: for example, on widows' pensions, the introduction of a flexible pensionable age, and the changes to the law on disability pensions. He therefore proposed that although the new law should eventually be approved in the Bundesrat, the SPD should try to achieve certain 'structural improvements'. However, since the alternative proposed by the SPD—namely, to introduce a Preliminary Pensions Law[106] bringing forward improvements for eastern pensioners to 1 January 1992 but otherwise delaying the transition until 1 January 1993—had no chance of being accepted, a compromise solution was found, after the committee stage, by a small group of insurance experts and politicians specializing in social policy.[107] The draft law was then approved by the Bundestag on 21 June and by the Bundesrat on 5 July 1991. This obviated the need for the Mediation Committee to become involved, which would have meant special sittings of both Bundestag and Bundesrat during the summer recess,[108] when in any case there was only just enough time to complete the administrative technicalities needed before the legislation came into force. Blüm also made it very clear to the CDU/CSU members in the Bundestag that if the Mediation Committee were to become involved, then there would be a pensions debate over the summer recess and the cross-party consensus on pensions that had so far prevailed might be put at risk.[109]

The unity that was achieved, not just within the governing coalition—which itself had been hard enough to secure—but between the coalition and the opposition, bordered, in the words of the FDP's spokeswoman Gisela Babel, on the miraculous. It was the product, she said, of the 'adroit negotiating skills, the tenacity, the determination and the courage of the political spokesmen [of the CDU/CSU, the FDP, and the SPD] Julius Louven, Julius Cronenberg, and Rudolf Dreßler'.[110] A key element of the compromise was a resolution of 21 June 1991, supported by the CDU/CSU, SPD, and FDP,[111] which extended the protection of eastern pensions from the originally planned termination date of 30 June 1995 to 31 December 1996 and declared that the intervening period should be used to 'improve the retirement protection of women within statutory pensions insurance' and, *inter alia*, give fuller recognition than previously to time devoted to the bringing up of children or the care of dependants. An enhancement of independent pension expectancies for women should play an important part in dealing with the question of poverty in old age. The guarantees regarding admittance to a pension under the old GDR rules were extended considerably beyond the terms in the draft law. The compromise also specified that the social allowance, which in the draft law was to be granted only until the end of 1991 for new pensions, could now be awarded until 31 December 1993; in addition, it would not be discontinued on 30 June 1995, as had been laid down in the Unification Treaty, but could be paid until 31 December 1996 at the latest. On the other hand, from 1 January 1992 it would continue to be paid only if the monthly income of a single person was less than 600 DM or that of a married couple less than 960 DM.[112] From 1 July 1992 the social allowance was raised in the new *Bundesländer* in line with the average increase in income support. There was particular difficulty and controversy over pensions and expectancies from the GDR systems of special and supplementary provision for particular groups, which were converted by legislation and not, as originally envisaged, by Federal government statutory order.[113] As has already been mentioned,[114] the low valuation put on these pensions, the administration of which was transferred to the Federal Insurance Office for White-Collar Workers, was strongly contested by those affected, and a number of increases were subsequently granted through legislation and legal judgements.

There was an especially delicate political issue with regard to so-called honorary pensions, which the GDR had awarded to a total of about 11,000 people and which were valued at 1,400 DM per month for 'victims of fascist persecution' and 1,700 DM for 'fighters against fascism'. There was disagreement whether these pensions should continue to be paid, should be reduced, or should be abolished. A working group from the Labour, Finance, Interior, and Justice Ministries and the Federal Chancellery had at first taken the view that honorary pensions on this scale were not justifiable in social policy terms, not only because they exceeded comparable benefits in the old *Bundesländer* but, more particularly, because they far exceeded the very low compensation payments available to 'victims of GDR injustice'. However, the initial hard-line attitude that these pensions should be either drastically reduced or eliminated altogether (although individuals should be able, where appropriate grounds existed, to apply for compensation in accordance with the Federal Compensation Law)[115] could not be sustained, partly for domestic political reasons but also as a result of criticism from abroad, especially from Jewish organizations.[116] After months of discussion involving the SPD, the Central Council of Jews in Germany, and the Claims Conference it was decided that existing pensions should continue to be paid, at a uniform rate of 1,400 DM. In individual cases a pension might be terminated or reduced, if there had been breaches of principles of humanity or legality or if the beneficiary had seriously abused his position, either to his own advantage or to the disadvantage of others. New compensatory pensions should be approved in cases where compensation payments had been illegally disallowed and withdrawn by the former GDR.[117]

The core of the Pensions Transition Law was a revaluation of pensions on the basis of the number of years that an individual had worked and of his or her average earnings during the previous twenty years, up to a contributions ceiling corresponding to that applicable in the old *Bundesländer*. If, up to 31 December 1996, the levels of pensions of pensioners and pre-pensioners assessed on this basis came below the amount to which they would have been eligible, without social allowance, under existing legislation, then so-called top-up payments would be made. These latter payments, however, were not indexed to earnings, and they would be phased out after 1996 in five stages of pension alignment. A total of 3.6 million pensions were revalued on 1 January 1992. In addition, there were about 200,000 cases for which no alignable figure could be established, owing to a lack of data, and in which pensions therefore initially continued to be paid at the same level as in December 1991. Top-up payments were made to about 2.4 million of the 3.6 million pensions, affecting 55.6 per cent of men's pensions and 96.7 per cent of women's pensions; about 120,000 widows' pensions were supplemented by top-up payments, and about 80,000 orphans' pensions.[118] Altogether, in 1992, as a result of the pensions transition and the 11.65 per cent pensions increase in the east on 1 January 1992, 96 per cent of pensioners received a higher pension. For women the average rise, also taking into account widows' pensions and top-up payments, was 21.1 per cent, while for men it was 14.8 per cent. Widows gained particularly from the new pensions law. For 780,000 widows, the widow's pension rose by about 270 DM per month, while 150,000 widows became able to claim a surviving dependant's pension for the first time.[119]

The smooth and punctual revaluation of pensions carried out under the Pensions Transition Law (to which some adjustments on points of detail were made in December 1991) was a 'masterly' administrative achievement on the part of the pensions insurance providers.[120] Within the space of a few weeks the necessary programmes had to be set up, pensioners had to be allocated to the appropriate pensions insurance providers, and new policy numbers had to be assigned. Over just a few days in November the providers had to reassess four million pensions on the computers at the Leipzig computer centre, and during a fortnight in December they had to print out the pension notifications and dispatch them from two specially established post offices. The first notifications of reassessments were sent out on 4 December 1991; the last on 23 December.[121] According to the *Frankfurter Allgemeine Zeitung* of 27 December 1991, the pensions insurance system won 'a battle against time, despite innumerable difficulties', and, in doing so, 'made an important contribution to social harmony'.[122]

The cessation of many of the allowances that had previously been paid was a particular cause of disquiet in the new *Bundesländer*: many married couples, for example, now lost the allowance that had earlier been received by one of the spouses. The overall number of people receiving social allowances fell by about 460,000. In addition, the size of payments was reduced, with the result that for 200,000 pensioners the sum they received from the combination of pension and social allowances was reduced, on average, by 92 DM per month.[123] Allowances for children, at 60 DM per month, were eliminated for about 66,000 pensioners. So too was the married couple's allowance, at 200 DM per month, previously payable in only 13,800 cases where the spouse had reached pensionable age and was an invalid, or had one child under the age of 3 or two children under the age of 8, and did not have an individual pension entitlement. The same applied to social care benefit, special social care benefit, and visual impairment benefit, which on 1 January 1991 had been paid to a total of over half a million pensioners, with monthly amounts ranging from 20 DM for the first level of social care to 240 DM for the highest level of visual impairment benefit.[124] (In the case of many benefits, however, claims could be made to other benefit providers from 1 January 1991 onwards.) The switch to Federal pensions law also meant that the extent to which added pensionable years were recognized was now much smaller. Many people, too, did not realize that because top-up payments, paid to protect existing levels of support, were not included in the general pensions increase of 11.65 per cent that took place on 1 January 1992, the increase for recipients of insurance-based pensions with top-up payments was smaller, with the average increase of insurance-based pensions rising only by 8.1 per cent.[125] Altogether, about 180,000 objections to the pension notifications were lodged, of which only a few had to do with incorrect calculations, the great majority being directed against the new provisions in the law.[126]

Over the following years the main challenges with regard to pensions insurance[127] were twofold. The first was the flood of new applications for pensions, arising from the fact that men could now opt to draw an early retirement pension from the age of 60 onwards and from the easing of the claim conditions for pensions for surviving dependants. The second was the transfer of claims from the supplementary and special provision systems, which, under the Pensions Transition Law, had at first simply been converted *en bloc* and were to be recalculated on a case-by-case basis later. Further tasks were the development of provision for rehabilitation, and the merger of the data processing systems in east and west.

Pensions insurance finances at first improved, as a result of the savings incurred through the pensions reform of 1989/92, but this favourable situation did not last. The reasons for the deterioration were the increase in the rate of early retirement,[128] the recession of 1993, and the high level of west-to-east transfer payments within pensions insurance, which rose from 4,500 million DM in 1992 to 16,000 million DM in 1995.[129] For the year 1994 the contribution rate for pensions insurance, paid jointly by employers and employees, had to be raised from 17.5 per cent of wages to 19.2 per cent. Even so, there was a deficit of 2,000 million DM.[130] Further rises in contributions would be necessary if a reduction in benefits was to be avoided. Altogether, the share of gross domestic product represented by statutory pensions insurance expenditure was about 10 per cent in the west but about 20 per cent in the east.[131]

The difficult economic situation, political pressures to reduce additional wage costs, and the demand, increasingly voiced in the media, for action to be taken about the 'demographic time bomb'—which meant that a proportionately smaller population of working age would have to support a proportionately larger population of the elderly—led from 1993/4 to a renewed debate on the fundamental principles of pensions insurance. In this debate, there were growing calls for a tax-financed basic pension to be introduced, or for the financing of statutory pensions insurance benefits through current contributions to be supplemented by private capital-funded systems. The Labour Minister, Blüm, tried to defuse the argument by insisting that people's pensions were secure[132] and spoke out strongly, in particular, against the suggestion of a basic pension, terming it a 'bonus for moonlighters and dropouts'.[133] It became clear, however, that during the forthcoming parliamentary term 1994–8 the political agenda would have to include not only the enhancement of independent pensions insurance expectancies for women—as heralded in the Bundestag's resolution of 21 June 1991—but fundamental reform of pensions insurance generally.

11.4.2 Accident insurance

Like pensions insurance, west German accident insurance was extended to the new *Bundesländer* in a series of steps. The State Treaty of 18 May 1990 had included the basic decision that a separate system of accident insurance would be established, and close cooperation subsequently began between the providers of accident insurance in the Federal Republic and the GDR government to build up such a system in the GDR, initially as a division of the Joint Social Insurance Provider.[134] Under the GDR's Social Insurance Law, responsibility for rehabilitation and accident prevention was at first undertaken by the Joint Provider; its responsibilities were later transferred to the professional cooperative associations of employers running accident insurance. Altogether, 125 centres of the Technical Control Service were set up[135] and the trade associations' industrial medicine service was expanded to take in the east.[136] With the Pensions Alignment Law of 28 June 1990 accident pensions were increased by a minimum of 90 per cent: a substantially higher rise than the rise in pensions from pensions insurance.[137] A section of Federal Republic accident insurance law was extended to the new *Bundesländer* through the Unification Treaty on 1 January 1991, and the remainder through the Pensions Transition Law on 1 January 1992. The new accident insurance providers, operating without pensions records, had to allocate roughly 300,000 existing accident pensions to the trade associations as industry-based cost-bearers and take over the old cases from 1 April 1991 with scant financial support from the Federal government. Leaving aside a Federal contribution of 400 million DM for conscripts, which was regarded as a continuing cost from the war, the providers also became responsible for the high costs of care and medical treatment of the workers (between 500,000 and 600,000 in number) who had been employed by Wismut AG during the period 1945–91 and who in the GDR had their own social insurance system. These uranium miners had been exposed to working conditions extremely damaging to their health, particularly during the period 1946–54.

The operational structure of accident insurance also underwent speedy alignment. On 1 January 1991 thirty industrial trade associations and four Federal executive authorities took over their responsibilities in east Germany. Two new agricultural trade associations, and a separate accident insurance provider in each *Bundesland* for public service employees in the new *Länder* and local authorities, began work. The accident insurance trade associations, among which the industrial associations alone provided €10,900 million in benefits for existing GDR accident pensioners between 1991 and 2005, increased their personnel by more than 8,700, to 28,742, between 1989 and 1994 as a result of expansion to the east.[138]

11.4.3 Health insurance and the health system

The Unification Treaty had stipulated that a multipartite system of health insurance would be introduced in the east on 1 January 1991. In a highly competitive process of territorial acquisition, the different health insurance providers spread out across the new *Bundesländer*,[139] the General Local Health Insurance Providers (AOK) enjoying something of a head start.

According to an assessment made by the Federal Ministry of Health on 18 June 1991,[140] of the total of roughly twelve million members of health insurance schemes in the new *Bundesländer*, through whom a further four million family members were also insured, 7.4 million were insured through the AOK. The AOK had an extensive coverage, with over 270 offices at local level and a further 100 part-time centres, for the most part in industrial enterprises. They employed 12,000 regular members of staff, all but 100 of whom were from the new *Bundesländer*, where they had mainly been employed by the GDR's social insurance system. The Substitute Sickness Funds (*Ersatzkassen*), with 500 offices and 6,200 members of staff, served nearly 2.7 million members; the two largest, the Barmer Ersatzkasse and the Deutsche Angestellten-Krankenkasse, had also built up comprehensive administrative networks. The company-based sickness funds employed 2,000 personnel and encompassed 1.3 million members, but the trade guild sickness funds (*Innungskrankenkassen*) were still in the process of expanding their activity. The Federal Miners' Insurance Institute had insured about 450,000 new members in the east, taking over 700 personnel on the spot in the mining districts and reinforcing these on occasion with up to 75 western members of staff. In addition, the Agricultural Health Insurers had set up a central office in Berlin for the few independent farmers in the east. Seamen were served either by a regional office of the Seamen's Health Insurers in Rostock or, in other regions, by the AOK. By 1995 over 90 per cent of the population in the east were insured with the statutory health insurers, and almost all of the insurers' 23,000 members of staff had been recruited within the new *Bundesländer*.[141]

The distribution of members between particular health insurers is significantly different in east and west. Private health insurance, used for full cover by somewhat less than one-tenth of the population in the west, plays even less of a role in the east, where there had been relatively few civil servants and self-employed. In October 1994, of the members of statutory health insurance schemes, 55.5 per cent in the east and 41.3 per cent in the west were insured through the AOK. The proportion of members of the Federal Miners' Insurance Institute in the east, 3.1 per cent, was higher than that in the west (2.2 per cent), whereas the proportions of members of the company-based sickness funds (7.1 per cent in the east versus 11.4 per cent in the west) and of the white- and blue-collar Substitute Sickness Funds (27.8 and 0.5 per cent in the east, versus 35.7 and 2.1 per cent in the west) were considerably lower in the east than in the west. The proportions in the trade guild sickness funds were roughly similar (5.5 per cent in the east, 5.7 per cent in the west).[142]

The central problem in the health system had not been caused by German unification. This was the greatly disproportionate rise in the system's costs, even in comparison with other areas of the welfare state. Between 1960 and 1992, costs in the Federal Republic had soared from 4.8 per cent to 8.7 per cent of gross domestic product.[143] The main reasons for this surge were the rise in the proportion of the elderly within the population, particularly the very old with their greater susceptibility to illness; the rise in the costs of medical advance, due in part to the acquisition of ever more expensive diagnostic and therapeutic equipment; and the high level of expenditure on labour-intensive health care, where increases in productivity were hard to achieve. A further factor was the difficulty of running a highly complex health care system efficiently, when the activities both of the providers of services (doctors, hospitals, the pharmaceutical industry, and pharmacists) and of patients were leading to increases in services and costs.[144] From the mid-1970s, in particular, there were repeated attempts in the Federal Republic—as in other countries—to bear down on costs, but such successes as were achieved were short-lived. The Federal government hoped that the Health Service Reform Law of 20 December 1988[145] would lead to a longer-term reduction in costs. The law, which specified fixed sums for drugs, other medication, and medical aids, imposed restrictions on charges for dentures, spectacles, and similar items, and called for an element of payment by patients, was passed after lengthy arguments within the governing coalition and in the face of fierce criticism by the opposition. Its effect was, indeed, to reduce expenditure by 4,700 million DM in 1989, partly as a result of treatments carried out before the new law came into effect, and surpluses of 9,400 million and 6,100 million DM were obtained in 1989 and 1990 respectively. Average health insurance contributions were reduced from 12.9 per cent of wages in 1989 to 12.2 per cent in 1991.[146]

The improvement, however, did not last. By 1991 there was already a deficit of 5,600 million DM, and this rose to 9,100 million DM in 1992. In the new *Bundesländer*, where the health insurers were able independently to set their own contribution rates from 1 January 1992 onwards, a surplus of 2,800 million DM in 1991 was transformed into a deficit of 260 million DM in 1992. In the old *Bundesländer* the average contribution rate had to be increased to 13.4 per cent until 1 January 1993.[147] Publicly, the Federal Ministry of Labour argued that the delayed implementation of the legislation was responsible for the reform's failure, maintaining that self-administration had been hampered by the process of expansion in the new *Bundesländer* and that powerful vested interests in the health system had been able to circumvent the law.[148] Internally, however, shortcomings on the part of the Health Ministry, which had been responsible for health insurance since the formation of the governing coalition in January 1991, were also identified.[149]

When Horst Seehofer was appointed as Federal Health Minister in place of Gerda Hasselfeldt at the beginning of May 1992, a thoroughgoing reform of the health system was immediately set in train. In a briefing to the CDU/CSU members of parliament, Seehofer emphasized the *political* need for reform, presenting three main arguments. First, there was no point in further talk about social care insurance if contributions to statutory health insurance were not stabilized. Secondly, any raising of health insurance contributions would be tantamount to a reduction in the increase in pensions, as pensioners had to pay a proportion of health insurance contributions. Thirdly, a failure to act would turn health policy into an election issue in 1994, and the coalition would suffer as a result.[150] The Health Service Structure Law[151] underwent a process of intensive political argument and negotiation, which reached a climax and a final resolution in discussions among leading experts on health policy in the governing parties and the SPD at Bad Lahnstein in October 1992.[152] The resulting 'well-balanced and workable compromise'[153] was passed by the Bundestag on 9 December 1992 with broad majority support from the CDU/CSU, the SPD, and the FDP, 455 members voting in favour and 54 against, with 21 abstentions.[154] In his detailed defence of the compromise to the CDU/CSU parliamentarians, Seehofer explained that contact with the SPD had been an 'absolute must', given that the law required the assent of the Bundesrat, where the opposition had a majority. He also argued that savings in excess of 10,000 million DM had to be made, and that the sixteen *Bundesländer*, which were also interested parties, had to be brought on board.[155]

The central provisions of the law dealt with budgeting, albeit time-limited, of the costs of drugs and other medical aids and of doctors' fees; the creation of an approved list of reimbursable drugs; limitations on the registration of new doctors in areas already over-supplied with physicians; and a reform of the financing of hospital services. A particularly important element, included largely as a result of pressure by the SPD, was the introduction of a reform of the organization of statutory health insurance. A risk structure equalization between the health insurance providers would take place on 1 January 1994, to even out the differences in the levels of members' earnings subject to statutory insurance, in the number of insured family members not liable to contributions, and in the sex and age of the insured. In addition, from 1996/7 onwards competition between insurance providers was to be encouraged by an extension and standardization of the entitlement of white- and blue-collar workers to choose freely between particular providers. Especially significant for the new *Bundesländer* was the Federal government's commitment to provide 700 million DM annually between 1995 and 2004 for investment in hospitals, this sum to be at least matched by the *Länder* and—over a twenty-year period—by the health insurance providers.[156]

It was unusual for a governing coalition and an opposition to forge a compromise in the area of health policy, in this instance prompted by the existence of an SPD majority in the Bundesrat.[157] It was also notable that the power of the doctors' organizations and the other providers of medical services had been held in check, while the position of the fragmented forces of the health insurers had been enhanced and the government had strengthened its ability to manage the health system.[158] The FDP, which wanted comprehensive care through statutory health insurance to be replaced by a system of basic provision, and greater account to be taken, through higher private payments, of the costs of medical services,[159] was pushed as far as it was prepared to go by the 'grand coalition' of health politicians in the CDU/CSU and SPD. Significantly, as well as twelve CDU/CSU members of the Bundestag and five SPD members, twelve FDP parliamentarians voted against the law and a further seven abstained; forty-one voted in favour.[160] It was clear that the FDP would not be prepared to make any further concessions over health policy.

At first, the Health Service Structure Law brought about the savings that had been expected. Surpluses of about 6,500 million DM were recorded both in 1993 and in 1994, and these enabled modest reductions in contribution rates to be made in the old *Bundesländer* in 1994 and 1995. However, in 1995 and 1996 deficits returned, partly because the law had still not been fully implemented, and the result was another rise in contributions, an increase in co-payments by the insured, and adjustments in benefits law.[161] Further structural reforms to the health system and to statutory health insurance were added to the political agenda.

11.4.4 The introduction of social care insurance

The most important achievement of the 'grand coalition' in social policy that prevailed in this area between 1991 and 1994—indeed, the most significant reform and institutional change in the German welfare state during the Kohl era altogether—was the creation of social care insurance as a fifth main branch of social insurance. Improved assistance for those in need of social care had been a topic of public debate since 1974, when the Board for Support for the Elderly in Germany had published a report on inpatient treatment of illnesses of the elderly. In the years between 1974 and 1990 further reports, surveys, and draft laws had been produced,[162] and under the Health Service Reform Law of December 1988, in a first step, the responsibility for the provision of certain outpatient services for roughly 600,000 people in serious and severe need of care was taken over by the health insurance providers.[163] The debate also assumed new momentum as a result of unification, since about 500,000 people in need of social care in the GDR had been in receipt of services through social insurance.[164]

There were several reasons why the problem of social care provision was becoming more urgent: the ageing of the population, which meant that there were very many more old people dependent on care; the decline in the number of people—usually women—available to provide home care, as a result of the fall in births and the fact that more women were seeking employment; and the heavy cost of income support, which at the beginning of the 1990s was being paid to 84 per cent of the over 450,000 people dependent on inpatient care.[165] Income support was payable only after the person's own financial resources had been exhausted, and on condition that relatives responsible for the person's maintenance should bear all or part of the costs. Roughly a further 1.2 million more people in need of social care lived at home, mainly looked after by relatives, neighbours, or outpatient care providers.

On 26 September 1990, at the annual conference of the Substitute Sickness Funds, the Federal Labour Minister, Blüm, took the surprising step of announcing that the provision of social care was to become a fifth pillar of social insurance.[166] Although the chairman of the FDP, Count Lambsdorff, in a television debate with Blüm before the December 1990 election, had dismissed the idea as a 'pipe-dream' which had not been agreed with the Finance Minister or mentioned in the CDU's election manifesto,[167] there was widespread demand for a 'draft law providing protection in the event of need of social care', and the proposed measure was included in the coalition agreement of 16 January 1991. In his inaugural statement of government policy on 30 January 1991[168] Kohl announced that a draft law would be presented to parliament by the summer of 1992. However, it was clear from a summary paper produced during the negotiations on the formation of the coalition, listing seven key points that would have to be addressed by a law dealing with the problem of social care,[169] that as yet there was no agreement on a particular model of social care insurance. The government, however, was opposed to a tax-financed benefits law of the sort that had originally been proposed by the Social Democrats, the trade unions, and some associations representing the disabled, on the grounds that that would merely add to the financial burden imposed by German unification. A solution based on the income support system, linking social care benefits to financial need, was also rejected. The remaining options were a voluntary scheme involving private insurance, based on an accumulated capital fund backed up by state subsidies or tax relief; a form of compulsory private social care insurance; or—the solution proposed by the Labour Ministry and tenaciously advocated by Blüm—a form of social care insurance with benefits paid from current contributions, under the aegis of the health insurance providers.[170] The project was vehemently opposed by the employers. Klaus Murmann, the president of the National Union of German Employers' Associations, said that he could not remember a proposed piece of legislation that had been 'so universally rejected, not just by business, but by the academic world and the Bundesbank'.[171] The employers and the business associations favoured a bipartite model. This would involve the establishment of a fund (without a capital fund) for the 1.65 million people already in need of social care and for people over the age of 60 (roughly 16.4 million). In addition, the entire residential population over the age of 25 would become members of a private social care insurance system that would be based exclusively on capital funds for the younger age-groups and would levy age-related contributions. The fund would be financed by contributions from those groups approaching the age when social care might be needed and, in the event of a shortfall, by subsidies from the employers. Benefits would deliberately be kept at a low level and, in the case of those already in need of social care, would be subject to a means test.[172] As late as February 1996—long after the law had been passed—the National Union of German Employers' Associations said in a statement that the absence of a means test was a major flaw in the system as established.[173]

Only after long and highly contentious arguments within the coalition about possible alternatives was a majority of the FDP won over to the Labour Ministry's social insurance scheme. The FDP's agreement, however, was conditional on the granting of adequate compensation to employers for their 50 per cent share of the insurance contributions. In the CDU/CSU, too, there was strong initial opposition to a form of social care insurance with benefits paid from current contributions, particularly among representatives of middle-class interests and in the business wing of the party.[174] On the other hand, the Labour Minister obtained support from an internal party commission on social care headed by Heiner Geißler, from the ministers of labour and social affairs of the CDU-led *Länder*, from the CDU social affairs committees chaired by Ulf Fink, and from the CDU Women's Union led by Rita Süssmuth.[175] The coalition parties began consulting on the development of social care insurance in November 1991 and finally reached agreement on social care insurance and on the principle of compensation for employers in a resolution on principles of 30 June 1992. There were further tough negotiations before it was decided, on 27 May 1993, that employees should bear a share in earnings compensation in the event of illness, so as to reduce the burden on employers.[176] Even then, however, elements in the CDU/CSU and within the coalition continued to attempt to thwart the project.

During the parliamentary term 1990–4 no piece of legislation was the subject of such intensive debate and controversy in the organizations and committees of the CDU and the CSU, and especially among the parties' members in the Bundestag, as the introduction of social care insurance. Throughout, Blüm stressed the importance of social care insurance from the point of view of political strategy. All the associations for the disabled, he said, all the Independent Welfare Associations, the Protestant church's welfare bodies, the Catholic Caritas organization, the war victims' associations, the four major doctors' bodies, the trade unions, the German Trade Union Federation, the German White-Collar Workers' Trade Union, and all the churches supported his proposal, and this alliance should not be put at risk.[177] On 27 May 1993, however, the coalition agreement was called into question within the CDU/CSU parliamentary party by Gerhard Stoltenberg, the former Federal Finance Minister (1982–9). In view of the cuts that had been necessary in the Federal budget, Stoltenberg said, and the rises in taxes and charges, he could not 'today' endorse the further charges that were being envisaged and therefore had to oppose the scheme for social care insurance as it stood.[178] The issue was finally resolved through the intervention of the Federal Chancellor, Kohl, who had held back during the preceding stages of the debate[179] but now—after years of argument at *Land* party conferences, in *Land* party committees, among local party associations, at the national conference of the CDU, and at the corresponding levels of the CSU—came out powerfully for a system of compulsory social care insurance involving compensation for employers. The German Trade Union Federation, he said, was in favour of the SPD model, and there was no doubt that if the SPD were to form a government with the Greens, or with the Greens and the FDP, then some non-compensatory form of social care insurance would be implemented. The FDP would not refuse to join such a coalition over the issue, and business interests would then naturally fall into line. The CDU and CSU would not be able to fight an election without addressing a subject which 'is not only a matter of rational sense but—and this applies particularly to the over-60s, who are a significant part of the electorate—which speaks to people's concerns about the solidarity of society, about working together'.[180] Kohl finally exerted his authority and stifled the argument within the CDU on 15 June 1993.[181]

According to Julius Cronenberg—who put on record his fundamental opposition to a system of social care insurance not based on a capital fund in statements in the Bundestag on 7 July and 22 October 1993[182] and resigned his post as his party's spokesman on social policy over the issue—the FDP approved the new law by majority vote only in order to avoid putting the coalition at risk. In the view of Count Lambsdorff, the party's chairman, the coalition might otherwise have collapsed.[183] Klaus Murmann, the president of the National Union of German Employers' Associations, later said that he regarded the way in which social care insurance was financed as 'the greatest fiasco' of his period in office, and criticized himself and his colleagues for not having developed an alternative model 'earlier and more intensively' in collaboration with the insurance industry.[184] Support for social care insurance came from the Social Democrats, who incorporated their own ideas in a draft law of 18 September 1991[185] and pressed the case for them with the trade unions.[186] There was also backing from the local authorities,[187] and, across parties, from the *Länder*,[188] which had a huge vested interest in reducing the burden of income support. In addition, most of the disability organizations were in favour.[189]

Nevertheless, the draft law that was finally introduced by the coalition parties at the end of June 1993[190] came close to foundering, since, along with the trade unions and the employers, the Social Democrats and the Bundesrat—which was controlled by a majority of SPD-led *Länder*—had strong reservations about it. The SPD and the unions were strongly opposed, in particular, to the employers' being compensated by the limiting of continued payment of wages in the event of illness, on the grounds that this was an intervention into free collective bargaining; the Christian Democratic Association of Employees also had great misgivings on this score.[191] It took two procedures by the Mediation Committee of the Bundestag and Bundesrat and repeated talks between the leaders of the coalition parties and the opposition and the SPD-led *Länder*, as well as a series of improvements in benefits, before agreement regarding compensation for employers was reached. Under the agreement, when the first stage of social care insurance, concerning home care, came into force on 1 January 1995, the *Länder* would cancel a public holiday that always fell on a working day. The Council of Economic Experts, responsible for monitoring the general progress of the economy, would establish whether the cancellation of a further holiday would be necessary when the second stage, involving benefits for inpatient care, came into force on 1 July 1996. If a *Land* did not provide compensation by abolishing a public holiday—or, where applicable, two holidays—then employees would have to cover the whole contribution, which was set at 1 per cent of wages for the first stage of implementation and at 1.7 per cent for the second.[192] This was done in Saxony.

The law laid down that home care was preferable to residence in a care home, and similarly stressed that preventive treatment and rehabilitation, enabling a person to require less social care, to cease to require it, or to avoid having the need for it in the first place, were preferable to dependence on social care benefits. It made significant changes to the social position of those in need of social care, created new jobs, and significantly eased the strain on the income support system.[193] The government's original aim of setting up a system of financing that would be homogeneous, unlike that in health insurance, with the running costs of care facilities and the investment costs financed jointly by price and paid by social care insurance, was not realized, owing to the united opposition of the *Länder*. Instead, a dual system of financing, like the system that existed for health insurance, was created: charges for inpatient care were covered by social care insurance, while investment costs for care facilities were borne by the *Länder*.[194] However, Federal money was made available to the new *Bundesländer* to enable them to put much-needed investment into care facilities: 800 million DM annually for eight years from 1995, which the *Länder* had to supplement by 200 million DM annually.[195]

The effect of the introduction of social care insurance—which was added to the Social Statute Book as Book XI[196]—was to entrench the basic concept of social insurance, in the face of what had been mounting criticism, and underline the path-dependency that has characterized the German system of social protection.[197] That said, social care insurance has certain features that distinguish it from other forms of German social insurance. First, members of the private health insurance schemes, making up roughly 10 per cent of the population, were also included in the system through compulsory private care insurance, with contractual obligations on the health insurers to provide for every member (including those already in need of care), identical sets of benefits, and stipulated premiums.[198] Social care insurance has thus become akin to a form of national insurance. Secondly, employers effectively withheld themselves from the financing of the system as a result of the granting of compensation for their contribution by the waiving of a public holiday. Thirdly, and more importantly, the linking of expenditure to income represented, much more clearly than in the case of similar changes in statutory health insurance, a switch from the principle of meeting demand to that of budgeting.[199] In the long run this situation will not be sustainable. Although social care insurance at first recorded surpluses, since 1999 it has been in deficit,[200] so that despite the introduction since 1 January 2005 of a special contribution of 0.25 per cent of wages for people without children, a fundamental reform of social care insurance has come under discussion: either through transition to a system partially covered by a capital fund, with the development of a demographic reserve to meet the additional costs caused by the ageing of the population, or through a gradual but complete shift to a system based on a capital fund. There has also been debate about rebalancing financial burdens between public and private social care insurance, which continues to yield surpluses.[201] In the event, contributions have increased, while at the same time people with dementia have been included in social care insurance.

11.5 THE BUILD-UP OF SUPPORT FOR WAR VICTIMS

Under the Unification Treaty of 31 August 1990 the Federal Social Provision Law, which specified benefits and care both for disabled ex-servicemen and their surviving dependants and for former political prisoners whose health had been damaged, was extended to the new *Bundesländer*. Altogether, it was planned to set up fifteen social provision offices, five *Land* social provision offices, and five main and ten subsidiary welfare offices.[202] Although talks between the GDR Ministry of Labour and Social Affairs and the regions (later the *Länder*) of the GDR about the rapid establishment of an administrative system for social provision for war victims had been under way since July 1990,[203] and though Blüm had pressed the east German *Land* Prime Ministers hard on the matter,[204] there were considerable initial delays in procuring buildings, equipping offices, and appointing staff, who then had to undergo intensive training in applying the new legislation. The Federal Labour Ministry had pointed out at an early stage that the east German *Länder*, which were responsible for setting up the administrative authorities and recruiting personnel, should be aware how influential the major war victims' associations were and how much political damage would be caused if no pensions were paid, under the Social Provision Law, at the beginning of 1991.[205] The suggestion by the president of the Association of War Victims, the Disabled, and Social Pensioners, Walter Hirrlinger, that the first notifications should be drawn up by the social provision offices in the western *Bundesländer* was rejected by the Social Affairs Ministers in the new *Länder*.[206]

On 12 October 1991 Hirrlinger drew to Blüm's attention the great delays that were occurring in dealing with applications for remuneration under social compensation law and severe disability law, in comparison with the speedy operation of Federal child benefit law, and emphasized that those affected 'are naturally not happy that they are possibly being discriminated against'.[207] A report of 9 August 1991 on the development of the administrative system for social provision for war victims in the new *Bundesländer* emphasized that the newly established social provision machinery—the social provision offices, the *Land* social provision offices, and the main and subsidiary welfare offices—was (with the exception of the subsidiary welfare offices) responsible, on grounds of administrative rationalization and cost saving, for the implementation both of social compensation law, under which the bulk of social provision for war victims fell, and of severe disability law. The report accepted that the new *Länder*, which were responsible for the application of the laws, had, with support from the western *Bundesländer*, fostered the training of members of staff in what were, for them, sometimes quite new areas of legislation, while the Federal Labour Ministry had helped develop the administrative machinery through regular coordinating meetings with responsible officials in the *Länder* and had mounted training courses for medical experts. Nevertheless, in view of the large number of applications, particularly in the areas of social provision for war victims and severe disability law, there was a backlog in the processing of cases and it was possible that some applications, especially those involving social provision for war victims, might not be dealt with for three or four years. It was therefore 'absolutely essential' for the new *Länder* and their western partners to 'redouble their previous efforts'. In the Labour Ministry's view, current posts in the administrative system and in the medical assessment service—the latter was the real bottle-neck as far as the processing of applications was concerned—needed to be quickly filled, and new posts had to be created and a sufficient number of additional qualified external medical assessors enlisted and trained. That should not, however, be done as a substitute for the appointment of doctors fully employed in the medical assessment service.[208] Finally, in a report to Chancellor Kohl on 19 November 1991, Blüm pointed out that although the administrative machinery for social provision had meanwhile been built up in the new *Länder*, the state of the system for processing applications was still desperate. Of about 300,000 applications, only 83,000 had been dealt with, and with most of these only a provisional payment decision had been made. However, it was 'particularly with regard to social provision for war victims', Blüm said, that 'a rapid and unconventional processing system should be insisted upon, as war victims were flagrantly discriminated against during the past four decades of the SED regime, despite the fact that they were the group most severely affected by the war. For many in this group, in view of their advanced age, making them wait means that they will never receive benefits.' Blüm's call for an expansion of posts, though, was strongly resisted by the Finance Ministers of the new *Länder*, several of whom were carrying out, or planning to carry out, across-the-board reductions in posts. Blüm accordingly asked Kohl to warn the Prime Ministers of the new *Länder* at the earliest opportunity that the delays, caused by staff shortages, in dealing with applications both for social provision for war victims and for the issue of passes for the severely disabled meant that 'social unrest could not be ruled out'.[209]

Almost exactly a year later the situation had improved markedly. The way in which applications were processed had been simplified, and contentious legal questions had been resolved; there had also been 'massive intervention by the Federal government' in the *Bundesländer*. Of the 342,000 applications that had been made up to the end of September 1992, decisions had been taken in 276,000 cases, of which 221,000 were decisions about payment.[210] According to a report by the Labour Ministry of January 1993,[211] the proportion of applications that had been handled had since risen to 87 per cent. The Ministry judged this an 'extraordinarily good' outcome, given that the administrative system for social provision for war victims in the new *Länder* had had to be built up from scratch, and given, too, the complexity of social compensation law and the problems inherent in clarifying factual questions and causal relationships, some of which went back sixty years. At the same time, however, the Ministry pointed out that a second stage of processing of applications was required, for which further specific training of staff was necessary, when provisional decisions on applications would have to be replaced by final ones, and questions, some of them difficult, to do with earnings-related benefits would have to be resolved. In addition, a temporary strengthening of numbers in the medical assessment service was needed, so that detailed medical reports for the large number of appeals, as well as reports relating to the law on severe disability, could be produced.

Of the approximately 26,400 applications for welfare for war victims, three-quarters of the cases had been dealt with. The comparative paucity of these applications was attributed to three main factors: a lack of information, the widespread 'prejudice against "welfare" in the sense of charity', and the fact that the people affected were relatively well placed in terms of income and wealth.[212] By the end of March 1996 a total of 440,000 applications for social provision had been made in the new *Bundesländer*, and of these, 238,000 cases resulted in war victim benefits or similar payments. Of a total of 141,000 applications for welfare for war victims, claims were granted in 131,000 cases.[213] Other resources were found in order to provide support to victims of injustice by the GDR whose health had suffered permanent damage, and to those who had been conscripted during the period of Soviet occupation—for example, uranium mine workers in Wismut AG—and had likewise suffered permanent health damage. The total amount of money paid out in social compensation between 1991 and 1995 came to 5,160 million DM.[214]

11.6 SUPPORT FOR THE DISABLED

Problems similar to those that occurred with social provision for war victims arose with the extension to the new *Bundesländer* of Federal law on severe disability as laid down in the Unification Treaty. Because of the lack of trained personnel in the administration of social provision, only 107,000 applications for a severe disability pass, out of a total of 531,000, had been dealt with by the end of October 1991. Since possession of a pass was required for obtaining an array of financial concessions improving the economic position of the severely disabled, many of whom were not well off, it was, as Blüm wrote to Chancellor Kohl on 19 November 1991,[215] 'not acceptable that the severely disabled should have to wait for years for their passes'. He noted that this applied particularly to passes for free travel: the transitional arrangements whereby old GDR free travel passes would remain valid for a limited period would benefit only a small number of people.

Eleven months later the situation had still not basically improved. Although the Labour Ministry had made all manner of simplifications to the way in which the law on severe disability was administered, only 461,000, or 53 per cent, of the approximately 867,000 applications for severe disability passes that had been received by the end of August 1992 had been fully processed. The Federal government's appeals to the new *Bundesländer* to build up staffing numbers in the administration dealing with severe disability law had largely been ineffective, owing to the restrictive personnel policies being pursued by the *Land* Finance Ministers. 'Temporary short-term contracts are coming to an end and not being extended,' Blum reported.[216] However, after the GDR's severe disability passes ceased to be valid on 31 December 1993, the backlog in handling applications began to diminish. By the summer of 1995 roughly 96 per cent out of a total of 1.5 million applications had been processed and about 922,00 passes had been issued.[217]

A further challenge was the creation of new facilities, or the modernization of the wholly inadequate existing facilities, in the new *Bundesländer* for medical rehabilitation of the disabled, and the provision of support for integrating the disabled into employment. On 28 November 1990 Blüm wrote to Regine Hildebrandt,[218] who was now Minister of Labour, Social Affairs, Health, and Women in Brandenburg, that since April 1990 a working group consisting of representatives from the GDR Ministry of Labour and Social Affairs, the Federal Labour Ministry, the rehabilitation providers and the providers of rehabilitation facilities had been developing 'plans for making available as soon as possible . . . provision for professional rehabilitation in the five new *Bundesländer* . . . equivalent to' that in the Federal Republic. He asked her to ensure that *Land* resources would also be included in the Brandenburg budget from 1991 to build up this provision. Two weeks later he sent Hildebrandt a development programme that had been agreed with the professional rehabilitation providers.[219] Under the scheme, an employment promotion facility, with around 400 places, would be set up in each of the new *Länder* to train adult disabled people, and also a special facility in Halle, with 128 places, for blind and visually impaired adults.

In addition, the Labour Ministry's plans included establishing six job training facilities, each with 250 places, to give initial training to disabled young people, creating 180 workshops for the disabled, with about 20,000 places, and modernizing 80 existing workshops with 10,000 places.[220] On 31 October 1991 Blüm wrote to the Social Affairs Ministers of the new *Bundesländer* that approximately 1,200 million DM in investment costs needed to be made available for the seven employment promotion facilities and eight job training facilities that were now being planned and approximately 2,000 million DM for the establishment of the residential facilities and workshops for the disabled. The Federal government and the providers of professional rehabilitation in the old *Bundesländer* would provide a share of the funds, but the new *Bundesländer* would have to contribute roughly one-third of the costs in the case of the employment promotion and job training facilities, 30–5 per cent for the workshops and about 40 per cent for the residential facilities for the disabled.[221] The planned employment promotion and job training facilities were up and running by the beginning of 1994, albeit some in temporary accommodation, but the workshops took longer to be set up and there was still a considerable backlog at the beginning of 1998.[222]

During the advance discussions on the Federal budget for 1993 the Labour Ministry presented an overview of those provisions for the disabled for which it was responsible.[223] Almost three-quarters of the full sum of 210 million DM was assigned to medical and professional rehabilitation in the new *Bundesländer*. Within medical rehabilitation, the main emphasis was placed on the building of facilities for geriatric rehabilitation and early neurological rehabilitation, in accordance with the principle, emphasized in the Health Service Reform Law and the coalition's decision on social care insurance, that rehabilitation should take precedence over social care. In the experts' view, roughly 30 per cent of the existing facilities for medical rehabilitation in the new *Bundesländer* were not worth preserving and a further 40 per cent were in need of renovation.

Between 1991 and 1996 the Federal government gave the new *Bundesländer* 835 million DM for the construction and modernization of workshops for the disabled and the residential facilities connected with them.[224] Nevertheless, while the situation of the disabled in the new *Bundesländer* improved in the sense that medical rehabilitation was enhanced and a professional rehabilitation network was created, the position of disabled people in the labour market dramatically worsened. Although on 1 October 1990 a main welfare office was set up in each of the new *Länder*, along with a total of ten subsidiary offices,[225] responsible for ensuring that the special protection against dismissal for the severely disabled was upheld and for advising the severely disabled in the event of problems in the workplace, in the last analysis these bodies were comparatively powerless to stem massive redundancies among the severely disabled. According to a report of 15 November 1991[226] there had been 69,000 proceedings against dismissals involving the severely disabled, of which 48,000 were settled. The number of proceedings was significantly higher than in west Germany, where on average there were 21,000 per year, and they took considerably longer to settle: between three and six months, as compared with one month in the west. In 1993, as a yearly average, 145,000 severely disabled people were without work in the old *Bundesländer*, while the figure for the east was 28,000.[227]

As has already been mentioned, the legal position of the disabled improved as a result of the adoption on 27 October 1994 of the ban on discrimination 'on grounds of disability' enshrined in the Basic Law. The law on disability, however, was not codified (in Book IX of the Social Statute Book) until 2001.

11.7 THE BUILD-UP OF INCOME SUPPORT AND OF THE INDEPENDENT WELFARE ASSOCIATIONS

Income support, which replaced the GDR's wholly marginalized system of social welfare, had to be built up in the new *Bundesländer*, and providers had to be established through the Independent Welfare Associations. The process began with the enactment of the GDR Income Support Law of 21 June 1990, which had been drafted in close cooperation with Federal Republic authorities and organizations[228] and required local authorities and cities to set up social services offices.[229] Benefits were largely confined to support with current living costs. Under the Unification Treaty, and the adoption on 1 January 1991 of the Federal Income Support Law, the responsibility for financing income support, previously in the hands of the central state, was transferred to local authorities and the *Länder*. Support for people in specific difficult life-situations now became increasingly important,[230] particularly after the Pensions Transition Law brought to an end the GDR's systems of social care benefit, special care benefit, and benefits for the blind. The Unification Treaty, however, stated that some of the benefits payable under the Federal Income Support Law for specific life-situations would not become available until after a transition period, during which the facilities necessary for delivering them would have to be built up.[231]

The establishment of the social services offices, which was predicated on the existence of effective local government, was initially beset with problems, despite assistance from a branch of the Federal Ministry for Young People, the Family, Women, and Health in east Berlin, the German Association for Public and Private Welfare, and individual welfare organizations. There was a shortage of office space and a lack of trained personnel capable of applying the Income Support Law, which was complicated and geared to individual cases.[232] Implementation regulations by the governments in Brandenburg, Saxony-Anhalt, and Thuringia created supra-local income support providers in those *Länder*, while in Saxony the provider's role was assigned to a *Land* welfare association and in Mecklenburg-West Pomerania the *Land* itself remained the supra-local provider, although the task of implementation was, with some exceptions, transferred to local providers.[233]

It was more difficult to set up and expand the Independent Welfare Associations, the promotion of which had been expressly prescribed by article 32 of the Unification Treaty. Here, only the religious associations—Caritas and the Protestant church's welfare organization—were able to continue to provide services and facilities in the way they had done during the GDR years, whereas the German Red Cross, for example, had to be transformed from a state-run mass organization to a non-state welfare association. The GDR's Volkssolidarität, primarily involved in providing care for the elderly, similarly had to adapt to the new conditions. It was one of the few east German organizations to survive reunification without merging with a west German partner organization. Its own organization became decentralized, but it remained a members' association, with local groups and 'with GDR features and with a well-attuned local culture'; after unification, it saw its role as representing the interests of older people.[234] The Volkssolidarität became a member of the German Parity Welfare Association, an umbrella body representing different organizations in the field of social welfare. This latter body, and the Workers' Welfare, had to be rebuilt from scratch.[235] In a joint statement in mid-1991 the Federal Minister for the Family and Senior Citizens and the presidents of the Independent Welfare Associations hailed the first achievements in the restructuring process: the creation of *Land* associations of Independent Welfare Associations in all of the new *Bundesländer*, and the establishment of regional and local branches in some of the *Länder*. At the same time, however, they stressed that there were still major problems regarding the acquisition of office space and the provision of training facilities, and they were particularly critical of the lack of support for the work of the Independent Welfare Associations from local government, which had taken over responsibility for public facilities in the areas of youth support, support for the disabled, support for the elderly, and care of the sick. They appealed to decision-makers in local government to 'transfer social welfare facilities to the Independent Associations, but not evade their share of the costs'. It was, they insisted, only through the creation of a plurality of providers and a range of different welfare facilities that citizens would be ensured freedom of choice—'a pillar' of the free system of the Federal Republic—and that the danger of the old structures' remaining in place would be averted.[236]

One of the chief difficulties was the urgent need to modernize the independent charities in the new *Länder*, a task which it was estimated would cost in excess of 10,000 million DM. The president of the Protestant welfare organization, Karl Heinz Neukamm, accordingly approached Kohl with a request that the Federal government take greater account of their concerns. The government's investment programme, he said, including the joint action plan for the rebuilding of the east, was going to neglect the Independent Welfare organizations, 'despite declarations of intent to the contrary'. 'According to provisional calculations, at most 10 per cent of the aid allocated to local authorities through the overall investment package has been put at the disposal of Independent Welfare Associations.' In addition, few if any of the welfare associations had been represented among the development staff. He warned that the bulk of Federal resources for investment in the areas of support for the elderly and the disabled was going to local authorities, to which the Independent Welfare Associations would then have to apply for grants. This way of proceeding was 'long-winded and bureaucratic', and the outcome, 'given the "sovereignty of decision-making" of local authorities, will be that resources will not reach independent charitable providers in adequate amounts'. It was absolutely vital that the Federal government should 'make further financial resources available on a substantial scale and launch a specific investment programme for the social welfare and health services in the new *Länder*, covering a period of several years, which will directly benefit the Independent Welfare Associations and enable them to use these resources in an effective and flexible way'.[237]

Because the system of welfare for the elderly, the disabled, and the poor in the east had been wholly state-run for decades, and because of the absence or weakness of the Catholic, Protestant and Social Democratic cultures with which some of the Independent Welfare Associations in the old *Bundesländer* were traditionally linked, the Independent Welfare Associations in the east did not become as significant as they were in the west, despite the efforts that were made to mobilize political support for them. The takeover of facilities and services by the welfare associations, which at first relied heavily on job creation schemes, was beset with many initial obstacles: financial problems, a lack of interest on the part of potential staff, departures by existing trained staff, and a lack of administrative experience and financial strength among the independent providers.[238] Nevertheless, the associations did eventually improve their position, particularly through the establishment of social centres. In addition, by 30 June 1993 the majority of residential care facilities for the elderly were in the hands of independent charitable organizations,[239] and between 1993 and 1995 the welfare associations almost doubled their care capacity, achieving a total of over 400,000 beds and residential places.[240]

The level of assistance with household tasks and the provision of midday meals, which had been important features of the GDR system—and were still exclusively provided by the Volkssolidarität in 1990—declined. This was partly because of the sudden rise in costs, from 0.30 marks to 5.50 DM per meal, and partly because the financing of household and other social care services, delivered through the Federal social security system, did not begin until the beginning of 1991 and then only on a limited scale. There was incomprehension and fierce disapproval when the costs of a place in an old people's home and a nursing home, which in June 1990 had been 105 marks and 120 marks per month respectively, were increased sharply to 1,800 DM per month in July 1991; and further increases took place in the following year.[241] As a consequence, the assets of the resident in the care home, or the income or assets of the relatives responsible for his or her maintenance, had to be drawn on before funding could be made available through income support.

During the first years after unification, there were considerably fewer claims on income support in the east than in the west. There were several reasons for this: a prejudice against income support, which was perceived as charity; the superior protection provided by social insurance, with the social allowances that were initially paid; and the low level of rents. People were also reluctant to involve their relatives in paying for their maintenance and lacked information about the benefits available through income support. Moreover, the relevant facilities and services were not yet fully in place.

An analysis conducted in 1994 by the Rhineland-Westphalia Institute of Economic Research concluded that in east Germany, unlike the west, the level of income support needed by families with several children and only one earner exceeded net earnings from employment, in breach of the principle that earnings from employment should be higher than income support. The Institute said, though, that the problems of income support seemed greater in the west than in the east, 'as there is a greater readiness to accept work there'.[242] Indeed, the new *Bundesländer*, with roughly one-fifth of the population of the Federal Republic, accounted for only 10.5 per cent of total spending on income support in 1992 and 12 per cent in 1996, even when the social allowance paid through pensions insurance was included.[243]

11.8 THE CREATION OF SEPARATE JURISDICTIONS IN EMPLOYMENT LAW AND SOCIAL LAW

In the GDR the employment courts lost their organizational independence in 1963, when decision-making in the area of employment law was brought within the jurisdiction of the ordinary courts and placed under the aegis of the Ministry of

Justice.[244] Although employment law chambers (*Kammern*) and senates (*Senate*) were established, in association with the local and regional courts respectively, to deal with employment law, most employment disputes were dealt with by 'conflict commissions' that had been set up in larger and medium-sized enterprises and administrative organizations under a law of 1953.[245] In the State Treaty the GDR committed itself to adopting important principles of Federal Republic employment law and accepted that until a separate jurisdiction in employment law had been established, legal disputes arising out of the employment relationship between employers and employees would be handled by newly created neutral arbitration panels.

The full extension to the new *Bundesländer* of the Federal system of employment and social security also entailed the formation, as specified in the Unification Treaty of 31 August 1990, of separate employment courts and social courts.[246] In the beginning, however, great difficulties arose. There was a flood of cases, particularly as people contested the mass redundancies, but the GDR had only a few judges with a specialization in employment law, and they came under great initial strain as they got to grips with Federal Republic employment law. Moreover, many judges either had to stand down, because they were politically compromised, or established their own practices as ordinary lawyers. Even though employment court judges, including some who had retired, were sent from the west on a temporary basis, and new judges, mostly younger and likewise from the west, were appointed, at first there were not enough of them to fill the gaps. It was also difficult to find honorary judges from among employees and, especially, employers.[247] In addition, the foundations of the system, the local and regional courts, were suffering from a 'catastrophic' shortage of personnel and lack of technical facilities.[248]

In accordance with the State Treaty, before a separate jurisdiction was established a system of 'employment law arbitration panels' was set up, under a GDR law of 29 June 1990, to serve as a form of replacement for the old conflict commissions. These panels were to have lay assessors chosen by the employer and the works council, who were to agree on the selection of a third person to act as chairman.[249] Contrary to the specifications of the law, not many of these panels were set up in enterprises employing more than 50 people, and those that were were often not accepted by the employees. They also came under strong criticism from the German Trade Union Federation, the National Union of German Employers' Associations, and the German Union of Judges. The only bodies to view them more favourably were the German White-Collar Workers' Trade Union, the Metal Workers' Union, and the Chemical Workers' Union.[250]

The dire state of decision-making in employment law was of considerable political significance. The law on dismissal, which was largely unfamiliar to employees in the new *Bundesländer*, at first could simply not be enforced. In addition, many employees felt unjustly treated, because redundancies had been ordered by the old managers, who had been closely linked to the SED, and there was no confidence in the existing judges.[251] According to a paper prepared by the relevant department of the Labour Ministry ahead of a discussion on 28 February 1991 between the Federal Chancellor and the Prime Ministers of the *Länder*, there was a danger that the 'more than disquieting state of the administration of justice in employment law in the five new *Bundesländer*' might give rise to unacceptable denials of justice and might be socially explosive.[252] Accordingly, in a letter to the Prime Ministers of the new *Länder* of 21 February 1991 the Labour Minister, Blüm, called for the building-up of a 'separate and functioning jurisdiction in employment law' as one of the 'most urgent tasks' and—echoing a suggestion by the president of the Federal Employment Court, Professor Kissel—proposed that second-instance jurisdiction should be transferred to *Land* employment courts in the old *Bundesländer*.[253]

In a discussion at the Labour Ministry with representatives of the new *Länder* on 26 August 1991 the experiment with the arbitration panels was judged to have been largely a failure. It was agreed that they had not eased the pressure on the courts in any significant way, and the quality of their decisions had been extremely dubious. The *Länder* accordingly urged that the panels be abolished by Federal legislation by the end of 1992 and that the *Länder* be enabled to abolish them earlier than that by the establishment of their own separate *Land* employment law jurisdictions.[254]

In east Berlin the arbitration panels had already been abolished, and decision-making in employment law taken over by the west Berlin employment court and *Land* employment court, by the time of German unification on 3 October 1990. On 1 July 1991 Brandenburg was the first of the east German *Bundesländer* to set up, by legislation, its own separate employment law jurisdiction with a *Land* employment court as a court of second instance, and by the end of 1992 the other four new *Länder* had also established their own separate employment law jurisdictions.[255] On 31 December 1992 the remaining employment law arbitration panels were abolished.[256] On 1 January 1993 258 judges were in post in the employment courts in the new *Länder*, of whom 143 had been newly installed from the west. A total of 43 judges from the old *Bundesländer* who were to have gone into retirement in the course of 1993 had been sent in from the west. After a process of vetting, 72 judges from the former GDR were retained in post.[257] However, there were still shortages of personnel among non-judicial staff.

The backlog of unsettled cases was gradually reduced. Whereas by the end of 1991, out of 283,564 first-instance proceedings, only 191,381 had been settled and, with cases going back to 1990 included, 140,489 were still pending, from 1992 onwards the number of cases settled exceeded the number of new proceedings, so that by 1994 only about 91,000 remained unsettled. At second instance, on the other hand, the number of cases settled did not outstrip the number of new proceedings until 1994.[258] Because of people's continuing reluctance, stemming from GDR days, to pursue arguments through the courts, a large majority of disputes were settled out of court, and the proportion of decisions that were contested in a court of higher instance was low in comparison with the old *Bundesländer*.[259]

As far as the build-up of the social courts in the new *Bundesländer* was concerned, in which judges from the old *Länder* again played a key role,[260] an excessive workload did not really build up until 1992. Of the 29,545 proceedings initiated in 1994, only 21,873 were settled, so that with the addition of cases carried over from previous years a total of 23,791 first-instance proceedings were still pending at the end of the year.[261]

Although the Federal Finance Minister, Waigel, was at first unwilling to give his consent,[262] the Federal government underpinned the development of the employment and social courts by providing annual funds of 23.1 million DM between 1991 and 1993.[263] More important still was the support in terms of personnel that came from the old *Bundesländer*, which enabled the protective functions of Federal employment and social law to became a reality in the new *Länder* in the east, despite the major initial difficulties.

11.9 CONCLUSIONS

As well as detailing the origins, content, and effects of some of the major pieces of new social legislation, this survey has focused on the way in which the institutions and actors of the welfare state in the Federal Republic were extended to the new *Bundesländer* in certain central areas of social policy. We have seen that although at first there were substantial problems in some areas, by 1992–3 the process had been, by and large, successfully completed. As a result, social policy was able to play its part in ensuring that the transformation from a planned to a market economy took place in a way that was socially acceptable to the population in the east. Nevertheless, the economic effects of the extension to the former GDR of the specific protective provisions of Federal Republic law in the area of social policy, and of the wide-ranging benefits available through the Federal welfare state, were of great concern to many people and were seen as partly responsible for the continuance of mass unemployment in the east.

Accordingly, in a paper prepared on the instructions of Staatssekretär Tegtmeier ahead of talks on 6 December 1993 between the Federal Chancellor and representatives of business and the trade unions on economic questions affecting the new *Bundesländer*, the Federal Ministry of Labour tried to set out which of the developments that had taken place in social policy had served to 'improve the infrastructure for investment by business and by local authorities', in order to make clear that 'more than mere transfers to boost consumption' had been involved.[264] The paper emphasized, in particular, that 'without the sizeable social transfers . . . circulation of money and goods in the new *Bundesländer* would have collapsed' and that 'without the speedy development of a functioning system of social administration . . . private investment activity would, at the least, have been severely impeded'.[265] In business circles and among economists, on the other hand, perceptions were different, and there was widespread criticism of the fact that a large proportion of the transfers from west to east had gone on consumer spending.

All told, the rapid and relatively smooth extension of the west German welfare state to the east was a *tour de force* of public administration, and a notable achievement on the part of the organizations of the other actors within social policy, which significantly reduced the social and political costs of unification. At the same time, however, it generated high economic costs, and imposed heavy extra burdens on the social insurance systems, particularly as a result of the huge encouragement of early retirement and the implementation of an active labour market policy. It remains an open question whether, had there been less forceful intervention through social policy and had market forces been allowed to prevail, the economic costs would on balance have been lower, or whether the story would have been one of continuing economic decline.

12

The Debates on Germany's Economic Position and on the Problems in Financial and Social Policy Resulting from German Unity

12.1 THE COMPETITIVENESS OF THE GERMAN ECONOMY

The German economy went through great difficulties in the early 1990s. Hopes that there would be a self-sustaining economic upturn in the east proved illusory, and, after early warning signs had appeared in the second half of 1991,[1] a recession set in during the late summer and autumn of 1992, becoming acute in 1993 and affecting the old *Bundesländer* as well as the new. In a clear indication of the seriousness of the situation, there was an intensive debate among politicians, economists, and economic actors and organizations about the threat to Germany's economic standing. Central to the debate were arguments about the scale and method of financing of German unity, the consolidation of the public finances, reforms of the welfare state to lower its running costs, and the reduction of unemployment through higher growth and the creation of new jobs. It was also argued by many that structural changes were needed, above all if Germany was to cope with changes in the economic framework in Europe and worldwide—changes summed up in the term 'globalization'. The defining features of globalization have already been discussed:[2] the growing integration of markets for products, finance, quality services, and, to an extent, labour; the internationalization of many firms and the increasingly free movement of business activity; mounting competition from the economies of eastern central Europe and the rapidly developing economies of south-east Asia; battles over the location of production; and, particularly, the worldwide dissemination of technical knowledge and skills through modern information and communications technologies, which were whittling away the competitive advantages that the German economy had traditionally enjoyed.

On top of these changes, German unity was imposing its own particular burdens. One was the huge transfer of economic resources from west to east Germany. Another, however, was the challenge to, and questioning of, the 'German model'—that is, the social compact whereby structural economic change was accompanied by corporate cooperation between the state and the social partners. It was apparent that while the west German model had been appropriate during a period when economic change was gradual, it was not well suited for dealing with the radical structural transformation that was taking place in the east, where the preconditions for competitive business enterprise, free collective pay bargaining orientated to increases in productivity, and economic growth were lacking. We have already discussed some of the consequences of the wholesale extension to the east of west German legislation, institutions, and actors: the excessive pay agreements, financed by taxpayers; the weakening of the trade unions, and the move away from employers' associations and regional collective agreements by entrepreneurs; the overburdening of the social insurance systems as a result of the massive transfer of funds from west to east; and the sharp increase in unemployment caused partly by rises in taxes and, most particularly, by social expenditure. In the light of these concerns, for many people the attempt to diagnose the crisis as an effect of 'globalization' was therefore merely a distraction from problems that had been manufactured at home,[3] and worries about Germany's competitiveness were merely a 'pretext for making cuts in the social protection system'.[4] In particular, social policy experts in the CDU/CSU, in the opposition parties, and in the trade unions repeatedly warned that the question of Germany's economic position should not be reduced to a question simply of wages and the costs of the welfare state.

An illustration of the flavour of the debate is given by the annual report of the Council of Economic Experts for 1995/6, entitled 'The Competition for Location'. The report posed the question whether Germany was still attractive as a location for investment, in comparison with other countries.[5] It was certainly the case that although German direct investment abroad had been increasing, foreign investment in Germany had remained at a much lower level.[6] Moreover, domestic investment by German entrepreneurs was devoted primarily to 'labour-saving rationalization', rather than the creation of new jobs.[7] The Council of Economic Experts' main proposals for improving the competitiveness of the German economy were a reduction in the level of public spending as a share of gross national product, cuts in taxes for businesses, a moderation in wage increases to below the rise in productivity, greater flexibility in pay agreements, with a wider spread of wage rates, effective hardship clauses, and more flexible working hours, and a reduction in the excessive burden of regulation governing entrepreneurial activity. More generally, the Council argued that there should be a move away from a social policy based on preserving and extending vested rights 'without taking account of efficiency and financial viability'.[8]

Many of the structural problems of the economy, however, were not addressed in the report. These included the fact that the pace of structural change was relatively slow and that certain forms of activity which were no longer economically competitive were being sustained artificially, for example through state subsidies. A further obstacle was the high level of corporate institutionalization[9] and the range of opportunities for blocking change that were built into the domestic political system. This favoured a politics of consensus in which solutions to economic and social problems tended to be sought along well-trodden paths and flexible adjustments to new situations tended to be avoided.

Similarly, the processes of schooling and higher education went on for too long and were not sufficiently responsive to changing needs. What had long been seen as the exemplary German dual system of vocational training, combining practical learning in the workplace with theoretical education in vocational schools, undoubtedly produced highly professional and specialized skilled workers who were extremely well qualified by international standards, and encouraged the production of standardized high-quality products. On the other hand, it also tended to make those in industry less ready to think in terms of processes and projects or to strike out in new directions, in contrast with workers in the Anglo-Saxon countries, where 'on-the-job training' was the norm.

German industry had been very successful in maintaining its competitiveness, and hence its position in export markets, in branches of industry with high levels of technology, such as chemicals, mechanical engineering, and motor manufacture. It had done so, primarily, by increasing productivity while upholding quality. However, in the motor industry, for example,[10] this had been achieved through rigorous downward pressure on costs and—since it would have been very difficult to implement short-term mass redundancies or wage reductions in the face of trade union and works council resistance—through the transfer of substantial portions of production and supply provision to other countries. Rises in exports thus had only a minor effect in reducing unemployment in Germany. In the service sector Germany had fallen behind the USA and Japan, in terms both of high-quality services that were exposed to international competition and of personal-based services in local markets, an area that remained relatively under-developed because of high labour costs.[11] Particularly disturbingly, Germany also lagged behind in the 'hi-tech' sector, where there was an especially high rate of growth and innovation in, for example, the USA and elsewhere.

The problems that flowed from structural economic change, the intensification of international competition, and Germany's 'industrial conservatism' and concentration on certain sectors of industry[12] were exacerbated by the challenges caused by unification. From the early 1990s onwards German industry was subject to heavy pressures in respect of costs and innovation, and these pressures were reflected in demands for a radical reform of the welfare state in the shape of reductions in the excessive amount of legal regulation of the changing world of work and cuts in the level of social benefits. Increasingly, what had been regarded as the strong points of the German system were lost sight of, or seen as drawbacks: the high standard of basic vocational training, which in turn provided the foundation for continuing advanced training and re-training; the way in which employees could be integrated, through the system of co-determination, into the process of structural change and motivated to increase economic performance; and the priority given to the search for consensus in solving social and political problems.

The political debate about the dangers to Germany's economic standing, and the consequences of economic decline for social policy, took on a new edge following a change of course on the part of the government. On 8 September 1992 Chancellor Kohl addressed the CDU/CSU members of the Bundestag to voice his concern about economic developments in Germany, urging, in particular, that pay settlements should return 'to the path of reason'.[13] Then, on 26 October 1992, in a widely reported keynote speech to the CDU party conference in Düsseldorf, Kohl declared that a reunited Germany needed 'something more than simply a continuation of tried and tested policies' and that a 'reassessment of priorities [was] urgently required'.[14] Reconstruction in the new *Bundesländer* would 'take longer' and 'become more expensive' than people had assumed in mid-1990, and the east German labour market was not going to be transformed in short order. Moreover, the fact that the threats to the economy were increasing—as a paper published by the Labour Ministry on 25 August 1992 had already made clear[15]—meant that the Social Market economy was facing a new test. Crucial objectives were at stake: 'completing the internal unity of Germany, securing Germany's economic standing', and 'adapting the social insurance systems to changing demographic circumstances',[16] even under conditions of a slowdown in economic growth (and indeed, there would be a fall of 2 per cent in gross domestic product in 1993).[17] Accordingly, Kohl said, he had issued invitations for 'discussions on a solidarity pact for Germany'. There was a challenge, not only to the trade unions and the employers, but to the Federal government, the *Länder* and local government, and to all groups in society. There was a challenge to everyone in Germany. 'We are also talking about a socially just distribution of burdens—including the burdens inherited from the GDR... We are talking about the future of our country.'[18]

Kohl's call for a solidarity pact was an attempt to induce the Social Democratic opposition—which could block any sizeable reforms, since the SPD-led *Länder* were in a majority position in the Bundesrat—into sharing the responsibility for unpopular decisions, and, with its cooperation, to bring the negotiations on the extraordinarily difficult financial settlement between the Federal government and the *Länder* to a satisfactory conclusion. The risks for Kohl were great, as his political standing was dependent on the success of the new policy. However, they were considerable for the Social Democrats too, as the dire state of the Federal finances and the wholly inadequate level of financial provision for the new *Länder* and the local authorities would make it very difficult for the Social Democrats to refuse to fall in line behind the government.

12.2 THE FEDERAL CONSOLIDATION PROGRAMME

The State Treaty of 18 May 1990 and the Unification Treaty of 31 August 1990 had left largely unresolved the question of how German unity was to be financed over the longer term.[19] The 'German Unity Fund' (*Fonds 'Deutsche Einheit'*) that was set up on the basis of the State Treaty had at its disposal 115,000 million DM for a period of five years—far too small an amount to meet the needs of the new *Länder*. Moreover, although the GDR's negotiators had striven in the negotiations on the Unification Treaty to have the new *Länder* included, immediately after accession to the Federal Republic, in the west German financial adjustment and the distribution of the share of the proceeds of the sales tax taken (on the basis of population) by the *Länder*, they had been thwarted by fierce resistance from the west German *Länder*.[20] Thus in 1991, in accordance with Article 7, paragraph 7 of the Unification Treaty, the east German *Länder* were to receive only 55 per cent of the average share of sales tax proceeds received per head of population by the *Länder*, because of their lower levels of income and consumption. This share would rise only gradually, reaching 70 per cent of the western level by 1994. Although the Federal and *Land* heads of government agreed in February 1991 that the new *Länder* should be wholly included in the distribution of sales tax proceeds on the basis of population, and the Federal government refrained from claiming the share of the resources of the 'German Unity Fund' that had initially been reserved for it, additional resources still had to be made available for the new *Länder* for the years 1992 to 1994. This was done through a joint 'Eastern Recovery Project' and by an increase in the size of the 'German Unity Fund' and was partly paid for by rises in taxes.[21]

However, decisions still remained to be taken about the shape that the financial adjustment between the *Bund* and the *Länder*, and between the rich and the poor *Länder*, would assume when the new *Bundesländer* were included in the adjustment from 1 January 1995, about the management of the heavy debts that had been incurred by the *Treuhand*, and about consolidation of the Federal finances through cost savings and/or tax increases. The policy-makers were also under pressure from the Bundesbank, which, in order to stem inflationary tendencies, had responded to the sharp rise in public debt and the large wage increases in east Germany by steadily raising the discount rate from 3.5 per cent in January 1989 to 8.75 per cent in July 1992.[22] In addition, a decision by the Federal Constitutional Court served notice that an amendment to the Federal financial adjustment was necessary in order to resolve budgetary difficulties in the Saarland and Bremen.[23]

At first, the positions of the Federal government and the *Länder* seemed irreconcilable, as did those of the ruling coalition and the opposition. Disagreement centred primarily on the distribution of financial burdens between the Federal government, the old and the new *Länder*, and the rich and the poor *Länder*. The coalition and the opposition were at odds whether the budget should be consolidated primarily through economies in social benefits or through increases in taxes. Waigel, the Finance Minister, attempted to divide the *Länder*, but failed, and the *Länder* agreed on a joint negotiating position at a conference of Prime Ministers in Potsdam on 26–7 February 1993.[24] Although the Federal government and the *Länder* were in accord that the new *Länder* needed roughly 60,000 million DM annually, they differed over how the money should be found. The Federal government proposed that of the estimated overall budget deficit of 105,000 million DM in 1995, 56,000 million should be assigned to the Federal government, 35,000 million to the old *Bundesländer* (of which 8,000 million should fall on local government), and 14,000 million to the new *Bundesländer* (including 5,000 million to local authorities). The *Länder*, on the other hand, proposed that the Federal government should carry a deficit of 88,000 million DM, the old *Bundesländer* nearly 5,000 million, and the new *Bundesländer* 12,000 million: in other words, that the old *Bundesländer* should bear a much less heavy burden. Addressing the CDU/CSU parliamentarians, Waigel maintained firmly that if the settlement proposed by the *Länder* were followed, either there 'could be no' financial policy at Federal level for the next ten years or 'colossal tax increases would be absolutely unavoidable, merely to allow the central state to continue to function'. However, he said, Germany, with a tax rate of 24 per cent and a contributions rate of 41.5 per cent, was already at the top of the international league table, and the German economy, which was facing fierce competition from other countries, would not be able to cope with further tax rises.[25]

The coalition parties and the Social Democrats were able to bridge their differences only by deferring the resolution of many of the contentious issues that divided them. The Social Democrats, broadly supported by the representatives of the Christian Democratic employees and the east German CDU Bundestag members, were not prepared to countenance deeper cuts in the area of social policy. Conversely, their call for a supplementary contribution by higher earners and a labour market contribution by civil servants and the self-employed was firmly opposed by the FDP and a majority of members of the CDU and CSU.

In the end, at the initiative of the Chancellor, a conference was held at the Federal Chancellery on 11–13 March 1993 between the Chancellor, the Federal Finance Minister, and the heads of government in the *Länder*—the parliamentary parties being effectively excluded—and a highly complex compromise package was put together. This set out a clear framework of financial support for the new *Länder* and the eastern local authorities by the Federal government and the western *Länder*, totalling around 56,000 million DM per year from 1 January 1995 onwards. For 1993 and 1994, the 'German Unity Fund' was to be replenished. The credit liquidation fund (*Kreditabwicklungsfonds*), totalling 140,000 million DM, the debts of the *Treuhand*, estimated to amount to 230,000 million DM, and a substantial portion of the debts of east German housing, running to 31,000 million DM, were put together into an inherited liabilities redemption fund (*Erblastentilgungsfonds*), with interest payments and the debt redemption to be undertaken by the Federal government alone.[26] On the other hand, the *Länder* and local authorities would have to play a greater role in servicing the 'German Unity Fund' debts. There would be programmes to encourage the building of housing and maintain a core of industrial production in east Germany.[27] The new *Länder*, in particular, would also benefit by the ending of the freeze, ordered on 26 February 1993 by the president of the Federal Institute of Labour, on new approvals of job creation schemes through the provision of additional funding of 2,000 million DM.[28] The *Länder*'s share in the proceeds of sales taxes was raised from 37 to 44 per cent, in compensation for the inclusion of the new *Länder* in the adjustment between rich and poor *Länder*.

The resultant new financial order, which altogether represented a reallocation in resources of 94,795 million DM,[29] was in line with the thinking of the Social Democrats and the SPD-led *Bundesländer* inasmuch as it placed the great bulk of the burden of additional expenditure caused by unification on to the Federal government and required it to take the main risk with regard to budgetary stability. Many of the Social Democrats' ideas were also reflected in the ways in which the expenditure was to be financed. Although there was to be no supplementary contribution by higher earners, and no labour market contribution by civil servants and the self-employed, the 7.5 per cent solidarity supplement on income and corporation tax that had already been in force for a year would be renewed, for an indefinite time period, from 1 January 1995. Certain tax concessions were reversed, and social regulatory benefits were excluded from the reduction, totalling 10,500 million DM in public expenditure. However, there was to be a crackdown on the abuse of social benefits, with projected savings of about 1,500 million DM annually.[30]

Speaking to the CDU/CSU members of parliament on 23 March 1993, the chair of the parliamentary party, Wolfgang Schäuble, standing in for the indisposed Finance Minister, hailed the agreement between the Federal government and the *Länder*, and between the leaderships of the parties inside and outside parliament, as a great achievement, and 'one that most people had not thought possible'.[31] In the debate on the Federal Consolidation Programme in the Bundestag two days later, Kohl stressed that the successful conclusion of the solidarity pact had 'reinforced confidence in the strength of German democracy, particularly abroad'.[32] He also said that the trend towards ever shorter working hours was a threat to Germany's competitiveness, as a 'successful industrial nation cannot be run like a collective amusement park'.[33] He expressed the hope that the Consolidation Programme would help to stimulate economic growth and combat unemployment, as well as improve Germany's position as a location of production.

Schäuble, for the CDU/CSU, said that the decisions achieved by the negotiations would be an 'important contribution to dealing with the economic, financial and social consequences of 40 years of socialism and the division of Germany', but regretted that the action of the Social Democratic majority in the Bundesrat had made it impossible to achieve bigger savings in the Federal budget.[34] For the FDP, Count Lambsdorff said that the old *Bundesländer* had done too well out of the new settlement: the Federal government was going to have to bear the main burden of a reasonable level of support for the new *Länder*, and its financial room for manoeuvre was approaching 'zero'. Like Schäuble, he bemoaned the fact that 'vital, and unavoidable, savings in the area of social expenditure' had not been made.[35]

On behalf of the east German Social Democrats, Wolfgang Thierse welcomed the compromise that had been reached, claiming that the Social Democrats had succeeded in halting the 'attack on the idea of the welfare state' that the Finance Minister, Waigel, had planned. Not only had the financial adjustment been achieved, but a core of east Germany's industries would be preserved and modernized, measures to promote the sale of east German products had been promised, programmes to build new housing, modernize the existing housing stock, and solve the problem of inherited housing debt had been agreed, and job creation schemes would be extended. On the other hand, there was no 'real future investment programme' for eastern Germany of the sort the Social Democrats had proposed, and nothing was being done to mitigate social conflict by distributing the burdens of unity more equitably.[36] Rudolf Dreßler of the SPD deplored the fact that the different groups in society had not been incorporated into the unification process and that there was no programme to combat the recession in the western part of Germany.[37]

Overall, the Federal Consolidation Programme was a demonstration of the 'adaptability' and 'political strength of Germany's federal system'[38] and showed that 'policy-making within the German system of government [had] a high degree of institutional flexibility'.[39] It had been achieved through informal procedures of decision-making by the Federal government and the heads of the *Länder* governments which had been conducted within the Federal Chancellery and had largely been shielded from pressures by the Bundestag, the Bundestag parties, and different interest groups.

Nevertheless, although the reforms were a significant attempt to resolve the difficult problem of providing the new *Länder* with financial resources and dealing with the financial burdens imposed by unification, their scope was limited. The Federal budget, as well as being required to carry too large a share of the financial costs of unification, had not really been put back on its feet, either through cost savings or through tax increases. Nor had the unfairly heavy responsibility placed on social insurance contributors for covering the costs of unification been lessened. The Bundesbank, however, did fulfil its side of the bargain. After the announcement of the offer of a solidarity pact and the government's demonstration that it was determined to make savings in the Federal budget, the bank made substantial cuts in base rates after September 1992 and then again, in particular, in March 1993, after the new settlement was agreed.[40] Monetary policy thus played its part in the stimulation of the economy.

12.3 THE PARTIAL FINANCING OF GERMAN UNITY THROUGH SOCIAL INSURANCE

In conjunction with the negotiations over the solidarity pact and the Federal Consolidation Programme there were also intensive discussions, both within the government and among politicians, about the possibility of lessening the specific burden that social insurance contribution payers—employers and employees—were carrying in order to pay for German unity. As has already been mentioned, between 1991 and 1995 140,000 million DM, or 23 per cent of the total quantity of financial transfers from west to east Germany, was raised through pensions and unemployment insurance.[41] This form of financing was criticized by the Social Democrats and the German Trade Union Federation for creating what the latter called a 'fairness gap';[42] they called instead for a labour market contribution by civil servants and the self-employed and/or a supplementary contribution by higher earners. The Labour Minister, Blüm, also repeatedly argued in interviews for a fairer way of financing the active labour market policy in the east and later urged that job training and re-training should be financed out of taxation, by analogy with the financing of school education.[43] Reinforcing the argument was a calculation by the Labour Ministry, based on Finance Ministry estimates, that from 1993 the burden carried by lower income groups would be far in excess of their share in disposable income, as a result of extra taxes and social insurance contributions introduced from 1991.[44]

Attempts to reduce the load on contribution payers, however, were repeatedly unsuccessful, in the face of concerns about constitutional law, opposition by interest groups—in particular civil servants, represented by the Federal Interior Ministry—and resistance from the Finance Ministry, which preferred to raise money by the relatively unobtrusive method of increasing social insurance contributions, rather than by putting up taxes, which was bound to generate powerful political tensions, not least within the governing coalition. Doubtless for similar reasons, the form of financing of the costs of unification through social insurance was at first not discussed intensively within government,[45] despite the fact that the demands placed on the social insurance systems by politicians and—through the use of early retirement—by business in the early 1990s were 'gigantic'.[46]

In October 1992, at the instigation of the Labour Ministry, the constitutionality of a labour market contribution was tested by the Ministries of Justice and the Interior. The Justice Ministry claimed that a separate labour market contribution for civil servants, the self-employed, and family members working alongside them was constitutionally inadmissible, on the grounds that 'no group-specific responsibility for the objective served by the contribution exists, nor is the contribution being used for the benefit of the group'. It argued in addition that a special fiscal contribution by all persons in employment, including payers of contributions to the Federal Institute of Labour, was 'not in accord with the requirements which the Federal Constitutional Court [places] on the legal admissibility of the introduction of a special contribution'.[47] In the view of the Interior Ministry—which also alluded to the solidarity payments made by civil servants through the two-month moratorium on salary increases in 1991, the poor competitive position of the public service within the labour market, and the large deployment of civil servants and judges to eastern Germany—a labour market contribution for civil servants would be a 'special tax', and would therefore be incompatible with Article 3 of the Basic Law, on equality before the law. Any form of subsidizing of the employment promotion programmes other than through the revenue from contributions would therefore have to come from taxation.[48]

The Labour Ministry did not give up immediately, however. It studied closely a wide range of alternative models for financing the active labour market policy and calculated their financial implications.[49] On one of the models, the 'fairness gap' in unemployment insurance and the gap in the financing of social care would be dealt with in a single package, with a reduction in employers' contributions to unemployment insurance being offset against compensation for the costs of their contributions to social care insurance.[50] Eventually a labour market contribution of one per cent of wages for all people in employment, combined with a one per cent reduction in employees' contributions to unemployment insurance, emerged as the Labour Ministry's preferred solution.[51] However, if this scheme were to be implemented, a constitutional amendment would be necessary, 'through inclusion in the Basic Law of an authorization to impose an earnings-dependent non-tax contribution as a time-limited and closely circumscribed special instrument for financing the costs of social security generated by unification'.[52]

In the political arena, three further models were under discussion. The first had been developed, at Wolfgang Schäuble's instigation, by Julius Louven, the chairman of the working group on labour and social affairs of the CDU/CSU parliamentary party.[53] On this proposal, existing unemployment contributions, at 6.5 per cent of wages, would be split into an insurance contribution of 4 per cent, with employers and employees providing one-half each, and a general contribution of 2.5 per cent, applicable not only to blue- and white-collar workers but also to civil servants and the self-employed, to provide separate financing of the labour market policy. Self-administration would thus be confined to unemployment insurance, while the active labour market policy would become the responsibility of a special branch of the Federal Institute of Labour, which would accordingly be brought directly under the Labour Ministry as a subordinate authority. As well as reducing the power of the social partners in the area of labour market policy, this proposal would lessen the burden on companies and thus reduce additional wage costs by 1.25 per cent while at the same time increasing by 1.25 per cent the burden on employees liable to social insurance contributions. The Labour Ministry's response to the proposal was that it would be very difficult to explain to the population that the way to remove a distortion in social transfer payments was to impose a heavier burden than before on to employees liable to social insurance, and also to require civil servants and the self-employed to make a long-term contribution of 2.5 per cent of their earnings.[54]

The Labour Ministry's views were much more closely echoed by the proposal put forward by Ottmar Schreiner, chairman of the labour and social affairs working group of the SPD in parliament. On this scheme, too, the existing single contribution would be split into two separate contributions. One contribution, to unemployment insurance, would continue to be levied from employers and employees liable to social insurance. At the same time, however, a contribution to cover the costs of the active labour market policy would be borne by employers and all people in employment, each providing one-half. The drawback to this proposal, in the Labour Ministry's eyes, was that the new liability to contributions on the part of civil servants went along with a corresponding liability on the part of public-service employers, which would create significant new burdens for government budgets. In addition, the distinction between employers (firms) and the self-employed (individuals) was not clear-cut: 'they are found on both sides of the divide as far as the funding of the active labour market policy is concerned.'[55]

A third model was put forward by the Council of Economic Experts. The Council argued that 'the heavy burden of unemployment insurance caused by structural change in the east, and the high level of unemployment with which it is linked, should be regarded as the legacy of the socialist regime' and that it should, 'essentially, be borne by the totality of taxpayers'. It proposed that the contribution rate should be lowered from 6.5 per cent to 4.5 per cent and that the resultant loss in revenue to the Federal Institute of Labour should be balanced by a corresponding Federal subsidy. This would be financed by a 'supplementary contribution of 7 per cent on income and corporation tax liability, limited to a five-year period and degressively structured'.[56] This was the only proposal of the three that could have been implemented without the need for a constitutional amendment.

None of the models outlined here was adopted. In a response to the Labour Ministry proposal, Professor Heinz-Dietrich Steinmeyer said that while there were no objections to the proposed constitutional amendment on grounds of constitutional *law*, there were objections on grounds of constitutional *policy*. The absence of a group-specific reference with regard to the planned special contribution would make the labour market contribution 'a tax for a particular purpose, which is actually meant to be ruled out under the Basic Law'. In addition, a problem involving federalism would arise, since the Federal government—in concrete terms, the administrative system for employment—would be obtaining a new source of revenue outside the categories specified in Article 106 of the Basic Law on the distribution of taxes, and, moreover, the resources would 'bypass' the Finance Ministry. 'This might set a precedent and might provoke other ministries to make similar demands, since in other areas there are special burdens similarly resulting from unification.'[57]

The influential director of the Association of German Pensions Insurance Providers, Professor Franz Ruland, also spoke out against the Labour Ministry's model and the proposed constitutional amendment, arguing that the '"non-tax *sui generis* contribution"—even if it can be unambiguously characterized in legal terms, which is debatable—relates, not to the ability to pay of those individuals affected by the contribution, but solely to the level of their income'. The principle of equality, however, could not be overridden, even by a constitutional amendment. There was therefore a danger that the Federal Constitutional Court would 'declare the proposed amendment invalid as an unconstitutional principle under Article 79, paragraph 3 of the Basic Law' (exempting the federal structure of the Republic, and the principles of basic rights, from the process of constitutional amendment). It would be more sensible and obvious for the 'necessary sharing of the burden of the costs of unification, which, though the responsibility of society as a whole, is being borne by social insurance providers', to be linked to the Federal subsidy for social insurance. He accordingly suggested the following addition to Article 120 of the Basic Law (on the sharing of burdens from the war): 'The Federation [*Bund*] is obliged to ensure a sharing of the special burdens borne by social insurance providers, including the Federal Institute of Labour, which arise from the alignment of living conditions in the process of unification but which should, as a matter of principle, be borne by all citizens. To finance the resources necessary for this purpose, the Federation may levy a time-limited supplement to wage and income tax (Article 106, paragraph 1, no. 6 of the Basic Law).'[58]

The Labour Ministry did not pursue its proposal further. It is not clear from the documentary sources whether it refrained because of legal considerations or owing to the opposition from other Federal ministries and from sections of the CDU/CSU and the FDP. Like Ruland's scheme—which would have entailed a much more far-reaching commitment by the Federal government—the Labour Ministry's proposal did not find favour with the Finance Ministry.[59] The latter obtained a source of additional non-ring-fenced funds through the solidarity supplement that had been agreed as part of the Federal Consolidation Programme. The problems of financing the costs of unity, however, remained unresolved.

12.4 SOCIAL POLICY, BUDGETARY CONSOLIDATION, AND THE EFFORT TO MAINTAIN GERMANY'S ECONOMIC STANDING, 1993/1994

On 29 June 1993, just three days after the law implementing the Federal Consolidation Programme had been promulgated,[60] the Finance Minister, Theo Waigel, the Economics Minister, Günter Rexrodt, and the Labour Minister, Norbert Blüm—in a departure from the previous policy of 'reluctant unification-led Keynesianism'[61]—reached agreement on a programme of cost-saving, consolidation and growth involving cuts of over 20,000 million DM. The programme was approved by the cabinet on 13 July and, after legal drafting, received its first reading in the Bundestag on 7 September 1993.[62] The principal reason for the introduction of the programme was the need, in view of the steep decline in tax revenues caused by the continuing recession, to limit Federal net borrowing, which would otherwise have risen to more than 90,000 million DM. From 1993 onwards, too, the fact that the government had to adhere to the Maastricht criteria—stipulating that public borrowing by the states planning to participate in European monetary union should not exceed 3 per cent of gross domestic product—played an increasingly important role in budgetary policy.[63] The planned cuts, which did not fall within the framework of the Federal Consolidation Programme, primarily affected social policy. Even so, the share in the Federal budget accounted for by social policy rose from 21 per cent in 1989 to 37 per cent in 1995, while the extent of the Federal government's indebtedness was reflected in an increase in the proportion of expenditure on interest payments from 11 to 21 per cent over the same period.[64]

In a number of working papers, produced partly to serve as information notes for discussions between the Chancellor and the east German CDU members of parliament on 6 September 1993 and with the Prime Ministers of the new *Länder* on 23 September, the Labour Ministry gave details of possible changes to the Employment Promotion Law and other laws within the Ministry's area of responsibility, the savings that it was hoped would result, and the groups of people affected by the cuts, both generally and in the east in particular.[65] The most important of the proposed economies was a reduction in unemployment benefit (*Arbeitslosengeld*) after payment had been received for a year, from 68 to 64 per cent of wages for recipients with children and from 63 to 59 per cent for those without children. In addition, short-time working and bad-weather benefit (due to be discontinued on 30 June 1994), integration benefit for the disabled, and Federally financed unemployment assistance (*Arbeitslosenhilfe*) and integration benefit for immigrants of German origin would all be reduced by three percentage points. The maximum duration of integration benefit for German-origin immigrants would be reduced from between nine and fifteen months to a standard period of six months. It was also proposed to reduce maintenance payments for participants in job re-training schemes who had children from 73 per cent of wages, and for participants without children from 65 per cent of wages, to the level of unemployment benefit, and to replace the legal right to maintenance payments with a discretionary decision. A particularly large cutback in the social protection net was the proposed abolition of primary unemployment assistance. In future, unemployment assistance would be provided only for people who had previously been in receipt of unemployment benefit; moreover, the period for which unemployment assistance could be received, which previously had been unlimited, would be restricted to two years. Recipients of pre-pension transitional benefit would be obliged, from 1995 onwards, to claim their old-age pension under statutory pensions insurance at the earliest possible opportunity, irrespective of the level of the pension, although if the pension was lower than the pre-pension transitional benefit, they would receive a compensatory payment equivalent to the difference between the previous pre-pension transitional benefit and the pension. The Labour Ministry succeeded in blocking a reduction in pensions and other benefits for war victims. Altogether, the volume of proposed savings in the area of Federal Institute of Labour and other labour market activity would rise from 13,700 million DM in 1994 to 16,200 million DM in 1996, taking increased pensions insurance spending into account.[66]

In a briefing document for Blüm for the talks between the Chancellor and the heads of government of the new *Länder* on 23 September 1993, the primary rationale given for the cuts in social spending was the weak overall state of the economy. It was also very clear, however, that in contrast with the period between 1990 and 1992, there was now less optimism about the usefulness of labour market and social policies in the east. These policies, the document said, were no substitute for 'effective policies for growth and jobs'. Given that citizens would be burdened with an increase in taxes and social contributions amounting to 116,000 million DM annually from 1991 to 1995, rigorous savings were the only option if the growth capacity of the economy was to be strengthened and inflation held at bay. Labour market policies could not serve as a substitute for the creation of 'lasting jobs capable of withstanding competition'. Moreover, the 'huge educational industry' that had been built up in the east in the fields of job training and re-training had not prevented 'many workers from being unable to find jobs after completing their training schemes'. With regard to the improvement of professional qualifications of the unemployed, therefore, 'high priority should be given to their prospects of being integrated into the labour market. The gaining of qualifications, at the expense of contribution payers, cannot be an end in itself for workers and training providers.' The document said that the percentage reduction in income replacement benefits, which the Labour Minister had long resisted, would not fall disproportionately on workers in the east. It conceded, however, that the reduction in income replacement benefits and the tightening of conditions on their receipt would lead indirectly to extra expenditure on income support by local authorities, amounting to as much as 4,000 million DM in 1994, though there would also be savings as a result of the Federal government's assumption of responsibility for covering extra costs through the Federal Consolidation Programme and through the prospective introduction of social care insurance.[67]

Since it was expected that the opposition would be vehemently opposed to the programme, the measures were divided into two separate bills, one of which would not require the consent of the Bundesrat. Coming so soon after agreement had been reached on the Federal Consolidation Programme, this was tantamount to a declaration of war on the opposition and was widely seen as heralding the end of cross-party cooperation and the attempt to forge German unity in a socially acceptable way. At a hearing of experts by the labour and social affairs committee of the Bundestag on 22 September 1993[68] serious reservations about the programme were expressed, not only by the Social Democrats but also by the trade unions, which fiercely criticized the cutbacks in the active labour market policy and the reductions in income replacement benefits, and by the leading local government organizations, which feared that the costs of income support would rise rapidly at a time when local authority revenues were falling 'dramatically'. The Protestant church said that the programme was too heavily influenced by fiscal considerations and did not pay sufficient regard to the impact of unemployment on the lives of those directly affected and on the life of the community generally. On the other hand, the National Union of German Employers' Associations and the Central Association of German Craft Trades, which were calling for a reduction in wages paid through job creation schemes, broadly supported the measures, while voicing criticisms on some specific points.

The two bills were approved by the Bundestag, with the backing of the governing parties, on 22 October 1993, but were then voted down in the Bundesrat, which objected, in particular, to the cutbacks in unemployment assistance. After tough negotiations in the Mediation Committee the Bundesrat and the Social Democrats obtained a number of amendments to the legislation. Unemployment benefit, short-time working and bad-weather benefit, and unemployment assistance for employees with children, were reduced by only 1 instead of 4 percentage points, and unemployment assistance for employees without children was reduced by 3 percentage points. More importantly, continuing unemployment assistance would remain paid on a non-time-limited basis and primary unemployment assistance was not abolished but merely restricted to one year. Bad-weather benefit would cease to be paid only after the winter of 1995/6. Instead of the proposed complete suspension of the increase in income support, there would be only a reduction in the increase. The local authorities succeeded in altering into a 'target requirement' the original provision that they should make job opportunities available to unemployed recipients of income support.[69] In their amended form the two laws[70] were approved by the Bundestag on 10 December 1993 and by the Bundesrat on 17 December, and came into force on 1 January 1994. The effect of the savings that were achieved, primarily by these laws, was that the Federal government's subsidy to the Federal Institute of Labour fell from 24,000 million DM in 1993 to 10,200 million DM in 1994 and 6,900 million DM in 1995.[71]

Meanwhile the government, after months of preparatory work and intensive inter-ministerial consultation, had produced a report on 'securing Germany's future economic standing'.[72] The report highlighted a number of urgent tasks: achieving further consolidation of the public finances; strengthening the competitiveness of the German economy, for instance through pay restraint, greater flexibility in employment law and with regard to working hours, and extending the operational life of machinery; improving the economy's tax framework; reducing unemployment; securing the long-term future of the social security systems; continuing with the policy of privatization; cutting back on over-regulation; enhancing Germany's position as a place of research and innovation; reforming education, higher education, and science to make them more orientated towards the future; creating well-functioning and attractive infrastructure; achieving environmental targets in an efficient way; developing an economical and environment-friendly energy policy; and fostering cooperation and a wider division of labour in the world economy.

For the Labour Ministry, the most important features in the report were, first, its statements on pay policy—on which the report said that as far as the new *Bundesländer* were concerned, account should be taken of the low levels of productivity, there should be greater differentiation in negotiated wages in line with the varying efficiency of enterprises, and special lower wage rates should be set for job creation schemes—and, secondly, its call for social insurance contributions to be stabilized and, if possible, reduced. On pensions insurance, the Ministry, while accepting that the costly trend towards early retirement had to be reversed, was concerned to protect the system from possible cuts, pointing out that expenditure had increased, not for demographic reasons, but because of unification.[73]

The report's proposals on safeguarding the future were strongly attacked by the Social Democrats on the grounds that they would cause social disruption. The proposals rekindled the debate on Germany's economic position and sparked off vigorous exchanges between government and opposition in the Bundestag on 21 October 1993.

Kohl, drawing an analogy with the years immediately following the founding of the Federal Republic, called for another great new departure, this time by a reunited Germany. There had to be profound changes in society and the economy, he said,[74] one of the aims of which should be the creation, through a palette of measures, of five million jobs capable of withstanding competition. He expressly defended the reform of the welfare state, arguing that more weight should once again be given to the role of the individual in safeguarding his own future. However, he said, the cuts in social benefits that had been proposed were still much smaller than the dramatic reductions in benefits that had taken place in countries such as Sweden, the Netherlands, France, and Italy—countries which had not had to face a challenge on the scale of German reunification.[75]

For the Social Democratic opposition, Lafontaine rejected the term 'collective amusement park', which the Chancellor had used again, and put forward a ten-point programme for modernization, jobs, and environmentally friendly growth. The central elements in the scheme were a national jobs programme to combat unemployment and the recession, the ecological modernization of the economy, a strengthening of research, education, and science, and a large-scale programme of reconstruction in the east. In addition, public 'investment in the future' and private demand should be strengthened, and the costs of work should be lessened by a reduction in statutory additional wage costs, in particular social insurance contributions. On financing, and on the creation of greater social justice, Lafontaine proposed the somewhat vague notion of nationwide 'burden-sharing with increased taxation of higher incomes and greater wealth'.[76]

Count Lambsdorff attacked Lafontaine's proposals, which he said were uncosted, and criticized the errors that had been committed in the implementation of the active labour market policy in the east. Lambsdorff also made it clear that the scheme that the Economics Minister, Rexrodt, had originally put forward had been 'watered down and weakened' in the course of the government's discussions and that 'the Federal Ministries, from the lower levels of civil servants to the Minister', had engaged in 'trench warfare' in order to generate delay. What was needed was not constantly new working groups, but decisions: 'deeds and not words'.[77]

Wolfgang Thierse, speaking for the eastern Social Democrats, also deplored the government's weak leadership and described the report on Germany's economic position as a 'documentation of failure'.[78] The problems of the economy had not been caused by unification: they were of the government's own making. He attacked the social and emotional division of Germany and the decline in social solidarity, and called for a new industrialization of the east. East German manufacturing firms should be given time, through measures such as wage cost subsidies, to 're-conquer the lost markets' and win new ones.[79]

The governing coalition parties finally spelled out their proposals for securing Germany's economic position in a thirty-point 'action programme for greater growth and employment' and a draft employment promotion law, based on this programme, which was introduced in the Bundestag at the beginning of February 1994. Along with further consolidation of government budgets, the programme and the draft law contained the following main points: support for the establishment of new businesses, to help the middle class; changes to the machinery of labour market policy, with an extension of productive employment promotion from the new *Bundesländer* to the regions in the old *Länder* that had been particularly affected by structural crises; a lowering of the assessment basis for wages from job creation schemes to 80 per cent of wages for comparable work in the primary labour market; deregulation measures; and a general authorization of private commercial employment agencies.[80]

When the Finance Minister, Waigel, and the Economics Minister, Rexrodt,[81] presented the programme to the Bundestag on 20 January 1994, the debate was coloured by the knowledge that 1994 was going to be an 'electoral super-year'. The opposition Social Democrats' spokeswoman on financial policy, Ingrid Matthäus-Maier, complained that the programme was 'political action for action's sake', designed to conceal the fact that the coalition was bereft of policies. It was clear, she said, that the government's days were numbered—privately, coalition members would be giving the programme the apt and succinct name 'Operation Evening Sun'.[82] The government was setting one negative record after another: it was responsible for the highest level of unemployment and the worst economic crisis in post-war German history, the greatest burden of taxation and contributions of all time, and the highest level of public debt and interest payments.[83] Rudolf Dreßler of the SPD condemned the government's concrete proposals as a 'wild conglomeration of disjointed individual measures', 'spawned' by the forthcoming elections.[84] He said that the measures would not achieve a reduction in the cost of labour as a factor of production, but would merely redistribute the cost of labour from entrepreneurs to employees. What the Federal government was really doing was 'destroying and disposing of our social insurance system . . . saying good-bye to the welfare state of the Federal Republic of Germany. At root, it is intent on a different kind of Republic.'[85]

Nevertheless, the huge opposition to the government's plans was not sufficient to prevent an eventual compromise. The government had originally assumed that the law would not need to be approved by the Bundesrat. The Bundesrat, however, judged that a proposed regulation amending the law to combat illicit work required its consent and it threatened to wreck the law as a whole, primarily because of the removal of the Federal Institute of Labour's exclusive rights over job-finding. There was also a possibility that with the end of the parliamentary term approaching, delay of any kind might threaten the passage of the law.[86] Accordingly, the bill was split into two separate parts, a bill requiring the consent of the Bundesrat and a bill not requiring such consent, and after the Mediation Committee of the Bundestag and the Bundesrat had been called into play the two bills, in altered form, were finally approved by both chambers and became law on 1 August 1994.[87]

In important changes to the government's draft, wages from job creation schemes were raised from 80 to 90 per cent of comparable wages, the proposed general upper limit on higher wages from job creation schemes was abandoned, and the implementation of the new regulation with regard to job creation schemes was deferred until 1 January 1995. The government's renewed attempt to confine to two years the claim to unemployment assistance in continuation of unemployment benefit, and thus to transfer the financial burden from the Federal government to local authorities, was defeated by resistance from the *Länder*. Structural short-time working benefit, introduced in 1988 and scheduled to be terminated in 1995 for specific trades and professions in the old *Länder* and on a general basis in the new *Länder*, was extended for a further two years by the Mediation Committee.[88] However, the legislation retained the authorization of private commercial employment agencies, the prolongation of regulations making it easier to time-limit the employment relationship, the increased scope for transferring from one firm to another those unemployed people who were finding it difficult to obtain work, the changes making it easier for the unemployed to receive unemployment benefit after reaching the age of 58, and measures to encourage part-time work and to help the unemployed make the transition to self-employment.

All told, from the autumn of 1992 onwards social policy had come under increasing pressure from business and the business associations, from a majority of economists and of CDU/CSU politicians specializing in economics and finance, and from the whole of the FDP. In a situation dominated by a rapid increase in public debt, the limits on borrowing imposed by the Maastricht criteria, the continuing steep decline in the economy in the east, the 1993 recession, the debate on the threat to Germany's economic standing, and mounting doubts about the effectiveness of the active labour market policy, critics had been calling for far-reaching changes to be made to the German welfare state through the removal of regulations on the world of work and reductions in social benefits. The 10th amendment to the Employment Promotion Law, enacted on 18 December 1992, certain aspects of the Federal Consolidation Programme of 1993, the laws passed in December 1993 implementing the savings, consolidation, and growth programme, and the Employment Promotion Law of 1994 were all products of this pressure.

In March and April 1994 there were intensive discussions at the highest level within the Labour Ministry about alternative future models of financing for the different systems of social insurance. The models considered included a negative income tax; the introduction of a tax-financed basic pension; tax financing of social insurance benefits unrelated to insurance; a net product contribution by firms; more involvement in the social insurance system by people in 'small-scale employment'; the raising or abolition of the contributions ceiling in social insurance; more generous burden-sharing within social insurance for families, by making contribution rates dependent on the number of children; giving greater account, in pensions insurance, to the time spent bringing up children; and even the replacement of the system of financing benefits from current contributions to one based on an accumulated capital fund.[89] However, although all these alternatives were carefully examined, no specific proposals for reforming the financing of social insurance were put forward.

The policies of making savings in the social security field and removing protective regulations within employment law continued to be applied in the next parliamentary term.[90] The Federal Minister of Labour, Blüm, his ministry, and some of the social policy specialists in the CDU/CSU maintained their opposition to the reduction in social benefits. Blüm, who was at first able to ward off budgetary cuts in the pensions insurance system as reformed in 1989, was criticized in business circles as a 'major threat to Germany's industrial position' and the chief obstacle to the reform of the welfare state.[91] He defended himself against attacks from Bundestag members of the CDU/CSU and FDP by arguing that in the area of responsibility of the Labour Ministry alone, from the start of the Kohl government in 1982 until 1997, savings amounting to 98,000 million DM had been achieved, and that many measures to promote job employment and greater flexibility had been introduced, particularly in the areas of employment law and the law on working time.[92] His argument, however, implying that there had been continuity in social policy over the whole period, and that cost savings had always been at its heart, did not acknowledge that policy in the Kohl era had in actuality passed through different phases. The period between 1982 and 1989 had indeed been one of financial consolidation, but it had been followed, during the eighteen months after 1990, by a spell of unlimited spending, when social policy had been called on to protect German unification. In the autumn of 1992, however, the cold winds had undoubtedly begun to blow once again.

13

Social Policy and its Actors, 1991–1994

13.1 THE FRAMEWORK

The political and economic framework within which the actors in the field of social policy had to operate, and the scope for action that was available to them, changed substantially as a result of German unification and the acceleration of European integration. Political conditions in sixteen, rather than eleven, *Bundesländer* now came into the reckoning, and the five new *Länder* in the east had specific common interests that transcended party divisions. A new political party, the PDS, with a strong following in eastern Germany, had been formed. The influence of European institutions, notably the European Commission and the European Court of Justice, had increased. The ability of the state to pursue independent national economic and social policies had declined, in face of the need to retain international competitiveness in an era of 'globalization' and the emergence of many major companies as 'global players'.

With the ending of the east–west conflict, and the emergence of new challenges—the need to manage the process of transformation from a planned to a market economy in east Germany, to respond appropriately to structural changes in the national economy and increased interdependence in the world economy, and to integrate new actors into the political process—policy-making had to become more sophisticated, but it had also become more confusing, and the consequences of decisions were now harder to foresee. Moreover, Germany's relative economic standing had weakened, with gross domestic product per head falling from 40,200 DM in west Germany in 1990 to 36,000 DM in a united Germany in 1991. In the OECD's league table of economies, Germany had fallen to twelfth place.[1] Economic decline also reduced the state's scope for making distributional decisions in social policy.

The Basic Law had not specified the form that the economic and social order should take in Germany. With the State Treaty of 18 May 1990, however, the Social Market economy was now expressly enshrined as the norm. This did not, though, entirely clarify the situation. Although both a socialist planned economy and a system of untrammelled laissez-faire capitalism were certainly ruled out, the precise nature of the Social Market economy was left undefined. In particular, it was not clear what the relative weightings of the social and the market components should be.

Relations between the state, the economy, and society were subject to countervailing processes. On the one hand, the state had become stronger. It had the primary role in 'Aufbau Ost' (reconstruction in the east), the partial takeover of east German industry through the *Treuhand*, the use of social policy to cushion the effects of economic transformation in the east, the rise in public spending as a proportion of gross national product, the introduction of social care insurance, the expansion of family policy, and the growing role of environmental policy. On the other hand, the neo-liberal policy of denationalization also remained in force. Under its aegis, private television companies were created, postal services, telecommunications, and the railways were privatized, and there was a general authorization of private commercial employment agencies. In addition, more groups in society were calling for greater individual self-provision within the social insurance system, for a relaxation of protective rules within employment law, and for reductions in state regulation and bureaucracy, and some of these demands, too, were translated into government policy.

13.2 THE FEDERAL CHANCELLERY AND THE COORDINATION OF POLICY

During the negotiations on the State Treaty and, to a slightly lesser extent, on the Unification Treaty, the Federal government and the ministerial bureaucracy had played the dominant role. Subsequently, however, in the processes of discussion and decision-making concerning policy, especially social policy, government and the bureaucracy yielded ground again to the complex and largely informal procedures of consultation and compromise that had come to characterize the German political system over the four decades since the founding of the Federal Republic.

At the centre of power were the Federal Chancellor and the Federal Chancellery. Significantly, for example, it was Chancellor Kohl, speaking at the party conference of the CDU at the end of October 1992, who took the initiative in calling for a 'reassessment of priorities'[2] in policy through renewed efforts to protect Germany's economic standing, restrict additional wage costs, and consolidate the public finances, and sought to bind the Social Democratic opposition more closely into support for this programme. It is noteworthy, too, that despite the urgings of de Maizière, no separate ministry for the new *Bundesländer* was set up. Rather, the coordination of 'Aufbau Ost' was handled by the Chancellor and the Chancellery, and issues relating to reconstruction in the east were central to the regular discussions that the Chancellor held with leading representatives of the employers' associations and trade unions.[3] In addition, besides the general meetings between the Chancellor and the Prime Ministers of all the *Bundesländer*, Kohl held frequent special talks with the heads of government in the eastern *Länder* at which problems specific to the east were discussed, with Kohl trying to win support for the Federal government's policy.[4] These events, which were widely reported in the media, also enabled the participants to promote their political image and win over public opinion.

Detailed soundings on the 'Aufbau Ost' policy took place in the working parties that were held roughly once a month and attended by the chief of the Federal

Chancellery, the state chancellery chiefs in the new *Länder*, and the chief of the senate chancellery in the *Land* of Berlin.[5] The Federal Chancellery was also kept informed on a weekly basis by individual government ministries about the concrete ways in which the State and Unification Treaties were being implemented and about the problems that had arisen. At the operational level, activities affecting the new *Bundesländer* were coordinated by the so-called 'Ludewig group', which consisted of the permanent Staatssekretäre in the participating ministries and Ministerialdirektor Johannes Ludewig, head of Department IV in the Chancellery, which was responsible for economic and financial policy and coordination for the new *Bundesländer*.[6]

Other bodies involved in the development of policy for east Germany were the cabinet committee for the new *Bundesländer*, which had been established by a cabinet decision on 29 January 1991,[7] and the Bundesrat committee on 'German unity', which was formed on 27 September 1991 under the chairmanship of the CDU Prime Minister of Saxony, Kurt Biedenkopf, with the SPD Prime Minister of Brandenburg, Manfred Stolpe, as the first deputy chairman.[8] Within the Federal Ministry of Labour a 'management staff for the new *Bundesländer*' was set up at a senior level by a decree of 9 April 1991, with Ministerialdirigent Dr Johannes Vöcking, who was also in charge of the ministerial office, as its head. Below Vöcking, Regierungsdirektor Werner Sasdrich, who in February 1990 had been put in charge of a working group planning the alignment of employment and social policy in the two German states, was tasked with providing 'support for the senior management of the Ministry in the area of labour market and social policy in the new *Bundesländer*'.[9] The designation of the staff group assigned to the Parlamentarische Staatssekretär Horst Günther by a decree of 24 July 1991 from now on included a reference to the 'link with the *Treuhand* agency'.[10]

Under Kohl's chancellorship—unlike that of Helmut Schmidt—the cabinet primarily had the notarial function of giving official blessing to initiatives and legislative plans of the government, and played only a minor role in the coordination of policy.[11] Kohl expected government ministers to coordinate and achieve agreement about policy before bills were brought to the cabinet. Initiatives in social policy that would cost money had to be cleared, first and foremost, with the Finance Minister. Proposals also had to be coordinated with other relevant ministries, particularly the Interior Ministry, the Economics Ministry, and the Justice Ministry, but for the most part these processes of coordination took place at the level of the permanent Staatssekretäre of the ministries concerned.[12]

Of course, the political chances of a particular piece of legislation's being enacted were also a crucial consideration. As far as the parliamentary term 1994–8 is concerned, it is clear that the experience of delays and failures of coordination in the preparation of legislative initiatives and proposals during the preceding parliamentary term caused the Federal Chancellery to become more heavily involved in the selection of legislative proposals, inter-ministerial coordination at draft stage, the dissemination of drafts to the *Länder*, policy experts and interest groups, and preliminary talks and negotiations with the *Länder* before and after the introduction of cabinet bills. The main aim was to provide a political 'early warning system' that would enable the Chancellery to test what prospects particular legislative proposals had of finding approval in the Bundestag and Bundesrat, given the political make-up of the two chambers.[13]

13.3 NORBERT BLÜM AND THE SOCIAL POLICY COALITION

After the formation of the government in January 1991, policy-making in the social field became more segmented. While policy for women and the family and housing policy continued to be dealt with primarily by their own ministries, responsibility for health insurance and, with it, the highly controversial issue of health service reform were now transferred from the Federal Ministry of Labour to the Federal Ministry of Health, so that the political responsibility for social insurance and supervision of the self-administered social insurance bodies was split. In addition, in 1992 the Health Ministry acquired, in Horst Seehofer—previously Parlamentarischer Staatssekretär in the Labour Ministry—a competent and effective minister with strong roots in the CSU and the CDU/CSU parliamentary party.

The Labour Minister, Norbert Blüm, was in a strong position as the longest-serving minister in Kohl's various cabinets. He was adept at crystallizing complex issues into simple terms, and his rhetorical gifts made him a brilliant electoral campaigner, but he also had great understanding of the nature of power and was a skilled tactician.[14] Moreover, his role as the leading representative of the working-class wing of the CDU and chairman of the party in North Rhine-Westphalia gave him a significant power base within the party. Within the government and the coalition his views carried special weight if there was conflict over policy (as in the case of the introduction of social care insurance), thanks to the fact that he had direct access to Kohl. The Chancellery did not intervene in social policy at the level of ideas: once Blüm had reached agreement with Waigel, the Finance Minister, and so long as no legal problems arose, then a measure was free to proceed, as far as the government side was concerned.[15]

As a politician, Blüm concentrated his efforts on central matters of policy, such as the pensions reform of 1989/92, the addition of a social union to monetary and economic union in 1990, and the introduction of social care insurance in 1991–4. He strove to keep a social policy coalition alive by maintaining close personal contacts with the leading social policy spokesmen in the parliamentary parties, such as Dreßler in the SPD and Cronenberg in the FDP. Similarly, either he or senior officials in his ministry preserved close ties with trade unions and management and with the most important social policy experts in the employers' associations and other bodies, such as the Association of German Pensions Insurance Providers (which was the source of data indispensable for the future planning of pensions policy). The members of this social policy coalition[16] had, in many cases, been socialized in similar ways through politics, were anxious to stand up against what they saw as the overweening influence of the budgetary policy experts, spoke with authority in a field that was becoming ever more complex, and were experienced in translating social polices into practice in collaboration with the self-governing social policy bodies.[17] Blüm's own views on social policy were rooted in the social doctrines of the Catholic church. For him, social policy was an ingredient of social solidarity generally: it was a tool for ensuring fairness and harmony in society, and hence for creating social cohesion. These beliefs also underlay his unqualified support for a full-fledged social union with the GDR, and later the new *Bundesländer*, and his refusal to reduce the question of Germany's economic position to one of wage levels and the dismantling of social benefits.[18]

On the issue of social care insurance Blüm pushed his political influence as far as it would go. He brought the coalition with the FDP to the brink of collapse and earned himself fierce and lasting criticism from business and its representative bodies, which branded him as a defender of an outdated conception of the welfare state. With the deterioration in the economic situation during the recession of 1993, the continuing high costs of unification, and the intensification of economic competition, the social policy coalition lost influence and began to crumble. This change was foreshadowed when Horst Günther, from the German White-Collar Workers' Trade Union, who had been chairman of the working group on labour and social affairs in the CDU/CSU parliamentary party, was appointed Parlamentarischer Staatssekretär in the Labour Ministry in the new government in January 1991 and replaced as chairman of the working group by Julius Louven, a politician identified with medium-sized business, who established a clear distance between himself and Blüm. The personal friendship between Blüm and Cronenberg of the FDP also suffered as a result of the strains imposed by the two men's sharp differences over the question of social care insurance.[19]

13.4 THE COORDINATION OF SOCIAL POLICY WITHIN THE GOVERNING COALITION

Nevertheless, one of the salient facts about the parliamentary term 1991–4 is that after some very fierce clashes, the major legislative projects of this period—the Pensions Transition Law of 1991, the Health Service Structure Law of 1992, and the introduction of social care insurance in 1994—together with the Federal Consolidation Programme of 1993 and the asylum compromise of 1992/3, were eventually implemented on the basis of cooperation and consensus between the governing coalition, the *Länder*, and the Social Democratic opposition.

As far as the governing coalition was concerned, the process of policy formation and decision-making involved restraining the influence of the relevant constitutional bodies by a combination of party politics and informal methods. In the coalition democracy of the Federal Republic a governing party could not be simply outvoted; moreover, individual ministries tended to be allocated, almost as hereditary fiefdoms, to particular parties within the government. Coordination between the coalition parties was based on a detailed coalition agreement, negotiated when the government was formed, and during the Kohl era took place primarily through meetings of the 'Elefanten'—senior figures in the national and parliamentary parties—who were in tune with Kohl's distinctive personality-centred style of leadership,[20] and through coalition working groups.[21] Typically, these elder statesmen and experts sought to resolve conflicts in advance of the meetings of the official decision-making bodies, with the result that the cabinet, parliament, and the parliamentary parties were left with little room for manoeuvre. Decisions taken by these informal groups of leading party figures or experts in particular fields were not easily amended later on.

In social policy, coalition working groups played a central role, especially, in the preparatory work on social care insurance, in the discussions on the structural reform of the health service, and in the efforts to reduce the abuse of social benefits by the unemployed. As far as the Labour Ministry's area of responsibility was concerned, Blüm sought to maintain his political influence by seizing the initiative and discussing problems publicly, as he did in the case of social care insurance, and by forming his own Labour Ministry staff group to shadow the coalition negotiations on social policy. (This approach was not followed in some other ministries, which were caught out by the results of the coalition negotiations.[22]) Blüm also tried to steer the activities of the coalition working groups by supplying working papers from his ministry, seeing to it that leading officials were involved in the discussions, and maintaining close contact with the members of the working groups.

13.5 THE BUNDESTAG, THE BUNDESRAT, AND THE SOCIAL DEMOCRATIC OPPOSITION

The Bundestag's involvement in the processes of decision-making on social policy primarily took the form of giving detailed scrutiny to, and adjusting the wording of, the draft legislation that came before its various social policy committees. With the Pensions Transition Law, significant changes were also made as a result of hearings with experts and representatives of interest groups by the committee on labour and social order. In plenary debates, on the other hand, parliamentarians were concerned less with trying to win over their political opponents than with publicly voicing their views, which were then reported on a wide and increasing scale in the mass media.

In some cases, notably that of social care insurance, the coalition parties in parliament—the CDU/CSU in particular—found it hard to form a united front. Wolfgang Schäuble, who became leader of the CDU/CSU parliamentary party on 25 January 1991, spelled out his view of the party's internal processes of policy debate and decision-making in a highly instructive speech to the party on 15 October 1992. He expressly rejected the idea that decisions on contentious issues should be reached through a vote. 'Recently we have taken a vote on most questions, but mainly for purposes of confirmation. Friends, if we use votes—controversial votes—to deal with conflicts, if we block off consensus-building, then we shall soon find ourselves in trouble, bitter trouble.' Differences between the CDU and the CSU, he said, or between the east German members of parliament and the west German members, or between representatives of medium-sized business and of employees, could not be resolved by majority vote. 'Prematurely cutting off the attempt to reach a common position, by trying to build a majority and taking a vote', would 'quickly endanger the unity of the parliamentary party and seriously impair its effectiveness'.[23]

Securing consensus, Schäuble added, could not be done simply at the plenary level of the parliamentary party, but was a much more complex matter. In his view, the party's executive committee should, as a general rule, try to sort out problems in advance and come up with a formula that would then work its way through *Land* and working groups to the full parliamentary party; that formula should then shape the party's discussion and take the pressure off it. However, the internal process of establishing a policy line also had to be confidential—unlike the existing situation, in which controversies were constantly being aired in public. Otherwise the parliamentary party's ability to influence events would 'go bust'.[24]

The process of decision-making on policy in the CDU/CSU parliamentary party involved the parliamentary party's executive committee—including the party's ministers, sometimes represented by their Parlamentarische Staatssekretäre—the *Land* groups, and the working groups for specific policy areas. The Union for Medium-Sized Business, the party's economics council, and the social committees (representing the interests of employees) also brought their influence to bear, as did external experts, mainly called in for hearings and discussions in the working groups. The interests of the new *Länder* were represented primarily by a committee on 'reconstruction in the new *Bundesländer*', which met weekly, and by groups of function-holders from the new *Länder*, which met weekly both among themselves and with the Chancellery Minister; the new *Länder* also made their voice heard through regular talks between the Federal Chancellor and all the CDU members of parliament from the east.[25] In addition, at the instigation of the coalition parties in east Germany ten working groups were set up by the Federal government in mid-September 1992, to address matters specific to the new *Länder*, including obstacles to investment, the promotion of structural change, housing construction, the labour market and training, finance, the infrastructure, agriculture, and the development of administrative machinery. Each of these working groups, which took their lead from particular ministries and whose deliberations were conducted at the level of Staatssekretäre, included two members of the coalition parliamentary parties: in the case of the CDU/CSU, one from the new *Länder* and one from the old.[26]

In Schäuble's eyes, it was essential, if the parliamentary party was to be effective, for it to work in a highly cooperative manner both internally and with its coalition partner, to be prepared to share responsibility for decisions jointly arrived at, and to support the government. He rejected the view that the party's main job was to monitor the government and exert as much influence on it as possible. The parliamentary party and the government, he argued, might not be an institutional unit, but they were a political one, since in a parliamentary system the government and the majority in parliament were politically identical. The leader of the parliamentary majority was the Chancellor.[27]

The process of decision-making, then, in social policy as in other areas, was a complicated one, in which the Bundestag, its committees, and the coalition parliamentary parties and their committees and experts were all involved to varying degrees. They did not, however, dominate the process.

On all questions on which the agreement of the Bundesrat was necessary, the Social Democrats also had to be brought into the process of establishing consensus. Inclusion of the *Länder* at an early stage was a key feature of decision-making on social policy during the period 1991–4. Coordination between the Federal government and the *Länder* over policy was at first a piecemeal affair, conducted at the level of Staatssekretäre of the *Land* governments, whether headed by the CDU/CSU or by the SPD.[28] Account had to be taken early on, in particular, of the financial interests of the *Länder*. After it conclusively lost its majority in the Bundesrat in the spring of 1991, the governing coalition had to obtain support from *Land* governments over and beyond those composed of the parties in power in Bonn: in other words, it had to win backing from all, or at least some, of the *Länder* in which the SPD was represented in government (whether within a Grand Coalition, as in Berlin or later in Baden-Württemberg, or in a coalition with the FDP, as in Brandenburg and later in Bremen and Rhineland-Palatinate), or it had to bring on board the Social Democratic Party as a whole. This was the case with the Pensions Transition Law and the structural reform of the health service, and subsequently with social care insurance and some of the consolidation legislation, when the relevant ministers in the *Länder*, leading social policy experts in the Bundestag parties, and—as far as particularly thorny issues were concerned—the heads of the national and parliamentary parties were incorporated into the process. When it came to overcoming differences between the coalition majority in the Bundestag and the SPD-dominated Bundesrat, the Mediation Committee of the two houses was also required to play a vital role.

The evolution of the Bundesrat from a chamber representing the *Länder* into an arena of party-political rivalry was reflected in social policy. However, even when the majorities in the two houses were at odds, because of the different complexions of the governing coalitions in the *Länder* and the mounting divergence of *Länder* interests in the wake of unification, the Bundesrat did not play a merely negative role.[29] Party divisions in the Bundesrat were powerful, but not all-pervasive, while at the same time opposition politics became increasingly federalized, in line with a move towards federalization on the part of the parties themselves. As we have seen,[30] the Social Democrats' response to the emerging Unification Treaty was led and coordinated by Wolfgang Clement, who was the chief of the state chancellery in North Rhine-Westphalia, the spokesman for the SPD-led *Länder*, and also, between October 1989 and October 1990, the senior representative of the state and senate chancelleries of all the *Länder*. On other questions, such as the Pensions Transition Law, the crucial compromises were negotiated by the Bundestag parties' social policy experts.[31] Ultimately, it was fear of political stalemate that compelled politicians to seek consensus or compromise, the FDP in particular being forced to sacrifice some important positions in areas of social policy in response to pressure from the social policy 'grand coalition' of the CDU/CSU and SPD.

In addition, across broad areas of social policy there was close cooperation between the Federal government and the *Bundesländer*, irrespective of the party-political make-up of the *Land* governments. This was true, in particular, as far as the extension of the institutions of the west German welfare state to the new *Länder* was concerned: for example, the introduction of a multipartite system of social insurance and of income support, the establishment of independent jurisdictions in employment law and social law, and the creation of an administrative service for social provision,[32] where the old *Bundesländer* contributed substantial support in addition to that of the Federal government.

The parliamentary term 1994–8 saw a sharper polarization in politics, as the creation of the administrative apparatus of the welfare state in the new *Länder* was completed, the FDP's position on social policy issues hardened, and the Social Democrats stepped up the level of political controversy, not least for electoral reasons. The result was a block on further significant reform, and this in turn was one of the reasons why the Kohl government, which anyway had come to be seen as exhausted in both personal and policy terms, was voted out of office in September 1998.

13.6 TRADE UNIONS AND EMPLOYERS' ASSOCIATIONS

Another reason for the increasing polarization was a growing tension between the government and the bodies representing the major interest groups. As we have seen,[33] during the negotiations on German unity the main organizations of the two sides of industry exercised very little influence over the actual shaping of ideas and taking of decisions. On the other hand, when it came to the operational implementation of the social union, the social partners played a crucial role, as self-administrators within social insurance and the bodies controlling, with government, the Federal Institute of Labour. It was primarily the social insurers themselves and their leadership organizations that had to carry out the politically uncontentious task of extending the Federal system of social insurance to the new *Bundesländer*. In the area of labour market policy the influence of the social partners was cut back when the 10th amendment to the Employment Promotion Law, passed in December 1992, gave the government the right to set the budget of the Federal Institute of Labour and, if it wished, to override the opposition of the self-administrators.[34]

In the core area of their activity, free collective bargaining, the social partners remained powerful, despite the weakening role of the employers' associations and the trade unions as a consequence of the move away from collective agreements and the decline in regional agreements in favour of company-based agreements. Even in this field, however, both sides believed that their positions were under threat. An example occurred over social care insurance, where the trade unions protested vehemently against compensation to employers through non-payment days within the continued payment of wages during illness, seeing this as interference with free collective bargaining.[35] In this instance they were supported in their stand by the employers, for tactical reasons.

Unlike the case of pensions reform in 1989/92, where they had been able to exert a great deal of influence on behalf of their members, the trade unions and the employers' organizations were not involved in the compromises that formed the basis of the major pieces of social policy legislation enacted between 1991 and 1994. The Health Service Structure Law was passed in the face of fierce opposition from the service providers' organizations, and social care insurance was introduced despite the hostility of business and its organizations and without the agreement of the trade unions. In addition, the mounting demand from business for reductions in additional wage costs and in the role of the welfare state made it harder for employers' associations and trade unions to reach common positions.

13.7 SUMMARY

The government's loss of its majority in the Bundesrat had a significant effect on social policy during the years 1991 to 1994. It led the Social Democratic opposition to become more heavily involved in the shaping of policy, made for greater interlocking between the Federal government and the *Länder*, and caused a loosening of the links between the parties and the bodies associated with them, the latter thereby losing some of their influence. The executive, though it did not retain the dominance it had enjoyed in 1990, was not sidelined in the political decision-making process. The ministerial bureaucracy was still able to pursue its own initiatives, thanks in part to its grasp of the issues and its close contacts with experts in the parties and other bodies, but mainly because it was able to exploit the room for manoeuvre within the political game that was created for it by strong ministers such as Norbert Blüm, Horst Seehofer, Wolfgang Schäuble, and Theo Waigel of the CDU/CSU. With the balance of political and economic forces constantly shifting, particularly in reference to less controversial issues, the bureaucracy also had considerable scope to exert influence through the detailed drafting of legislation and the translation of policy into administrative action.

As we have seen,[36] the Federal Constitutional Court had an important impact on social policy. The Bundesbank likewise influenced social policy, at least indirectly, through its policy on interest rates: this was an important contributory factor, for example, in enabling the government and the opposition to reach agreement over the Federal Consolidation Programme.[37] It is also worth noting that in the case of social care insurance, the highly controversial question whether employers should receive further compensation when the second stage of the policy (involving benefits for inpatient care) was introduced was resolved only because the decision was effectively left to the Council of Economic Experts and thus politically neutralized.

Our study of the actors in the field of social policy during the period 1991–4 has also shown that in sharp contrast with the decision-making processes that accompanied the establishment of the social union in 1990, the behaviour of actors was strongly conditioned by the relative strengths of the parties in the Bundesrat, the specific nature of the different issues involved, the wider political and economic climate, the Chancellor's governing style, the interplay of different institutions and organizations, and the role of particular individuals and the networks of connections between them. The system of decision-making was thus in a constant state of flux.

Concluding Reflections

1. GERMAN SOCIAL POLICY IN THE CONTEXT OF GERMAN UNIFICATION AND THE ATTEMPT TO MAINTAIN GERMANY'S ECONOMIC STANDING, 1989–1994: GENERAL OUTLINE, ACTORS, AND PROBLEMS

The overriding factor that influenced social policy in the period between the fall of the Wall in November 1989 and the end of the 12th parliamentary term in October 1994 was the forging of German unity and the extension to the new *Bundesländer* in the east of the institutions, norms, and actors of the welfare state of the west. In addition, as the economic recession began to make its impact on the Federal Republic in the autumn of 1992, the threats to Germany's economic position caused by the advance of European unification and the exacerbation of international competition through 'globalization'—threats which were at first ignored—began to loom more largely. The central policy aims that the government had pursued during the years 1982 to 1989—the consolidation of state budgets, the reduction of the proportion of gross national product claimed by social expenditure, and a stronger emphasis on private provision within the system of social security—effectively had to be abandoned in the face of the high transfer payments that were made to finance the transformation of the economy of east Germany from a planned to a market system and to cushion the effects of the change by means of social policy within the framework of the social union. Between 1989 and 1995 public debt more than doubled. The share of gross national product allocated to expenditure on social policy, the share allocated to public spending generally, and additional wage costs all rose sharply. Although the policy of privatization remained in place, the demands made on the state—which was the most important actor in the transformation process, and on which the east Germans were counting to fulfil their expectations of a rapid improvement in their living standards—had grown greater than ever.

The huge effort that was made after the autumn of 1992 to reverse these trends and give a new impetus to employment and economic growth was ultimately unsuccessful, as the conditions that would have made possible the development of a competitive economy in the east were lacking and the costs of mass unemployment rose inexorably. Social policy helped to mitigate the effects of the change, but did little to overcome the economic crisis itself. The active labour market policy largely failed to provide a bridge to the emergence of a labour market in the east, and the removal of burdens on the labour market through the easing of early retirement and the provision of pre-pension transitional benefits merely made the financial problems of the pensions insurers and the Federal Institute of Labour more acute. Social security benefits certainly saved east Germany from mass poverty, but, by driving up additional wage costs, they also sent the cost of labour soaring and thus depressed employment.

Unification made the system within which social policy actors operated even more complex than before, and it gave rise to an even more heterogeneous set of vested interests that needed to be accommodated. During the reunification phase, and particularly until the signing of the State Treaty on monetary, economic, and social union, the Federal government unambiguously dominated the political process, as the leading party to the negotiations and the representative of German interests *vis-à-vis* the victorious powers. This gave it considerable room for manoeuvre, which it exploited to the full. The situation changed fundamentally, however, when the governing coalition of Christian Democrats, the Bavarian Christian Social Union, and liberals finally lost its majority in the Bundesrat at the beginning of 1991. Two separate majorities now had to be assembled for all important pieces of proposed legislation, one within the coalition and another in the Bundesrat: in practice, the government had to reach compromises with the Social Democratic opposition. The political game had become more complicated, and the government's freedom of action had become more limited.

The scope for change, however, differed from one area of social policy to another. The rapid extension of the west German welfare state to the new *Bundesländer* was an inevitability, owing to the wide-scale collapse of industry and employment in agriculture in the east, and though there was a wide range of views about the degree to which the west German social security system itself needed to be reformed, it took place, essentially, with the consent of the main political and social forces in Germany. Those neo-liberals who wanted merely a slimmed-down version of the Federal Republic welfare state to be established in the east, with fewer social benefits and employment law regulations protecting employees, in order to ease the process of economic transformation, had no chance of seeing their ideas implemented. Equally fated to be disappointed, given the balance of political forces and the pressures of time, were Social Democrats and trade unionists who hoped that some of the structural weaknesses in the west German welfare system—for example, in the health service, or in social insurance, with its divisions into a multiplicity of institutions—would not be extended to the east, and that the system in the west might be improved through the adoption of some of the features of the GDR system, such as the rights to work and to housing, and a scheme of basic protection within pensions law. Speedy action was also required because the industrial enterprises in the east were no longer fulfilling their role in supporting the social security system. With many enterprises going bankrupt, the guarantee of employment that they had previously represented now expired too. Those enterprises that were able to keep functioning had to make drastic reductions in personnel and cut their social costs in order to remain competitive.

In some areas vital reforms were carried out on the basis of compromise, in a number of instances after fierce argument. This was the case with the difficult issue of the financing of German unity through the Federal Consolidation Programme, the temporary containment of the costs of the health service in the Health Service Structure Law, and, especially, the introduction of social care insurance, the purpose of which was to address one of the central problems of an ageing society in the Federal Republic. On the other hand, after the major pensions reform of 1989/92 the task of dealing with the problems of protection for the elderly was put on hold until 1994.

Although savings were made in other areas of social policy, benefits for families were expanded, with the increase in child benefit in 1996, the recognition within social care insurance of care work done for relatives and friends, and the rewarding of work within the family in pensions insurance; these extensions of benefits were obtained at the expense, primarily, of the recognition of time devoted to training. Within unemployment insurance, benefits became more differentiated according to family circumstances, with the benefit rate for single persons being reduced further than that for parents.[1] In the case of support for families and measures to ease the combination of work with family life, particularly for women, there was little progress, mainly as a result of lack of funds. There was no consensus, either, about the best way to promote employment and economic growth. The government believed in a policy of deregulation and the removal of burdens from businesses through a lowering of statutory social benefits, while the opposition favoured large-scale state-financed employment programmes, and so those measures and laws that were eventually adopted were half-hearted in character and did little to stimulate the economy.

In comparison with earlier years, the role of the organizations of the major social interest groups in the decision-making processes affecting social policy declined. The interest-group bodies made few distinctive contributions to the debate on unification policy. Nor were they able to put their imprint on the most important pieces of social policy legislation of the period, the Health Service Structure Law and the Social Care Insurance Law. This was partly because the government and the Social Democratic opposition were not prepared to jeopardize the hard-won compromises they themselves had achieved, and partly, too, because the interest-group organizations were largely unsuccessful in developing institutions capable of adequately representing the particular interests of east Germans. On the other hand, as social insurers, as the bodies controlling (with government) the Federal Institute of Labour, and, in the case of the welfare associations, as providers of welfare facilities, the interest-group organizations played an indispensable role in the implementation of social policy and the concrete development of the welfare state in the east. In addition, the social partners had a vital influence on the economic framework, and hence on investment decisions by business, through the process of collective pay bargaining. Chancellor Kohl met regularly with leading representatives of the trade unions and the employers' associations in order to seek their support, notably over the implementation of 'Aufbau Ost', the policy of economic reconstruction in the east.

There was no comprehensive vision of social policy that was, at the same time, politically viable. This was partly because there were so many different actors and vested interests in the social policy field, and partly because the making and implementation of policy in Germany is distributed among so many different institutions.[2] Within government, social policy is the responsibility of different ministries. In turn, social insurance is divided into different branches according to the nature of the risks insured. Even within statutory health insurance, there is fierce competition for lower-risk clients between individual insurance companies and types of company, while within pensions insurance major problems have been caused by anachronistic organizational overlaps (though these were removed by the reform of 1 October 2005) and by the competing interests of the Federal Insurance Office for White-Collar Workers, the *Land* insurance bodies for blue-collar workers, and the miners' guilds.

Repeatedly, problems were not resolved, but merely shifted from one institution to another. Thus, the widespread granting of early retirement certainly made it easier for firms to rationalize and to trim production and administration by shedding older members of the workforce in a socially acceptable way, and it reduced some of the burdens on the labour market, which was in the interest of the trade unions. However, it also placed extra burdens on unemployment insurance and, especially, on pensions insurance. Similarly, the splitting of the financing of the welfare state between the Federal government, the *Länder*, the local authorities, and the providers of social insurance through contributions revenue only added to the difficulties of any prospective reform of the system. Reductions in unemployment benefit and unemployment assistance, or in pensions, placed an additional burden on local authorities in the form of income support; on the other hand, the introduction of social care insurance made for substantial savings as far as the same benefits were concerned. Several questions, then, required answers. Who ought to have financial responsibility for the subsidizing of a low-income sector out of public funds, as was being widely demanded? Who would benefit, apart from businesses? Who would be the gainers as a result of possible changes, and who the losers?

It would certainly have made economic sense to transfer the investment costs of hospitals and health care facilities from the *Länder* to health and social care insurance, but that would have reduced the influence of the *Länder* over the health care system and social care facilities, and would also have led to a rise in contribution rates and thus in additional wage costs.

It was a particularly serious failure that German unification had come about without a proper coordination of economic, financial, and social policy. It made no sense that a substantial proportion of the cost of unity was simply shifted on to the mutualist systems of unemployment, pensions, and accident insurance (and, after 1999, health insurance). Fiscal anxieties on the part of the Finance Ministry; legal anxieties on the part of the Justice Ministry; efforts by the Interior Ministry to protect the interests of civil servants, and by the Economics Ministry to protect those of the self-employed; the governing coalition's calculation that increases in social insurance contributions would be politically very much easier to implement than tax increases—these were the decisive factors that led to this inappropriate decision. The over-burdening of the social insurance systems, when society as a whole should have borne the brunt, the sharp resultant rise in statutory additional wage costs, and the disproportionate load that was imposed on the lower social classes[3] were not necessary consequences of German unity: they were a product of the mistaken way in which unity was financed.

In view of the fundamental changes in the political, economic, and social framework that were brought about by German unity, it is remarkable that there has been such a degree of continuity in social policy in the Federal Republic. The welfare state that had evolved over a long period of time, with its traditional institutions, norms, and actors, and with its traditional funding sources, proved to be the sole common ground on which the country's political and social forces could find agreement. Little of the institutional structure for social security that had been specific to the GDR remained in place, and ideas emanating from the new *Bundesländer* had very limited impact on social policy, except in a few cases—for example, the expansion of child care facilities, with the enshrinement in 1996 of the legal right to a kindergarten place. In practice, the existing welfare state became yet more deeply entrenched as a result of unification, being seen to have 'proved its worth', and the debate about the reform of the system was deferred for several years. The sheer weight of the burdens that were placed on the government, the state's administrative machinery, the legislative bodies, and the social insurance providers by the extraordinary and unforeseen problems posed by German unification, and the increased complexity of the tasks that followed in unification's wake, meant, too, that the German welfare state was slow to adapt to the changing international conditions within which it had to function.

2. THE EFFECTS OF UNIFICATION ON THE POPULATION IN THE EAST

For most citizens in the new *Bundesländer*, the political and economic structural changes brought about by unification made for an almost total re-shaping of their lives. Old certainties vanished, and people had to find their feet in a very different world: one that was governed according to complex new rules and that required them to take many more initiatives on their own behalf. The extension to the former GDR of the west German welfare state, with its dense network of different forms of social protection, helped make the population more ready to accept the transformation in their circumstances.

The effects of unification on the lives of individuals and social groups were very varied. Everyone benefited from the improvements in the range of available goods and from the opportunity to travel to the west. Everyone was adversely affected, if in different degrees, by the rise in rents and the dismantling of subsidies on essentials. Nevertheless, the increases in living costs were more than offset by the sharp rise in wages and salaries and in average private household income generally, so that living standards for most people in the east improved significantly in comparison with the period before unification, even if they remained well below those of the population in the old *Bundesländer*.

The gainers from unification were the majority of pensioners, who had been in a very disadvantageous position in the GDR, along with almost everyone not directly involved in the production process. Average pensions in the east rose in nominal terms from 475 marks in June 1990 to 1,214 DM in July 1994: in other words, by more than two and a half times.[4] In real terms, too—i.e. taking into account the increase in living costs—the incomes of pensioner households in the east in 1994 were roughly twice the level they had been in 1989.[5] Only a fairly small number of pensioners failed to benefit from this clear rise in living standards: for example, some of those who had been particularly closely associated with the regime had their supplementary or special provision payments reduced, or had their previous income taken only partially into account in the calculation of their pensions. As we have seen, however,[6] these reductions were partly reversed by later legislation and legal judgements.

The position of widows changed considerably. In the GDR, widows who had not reached the pensionable age of 60 received no form of pension, except under highly restricted circumstances (for example, if they were bringing up two children under the age of 8), and even when they reached pensionable age they received a widow's pension only as a secondary benefit, worth 50 marks per month, because of their entitlement to their own pension. Although provision for surviving dependants was improved after 1 July 1990 by the GDR's own Pensions Alignment Law, the more decisive change came with the Pensions Transition Law, which raised widows' pensions for 780,000 widows by an average of 270 DM per month from 1 January 1992, and for the first time gave about 150,000 widows the entitlement to claim a surviving dependant's pension.[7] Overall, the average widow's pension of 100 east German marks on 30 June 1990 rose to 943 DM on 1 July 1997[8]—a near-tenfold increase in nominal terms (treating the two currencies as equivalent), and a fivefold increase in real terms. Even though the incomes of households of older people in the east remained well below the incomes of comparable households in the west, owing to the widespread lack of other sources of income other than the statutory pension (though by 1994 this had, on average, nearly reached the western level),[9] most elderly people in the east were no longer living on the edge of poverty, as had been the case under the GDR, and they could now also afford some non-essentials and foreign travel. This applied, in particular, to pensioner couples who received two higher pensions by virtue of both partners' having been in full-time employment for many years, the normal situation during the GDR years. Whereas on 1 July 1996 almost half of all women pensioners in the old *Bundesländer* were receiving pensions of less than 500 DM per month through blue-collar workers' pensions insurance, because they had not had long periods of employment, this applied to only about 5 per cent of female blue-collar pensioners in the new *Bundesländer*.[10]

The position of war victims improved even more markedly as a result of unification. Under the GDR they had been at the bottom of the social scale and most of them had received only minimum pensions. In 1996 about 200,000 people in the new *Bundesländer* who were entitled to provision now received regular payments on grounds of disability or as surviving dependants, thanks to the much more generous regulations of the Federal Social Provision Law.[11]

People with disabilities had been a marginal group in the GDR and came well towards the end of the queue as far as the allocation of social resources was concerned. Many of them were cared for in residential homes that were often insanitary and in a bad state of repair, and in any event the demand for places far outstripped the supply. After unification, residential homes were refurbished and modernized, albeit slowly, care improved in quality and was eventually made available through social care insurance, and better medical treatment and rehabilitation were also provided. On the other hand, the disabled were excluded from the labour market in much larger numbers than had been the case under the GDR.[12] The residents of old-age homes and the mainly elderly residents of care homes also found it very difficult to learn how to deal with the new system, and there was dismay at the drastic increases in the costs of a place in an old-age or care home.[13] Many residents felt great anguish at having to spend their carefully accumulated savings before they could claim income support and, if their own money was insufficient, at having to ask their children to help support them.[14]

As far as people in employment were concerned, the decisive factors were, of course, whether they were able to maintain their career, whether they were experiencing a move up or down the social scale, and how seriously they were affected by mass unemployment. As a general rule, those with qualifications fared better than those without, and the young and the mobile had less cause to fear long-term unemployment than those who were older or who—like many women—were tied to their place of residence for family reasons. It is difficult to overstate the dramatic impact that the collapse in the world of work had on people who had become accustomed to thinking that they had total job security. At the end of 1993 only 29 per cent of people who had been in employment in November 1989 had remained uninterruptedly employed in the same place of work since that date.[15] By November 1994 57 per cent of east Germans of working age had taken part in job creation schemes, many of them more than once, and if re-training measures provided within enterprises and not supported by public funds are also included, this proportion rises to 81 per cent.[16] Huge adjustments to the new conditions accordingly had to be made.

Women were especially seriously affected by the structural transformation of the economy and the collapse in employment. The rate of unemployment among women in 1993/4, at over 20 per cent, was roughly twice as high as that among men,[17] and the rate of participation of women in the active labour market policy was also much lower until the shift in economic policy that took place in 1993. The situation of single parents and women with young children was particularly difficult, as companies were becoming increasingly unwilling to adjust terms and conditions of work to their specific needs. Nevertheless, women—including single parents and mothers of young children—remained very eager to work.[18] Moreover, it would be wrong to imply that unification caused a general deterioration in the position of women. Many women availed themselves of new opportunities, such as the increase in jobs in the service sector. In many cases, too, women now gave greater priority to material considerations than they had done under the GDR and sought to improve their chances on the labour market by deferring the moment when they had children.

By and large, surveys of attitudes in the east have shown that most people believe that their own particular material situation has improved since unification. At the same time, they think that the general situation is worse than their own individual one, and they especially lament the disappearance of the sense of social safety and certainty[19] that the GDR provided, albeit at a lower level of prosperity. To a far greater degree than people in the west, they see the state as having the primary responsibility for rectifying these shortcomings.

3. THE GERMAN WELFARE STATE: INTERNATIONAL COMPARISONS

In comparison with other democratic states, economic and social policy in Germany have followed a 'middle way'.[20] Within a typology of developed democratic states,[21] German policy is situated at a mid-point between, on the one hand, the elaborate welfare states of northern Europe and, on the other, the market-orientated capitalism of north America. The first broad type of social policy system, seen in its clearest form in the Scandinavian countries, was primarily the creation of social democratic movements and, in the early years, also of farmers' groups. As an 'ideal type', it embodies the aspiration that the members of society should be included, on as near a universal basis as possible, within a system of social security that is regarded as a social entitlement of citizenship and that offers a high degree of social protection. The distinctive features of such systems are comprehensive social insurance, substantial income transfers for social security, highly developed social services (largely financed out of taxation, rather than through contributions), and a significant degree of 'de-commodification'[22] of work, which largely ceases to have the character of a product. Under the model there is a high level of redistribution and a considerable evening-out of social inequalities.

Welfare capitalism (also termed a 'residual' welfare model), the system most clearly exemplified in north America, is based on the dominance of market-orientated liberal and conservative forces. As an ideal type, it seeks to solve social problems through the market and by means of subsidiary social forces, in particular the family, local social networks, and private charities. State support is provided, if at all, only on a short-term basis and is subject to strict tests of need. The distinctive features of such systems are a highly flexible and very lightly regulated labour market, a low level of social security not founded on explicit legal rights, a wide range of incomes, and a high degree of social inequality.

The Federal Republic of Germany, by contrast, is commonly seen as the prime example of a conservative, corporatist, welfare state: a type found mainly in continental Europe and usually characterized by the dominance of both authoritarian conservative and Christian Social ideas. The German system combines relatively extensive social benefits with a high level of regulation and 'de-commodification' of work. Its distinctive social policy institution is a system of social insurance linked to employment, financed primarily through contributions from employers and employees, and strictly differentiated on the basis of different kinds of risk and different groups of jobs and professions; those in need who are not covered by social insurance are provided with income support.

The German system offers fairly comprehensive social security, but, unlike the Scandinavian model, its redistributive effects are small, because social insurance contributions, and hence the benefits derived from them—particularly in respect of pensions insurance—vary very considerably. The system is based on the principle that differences in income and social status should be retained in old age or in the event of invalidity, illness, or unemployment. Alongside social insurance and income support, the concept of subsidiarity—the provision of support by the family, by smaller community bodies, and by larger welfare associations—plays a significant role.

In practice, however, all existing welfare states are hybrids. Thus, in the Scandinavian countries basic provision for all citizens through comprehensive insurance is supplemented by earnings-related contributions by, and benefits for, people in employment in order to protect living standards attained during working life, and the labour market has become highly flexible in order to maintain economic competitiveness. In the United States the popular system of contributions-based, earnings-related old-age pensions, introduced in 1935 as part of the New Deal and strongly defended by the lobbying organization the American Association of Retired Persons, is a vital part of the system as a whole. In the United Kingdom, which, since the period of government of Margaret Thatcher, has often been seen as another example of a 'residual' welfare state, an extensive system of company-based retirement provision has developed within the general framework of statutory state provision, yet at the same time the National Health Service, available to all citizens, has been preserved.[23] In continental European states such as Germany, France, and Italy there have been powerful trends towards universalism and the levelling-out of job- and profession-based differences, and also towards the redistribution of resources.

In the Federal Republic these changes have found expression in the inclusion within social insurance of more and more groups in the population over and beyond employees, and in financial burden-sharing between the various funders of pensions insurance, the latter undertaking responsibility for provision for surviving dependants without rises in contributions. Within statutory health insurance, too, there is now a sharing of risk structures between the various insurers. There has also been a large-scale transfer of social benefits within social insurance from the west to the east of the country. In addition, redistribution through statutory health insurance and social care insurance has been substantial, with earnings-related contributions paying for the same medical care and social care benefits both for members of the insurance company schemes and for their dependent relatives, the latter being co-insured without supplementary charges. Income support, too, although conditional on a test of need, gives the country's inhabitants a legally enforceable entitlement to social protection, as the lowest tier of the social security system. However, in 1993 support for asylum seekers who had lost the legal right to income support was cut back significantly when cash benefits were reduced by about one-fifth and a switch was made to benefits in kind as the standard form of benefits, in order to contain costs and lessen incentives to potential immigrants.

The policy of the 'middle way' has the firm support of the two main parties associated with the welfare state in Germany, the CDU/CSU and the Social Democrats, and of the trade unions, though there are differences of emphasis on points of detail. At its centre are the priority given to price stability, powerfully backed by the Bundesbank, and the balance between economic efficiency and a strong social policy that define the concept of the Social Market economy—a balance that is admittedly subject to many tensions and that has constantly to be renegotiated. At the same time, the 'middle way' is characterized by a high degree of delegation of tasks to non-governmental institutions: to the social partners, as largely autonomous actors within the industrial relations system; to the self-administered organizations of the social insurance system; to the complex network of benefits providers and the insured within the health insurance system; and, within the systems of income support and provision for the elderly and the young, to the Independent Welfare Associations. Even though the proportion of people involved in the operation of social policy who are employed by the Federal government, the *Länder*, and the local authorities is lower, in particular, than in the Scandinavian countries, the scale of the financial transfers that take place in the German welfare state is considerable.

This analysis of German economic and social policy as a policy of the 'middle way' is confirmed by a comparison of German social benefits with those of other countries.[24] According to OECD criteria, the share of gross domestic product allocated to social policy expenditure in the Federal Republic in 1989, at 23.9 per cent, was only a little above the mean value of 21.5 per cent in eighteen selected democracies.[25] In 1994, in the old *Bundesländer*, the proportion was again only a little above the average for the states of the European Union.[26] In 1990 the level of pensions of married people relative to net salary of couples in 1989 was below the average figure for European Union states, while the income replacement rate for married people through unemployment insurance in 1994/5 was only marginally above the mean value. Among EU states, Germany came second to Denmark in the fight against poverty.[27]

The German situation does have some distinctive features, owing in part to the policy of consolidation pursued by the Kohl government since 1982 and in part to the consequences of German unification. Between 1980 and 1990 the Federal Republic was one of the few European states to reduce the share of its gross domestic product devoted to social expenditure, as a result of favourable economic and social conditions and deliberate policies of consolidation on the part of the government.[28] With unification, however, the situation changed radically. Whereas between 1980 and 1994 the Federal Republic (and later the old *Bundesländer*) had dropped from second place to the midway position of sixth place among the EU states in terms of the social expenditure ratio, the reunited Germany moved up to third place behind Denmark and the Netherlands, ahead of the other large EU states, France, the United Kingdom, and Italy.[29]

Another distinguishing characteristic of the German system is the relatively high share in the financing of the welfare state that employers and the insured are required to furnish in the form of contributions. Moreover, that high share rose from about 55 per cent in 1960 to almost two-thirds (65 per cent) in 1994.[30] This easing of the burden on the public purse, at the expense of employers and the insured, was at odds with the general trend in the member states of the European Union, where, according to a report on social security by the European Commission, there was a perceptible 'trend towards taxation and away from contributions'.[31] After 1998, however, the share of the financing of the German welfare state borne by taxation likewise rose, primarily because of the sharp increase in the Federal government's subsidy of pensions insurance,[32] though also, more recently, as a result of support for health insurance and the public defraying of the relative increase in the cost of unemployment and short-time working.

With regard to the distribution of social benefits in terms of function or type of benefit, in 1994/5 the Federal Republic recorded mid-ranking values in expenditure (as a share of gross domestic product) in benefits for the elderly and surviving dependants, benefits for the unemployed and those seeking re-entry into the labour market, and benefits for families and children. However, it achieved top place among the countries of the European Union for expenditure on health services.[33]

Since the mid-1970s the Federal Republic has made strenuous efforts, in a succession of policy initiatives, to contain the explosion in health service costs, which had soared from 4.8 per cent of gross domestic product in 1960 to 8.1 per cent in 1975.[34] In comparison with some other countries it has been fairly successful in this attempt, confining the share of gross domestic product devoted to health expenditure to 8.7 per cent in 1992. By contrast, between 1972 and 1992 expenditure on health continued to rise sharply in the United States (from 7.6 to 14 per cent), in France (from 6.2 to 9.4 per cent), in Italy (from 5.6 to 8.5 per cent), and in the United Kingdom (from 4.7 to 7.1 per cent).[35] However, a comparative analysis of member states of the OECD for the year 1997 showed that the proportion of gross domestic product allocated to health expenditure in Germany, at 10.4 per cent, was the second highest after that of the USA (at 14 per cent), and that Germany's figure of 8.1 per cent for the share of *public* spending on health was the highest of the group.[36] Plainly, the government's drive to reduce costs had not succeeded over the longer term. That said, the example of the USA—where the Obama administration's plan to include a sizeable proportion of the population into health insurance for the first time has been a matter of extreme controversy—shows that a primarily market-based system of health care is not necessarily either more efficient or cheaper.

Many of the causes of the cost increases in the health system in Germany also apply to other countries: advances in medicine, the ageing of the population, the transference of health services from underpaid domestic workers to the market or the state as more women enter the job market, and the limited scope for rationalization and increases in productivity in health care provision, a service that is necessarily highly labour-intensive. However, in Germany there are also especially serious shortcomings in the way the excessively complex health care system has been managed. For example, the behaviour both of the providers of medical services (doctors, hospitals, the pharmaceutical industry, etc.) and of patients, as the consumers of such services, has tended to lead to a multiplication of services and hence of costs.[37] The German system is one in which the providers of health services exert a considerable amount of power, and it has been top-heavy with doctors, who, at the start of the 1990s (contrary to the present situation, particularly in the east), were still able to command relatively generous incomes.[38] Reform, though, has been politically hard to achieve, because of the high value that people place on health, their fears—not unjustified—that a two-tier health service might develop, and the scope for rallying political support that issues of health policy give to the doctors' organizations, trade unions, and political parties.

In the field of pensions, similarly, the potential electoral power of pensioners has weighed heavily with policy-makers. Although the ageing of the population, and hence the pressure to find a fair balance between the needs of the different generations, are features of all modern industrial societies, the problems are particularly acute in Germany, which, according to forecasts of the demographic situation in 2030, will be more severely affected by the 'greying' of society than any other OECD country.[39] In addition, the strongly employment-centred nature of pensions insurance in Germany, the fact that the existing system of financing in statutory pensions insurance is based mainly on current contributions, and the unsatisfactory way in which the various systems of old-age provision, with their links to huge vested interests, are harmonized have made any fundamental reform all the more difficult to secure. Because of the great political risks attendant on change, reforms were implemented on the basis of consensus among the political parties and the major social organizations until fierce arguments broke out over the abortive attempt at pensions reform in 1998 and the pensions reform carried out by the Federal Minister of Labour, Walter Riester, in 2001.

Although the Federal Republic largely continued to adhere to the policy of the 'middle way' after unification, the enormous scale of the transfer of economic resources from west to east, the recession of 1992/3, and the intensification of international competition for economic advantage exacerbated disputes over policy goals and made the policy more expensive.

This was particularly evident in employment policy. The host of active labour market measures that were deployed in the east did little more than cushion the effects of mass unemployment following the collapse of the GDR; they did not really combat unemployment itself. The German model of structural change based on consensus and close cooperation between the social partners within a framework of statutory regulation was not equipped to deliver the huge transformations that were needed in the east—transformations the scale of which was in any case initially underestimated. The pay increases that were negotiated by the two sides of industry in the early 1990s were far in excess of the sluggish rise in productivity: they merely aggravated the economic crisis and eventually had to be borne by taxpayers.[40] This, together with the wide-scale departures of employers from employers' associations and the move away from collective agreements, was a sign that the ability of the social partners to influence the management of the economy, which had been a central element of the 'middle way', had become significantly weaker.

In 1980 Germany's rate of unemployment had been well below the average level of the OECD states; by 1994 it was well above.[41] The decline in the number of jobs after 1992 was also particularly pronounced in Germany.[42] The fall in job numbers and the rise in unemployment are especially striking in comparison with the record of countries that were most successful in this area: the United States, the United Kingdom, Denmark, and the Netherlands. Although Germany still had the lowest unemployment rate among these states at the beginning of the 1990s, and had been in third place for employment growth since 1983, by 1997 unemployment was much higher than in any of these countries and the growth of employment much lower. However, in more recent years Germany has been fairly successful in reducing unemployment, bringing the number down from about 5 million to less than 3.5 million. Even in the current severe financial and economic crisis, the number of unemployed has risen relatively little in the west (largely because of the widespread prevalence of short-time work) and has actually fallen slightly in the east. Since real wages in industry in the east now stand at about two-thirds of those in the west, while productivity has reached nearly 80 per cent, east German industry at present has lower unit labour costs than west German industry and, despite having started at a low level, is slowly catching up with industry in the west.[43]

There were significant differences between the various countries that did particularly well in terms of employment during the 1990s. The United States and the United Kingdom were market-orientated states with weak trade unions, very broad spreads of income levels, a wide use of company-based or individual pay settlements, very flexible labour markets, and weak forms of protection against dismissal. Denmark and the Netherlands, by contrast, had high levels of trade union organization, narrow ranges of earnings, very active labour market policies, and high levels of income replacement benefits in the event of unemployment. It is true, however, that the labour markets in both Denmark and the Netherlands were extremely flexible, in the former case as a result of the wide prevalence of part-time working, and in the latter because of the strong pressure put on the unemployed either to accept paid employment or to take part in job re-training schemes.

4. CONCLUSIONS AND PROSPECTS

Compared with the welfare states of other countries, the German welfare state has been remarkable for continuity and path-dependency since its establishment in the 1880s. The degree of continuity is all the more striking when one considers the huge political upheavals that took place in Germany in 1918, in 1933, in 1945, and in 1989/90, and the divergences from the principles of social welfare that occurred during the National Socialist period and under the GDR. There are several reasons why the welfare state has retained its character: the robustness of the social policy institutions and norms that were originally created; the multiplicity of political and social interests involved in the formulation of social policy, and of organizations involved in implementing it; the highly complex structure of financing that has underpinned the system; and the great electoral significance of the welfare state's client groups. These factors have all served as impediments to fundamental alterations of the system.

Social security systems financed through taxation are easier to change than systems, like the German, which are based primarily on contributions creating clear and legally enforceable entitlements. Similarly, centralized democratic states are able to alter the course of social policy more quickly and extensively after a change of government than are federal democracies. Despite the fact that the Federal government is responsible for the great bulk of social policy legislation in Germany, federalism, and its most important instrument, the Bundesrat, have exerted a strong influence over social policy, particularly since 1949. When the majority party in the Bundesrat is different from that in the Bundestag, the opposition has to be brought into the policy-making process so that a Bundesrat majority can be achieved, or, alternatively, agreements have to be sought with individual *Länder* in which an opposition party heads, or is a participant in, the government. Support from the *Länder*, moreover, is rarely achieved if account is not taken of their vital financial interests. If that is done, however—as happened, for example, with the introduction of social care insurance, when local authority payments to finance income support were reduced and the burden on the *Länder* was eased—then the *Länder* can provide a backing for reform efforts.

The fact that tasks which affect the entire community are delegated to certain particular bodies within society makes it difficult to shift the prevailing balance of interests in any fundamental way or to pursue a social policy in the face of massive opposition from powerful social organizations. The need for the political parties within a governing coalition to reach agreement among themselves, and the powerful influence of the Bundesbank and the Federal Constitutional Court, are further significant factors serving to stabilize the existing system. That said, the present study has shown that both the Bundesbank and the Federal Constitutional Court have also given significant impetus to reform, the Bundesbank through its insistence on a restructuring of the German financial system after reunification, and the Court through its support for an extension of financial support for families.

Our analysis of social policy during the period between 1989/90 and 1994 has made clear that the German welfare state is well capable of resolving problems and adjusting to change. The creation of the social union, the reform of pensions insurance in 1989, the structural reforms of statutory health insurance, and the introduction of social care insurance all demonstrate that the system is susceptible of large-scale reform, albeit within the existing framework and in keeping with the principles underlying it. On the other hand, the following parliamentary term, from 1994 to 1998, was dominated by fierce disagreements between government and opposition and between trade unions and employers' associations, and most attempts at major reform were blocked. These difficulties were, in part, a symptom of the fact that German society had been undergoing sweeping changes—as a result of unification, the growth of constraints on national social policy through globalization and growing European integration, the ageing of the population, the erosion of established patterns of full-time employment subject to compulsory insurance, the increase in the number of couples living together outside marriage, and the call for a better balance between work and family life as far as women are concerned. In addition, though, during the 1990s the German welfare state underwent a structural crisis, resulting from low economic growth, de-industrialization, low levels of economic performance and productivity in many parts of the new *Bundesländer*, and continuing mass unemployment, and this crisis posed enormous, complex and long-term challenges to the political system, the economy, and society. It was not clear whether the old ways of resolving problems within the system by taking 'little steps',[44] ideally through cooperation and consensus among the different groups in politics and society, and thus circumventing the obstacles in the way of reform, were still appropriate. What was not in doubt was that although it is relatively easy to reform the welfare state if proceeds of growth are available to be shared, it is extremely hard to do so when incursions have to be made into the wealth and power of vested social interests.

The German political system, operating through consensus rather than confrontation, is such that far-reaching reform is not easy to achieve. Unlike other countries—for example, the United Kingdom or Sweden, where there is only one major party fully identified with the welfare state—the two main parties in Germany, the CDU/CSU and the Social Democrats, compete for electoral favour as 'welfare state parties', and since 1990 the populist party The Left (the former PDS) has been added to their number. Cuts in social benefits are unpopular with the voters and can easily cause parties to do badly in elections, at which problems of social policy are increasingly being instrumentalized for political purposes. This reinforces the trend—encouraged by the continuous round of elections—towards short-termism in politics and a preoccupation with speedy results. Social issues play an important role, not only in the quadrennial elections to the Bundestag, but in elections to the European parliament and in elections within the *Bundesländer*, now sixteen in all, when questions of national policy are generally to the fore. The actual outcomes of reforms in social policy, however, are often not evident until many years have passed.

A further factor is that the German political system contains an unusually large number of institutions capable of exercising a veto over policy. The most important of these is the Bundesrat, particularly when the political majority within it differs from that in the Bundestag. The reform of the federal structure implemented by the Grand Coalition government that was formed in November 2005, which gave the *Länder* greater authority over legislation and wider scope in determining their own financial policies while at the same time reducing drastically their rights of approval over Federal legislation, may prove to be an important step towards removing obstacles to reform. However, reforms of the federal structure will remain half-baked if they are not complemented by a reordering of the financial relations between the Federal government, the *Länder*, and the local authorities, so that the close financial alliance between these three tiers of the state is at least partially broken up. Achieving this, though, will be extremely difficult.

Other institutions with veto powers include the organizations of employers and employees, which exert considerable influence on policy, both in their own right and as institutions involved in the implementation of areas of social policy. Likewise, the government has to adhere to conditions laid down by the Federal Constitutional Court, as well as to the Maastricht treaty rules limiting the size of deficits in public budgets (though these rules have often been relaxed). More recently, the Basic Law has been amended so as to impose strict limitations on deficits.

Until the first years of the twenty-first century, owing to the traditions of its welfare state and the complexities of its political system, Germany did less well than most industrial nations in carrying out the reforms that were needed if the country was to adjust to the ageing of the population and the changes in the international framework. As a result, it was in danger of forfeiting its position as one of the world's leading economies. In more recent times, however, there have been hopeful signs that the urgency of the need to solve the problems of the welfare state is being more widely recognized. Germany has also been more successful than most other industrial countries in stabilizing, and even reducing, unit labour costs and maintaining its strong position as one of the leading exporting nations. Moreover, it has recovered better and more quickly from the financial and economic crisis of 2008–9 than most western economies.

Although there is a widespread feeling among politicians, experts, and officials of the major social institutions that the welfare state needs to be comprehensively reformed if its guiding principles—helping to meet life's risks, and strengthening the solidarity of the community—are to be preserved, it is difficult to win majority electoral backing for measures that in many cases entail reductions in benefits and other forms of support. Reform, moreover, cannot be delivered overnight. If short-term accommodations are to be avoided, and long-term solutions found, politicians will need to display staying power, a capacity for innovation, good judgement, and a command of the issues—and, not least, the political skill to present reform proposals in the media, obtain majorities in parliament, and strike the right balance between conflict and cooperation.

Ultimately, the survival of the German welfare state, as of any welfare state, will turn on whether policy-makers can take full account of the constant changes that are taking place not only in the state, the economy, and society but in the international framework, whether they can continue to renegotiate the balance between self-provision and mutualist provision, either by society as a whole or by a combination of smaller bodies and the state, and whether they can create the conditions for economic growth without jeopardizing social cohesion and political freedom.[45]

Notes

(For abbreviations and other terms, with translations, see Glossary)

Introduction

1. Prot. BT, 11. WP, p. 13221.
2. ibid., pp. 13016–17.
3. Reproduced in *Bulletin des Presse- und Informationsamtes der Bundesregierung*, no. 134/89, 28 November 1989, pp. 1141–8.
4. For this timescale, cf. *Sozialbericht 1993*, BMA, Bonn 1994, p. 9.
5. cf. Kohl in the Bundestag on 8 November 1989, Prot. BT, 11. WP, p. 13017.
6. This was the case even with the Ministry for Internal German Relations. Cf. Lothar de Maizière, *Die deutsche Einheit—eine kritische Betrachtung*, Fürstenfeldbruck 1994, p. 8.
7. cf. Gerd Lehmbruch, 'Die improvisierte Vereinigung: Die Dritte deutsche Republik. Unentwegter Versuch, einem japanischen Publikum die Geheimnisse der deutschen Transformation zu erklären', in *Leviathan*, 18 (1990), pp. 462–86.
8. *Sozialbericht 1990*, BMA, Bonn 1990, p. 12.
9. BMWi, Referat I D 5, Zur wirtschaftlichen Situation in der DDR, 7 August 1990, BArch, B 136/20252.
10. *Der Vertrag über die Schaffung einer Währungs-, Wirtschafts- und Sozialunion zwischen der Bundesrepublik Deutschland und der Deutschen Demokratischen Republik. Erklärungen und Dokumente* (hereafter, Staatsvertrag), Presse- und Informationsamt der Bundesregierung, Bonn, June 1990, Artikel 10, Absatz 6, p. 80. On the idea of the privatization of a proportion of nationally owned assets through the issue of share certificates to the citizens of the GDR (which played a role in the campaign for the Volkskammer elections of 18 March 1990), cf. Dieter Grosser, *Das Wagnis der Währungs-, Wirtschafts- und Sozialunion. Politische Zwänge im Konflikt mit ökonomischen Regeln*, Stuttgart 1998, pp. 121–3.
11. Rudi Schmidt, 'Restrukturierung und Modernisierung der industriellen Produktion', in *Arbeit, Arbeitsmarkt und Betriebe*, ed. Burkart Lutz, Hildegard M. Nickel, Rudi Schmidt *et al.*, Opladen 1996, pp. 227–56 (here, p. 240). In the Volkskammer on 20 February 1990 Modrow had actually estimated the national assets of the GDR in 1988 at 1.4 billion marks, made up of 980,000 million marks of state assets, 140,000 million marks held by cooperatives, and 280,000 million marks held in private hands (Prot. VK, 9. WP, 17. Tagung, 20 February 1990, p. 473).
12. *Süddeutsche Zeitung*, 21 July 2000. This was a corrected version of the original balance sheet, which had actually shown a deficit of 256,000 million DM.
13. Jens Alber, 'Der deutsche Sozialstaat in der Ära Kohl. Diagnosen und Daten', in *Der deutsche Sozialstaat. Bilanzen—Reformen—Perspektiven*, ed. Stephan Leibfried and Uwe Wagschal, Frankfurt/New York 2000, pp. 235–75; Manfred G. Schmidt, 'Sozialpolitische Denk- und Handlungsfelder', in *Geschichte der Sozialpolitik in Deutschland seit 1945*, vol. vii, *1982–1989. Bundesrepublik Deutschland. Finanzielle Konsolidierung und institutionelle Reform*, ed. Manfred G. Schmidt, Baden-Baden 2005, esp. pp. 63–72.

14. Grosser, *Wagnis*, pp. 74 f.; *Statistische Übersichten zur Sozialpolitik in Deutschland seit 1945*, Bundesministerium für Arbeit und Sozialordnung, West vol., ed. Hermann Berié, Bonn 1999, pp. 24, 110, 121.
15. cf. Hans-Werner Sinn, *Volkswirtschaftliche Probleme der deutschen Vereinigung*, Opladen 1996, esp. pp. 7–12.
16. cf. Johannes Frerich and Martin Frey, *Handbuch der Geschichte der Sozialpolitik in Deutschland*, vol. iii, *Sozialpolitik in der Bundesrepublik Deutschland bis zur Herstellung der Deutschen Einheit*, 2nd edn., Munich/Vienna 1996, p. 598.
17. Federal Minister of Labour Norbert Blüm, in BMA, *Sozialpolitische Informationen*, vol. 28, no. 6, 22 April 1994.
18. cf. Blüm's comments during a visit to the Federal Institute of Labour in Nuremberg, quoted in BMA, *Sozialpolitische Informationen*, vol. 26, no. 7, 23 April 1992.
19. In a stock-taking on social policy on the first anniversary of German unity, Blüm said that the rapid establishment and expansion of the welfare state in the new *Bundesländer* bordered 'on the miraculous'. Cf. BMA, *Sozialpolitische Informationen*, vol. 25, no. 11, 21 October 1991.
20. cf. Alber, 'Der deutsche Sozialstaat in der Ära Kohl', pp. 254–9.
21. Publications by the Kommission für die Erforschung des sozialen und politischen Wandels der neuen Bundesländer (KSPW) have been especially important.

I GERMAN UNITY: THE FRAMEWORK

1 The Political Framework

1. Election results in Gerhard A. Ritter and Merith Niehuss, *Wahlen in Deutschland 1946–1991. Ein Handbuch*, Munich 1991, p. 102.
2. cf. Klaus Dreher, *Helmut Kohl. Leben mit Macht*, Stuttgart 1998, pp. 388–431, esp. p. 414. On the 'failed putsch', cf. also Helmut Kohl, *Erinnerungen 1982–1990*, Munich 2005, pp. 924–40.
3. *Fortschritt 90. Fortschritt für Deutschland*, ed. Rudolf Dreßler, Ingrid Matthäus-Maier, Wolfgang Roth *et al.*, Munich 1990, esp. part II, 'Für den ökologischen Umbau der Industriegesellschaft'.
4. On the Greens' policy on the future of Germany, cf. Wolfgang Jäger in collaboration with Michael Walter, *Die Überwindung der Teilung. Der innerdeutsche Prozess der Vereinigung 1989/90*, Stuttgart 1998, pp. 108–95.
5. Grosser, *Wagnis*, pp. 136–9, 189 f. On the SPD's policy on the future of Germany in 1989/90, cf. also Jäger, *Überwindung*, pp. 141–79; Ilse Fischer (ed.), *Die Einheit sozial gestalten. Dokumente aus den Akten der SPD-Führung 1989/90*, Bonn 2009.
6. Quoted in Egon Bahr, *Zu meiner Zeit*, Munich 1998, p. 579.
7. Prot. VK, 9. WP, 12. Tagung, 17/18 November 1989, pp. 272–82.
8. cf. Siegfried Mampel, 'Das Ende der sozialistischen Verfassung der DDR', in *DA*, 23 (1990), pp. 1377–96 (here, pp. 1378 f.); Thomas Würtenberger, 'Die Verfassung der DDR zwischen Revolution und Beitritt', in *Handbuch des Staatsrechts der Bundesrepublik Deutschlands*, ed. Josef Isensee and Paul Kirchof, vol. viii, *Die Einheit Deutschlands: Entwicklung und Grundlage*, Heidelberg 1995, pp. 101–30 (here, pp. 108 f.). A motion by the CDU parliamentary party that the words 'der Arbeiter und Bauern' ('of workers and peasants') be deleted was not approved.
9. On the origins, organization, and political role of the Round Table, and on its work, cf. Uwe Thaysen, *Der Runde Tisch. Oder: Wo blieb das Volk? Der Weg der DDR in die*

Demokratie, Opladen 1990; also *Der Zentrale Runde Tisch der DDR. Wortprotokolle und Dokumente*, ed. Uwe Thaysen, 5 vols., Wiesbaden 2000.

10. Inaugural government statement by Modrow in the Volkskammer on 11 January 1990, in Prot. VK, 9. WP, 14. Tagung, 11/12 January 1990, pp. 361–9 (here, p. 362).
11. On the economic views of the new parties and movements, cf. Isolde Stark, 'Wirtschafts- und sozialpolitische Vorstellungen der neuen Parteien und Bewegungen in der Zeit vom Sommer 1989 bis zum Oktober 1990' and Uwe Thaysen, 'Wirtschafts- und sozialpolitische Vorstellungen der neuen Parteien und Bewegungen in der DDR zur Zeit des Zentralen Runden Tisches (1989/90)', both in *Materialien der Enquete-Kommission 'Überwindung der Folgen der SED-Diktatur im Prozess der deutschen Einheit'*, Deutscher Bundestag, vol. iii, *Wirtschafts-, Sozial- und Umweltpolitik*, Baden-Baden 1999, pp. 2630–715 and 2716–805.
12. ACDP, Fraktionsprotokolle, 7 November 1989.
13. Prot. BT, 11. WP, 16 November 1989, p. 13332.
14. Argumentationspapier Über Maßnahmen für die DDR an die Mitglieder der CDU/CSU Bundestagsfraktion, 7 December 1989, in BArch, B 149/74916.
15. Grosser, *Wagnis*, pp. 136 f.
16. Prot. BT, 11. WP, 28 November 1989, p. 13512. On the origins of the programme, interpretations of it, and reactions to it, cf. Kohl, *Erinnerungen 1982–1990*, pp. 988–1000, 1002 f.; Horst Teltschik, *329 Tage. Innenansichten der Einigung*, Berlin 1991, pp. 42–86; Werner Weidenfeld with Peter M. Wagner and Elke Brock, *Außenpolitik für die deutsche Einheit. Die Entscheidungsjahre 1989/90*, Stuttgart 1998, pp. 97–173.
17. ACDP, Fraktionsprotokolle, 27 November 1989.
18. cf. Jäger, *Überwindung*, p. 68 f.
19. Preface by Patrick Salmon to *German Unification, 1989–1990, Documents on British Policy Overseas*, series 3, vol. vii, ed. P. Salmon, K. A. Hamilton, and S. R. Twigge, London 2010, pp. IX–XXXV (here, p. X).
20. Hans-Dietrich Genscher, *Erinnerungen*, Berlin 1995, pp. 677–81. It is clear from French and British sources that Genscher, who assumed after the discussions that Germany could count on understanding and support from France, underestimated the extent of Mitterrand's reservations about German unification.
21. Jacques Attali, *Verbatim*, vol. iii, *Chronique des années 1988–1991*, Paris 1995, esp. pp. 350, 353 f., 358–72, 389 f.; Salmon *et al.* (eds.), *German Unification, 1989–1990*. François Mitterrand's posthumously published book, *De l'Allemagne, de la France* (Paris 1996), challenges Attali's claim that the French President tried first to prevent and then to delay unification. Tilo Schabert's *Wie Weltgeschichte gemacht wird. Frankreich und die deutsche Einheit* (Stuttgart 2002), a detailed account based on a wider range of previously unpublished sources, has a similar thrust. It is clear, however, that Mitterrand had at least a divided attitude towards Germany and that his views on German unity were ambivalent from the fall of the Wall until the end of January 1990. Kohl himself believed that Mitterrand was initially playing a 'double game' and that his position was 'at the least, opaque': cf. Kohl, *Erinnerungen 1982–1990*, pp. 956, 1033. On French public attitudes towards German unity and, especially, the approach of the French press, cf. Ines Lehmann, *Die deutsche Vereinigung von außen gesehen. Angst, Bedenken und Erwartungen in der ausländlischen Presse*, vol. i, *Die Presse der Vereinigten Staaten, Großbritanniens und Frankreichs*, Frankfurt a. M./Berlin/Berne etc. 1995, pp. 431–740.

22. In his talks with Kohl on 4 January 1990 Mitterrand voiced the view that Gorbachev's fate was more dependent on the actions of Kohl than on those of his fiercest internal Soviet adversary, Yegor Ligachev. Cf. *Dokumente zur Deutschlandpolitik. Deutsche Einheit. Sonderedition aus den Akten des Bundeskanzleramtes 1989/90*, ed. Hanns Jürgen Küsters and Daniel Hofmann, Munich 1998, Gespräch des Bundeskanzlers Helmut Kohl mit Staatspräsident Mitterrand, Latché, 4 January 1990, pp. 683–90 (here, p. 686).
23. cf. Attali, *Verbatim*, vol. iii, pp. 360–7; Weidenfeld, *Außenpolitik*, pp. 135–59.
24. Weidenfeld, *Außenpolitik*, pp. 159–63.
25. Records of the meeting in Attali, *Verbatim*, pp. 368–70; Salmon *et al.* (eds.), *German Unification*, Letter from Mr Powell to Mr Well, 8 December 1989, no. 71, pp. 164–6. Charles D. Powell was Private Secretary for Foreign Affairs to the Prime Minister, 1983–91; J. Stephen Well was Private Secretary to the Secretary of State for Foreign and Commonwealth Affairs, 1988–91. The meeting is not mentioned in Schabert, *Weltgeschichte* or in Frédéric Bozo, *Mitterrand, la fin de la guerre froide et l'unification allemande. De Yalta à Maastricht*, Paris 2005. There was a second meeting in Strasbourg, no records of which have so far been located.
26. Record of the meeting in Salmon *et al.* (eds.), *German Unification*, Letter of Mr Powell to Mr Well, 20 January 1990, no. 103, pp. 215–19.
27. On this, and on her opposition to German unification, see Margaret Thatcher, *The Downing Street Years*, London 1993, pp. 791–9; Gordon Craig, 'Die Chequers Affäre von 1990', in *VfZ*, 39 (1991), pp. 611–23. See also Klaus-Rainer Jackisch, *Eisern gegen die Einheit. Margaret Thatcher und die deutsche Wiedervereinigung*, Frankfurt a.M. 2004.
28. Salmon *et al.* (eds.), *German Unification*, no. 71, pp. 164–6.
29. ibid., no. 103, pp. 215–19.
30. *Bulletin of the European Communities*, supplement 1/90, Luxembourg 1990, p. 9.
31. Thatcher, *The Downing Street Years*, p. 798.
32. Brief von Kohl an Mitterrand, 5 December 1989; Gespräch von Kohl und Mitterrand, 4 January 1990: both in *Dokumente zur Deutschlandpolitik*, pp. 614 f. and 682–90.
33. Weidenfeld, *Außenpolitik*, p. 146.
34. For this, and for the German analysis of Thatcher's position, cf. *Dokumente zur Deutschlandpolitik*, no. 148, Vorlage des Ministerialdirektors Teltschik an Bundeskanzler Kohl, Bonn, 25 January 1990, with the key passages of the interview and an assessment, pp. 719 f.
35. Salmon *et al.* (eds.), *German Unification*, Letter from Mr Powell to Mr Well, no. 153, pp. 305 f.
36. Salmon *et al.* (eds.), *German Unification*, Mr Hurd to HM Representatives Overseas, 28 February 1990, no. 159, pp. 319–21.
37. Jackisch, *Eisern gegen die Einheit*, pp. 227–56.
38. See, for example, Mallaby's telegrams to the Foreign Secretary, Douglas Hurd, of 9 November, 30 November 1989, and 5 January 1990, in Salmon *et al.* (eds.), *German Unification*, nos. 35, 63, and 85, pp. 98 f., 145 f. and 190 f. Mrs Thatcher commented critically on a telegram of Mallaby to Hurd of 29 November, 'Christopher Mallaby seems to welcome reunification' (ibid., no. 61, pp. 142 f.). Concerning the telegram of 30 November 1989 pleading for an early public statement by Hurd on Kohl's Ten Points, she remarked: 'Most inadvisable.' The publication of the official British documents on German unification brings out the far more moderate and nuanced approach to unification on the part of the Foreign Office and the Foreign Secretary. Cf. the rather

discreet account by Douglas Hurd, *Memoirs*, London 2003, pp. 381–9. On the attitudes of the British government and British public opinion towards German unification, cf. Lothar Kettenacker, 'Britain and German Unification, 1989/90', in *Uneasy Allies: British-German Relations and European Integration since 1945*, ed. K. Larres and E. Meehan, Oxford 2000, pp. 99–123; Lehmann, *Deutsche Vereinigung*, pp. 269–430; Günther Heydemann, 'Die britisch-deutschen Beziehungen und das Deutschlandbild Großbritanniens. Zwischen Margaret Thatcher und Tony Blair.—Eine kritische Rückblende', in *Wiedervereinigung Deutschlands. Eine Festschrift zum zwanzigjährigen Bestehen der Gesellschaft für Deutschlandforschung*, ed. Karl Eckart, Jens Hacker, and Siegfried Mampel, Berlin 1989, pp. 627–47; Yvonne Klein, 'Obstructive or Promoting? British Views on German Unification, 1989/90', in *German Politics*, 5 (1996), pp. 403–31.

39. Salmon, preface to Salmon *et al.* (eds.), *German Unification*, p. XXVII.
40. cf. Philip Zelikow and Condoleeza Rice, *Germany Unified and Europe Transformed: A Study in Statecraft*, Cambridge, Mass., 1995, pp. 24–32. The main emphasis in this excellent account (based on a wide range of unpublished sources, primarily from the American State Department and the White House) is on the policy of the United States, but attention is also paid to developments in the Federal Republic and the Soviet Union and, to a lesser degree, France and the United Kingdom. On American policy, cf. also, especially, the book by President George Bush and his National Security Adviser Brent Scowcroft, *A World Transformed*, New York 1998, and the memoirs of the American Secretary of State James A. Baker, *The Politics of Diplomacy: Revolution, War and Peace, 1989–1992*, New York 1995. Cf. also Robert Hutchings, *American Diplomacy and the End of the Cold War: An Insider's Account of U.S. Policy in Europe, 1989–1992*, Washington, DC, 1997, pp. 131–203.
41. For this statement, cf. Vorlage des Ministerialdirektors Teltschik an Bundeskanzler Kohl, Bonn, 30 November 1989, in *Dokumente zur Deutschlandpolitik*, pp. 574–577 (here, p. 574).
42. Zelikow and Rice, *Germany Unified*, pp. 132 f.
43. Genscher, *Erinnerungen*, p. 683 f.
44. cf. Rafael Biermann, *Zwischen Kreml und Kanzleramt. Wie Moskau mit der deutschen Einheit rang*, Paderborn/Munich/Vienna etc. 1997, p. 341. The quotation is from a Soviet record of the discussions. Biermann's study is fundamental for an understanding of Soviet attitudes. See also the analysis of Soviet sources, some of them previously unknown, in Alexander von Plato, *Die Vereinigung Deutschlands—ein weltpolitisches Machtspiel. Bush, Kohl, Gorbatschow und die geheimen Moskauer Protokolle*, Berlin 2002.
45. Schreiben des Bundeskanzlers Kohl an Generalsekretär Gorbatschow, Bonn, 14 December 1989, in *Dokumente zur Deutschlandpolitik*, pp. 645–50.
46. Biermann, *Zwischen Kreml und Kanzleramt*, p. 368 f.
47. cf. Kohl, *Erinnerungen 1982–1990*, pp. 1020–8; Helmut Kohl, *'Ich wollte Deutschlands Einheit'*, presented by Kai Diekmann and Ralf Georg Reuth, Berlin 1996, p. 213.
48. Aufzeichnung über das 'Gespräch des Bundeskanzlers Kohl mit Ministerpräsident Modrow im erweiterten Kreis Dresden, 19. Dezember 1989', in *Dokumente zur Deutschlandpolitik*, pp. 668–73. A 'joint communiqué' on the discussions was published in *Bulletin*, no. 148, 20 December 1989, pp. 1249–52.
49. Absichtserklärung, BArch, B 149/7924.
50. Prot. VK, 9. WP, 14. Tagung, 11/12 January 1990, pp. 368, 363.
51. Jäger, *Überwindung*, p. 91.

52. cf. Gespräch des Bundesministers Seiters mit Ministerpräsident Modrow, east Berlin, 25 January 1990; Entwurf der Regierung der DDR, Vertrag über 'Zusammarbeit und gute Nachbarschaft zwischen der Deutschen Demokratischen Republik und der Bundesrepublik Deutschland'; both in *Dokumente zur Deutschlandpolitik*, pp. 707–16.
53. cf. Teltschik, *329 Tage*, pp. 107 f. See also Kohl's address to the meeting of the CDU/CSU parliamentary party, 16 January 1990, in ACDP, Fraktionsprotokolle.
54. Figures from an undated paper by Dr Detlev Grieswelle, BMA, Auf dem Weg zur Sozialunion im Deutschen Einigungsprozess. Sozialgemeinschaft versus Abschottung, in BMA, I a 7, 12411.
55. On the age, sex, and job qualifications of new arrivals during this period, and on their motives for moving to the Federal Republic (the most important of which was their lack of confidence in the policies of the GDR leadership), cf. Sabine Meck, Hannelore Belitz-Demiriz, and Peter Brentzke, 'Sozialdemographische Struktur und Einstellungen von DDR-Fl/Üchtlingen/Übersiedlern. Eine empirische Analyse der innerdeutschen Migration im Zeitraum Oktober 1989 bis März 1990', in *Minderheiten in und Übersiedler aus der DDR*, ed. Dieter Voigt and Lothar Mertens, Berlin 1992, pp. 9–38.
56. Blüm to Vasso Papandreou, 8 February 1990, in ACDP, Bestand Blüm I 504/60.
57. cf. Sachverständigenrat zur Begutachtung der gesamtwirtschaftlichen Entwicklung, *Auf dem Wege zur wirtschaftlichen Einheit Deutschlands. Jahresgutachten 1990/91*, Stuttgart 1990, pp. 108–11.
58. Findings of a survey by the Forsa-Institut, 21–3 February 1990, in Jäger, *Überwindung*, p. 139.
59. cf. Grosser, *Wagnis*, pp. 137–9.
60. cf. statement by Schäuble, 17 January 1990, Das Tor zur Bundesrepublik bleibt offen. Ein geordnetes Verfahren zur Aufnahme der Aussiedler ist unerlässlich, BArch 149/400001. See also Schäuble's impassioned argument, to the CDU/CSU parliamentary party on 6 February 1990, against administrative measures to halt the flow of arrivals: German unity, he said, would not be 'bought with small change . . . If we give a signal that we no longer feel responsible, and do not accept any more people, we shall not achieve unity . . . After all, the only reason we have got this far is that people have been walking out on the GDR because change there has been so slow.' In ACDP, Fraktionsprotokolle.
61. Text of the announcement in *Dokumente zur Deutschlandpolitik*, pp. 768–70.
62. cf. Grosser, *Wagnis*, pp. 159–89.
63. Prot. VK, 9. WP, 17. Tagung, 20/21 February 1990, pp. 471–4.
64. Teltschik, *329 Tage*, p. 145.
65. On the disputes in Moscow over possible alternative Soviet policies on Germany, cf. Biermann, *Zwischen Kreml und Kanzleramt*, pp. 388–92; Plato, *Vereinigung*, pp. 187–99.
66. Biermann, *Zwischen Kreml und Kanzleramt*, p. 392.
67. ibid., pp. 393–9; Plato, *Vereinigung*, pp. 223–36. On the discussions, cf. also Michail Gorbatschow, *Wie es war. Die deutsche Wiedervereinigung*, Berlin 1999, pp. 97–101; Hans Modrow, *Die Perestroika. Wie ich sie sehe. Persönliche Erinnerungen und Analysen eines Jahzehntes, das die Welt veränderte*, 2nd edn., Berlin 1998, esp. pp. 110 f.
68. Hans Modrow, *Aufbruch und Ende*, Hamburg 1991, p. 121.
69. On the contents of the plan, cf. ibid., appendix 6, pp. 186–8.
70. Teltschik, *329 Tage*, pp. 123 f.
71. cf. Gespräch des Bundeskanzlers Kohl mit Generalsekretär Gorbatschow, Moscow, 10 February 1990; Delegationsgespräch des Bundeskanzlers Kohl mit Generalsekretär

Gorbatschow, Moscow, 10 February 1990; both in *Dokumente zur Deutschlandpolitik*, pp. 795–811. See also Kohl, *Erinnerungen 1982–1990*, pp. 1062–70; Teltschik, *329 Tage*, pp. 138–42; Plato, *Vereinigung*, pp. 258–73.

72. Interview with Teltschik in Ekkehard Kuhn, *Gorbatschow und die deutsche Einheit. Aussagen der wichtigsten russischen und deutschen Beteiligten*, Bonn 1993, p. 108.
73. cf. Non-Paper der Regierung der UdSSR, 19 April 1990, in *Dokumente zur Deutschlandpolitik*, pp. 1023 f.; Biermann, *Zwischen Kreml und Kanzleramt*, pp. 437–41.
74. Zelikow and Rice, *Germany Unified*, pp. 167–72.
75. Weidenfeld, *Außenpolitik*, p. 224.
76. Genscher, *Erinnerungen*, p. 729.
77. Zelikow and Rice, *Germany Unified*, pp. 192 f.
78. On the origins and development of the new party system in the GDR, cf. Andrea Volkens and Hans-Dieter Klingemann, 'Die Entwicklung der deutschen Parteien im Prozess der Vereinigung', in *Die Gestaltung der deutschen Einheit. Geschichte—Politik—Gesellschaft*, ed. Eckhard Jesse and Armin Mitter, Bonn/Berlin 1992, pp. 189–214; Rainer Linnemann, *Die Parteien in den neuen Bundesländern. Konstituierung, Mitgliederentwicklung, Organisationsstrukturen*, Münster 1994; Oskar Niedermayer, 'Das intermediäre System', in *Politisches System*, ed. Max von Kaase, Andreas Eisen, Oscar W. Gabriel, *et al.*, Opladen 1996, pp. 155–230, esp. pp. 167–88; *Parteien und Wähler im Umbruch. Parteiensystem und Wählerverhalten in der ehemaligen DDR und den neuenBundesländern*, ed. Oskar Niedermayer and Richard Stöss, Opladen 1994; Stefan Grönebaum, 'Wird der Osten rot? Das ostdeutsche Parteiensystem in der Vereinigungskrise und vor den Wahlen 1998', in *ZParl* 28 (1997), pp. 407–25; Jäger, *Überwindung*, pp. 197–297.
79. On the SDP, and on further developments within east German Social Democracy, cf. Jens Walter, 'Von der Gründung der SDP in der DDR zum SPD-Vereinigungsparteitag—356 Tage ostdeutsche Sozialdemokratie im Spannungsfeld der deutschen Einheit', in *Revolution und Transformation in der DDR 1989/90*, ed. Günther Heydemann, Gunther Mai, and Werner Müller, Berlin 1999, pp. 407–28; Petra Schenk and Bianca von der Weiden, *Die deutsche Sozialdemokratie 1989/90. SDP und SPD im Einigungsprozess*, Munich 1997; Gero Neugebauer, 'Die SDP/SPD im Einigungsprozess: Zur Geschichte und Entwicklung einer unvollendeten Partei', in Niedermayer and Stöss (eds.), *Parteien*, pp. 75–104; Jäger, *Überwindung*, pp. 252–68.
80. Protokoll der Delegiertenkonferenz der Sozialdemokratsichen Partei in der DDR, 12.1.–14.1.1990, publ. Vorstand der Sozialdemokratischen Partei in der DDR, Berlin 1990, pp. 131, 240.
81. cf. Lehmbruch, 'Improvisierte Vereinigung', p. 469.
82. cf. Lothar de Maizière, *Anwalt der Einheit. Ein Gespräch mit Christine de Maizière*, Berlin 1996, pp. 66–76; Kohl, *Erinnerungen 1982–1990*, pp. 1038 f., 1045; Kohl, *'Ich wollte Deutschlands Einheit'*, pp. 283–90; Wolfgang Schäuble, *Der Vertrag. Wie ich über die deutsche Einheit verhandelte*, ed. Dirk Koch and Klaus Wirtgen, paperback edn., Munich 1993, pp. 30–3, 37–50; Dreher, *Kohl*, pp. 498–504, 509 f. On the development of the CDU in the east, see also Ute Schmidt, 'Die CDU', in *Intermediäre Strukturen in Ostdeutschland*, ed. Oskar Niedermayer, Opladen 1996, pp. 13–39; Ute Schmidt, 'Transformation einer Volkspartei.—Die CDU im Prozess der deutschen Vereinigung', in Niedermayer and Stöss (eds.), *Parteien*, pp. 37–74; Jäger, *Überwindung*, pp. 216–32.

83. cf. Kohl's criticism of the eastern CDU for its participation in government, voiced at a meeting of the CDU/CSU parliamentary party, 16 January 1990, in ACDP, Fraktionsprotokolle.
84. cf. Genscher, *Erinnerungen*, pp. 698–702, 719–21; Hans Vorländer, 'Die FDP: Entstehung und Entwicklung' and Theo Schiller and Kerstin Weinbach, 'Die FDP: Wahlen und Wähler', both in Niedermayer (ed.), *Intermediäre Strukturen*, pp. 113–33 and 135–150; Jäger, *Überwindung*, pp. 232–46.
85. Siegfried Suckut and Dietrich Staritz, 'Alte Heimat oder neue Linke? Das SED-Erbe und die PDS-Erben', in Niedermayer and Stöss (eds.), *Parteien*, pp. 169–94; Hasko Hünig and Gero Neugebauer, 'Die PDS', in Niedermayer (ed.), *Intermediäre Strukturen*, pp. 67–85; Jäger, *Überwindung*, pp. 197–215; Gero Neugebauer and Richard Stöss, *Die PDS. Geschichte. Organisation. Wähler. Konkurrenten*, Opladen 1996, esp. pp. 34–47.
86. cf. Thaysen, *Der Runde Tisch*, p. 136 f.
87. cf. Kohl's address to the CDU/CSU parliamentary party, 13 February 1990, in ACDP, Fraktionsprotokolle. See also his comments on the problems and special features of the election campaign in the GDR, at the meeting of the CDU/CSU parliamentary party, 12 February 1990: 'Anxieties in the GDR [are] based primarily on problems with pensions, anxieties in the Federal Republic [are] based on fears of inflation.' ACDP, Protokolle des Fraktionsvorstandes.
88. *Parteitag in Leipzig 22. bis 25. Februar 1990. Ja zur deutschen Einheit—Eine Chance für Europa. Wahlprogramm der SPD zum ersten frei gewählten Parlament der DDR*, publ. Vorstand der SPD, February 1990.
89. Walter, 'Gründung', p. 420.
90. For the PDS, cf. the party's electoral manifesto, in *Wahlparteitag der Partei des Demokratischen Sozialismus PDS, 24./25. Februar 1990*, Berlin 1990, pp. 67–77.
91. On the origins of the electoral law and arguments about the date of the election, cf. Michael Kloth, *Vom 'Zettelfalten' zum freien Wahlen. Die Demokratisierung der DDR 1989/90 und die 'Wahlfrage'*, Berlin 2000, esp. pp. 426–717.
92. Cf. Matthias Jung, 'Parteiensystem und Wahlen in der DDR. Eine Analyse der Volkskammerwahl vom 18. März 1990 und der Kommunalwahlen vom 6. Mai 1990', in *APuZG*, B 27/90, pp. 3–15; Dieter Roth, 'Die Wahlen zur Volkskammer in der DDR. Der Versuch einer Erklärung', in *PVS*, 31 (1990), pp. 369–92.
93. Walter, 'Gründung', p. 420.
94. cf. Ritter and Niehuss, *Wahlen 1946–1991*, p. 259.
95. 'Grundsätze der Koalitionsvereinbarungen zwischen den Fraktionen der CDU, der DSU, der DA, der Liberalen (DFD, BFD, FDP) und der SPD', in *Informationen*, 24 April 1990, no. 8 (supplement), published by BMB.
96. Prot. VK, 10. WP, 3. Tagung, 19 April 1990, pp. 41–51.
97. ibid., p. 44.
98. Vorlage des Ministerialdirigenten Duisberg an Bundeskanzler Kohl, Bonn, 19 April 1990, in *Dokumente zur Deutschlandpolitik*, pp. 1018–20.
99. For the Chancellery's assessment of the coalition agreement, cf. Vorlage des Ministerialdirigenten Duisberg an Bundeskanzler Kohl, Bonn, 17 April 1990, and Vorlage des Regierungsdirektors Nehring an Bundeskanzler Kohl, Bonn, 17 April 1990, both in *Dokumente zur Deutschlandpolitik*, pp. 1012–16.
100. cf. Vorlage des Ministerialdirigenten Hartmann an Bundeskanzler Kohl, 'zur Bewertung der außen- und sicherheitspolitischen Aussagen' in the inaugural government statement, Bonn, 19 April 1990, in ibid., pp. 1021–3. Peter Hartmann was head of

group 21 (Foreign Office, Federal Ministry for Economic Cooperation) in the Federal Chancellery and a member of the west German 'Two-Plus-Four' delegation.

101. Prot. VK, 10. WP, 15. Tagung, 17 June 1990, pp. 534–43.
102. In the analysis of the 'bitter' election result in Lower Saxony that he presented to the CDU/CSU parliamentary party on 15 May 1990, Kohl singled out, as one of the main reasons for this defeat, the 'unfortunate timing, because we were, so to speak, in the thick of the negotiations on the State Treaty and there was a host of things that we simply could not bring into the discussion'. Cf. ACDP, Fraktionsprotokolle.
103. cf. Jürgen W. Falter, 'Wahlen 1990. Die demokratische Legitimation für die deutsche Einheit mit großen Überraschungen', in Jesse and Mitter (eds.), *Die Gestaltung der deutschen Einheit*, pp. 163–88 (here, pp. 174 f.).
104. cf. the interview by Romberg in the *taz*, 8 August 1990, which gave rise to fierce arguments within the GDR Council of Ministers; BArch, DC 20/I/3–3038.
105. Peter Schindler, *Datenhandbuch zur Geschichte des Deutschen Bundestages 1983 bis 1991*, with appendix, *Volkskammer der Deutschen Demokratischen Republik*, Baden-Baden 1994, p. 1569.
106. Richard Schröder, 'Zum Bruch der Großen Koalition der letzten DDR-Regierung', in *ZParl*, 22 (1991), pp. 473–80. Cf. ibid. (pp. 478–80) for the manuscript draft of the proposed speech.
107. Prot. VK, 10. WP, 30. Tagung, 22/23 August 1990, pp. 1371–85. The CDU/DA, the FDP, the DSU, and the DBD/DFD voted unanimously in favour. In the SPD there were 2 votes against and 2 abstentions. In the group Alliance 90/The Greens there were 2 votes in favour, 8 votes against, and 4 abstentions. The PDS voted unanimously against. Of the 4 members of parliament not belonging to a party group, 3 voted in favour and 1 abstained (ibid., pp. 1385–8). On the background to the decision, cf. Johannes Leithäuser, ' "Wir sind einfach müde geworden" ', in *FAZ*, 22 August 2000; Richard Schröder, 'Zeitverschobene Vernunft. Schritt für Schritt zum 3. Oktober', in *FAZ*, 5 October 2000.
108. cf. Erstes Treffen der Außenminister der Zwei-plus-Vier, Bonn, 5 May 1990, in *Dokumente zur Deutschlandpolitik*, pp. 1090–4.
109. Weidenfeld, *Außenpolitik*, pp. 435–9; Zelikow and Rice, *Germany Unified*, p. 251 f.
110. Text of Genscher's government statement in *Auf dem Weg zur deutschen Einheit II. Deutschlandpolitisiche Debatten im Deutschen Bundestag vom 30. März bis 10. Mai 1990*, Deutscher Bundestag, Bonn 1990, pp. 218–25.
111. Zelikow and Rice, *Germany Unified*, pp. 275–81; Anatoli Tschernajew, *Die letzten Jahre einer Weltmacht. Der Kreml von innen*, Stuttgart 1993, p. 298.
112. On the proposal, cf. Zweites Treffen der Außenminister der Zwei-plus-Vier, Berlin-Niederschönhausen, 22 June 1990, with attachments 1–3, in *Dokumente zur Deutschlandpolitik*, pp. 1249–56; cf. also Weidenfeld, *Außenpolitik*, pp. 473–6; Zelikow and Rice, *Germany Unified*, pp. 295–8.
113. On GDR foreign policy and its principal figures during the period of the de Maizière government, cf. Weidenfeld, *Außenpolitik*, pp. 316–36; Hans Misselwitz, 'Die Außenpolitik der letzten DDR-Regierung und ihre Rolle bei den Zwei-plus-Vier-Verhandlungen', in *Wege zum '2+4'-Vertrag. Die äußeren Aspekte der deutschen Einheit*, ed. Elke Bruck and Peter M. Wagner, Munich 1996, pp. 40–69; Ulrich Albert, *Die Abwicklung der DDR. Die '2+4-Verhandlungen'. Ein Insiderbericht*, Opladen 1992.
114. Weidenfeld, *Außenpolitik*, pp. 329–33; Albrecht, *Abwicklung*, pp. 29–35.
115. Weidenfeld, *Außenpolitik*, pp. 333–6.

116. Vorlage des Ministerialdirektors Teltschik an Bundeskanzler Kohl, Bonn, 28 June 1990, *Dokumente zur Deutschlandpolitik*, p. 1281.
117. ibid.
118. On the CPSU conference, cf. Biermann, *Zwischen Kreml und Kanzleramt*, pp. 665–76.
119. cf. Gespräch des Bundeskanzlers Kohl mit Präsident Gorbatschow, Moscow, 15 July 1990; Delegationsgespräch des Bundeskanzlers Kohl mit Präsident Gorbatschow, Moscow, 15 July 1990; Gespräch des Bundeskanzlers Kohl mit Präsident Gorbatschow im erweiterten Kreis Archys/Bezirk Stawropol, 16 July 1990; all in *Dokumente zur Deutschlandpolitik*, pp. 1340–8, 1352–67. See also Teltschik, *329 Tage*, pp. 316–42; Michail S. Gorbatschow, *Gipfelgespräche. Geheime Protokolle aus meiner Amtszeit*, Berlin 1993, pp. 161–77.
120. Teltschik, *329 Tage*, pp. 10 f.
121. ibid., pp. 220 f., 231–5; Biermann, *Zwischen Kreml und Kanzleramt*, pp. 647–50.
122. Weidenfeld, *Außenpolitik*, pp. 525 f.; on the United States' careful preparations for the London summit and the course of the talks, cf. Zelikow and Rice, *Germany Unified*, pp. 303–24. On the position of the Federal Republic, cf. Gesprächsunterlagen des Bundeskanzlers Kohl für das Gipfeltreffen der Staats- und Regierungschefs der Mitgliedsstaaten der NATO London, 5./6.Juli 1990, in *Dokumente zur Deutschlandpolitik*, pp. 1309–23.
123. cf. Teltschik, *329 Tage*, pp. 205–7. For the thinking of the Soviet Union, cf. Überlegungen zum Inhalt eines Vertrages über Partnerschaft und Zusammenarbeit zwischen der Union der Sozialistischen Sowjetrepubliken und Deutschland, 15 July 1990, presented to Kohl on 15 July 1990, in *Dokumente zur Deutschlandpolitik*, pp. 1348–52.
124. On this, cf. Weidenfeld, *Außenpolitik*, pp. 479–509.
125. cf. Kohl's comments in his interview with Ekkehard Kuhn, in Kuhn, *Gorbatschow*, pp. 172 f.
126. Telefongespräch des Bundeskanzlers Kohl mit Präsident Gorbatschow, 7 September 1990, in *Dokumente zur Deutschlandpolitik*, pp. 1527–30; Teltschik, *329 Tage*, pp. 359–63.
127. Weidenfeld, *Außenpolitik*, pp. 593–602.
128. A detailed summary and analysis of the treaty is in Christoph-Matthias Brand, *Souveränität für Deutschland. Grundlagen, Entstehungsgeschichte und Bedeutung des Zwei-plus-Vier-Vertrages vom 12. September 1990*, Cologne 1993, pp. 254–65.
129. Biermann, *Zwischen Kreml und Kanzleramt*, pp. 757–67.
130. Weidenfeld, *Außenpolitik*, pp. 613–15.
131. Prot. BT, 11. WP, 5 October 1990, pp. 18087–99 (here, p. 18099). See also the amended electoral law in *Rechtsgrundlagen für die Wahl zum 12. Deutschen Bundestag*, 2nd edn., publ. Bundeswahlleiter, October 1990.
132. cf. Klaus Joachim Grigoleit, *Bundesverfassungsgericht und deutsche Frage. Eine dogmatische und historische Untersuchung zum judikativen Anteil an der Staatsleitung*, Tübingen 2004, pp. 311–18.
133. cf. Mampel, 'Ende der sozialistischen Verfassung', pp. 1391–6; Würtenberger, 'Verfassung der DDR', pp. 118 f.
134. On the problems and sometimes bitter arguments that arose over the establishment of the new *Bundesländer* in the east, cf., with reference to the case of Saxony, Michael Richter, *Die Bildung des Freistaates Sachsen. Friedliche Revolution, Föderalisierung, deutsche Einheit 1989/90*, Göttingen 2004.

135. cf. Ursula Feist and Hans-Jürgen Hoffmann, 'Landtagswahlen in der ehemaligen DDR am 14. Oktober 1990: Föderalismus im wiedervereinigten Deutschland—Tradition und neue Konturen', in *ZParl*, 22 (1991), pp. 5–34.
136. *Ja zu Deutschland—Ja zur Zukunft. Wahlprogramm der Christlich Demokratischen Union Deutschlands zur gesamtdeutschen Bundestagswahl am 2. Dezember 1990*, CDU-Bundesgeschäftsstelle.
137. *Heimat Bayern. Zukunft Deutschland. Mit uns. CSU. Programm der Christlich-Sozialen Union zur Bundestagswahl am 2. Dezember 1990*, adopted by the steering committee of the CSU, 29 October 1990.
138. cf. the messages on social policy in the FDP's manifesto for the 1990 Bundestag elections, *Das liberale Deutschland*, pp. 57–68.
139. cf. Monika Toman-Banke, 'Die Wahlslogans von 1949 bis 1994', in *APuZG*, B 51–52/94, pp. 47–55 (here, p. 54).
140. Hans-Jochen Vogel, 'Die SPD vor der Bundestagswahl', preface to Dreßler *et al.* (eds.), *Fortschritt 90*, p. 9.
141. *Regierungsprogramm 1990–1994. Der Neue Weg, ökologisch, sozial, wirtschaftlich stark*, approved by the SPD party conference in Berlin, 28 September 1990.
142. *DIE GRÜNEN. Das Programm zur 1. gesamtdeutschen Wahl 1990.*
143. Ritter and Niehuss, *Wahlen 1946–1991*, p. 125.
144. For the attitude of the member states of the Warsaw Pact see, in particular, Biermann's account, *Zwischen Kreml und Kanzleramt*, esp. pp. 264–80, 780.
145. Weidenfeld, *Außenpolitik*, p. 420.
146. cf. his interview in the *Irish Times*, 6 January 1990, referred to in Teltschik, *329 Tage*, p. 101. The role of Delors in supporting German unification and the full incorporation of what were to become the new *Bundesländer* into the European Community is strongly emphasized by Kohl, *Erinnerungen 1982–1990*, p. 115 f.
147. Weidenfeld, *Außenpolitik*, p. 385.
148. cf. the outstanding account in Grosser, *Wagnis*, esp. pp. 399–401, 405–8.
149. cf. the conclusions of the Presidency of the European Council at the 83rd council session (special meeting) on 28 April 1990 in Dublin, reprinted in *Jahrbuch der Europäischen Integration 1990/91*, ed. Werner Weidenfeld and Wolfgang Wessels, Bonn 1991, pp. 402–7, esp. pp. 402 f.
150. Grosser, *Wagnis*, p. 403.
151. ibid., pp. 403 f., 407 f.
152. ibid., pp. 394, 408 f.; Weidenfeld, *Außenpolitik*, pp. 401–11.
153. Accounts of the Federal Republic's foreign policy with regard to unification have suffered from the drawback that while the role of the Federal Chancellor, which was unquestionably very significant, has emerged very clearly, owing not least to the fact that documents of the Federal Chancellery for 1989/90 have been made available on an extensive scale, the activities of the Foreign Office have remained less well known, as there has been no access to the relevant sources. In the absence of those sources, Genscher's memoirs, which are very interesting but plainly gloss over some points out of consideration for Germany's allies (notably France), provide a substitute, though only a partial one.
154. There is a full discussion of the power relations and the actors as these affected the unification process in Chapter 10.
155. Interview with Kohl in *Newsweek*, October 1986. On this, and on the Soviet reaction, cf. Biermann, *Zwischen Kreml und Kanzleramt*, p. 101.
156. cf. Kuhn's interview with Kohl in Kuhn, *Gorbatschow*, pp. 32–4.

157. cf. Genscher, *Erinnerungen*, pp. 805–15.
158. Delegationsgespräch des Bundeskanzlers Kohl mit Präsident Bush, Washington, 17 May 1990, in *Dokumente zur Deutschlandpolitik*, pp. 1126–32 (the quotation, p. 1127).
159. Genscher, *Erinnerungen*, p. 813.
160. Interview with Teltschik in Kuhn, *Gorbatschow*, pp. 174 f. See also Teltschik, *329 Tage*, pp. 350–4. The significance of the fact that the most important foreign-policy questions concerning German unity were resolved quickly, *before* the outbreak of the Gulf War, and the role of the time factor generally, are also strongly emphasized by Zelikow and Rice, *Germany Unified*, pp. 345 f., 366.
161. This figure does not include the twenty-two Bundestag members elected by the House of Representatives of west Berlin. The voting rights of the Berlin representatives were limited by Allied provisos which were lifted only when a Note was issued by the United States, the United Kingdom, and France on 8 June 1990. The representatives were not entitled to take part in votes for the Federal Chancellor, votes of confidence, votes on the second and third readings of items of legislation, final votes, votes on proposals by the mediation committee, or votes on objections by the Bundesrat. On the other hand, they were entitled to take part in votes on internal Bundestag affairs (such as the election of the president and his or her deputies), votes on standing orders, votes on Bundestag resolution proposals, and votes in committees. Cf. Peter Schindler, *Datenhandbuch zur Geschichte des Deutschen Bundestages 1949–1999*, 3 vols., Baden-Baden 1999, vol. iii, pp. 1973–5.
162. cf. *Vertrag zwischen der Bundesrepublik Deutschland und der Deutschen Demokratischen Republik über die Herstellung der Einheit Deutschlands* (hereafter, Einigungsvertrag), *BGBl II*, no. 35, 28 September 1990; Artikel 4, p. 890.
163. 'Koalitionsvereinbarung für die 12. Legislaturperiode des Deutschen Bundestages', in *Union in Deutschland*, Informationsdienst der CDU, no. 2, 17 January 1991.
164. For their position, cf. Waigel's address to the CDU/CSU parliamentary party, 14 January 1991, in ACDP, Fraktionsprotokolle.
165. cf. Genscher, *Erinnerungen*, pp. 1000–2; Antje Vorbeck, 'Regierungsbildung 1990/1991: Koalitions- und Personalentscheidungen im Spiegel der Presse', in *ZParl*, 22 (1991), pp. 377–89.
166. 'Koalitionsvereinbarung', pp. 3, 24.
167. Address by Blüm to the CDU/CSU parliamentary party, 13 December 1990, in ACDP, Fraktionsprotokolle.
168. Address by Blüm to the CDU/CSU parliamentary party, 14 January 1991, in ACDP, Fraktionsprotokolle.
169. Address by Kohl to the CDU/CSU parliamentary party, 14 January 1991, in ACDP, Fraktionsprotokolle.
170. 'Koalitionsvereinbarung', p. 41.
171. ibid., p. 22. The contribution rate was to be lowered to 6.3 per cent on 1 January 1992.
172. Vorbeck, 'Regierungsbildung', p. 383. Cf. also the undated SPD document, Koalitionsvertrag zur Sozialpolitik: Die kleinen Leute müssen die Kosten der Einheit tragen, in AdsD, 19804. For the German Trade Union Federation, cf. the letter of 8 January 1991 from the chairman, Heinz-Werner Meyer, and deputy chairwoman, Ursula Engelen-Kefer, to the Federal Chancellor, opposing Waigel's endeavours. BArch, B 149/401173.

173. Prot. BT, 12. WP, 30 January 1991, pp. 67–94; comments on social policy, pp. 75 f., 81–3. Cf. also the much more detailed groundwork by the Labour Ministry, Beitrag des Bundesministers für Arbeit und Sozialordnung zur Regierungserklärung über das Arbeitsprogramm der Bundesregierung in der neuen Legislaturperiode. Den Sozialstaat Deutschland weiterbauen und ihn zukunftsorientiert gestalten, in ACDP, Bestand Blüm I 504/74.
174. Prot. BT, 12. WP, 31 January 1991, pp. 95–107.
175. ibid., pp. 204–6.
176. Election results from Ritter and Niehuss, *Wahlen 1946–1991*, pp. 168–71. See also Werner Billing, 'Die rheinland-pfälzische Landtagswahl vom 21. April 1991: Machtwechsel in Mainz nach 44 Jahren', in *ZParl*, 22 (1991), pp. 584–601.
177. During the 12th parliamentary term, 56.6 per cent of bills were consent bills. Cf. Schindler, *Datenhandbuch*, vol. ii, p. 2430. With other bills, the Bundesrat had merely the right to register an objection, which could be rejected by an absolute majority of members of the Bundestag. Since an absolute majority of members of the Bundesrat was necessary for the registering of an objection, abstentions in the case of government bills—in contrast to consent bills—served to favour the government.
178. ibid., pp. 2450 f.
179. The other members of the governing coalition were the Greens and the FDP.
180. cf. Thomas König and Thomas Bräuninger, 'Wie wichtig sind die Länder für die Politik der Bundesregierung bei Einspruchs- und Zustimmungsgesetzen?', in *ZParl*, 28 (1997), pp. 605–28 (here, p. 608).
181. Election results from Gerhard A. Ritter and Merith Niehuss, *Wahlen in Deutschland 1990–1994*, Munich 1995, pp. 27–30.
182. cf. Thomas Emmert and Andrea Stögbauer, 'Volksparteien in der Krise. Die Wahlen in Baden-Württemberg, Schleswig-Holstein und Hamburg', in *Das Superwahljahr. Deutschland vor unkalkulierbaren Regierungsmehrheiten?*, ed. Thomas Bürklin and Dieter Roth, Cologne 1994, pp. 86–110; Ursula Feist and Hans-Jürgen Hoffmann, 'Die Hamburger Bürgerschaftswahl vom 19. September 1993: Rundumangriff auf die Etablierten', in *ZParl*, 25 (1994), pp. 217–34; Jürgen W. Falter in collaboration with Markus Klein, *Wer wählte rechts? Die Wähler und Angehörigen rechtsextremischer Parteien im vereinigten Deutschland*, Munich 1994; Elmar Wiesendahl, 'Volksparteien im Abstieg. Nachruf auf eine zwiespältige Erfolgsgeschichte', in *APuZG*, B 34–35/92, pp. 3–14; '1994—Das Jahr der 19 Wahlen. Vier Jahre nach der Vereinigung sind die großen Volksparteien in Bedrängnis', in *FAZ*, 20 December 1993.
183. Franz Walter, 'Die SPD nach der deutschen Vereinigung—Partei in der Krise oder bereit zur Regierungsübernahme?', in *ZParl*, 26 (1995), pp. 85–112.
184. Thomas Emmert, 'Politische Ausgangslage vor der Bundestagswahl 1994. Entwicklung der Parteien, Themen und Kandidaten in Ost und West', in Bürklin and Roth (eds.), *Superwahljahr*, pp. 54–85.
185. cf. also the debate in the Bundestag on 28 April 1994, Prot. BT, 12. WP, pp. 19373–403.
186. Renate Köcher, 'Auf einer Woge der Euphorie. Veränderungen der Stimmungslage und des Meinungsklimas im Wahljahr 1994', in *APuZG*, B 51–52/94, pp. 16–21.
187. Election results from Ritter and Niehuss, *Wahlen 1990–1994*, p. 36.
188. *Wir sichern Deutschlands Zukunft*, CDU and CSU manifesto, Bonn 1994.
189. Toman-Banke, 'Wahlslogans', p. 55.
190. ibid., p. 54.
191. *Reformen für Deutschland*, SPD manifesto.

192. cf. Ritter and Niehuss, *Wahlen 1990–1994*, pp. 27–34, 36.
193. Toman-Banke, 'Wahlslogans', p. 55.
194. *Liberal denken. Leistung wählen*, FDP Bundestag election manifesto, 1994.
195. *Opposition gegen Sozialabbau und Rechtsruck*, PDS manifesto, 1994, adopted at the 3rd conference of the PDS, 3rd session, Berlin, 13 March 1994.
196. *Nur mit uns: Bündnis 90/DIE GRÜNEN*, Bundestag election manifesto, 1994, adopted at the Federal delegates' conference, Mannheim, February 1994.
197. As Table 4 shows, in the old *Bundesländer* and west Berlin the FDP received 3.4 per cent of first votes and 7.7 per cent of second votes.
198. cf. Ursula Birsl and Peter Lösche, 'Parteien in West- und Ostdeutschland: Der gar nicht so feine Unterschied', in *ZParl*, 29 (1998), pp. 7–24.
199. Results of an exit-poll survey conducted on election day, in 'Bundestagswahl 1994. Eine Analyse der Wahl zum 13. Deutschen Bundestag am 16.10.1994', *Berichte der Forschungsgruppe Wahlen e.V.*, no. 76, 21 October 1994, Mannheim, p. 22.
200. On the PDS, cf. Jürgen Lang and Patrick Moreau, 'Das Erbe der Diktatur', special edn. of *Politische Studien*, vol. 45, September 1994; Jürgen W. Falter and Markus Klein, 'Die Wähler der PDS bei der Bundestagswahl 1994. Zwischen Ideologie, Nostalgie und Protest', in *APuZG*, B 51–52/94, 23 December 1994, pp. 22–34; Henry Kreikenbom, 'Nachwirkungen der SED-Ära. Die PDS als Katalysator der Partei- und Wahlpräferenzen in den neuen Bundesländern', in *ZParl*, 29 (1998), pp. 24–46.

2 German Unity and Social Policy: The Legal Framework

1. BVerfGE 36, pp. 1–37 (Urteil zum Grundlagenvertrag, 31 July 1973).
2. Einigungsvertrag, *BGBl II*, 1990, pp. 890 f. See also articles 5 and 6 of the Unification Treaty. Cf. further Hans H. Klein, 'Kontinuität des Grundgesetzes und seine Änderung im Zuge der Wiedervereinigung', in *Handbuch des Staatsrechts*, ed. Josef Isensee and Paul Kirchhof, vol. viii, *Die Einheit Deutschlands. Entwicklung und Grundlagen*, Heidelberg 1995, pp. 557–602.
3. cf. Detlef Merten, *Grundlagen des Einigungsvertrages unter Berücksichtigung beamtenrechtlicher Probleme. Zur Verfassungsmäßigkeit des Art.6 EinigungsV.*, Berlin 1991.
4. cf. Paul Kirchhof, '§221. Der demokratische Rechtsstaat—die Staatsform der Zugehörigen', in *Handbuch des Staatsrechts*, vol. ix, ed. Josef Isensee and Paul Kirchhof, *Die Einheit Deutschlands. Festigung und Übergang*, Heidelberg 1997, esp. pp. 1029–35.
5. Staatsvertrag, Artikel 1, Absatz 3.
6. cf. Hans F. Zacher, 'Was kann der Rechtsstaat leisten?', in *Verfassungsstaatlichkeit. Festschrift für Klaus Stern zum 65. Geburtstag*, ed. Joachim Burmeister, Munich 1997, pp. 394–406, esp. pp. 394 f.
7. Peter Lerche, '§194. Der Beitritt der DDR—Voraussetzungen, Realisierung, Wirkungen', in Isensee and Kirchhof (eds.), *Handbuch des Staatsrechts*, vol. viii, pp. 403–46.
8. Martin Ammermüller, 'Deutscher Einigungsprozess', in *Sozialstaat im Wandel*, Bundesministerium für Arbeit und Sozialordnung, Bonn 1994, pp. 107–20 (here, p. 109 f.).
9. *BGBl II*, 1990, p. 899.
10. Ammermüller, 'Deutscher Einigungsprozess', pp. 110 f.
11. cf. below, pp. 252–6.
12. Only in two instances (with regard to the additional social allowance for pensions and the special law on housing benefit) was it specified that special rights in the new *Bundesländer* should be part of the Social Statute Book. Cf. Gesetz über die

Einführung eines Wohngeldsondergesetzes für das in Art.3 des Einigungsvertrages genannte Gebiet usw., 20 July 1991, *BGBl I*, p. 1250; Art.40 des Renten-Überleitungsgesetzes, 25 June 1991, *BGBl I*, p. 1606; Art.5 des Renten-Überleitungs-Ergänzungsgesetzes, 24 June 1996, *BGBl I*, p. 1038.

13. cf. Mampel, 'Ende', p. 1385.
14. ibid., pp. 1378–81.
15. Würtenberger, 'Verfassung', pp. 113 f.
16. Thaysen, *Der Runde Tisch*, pp. 143–5.
17. ibid., p. 148 f.; *Der Zentrale Runde Tisch*, ed. Thaysen, vol. iv, pp. 1096–112.
18. *Verfassungsentwurf für die DDR*, Arbeitsgruppe 'Neue Verfassung der DDR' des Runden Tisches, Berlin 1990. For a critique, cf. Klaus Michael Rogner, *Der Verfassungsentwurf des Zentralen Runden Tisches der DDR*, Berlin 1993.
19. Grundsätze der Koalitionsvereinbarungen, 12 April 1990.
20. Prot. VK, 10. WP, 3. Tagung, 19 April 1990, pp. 51–9.
21. Prot. VK, 10. WP, 5. Tagung, 26 April 1990, pp. 123–6.
22. Olaf Winkel, 'Die deutsche Einheit als verfassungspolitischer Konflikt', in *ZParl*, 28 (1997), pp. 474–501 (here, p. 487).
23. Gesetz zur Änderung und Ergänzung der Verfassung der Deutschen Demokratischen Republik (Verfassungsgrundsätzegesetz), 17 June 1990, *GBl I*, pp. 299–303.
24. On criticism of this, cf. Mampel, 'Ende', pp. 1390 f.
25. Verfassungsgesetz zur Bildung von Ländern in der Deutschen Demokratischen Republik—Ländereinführungsgesetz, 22 July 1990, *GBl I*, pp. 955–9.
26. Gerhard A. Ritter, *Über Deutschland. Die Bundesrepublik in der deutschen Geschichte*, 2nd edn., Munich 2000, p. 150.
27. Rogner, *Verfassungsentwurf*, pp. 97–100.
28. Grundsätze der Koalitionsvereinbarungen, 12 April 1990.
29. Einigungsvertrag, Artikel 5, *BGBl II*, 1990, p. 881.
30. On the outcome of the discussions, cf. *Bericht der Gemeinsamen Verfassungskommission*, BTDrs 12/6000, 5 November 1993. See also *APuZG*, B 52–53/93, 24 December 1993, containing a series of articles on individual aspects of the work of the Joint Constitutional Commission, as well as the wording of the proposals for amending and amplifying the Basic Law.
31. The ban on discrimination on the basis of disability, which had not been included in the proposals of the Joint Constitutional Commission, was plainly added to the Basic Law as a result of pressure from the War Victims' Association, which had gained Kohl's support. Cf. VdK Deutschland, *12. Bundesverbandstag, 18. bis 20. Mai 1994, Bonn. Geschäftsbericht 1990–1994. Aufgabe und Leistung*, Bonn-Bad Godesberg 1994, pp. 234 f.; Sozialverband VdK Deutschland, *Jahresbericht 95*, Bonn-Bad Godesberg, p. 8.
32. The constitutional amendments relevant to social policy, including the new distribution of responsibilities of the Federal and *Land* governments with regard to competing legislation and the supervision of social insurance providers, are discussed by Gerald Becker-Neetz, 'Verfassungsreform. Sozialpolitischer Spielraum gewahrt', in *BArbBl* (1995), vol. 5, pp. 5–8.
33. *BGBl I*, 1993, p. 1002.
34. cf. Hans von Mangoldt, *Die Verfassungen der neuen Bundesländer. Einführung und synoptische Darstellung. Sachsen, Brandenburg, Sachsen-Anhalt, Mecklenburg-Vorpommern, Thüringen*, 2nd edn., Berlin 1997. On the influence of the draft constitution

of the Round Table on the constitutions of the new *Länder*, cf. Rogner, *Verfassungsentwurf*, pp. 156–77.

35. cf. Christian Starck, 'Die Verfassungen der neuen Länder', in Isensee and Kirchhof (eds.), *Handbuch des Staatsrechts*, vol. ix, pp. 353–402, esp. pp. 383–9.
36. Hans-Jürgen Papier, 'Der Einfluß des Verfassungsrechts auf das Sozialrecht', in *Sozialrechtshandbuch*, ed. Bernd Baron von Maydell and Franz Ruland, 2nd edn., Neuwied/Kriftel/Berlin 1996, pp. 73–124, esp. pp. 104 f.
37. For an overview, cf. the reports by Wolfgang Rüfner, 'Das Sozialrecht in der Rechtsprechung des Bundesverfassungsgerichts', in *JBSozRG*, vols. 12–21, 1990–1999.
38. BVerfGE 53, pp. 257–313 and BVerfGE 58, pp. 81–136.
39. BVerfGE 100, pp. 1–195 (here, p. 39). On the scope available for legislation, cf. Hans-Jürgen Papier, 'Das Rentenversicherungsrecht vor dem Grundgesetz. Eigentum, Gleichheit und Schutz der Familie', in *FAZ*, 11 June 2001.
40. cf. Detlef Merten, 'Rentenversicherung und deutsche Wiedervereinigung', in *Geschichte und Gegenwart der Rentenversicherung in Deutschland. Beiträge zur Entstehung, Entwicklung und vergleichenden Einordnung der Alterssicherung im Sozialstaat*, ed. Stefan Fisch and Ulrike Haerendel, Berlin 2000, pp. 317–32.
41. BVerfGE 100, pp. 1–195.
42. On the consequences of the judgements for those affected, cf. Klaus Schroeder, *Der Preis der Einheit. Eine Bilanz*, Munich/Vienna 2000, pp. 227 f.
43. BVerfGE 84, pp. 133–60 (here, p. 133).
44. cf. Eckart Klein, 'Die verfassungsrechtliche Bewältigung der Wiedervereinigung', in Eckart *et al.* (eds.), *Wiedervereinigung Deutschlands*, pp. 417–28; cf. also id., 'Deutsche Einigung und Rechtsprechung des Bundesverfassungsgerichts. Vorläufiger Überblick mit Anmerkungen', in *Verfassungsrecht im Wandel. Wiedervereinigung Deutschlands. Deutschland in der Europäischen Union. Verfassungsstaat und Föderalismus. Zum 180jährigen Bestehen der Carl Heymanns Verlag KG*, ed. Jörn Ipsen, Hans-Werner Rengeling, Jörg-Manfred Mössner and Albrecht Weber, Cologne/Berlin/Bonn/Munich 1995, pp. 91–107.
45. cf. below, pp. 80–2.
46. Klein, 'Verfassungsrechtliche Bewältigung', p. 426.
47. Gesetz zur Neuregelung der einkommenssteuerrechtlichen Behandlung von Altersvorsorgeaufwendungen und Altersbezügen (Alterseinkünftegesetz), 5 July 2004, *BGBl I*, pp. 1427–47.
48. BVerfGE 81, pp. 156–207.
49. Rüfner, 'Sozialrecht', in *JBSozRG*, vol. 13 (1991), pp. 65 f.
50. *BGBl I*, 1992, pp. 2044–57.
51. BVerfGE 92, pp. 365–411.
52. On the law, and the arguments preceding its passage, cf. Frerich and Frey, *Handbuch*, vol. iii, pp. 226–8.
53. cf. the critical comments by Rüfner, 'Sozialrecht', in *JBSozRG*, vol. 18 (1996), pp. 37 f.
54. BVerfGE 82, pp. 60–126. The Court's judgement of 12 June 1990 tallied with the principles of this decision: cf. ibid., pp. 198–208.
55. ibid., p. 85.
56. BVerfGE 87, pp. 1–68.
57. ibid., p. 41.
58. cf. Rüfner, 'Sozialrecht', in *JBSozRG*, vol. 21 (1999), pp. 88–90.
59. cf. Deutsche Bundesbank, *Monatsbericht April 2002: Staatliche Leistungen für die Familien*, pp. 15–32.

60. cf. Jörg Mohn, 'Die Rechtsentwicklung der Überführung der Ansprüche und Anwartschaften aus Zusatz- und Sonderversorgungssystemen der ehemaligen DDR in der Rentenversicherung', in *DAngVers*, 12/1993, pp. 438–47; Michael Mutz, 'Renten der Zusatzversorgung der Intelligenz in der DDR—Chronik der Überführung in die gesetzliche Rentenversicherung', in *DAngVers*, 12/1995, pp. 426–32; Michael Mutz, 'Aufstieg und Fall eines Konzepts. Die Zusatz- und Sonderersorgungssysteme der DDR und ihre Überführung', in *DAngVers*, 11/1999, pp. 509–19; Ralf-Peter Stephan, 'Das Zusammenwachsen der Rentenversicherungen in West und Ost.—Eine Zwischenbilanz im zehnten Jahre der Deutschen Einheit', in *DAngVers*, 12/1999, pp. 546–56.
61. BSGE 81, pp. 276–88.
62. *The Treaty Establishing the European Economic Community*, 25 March 1957, Articles 117 and 123.
63. This is particularly clear in Regulation 1408/71 of 1971: quoted in Hans F. Zacher, 'Grundfragen des internationalen Sozialrechts', in *Mitteilungen der Landesversicherungsanstalten Oberfranken und Mittelfranken*, 12 (1983), pp. 481–92 (here, p. 487).
64. cf. Winfried Schmähl, 'Europäische Sozialpolitik und die sozialpolitische Bedeutung der europäischen Integration', in *Europäische Sozialpolitik*, ed. Winfried Schmähl and Herbert Rische, Baden-Baden 1997, pp. 9–37; see also Heinz Dietrich Steinmeyer, 'Akteure, Instrumente und Maßnahmen europäischer Sozialpolitik.—Ein Überblick', in ibid., pp. 39–57; Jochen C. K. Ringler, *Die Europäische Sozialunion*, Berlin 1997.
65. cf. *Sozialbericht 1993*, p. 111.
66. cf. Eberhard Eichenhofer, 'Das Sozialrecht in der Rechtsprechung des Europäischen Gerichtshofes. Zur Genealogie der Thematisierung des Sozialrechts durch den EuGH', in *ZeS-Arbeitspapiere*, no. 9/96. See also the annual reports by Bernd Schulte, 'Das Sozialrecht in der Rechtsprechung des Europäischen Gerichtshofs', in *JBSozRG*, vols. 10 (1988) to 20 (1998), and the contributions in *Zukunftsperspektiven des Europäischen Sozialrechts*, ed. Bernd Baron von Maydell and Bernd Schulte, Berlin 1995.
67. cf. *FAZ*, 25 October 2000; Norbert Blüm, 'Rücksicht auf Tradition nehmen', in SPI 18/1992, 19 December 1992. Blüm's comments were made at a symposium entitled 'Sozialraum Europa—Fortschritt oder gefährlicher Irrweg?' For Blüm's criticisms of the European Court of Justice, cf. also his address to the CDU/CSU parliamentary party, 13 October 1992, in ACDP, Fraktionsprotokolle. See further Werner Tegtmeier, 'Wechselwirkungen zwischen dem Europäischen Sozialrecht und dem Sozialrecht der Bundesrepublik Deutschland', in *Wechselwirkungen zwischen dem Europäischen Sozialrecht und dem Sozialrecht der Bundesrepublik Deutschland*, ed. Bernd Schulte and Hans F. Zacher, Berlin 1991, pp. 27–43; Peter Clever, 'Rechtsprechung und Akzeptanz—Gedanken zur Rechtsprechung des EuGH im Sozialbereich anhand einiger ausgewählter Fälle jüngster Zeit', in *ZfSGB*, 30 (1991), pp. 561–71. Peter Clever was head of the department of international social policy in the Labour Ministry.
68. cf. Stephan Leibfried, 'Grenzen deutscher Sozialstaatlichkeit. Vom gemeinsamen Arbeitsmarkt zu erzwungener europäischer Sozialreform', in *Grenzen des Sozialversicherungsstaates*, ed. Barbara Riedmüller and Thomas Olk, Opladen 1994, pp. 313–23 (here, p. 317).
69. cf., for example, Blüm's comments to the German unity committee, 14 September 1990: 'We believe that in the case of minimum protections under the umbrella of pensions insurance, there is a danger that they will have to be exportable as part of the process of European unity and will be a positive invitation to people to acquire minimum insurance entitlements with short insurance periods, which they can then bring back home.' Prot. BT, Ausschuß Deutsche Einheit, p. 600.

70. Helmut Linhart and Olgierd Adolph, 'Einstieg in die Sozialhilfewanderung in der Europäischen Union?', in NDV, August 2004, pp. 282–285.
71. cf. Bernd Schulte, 'Die Entwicklung der Europäischen Sozialpolitik', in *Nationalismus—Nationalitäten—Supranationalität,* ed. Heinrich August Winkler and Hartmut Kaelble, Stuttgart 1993, pp. 261–87, esp. pp. 281 f.; on the still relatively small extent of Europeanization in the area of social policy, cf. Manfred G. Schmidt, 'Die Europäisierung der öffentlichen Aufgaben', in *50 Jahre Bundesrepublik Deutschland. Rahmenbedingungen—Entwicklungen—Perspektiven,* ed. Thomas Ellwein and Everhard Holtmann, Opladen 1999, pp. 385–94.

3 The German Economy and the Process of Unification

1. Staatsvertrag, Artikel 1, 11, 17.
2. cf. Sven Jochem and Nico A. Siegel, 'Wohlfahrtskapitalismus und Beschäftigungsperformanz—Das "Modell Deutschland" im Vergleich', in *ZSR,* 46 (2000), pp. 38–64; Roland Czada, 'Vereinigungskrise und Standortdebatte. Der Beitrag der Wiedervereinigung zur Krise des westdeutschen Modells', in *Leviathan,* 1998, pp. 24–59. For the recent debate on the validity of the German model, see *Modell Deutschland. Erfolgsgeschichte oder Illusion?,* ed. Thomas Hertfelder and Andreas Rödder, Göttingen 2007.
3. Rudi Schmidt, 'Restrukturierung und Modernisierung der industriellen Produktion', in *Arbeit, Arbeitsmarkt und Betriebe,* ed. Burkart Lutz, Hildegard M. Nickel, Rudi Schmidt *et al.*, Opladen 1996, pp. 227–56 (here, p. 235). On the work of the *Treuhand,* cf. Wolfgang Seibel in collaboration with Hartmut Maaßen, Jörg Raab, and Arndt Oschmann, *Verwaltete Illusionen. Die Privatisierung der DDR-Wirtschaft durch die Treuhandanstalt und ihre Nachfolger 1990–2000,* Frankfurt a.M./New York 2005.
4. cf. Ingrid Artus, 'Tarifpolitik in den neuen Bundesländern. Akteure, Strategien, Problemlagen', in *Industrielle Beziehungen. Institutionalisierung und Praxis unter Krisenbedingungen,* ed. Joachim Bergmann and Rudi Schmidt, Opladen 1996, pp. 71–100.
5. Czada, 'Vereinigungskrise', p. 30.
6. cf. below, pp. 248 f.
7. cf. Nico A. Siegel and Sven Jochem, 'Zwischen Sozialstaats-Status quo und Beschäftigungswachstum. Das Dilemma des Bündnisses für Arbeit im Trilemma der Dienstleistungsgesellschaft', *ZeS-Arbeitspapier* no. 17/99, Bremen 1999, p. 15.
8. cf. below, pp. 91 ff.
9. cf. below, pp. 91–101.
10. cf. Hartmut Kaelble, *Auf dem Weg zu einer europäischen Gesellschaft. Eine Sozialgeschichte Westeuropas 1880–1980,* Munich 1987; Peter Flora, *State, Economy and Society in Western Europe, 1815–1975: A Data Handbook in Two Volumes,* vol. i, *The Growth of Mass Democracies and Welfare States,* Frankfurt a.M./London 1983; vol. ii (with Franz Kraus and Werner Pfennig), *The Growth of Industrial Societies and Capitalist Economies,* Frankfurt a.M./Chicago 1987; *Growth to Limits: The Western European Welfare States since World War II,* ed. Peter Flora, vols. i, ii, and iv, Berlin/New York 1986/7; Peter Flora, Jens Alber, and Jürgen Kohl, 'Zur Entwicklung der westeuropäischen Wohlfahrtsstaaten', in *PVS,* 18 (1977), pp. 707–72.
11. cf. Gerhard A. Ritter, *Der Sozialstaat. Entstehung und Entwicklung im internationalen Vergleich,* 3rd edn., Munich 2010, pp. 202–4.
12. cf. above, pp. 66–8.
13. These trends are highlighted by Elmar Rieger and Stephan Leibfried, 'Welfare State Limits to Globalization', in *Politics and Society,* 26 (1998), pp. 363–90.

14. However, on the limited success of attempts to reduce the scale of the welfare state in the USA and the United Kingdom, cf. Paul Pierson, *Dismantling the Welfare State? Reagan, Thatcher and the Politics of Retrenchment*, Cambridge 1994.
15. Among the now extensive literature, cf. *Internationalisierung von Wirtschaft und Politik—Handlungsspielräume der nationalen Sozialpolitik*, ed. Winfried Schmähl and Herbert Rische, Baden-Baden 1995; *States against Markets: The Limits of Globalisation*, ed. Robert Boyer and Daniel Drache, London/New York 1996; James Midgley, *Social Welfare in Global Context*, Thousand Oaks, Calif., 1997. See also Elmar Rieger and Stephan Leibfried, 'Globalisation and the Western Welfare State: An Annotated Bibliography', *ZeS-Arbeitspapier* no. 1/95, Bremen 1995.
16. cf. Hans F. Zacher, 'Grundlagen der Sozialpolitik in der Bundesrepublik Deutschland', in *Geschichte der Sozialpolitik in Deutschland seit 1945*, vol. i, *Grundlagen der Sozialpolitik*, Baden-Baden 2001, pp. 333–684 (here, p. 592).
17. On the weaknesses of the GDR economy, cf. André Steiner, *Von Plan zu Plan. Eine Wirtschaftsgeschichte der DDR*, Munich 2004; Grosser, *Wagnis*, pp. 39–67; Johannes Bähr, 'Institutionenordnung und Wirtschaftsentwicklung. Die Wirtschaftsgeschichte der DDR aus der Sicht des zwischendeutschen Vergleichs', in *GuG*, 25 (1999), pp. 530–55; Theo Pirker, M. Rainer Lepsius, Rainer Weinert, *et al.*, *Der Plan als Befehl und Fiktion. Wirtschaftsführung in der DDR. Gespräche und Analysen*, Opladen 1995; *Am Ende des realen Sozialismus*, vol. ii, *Die wirtschaftliche und ökologische Situation der DDR in den 80er Jahren*, ed. Eberhard Kuhrt, Gunter Holzweißig, and Hannsjörg F. Buck, Opladen 1996; *Unterrichtung durch die Bundesregierung. Materialien zur deutschen Einheit und zum Aufbau in den neuen Bundesländern*, BTDrs 13/2280, 8 September 1995, esp. pp. 90–5; Jahresgutachten 1990/91 des Sachverständigenrates zur Begutachtung der gesamtwirtschaftlichen Entwicklung, *Auf dem Wege zur wirtschaftlichen Einheit Deutschlands*, BTDrs 11/8472, 13 November 1990, pp. 62–5, 80–2; OECD, *OECD Economic Surveys: Germany*, Paris 1990, pp. 49–52.
18. cf. Wolfgang Zank, *Wirtschaft und Arbeit in Ostdeutschland 1945–1949. Probleme des Wiederaufbaus in der Sowjetischen Besatzungszone Deutschlands*, Munich 1987; Lothar Baar, Rainer Karlsch, and Werner Matschke, 'Kriegsschäden, Demontagen und Reparationen', in *Materialien der Enquete-Kommission 'Aufarbeitung von Geschichte und Folgen der SED-Diktatur in Deutschland'*, Deutscher Bundestag, vol. ii, *Machtstrukturen und Entscheidungsmechanismen im SED-Staat und die Frage der Verantwortung*, Baden-Baden 1995, pp. 868–988; Christoph Buchheim, 'Kriegsschäden, Demontagen und Reparationen. Deutschland nach dem Zweiten Weltkrieg', in ibid., pp. 1030–69.
19. On this, cf. Helge Heidemeyer, *Flucht und Zuwanderung aus der SBZ/DDR 1945/1949–1961. Die Flüchtlingspolitik der Bundesrepublik Deutschland bis zum Bau der Berliner Mauer*, Düsseldorf 1994.
20. Barbara Janke and Manfred Ebert, 'Von "jeder zweiten" Frau zu "neun von zehn" Frauen—der Arbeitsmarkt gekennzeichnet durch viele berufstätige Frauen', in *Im Trabi durch die Zeit—40 Jahre Leben in der DDR*, ed. Egon Hölder, Wiesbaden 1992, pp. 77–95 (here, p. 89); Doris Schwarzer, *Arbeitsbeziehungen im Umbruch gesellschaftlicher Strukturen. Bundesrepublik Deutschland, DDR und neue Bundesländer im Vergleich*, Stuttgart 1995, p. 105.
21. Hans Günter Hockerts, 'Soziale Errungenschaften? Zum sozialpolitischen Legitimitätsanspruch der zweiten deutschen Diktatur', in *Von der Arbeiterbewegung zum modernen Sozialstaat. Festschrift für Gerhard A. Ritter zum 65. Geburtstag*, ed. Jürgen Kocka, Hans-Jürgen Puhle, and Klaus Tenfelde, Munich/New Providence/London etc. 1994, pp. 790–804 (here, p. 794 f.).

22. Gerhard Schürer, 'Planung und Lenkung der Volkswirtschaft der DDR—Ein Zeitzeugenbericht aus dem Zentrum der DDR-Wirtschaftslenkung', in *Am Ende des realen Sozialismus. Beiträge zu einer Bestandsaufnahme der DDR-Wirklichkeit in den 80er Jahren*, vol. iv, *Die Endzeit der DDR-Wirtschaft—Analysen zur Wirtschafts-, Sozial- und Umweltpolitik*, ed. Eberhard Kuhrt in collaboration with Hannsjörg F. Buck and Gunter Holzweißig for Bundesministerium des Innern, Opladen 1999, pp. 61–98 (here, p. 89).
23. Grosser, *Wagnis*, p. 53.
24. Holle Grünert, 'Das Beschäftigungssystem der DDR', in Lutz *et al.* (eds.), *Arbeit, Arbeitsmarkt und Betriebe*, pp. 17–68 (here, pp. 62–6).
25. Joachim Bergmann, 'Industrielle Beziehungen in Ostdeutschland: Transferierte Institutionen im Deindustrialisierungsprozeß', in Lutz *et al.* (eds.), *Arbeit, Arbeitsmarkt und Betriebe*, pp. 257–94 (here, p. 259).
26. Grünert, 'Beschäftigungssystem', p. 49.
27. In July 1990 the Ifo-Institut für Wirtschaftsforschung concluded, on the basis of surveys of enterprises, authorities, and scientific facilities in the GDR, that production and work conditions in the GDR were such that hidden unemployment ran to about 1.4 million employees, or 15 per cent of those in employment. It calculated that there was a potential redundancy pool of about three million under market conditions. See also *Unterrichtung durch die Bundesregierung*, BTDrs 13/2280, 8 September 1995, p. 90.
28. Günter Schabowski, *Der Absturz*, Berlin 1991, p. 126.
29. Grosser, *Wagnis*, p. 40.
30. *Unterrichtung durch die Bundesregierung*, BTDrs 13/2280, 8 September 1995, p. 90.
31. Grosser, *Wagnis*, p. 45.
32. Andreas Herbst, Winfried Ranke, and Jürgen Winkler, *So funktionierte die DDR*, Hamburg 1994, p. 479.
33. Details of the scale of the GDR's debts in western countries have been adjusted in the light of subsequent research. At the end of October 1989 a group of leading GDR economists told the Politburo of the SED that indebtedness at the end of the year would amount to 49,000 million foreign exchange marks (26,500 million dollars), but as a result of the uncovering of secret reserves the deficit has been reduced to 38,000 million foreign exchange marks (20,600 million dollars). Since then the German Bundesbank has calculated that net indebtedness at the end of 1989 amounted to 19,900 million foreign exchange marks (10,800 million dollars). Cf. Deutsche Bundesbank, *Die Zahlungsbilanz der ehemaligen DDR 1975 bis 1989*, Frankfurt a.M., August 1999, p. 59. See also Arnim Volze, 'Zur Devisenverschuldung der DDR—Entstehung, Bewältigung und Folgen', in Kuhrt *et al.* (eds.), *Am Ende des realen Sozialismus*, vol. iv, *Die Endzeit der DDR-Wirtschaft*, pp. 151–87 (here, p. 161 f.).
34. cf. 'Schürers Krisen-Analyse', in *DA*, 25 (1992), pp. 1112–20.
35. cf. also Richard Hauser, Wolfgang Glatzer, Stefan Hradil *et al.*, *Ungleichheit und Sozialpolitik*, Opladen 1996, pp. 4–7.
36. Norbert Kloten, 'Deutsche Einheit: Die wirtschaftliche Last der Folgen für Ost und West', in Deutsche Bundesbank, *Auszüge aus Presseartikeln*, no. 8, 5 February 1996, pp. 11–17.
37. Gerlinde Sinn and Hans-Werner Sinn, *Kaltstart. Volkswirtschaftliche Aspekte der deutschen Vereinigung*, 3rd edn., Munich 1993.
38. cf. Hellmut Wollmann, 'Institutionenbildung in Ostdeutschland: Neubau, Umbau und "schöpferische Zerstörung"', in Kaase *et al.* (eds.), *Politisches System*, pp. 47–153;

Hans-Ulrich Derlien, 'Kommunalverfassung zwischen Reform und Revolution', in *Kommunalwissenschaftliche Analysen*, ed. Oscar W. Gabriel and Rüdiger Voigt, Bochum 1994; Hellmut Wollmann and Wolfgang Jaedicke, 'Neubau der Kommunalverwaltung in Ostdeutschland—zwischen Kontinuität und Umbruch', in *Verwaltungsreform und Verwaltungspolitik im Prozess der deutschen Einigung*, ed. Wolfgang Seibel, Arthur Benz, and Heinrich Mäding, Baden-Baden 1993, pp. 98–116.

39. On pay policy, cf. Gerlinde Sinn, 'Lohnentwicklung und Lohnpolitik in den neuen Bundesländern', in *Wiedervereinigung nach sechs Jahren: Erfolge, Defizite, Zukunftsperspektiven im Transformationsprozess*, ed. Karl Heinrich Oppenländer, Berlin/Munich 1997, pp. 253–80.
40. SPI 31, no. 4, 1 April 1997, p. 4.
41. cf. *Unterrichtung durch die Bundesregierung. Jahresbericht der Bundesregierung zum Stand der Deutschen Einheit 1998*, BTDrs 13/10823, 27 May 1998, pp. 19 f.
42. Deutsche Bundesbank, *Zur Entwicklung der Produktivität in Deutschland*, monthly report, September 2002, pp. 49–63 (here, pp. 58 f.).
43. Hauser *et al.*, *Ungleichheit*, p. 6.
44. cf. Fred Oldenburg, 'Gorbatschows Deutschlandpolitik und die Implosion der DDR', in Eckart *et al.* (eds.), *Wiedervereinigung Deutschlands*, pp. 259–82 (here, p. 263); Biermann, *Zwischen Kreml und Kanzleramt*, p. 643.
45. cf. Non-Paper der Regierung der UdSSR, 19 April 1990, in *Dokumente zur Deutschlandpolitik*, pp. 1023 f.; cf. also the assessments of this Soviet *démarche* in Vorlage des Ministerialdirigenten Duisberg an Bundeskanzler Kohl, Bonn, 19 April 1990 and Vermerk des Ministerialrats Ludewig, Bonn, 20 April 1990, both in *Dokumente zur Deutschlandpolitik*, pp. 1024–6.
46. Biermann, *Zwischen Kreml und Kanzleramt*, pp. 644 f.
47. Staatsvertrag, Artikel 13.2, 18 May 1990.
48. Biermann, *Zwischen Kreml und Kanzleramt*, p. 745.
49. ibid., p. 747.
50. Text of the treaty in *Bulletin des Bundespresse- und Informationsamtes der Bundesregierung*, 15 November 1990.
51. Schreiben des Ministerpräsidenten Modrow an Bundeskanzler Kohl, Berlin, 2 March 1990, with attachment, Erklärung der Regierung der Deutschen Demokratischen Republik zu den Eigentumsverhältnissen, in *Dokumente zur Deutschlandpolitik*, pp. 906–8.
52. cf. Grosser, *Wagnis*, p. 227.
53. Jäger, *Überwindung*, p. 508.
54. cf. the statement published by TASS on 27 March 1990 concerning the GDR's statement of 1 March 1990, in *Dokumente zur Deutschlandpolitik*, p. 989.
55. According to a statement by the Federal Ministry of Justice, however, the property guarantee in the Basic Law applied only to measures of the Federal German authorities, not to measures of the GDR. Cf. Grosser, *Wagnis*, p. 235.
56. Kurzbericht über die zweite Sitzung der Expertengruppe Klärung offener Vermögensfragen, Bonn, 29/30 March 1990, with attachment, Sprachregelung zu den offenen Vermögensfragen, in *Dokumente zur Deutschlandpolitik*, pp. 989–93.
57. cf. Grosser, *Wagnis*, p. 330.
58. Schäuble, *Vertrag*, p. 103.
59. Text of declaration in Einigungsvertrag, *BGBl II*, 1990, p. 1237 f.
60. cf. Grosser, *Wagnis*, p. 335.

61. The letter was added to the appendix to the 'Two-Plus-Four' treaty. Cf. Genscher, *Erinnerungen*, pp. 857–861.
62. Schäuble, *Vertrag*, pp. 104, 259 f.
63. cf., in particular, Constanze Paffrath, *Macht und Eigentum. Die Enteignungen 1945–1949 im Prozess der deutschen Wiedervereinigung*, Cologne/Weimar/Vienna 2004. Paffrath goes so far as to say that the Federal government, which she accuses of breaching the Basic Law and of deliberately deceiving the public and the legislature with regard to the actual position of the Soviet Union, should not have accepted the expropriations even if that would have caused reunification to fail (pp. 375 f.).
64. Grosser, *Wagnis*, p. 343. See also Genscher's 'statement . . . concerning the discussions on the expropriations in the former Soviet zone of occupation in the period 1945–1949', in Genscher, *Erinnerungen*, pp. 859 f.
65. BVerfGE 84, pp. 90–132; 94, pp. 12–49.
66. *BGBl I*, pp. 2624–39. Cf. also Gesetz zur Regelung offener Vermögensfragen, 2 December 1994, *BGBl I*, 1994, pp. 3610–29.
67. Grosser, *Wagnis*, p. 344.
68. Erklärung der Regierungschefs der SPD-geführten Bundesländer, 19 August 1990; Vorlage des Ministerialdirigenten Busse und des Ministerialdirigenten Stern an den Chef des Bundeskanzleramtes Seiters, Bonn, 23 August 1990 on an internal discussion with the representatives of the *Bundesländer*: in *Dokumente zur Deutschlandpolitik*, pp. 1478 f., 1490–2.
69. cf. Schäuble, *Vertrag*, p. 212.
70. Einigungsvertrag, Artikel 41.2.
71. Gesetz zur Beseitigung von Hemmnissen bei der Privatisierung von Unternehmen und zur Förderung von Investitionen, *BGBl I*, 1991, pp. 766–89.
72. cf. Grosser, *Wagnis*, pp. 485–8.
73. Hans-Werner Sinn, *Volkswirtschaftliche Probleme der deutschen Vereinigung*, Opladen 1996, p. 23. The figure relates to people in regular employment, but not to those participating in programmes under the active labour market policy.
74. Altogether, between 1989 and 1994 approximately 1.6 million people left east Germany and nearly 0.5 million moved there, so that there was a net outflow of approximately 1.1 million (Hauser *et al.*, *Ungleichheit*, p. 26). On the changes in the labour market and on labour market policy in east Germany, cf. also Bundesanstalt für Arbeit, Institut für Arbeitsmarkt- und Berufsforschung, 'Arbeitsmarkt und Arbeitslosigkeit in den neuen Bundesländern—Ausgangsbedingungen und Einsatz aktiver Arbeitsmarktpolitik im ostdeutschen Transformationsprozess', in *Enquete-Kommission 'Überwindung der Folgen der SED-Diktatur'*, vol. iii, pp. 2806–74.
75. cf. Werner Tegtmeier, 'Die Zusammenführung der beiden deutschen Sozialsysteme—Probleme und mögliche Folgerungen für den Umwandlungsprozess in Mittel- und Osteuropa', in *Probleme der Umwandlung der Sozialordnungen der Staaten Mittel- und Osteuropas*, Gesellschaft für Versicherungswissenschaft und –gestaltung e.V., Cologne/Bergisch-Gladbach 1994, pp. 10–46, esp. p. 42. For the scope of the policy, see also *Sozialbericht 1993*, Bonn 1994, p. 29; *Sozialbericht 1997*, Bonn 1998, p. 19.
76. For these and the following figures on unemployment, cf. BMA, *Statistische Übersichten*, West volume, tables 90–3, 'Arbeitslose in Prozent der abhängigen zivilen Erwerbspersonen'. The unemployment rate accordingly differs slightly from that in Table 5 here, which shows the unemployed as a percentage of all persons capable of gainful employment.

77. cf. also statistics of persons included in the active labour market policy in *Sozialbericht*, BMA, 1993. According to these figures, the active labour market policy eased pressure on the labour market in the east by including 1,881,000 people in 1991, 1,972,000 in 1992, and 1,618,000 in 1993.
78. *Unterrichtung durch die Bundesregierung*, BTDrs 13/2280, 8 September 1995, p. 242; Hauser *et al.*, *Ungleichheit*, p. 329 f.
79. Hauser *et al.*, *Ungleichheit*, p. 329.
80. Joachim Rosenow, 'Die Altersgrenzenpolitik in den neuen Bundesländern: Trends und Regulationsmechanismen im Transformationsprozess—Differenzen zur Entwicklung in den alten Bundesländern', in *ZSR*, 38 (1992), pp. 682–97 (here, p. 683).
81. Anne Hampele and Stefan Naevecke, 'Erwerbslosigkeit von Frauen in den neuen Bundesländern—Lebensmuster unter Druck', in *Der schwierige Weg zur Demokratie. Vom Ende der DDR zur Deutschen Einheit*, ed. Gert-Joachim Glaeßner, 2nd edn., Opladen 1992, pp. 107–41.
82. Klaus-Peter Schwitzer, 'Die Rentner sind die Gewinner der Einheit', in *Das Parlament*, 17/24 January 1997, p. 2.
83. Bundesanstalt für Arbeit, Institut für Arbeitsmarkt- und Berufsforschung, 'Arbeitsmarkt', in *Enquete-Kommission 'Überwindung'*, vol. iii, p. 2821.
84. GDR gross domestic product figures (substantially revised from earlier calculations) taken from Bundesministerium für Gesundheit und Soziale Sicherung, *Sozialbericht 2005*, Bonn 2005, p. 194.
85. BMA, *Statistische Übersichten*, West volume, tables 17 and 18.
86. ibid., tables 6 and 90.
87. ibid., tables 17 and 18.
88. ibid., tables 18 and 6.
89. ibid., table 90.
90. ibid., tables 18 and 93. For developments since 1997, cf. *FAZ*, '15 Jahre deutsche Einheit. Die Aufholjagd des Ostens stockt schon seit Jahren', 1 October 2005.
91. *Unterrichtung durch die Bundesregierung*, BTDrs 13/10823, 27 May 1998, p. 20.
92. ibid., pp. 20 f., 110.
93. Grosser, *Wagnis* pp. 76–9.
94. cf. Frieder Naschold, 'Ökonomische Leistungsfähigkeit und institutionelle Innovation. Das deutsche Produktions- und Politikregime im globalen Wettbewerb', in *Ökonomische Leistungsfähigkeit und institutionelle Innovation. Das deutsche Produktions- und Politikregime im globalen Wettbewerb*, ed. Frieder Naschold, David Soskice, Bob Hancké *et al.*, WZB-Jahrbuch 1997, Berlin 1997, pp. 19–62, esp. pp. 29 f.
95. cf. Jahresgutachten 1988–1989 des Sachverständigenrates zur Begutachtung der gesamtwirtschaftlichen Entwicklung, *Arbeitsplätze im Wettbewerb*, BTDrs 11/3478, 24 November 1989, pp. 101 ff.; Wolfgang Gerstenberger, *Grenzen fallen—Märkte Öffnen sich. Die Chancen der deutschen Wirtschaft am Beginn einer neuen Ära*, Berlin/Munich 1990, pp. 169–97.
96. cf. Rainer Geißler, *Die Sozialstruktur Deutschlands. Zur gesellschaftlichen Entwicklung mit einer Zwischenbilanz zur Vereinigung*, 2nd edn., Opladen 1996, pp. 27, 29.
97. OECD, *OECD Economic Surveys: Germany 1989/1990*, appendix, 'Basic Statistics—International Comparisons'.
98. Grosser, *Wagnis*, pp. 78 f. In 1990, 33 out of 1,000 inhabitants of employment age were employed in retail trades in the Federal Republic, compared with 49 per 1,000 in the USA.
99. cf. Doris Schwarzer, *Arbeitsbeziehungen*, p. 116.

100. cf. Bernhard Pieper, 'Industrie. Rasche Angleichung an die westdeutsche Beschäftigungsstruktur', in Oppenländer (ed.), *Wiedervereinigung*, pp. 401–18 (here, p. 413).
101. cf. Burkart Lutz and Holle Grünert, 'Der Zerfall der Beschäftigungsstruktur der DDR 1989–1993', in Lutz *et al.* (eds.), *Arbeit, Arbeitsmarkt und Betriebe*, pp. 69–120 (here, p. 76).
102. Rüdiger Meimberg, 'Landwirtschaft: Großbetriebe prägen den ländlichen Raum', in Oppenländer (ed.), *Wiedervereinigung*, pp. 383–400 (here, p. 384).
103. Walter Schaefer-Kehnert, 'Die LPG-Nachfolger sind für den Staat ein Fass ohne Boden', in *FAZ*, 3 January 2000.
104. After 1993, levels of both public and private investment per employee were higher than those in west Germany: cf. *Unterrichtung durch die Bundesregierung*, BTDrs 13/2280, 8 September 1995, p. 413.
105. cf. Markus Pohlmann and Rudi Schmidt, 'Management in Ostdeutschland und die Gestaltung des wirtschaftlichen und sozialen Wandels' and Rudi Schmidt, 'Restrukturierung und Modernisierung der industriellen Produktion', both in Lutz *et al.* (eds.), *Arbeit, Arbeitsmarkt und Betriebe*, pp. 191–226, 227–56.
106. Statistisches Bundesamt, *Tabellensammlung*, 3/97, pp. 16, 18.
107. Wollmann, 'Institutionenbildung', pp. 131–5.
108. Statistisches Bundesamt, *Tabellensammlung*, 3/97, p. 17.
109. Statistisches Bundesamt, *Tabellensammlung*, 3/97, p. 15.
110. cf. Hasko Hünig and Hildegard Maria Nickel, 'Großbetriebliche Dienstleistungen. Rascher Aufbau und harte Konsolidierung', in Lutz *et al.* (eds.), *Arbeit, Arbeitsmarkt und Betriebe*, pp. 297–346.
111. *Unterrichtung durch die Bundesregierung*, BTDrs 13/10823, 27 May 1998, p. 114.
112. cf. Pieper, 'Industrie', p. 413.
113. The following figures are based, in the case of the GDR in 1989, on *Statistisches Jahrbuch der DDR 1990*, Freiburg/Berlin 1990, pp. 129 f., and, for 1994, on a summary of results of a micro-census conducted in the former territory of the Federal Republic and in the new *Bundesländer*, in *Arbeits- und Sozialstatistik. Hauptergebnisse 1996*, BMA, Bonn 1996, pp. 23 f.
114. cf. Ingrid Haschke and Udo Ludwig, 'Produktion und Nachfrage', in *Herausforderung Ostdeutschland*, ed. Rüdiger Pohl, Berlin 1995, pp. 95–106 (here, p. 104); *Sozialbericht 2005*, p. 193.
115. *FAZ*, 1 October 2005, using figures from the Institut für Wirtschaftsforschung, Halle; cf. also Karl-Heinz Paqué, *Die Bilanz. Eine wissenschaftliche Analyse der Deutschen Einheit*, Munich 2009, p. 184.
116. Interview with Weber in the *Guardian*, 10 September 2005.
117. Jahresgutachten 1997/1998 des Sachverständigenrates zur Begutachtung der gesamtwirtschaftlichen Entwicklung, *Wachstum, Beschäftigung, Währungsunion—Orientierungen für die Zukunft*, BTDrs 13/9090, 18 November 1997, p. 349. On the drastic changes in the key financial figures caused by unification and cyclical factors, cf. also the address by Federal Finance Minister Waigel to the CDU/CSU parliamentary party, 25 May 1993. According to Waigel the deficit in the Federal budget, including special budgets, rose from 1.2 per cent of gross national product in 1989 to 6.5 per cent. See ACDP, Fraktionsprotokolle.
118. *Statistisches Taschenbuch 1998. Arbeits- und Sozialstatistik*, BMA, Bonn 1998, table 1.27. See also 'Die Entwicklung der Staatsverschuldung seit der deutschen Vereinigung', in Deutsche Bundesbank, *Monatsbericht März 1997*, vol. 49, no. 3, pp. 17–32.

119. BMA, *Statistisches Taschenbuch 1998*, table 1.21. See also 'Zum Stand der außenwirtschaftlichen Anpassung nach der deutschen Vereinigung', in Deutsche Bundesbank, *Monatsbericht Mai 1996*, vol. 48, no. 5, pp. 49–62.
120. cf. the table in *FAZ*, 21 July 2000. Because of variations in contribution rates for health insurance, social insurance rates in the new *Bundesländer* were somewhat higher in 1990–2 and 1997 and somewhat lower in 1993–5.
121. *Zweiter Zwischenbericht der Enquete-Kommission Demographischer Wandel—Herausforderungen unserer älter werdenden Gesellschaft an den einzelnen und die Politik*, BTDrs 13/11460, 5 October 1998, p. 102.
122. *Sozialbericht 1997*, p. 292.
123. A further 3.4 per cent of receipts in 1990 and 2.4 per cent in 1994 were other allocations and receipts.
124. Carola Kaps, 'Welches Rezept steckt hinter dem Job-Wunder in Amerika?', in *FAZ*, 3 January 2000.
125. Fritz W. Scharpf, 'Wege zu mehr Beschäftigung', in *Gewerkschaftliche Monatshefte*, 48 (1997), pp. 203–16; Scharpf, 'The Viability of Advanced Welfare States in the International Economy: Vulnerabilities and Options', Max-Planck-Institut für Gesellschaftsforschung, Working Paper 99/9, September 1999; on the effects of welfare-state benefits on employment, cf. also Siegel and Jochem, 'Zwischen Sozialstaats-Status quo und Beschäftigungswachstum'; Sven Jochem, 'Sozialpolitik in der Ära Kohl: Die Politik des Sozialversicherungsstaates', in *ZeS-Arbeitspapier* no. 12/99.
126. cf. Scharpf, 'Viability', p. 7. Between 1980 and 1996 the proportion of such employees in Germany fell from 39.5 to 35.8 per cent of the population aged between 15 to 64, but in 1996 it remained well above the average of 32.7 per cent across 18 OECD countries.
127. The German share of world exports fell from 11.4 per cent in 1991 to 8.7 per cent in 2001, well below the long-term average level of 10.6 per cent during the period 1975–89. Cf. Horst Siebert, 'Drei deutsche Schwächen', in *FAZ*, 11 March 2002.
128. Scharpf, 'Viability', p. 8. In Germany the proportion rose from 25.5 to 28.4 per cent between 1980 and 1996. The average proportion across 18 OECD countries rose much more sharply, from 28.4 to 34.4 per cent.
129. cf., for example, Scharpf, 'Wege', esp. pp. 212–16.
130. *Zweiter Zwischenbericht der Enquete-Kommission Demographischer Wandel*, p. 142 f. The report was not talking in terms merely of new jobs. A not inconsiderable number of the additional possible jobs to be created in the service sector were substitutional in nature, since, with outsourcing of services and research and development, jobs in industry were disappearing or would be changing in character.
131. cf. Roland Czada, 'Vereinigungskrise'.
132. Jahresgutachten 1995/96 des Sachverständigenrates zur Begutachtung der gesamtwirtschaftlichen Entwicklung, *Im Standortwettbewerb*, BTDrs 13/3016, 15 November 1995, p. 348. The real-terms rise in incomes, however, was much smaller, as there were simultaneous rises in living costs of 27 per cent in the east, compared with 11 per cent in the west. In west Germany in 1994, net wages and salaries had fallen by almost 3 per cent in terms of 1991 prices, whereas in the east they had risen by about 21 per cent (cf. *Sozialbericht 1997*, pp. 203 f.).
133. Hauser *et al.*, *Ungleichheit*, p. 50.
134. ibid., p. 142. On changes in income and income distribution in east and west Germany, cf. also Richard Hauser and Gert Wagner, 'Die Einkommensverteilung

in Ostdeutschland: Darstellung und Determinanten im Vergleich zu Westdeutschland für die Jahre 1990 bis 1994', in *Wohlstand für alle?*, ed. Wolfgang Glatzner and Gerhard Kleinhenz, Opladen 1997, pp. 11–61.

135. BMA, *Statistische Übersichten*, West volume, p. 60. For white-collar workers, negotiated weekly working hours fell from 38.4 to 37.8 hours between 1990 and 1994 in the west, and from 40.2 to 39.9 hours in the east (ibid., p. 62).
136. ibid., p. 73.
137. Hauser *et al.*, *Ungleichheit*, pp. 203–5.
138. BMA, *Statistische Übersichten*, West volume, p. 297. The figures relate to two-person households of recipients of pensions and income support and four-person households of employees on mid-level incomes. In fact, in the east in 1990, owing to the GDR's strict fixing of rents, the proportion accounted for by rents had been even lower, at 6.1 per cent for pensioners and 4 per cent for people in employment.
139. *Zweiter Zwischenbericht der Enquete-Kommission Demographischer Wandel*, p. 296, which also gives figures for average net wealth for different categories of family.
140. Hauser *et al.*, *Ungleichheit*, p. 168.
141. Geißler, *Sozialstruktur*, pp. 67 f. According to figures in Schroeder, *Preis der Einheit*, in 1996 just under half of all employees were employed in mainly smaller or medium-sized enterprises with east German owners, and roughly a quarter in enterprises with west German or foreign owners, while the remainder were in public employment.
142. Frerich and Frey, *Handbuch der Geschichte der Sozialpolitik*, vol. ii, *Sozialpolitik in der Deutschen Demokratischen Republik*, 2nd edn., Munich/Vienna 1996, p. 345.
143. *Sozialbericht 1997*, p. 310.
144. 'Zur Finanzentwicklung der gesetzlichen Rentenversicherung seit Beginn der neunziger Jahre', in Deutsche Bundesbank, *Monatsbericht März 1995*, vol. 47, no. 3, pp. 17–31 (here, p. 24). Average recorded insurance years for women in the east were 38, for women in the west 24.5.
145. *Sozialbericht 1997*, pp. 51 f.; cf. also Winfried Schmähl and Uwe Fachinger, 'Einkommen und Vermögen älterer Haushalte. Anmerkungen zur heutigen Situation und zur künftigen Entwicklung', in *Lebenssituation älterer Menschen. Beschreibung und Prognose aus interdisziplinärer Sicht*, ed. Dieter Farny, Peter Lütke-Bornefeld, and Gertrud Zellenberg, Berlin 1996, pp. 93–124, esp. pp. 104–6.
146. *Sozialbericht 2001*, pp. 124 f.
147. Winfried Schmähl, 'Einkommenslage und Einkommensverwendungspotential Älterer in Deutschland', in *Wirtschaftsdienst*, 85, March 2005, pp. 156–65 (here, p. 158).
148. Hauser *et al.*, *Ungleichheit*, p. 379. There were no significant shifts in the west between 1990 and 1994 (ibid., p. 380).
149. cf. Roland Merten, 'Junge Familien in den neuen Bundesländern: die vergessenen Verlierer im Prozess der deutschen Vereinigung', in *Sozialer Fortschritt*, 42 (1993), pp. 295–300; 43 (1994), pp. 18 f.
150. ibid., p. 287.
151. *Zweiter Zwischenbericht der Enquete-Kommission Demographischer Wandel*, p. 321.
152. On what follows, cf., in particular, Hans F. Zacher, 'Der Wandel der Arbeit und der sozialen Sicherung im internationalen Vergleich', in *ZIAS*, 13 (1999), pp. 1–47; Ralf Dahrendorf, *Fragmente eines neuen Liberalismus*, ch. 11, 'Die Arbeitsgesellschaft in der Krise', Stuttgart 1987, pp. 161–72; Rainer Dombois, 'Der schwierige Abschied vom Normalarbeitsverhältnis', in *APuZG*, B 37/99, pp. 13–20.
153. cf. Kommission für Zukunftsfragen der Freistaaten Bayern und Sachsen, *Erwerbstätigkeit und Arbeitslosigkeit in Deutschland. Entwicklung, Ursachen und Maßnahmen*,

part I, *Entwicklung in Erwerbstätigkeit und Arbeitslosigkeit in Deutschland und anderen frühindustrialisierten Ländern*, Bonn 1996, pp. 62–4. On the decline in the normal employment relationship and the reasons for it, cf. also Edeltraut Hoffmann and Ulrich Walwei, *Beschäftigung: Formenvielfalt als Perspektive?*, part 1, 'Längerfristige Entwicklung von Erwerbsformen in Westdeutschland', IAB Kurzbericht, no. 2, 27 January 1998; Ulrich Walwei, part 2, 'Bestimmungsfaktoren für den Wandel von Erwerbsformen', IAB Kurzbericht, no. 3, 28 January 1998.

154. *WZB-Mitteilungen*, 97, September 2002, p. 6.
155. Deutsche Bundesbank, 'Rascher Wandel der Erwerbsarbeit', in *Monatsbericht Juli 2005*, vol. 57, no. 7, pp. 15–27.
156. cf. Franz-Xaver Kaufmann, 'Sozialstaatlichkeit unter den Bedingungen moderner Wirtschaft', in *Handbuch der Wissenschaftsethik*, vol. i, *Verhältnisbestimmung von Wirtschaft und Ethik*, ed. Wilhelm Korff (for the Görresgesellschaft), Gütersloh 1999, pp. 800–30. According to a representative survey of time budgeting by the Statistisches Bundesamt cited by Kaufmann (ibid., p. 807), the annual volume of paid and unpaid work in Germany in 1992 was made up of 60,000 million hours of gainful employment (36 per cent), 10,000 million hours of journey time (6 per cent), and 95,500 million hours of unpaid work (58 per cent). Unpaid work included household work, network support work, and voluntary activities.

4 The Social Structure and Expectations from Social Policy

1. *Erster Zwischenbericht der Enquete-Kommission Demographischer Wandel—Herausforderungen unserer älter werdenden Gesellschaft an den einzelnen und die Politik*, BTDrs 12/7876, 14 June 1994, p. 15. On the relationship between demography and the welfare state in Germany since 1949, cf. Thomas Olk and Heinz Rothgang, 'Demographie und Sozialpolitik', in Ellwein and Holtmann (eds.), *50 Jahre Bundesrepublik Deutschland*, pp. 258–78.
2. Statistisches Bundesamt, *Bevölkerung Deutschlands bis 2050. 10. Koordinierte Bevölkerungsvorausberechnung*, Wiesbaden 2003; cf. also Herwig Birg, *Die demographische Zeitenwende. Der Bevölkerungsrückgang in Deutschland und Europa*, 2nd edn., Munich 2002.
3. Enquete-Kommission Demographischer Wandel, *Erster Zwischenbericht*, p. 13.
4. Enquete-Kommission Demographischer Wandel, *Zweiter Zwischenbericht*, pp. 32 f.
5. ibid., p. 37. In the new *Bundesländer*, however, the proportion of childless women born in 1960 was considerably lower, at about 10 per cent.
6. Herwig Birg, 'Deutschlands Weltrekorde', in *FAZ*, 22 February 2005.
7. Enquete-Kommission Demographischer Wandel, *Zweiter Zwischenbericht*, pp. 32 f.
8. Statistisches Bundesamt, *Datenreport 1994. Zahlen und Fakten über die Bundesrepublik Deutschland*, Bonn 1994, p. 30.
9. Enquete-Kommission Demographischer Wandel, *Zweiter Zwischenbericht*, p. 33.
10. cf. Enquete-Kommission Demographischer Wandel, *Erster Zwischenbericht*, pp. 24 f. On the debate on the causes of the decline in births in the GDR and prospects for the future, cf. Christopher Conrad, Michael Lechner, and Welf Werner, 'East German Fertility after Unification: Crisis or Adaptation?', in *Population and Development Review*, 22 (1996), pp. 331–58.
11. Enquete-Kommission Demographischer Wandel, *Erster Zwischenbericht*, p. 101.
12. Unless otherwise indicated, all figures on labour-force participation rates by sex and age are taken from ibid., p. 102 and Enquete-Komission Demographischer Wandel, *Zweiter Zwischenbericht*, p. 88.

13. *Schlussbericht der Enquete-Kommission Demographischer Wandel*, BTDrs 14/8800, 28 March 2002, p. 81.
14. 'Zur Finanzentwicklung der gesetzlichen Rentenversicherung seit Beginn der neunziger Jahre', in Deutsche Bundesbank, *Monatsbericht*, vol. 47, March 1997, pp. 17–31 (here, p. 21).
15. Werner Tegtmeier, 'Beschäftigung, Arbeitsmarkt und Sicherung bei Arbeitslosigkeit', in BMA, *Sozialstaat im Wandel*, pp. 85–105 (here, p. 92). On the effects of the attempts to deflect the trend towards early retirement by making admittance to a pension more difficult, cf. Alber, 'Der deutsche Sozialstaat', pp. 235–75 (here, pp. 268 f.).
16. Enquete-Kommission Demographischer Wandel, *Zweiter Zwischenbericht*, pp. 137–9.
17. Subsequently, labour-force participation rates rose again with the expiry of the early-retirement regulations, reaching, for example, 78 per cent in 1997 in the case of men aged between 55 and 60: cf. ibid., p. 88.
18. ibid., pp. 93 f., 135. At the end of September 1995 one in every two long-term unemployed people was over 45 years old: cf. Hauser *et al.*, *Ungleichheit*, p. 344.
19. cf. 'Gemeinsam für Deutschland—mit Mut und Menschlichkeit', coalition agreement between the CDU, CSU, and SPD, 11 November 2005, pp. 82 f.
20. cf. the article 'Deutschland ist auf das Ende der Frühverrentung nicht vorbereitet', in *FAZ*, 29 August 2005.
21. Enquete-Kommission Demographischer Wandel, *Erster Zwischenbericht*, p. 111.
22. ibid., pp. 110–24.
23. Enquete-Kommission Demographischer Wandel, *Zweiter Zwischenbericht*, pp. 121–4.
24. *Schlussbericht der Enquete-Kommission Demographischer Wandel*, p. 76.
25. Enquete-Kommission Demographischer Wandel, *Erster Zwischenbericht*, p. 38.
26. The Statistical Office posits an increase in life expectancy of about 6 years by 2050, to 81.1 years for boys and 86.6 years for girls, and a net increase in immigration of 200,000 people per year. As far as those over 65 are concerned, the age quotient would rise, on these assumptions, from 27.5 per cent in 2001 to 47.3 per cent in 2030 and 54.5 per cent in 2050. Cf. Statistisches Bundesamt, *Bevölkerung Deutschlands bis 2050*, p. 32.
27. According to the calculations of the Federal Statistical Office, the proportion of those over 80 within the overall population, which stood at about 1 per cent in 1950, will rise from 3.8 per cent in 1990 to 5.0 per cent in 2010, 7.3 per cent in 2030 and 12.1 per cent in 2050: ibid., p. 31.
28. cf. Enquete-Kommission Demographischer Wandel, *Zweiter Zwischenbericht*, p. 281.
29. cf. for example, Bert Rürup and Werner Sesselmeier, 'Die demographische Entwicklung Deutschlands: Risiken, Chancen, politische Optionen', in *APuZG*, B 44/93, pp. 3–15.
30. Statistisches Bundesamt, *Bevölkerung Deutschlands bis 2050*, p. 42.
31. Coalition agreement, 11 November 2005, p. 83.
32. cf. the reports of the Rürup commission (named after the commission's chairman, Bert Rürup), appointed by the Federal Minister for Health and Social Security, Ulla Schmidt, and of the Herzog commission (named after the commission's chairman, Roman Herzog), appointed by the CDU: Bundesministerium für Gesundheit und soziale Sicherung, *Nachhaltigkeit in der Finanzierung der sozialen Sicherungssysteme. Bericht der Kommission*, Berlin 2003, and *Bericht der Kommission 'Soziale Sicherheit' zur Reform der sozialen Sicherungssysteme*, Berlin, 29 September 2003. The two reports rested on quite different sets of assumptions. The Rürup commission, for example,

posited a much higher labour-force participation rate, particularly for women, and annual immigration of 200,000, as against the Herzog commission's assumption of 100,000. In addition, it assumed an unemployment rate of 4.4 per cent in 2030 (as against the Herzog commission's assumption of a long-term rate of 9.6 per cent), a higher level of labour productivity, a considerably greater increase in gross domestic product, and a less sharp decrease in the population. The Herzog commission, which made much more pessimistic assumptions, concluded that the need for additional financial resources was very much greater and made correspondingly more radical reform proposals.

33. cf. the discussion of the various options for reform of the old-age protection system in Enquete-Kommission Demographischer Wandel, *Zweiter Zwischenbericht*, pp. 189–212. Of the many other publications on this question, cf. also Winfried Schmähl, 'Alterssicherung in Deutschland an der Jahrtausendwende—Konzeptionen, Maßnahmen und Wirkungen', in *Deutsche Rentenversicherung*, 1–2/2000, pp. 50–71; Bert Rürup, 'Alterndes Deutschland. Herausforderung des demographischen Wandels', in ibid., pp. 72–81.
34. cf. Enquete-Kommission Demographischer Wandel, *Zweiter Zwischenbericht*, pp. 218–60.
35. cf. the analysis by Winfried Schmähl, 'Migration und soziale Sicherung. Über die Notwendigkeit einer differenzierten Betrachtung: das Beispiel der gesetzlichen Kranken- und Rentenversicherung', in *Hamburger Jahrbuch für Wirtschafts- und Gesellschaftspolitik*, 14 (1995), pp. 247–71.
36. *Familien und Familienpolitik im geeinten Deutschland.—Zukunft des Humanvermögens. Fünfter Familienbericht*, Bundesministerium für Familie, Senioren, Frauen und Jugend, Bonn 1994, p. 70 (BTDrs 12/7560, 15 June 1994).
37. Enquete-Kommission Demographischer Wandel, *Zweiter Zwischenbericht*, p. 269.
38. Enquete-Kommission Demographischer Wandel, *Erster Zwischenbericht*, p. 63.
39. Enquete-Kommission Demographischer Wandel, *Zweiter Zwischenbericht*, p. 273.
40. Enquete-Kommission Demographischer Wandel, *Erster Zwischenbericht*, p. 66.
41. ibid., p. 67.
42. Bundesinstitut für Bevölkerungsforschung, *Bevölkerung, Fakten—Trends—Ursachen—Erwartungen*, Wiesbaden 2000, p. 13.
43. cf. Johannes Huinink, 'Sozialpolitik und individuelles Handeln. Zu unbeabsichtigten Folgen politischer Intervention am Beispiel der DDR', in *Zeitschrift für Sozialreform*, 42 (1996), pp. 1–16, esp. pp. 6 f.
44. Enquete-Kommission Demographischer Wandel, *Zweiter Zwischenbericht*, p. 265. The figure includes children of non-married partners.
45. Hauser *et al.*, *Ungleichheit*, p. 267.
46. Enquete-Kommission Demographischer Wandel, *Zweiter Zwischenbericht*, p. 294. Among single parents with children below the age of 3, the proportion of those receiving income support was over 60 per cent in the west, while in the east it was about 45 per cent.
47. Petra Drauschke and Margit Stolzenburg, 'Familie', in *Sozialreport 1995. Daten und Fakten in den neuen Bundesländern*, ed. Gunnar Winkler, Berlin 1995, pp. 276–328 (here, p. 310).
48. Enquete-Kommission Demographischer Wandel, *Zweiter Zwischenbericht*, p. 321.
49. ibid., p. 295.
50. ibid., p. 262.
51. ibid.

52. On the transformation of the east German elites after unification, cf. Wilhelm Bürklin, Hilke Rebenstorf *et al.*, *Eliten in Deutschland. Rekrutierung und Integration*, Opladen 1997.
53. Lutz and Grünert, 'Zerfall', in Lutz *et al.* (eds.), *Arbeit, Arbeitsmarkt und Betriebe*, pp. 69–120.
54. Burkart Lutz, 'Einleitung', in Lutz *et al.* (eds.), *Arbeit, Arbeitsmarkt und Betriebe*, pp. 4 f.; Pohlmann and Schmidt, 'Management', in ibid., pp. 191–226.
55. Enquete-Kommission Demographischer Wandel, *Zweiter Zwischenbericht*, p. 321. At the end of 1996, 2.9 per cent of Germans, as against 8.5 per cent of foreigners, were receiving regular assistance with living costs.
56. Hauser *et al.*, *Ungleichheit*, pp. 323–5.
57. cf. above, pp. 95–9.
58. *Datenreport 1994*, pp. 579–81.
59. The findings of the surveys naturally depend on the exact wording of the questionnaires used and should not be over-interpreted. However, they reveal clear differences between east and west Germany and, in some measure, changes between 1989/90 and 1994. The most important surveys that have been consulted here are the survey of welfare in the east conducted by the Wissenschaftszentrum Berlin für Sozialforschung (WZB) in October/November 1990, a welfare survey conducted jointly in the spring of 1993 by the WZB and the Zentrum für Umfragen, Methoden und Analysen (ZUMA), Mannheim, the Allgemeine Bevölkerungsumfrage der Sozialwissenschaften (ALLBUS) conducted by the ZUMA, and surveys (some unpublished) conducted by the Institut für Demoskopie Allensbach.
60. Statistisches Bundesamt, *Datenreport 1992. Zahlen und Fakten über die Bundesrepublik Deutschland*, Bonn 1992, p. 640; id., *Datenreport 1994*, p. 425.
61. id., *Datenreport 1994*, p. 483.
62. ibid., p. 485. In 1990 as many as 71 per cent of those questioned in the east had regarded financial protection against unemployment as inadequate.
63. ibid., p. 441.
64. ibid., p. 491.
65. Wolfgang Thierse, 'Fünf Jahre deutsche Vereinigung: Wirtschaft—Gesellschaft—Mentalität', in *APuZG*, B 40/41, pp. 3–7; *Allensbacher Jahrbuch der Demoskopie 1984–1992*, vol. ix, ed. Elisabeth Noelle-Neumann and Renate Köcher, Munich/New York/London etc. 1993, pp. 516, 833; *Allensbacher Jahrbuch der Demoskopie 1993–1997*, vol. x, ed. Elisabeth Noelle-Neumann and Renate Köcher, Munich 1997, pp. 122–5, 961 f.; Detlef Pollack, 'Zwischen alten Verhaltensdispositionen und neuen Anforderungsprofilen. Bemerkungen zu den mentalitätsspezifischen Voraussetzungen des Operierens von Interessenverbänden und Organisationen in den neuen Bundesländern', in *Organisierte Interessen in Ostdeutschland*, ed. Volker Eichener, Ralf Kleinfeld, Detlef Pollack, *et al.*, 2 half-vols., Marburg 1992, pp. 489–508, esp. pp. 495 f.
66. cf. Ronald Inglehart, *The Silent Revolution: Changing Values and Political Styles*, Princeton 1977; Ronald Inglehart, *Culture Shift in Advanced Industrial Society*, Princeton 1990; Ronald Inglehart, *Modernization and Postmodernization: Cultural, Economic and Political Change in 43 Societies*, Princeton 1997; Dieter Fuchs, 'Zum Wandel politischer Konfliktlinien: Ideologische Gruppierungen und Wahlverhalten', in *Die Bundesrepublik in den achtziger Jahren. Innenpolitik, politische Kultur, Außenpolitik*, ed. Werner Süß, Opladen 1991, pp. 69–86.
67. *Datenreport 1992*, pp. 631 f., 640; *Datenreport 1994*, p. 426.

68. Hauser *et al.*, *Ungleichheit*, pp. 441 f.; *Allensbacher Jahrbuch 1993–1997*, pp. 1055, 1066.
69. cf. Ritter, *Über Deutschland*, pp. 176–178.
70. cf. Schwarzer, *Arbeitsbeziehungen*, p. 105.
71. cf. Heike Tappe, *Emanzipation oder Zwang? Frauen in der DDR zwischen Beruf, Familie und Sozialpolitik*, Berlin 1995, pp. 89–91.
72. cf., for example, Walter Heering and Klaus Schröder, 'Die DDR war kein Bollwerk der Emanzipation. Legenden und Wirklichkeit im ostdeutschen Emanzipationsprozess: Das Beispiel Frauenbeschäftigung', in *FAZ*, 21 December 1995.
73. Statistisches Bundesamt, *Datenreport 1994*, p. 481. The proportion of those in the east who intended to take up a job within three years was higher still, at 89 per cent, as compared with 31 per cent in the west.
74. Land Brandenburg, Ministerium für Arbeit, Soziales Gesundheit und Frauen, Die Ministerin, Arbeitspapier für die Referentenbesprechung zur Vorbereitung der Konferenz der Arbeits- und Sozialminister am 13. März 1991, 8 February 1991, in BMA VIII/Ia2/17666.
75. For a typical example, see the symposium of the Ludwig-Erhard-Stiftung, 18 October 1993, published under the title *Umbau der Sozialsysteme*, Ludwig-Erhard-Stiftung, ed. Martin Lambert, Krefeld 1994. Cf. especially the introduction by the retired Staatssekretär and chairman of the foundation, Otto Schlecht, presenting for discussion ten theses on a 'social policy in conformity with the Social Market economy': 'Soziale Sicherung als Aufgabe der Sozialen Marktwirtschaft', pp. 7–14.
76. Statistisches Bundesamt, *Datenreport 1992*, p. 642. The survey in the east was conducted two months after unification, in December 1990.
77. Institut für Demoskopie Allensbach, 'Probleme und Stimmungslage der Bevölkerung in den neuen Bundesländern. Eine aktuelle Bestandsaufnahme im Herbst 1991', pp. 81–4. 59 per cent of people wanted additional state resources to be provided, 57 per cent wanted temporary jobs to be created through job creation schemes, and 30 per cent still wanted enterprises to be taken over by the state. The survey was carried out and the results analysed by the Institut under commission from the Federal Ministry of Economics. The paper is held in BMA files, VIII/Ie7/17700 (1).
78. cf. Jörg Maschatzke, 'Einstellungen zum Umfang staatlicher Verantwortung.—Zum Staatsverständnis der Eliten im vereinten Deutschland', and Viktoria Kaina, 'Wertorientierung im Eliten-Bevölkerungsvergleich: Vertikale Distanzen, geteilte Loyalitäten und das Erbe der Trennung', both in Bürklin *et al.* (eds.), *Eliten*, pp. 321–50 and 351–89.
79. Carsten G. Ullrich, Ingrid Wemken, and Heike Walter, 'Leistungen und Beiträge als Determinanten der Zufriedenheit mit der gesetzlichen Krankenversicherung. Ergebnis einer empirischen Untersuchung zur Akzeptanz des Krankenversicherungssystems bei den gesetzlich Versicherten', *ZeS-Arbeitspapier* no. 3/94.
80. cf. Edeltraud Roller, *Einstellungen der Bürger zum Wohlfahrtsstaat der Bundesrepublik Deutschland*, Opladen 1992, esp. pp. 69–72.
81. ibid., p. 199; *Allensbacher Jahrbuch 1993–1997*, esp. pp. 702, 711–13.
82. Edeltraud Roller, 'Kürzungen von Sozialleistungen aus der Sicht der Bundesbürger', in *ZSR*, 42 (1996), pp. 777–88 (here, p. 781). For criticism of social policy and cuts in social benefits for older people, cf. also *Sozialreport 50+ 1996. Daten und Fakten zur sozialen Lage von Bürgern ab dem 50. Lebensjahr in den neuen Bundesländern*, Sozialwissenschaftliches Forschungszentrum Berlin-Brandenburg e.V., Berlin 1996, esp. pp. 203–38.

83. cf. Edeltraud Roller, 'Sozialpolitische Orientierungen nach der deutschen Vereinigung', in *Politische Orientierungen und Verhaltensweisen im vereinigten Deutschland*, ed. Oscar W. Gabriel, Opladen 1997, pp. 115–46 (here, pp. 126 f.). On changing attitudes towards the welfare state after German unification, cf. also Edeltraud Roller, 'Staatsbezug und Individualismus: Dimensionen des sozialkulturellen Wertwandels', in Ellwein and Holtmann (eds.), *50 Jahre Bundesrepublik Deutschland*, pp. 229–46.
84. Roller, 'Sozialpolitische Orientierungen', pp. 138 f.
85. ibid., p. 133. The remaining 19 per cent were undecided.
86. Katja Neller, '"Auferstanden aus Ruinen?" Das Phänomen der "DDR-Nostalgie"', in *Wächst zusammen, was zusammengehört? Stabilität und Wandel politischer Einstellungen im wiedervereinigten Deutschland*, ed. Oscar W. Gabriel, Jürgen W. Falter, and Hans Rattinger, Baden-Baden 2005, pp. 339–81, esp. p. 351.
87. The greater importance of the consequences of unification *vis-à-vis* socialization in the GDR is argued by Detlef Pollack and Gert Pickel, 'Die ostdeutsche Identität—Erbe des DDR-Sozialisimus oder Produkt der Wiedervereinigung? Die Einstellung der Ostdeutschen zu sozialer Ungleichheit und Demokratie', in *APuZG*, B41–42/98 pp. 9–23.
88. Thomas Bulmahn, 'Das vereinte Deutschland—Eine lebenswerte Gesellschaft? Zur Bewertung von Freiheit, Sicherheit und Gerechtigkeit in Ost und West', in *Kölner Zeitschrift für Soziologie und Sozialpsychologie*, 52 (2000), pp. 405–27 (here, pp. 406 f.). Typically, too, there are disparities in the new *Bundesländer* between people's estimates of their own economic situation, of their own future economic situation, and of the economic position of the country. The proportion of those with a positive estimate of their own economic situation rose from 17 to 48 per cent between 1990 and 1994, while during the same period the proportions of those with positive estimates of their own future economic situation and of the economic position of the country fell from 59 to 25 per cent, and from 89 to 12 per cent, respectively. Cf. Oskar W. Gabriel, 'Einleitung: politische Orientierungen und Verhaltensweisen im Transitionsprozeß', in Gabriel (ed.), *Politische Orientierungen*, pp. 9–33 (here, p. 26).
89. cf. *Allensbacher Jahrbuch 1984–1992*, pp. 426 f.; *Allensbacher Jahrbuch 1993–1997*, pp. 544, 558. In the new *Bundesländer* in November 1991, 90 per cent of those questioned declared themselves in favour of the incorporation of the right to housing into the Basic Law, and 85 per cent in favour of the enshrinement of the right to work: cf. *Allensbacher Jahrbuch 1984–1992*, p. 567.
90. Oskar W. Gabriel, 'Politische Orientierungen und Verhaltensweisen', in Kaase *et al.* (eds.), *Politisches System*, pp. 231–312 (here, p. 251).
91. Hauser *et al.*, *Ungleichheit*, p. 444.
92. Gabriel, 'Politische Orientierungen', p. 255; cf. also Dieter Fuchs, 'Welche Demokratie wollen die Deutschen? Einstellungen zur Demokratie im vereinigten Deutschland', in Gabriel (ed.), *Politische Orientierungen*, pp. 81–113.
93. Jens Reich, 'Bescheidenheit war politisches Programm', in *Die Zeit*, 18 October 1996.
94. Hauser *et al.*, *Ungleichheit*, p. 445. According to another source, favourable attitudes towards the market economy fell further from 38 per cent in 1994 to 23 per cent in 1998: cf. Bulmahn, 'Das vereinte Deutschland', p. 407.
95. Bulmahn, 'Das vereinte Deutschland', esp. pp. 414–25.
96. Gabriel, 'Politische Orientierungen', p. 243. Cf. also Elisabeth Noelle-Neumann, 'Die PDS als Kristallisationspunkt der Unterschiede', in *FAZ*, 16 December 1997.
97. Kai Arzheimer, '"Freiheit oder Sozialismus?" Gesellschaftliche Wertorientierungen, Staatszielvorstellungen und Ideologien im Ost-West-Vergleich', in Gabriel *et al.* (eds.), *Wächst zusammen, was zusammengehört?*, pp. 285–313 (here, p. 296). This article, like

most of the articles in that volume, is based on analyses of surveys conducted in the context of the Bundestag elections of 1994, 1998, and 2002.

98. In March 1990—i.e. during the period of the first free Volkskammer elections—61 per cent of east Germans questioned said that they saw themselves as Germans, as against only 32 per cent who saw themselves as east Germans, while in January 1992 only 35 per cent saw themselves primarily as Germans, compared with 60 per cent who saw themselves as east Germans: cf. *Allensbacher Jahrbuch 1984–1992*, p. 486. In 1997 67 per cent saw themselves primarily as east Germans, and 28 per cent as Germans: cf. *Allensbacher Jahrbuch 1993–1997*, p. 560.
99. cf. Leo Montada, 'Gerechtigkeitsansprüche und Ungerechtigkeitserleben in den neuen Bundesländern', in *Arbeit und Gerechtigkeit im ostdeutschen Transformationsprozess*, ed. Walter R. Heinz and Stefan E. Hormuth, Opladen 1997, pp. 231–74; Hauser *et al.*, *Ungleichheit*, p. 448. In a survey conducted five years after unification, roughly 70 per cent of east Germans felt that they were second-class citizens: cf. Manfred Schmitt and Leo Montada, 'Psychologische, soziologische und arbeitswissenschaftliche Analysen der Transformation nach der deutschen Wiedervereinigung', in *Gerechtigkeitserleben im wiedervereinigten Deutschland*, ed. Manfred Schmitt and Leo Montada, Opladen 1999, pp. 7–18 (here, p. 13); Institut für Demoskopie, 'Probleme', pp. 61–3. The study of changes in political attitudes in east and west Germany between 1994 and 2002 cited above (note 86) comes to the conclusion that there has not yet been 'a general convergence of political attitudes of east and west Germans' and that 'above all, in the central area of political culture, namely attitudes towards democracy, . . . the differences have widened rather than narrowed': cf. Oskar W. Gabriel, 'Wächst zusammen, was zusammengehört?', in Gabriel *et al.* (eds.), *Wächst zusammen, was zusammengehört?*, pp. 385–423 (here, p. 419).
100. Institut für Demoskopie, 'Probleme', pp. 61–3. In November 1996, 74 per cent of east Germans and 29 of west Germans declared themselves in favour of equal pay for equal work: cf. *Allensbacher Jahrbuch 1993–1997*, p. 613.

II THE CREATION OF THE SOCIAL UNION

5 The Central Features of the Social Union: The Legislation and Institutions Governing Social Policy in the Federal Republic and the GDR Compared

1. *Sozialbericht 1990*, BMA, pp. 6 f.
2. Interviews by the author with the Federal Minister of Labour, Norbert Blüm, 8 June 2000, and with Staatssekretär Bernhard Jagoda, 5 July 2000.
3. cf. the handwritten manuscript of an undated speech by Martin Ammermüller entitled 'Die Herausforderung der Sozialversicherung in den neuen Bundesländern', p. 1. I am grateful to Dr Ammermüller for providing me with a copy of the manuscript.
4. *Sozialbericht 1993*, preface.
5. ibid, p. 8.
6. cf. *Sozialstaatlichkeit in der DDR. Sozialpolitische Entwicklungen im Spannungsfeld von Diktatur und Gesellschaft 1945/9–1989*, ed. Dierk Hoffmann and Michael Schwartz, Munich 2005, esp. Gerhard A. Ritter, 'Thesen zur Sozialpolitik der DDR', pp. 11–29.
7. cf. Hockerts, 'Soziale Errungenschaften?', pp. 791–4.
8. On 'externalization' and 'internalization' of social costs, cf. Hans F. Zacher, 'Grundtypen des Sozialrechts', in id., *Abhandlungen zum Sozialrecht*, ed. Bernd Baron von Maydell and Eberhard Eichenhofer, Heidelberg 1993, pp. 257–78, esp. pp. 262–4.

9. M. Rainer Lepsius, 'Die Rolle der Sozialpolitik in der Bonner Republik und in der DDR', in *Soziale Konflikte, Sozialstaat und Demokratie in Deutschland*, ed. Helga Grebing and Hans Otto Hemmer, Essen 1996, pp. 41–50, esp. pp. 47 f.
10. For the period before the fall of the Wall, cf. Heinz Niemann, *Meinungsforschung in der DDR. Die geheimen Berichte an das Politbüro der SED*, Cologne 1993, pp. 277 f. For the position after unification, cf. note 89 to Chapter 4 above.
11. cf. Matthias Zeng, *'Asoziale' in der DDR. Transformation einer moralischen Kategorie*, Münster 2000, esp. pp. 34–43.
12. cf. Beatrix Bouvier, *Die DDR—ein Sozialstaat? Sozialpolitik in der Ära Honecker*, Bonn 2002, esp. pp. 130–8.
13. *GBl I*, 1961, pp. 27 ff.
14. *GBl I*, 1977, pp. 188–227.
15. cf. above, p. 57.
16. *GBl I*, 1990, pp. 371–81, Gesetz zur Änderung und Ergänzung des Arbeitsgesetzbuches, 22 June 1990; cf. also Rolf Schwedes, 'Arbeitsgesetzbuch der DDR und seine Neufassung 1990', in *Entwicklung von Arbeitsrecht und Arbeitsschutzrecht. Festschrift für Gottfried Wlotzke zum 70. Geburtstag*, ed. Rudolf Anzinger and Rolf Wenk, Munich 1996, pp. 145–72.
17. cf. Peter Hübner, *Konsens, Konflikt und Kompromiss. Soziale Arbeiterinteressen und Sozialpolitik in der SBZ/DDR 1945–1970*, Berlin 1995, esp. pp. 211–45; Jörg Roesler, 'Die Produktionsbrigaden in der Industrie der DDR. Zentrum der Arbeitswelt?', in *Sozialgeschichte der DDR*, ed. Hartmut Kaelble, Jürgen Kocka, and Hartmut Zwahr, Stuttgart 1994, pp. 144–70.
18. The supplementary pension, which, following a decree of 9 March 1954, was paid to employees of the most important state-owned enterprises after a minimum of twenty years' uninterrupted employment, is classed here as a supplementary provision rather than an enterprise-based pension. Cf. Frerich and Frey, *Handbuch*, vol. ii, p. 358.
19. cf. Marcel Boldorf, *Sozialfürsorge in der SBZ/DDR 1945–1953. Ursachen, Ausmaß und Bewältigung der Nachkriegsarmut*, Stuttgart 1998.
20. Frerich and Frey, *Handbuch*, vol. ii, p. 369. On social welfare in the GDR, and the development of income support after unification, cf. also Manfred Wienand, Volker Neumann, and Iris Brockmann, *Fürsorge*, Opladen 1997.
21. Heinz Aulmann, 'Die Verhütung und Entschädigung von Arbeitsunfällen und Berufskrankheiten in der DDR unter Berücksichtigung des Staatsvertrages', in *Kompaß* (1990), vol. 7, pp. 343–5.
22. cf. Dierk Hoffmann, *Sozialpolitische Neuordnung in der SBZ/DDR. Der Umbau der Sozialversicherung 1945–1956*, Munich 1996.
23. Frerich and Frey, *Handbuch*, vol. ii, p. 285.
24. ibid., pp. 291 f.
25. ibid., p. 345.
26. Günter Manz, *Armut in der 'DDR'-Bevölkerung. Lebensstandard und Konsumptionsniveau vor und nach der Wende*, Augsburg 1992, pp. 86 f., 88, 106.
27. cf. Dierk Hoffmann, 'Rentenversicherung und SED-Rentenpolitik in den achtziger Jahren', in Kuhrt *et al.* (eds.), *Am Ende des realen Sozialismus*, vol. iv, pp. 375–419.
28. cf. Hans Günter Hockerts, 'Grundlinien und soziale Folgen der Sozialpolitik in der DDR', in Kaelble *et al.* (eds.), *Sozialgeschichte*, pp. 519–44 (here, p. 528).
29. cf. Winfried Schmähl, 'Alterssicherung in der DDR und ihre Umgestaltung im Zuge des deutschen Einigungsprozesses', in *Sozialpolitik im vereinten Deutschland I*, ed. Gerhard Kleinhenz, Berlin 1991, pp. 49–95 (here, p. 70).

30. Hoffmann, 'Rentenversicherung', p. 395.
31. The shift in the GDR from a unified system of social insurance to a system that was very heterogeneous in terms of structure and of benefit rights, during a period when there was a trend towards greater homogeneity within social insurance in the Federal Republic, is discussed in Philip Manow-Borgwardt, 'Die Sozialversicherung in der DDR und BRD, 1945–1990: Über die Fortschrittlichkeit rückschrittlicher Institutionen', in *PVS*, 35 (1994), pp. 40–61.
32. Hockerts, 'Grundlinien', p. 529; cf. also Winfried Schmähl, 'Sicherung bei Alter, Invalidität und für Hinterbliebene', in *Geschichte der Sozialpolitik in Deutschland seit 1945*, vol. xi, *1989–1994. Bundesrepublik Deutschland. Sozialpolitik im Zeichen der Vereinigung*, ed. Gerhard A. Ritter, Baden-Baden 2007, p. 554.
33. Stefan Böhm and Arno Pott, 'Verteilungspolitische Aspekte der Rentenüberleitung. Eine Analyse ausgewählter Verteilungswirkungen der Übertragung des bundesdeutschen Rentenrechts auf die neuen Bundesländer', in Winfried Schmähl (ed.), *Sozialpolitik im Prozeß der deutschen Vereinigung*, Frankfurt a.M. 1992, pp. 166–227 (here, p. 173).
34. Frerich and Frey, *Handbuch*, vol. ii, pp. 417 f., 421.
35. Manfred G. Schmidt, 'Grundzüge der Sozialpolitik in der DDR', in Kuhrt *et al.* (eds.), *Am Ende des realen Sozialismus*, vol. iv, pp. 273–319 (here, p. 294).
36. Schwarzer, *Arbeitsbeziehungen*, p. 105.
37. ibid., p. 107. In the Federal Republic in 1988, blue- and white-collar female workers in full-time employment earned only 70 and 64 per cent, respectively, of the average gross earnings of their male counterparts.
38. Heike Trappe, *Emanzipation oder Zwang? Frauen in der DDR zwischen Beruf, Familie und Sozialpolitik*, Berlin 1995, p. 197.
39. Philip Manow, 'Entwicklungslinien ost- und westdeutscher Gesundheitspolitik zwischen doppelter Staatsgründung, deutscher Einigung und europäischer Integration', in *ZSR*, 43 (1997), pp. 101–31.
40. At the end of 1989 only 341 out of the 20,570 doctors active in outpatient care were working as independent practitioners: cf. Jürgen Wasem, *Vom staatlichen zum kassenärztlichen System. Eine Untersuchung des Transformationsprozesses der ambulanten ärztlichen Versorgung in Deutschland*, Frankfurt/New York 1997, p. 49. Between 7 and 8 per cent of hospital beds were in hospitals owned by religious institutions (Hockerts, 'Grundlinien', p. 539).
41. Manow, 'Entwicklungslinien', p. 117.
42. Hockerts, 'Grundlinien', p. 525.
43. Winfried Süß, 'Gesundheitspolitik', in *Drei Wege deutscher Sozialstaatlichkeit. NS-Diktatur, Bundesrepublik und DDR im Vergleich*, ed. Hans Günter Hockerts, Munich 1998, pp. 55–97 (here, pp. 79 f.).
44. For an analysis of the strengths and weaknesses of the GDR health system, cf. Sachverständigenrat für die Konzertierte Aktion im Gesundheitswesen, Jahresgutachten 1991, *Das Gesundheitswesen im vereinten Deutschland*, Baden-Baden 1992, pp. 102–51.
45. cf. Süß, 'Gesundheitspolitik', p. 89.
46. cf. Informationen über die Arbeit des Ministeriums für Gesundheits- und Sozialwesen seit November 1989, 14 March 1990, BArch, DQ 1, 14119.
47. Sachverständigenrat für die Konzertierte Aktion im Gesundheitswesen, Jahresgutachten 1991, p. 113; BMFuS, *Fünfter Familienbericht*, p. 39.

48. cf. Philip Manow, *Gesundheitspolitik im Einigungsprozess*, Frankfurt/New York 1994; Wasem, *Vom staatlichen zum kassenärztlichen System.*
49. Schmidt, 'Grundzüge der Sozialpolitik', p. 295.
50. On the *nomenklatura* system in the GDR, based on the Soviet model, cf. Matthias Wagner, 'Gerüst der Macht. Das Kadernomenklatursystem als Ausdruck der führenden Rolle der SED', in *Gesellschaft ohne Eliten? Führungsgruppen in der DDR*, ed. Arnd Bauerkämper, Jürgen Danyel, Peter Hübner, and Sabine Roß, Berlin 1997, pp. 87–108; Sabine Roß, '"Karriere auf der Lochkarte". Der Zentrale Kaderdatenspeicher des Ministerrats der DDR', ibid., pp. 109–30; Hartmann Zimmermann, 'Überlegungen zur Geschichte der Kader und der Kaderpolitik in der SBZ/DDR', in Kaelble *et al.* (eds.), *Sozialgeschichte*, pp. 322–56.
51. *Die Umgestaltung der Systeme sozialer Sicherung in den Staaten Mittel- und Osteuropas. Fragen und Lösungsansätze. Kolloquium des Max-Planck-Instituts für Ausländisches und Internationales Sozialrecht in Tutzing vom 9.–12. Februar 1993*, ed. Bernd Baron von Maydell and E.-M. Hohnerlein, Berlin 1993; *Probleme der Umgestaltung der Sozialordnungen Mittel- und Osteuropas*, Gesellschaft für Versicherungswissenschaft und- gestaltung e.V. Köln, Bergisch-Gladbach 1994. On the transformation of the welfare systems in central and eastern Europe between 1989 and 1995, with reference to Bulgaria, Poland, Slovakia, the Czech Republic, and Hungary, cf. also *Transformation der Wohlfahrtsstaaten in Mittel- und Osteuropa. Eine Zwischenbilanz*, ed. Ulrike Götting, Opladen 1998.

6 The Social Policy of the Modrow Government

1. Prot. VK, 9. WP, 12. Tagung, 17/18 November 1989, pp. 272–81.
2. cf. Hoffmann, 'Rentenversicherung', pp. 391 f., 416–19.
3. cf. Patrick Moreau (in collaboration with Marcus Overmann), Walter Süß, Annette Weinke *et al.*, 'Die Politik der letzten DDR-Regierung und ihre Folgen', in *Materialien der Enquete-Kommission 'Überwindung'*, vol. viii/3, *Das geteilte Deutschland im geteilten Europa*, Deutscher Bundestag, Baden-Baden 1999, pp. 2008–173 (here, p. 2017).
4. cf. Information über die Arbeit des Ministeriums für Gesundheits- und Sozialwesen seit November 1989, 14 March 1990, BArch, DQ 1, 14919.
5. BArch, DQ 1, 13004.
6. Analyse und Vorschläge, wie in Fortführung der Gesundheitspolitik der Partei durch höhere Qualität und Effekivität der Arbeit die medizinische und soziale Betreuung der Bevölkerung im Fünfjahresplanzeitraum bis 1995 gesichert wird, 11 August 1989, BArch, DQ 1, 12097.
7. Arbeitsgruppe 'Sanierung von Einrichtungen des Gesundheits- und Sozialwesens', Leitung Prof. Dr Ing. habil. Peter Korneli, BMG, 221-48120/5, vol. i.
8. In addition to the letter referred to below, cf. also letters to Prof. Kurt Hager, member of the Politburo and secretary of the Central Committee of the SED, 11 October 1989; to Willi Stoph, chairman of the Council of Ministers of the SED, 24 and 26 October 1989; to Günther Kleiber, first deputy chairman of the Council of Ministers, 7 November 1989; to Prof. Dr Christa Luft, deputy chairwoman of the Council of Ministers for Economics, 15 January 1990; and to Kurt Singhuber, Minister for Heavy Industry, 17 January 1990: copies of all letters in BArch, DQ 1, 14919. In the letter to Kleiber, Thielmann demands that the 'capacity in the special clinics of the Ministries of State Security and of the Interior and medical facilities of the National People's Army should also be opened up so as to provide medical care for the population'. He also argued that government hospitals should be made available for use by a wider public.

9. Letter of Thielmann to the General Secretary of the Central Committee of the SED and Chairman of the State Council of the GDR Egon Krenz, 7 November 1989, BArch, DQ 1, 14919.
10. Thielmann to Modrow, 20 November 1989, BArch, DQ 1, 14919.
11. Thielmann to Modrow, 21 January 1989, BArch, DQ 1, 14919.
12. cf. Thielmann to the Oberbürgermeister of Berlin E. Krack, 5 February 1990; Information über die Arbeit des MfG, BArch, DQ 1, 14919.
13. Thielmann to Modrow, 21 January 1990, BArch, DQ 1, 14919.
14. Letter of Thielmann to regional medical officers in the Abteilungen Gesundheits- und Sozialwesen des Rates der Bezirke, 14 February 1990, BArch, DQ 1, 14919.
15. cf. the similarly worded letters to all regional medical officers, 26 February 1990, with copies to Modrow and the heads of regional councils, and also Stellungnahme des Ministers für Gesundheits- und Sozialwesen zu Niederlassungen von Ärzten und Zahnärzten in eigener Praxis, 26 Feburary 1990, BArch, DQ 1, 14919.
16. Thielmann to the chairmen of the Rat der Bezirke, 28 February 1990, BArch, DQ 1, 14919.
17. Letter to six ministers with a copy to Ministerpräsident Modrow *et al.*, 28 February 1990, BArch, DQ 1, 14919.
18. Letter of Thielmann to Ministerin für Arbeit und Löhne, Hannelore Mensch, and those primarily responsible for the development of the Social Charter, Ministerin Tatjana Böhm and Minister Gerd Poppe, 13 March 1990, BArch, DQ 1, 14919.
19. cf. European Parliament, Directorate-General for Research, Mitteilung an die Mitglieder des nichtständigen Ausschusses für die Prüfung des Prozesses der Vereinigung Deutschlands auf die Europäische Gemeinschaft: Die soziale Lage in der DDR, 8 May 1990, BArch, DQ 3, 1882, p. 4.
20. cf. Horst Kinitz, *Aufbau der Arbeitsverwaltung in den neuen Bundesländern und die Entwicklung des Arbeitsförderungsrechts seit 1989*, Opladen 1997, p. 10.
21. ibid., esp. pp. 17 f., 44. At regional level there were so-called labour and wages offices.
22. cf. Dr Detlev Grieswelle, head of Referat I a 1, Grundfragen der Sozial- und Gesellschaftspolitik, BMA, paper, Auf dem Weg zur Sozialunion im Deutschen Einigungs prozess. Sozialgemeinschaft versus Abschottung, pp. 15 f., not dated, BMA, I a 7, 12411.
23. Direktive für die Tätigkeit der Delegation des Ministeriums für Arbeit und Löhne beim Kennenlernen der Beschäftigungspolitik der Republik Österreich, 2 January 1990, BArch, DQ 3, 1836.
24. Verordnung, 8 February 1990, *GBl I*, 1990, p. 41.
25. Regierungserklärung von Modrow in der Volkskammer, 20 February 1990, Prot. VK, 9. WP, 17. Tagung, 20/21 February 1990, p. 472.
26. Verordnung über die Gewährung von Vorruhestandsgeld, 8 February 1990, *GBl I*, 1990, p. 42.
27. Verordnung Über die Umschulung von Bürgern zur Sicherung einer Berufstätigkeit, 8 February 1990, *GBl I*, 1990, pp. 83 f.
28. Text in BMA VIII/I a 7, 17000, vol. ii. Cf. also Kinitz, *Aufbau*, pp. 27–9.
29. Verordnung über die Aufgaben, Rechte und Pflichten der Arbeitsämter und der Betriebe zur Sicherung des Rechts auf Arbeit, 8 March 1990, *GBl I*, 1990, pp. 161–4.
30. Heinrich Franke, 'Aufbau in den neuen Ländern', in *BArbBl* (1990), vol. 1, pp. 5–9 (here, p. 6). For the preparatory talks between the two ministries, cf. Karl Pröbsting and Gerhard Gröbner, Ergebnisse der Gespräche mit Vertretern des Ministeriums für Arbeit und Löhne der DDR, 6 February 1990, in BMA VIII/I a 7, 17000, vol. ii;

Ministerium für Arbeit und Löhne, Abteilung Arbeitskräfte, Protokoll der Beratung von Vertretern des Ministeriums für Arbeit und Löhne mit Vertretern des Bundesministeriums für Arbeit und Sozialordnung vom 6.2.1990, Berlin, 7 February 1990, BArch, DQ 3, 1836.

31. Kinitz, *Aufbau*, p. 45. There had been intensive preparatory deliberations about this on the Federal government side since February 1990. Cf., for example, express letter, BMA, signed by Ministerialdirektor Rosenmüller, head of Abteilung II Arbeitsmarktpolitik, Arbeitslosenversicherung und Ausländerpolitik, to Bundesministerien des Innern, der Finanzen und der Wirtschaft, with a consultative attachment, Aufbau eines Systems der Arbeitsförderung und der Arbeitslosenversicherung in der DDR, 21 February 1990. Alternatives considered were that the GDR, after the Volkskammer elections of 18 March 1990, should transfer labour market policy (including unemployment insurance) to the Federal Institute of Labour, or that a separate system should be created 'that [would] nevertheless lean as closely as possible on the systems of the Employment Promotion Law'. In the medium term, 'after a period of transition', the systems of the two states should be 'identical'. Since contribution revenues would not be adequate, the Federal government would have to assume liability for the predicted deficit of 6,770 million DM. This figure assumed administrative expenses of 1,500 million DM and 1.2 million recipients of benefits, including 450,000 recipients of unemployment benefit, 550,000 short-time workers, 120,000 people involved in job creation schemes, and 80,000 people undergoing job training. Cf. BMA VIII/I a 7, 17000, vol. ii.
32. Abteilungsleiter II (Arbeitsmarktpolitik, Arbeitslosenversicherung), BMA, Sitzung des Vorstandes der Bundesanstalt für Arbeit am 2./3.5.1990 in Berlin, 7 May 1990, BArch, B 149/400014. Regine Hildebrandt was a participant in the session.
33. Franke, 'Aufbau', p. 6; Hans-Ulrich Spree, *Der Sozialstaat eint. Zur sozialen Einheit Deutschlands—Entwicklungen und Eindrücke*, Baden-Baden 1994, esp. pp. 41–8.
34. On the problems arising with the restructuring—in particular, the lack of suitable buildings and offices and of 7,000 urgently needed additional members of staff—cf. Kittner, acting chairman of the Komitee für Volkskontrolle der DDR, to Ministerin Hildebrandt, 9 May 1990, with attachment, Prüfungsbericht über die Neugestaltung und Wirksamkeit der Arbeitsämter, 9 May 1990, BArch, DQ 3, 1836a.
35. cf. GDR Ministry of Health note, 8 March 1990, Sozialfürsorgeunterstützung als Mindestsicherung für Bürger ohne Anspruch auf Arbeitslosengeld, in BArch, DQ 1, 14919.
36. 4. Verordnung über Leistungen der Sozialfürsorge—4. Sozialfürsorgeverordnung, 8 March 1990, *GBl I*, 1990, pp. 165 f. Single persons were paid monthly support of 300 marks and married couples 500 marks, with a supplement of 60 marks for each dependent child.
37. *GBl I*, 1990, p. 107 f. According to §9 of the decree, four of the nine members of the supervisory board of a company, including one managerial employee, were to be nominated by the workforce, and another four by the shareholders; one member was to be selected by the representatives of the workforce and the shareholders on the supervisory board: March 1990, AdsD, 5/DGAi 002181.
38. Hans-Detlev Küller to Ernst Breit, 30 March 1990, with attachment of 29 March 1990, Gesetzgebung zur Unternehmensmitbestimmung in der DDR. §9 on co-determination was annulled by the State Treaty of 18 May 1990: cf. Staatsvertrag, Anlage III, p. 121.

39. cf. Peter Sander, *Interessenvertretung der Arbeitnehmer im Betrieb*, Opladen 1997, pp. 83 f.
40. ibid., pp. 90–3.
41. The representatives of the Trade Union Federation withdrew, as they failed to win support for their demands for a strengthening of works councils and of the position of trade unions within enterprises—demands which went much further than the regulations contained in the west German Works Constitution Law (*Betriebsverfassungsgesetz*). On this, and on the attempts by the Trade Union Federation and the Metal Workers' Union to obtain 'more co-determination' through GDR legislation, cf. Sander, *Interessenvertretung*, pp. 104–10.
42. Discussion of the draft law and copy of the text ibid., pp. 109–18, 239–53.
43. Staatsvertrag, Anlage III, p. 129.
44. cf. Rainer Weinert and Franz-Otto Gilles, *Der Zusammenbruch des Freien Deutschen Gewerkschaftsbundes (FDGB). Zunehmender Entscheidungsdruck, institutionalisierte Handlungsschwäche und Zerfall der hierarchischen Organisationsstruktur*, Wiesbaden 1999, pp. 71, 75–81; Walter Hantsche and Stefan Otte, 'Die Situation der Gewerkschaften der DDR nach der Wende und der Einfluss der gewerkschaftlichen Tätigkeit auf die Arbeits- und Sozialordnung', in *Aufbau der Verbände und Arbeitsgerichte*, ed. Walter Hantsche, Stefan Otte, Günter Hoffmann, *et al.*, Opladen 1997, pp. 9–87, esp. pp. 62–6; Schwarzer, *Arbeitsbeziehungen*, pp. 202–14.
45. Weinert and Gilles, *Zusammenbruch*, pp. 71 f., 92–7.
46. Hantsche and Otte, 'Situation', pp. 42–6.
47. Text of the constitutional amendments recommended by the conference and of the draft of a trade union law in Schwarzer, *Arbeitsbeziehungen*, pp. 477–84.
48. ibid., §§8, 11, 12, 20.
49. ibid., §§23, 25, 26.
50. ibid., §§5, 10.
51. Prot. VK, 9. WP, 18. Tagung, 6/7 March 1990, pp. 520–6; Gesetz zur Änderung der Verfassung der Deutschen Demokratischen Republik, 6 March 1990, *GBl I*, 1990, p. 109; Gesetz über die Rechte der Gewerkschaften in der Deutschen Demokratischen Republik, 6 March 1990, *GBl I*, pp. 110 f.
52. Manfred C. Hettlage, 'DDR—Gewerkschaftsgesetz. Ein Handstreich gegen das Volk. FDGB sichert seine Machtpositionen', in *Bayernkurier*, 17 March 1990; employers' president Murmann, 'DDR—Gewerkschaftsgesetz ohne Perspektive', in PDA, *Pressedienst der BDA*, no. 8, 7 March 1990; *Sozialbericht 1990*, p. 14. In an interview with Deutschlandfunk on 2 March 1990 Blüm described the draft trade union law approved by the trade union conference as a 'survival aid for the socialist planned economy', an 'obstacle to social unity', and an attempt to 'rescue the relics of socialism': cf. *BPA-Dok*, Text-Bull-RFTV-AA (87–95). On 24 April 1990 Blüm wrote to the former president of the Federal Employment Court, Gerhard Müller, that the trade union law 'constitutes an inappropriate attempt to prop up power that has not been democratically legitimized, and to carry it over into the new democracy': cf. ACDP, Bestand Blüm I 504/63.
53. Prot. VK, 9. WP, 18. Tagung, 6/7 March 1990, p. 548; cf. 'Grundlinie und Standpunkte für eine Sozialcharta', *Drucksache der VK*, 83, which was adopted with four minor amendments. Additional initiatives and proposed amendments by the individual groups of the Round Table were conveyed to the government for consideration. On the Social Charter, cf. also Thaysen (ed.), *Der Zentrale Runde Tisch der DDR*, esp. vol. iv, *Identitätsfindung*, pp. 963–95, and vol. v, *Dokumente*, pp. 493–608.

54. Prot. VK, 9. WP, 17. Tagung, 20/21 February 1990, pp. 471–4.
55. cf. Standpunkte der Regierung der Deutschen Demokratischen Republik zu sozialen Grundrechten im Sozialverbund Deutsche Demokratische Republik—Bundesrepublik Deutschland—Sozialcharta, BArch, DQ 3, 1884. The preamble to the Charter was the basis of the 'positions' (*Standpunkte*).
56. Böhm, speaking in the Volkskammer, Prot. VK, 9. WP, 18. Tagung, 6/7 March 1990, p. 546. Emphasis in the original.
57. Horst Seehofer, 'Das faule Ei vom Runden Tisch. Sozialisten lernen nichts dazu', in *Bayernkurier*, 17 March 1990.
58. Prot. VK, 9. WP, 18. Tagung, 6/7 March 1990, pp. 546 f.

7 The State Treaty on Monetary, Economic, and Social Union

1. Interview with Lafontaine headed 'Nicht das Weggehen prämieren, sondern das Dableiben', *Süddeutsche Zeitung*, 25/26 November 1989.
2. Schäuble, *Vertrag*, pp. 65–78.
3. cf. above, pp. 14 f.; *Der Tagesspiegel*, 11 November 2006.
4. Arbeitspapier, Projektgruppe 'Sozialpolitische Aspekte des Wandels im deutsch-deutschen Verhältnis', 1 December 1989, BMA VIII/I a 7, 17000, vol. i. Cf. also head of Abteilung IV, BMA, Niemeyer to Abteilung I, with attachment, Aktuelle sozialversicherungsrechtliche Probleme in Berlin und in den Grenzgebieten zur DDR durch Öffnung der deutsch-deutschen Grenze, BArch, B 149/78941.
5. Punktation für Gespräche zwischen beiden deutschen Staaten im Bereich der Sozialpolitik, 22 December 1989, BArch, B 149/78950. Cf. also Sasdrich, Abteilung IV, BMA, to Abteilung I, 22 December 1989, BArch, B 149/78950.
6. Telex from Dr Lucas, Ständige Vertretung der Bundesrepublik in Ostberlin etc. to Staatssekretär Jagoda, BMA, on 'Gespräche zwischen den Arbeitsministerien der Bundesrepublik Deutschland und der DDR am 3. Januar 1990 in Berlin (Ost)', 8 January 1990, BArch, B 136/21660.
7. cf. Staatssekretär Bernhard Jagoda, BMA, to the GDR deputy Minister für Arbeit und Löhne, Dr Jürgen Kaminski, 24 January 1990, BArch, B 149/78950.
8. Abteilung I, BMA, Vermerk über 'Verhandlungskonzeption für das 2. Gespräch mit Vertretern des Ministeriums für Arbeit und Löhne der DDR am 30./31. Januar 1990', 29 January 1990, BArch, 149/78950.
9. Ministerialdirektor Niemeyer, head of Abteilung IV, Sozialversicherung, Sozialgesetzbuch des BMA, to Staatssekretär Jagoda, BMA, on the meeting of Arbeitsgruppe 'Grenzüberschreitende Beschäftigung' on 12/13 February 1990 in east Berlin, 14 February 1990, BArch, B 149/78950, with record of session of 12 February 1990.
10. Blüm to Kohl, 12 December 1989, ACDP, Bestand Blüm I 504/57.
11. Parlamentarischer Staatssekretär, BMA, Wolfgang Vogt, to Kanzleramtsminister Rudolf Seiters, 9 January 1990, BArch, 136/21660.
12. Seiters to Blüm, 31 January 1990, BArch, B 136/21660.
13. On the make-up and work of the 'Leistungsgesetze' working group, cf. the letter from Blüm to the chairman of the CDU/CSU parliamentary party in the Bundestag, Alfred Dregger, 5 February 1990, ACDP, Bestand Blüm I 504/60, and the working paper, Auf dem Weg zur Sozialunion, BMA, I a 7, 12411.
14. cf. Grosser, *Wagnis*, esp. pp. 149–88; Erik Gawel in collaboration with Markus Grünewald and Michael Thöne, *Die deutsch-deutsche Währungsunion. Verlauf und geldpolitische Konsequenzen*, Baden-Baden 1994, esp. pp. 148–60. For contemporary criticisms by economists, cf. letter of the Council of Economic Experts to the Federal Chancellor,

9 February 1990, in Jahresgutachten 1990/91 des Sachverständigenrates zur Begutachtung der gesamtwirtschaftlichen Entwicklung, *Auf dem Wege zur wirtschaftlichen Einheit Deutschlands*, BTDrs 11/8472, n.d. (13 November 1990), pp. 306–8.

15. An otherwise over-optimistic working paper of the Federal Ministry of Economics, 7 August 1990 noted: 'If wages run ahead of the expected sharp rise in production, then the basis for an atmosphere of a new start in the GDR will be removed. From this point of view, current pay agreements very questionable.' BArch, B 136/20252.
16. Interview with Pöhl headed 'Wir sind im Jahre 1990 überrumpelt worden', in *Süddeutsche Zeitung*, 29 June 2000; report of a symposium on the process of transformation in east Germany held at the Akademie für Politische Bildung, Tutzing, under the title 'Blühende Landschaften?', in *Süddeutsche Zeitung*, 30 May 2000.
17. cf. Grosser, *Wagnis*, pp. 496–504, which argues that abandonment of unification would have been the only alternative to the policy of the Federal government. Norbert Kloten, president of the *Land* central bank of Baden-Württemberg, similarly held that in February 1990 there was 'no realistic alternative' to the government's proposal: cf. 'Vortrag von Prof. Norbert Kloten im Rahmen einer Ringvorlesung an der Universität Tübingen am 11. Januar 1996', in Deutsche Bundesbank, *Auszüge aus Presseartikeln*, no. 8, 5 February 1996, pp. 11–17.
18. Hans Tietmeyer, 'Erinnerungen an die Vertragsverhandlungen', in *Tage, die Deutschland und die Welt veränderten. Vom Mauerfall zum Kaukasus. Die deutsche Währungsunion*, ed. Theo Waigel and Manfred Schell, Munich 1994, pp. 57–117 (here, p. 66).
19. Blüm to Federal Chancellor Kohl, 9 February 1990, with attachment, Entwurf von Fragen des Bundeskanzlers an Ministerpräsident Modrow, Bereich: Sozial-Union, BArch, B 136/21660. Both Staatssekretär Tegtmeier, in an interview with the author on 13 July 2000, and Bernhard Jagoda, in an interview with the author on 5 July 2000, said emphatically that it was Blüm who had been primarily responsible within the Federal government for securing the addition of the social union to the offer to the GDR. 'Without Blüm', Jagoda said, 'the social union would not have happened at that time—later, perhaps.' Blüm himself, in an interview with the author on 8 June 2000, stressed that the model of the Social Market economy that was offered to the GDR would not have been able to function without the social components. A letter of 12 February 1990 from the head of the private office of the Labour Ministry, Johannes Vöcking, to Manfred Oßwald states that Blüm had proposed that the Federal Chancellor's initiative for the creation of a monetary union should be 'complemented by a social reform, within the framework of which the GDR could follow our system of social security': ACDP, Bestand Blüm I 504/60.
20. 'Anschubfinanzierung durch den Steuerzahler', in *Handelsblatt*, 12 February 1990.
21. Rudolf Kolb and Franz Ruland, 'Die Rentenversicherung in einem sich einigenden Deutschland', in *DRV*, vol. 3, March 1990, pp. 141–53.
22. ibid., p. 148.
23. ibid., p. 150. Through compensation for migration, account would be taken of the fact that west German pensions insurance had received an increase in contributions of more than 500 million DM as a result of the arrival of predominantly young and well-trained people in 1989, the increase being offset by relatively small expenditures for pensioners who had arrived in 1989.
24. ibid., p. 149.
25. On the establishment and work of the commission, cf. Thilo Sarrazin, 'Die Entstehung und Umsetzung des Konzepts der deutschen Wirtschafts- und Währungsunion', in *Tage*, pp. 160–225 (here, pp. 192–8).

26. cf. Zentralabteilung Referat ZbI, BMA, to the departments and other organizational units of the BMA, with an Erlass zur Errichtung des Arbeitsstabes von Staatssekretär Jagoda vom 18.2.1990, 27 February 1990, BMA VIII I a 7, 17000, vol. 2.
27. Norbert Blüm, 'Schritt für Schritt—Die Netze müssen langsam verknüpft werden', in *Die Welt*, 2 March 1990.
28. Zwischenbericht der Expertenkommission zur Vorbereitung einer Währungsunion und Wirtschaftsgemeinschaft zwischen der Deutschen Demokratischen Republik und der Bundesrepublik Deutschland, 13 March 1990, signed by the Minister Dr Romberg as head of the GDR delegation and Staatssekretär Dr Köhler as head of the Federal Republic delegation, BArch, B 149/78925.
29. In addition to the Zwischenbericht, cf. Vermerk über das Gespräch zwischen Herrn Dr. Barleben und Frau Dr. Wenzel (Gesundheitsministerium der DDR), Herrn Dr. Noack (zeitweise) und Herrn Steiniger and Herrn Streppel (BMJFFG) am 1.3.1990, 2 March 1990, signed by Streppel and Steiniger, BArch, B 149/78930.
30. cf. Frerich and Frey, *Handbuch*, vol. ii, p. 369.
31. Report by Arbeitsgruppe 'Angleichung der Arbeits- und Sozialordnung sowie der Bildung und Ausbildung' for the cabinet committee 'Deutsche Einheit', 6 March 1990, BArch, B 136/20251. For the negotiations, cf. Ergebnisvermerk über die erste Sitzung der Arbeitsgruppe 'Angleichung der Arbeits- und Sozialordnung sowie der Bildung und Ausbildung' am 14.2.1990 im BMA, BArch, B 149/78960; Referat I a 1 des BMA, mit 'Niederschrift der Sitzung der Arbeitsgruppe am 28.2.1990', 23 March 1990, BArch, B 149/78963; Entwurf einer Vorlage der vorbereitenden Arbeitsgruppe: 'Angleichung der Arbeits- und Sozialordnung sowie der Bildung und Ausbildung' für den Kabinettsausschuss 'Deutsche Einheit', 1 March 1990, BMA VIII, I a 7, 17000, vol. ii.
32. Working paper, 'Arbeitslosenversicherung', 24 February 1990, BMF, Referat II c 1, BArch, B 126/114047.
33. cf. working paper, 'Rentenversicherung', BMF, Referat II c 1, and the added Überlegungen zum finanziellen Ausgleich der bundesdeutschen Rentenversicherung und zugunsten der ostdeutschen Rentenversicherung. The paper, dated February 1990, is a response to the Labour Ministry draft of 20 February 1990: BArch, B 126/114047. On the attitude of the Finance Ministry, cf. also '*Vermerk*' für die Sitzung des Kabinettsausschusses 'Deutsche Einheit am 7.3.1990', Referat II c 1, BMF, 6 March 1990. For the initial position of the Finance Ministry at the beginning of February, cf. Umgestaltung in der DDR und dort resultierende soziale Belastungen—Abhilfe durch die Bundesrepublik?, Referat I a 8, 2 February 1990, BArch B 126/114047 and working paper, Kabinettsauschuss 'Deutsche Einheit', Referat II c 1, BMF, 12 February 1990, BArch, B 126/114047.
34. Ergebnisvermerk über die Sitzung vom 14.2.1990, BArch, B 149/78960.
35. Bundesminister des Innern, VtK I 6, Stellungnahme zur Frage der rentenrechtlichen Gleichbehandlung von Übersiedlern und Aussiedlern, 1 March 1990, BArch, B 136/20251. Cf. also paper by Gerhard Schulte, head of Gruppe 31 (Grundfragen der Sozial- und Gesellschaftspolitik), Bundeskanzleramt, Zur Vorbereitung des Koalitionsgesprächs am 6.3.1990 für die von der CSU angemeldeten Fragen zu Aus- und Übersiedlern, sent to Chef des Bundeskanzleramtes, 5 March 1990, BArch, B 136/20251; Blüm to Kohl, 15 March 1990, with attachment, Positions- und Entscheidungspapier zu Änderungen im Fremdrentenrecht und in der Arbeitslosenversicherung für Aus- und Übersiedler, BArch, B 136/20251.
36. BMF, Referat II c 1, Gesetzliche Krankenversicherung, 23 February 1990, BArch, B 126/114047.

37. Ergebnisvermerk über die Sitzung vom 14.2.1990, BArch, B 149/78960. Cf. also KOV/KOF. Stellungnahme des BMF zum BMA-Papier vom 22 Februar 1990, 23 February 1990, BArch, B 126/114047.
38. cf. Grosser, *Wagnis*, pp. 245–51.
39. On this, and the following points, cf. Bericht über 'Meinungen und Fakten zum Umstellungskurs M:DM' des Referatsleiters, MinRat Sykora, an den Leiter der Gruppe 51 (Gesellschaftliche und politische Analysen) im Bundeskanzleramt, Dr. Gotto, 4 April 1990, BArch, B 136/24454.
40. cf. *Frankfurter Rundschau*, 31 March 1990.
41. Blüm to Kohl, 27 March 1990, with attachment, Zum Umtauschverhältnis für Löhne und die Folgen für die soziale Sicherung, ACDP, Bestand Blüm I 504/62. The letter is published in *Dokumente zur Deutschlandpolitik*, pp. 979 f., but without the attachment (not held in the relevant files, but contained among Blüm's papers). On Blüm's commitment on the question of the conversion, cf. also his letter to the president of the German Industry and Commerce Conference, Hans Peter Stihl, 4 May 1990, in which he cites the 37:100 ratio in labour costs between the GDR and the Federal Republic as a further justification for his view: ACDP, Bestand Blüm I 504/64.
42. Interview with Blüm by the author, 8 June 2000.
43. Attachment, Zum Umtauschverhältnis.
44. Introduction to *Dokumente zur Deutschlandpolitik*, p. 143.
45. Interview with Jagoda by the author, 5 July 2000.
46. Grosser, *Wagnis*, pp. 288 f., with the text of the 12-point declaration of the two governments. The arithmetical average overall conversion rate was 1.8:1: this corresponded to 14.7 per cent of the west German M3 money supply, higher than the 10 per cent proportion regarded as appropriate. The M3 money supply includes money in savings accounts and bank credits as well as cash. Cf. Gawel, *Die deutsch-deutsche Währungsunion*, pp. 163–5.
47. Charles S. Meier, *Dissolution: The Crisis of Communism and the End of East Germany*, Princeton 1997, pp. 237 f.
48. Abteilung III, BMA, to Abteilung I, 26 March 1990, BArch, B 149/405234.
49. BMF, Referat II c 1, Positionspapier zur Angleichung der Arbeits- und Sozialordnung, 29 March 1990, BArch, B 126/114047.
50. Erste Skizze für einen Vorschlag an die DDR. Vertrag über die Schaffung einer Währungsunion, Wirtschafts- und Sozialgemeinschaft zwischen der Bundesrepublik Deutschland und der Deutschen Demokratischen Republik, 4 April 1990, BArch, B 136/21664. In the sketch the controversial points are enclosed within square brackets.
51. Copy of working paper in *Dokumente zur Deutschlandpolitik*, pp. 1034–44. The text of the joint Protokoll über Leitsätze zum Vertrag über die Schaffung einer Währungsunion, Wirtschafts- und Sozialgemeinschaft used here is not that reproduced in *Dokumente zur Deutschlandpolitik* (pp. 1045–9), which gives the state of the document on 17 April 1990, but that in a paper in the Archiv der Sozialen Demokratie (AdsD) of the Friedrich-Ebert-Stiftung, Bestand: SPD-Fraktion in der Volkskammer der DDR, Mappe 26. The latter, unlike the former, includes, as attachment II, the list of 'In der Deutschen Demokratischen Republik anzuwendenden Rechtsvorschriften' (legal provisions to be applied in the GDR) that were important with regard to questions concerning the 'social community' (*Sozialgemeinschaft*).
52. 'Informationsvermerk über den Stand der Besprechungen zum Staatsvertrag' to the Minister, with copies to the Parlamentarische Staatssekretäre and Staatssekretäre, BMA, 3 April 1990, BArch, B 149/78837. Cf. also draft of letter from Blüm to Waigel,

3 April 1990, BArch, B 149/78837. For the position of the Finance Ministry, cf. the undated 'Non-paper', with handwritten heading 'Stellungnahme BMF', which was noted by Sasdrich on 18 April: BArch, B 149/78841.

53. Referat II c 1, Vertrag über die Schaffung einer Währungsunion, Wirtschafts- und Sozialgemeinschaft D/DDR (Stand 4.4.1990): here, Kapitel IV-Sozialgemeinschaft, 3 April 1990. The paper lists the points at dispute between the Finance and Labour Ministries, BArch, B 126/1140048.
54. cf. Ergebnisvermerk der Besprechung der Staatssekretäre zum Staatsvertrag am 11. April 1990 im Kanzleramt, meeting chaired by Tietmeyer, BArch, B 149/78840. Cf. also Positionspapier zur Vorbereitung des Ministergesprächs am 19.4., sent by head of Unterabteilung I b, BMA, Ministerialdirigent Dr Peter Rosenberg, with accompanying letter of 19 April to Blüm; the position paper contains a 'Verzeichnis der streitigen Punkte' regarding the chapter on the social community in the State Treaty; BArch, B 149/78840. A revised version of this paper, 20 April, including *inter alia* a table on 'Höhe der Versichertenrenten 1990 in der DDR nach Altersjahren und Zugangsjahren': BArch, B 149/78840.
55. Tietmeyer, 'Errinerungen', in Waigel and Schell (eds.), *Tage*, p. 72; Grosser, *Wagnis*, p. 264.
56. BMF, Referat II c 1, Entwurf eines Vertragsgesetzes zu dem Vertrag über die Schaffung einer Währungs-, Wirtschafts- und Sozialunion zwischen der Bundesrepublik Deutschland und der Deutschen Demokratischen Republik, 9 May 1990, BArch, B 126/114048.
57. Staatsvertrag, Artikel 20.
58. cf. above, p. 63.
59. Working paper, attachment II: In der DDR in Kraft zu setzende Rechtsvorschriften, Teil IV: Sozialgemeinschaft, No. 4 and No. 12, 24 April 1990. In the final text these exceptions were eliminated.
60. Tietmeyer, 'Erinnerungen', in Waigel and Schell (eds.), *Tage*, pp. 106 f.
61. Grundsätze der Koalitionsvereinbarung. For the Labour Ministry's assessment of the coalition agreement of 12 April 1990, cf. Abteilung I to the Minister, with copies to the Staatssekretäre, Synoptische Darstellung der Positionen zur Sozialunion in der Koalitionsvereinbarung der DDR-Regierungsparteien und in dem zu diesem Zeitpunkt vorliegenden Entwurf der Bundesregierung zum Staatsvertrag, 17 April 1990. This synopsis was to serve as preparation for discussions between Blüm and Hildebrandt; BArch, B 149/78840.
62. cf. Articles 24, 25, and 37, in *Die neue Verfassung der DDR mit einem einleitenden Kommentar von Dietrich Müller-Römer*, Cologne 1974.
63. cf. above, pp. 61 f.
64. Referat III a 1, BMA, Koalitionsvereinbarung der neuen DDR-Regierung: Arbeitsrechtlicher Teil, sent to Blüm with copies to the Staatssekretäre and Abteilung I, 20 April 1990, BArch, B 149/78840.
65. See the attachment to the note on the coalition agreement (cf. note 64 above), Bericht über 'Gespräche mit Vertretern des Ministeriums für Arbeit und Löhne' vom 9.–11. April 1990 im BMA, BArch, B 149/78840.
66. Stellungnahme des BMF, BArch, B 149/78841.
67. cf. undated note on Sitzung der Arbeitsgruppe 'Sozialpolitik' zur Vorbereitung des Koalitionsvertrages, AdsD, Bestand: SPD-Fraktion in der Volkskammer der DDR, Mappe 5.

68. Letter, Bundesrechnungshof to Bundesminister für Arbeit und Sozialordnung, 24 April 1990, BArch, DQ 3, 1881. In its call for the merging of the white- and blue-collar insurance organizations, the Federal Audit Office also expressly refers to the support of 'the Federal Commissioner for Economy in Administration'.
69. ibid.
70. cf. 'Bye, bye BfA!', in *Der Tagesspiegel*, 19 September 2005.
71. In addition to the coalition agreement, cf. notes by the Arbeitsgruppen 'Soziales und Gesundheit' and 'Sozialpolitik' on the preparation of the treaty, AdsD, Bestand: SPD-Fraktion in der Volkskammer der DDR, Mappe 5.
72. Arbeitsgruppe Innerdeutsche Beziehungen, Regierungsdirektor Radermacher, Abteilung I, Bewertende Zusammenfassung der Koalitionsvereinbarung der Regierungsparteien der DDR, BArch, B 126/114048.
73. Dietrich Stobbe, note of 17 April 1990, concerning Entscheidungs- und Handlungsbedarf für die Sozialdemokraten in der Bundesrepublik und in der DDR nach Bildung der Koalitionsregierung in Berlin (Ost), AdsD, Bestand: SPD-Fraktion in der Volkskammer der DDR, Mappe 113.
74. Ergebnisprotokoll der Sitzung des Geschäftsführenden Vorstandes der SPD am 12. März 1990 im Reichstagsgebäude Berlin, AdsD, 15624. For Stobbe's close cooperation with the east German Social Democrats, cf. his letter of 25 April 1990 to the GDR Foreign Minister, Markus Meckel, and to the chairman of the SPD party in the Volkskammer, Richard Schröder, and the list, sent by Schröder to Vogel on 26 April 1990, of members of the Volkskammer party responsible for 'cooperation on State Treaty matters': AdsD, Bestand: SPD-Fraktion in der Volkskammer der DDR, Mappen 113 and 132.
75. cf. Stobbe's letter of 30 May 1990 to the chairman of the SPD party in the Volkskammer, Richard Schröder, in which he complains about the lack of contact between the GDR Minister of Labour and Social Affairs, Regine Hildebrandt, and the SPD party in the Bundestag during her previous three visits to Bonn: 'Rudolf Dreßler is very put out about it—particularly as he has helped your Social Affairs Minister so very closely. This applies to the social area in the coalition agreement—just as to the State Treaty. Rudolf Dreßler also objects to the fact that Regine has publicly thanked Blüm several times for his help without also mentioning the help given by the SPD party in the Bundestag.' AdsD, Bestand: SPD-Fraktion in der Volkskammer der DDR, Mappe 113.
76. Rudolf Dreßler, Sozialpolitische Folgeprobleme der Entwicklung in der DDR. Erste Überlegungen. Stand: 21. Dezember 1989—Vorlage für die Sitzung der SPD-Bundestagsfraktion am 23.1.1990, AdsD, 17652.
77. Rudolf Dreßler, Diskussionspapier: Vereinheitlichung der Rentenversicherung von Bundesrepublik und DDR, 20 February 1990, AdsD, 17652.
78. Rudolf Dreßler, Erste Schritte zur Sozialunion Bundesrepublik Deutschland—DDR, Diskussionspapier, Stand: 5 Marz 1990. The paper carries the annotation, Vorlage für die Sitzungen der Fraktion am 12./13.3.1990 in Berlin; AdsD, 17652. At the meeting of the executive committee of the SPD on 12 March 1990 the draft was 'noted, with agreement, as a discussion paper' and it was decided to present it to the parliamentary party leadership and the parliamentary party. At the meeting Dreßler also reported on a conversation with Blüm 'on the state of the Federal government's thinking with regard to the development of a common employment and social order between the two German states': Ergebnisprotokoll der Sitzung, AdsD, 15624.
79. Dreßler to Hildebrandt, 26 April 1990, with attachment, Änderungsvorschläge zum Bereich 'Sozialunion' im Entwurf des Staatsvertrages BRD/DDR (endgültiger Stand

24. April 1990), AdsD, Bestand: SPD-Fraktion in der Volkskammer der DDR, Mappe 5. Dreßler spoke in similar terms in the Bundestag on 27 April 1990. It was understandable, he said, that the GDR government would not accept this draft 'just like that', seeing that real wages would be 'cut by one-quarter': Prot. BT, 11. WP, p. 16423.

80. cf. letter of 10 May 1990, from Dieter-Julius Cronenberg, member and vice-president of the Bundestag, to the director of the Bundesbank, Dr Tietmeyer, concerning the ideas on social policy that the FDP wanted to see taken into account in the State Treaty. A carbon copy of this letter, with additional comments on works constitution regulations and on co-determination law, was sent to Staatssekretär Jagoda at the Labour Ministry, also on 10 May. Both letters in BArch, B 149/78841.
81. According to the note, there was effectively no trace of the spirit of overcoming 'division [*Teilung*] through sharing [*Teilen*]' that Prime Minister de Maizière had called for. 'Rather, the Federal Republic was to be released from as many burdens as possible.' The note recommended that the negotiations on the draft treaty should be conducted under the proviso that a state treaty not containing clarifications of the central questions itemized, including a sharing of burdens between the populations of the Federal Republic and the GDR, would not be meaningful. Cf. Vermerk: Betr. Arbeitspapier für die Gespräche mit der DDR pp. vom 24.4.90, BArch, DC-20/6007.
82. cf. a document with the handwritten heading 'Gegenvorschläge der DDR zum Staatsvertrag', in which the amendments and additions to chapter V of the draft of 24 April 1990 sought by the GDR are indicated by underlinings: BMA VIII, 17000, vol. 2.
83. cf. revised record of the parliamentary party meeting of 8 May 1990, with report by Vogel, Zum Stand der Verhandlungen und Diskussionen über den Staatsvertrag, AdsD, 9602.
84. cf. Grosser, *Wagnis*, p. 292.
85. Zuarbeit aus dem Kreis der SPD-Minister für die Erarbeitung einer gemeinsamen Verhandlungsposition des Ministerrates der DDR zum Vertrag über die Schaffung einer Währungsunion, Wirtschafts- und Sozialgemeinschaft zwischen der Bundesrepublik Deutschland und der Deutschen Demokratischen Republik, 2 May 1990, AdsD, Bestand: SPD-Fraktion in der Volkskammer der DDR, Mappe 27. This 'Zuarbeit' (groundwork) largely took over the GDR's 'counter-proposals' previously mentioned, but went beyond them in some respects, particularly regarding the burden to be placed on the Federal Republic. On the evolution of the eastern SPD's policy towards the State Treaty, cf. also Stobbe's report to Vogel and the chairman of the SPD parliamentary party, Gerhard Jahn, 30 April 1990. This letter indicates that a coordinating group comprising three representatives each of the party council, the party executive and the parliamentary party, a standing coordinating group of SPD cabinet members under the chairmanship of Markus Meckel and attended by the parliamentary party leader Richard Schröder, the parliamentary party executive, and the parliamentary party were to discuss the state of the negotiations on the State Treaty between 30 April and 2 May: AdsD, Bestand: SPD-Fraktion in der Volkskammer der DDR, Mappe 113.
86. Abteilung I, BMA, signed by Abteilungsleiter Ministerialdirektor Stahl, to the Minister, with copies to the Staatssekretäre, 7 May 1990, BArch, B 149/78841. A note of 8 May 1990 by Tietmeyer and Johannes Ludewig (the Ministerialrat responsible, as head of Gruppe 42, for economic policy in the Federal Chancellery), written in preparation for a coalition discussion of 9 May on the State Treaty, says with regard to the social union: 'Owing to differences of opinion within the GDR government (SPD resistance!), important points in this chapter remain unresolved. The central problem is that although the GDR SPD wishes to adopt in full the benefits in our social insurance

system, it wants to move only gradually to our level of corresponding contributions. At the same time, the GDR would like to retain in full all existing social benefits in the GDR. The SPD is opposed to *berufsständische Versorgungswerke* [organizations for support of the elderly in particular professions].' In *Dokumente zur Deutschlandpolitik*, pp. 1098–100.

87. cf. Grosser, *Wagnis*, pp. 291 f.
88. On the local government elections of 6 May 1990, cf. Falter, 'Wahlen 1990', pp. 174 f.
89. cf. the compilation of the positions of the GDR government on the State Treaty 'auf der Grundlage der Koalitionsvereinbarung' in the area of social policy, sent by Hildebrandt to de Maizière on 7 May 1990, BArch, DC-20/6008; Vermerk, 3 May 1990, for the meeting of Staatssekretäre on 7 May 1990 on 'wesentliche Problempunkte mit der DDR im Bereich des Arbeits- und Sozialrechts', BArch, B 136/21660; Strittige Punkte bei den Staatsvertragsverhandlungen/Thema Sozialunion zwischen BRD und DDR, 10 May 1990, AdsD, 9602 (the latter document probably relates to a paper by the SPD parliamentary party in the Bundestag). See also 'Wesentliche Veränderungen' im Vertragsentwurf, Stand 12.5.1990, BArch, DC-2-/6007; Vorlage von Tietmeyer und Ludewig an Bundeskanzler Kohl für die Tagung der CDU-Gremien am 14.5. und Kohls Gespräch mit de Maizière, 13 May 1990, with three attachments, including a compilation of the most important points of compromise in the State Treaty, in *Dokumente zur Deutschlandpolitik*, pp. 1108–18; 'Informationsvermerk' zum Entwurf eines Staatsvertrages mit der DDR über die Errichtung einer Währungs-, Wirtschafts- und Sozialunion, 14 May 1990, BArch, B 149/78842; Besprechung des Bundeskanzlers Kohl mit den Regierungsschefs der Länder, 16 May 1990, in *Dokumente zur Deutschlandpolitik*, pp. 1122–5.
90. cf. above, pp. 55 f.
91. DGB-Bundesvorstand, 30 April 1990, Erste Bewertung des Entwurfs der Bundesregierung für einen Staatsvertrag mit der DDR: 'The Federation is firmly opposed to the admission, for the first time, of lockouts, which, even within the legal system of the Federal Republic, are not permitted by legislation but only through court decisions'; AdsD, Bestand: SPD-Fraktion in der Volkskammer der DDR, Mappe 27.
92. Following the 10 May 1990 coalition meeting on the State Treaty, Cronenberg of the FDP, at the Chancellor's request, informed Tietmeyer of the important points as the FDP saw them. These included the fact that 'the Federal government is seeking the very rapid establishment of a multipartite social insurance system based on Federal German criteria. This means that a division between white- and blue-collar workers will have to be effected in the GDR, corresponding to our social insurance system.' 'We also believe that the creation of a multipartite health insurance system by 31 December 1990 is absolutely necessary.' BArch, B 149/78841.
93. The paragraph on organizations for pensions in certain professions was included in the draft treaty following the intervention of Tietmeyer with Staatssekretär Jagoda of the Labour Ministry: cf. Ministerialdirektor Niemeyer, head of Abteilung IV, BMA, to Regierungsdirektor Sasdrich, 24 April 1990, BArch, B 149/78841.
94. cf. letter, chairman of the Arbeitsgruppe 'Arbeit und Soziales' of the CDU/CSU parliamentary party, Horst Günther, to Staatssekretär Jagoda, BMA, 10 May 1990, BArch, B 149/78841. The demand that in addition to a contributions ceiling, a ceiling for compulsory membership be set, 'in accordance with the principles of social insurance law of the Federal Republic', had not been included in the draft.

95. cf. Überlegungen zur Notwendigkeit eines personenbezogenen Preisausgleichs für die unteren Einkommensgruppen, vor allem Rentner, 29 April 1990, BArch, DC-20/6007.
96. Article 20, paragraph 2 of the treaty stated that claims and expectancies relating to these systems should be scrutinized, with the aim of 'abolishing unwarranted benefits and reducing the levels of excessive benefits. Additional expenditures on the part of [statutory] pensions insurance arising as a result of transfers [from these systems] shall be reimbursed out of the state budget.'
97. cf. Rentenangleichungsgesetz, 28 June 1990. Appendix to §§2 and 10 of the law in *GBl I*, 1990, p. 500.
98. cf. point 4 of the two governments' 12-point declaration on the currency changeover, 2 May 1990, reproduced in Grosser, *Wagnis*, pp. 288 f.; interview with Jagoda by the author, 5 July 2000, and with Hildebrandt, 31 May 2000.
99. Frerich and Frey, *Handbuch*, vol. iii, p. 527.
100. It was clearly assumed at first by the Federal government that the requirement placed on the GDR in the State Treaty (though not in the working paper of 24 April 1990) to introduce an income support law would obviate the need for compensatory payment for those on small pensions. Cf. Vorlage von Tietmeyer und Ludewig an Bundeskanzler Kohl für die Tagung der CDU-Gremien am 14.5. und Kohls Gespräch mit de Maizière, 13 May 1990, with three attachments, including a compilation of the most important points of compromise in the State Treaty, in *Dokumente zur Deutschlandpolitik*, pp. 1108–14. In fact, even after the introduction of an income support law in the GDR, the social allowance initially remained in place.
101. Frerich and Frey, *Handbuch*, vol. iii, pp. 603, 624. In her interview with the author (31 May 2000), Regine Hildebrandt stated that she was responsible for implementing this regulation.
102. On the effects of the currency changeover, cf. Beispiele für die Änderung von Nettolöhnen bei der Umstellung von 1:1 und gleichzeitiger Anwendung des Steuer- und Sozialversicherungsrechts der Bundesrepublik Deutschland, BArch, B 149/74907. The formulations were circulated on 15 May 1990.
103. Minister Kleditzsch to Parlamentarische Staatssekretär Krause, 3 May 1990, BArch, DQ 1, 14920.
104. Kohl, meeting of CDU/CSU parliamentary party, 15 May 1990, ACDP, Fraktionsprotokolle.
105. Heinrich August Winkler, *Der lange Weg nach Westen*, vol. ii, *Deutsche Geschichte vom 'Dritten Reich' bis zur Wiedervereinigung*, Munich 2000, p. 571. For Lafontaine's attitude, cf. also Oskar Lafontaine, *Deutsche Wahrheiten. Die nationale und die soziale Frage*, Hamburg 1990, esp. pp. 174–84, 187–215.
106. Hans-Jochen Vogel, *Nachsichten. Meine Bonner und Berliner Jahre*, paperback edn., Munich/Zurich 1997, pp. 332 f.
107. Grosser, *Wagnis*, p. 316.
108. Stobbe to Vogel and Jahn, 30 April 1990, AdsD, Bestand: SPD-Fraktion in der Volkskammer der DDR, Mappe 113. However, the coordinated approach by the Social Democrats in the two states urged by Stobbe and Richard Schröder did not materialize. If the west German Social Democrats had rejected the treaty after it had been signed by the coalition government in the GDR, that would have been tantamount to a disavowal of their sister party in the east.
109. Presseservice der SPD, 21 May 1990, 205/90. Cf. also the text of the interview of Vogel with Deutschlandfunk, 22 May 1990, in Presseservice der SPD, 206/90.

110. For the opposing position, cf. the working paper sent to the SPD members of parliament by Andreas von Bülow and Norbert Wieczorek on 21 May 1990, in which they set out, in the form of 17 points, their view that the introduction of a market economy without a transition period would be a 'hysterectomy' carried out on a 'patient reduced to a critical condition' by the SED leadership and would hence be 'irresponsible': AdsD, 9604.
111. Winkler, *Weg*, vol. ii, p. 572. Text of the unsent letter in Oskar Lafontaine, *Das Herz schlägt links*, Munich 1999, pp. 18–21.
112. On the negotiations, cf. Grosser, *Wagnis*, pp. 317–19; text of an interview with Vogel by the Bonn correspondent of the Bayerischer Rundfunk, Dietmar Merten, reproduced under the title 'Unsere energischen Forderungen zum Staatsvertrag haben deutliche Bewegungen erbracht', in Die SPD im Deutschen Bundestag 1221, 1 June 1990, AdsD, 9608; Gespräch des Bundesministers Schäuble und des Bundesministers Waigel mit Vertretern der SPD, 6 June 1990, *Dokumente zur Deutschlandpolitik*, pp. 1182–4; Besprechung des Chefs des Bundeskanzleramtes, Seiters, mit den Chefs der Staats-und Senatskanzleien der Länder, 7 June 1990, ibid., pp. 1184–9; 'Mitteilung für die Presse' with comments by Vogel following a meeting of the SPD Presidency of 11 June 1990, no. 248/90, 11 June 1990, AdsD, 9608; Erklärung von Seiters nach einem Gespräch des Bundeskanzlers mit Vertretern der SPD am 12.6.1990, Presse- und Informationsamt der Bundesregierung, 12 June 1990, no. 250/90, in AdsD, 9608.
113. Stellungnahme des Bundesrates, BTDrs 11/7351, 7 June 1990, p. 2.
114. cf. Ergebnisprotokoll der Sitzung des Fraktionsvorstandes, 14 June 1990, AdsD, 17638; also 'Argumentationshilfe zum Staatsvertrag', signed by Gerhard Jahn and Eckhart Schlemm, 16 June 1990, entitled 'Von der SPD bewirkte Ergebnisse auf dem Weg zu einem sozialverträglichen und ökologisch orientierten einigen Deutschland', AdsD, Bestand: SPD-Fraktion in der Volkskammer der DDR, Mappe 74.
115. For the position of the majority of the parliamentary party, cf. the 'Erklärung der SPD-Bundestagsfraktion' made by Gerhard Jahn on 21 June 1990; for the minority, cf. their 'Erklärung zur Abstimmung gemäß §31 der Geschäftsordnung des Deutschen Bundestages', Prot. BT, 11. WP, pp. 17272 f.
116. All members of the CDU/CSU and the FDP who were present, together with two members of the Greens and one independent member, voted in favour of the treaty; the single abstention was by a member of the Greens: cf. Prot. BT, 11. WP, p. 17281. For the attitude of the Volkskammer, cf. Prot. VK, 10. WP, 16. Tagung, 21 June 1990, p. 625. The CDU/DA, the DSU, and the Liberals came out unanimously in support of the treaty. All of the SPD members voted in favour, except for the former leader, Ibrahim Böhme. Of the DBD/DFD group, 6 voted in favour and 2 against the treaty. Alliance 90/The Greens and the PDS (apart from Dr Herbert Richter, who abstained), voted against the treaty. The single member of the United Left also voted against. Cf. ibid., pp. 625–30.
117. For the election results, cf. above, pp. 31, 33.
118. August Bebel, 1840–1913: founder, with Wilhelm Liebknecht, of the Social Democratic Workers' Party (SDAP) in Eisenach in 1869, co-author of the 'Erfurt Programme' of the SPD in 1891, chairman of the SPD from 1892 to 1913.
119. Kurt Schumacher, 1895–1952: member of the SPD from 1918, imprisoned for many years in different concentration camps as a fierce opponent of the NSDAP, architect of the revival of the SPD in Hanover after 1945, chairman of the party from 1946 to 1952, leader of the opposition in the Bundestag from 1949 to 1952.

120. Copy of the letter in AdsD, Bestand: SPD-Fraktion in der Volkskammer der DDR, Mappe 42.

8 The Social Legislation of the de Maizière Government

1. Bundesarbeitsminister Blüm to Ministerin für Arbeit und Soziales der DDR Regine Hildebrandt, 24 April 1990, in ACDP, Bestand Blüm 1 504/63.
2. Interviews by the author with Regine Hildebrandt, 31 May 2000, and Alwin Ziel, 13 July 2000.
3. Spree, *Der Sozialstaat eint*, p. 103.
4. Gesetz über die Inkraftsetzung von Rechtsvorschriften der Bundesrepublik Deutschland in der Deutschen Demokratischen Republik, *GBl I*, 1990, pp. 357–63.
5. Gesetz zur Änderung und Ergänzung des Arbeitsgesetzbuches, *GBl I*, 1990, pp. 371–81. On the alterations, cf. also the fundamental contribution by Rolf Schwedes, who played a decisive role in the revision of the Labour Statute Book: 'Arbeitsgesetzbuch der DDR und seine Neufassung 1990', in *Entwicklungen im Arbeitsrecht und Arbeitsschutzrecht. Festschrift für Otfried Wlotzke zum 70. Geburtstag*, ed. Rudolf Anzinger and Rolf Wenk, Munich 1996, pp. 145–72.
6. cf. BMA, Abteilung III a 1 to Abteilung I, Konformität von DDR-Gesetzentwürfen mit dem Staatsvertrag (here, Gespräch des Ministers und Ministerin Hildebrandt am heutigen Tage), 31 May 1990, BArch, B 149/405234; BMA, Abteilung III a 1, to Staatssekretär Jagoda, with copies to the Minister and the Staatssekretäre, Abteilung I and Referat 6/I, Vergleich des DDR-Arbeitsrechts mit dem bundesdeutschen Arbeitsrecht, 31 May 1990, BArch, B 149/405234.
7. The conditions were that the woman should be married, or that the household should include children under 18 or family members needing care, or that the woman should have completed her 40th year (§185).
8. cf. speech by Hildebrandt introducing the draft law in the Volkskammer, in Prot. VK, 10. WP, 10. Tagung, 1 June 1990, p. 398.
9. cf. the speeches by Marlies Deneke for the PDS and Prof. Jens Reich for Alliance 90/ The Greens, ibid., pp. 399, 400 f.
10. Prot. VK, 10. WP, 10. Tagung, 1 June 1990, p. 402.
11. §613a of the Civil Code does not accept, in particular, change of ownership of an enterprise as a valid reason for dismissal. On the problems involved, cf. Blüm's letter to Cronenberg of 18 June 1990, which indicates that Cronenberg had criticized Blüm in a letter of 1 June 1990. In his reply Blüm pointed out that in crucial respects §613a of the Civil Code was based on the directive of the European Community Council on Harmonization of Regulations of Member States concerning the maintenance of claims and privileges of employees in the case of the transfer of undertakings (BTDrs 7/2312) and that the GDR had committed itself to 'gradually adapting its policy to European community law': ACDP, Bestand Blüm I 504/66. He made a similar point in his reply of 21 August 1990 to a letter of 13 July 1990 (sent as a copy) by the president of the Federal Association of German Industry, Dr Tyll Necker, to de Maizière: ACDP, Bestand Blüm I 504/67. The idea, later entertained by the Federal government (and included in the coalition agreement of January 1991), that the provisions in §613a might be suspended in the five new *Bundesländer* did not come to fruition, as this would have conflicted with European Community law. However, some modifications of §613a limiting employee protection were implemented, notably through the Law on the Break-Up of *Treuhand* Enterprises of 5 April 1991. Cf. BMA, Sasdrich to Ministerialdirigent Ludewig, BK, 15 February 1991, BArch, B 149/74923; Bernd Baron von

Maydell, Winfried Boecken, Wolfgang Heine, *et al.* (eds.), *Die Umwandlung der Arbeits- und Sozialordnung*, Opladen 1996, pp. 119–37.

12. BMA-AS, I DDR-Regelungen, die Abweichungen vom Staatsvertrag enthalten, and II Sonstige politisch sensible Probleme, 11 June 1990, BArch, B 149/78844; similarly, BMA, Abteilung I, Umsetzung des Staatsvertrages durch die DDR, 29 June 1990, BArch, B 136/21666.
13. Blüm to Cronenberg, 18 June 1990, ACDP, Bestand Blüm I 504/66.
14. *GBl I*, 1990, pp. 403–45.
15. The Federal government expressly offered its assistance in drafting the law. Cf. BMA, Unterabt. II b, Einführung der Arbeitsförderung der Bundesrepublik Deutschland in der DDR, and attached Arbeitspapier, Konzeption für die Einführung der Arbeitsförderung in der DDR mit Ausführungen, wie man bei wörtlicher Übernahme des bundesdeutschen Arbeitsförderungsgesetzes den Besonderheiten der DDR durch *Übergangsvorschriften* Rechnung tragen könne. The relevant sections of the Labour Ministry were asked to provide fully formulated contributions to the draft law. Cf. BArch, B 149/400012.
16. Horst Kinitz, one of the Staatssekretäre in the GDR Ministry of Labour and Social Affairs, was additionally appointed director of the newly created GDR Central Labour Administration on 6 June 1990: cf. Kinitz, *Aufbau*, p. 47.
17. On the responsibilities and make-up of the advisory councils, cf. §§190–206a of the Employment Promotion Law.
18. For the differences between the Employment Promotion Laws of the GDR and the Federal Republic, cf. Kinitz, *Aufbau*, pp. 30–43.
19. §§63–72 of the Employment Promotion Law.
20. cf. BMA, Referat II b 2 (Arbeitslosenversicherung), Zur Einführung einer Arbeitslosenversicherung einschließlich der Arbeitsförderung in der DDR, 25 May 1990, in BMG, 222-48120, vol. i; Klaus Leven, 'Für weniger als 100 Tage', unpubl. paper.
21. Frerich and Frey, *Handbuch*, vol. iii, p. 598. In 1991 nearly 60 per cent of short-time workers experienced losses of more than half their working time.
22. This regulation was opposed by the relevant officials in the Labour Ministry in Bonn. After unification, however, it was extended until the autumn of 1992: interview with Klaus Leven by the author, 18 May 2000.
23. Frerich and Frey, *Handbuch*, vol. iii, pp. 512 f.
24. cf. 'Sozialpolitische Forderungen des DGB für den deutschen Einigungsprozess', in Informationsdienst des DGB, 19, 20 July 1990.
25. cf. letter from Engelen-Kefer to Blüm, 10 July 1990, AdsD, 5/DGAi 002107. Cf. also R. Hildebrandt to Konrad Carl, Bundesvorstand der IG Bau-Steine-Erden in Frankfurt a. Main, 16 July 1990, BArch, DQ 3, 1889b.
26. cf. Referat II b 2 (Arbeitslosenversicherung), Zur Problematik der Einführung einer Mindestsicherung bei den Lohnersatzleistungen des AFG in der DDR, BArch, B 149/78844.
27. Prot. VK, 10. WP, 16. Tagung, 21/22 June 1990, pp. 678 f. In an interview with the author on 18 May 2000, Klaus Leven mentioned that he had known nothing of the 'surprise coup' at the second reading of the law. The Federal Labour Ministry regarded the removal of the prohibition as a contravention of Articles 17 and 19 of the State Treaty of 18 May 1990, in which the GDR had undertaken to adopt Federal Republic law on industrial action and the regulations of the Federal Republic Employment Promotion Law: cf. BMA, Abteilung I, Umsetzung des Staatsvertrages durch die DDR, 29 June 1990, BArch, B 136/21666.

28. cf. letter from deputy chairwoman of the DGB, Ursula Engelen-Kefer, to Krause, 16 July 1990, in BArch, DC-20/6006; Engelen-Kefer and Marianne Sanding, Sprecherrat der Gewerkschaften der DDR, to de Maizière, 8 August 1990, AdsD, 5/DGAi 002110. Letters obviously containing the same wording were sent to Hildebrandt and to the leaders of the SPD and CDU/DA parliamentary parties in the Volkskammer. Cf. also letter of Engelen-Kefer to the Vorstände und Hauptvorstände der Gewerkschaften und der Industriegewerkschaften and to the DGB-Landesbezirke, ibid. See also the letter of the leader of the SPD in the Volkskammer, Wolfgang Thierse, to Engelen-Kefer, in which he explained that although he shared her point of view, 'in view of the hard negotiating line taken by the Federal government on this particular question' the only option for the parliamentary party would be 'not to vote for the Unification Treaty as a whole. You will understand that I regard that as problematical.' In AdsD, Bestand: SPD-Fraktion in der Volkskammer der DDR, Mappe 116.
29. Krause to Ziel, 29 June 1990. A copy of the letter, with the assurance that they would 'continue to try to do everything . . . in order to arrive as soon as possible at a regulation for §116 and §119 of the Employment Promotion Law corresponding to the legal position in the Federal Republic', was sent to Staatssekretär Jagoda. Carbon copies were received by the chief of the Federal Chancellery, Seiters, and the Federal Justice Minister, Kinkel: BArch, B 149/400012.
30. Blüm to Cronenberg, 4 July 1990, in reply to the latter's letter of 8 June 1990: ACDP, Bestand Blüm I 504/66. The question of the alteration to §116 of the Employment Promotion Law, which had not yet taken place when Cronenberg's letter was written, is not touched on in Blüm's letter.
31. On the programme, cf. letter of President of the BA, Heinrich Franke, to Hildebrandt, 12 June 1990, BArch, B 149/85487.
32. On the development and significance of the active labour market policy after unification, cf. Bernd Ehlers, *Arbeitsmarktpolitik im Transformationsprozess. Einsatz und Neuorientierung des aktiven arbeitsmarktpolitischen Instrumentariums des Arbeitsförderungsgesetzes in den neuen Bundesländern*, Edewecht 1996; Hubert Heinelt and Michael Weck, *Arbeitsmarktpolitik vom Vereinigungskonsens zur Standortdebatte*, Opladen 1998; *Arbeitsmarktpolitik nach der Vereinigung*, ed. Hubert Heinelt, Gerhard Bosch, and Bernd Reissert, Berlin 1994; Bernd Keller, *Einführung in die Arbeitspolitik. Arbeitsbeziehungen und Arbeitsmarkt in sozialwissenschaftlicher Perspektive*, 5th edn., Munich/Vienna 1997, esp. chs. 12–14.
33. cf. also the letter from Heinrich Franke to Blüm, 4 May 1990, Einführung des AFG in der DDR am 1.7.1990, BArch, B 149/400014.
34. cf. Klaus Leven, 'Nach der Revolution im Osten Deutschlands—Arbeitsämter zwischen Norm und Wirklichkeit', in *Europa und Deutschland—Zusammenwachsende Arbeitsmärkte und Sozialräume. Festschrift für Heinrich Franke zum 65. Geburtstag, 26. Januar 1993*, ed. Friedrich Buttler, Heinrich Reiter, and Horst Günther, Stuttgart/Berlin/Cologne 1993, pp. 235–42 (the quotation on p. 238 f.).
35. cf. Martin G. Ammermüller and Udo Diel, 'DDR-Sozialversicherung wird angeglichen', in *Kompaß* (1990), vol. 7, pp. 333–42, esp. p. 335. Udo Diel was head of Referat 3 b 1 'Grundsatzfragen, Leistungsrecht' in the GDR Ministry of Labour and Social Affairs.
36. Gesetz über die Sozialversicherung (SVG), 28 June 1990, *GBl I*, 1990, pp. 486–95.
37. Ammermüller and Diel, 'DDR-Sozialversicherung', p. 335.
38. cf. Begründung zum Entwurf des Gesetzes über die Sozialversicherung, BArch, DQ 1, 13166.

39. SVG, §§70–3.
40. ibid., §33.
41. From 1 April 1991 the accident levy was calculated by multiplying the levy rate of 0.3 per cent of the employment income of those employed in the enterprise by the class of risk.
42. cf. Kleditzsch to Parlamentarischer Staatssekretär (Krause) to the Ministerpräsident, 20 May 1990, BArch, DQ 1, 13168a.
43. SVG, §16(2) (Krankenversicherung); Hildebrandt to Kleditzsch, 12 June 1990, BArch, DQ1, 13168a.
44. Kleditzsch to Hildebrandt, 6 June 1990; Hildebrandt to Kleditzsch, 12 June 1990; both BArch, DQ 1, 13168a.
45. cf. BMA, AS, I DDR-Regelungen, die Abweichungen vom Staatsvertrag enthalten, and II Sonstige politisch sensible Probleme, 11 June 1990, BArch, B 149/78844.
46. *GBl I*, 1990, pp. 495–500.
47. §1 of the law.
48. cf. Ammermüller and Diel, 'DDR-Sozialversicherung', p. 340.
49. cf. appendix to §§2 and 10 of the law, with a table showing pensions increases, *GBl I*, 1990, p. 500.
50. §3 of the law.
51. cf. Ammermüller and Diel, 'DDR-Sozialversicherung', p. 341.
52. For an indication of the reaction of those affected, cf. a note of 11 July 1990 to Hildebrandt by the director and deputy director of GDR social insurance for the city of Dresden, Naumann and Weber. According to the note, considerably more than 1,000 people had been in contact during the previous ten days and a further 800 objections by pensioners had been lodged. These objections, Naumann and Weber said, would be directed primarily against the fact that the increased provision of 90 DM for surviving dependants and the supplementary pension based on voluntary supplementary insurance contributions were being offset against the minimum figure of 495 DM, which fell short of the subsistence level for a one-person household. A female pensioner, for example, in a letter of 3 July 1990, forwarded to Hildebrandt on 10 July 1990, complained that after her widow's pension had been taken into account, her 'social compensation' was being limited to 15 DM. The extra 46 DM that she was now receiving was not enough to enable her to absorb the full effect of the elimination of subsidies: 'It is bringing me to the brink of poverty. I was better off before.' Hildebrandt replied that she personally was very sorry that 'we have so far not managed to treat the widow's pension as additional to the 495 DM basic amount' and that her ministry would do all it could to 'index the pension as fully as is possible' (BArch, DQ 3, 1889b). It should be said that the same source includes, *inter alia*, a letter of thanks from a widowed pensioner whose pension had been increased from 571 to 781 DM.
53. cf. BMA, Abt. I, Umsetzung des Staatsvertrages durch die DDR, 29 June 1990, BArch, B136/21666. The Ministry was also critical of the fact that even according to the amended version of the GDR Labour Statute Book, 'the regulations on the employer's liability in the case of industrial accidents and occupational diseases [had not been] annulled'. In addition, under the new §269a the employer was obliged to take out liability insurance.
54. §4 of the law.
55. §12 of the law.
56. cf. Hildebrandt to Reichenbach, 22 May 1990, with paper, Überprüfung der gesellschaftlichen Rechtfertigung von Leistungen aus Sonder- und Zusatzversorgungssystemen.

Cf. also Übersicht zur Höhe der zusätzlichen Versorgungen and Vorschläge zur Behandlung von Sonderregelungen im Zusammenhang mit der Währungsunion, BMA VIII, I a 7/17000 (1).

57. §§22 and 23 of the law. Cf. also paper by BMA, Abteilung IV (Sozialversicherung, Sozialgesetzbuch), 9 November 1990, which states, *inter alia*, that the Federal government statutory order necessary for the transfer of supplementary provisions into pensions insurance has still to be issued. 'Work on this statutory order, in conjunction with which various difficult legal and political questions will have to be resolved, has begun. However, it is very unlikely that the administration will be able to manage the actual transfer of claims from supplementary provision systems to pensions insurance before the end of 1991.' BArch, B 149/74922.
58. cf. Vermerk über die Beratung vom 29.6.1990 mit dem Ministerium für Abrüstung und Verteidigung und dem Ministerium des Innern über die Begrenzung der Versorgungen, which called unsuccessfully for an additional social insurance pension of 510 DM: BArch, DQ 3, 1984.
59. *GBl I*, 1990, p. 501.
60. Frerich and Frey, *Handbuch*, vol. iii, p. 529.
61. §§30–2 of the law. Cf. also Ammermüller and Diel, 'DDR-Sozialversicherung', p. 342.
62. Prot. VK, 10. WP, 17. Tagung, 22 June 1990, p. 656.
63. cf. BMA, Außenstelle Berlin, AB I.1, 12 November 1990, Entwurf zu den Hauptergebnissen der Rentenangleichung v. 1.6.1990, BArch, B 149/74940. Cf. also BTDrs 11/8504, pp. 47, 56.
64. cf. Werner Niemeyer, 'Ab sofort einheitliches Recht', in *BArbBl* (1992), vol. 1, pp. 7–12 (here, p. 7).
65. *GBl I*, 1990, pp. 392–7, Gesetz über den Anspruch auf Sozialhilfe—Sozialhilfegesetz.
66. §1 of the law.
67. cf. the statement by the Minister for the Family and Women, Dr Christa Schmidt (CDU), when introducing the law in the Volkskammer, in Prot. VK, 10. WP, 10. Tagung, 1 June 1990, p. 389.
68. §21 of the law.
69. cf. Wienand, Neumann, and Brockmann, *Fürsorge*. See also, as an example of the rebuilding of the Independent Welfare Associations, the letter of 12 July 1990 to Hildebrandt by the chairman of the Workers' Welfare, Otto Fichtner, BArch, DQ 3, 1889b.
70. Blüm to Thomas, 21 May 1990, ACDP, Bestand Blüm I 504/65. Blüm was replying to a letter by Thomas of 24 April 1990 and to the declaration of 8 April 1990 by the Hartmann Alliance (a German doctors' organization), enclosed with the letter, on the future form of the health system in a united Germany.
71. Rudolf Dreßler, 'Erste Schritte zur Sozialunion. Bundesrepublik Deutschland—DDR Diskussionspapier', in *Dienst für Gesellschaftspolitik*, 11–90 (1990), pp. 5–10. Cf. also Manow, 'Entwicklungslinien ost- und westdeutscher Gesundheitspolitik', pp. 119 f.
72. AOK-Bundesverband, 'Die deutsch-deutsche Entwicklung und mögliche Auswirkungen auf die AOK', in *Dienst für Gesellschaftspolitik*, 10–90 (1990), pp. 5–10.
73. Draft of a 'Verordnung über die vertraglichen Beziehungen der Krankenversicherung zu den Leistungserbringern—Kassenvertragsverordnung', extracts reproduced in *Dienst für Gesellschaftspolitik*, 25–90 (1990), p. 5. Cf. also Manow, 'Gesundheitspolitik', pp. 149–51.
74. Manow, 'Gesundheitspolitik', pp. 150–3; Frerich and Frey, *Handbuch*, vol. iii, pp. 538 f.

75. On the course of the conference, cf. Prof. Steinbach to the political heads and leading officials of the BMJFFG, 1 June 1990, with attachment, Ergebnis- und Verlaufsniederschrift der konstituierenden Sitzung der gemeinsamen Gesundheitskommission und der Arbeitsgruppen am 12./13.5.1990 in Bad Honnef (Klausurtagung), BMG, 221-48120/5, vol. i.
76. Telefax, Ministerialrat Dr Stein, BMJFFG, to Ministerialrat Dr Zipperer, head of Referat V B 1, on Grundsatzfragen der gesetzlichen Krankenversicherung im BMA, 18 May 1990, with draft of a letter of Werner Chory, BMJFFG, to the Vorsitzende der Konferenz der für das Gesundheitswesen zuständigen Minister und Senatoren der Länder, Günther Jansen, on Die Organisation der gemeinsamen Gesundheitskommission und die Bildung von elf Arbeitsgruppen.
77. Jung to the Unterabteilungsleiter and Referatsleiter of his Abteilung, 5 June 1990, with attachment, Gemeinsame Arbeitsgruppen des Ministeriums für Gesundheitswesen der DDR and des BMA zu den Aufgabengebieten 'Gesetzliche Krankenversicherung/ Gesundheitliche Versorgung', BMG, 221-48120/5, vol. i. The members of the working groups of the two sides are named, as are the topics to be dealt with by the working groups. The topics specifically mentioned are 'Entwurf eines Krankenkassen-Errichtungsgesetzes', 'Aufbau eines gegliederten Systems der Krankenversicherung', 'Finanzausgleich der GKV', 'Investitionsförderungsprogramm', 'Anschubfinanzierung für die GKV', 'Entwurf eines Krankenhausfinanzierungsgesetzes'.
78. Jung, telefax of 5 June 1990 to the leading associations of the GKV, the vice-President of the BVA, Frau Dr Meurer, and the Verband der privaten Krankenversicherung, with an invitation to the constituent meeting of the 'Arbeitsgruppe Sozialunion mit der DDR' at the BMA on 13 June 1990, BMG, 221-48120/5, vol. i.
79. For the view of the General Local Health Insurance Providers, cf. Franz Knieps, head of association policy planning, AOK-Bundesverband, Bonn, Problemschwerpunkte einer Harmonisierung der Gesundheits- und Krankenversicherungssysteme der Bundesrepublik Deutschland und der DDR, 19 June 1990; id., Statement zum DDR-Hearing in Hamburg, 15 June 1990; id., Die Reform der Kassenorganisation unter dem Blickwinkel der aktuellen deutschlandpolitischen Entwicklung, speech, 11 June 1990: BArch, DQ 3, 1881a. Cf. also Manow, 'Gesundheitspolitik', esp. pp. 126–30.
80. cf. Manow, 'Gesundheitspolitik', esp. pp. 129–31. For the attitude of the company sickness funds, see also the eight-page letter of 2 August 1990 to Kleditzsch from the deputy chairman of the Federal Association of Company Sickness Funds, opposing financial compensation between all forms of statutory health insurance organizations and compulsory state subsidies for GDR health insurance, as well as a unitary contribution rate. The Association also argued for the retention of reconstituted enterprise-based polyclinics in the GDR. 'The company sickness funds are prepared to convert a number of enterprise-based polyclinics in the GDR, along with management partners and investors, into, for example, polyclinic limited companies. Relevant plans showing that the same organizational structures are also appropriate for a unified health system in Germany in the long term have already been drawn up. Company sickness funds in the GDR might also be prepared, at least during a transition period, to take over polyclinics and ambulatories as "independent facilities".' BArch, DQ 1, 14339.
81. Gesetz zur Errichtung von Krankenkassen, 13 September 1990, *GBl I*, 1990, pp. 1538–44.
82. *GBl I*, 1990, pp. 1533–7.
83. Circular letter by head of Außenstelle des BMA, Ministerialdirektor Jung, to heads of regional departments of health and social affairs and heads of city and district

departments of health and social affairs, 29 October 1990. Blüm defended this circular against criticism by the chairman of the Association of Statutory Health Insurance Physicians for Lower Saxony, K. H. Schibort, in a letter of 12 December 1990, ACDP, Bestand Blüm I 505/73.

84. Blüm to former Minister Bergmann-Pohl, MdB, 22 January 1991, ACDP, Bestand Blüm I 504/75.
85. cf. Wasem, *Vom staatlichen zum kassenärztlichen System*, pp. 85 f.
86. *GBl I*, 1990, pp. 1428–30.
87. cf. Kleditzsch to chairmen of the Rat der Bezirke, 2 May 1990, BArch, DQ 1, 14918.
88. *GBl I*, 1990, pp. 711 ff., 1533–7.
89. The files of the GDR Ministry of Health (BArch, DQ 3) contain dozens of detailed responses to particular items of proposed legislation.
90. Kleditzsch to Parlamentarischer Staatssekretär to the Ministerpräsident, Dr Günther Krause, with Formulierungsvorschlägen zu einem neuen Kapitel X über 'Gesundheitswesen und Krankenversicherung' im Einigungsvertrag, 1 August 1990, BArch, DQ 1, 13657.

9 The Unification Treaty

1. Schäuble, *Vertrag*, pp. 53–7, 140, 151 f.
2. ibid., p. 112.
3. ibid., pp. 136 f.
4. cf. Aufzeichnung des Bundesministers des Innern, 28 May 1990; Grundstrukturen eines Staatsvertrages zur Herstellung der Deutschen Einheit; both in *Dokumente zur Deutschlandpolitik*, pp. 1151–4.
5. Diskussionspapier des Bundesministers des Innern mit Elementen einer zur Herstellung der deutschen Einheit zu treffenden Regelung, in ibid., pp. 1267–74.
6. Schäuble, *Vertrag*, p. 137. The list was agreed with the Federal Republic: cf. Abgestimmter Katalog der Verhandlungsthemen zum Vertrag über die Herstellung der Einheit Deutschlands (Einigungsvertrag), in *Dokumente zur Deutschlandpolitik*, 9 July 1990, pp. 1328–31. Questions of social policy were not mentioned in this list of topics.
7. cf. Erste Verhandlungsrunde über den Vertrag zur Herstellung der Einheit Deutschlands (Einigungsvertrag), Berlin, 6.7.1990. Ergebnisprotokoll. In *Dokumente zur Deutschlandpolitik*, pp. 1324–8.
8. *BGBl II*, 1990, pp. 1239–45.
9. Schäuble, *Vertrag*, pp. 120, 138, 150–5.
10. Stellungnahme der Bundesvereinigung der Deutschen Arbeitgeberverbände zum Entwurf des Einigungsvertrages, sent with accompanying letter by Dr Himmelreich and Dr Doetsch, Hauptgeschäftsführung der BDA, to Blüm, 15 August 1990, BMG, 221-48123-5/1, vol. i.
11. Blüm to Schäuble, 28 June 1990, ACDP, Bestand Blüm I 504/66.
12. Schäuble, *Vertrag*, p. 154.
13. ibid., pp. 154 f. For Schäuble's criticism of this decision, cf., in addition to his book on the treaty, Wolfgang Schäuble, 'Ich habe einen Traum', account by Mark Kayser, in *Die Zeit*, 30 September 1999.
14. Schäuble, *Vertrag*, p. 156. He says that 'in the initial phase [such attempts] were blocked at lower working levels'.
15. Vermerk des Regierungsdirektors Lehnguth für die Sitzung des Kabinettsausschusses Deutsche Einheit am 24.7.1990, 23 July 1990, in *Dokumente zur Deutschlandpolitik*,

pp. 1406–9, esp. p. 1409. Gerold Lehnguth was head of Referat 332 (Verfassungsrecht) in the Federal Chancellery.

16. Vorlage des Ministerialdirigenten Busse an den Chef des Bundeskanzleramtes Seiters, 17 August 1990, in ibid., pp. 1464 f. Volker Busse was head of Gruppe 33 (Recht, Staatliche Organisation) in the Federal Chancellery.
17. BMA, Unterabteilung I b, to the Minister, the Staatssekretäre and Abteilungsleiter, BMA, with Ergebnisvermerk über die Sitzung der 'Arbeitsgruppe Soziales' am 2.8.1990, 6 August 1990; the participants in the negotiations are listed by name. Bavaria was represented by Staatssekretär Dörfler, Berlin by the Senator for Health, Freier. For the BMA, Ministerialdirigent Dr Peter Rosenberg, head of Unterabteilung I b, 'Mathematische und finanzielle Fragen der Sozialpolitik und das Sozialbudget', was also present at the session; BMG, 221-48123-5/1, vol. i. In an interview with the author on 5 May 2000 Rosenberg emphasized that different officials from different administrative levels were present at the negotiations, depending on the topics under discussion.
18. cf. above, p. 170; also Schwedes, 'Arbeitsgesetzbuch', pp. 145–72.
19. cf. Zwischenbericht über die Ergebnisse der Fachgespräche zwischen dem Ministerium für Arbeit und Soziales (MfAS) und dem Bundesministerium für Arbeit und Sozialordnung (BMA) zum Einigungsvertrag, 20 July 1990, BMG, 221-48123-5/3, vol. 1. This interim report was sent to Krause and, with a note of 31 July 1990, to all departmental heads in the Federal Labour Ministry. Cf. also BMA, Abteilung III, Offene Punkte mit der DDR (Abt. III), 13 August 1990, BArch, B 149/78875; MfAS, Entwurf von Artikeln für den Einigungsvertrag, BMG, 221-48123/2, vol. i. (This undated draft was distributed at the beginning of August.)
20. Zwischenbericht, 20 July 1990, BMG, 221-48123-5/3, vol. i.
21. ibid.
22. BMA, Aufzeichnung über eine erste Gesprächsrunde zwischen Vertretern des DDR-Arbeitsministeriums und dem BMA zum Bereich Arbeitsrecht/Sozialer Arbeitsschutz, 11 July 1990; Anhang zu einem Schreiben des Referats III a 1 an die Unterabteilung III b and die Referate III a 2–III a 7, 12 July 1990; BArch, B 149/405236.
23. Zwischenbericht, 20 July 1990, BMG, 221-48123-5/3, vol. i.
24. BMA, Abteilung III, Argumentationspapiere zu den Themen 'Arbeitsgesetzbuch der DDR', 'Arbeitsgerichtsbarkeit', 'Befristete Arbeitsverträge nach dem Beschäftigungsförderungsgesetz 1985', 'zum Kapitel "Berufliche Weiterbildung" im Arbeitsgesetzbuch der DDR', 'zur Vorschrift über die Freistellung zur Pflege erkrankter Kinder (§186 AGB)', 'zum Kapitel "Soziale Betreuung" im Arbeitsgesetzbuch', 'zur Arbeitnehmerhaftung', 'zum Thema "Kündigungsfristen für Arbeiter und Angestellte"', 'zur Entgeltfortzahlung im Krankheitsfall', 27 July 1990, BArch, B 149/405237.
25. Argumentationspapier zum Thema 'Arbeitsgesetzbuch der DDR', BArch, B 149/405237.
26. Zwischenbericht, 20 July 1990, BMG, 221-48123-5/3, vol. i.
27. Einigungsvertrag, Artikel 30, Absatz (1) 1.
28. Judgement of Federal Constitutional Court, 30 May 1990, BVerfGE 82, pp. 126–56. On the regulations in the Unification Treaty, cf., in addition to the treaty itself, BMA, Abt. I, Inhalt des Einigungsvertrages (Stichwortliste), 5 September 1990, in BMA VIII/I a 1/15101.2.
29. Blüm to Minister Riesenhuber, 7 January 1991, ACDP, Bestand Blüm I 504/74.
30. Blüm to the President of the Bundesärztekammer Karsten Vilmar, 11 January 1991, ACDP, Bestand Blüm I 504/74.

31. Blüm to Herr Hinne and Herr Kleinherne, Vorstand der gewerblichen Berufsgenossenschaften, 11 January 1991, ACDP, Bestand Blüm I 504/74.
32. BMA, Abt. III a 1 to Staatssekretär Jagoda, 16.8.1990, with copies to the Ministers, Staatssekretäre and Abteilung I, regarding Einigungsvertrag (here, Streitpunkte mit den Ressorts, attachment 2, Rationalisierungsschutzabkommen 'der letzten Stunde' in der DDR, 16.8.1990, in which the agreements on protection measures against rationalization forwarded by the Ministry of Labour and Social Affairs are examined and summarized), BArch, B 149/78875. A further eleven agreements were not registered. The agreements on protection measures against rationalization concluded after 1 July, which also entailed significant burdens for employers, were not contested. The note argued—contrary to the position of the Economics Ministry—that the agreements should continue in force until they were replaced by new collective agreements or, if this recommendation were not adopted, that they should simply lapse on 31 December 1990.
33. Ministerin für Arbeit und Soziales, R. Hildebrandt, to DGB-Vorsitzende Heinz-Werner Meyer, 13 June 1990, BArch, DQ 3, 1882b.
34. DGB-Vorsitzende Meyer to Ministerin Hildebrandt, 9 July 1990, BArch, DQ 3, 1879.
35. Vorsitzende der 'Gewerkschaft öffentliche Dienste', Jürgen Kaiser, to the Parlamentarischer Staatssekretär to the Ministerpräsident and chairmen of the CDU/DA Volkskammer parliamentary party, Günther Krause, 18 July 1990, BArch, DC-20/8952.
36. Dr Steinpaß, personal assistant to Staatssekretär Otto Schlecht, BMWi, on Schlecht's instructions, to Parlamentarischer Staatssekretär Krause with copy to GDR Wirtschaftsminister Dr Gerhard Pohl, with note, Fortgeltung von Rationalisierungsschutzabkommen in der DDR, 9.7.1990, 10 July 1990, BArch, DC-20/6006.
37. Stellungnahme für Herrn Staatssekretär Dr. Krause zum Schreiben des Bundesministeriums für Wirtschaft vom 10.7.1990 zur 'Fortgeltung von Rationalisierungsschutzabkommen in der DDR', 13 July 1990, BArch, DC-20-6006.
38. Bundesarbeitsminister Blüm to Präsident des Bundesverbandes der Deutschen Industrie Dr Tyll Necker, 21 August 1990, ACDP, Bestand Blüm I 504/67. According to the letter, Blüm had instigated the Economics Ministry's intervention.
39. In a letter of 1 October 1990 to the chief representatives of the Metal Workers' Union, Franz Steinkühler and Klaus Zwickel, Blüm defended this position on the grounds, first, that there had not been free collective bargaining, and a guarantee thereof, in the GDR until 1 July 1990, with the State Treaty, and, secondly, that the GDR had not possessed the instruments newly created by the Employment Promotion Law: 'I also think it is questionable to seek to invoke collective bargaining and the basic right of free association in order to protect agreements on protection measures against rationalization made under the old law. As a rule, the contracting party on the employer's side was the GDR government and hence, in the final analysis, the state budget.' ACDP, Bestand Blüm I 504/69. Blüm's letter was in reply to a letter of 19 September 1990.
40. cf. Zwischenbericht, 20 July 1990, in BMG, 221-48123-5/3, vol. i; BMA, Unterabteilung I b, Ergebnisvermerk über 'Arbeitsgruppensitzung 2.8.1990 im Rahmen Regierungsverhandlungen zum Einigungsvertrag', 6 August 1990, in BMG, 221-48123-5/1, vol. i; Referat 332, Bundeskanzleramt, Entwurf des Einigungsvertrages, 13 August 1990, in BArch, B 136/20252.
41. cf. the draft of the corresponding section on pre-pension transitional benefit, sent by Ziel to Jagoda on 16 August 1990, and a note of 17 August 1990 for Jagoda by Abteilung II of the Labour Ministry for a telephone conversation on the issue with Ziel on 17 August 1990: BArch, B 149/78873.

42. cf. Einigungsvertrag, Artikel 30, and, for the details, Anlage I, Kapitel VII, Sachgebiet E, Abschnitt II, §249e; Anlage II, Kapitel VIII, Sachgebiet E, Abschnitt II; *BGBl II*, 1990, pp. 1037 f. and 1210.
43. Interview with Leven by the author, 18 May 2000.
44. Frerich and Frey, *Handbuch*, vol. iii, p. 611. Cf. also interview with Blüm, 7 May 1991, in *BPA-DoK*, Text-Bull-RFTV-AA (87–95).
45. Einigungsvertrag, Anlage I, Kapitel VIII, Sachgebiet E, Abschnitt II, *BGBl II*, 1990, pp. 1036 f. Cf. also the unsigned article, 'Arbeits- und Sozialrecht im einigen Sozialstaat Deutschland', in SPI, no. 10, 14 September 1990.
46. cf. Einigungsvertrag, Artikel 30.
47. ibid., Anlage II, Kapitel VIII, Sachgebiet H, Abschnitt III, Nr. 9, *BGBl II*, 1990, pp. 1215 f.
48. *BGBl I*, p. 1038.
49. cf. Zwischenbericht, 20 July 1990, BMG, 221-48123-5/3, vol. i; Ergebnisvermerk über die Sitzung der Arbeitsgruppe 'Soziales', 2 August 1990, BMG, 221-48123-5/1, vol. i; Formulierungsvorschlag des Ministeriums für Arbeit und Soziales der DDR mit Zeichen über dessen Kenntnisnahme, 9 August 1990, BMG, 221-48123/2, vol. i; Aufzeichnung des Arbeitsstabes Deutsche Einheit im Bundesministerium des Innern, 30 July 1990: Zusammenstellung der Textvorschläge aus den Ressortverhandlungen für den Einigungsvertrag, in *Dokumente zur Deutschlandpolitik*, pp. 1425–44. Article 22 on 'Finanzierung von Sozialleistungen' in the latter compilation says, still broadly in line with the GDR's demands, that the social allowance will 'be retained for a transition period until 31 December 1995' and 'increased in accordance with the adjustment in pensions' (p. 1435).
50. Blüm to Günther, 17 September 1990, ACDP, Bestand Blüm I 504/68.
51. Regierungsdirektor Boldorf, head of Spiegelreferat zum BMA 311 im Bundeskanzleramt, Einigungsvertrag. Strittige Punkte im Zuständigkeitsbereich des BMA, Anlage I, Kap. VII, 16 August 1990, BArch, B 136/20252. In the Unification Treaty, the relevant chapter was chapter VIII. Cf. also Blüm to Schäuble, 28 August 1990, indicating that although the coalition meeting of 21 August 1990 was agreed that pensions insurance should receive financial compensation from the public purse for the pensions claims of people with assigned civil-servant status, this should take place, not 'within the framework of the Unification Treaty, but at a later date, when the reconstruction phase of a tenured civil service begins': ACDP, Bestand Blüm I 504/68.
52. Waigel to Blüm, 16 August 1990, BArch, B 149/78915.
53. BMA, Abteilung IV b 2, concerning Einigungsvertrag mit der DDR (here, Finanzverbund in der Rentenversicherung), 17 August 1990, BArch, B 149/78915.
54. According to an 'internal' paper, BMA, Abt. I, Inhalt des Einigungsvertrages (Stichwortliste), 5 September 1990, 5,700 million DM had been found from public resources, including 2,300 million DM Federal capital loans, in order to finance GDR pensions insurance. A further 1,700 million DM, at least, would be necessary in the second half of 1990. Cf. BMA VIII/I a 1/15105.2.
55. BMA, Finanzverbund in der Rentenversicherung, 17 August 1990, BArch, 149/78195.
56. cf. above, p. 43.
57. The level of pensions benefits under social provision for war victims would depend on the relation of pensions from east Germany's pensions insurance to those in west Germany. The rate was initially 40.3 per cent and was raised to 75.3 per cent by 1 January 1994. Cf. *Sozialbericht 1993*, pp. 82, 271.
58. Waigel to Blüm, 16 August 1990, BArch, B 149/78915.

59. BMA, Abteilung I, Inhalt des Einigungsvertrages (Stichwortliste), 5 September 1990, BMA VIII/I a 1/15105.2.
60. Blüm's words to the national chairman of the Alliance of War-Blind of Germany, Dr Franz Sonntag, 12 September 1990, ACDP, Bestand Blüm I 504/68.
61. Mitteilung des Sprechers der Bundesregierung, Bundesminister Hans Klein, über einen Empfang des Präsidenten des VdK, Walter Hirrlinger durch Kohl, 6 September 1990, BArch, B 136/21660.
62. cf. Blüm to the Landesbevollmächtigte für das Land Brandenburg, Joachim Wolf, 16 October 1990; Blüm to the Präsident des VdK Deutschland, Minister a.D. Walter Hirrlinger, 9 November 1990; Blüm to the Ministerpräsident des Freistaates Sachsen, Prof. Dr Kurt Biedenkopf, 13 November 1990; ACDP, Bestand Blüm I 504/69 and 504/71. In addition to Biedenkopf, the Prime Ministers of the other four new *Bundesländer* received a similar letter. During a transition period the first notifications to those entitled to provision were prepared, through arrangement with the *Länder*, by partner *Länder* in the west.
63. *Sozialbericht 1993*, p. 82.
64. cf. BMA, Abteilung V b, Übersicht über Leistungsunterschiede in der gesetzlichen Krankenversicherung, 8 June 1990, BArch, B 149/78845.
65. I. Sachstandsbericht über die Verhandlungen mit der DDR, undated, with a Zwischenbericht über die Fachgespräche zum Einigungsvertrag zwischen dem Bundesministerium für Arbeit und Sozialordnung und den Ministerien für Arbeit und Soziales sowie für Gesundheit; no indication of source department given. The document was probably written on 20 July 1990 or soon thereafter. AdsD, Bestand: SPD-Fraktion in der Volkskammer der DDR, Mappe 295. Cf. also letter of Staatssekretär Tegtmeier, BMA, to Staatssekretär Dr Schönfelder, Ministerium für Gesundheitswesen, GDR, 31 July 1990, on the high level of the deficit in GDR health insurance in 1990. The letter said that there should be unequivocal opposition to all 'price and fee increases', especially in the area of drugs. BArch, DQ 1, 13166.
66. BMA, Abteilung V, GKV-Defizitausgleich durch den Bund, 8 September 1990, BArch, B 149/78915.
67. Sachstandsbericht (cf. note 65 above). Cf. also Regierungsdirektor Boldorf, Referat 311, Bundeskanzleramt, Einigungsvertrag. Strittige Punkte im Zuständigkeitsbereich des BMA. Krankenversicherung, 16 August 1990. According to this source, the position of the Labour Ministry was supported by the Ministry for Young People, the Family, Women, and Health and the *Bundesländer*; BArch, B 136/20252. The Labour Ministry document cited in note 66 above states that on the main issue of the covering of the deficit, no compromise is possible, 'as any kind of financial settlement affecting all categories of health insurer (or each category separately) for the whole of Germany would ignite the smouldering problem of health insurance structural reform. The result would be conflict within the coalition, but also serious conflict within the CDU and CSU.' A possible concession to the Finance Ministry, the document says, is that Federal government covering of the deficit might be confined to the period up to 31 December 1993. BArch, B 149/78915. The Finance Ministry was supported by the FDP and the Private Health Insurance Association, the director of which, Dr Uleer, voiced his strong opposition to state subsidies for statutory health insurance in a letter to Seehofer of 25 July 1990.
68. cf. Einigungsvertrag, Anlage I, Kapitel VIII, Sachgebiet G, Abschnitt II, *BGBl II*, 1990, pp. 1049, 1052.

69. The managing director of the Federal Association of General Local Health Insurance Providers, Dr Oldiges, in a letter to Jagoda of 23 August 1990, urged the latter to 'defend the state subsidy in the interests of social harmony', since otherwise there would be a difference in the levels of contributions in the GDR 'going beyond what is socially acceptable'. In his reply of 21 September 1990, after the treaty had been signed, Jagoda had to say that there had been 'no consensus for a regulation making the Federal government liable for the deficit'. Establishing a unitary contribution rate of 12.8 per cent in the region of the current GDR would, he maintained, serve the 'interests of the local health insurers, because it ensures equal competition, including in contribution rates, in the important phase of the introduction of the multipartite system'. BMG, 222-48120, vol. i.
70. cf. 'Bemerkungen des Bundesrechnungshofes 1992 zur Haushalts- und Wirtschaftsführung (einschließlich der Feststellungen zur Jahresrechnung des Bundes 1990)', BTDrs 12/3250, 21 September 1992.
71. cf. Einigungsvertrag, Anlage I, Kapitel VIII, Sachgebiet G, Abschnitt II, *BGBl II*, 1990, p. 1049.
72. ibid., pp. 1049 f.
73. cf. Frerich and Frey, *Handbuch*, vol. iii, pp. 572 f.
74. Blüm to Herr Loeper and Herr Stürzbecher, ACDP, Bestand Blüm I 504/73.
75. For the different points of view, cf. Blüm to the Geschäftsführung der Pharmed GmbH in Ostberlin, 21 September 1990, ACDP, Bestand Blüm I 504/68; Diskussion von Blüm mit Dr. Michael Vogt vom Bundesvorstand der Pharmazeutischen Industrie und Hans-Jürgen Nelde als Sprecher der Pharmaindustrie des Ostens, 'Plus-minus', 5 October 1990, in *BPA-Dok*, Text-Bull-RFTV-AA (87–95). Strong emphasis was placed on the arguments with the pharmaceutical industry in the interviews of the author with Blüm on 8 June 2000 and Jagoda on 5 July 2000.
76. For the details, cf. Frerich and Frey, *Handbuch*, vol. iii, pp. 614 f. On the compromise, see also interview with Blüm, 'Heute-Journal', 4 January 1991, in *BPA-Dok*, Text-Bull-RFTV-AA (87–95).
77. Entwurf von Artikeln des Einigungsvertrages, übersandt am 14.8.1990 zur Vorbereitung von Abstimmungsgesprächen auf Arbeitsebene im BMI am 16.8.1990, BMG, 221-48123/2, vol. i; cf. also Referat 332, Bundeskanzleramt, Entwurf des Einigungsvertrages, 17.8.1990 mit den Problemen, in denen noch politischer Abstimmungsbedarf bestünde, BArch, B 136/20256.
78. Waigel to Blüm, 16 August 1990, BArch, B 149/78915.
79. Einigungsvertrag, Anlage I, Kapitel VIII, Sachgebiet G, Abschnitt II, *BGBl II*, 1990, pp. 1053 f.
80. *Sozialbericht 1993*, p. 64. See also below, p. 261.
81. cf. Einigungsvertrag, Anlage I, Kapitel VIII, Sachgebiet G, Abschnitt II, *BGBl II*, 1990, p. 1050. Licences could be revoked prematurely or prolonged.
82. cf. above, p. 183.
83. Sachstandsbericht über die Verhandlungen mit der DDR (cf. note 65 above) and Aufzeichnungen über 'Gespräche mit dem Ministerium für Gesundheit', AdsD, Bestand: SPD-Fraktion in der Volkskammer der DDR, Mappe 295. Astonishingly, there is no demand for the preservation of state, local-government, and workplace-based outpatient health care institutions even in the very detailed 'position papers' of the SPD party in the Volkskammer of 7 July and 16 July 1990: AdsD, Bestand: SPD-Fraktion in der Volkskammer der DDR, Mappen 133, 135.
84. cf. Schäuble, *Vertrag*, esp. pp. 229–50.

85. Vergleichende Betrachtungen DDR/BRD Frauen und Familie, undated, AdsD, Bestand: SPD-Fraktion in der Volkskammer der DDR, Mappe 74. Renate Schmidt, deputy chairwoman of the SPD parliamentary party and head of the Arbeitskreis 'Gleichstellung von Frau and Mann', 28 May 1990 to Dr Herta Däubler-Gmelin, another deputy chairwoman of the SPD parliamentary party, with attachment, Tischvorlage zur Sitzung der AG Fortschritt '90 am 9. und 10.3.1990: Vergleich der familienpolitischen Maßnahmen in der DDR und der Bundesrepublik. This paper also sets out the commitments in *Fortschritt 90* and the additional costs, compared with the proposals of *Fortschritt 90,* if GDR regulations were adopted; AdsD, 9613. BMA, Sasdrich to Bauer, BMJFFG with accompanying letter, 1 October 1990; Synopse (Entwurf) der Ausgangsperspektiven der wirtschaftlichen Familienförderung in der Bundesrepublik und der DDR bei der staatlichen Vereinigung, 2 August 1990; document drafted by Bauer with corrections by the BMA, BArch, B 149/78930.
86. cf., and for what follows, Ministerium für Familie und Frauen, Parlamentarischer Staatssekretär Dr. Hans Geisler: Koordinierungsstab Deutsche Einheit. Bericht zu Punkt 1.5. des Verhandlungskataolgs zum Einigungsvertrag (Stand 26.7.1990), 26 July 1990, BArch, DC-20/6043. On the judgement of 29 May 1990 by the Federal Constitutional Court, cf. above, p. 65.
87. Gesetz zur Änderung des Familiengesetzbuches der DDR (1. Familienänderungsgesetz), 20 July 1990, *GBl I,* 1990, pp. 1038–42.
88. *GBl I,* 1966, pp. 1–18.
89. Geisler, Bericht (cf. note 86 above).
90. ibid.
91. ibid.
92. ibid. The financing was to be effected either through the budget of the Ministry for the Family and Women or through that of the Ministry of Health. Altogether, including the aid for the Independent Welfare Associations, funds totalling 15,800 million DM had to be allowed for in the budget of the Ministry for the Family and Women in 1991 as far as the region of the former GDR was concerned. Of the total, 1,400 million DM were allocated to child-raising allowance and support for mothers, 6,300 million DM to child benefit, 3,000 million DM to child care facilities, and 3,500 million DM to income support.
93. Ursula Lehr, 'Deutsche Einheit heißt auch mehr Chancen für Frauen', undated, BArch, B 149/78930.
94. Staatssekretär Werner Chory, BMJFFG, to Bundesminister des Innern, 10 August 1990, BMG, 211-48123/2, vol. v. Copies of this document were also sent to the other ministries. Cf. also the Ministry's concrete proposed formulations of 14 August 1990 on the relevant articles of the Unification Treaty and their rationale: BMG, 221-48123/2, vol. i.
95. Erklärung der Vorsitzenden des Volkskammer-Ausschusses für Frauen und Familie, Angelika Barbe, und der Stellvertretenden Vorsitzenden der SPD-Bundestagsfraktion und Vorsitzenden des Arbeitskreises 'Gleichstellung von Frau und Mann', Renate Schmidt: Frauen der SPD-Ost und der SPD-West stellen Forderungen an den deutschen Einigungsprozess, 3 June 1990, AdsD, Bestand: SPD-Fraktion in der Volkskammer der DDR, Mappe 288; chairman of the DAG, Roland Issen, to Bundeskanzler Kohl, 18 June 1990, AdsD, DAG-Buvo (Bundesvorstand), Abt. Vorsitzender—A. Reuer; Dr Ursula Engelen-Kefer, deputy chairwoman of the DGB, to Präsidentin der Volkskammer der DDR, Dr Sabine Bergmann-Pohl, 17 August 1990, with attachment, 16 August 1990. In the latter document Engelen-Kefer reports

on a meeting on 16 August with Hildebrandt, Helga Kreft, Staatssekretär in the GDR Ministry for the Family and Women, Konstanze Krehl, deputy chairwoman of the SPD in the Volkskammer, and six leading trade unionists from both the GDR and the Federal Republic to coordinate views on the 'rights and concerns of women in the process of German unification': BArch, DC-20/6025.

96. Bundeskanzleramt, Referat 332, Entwurf des Einigungsvertrages mit den zwischen den Ressorts offenen Punkten, 17 August 1990, BArch, B 136/20252.
97. Einigungsvertrag, Anlage II, Kapitel X, Sachgebiet H, Abschnitt II, *BGBl II*, 1990, p. 1220.
98. cf. above, p. 61.
99. de Maizière on the law on the Unification Treaty, in Prot. VK, 10. WP, 34. Tagung, 6 September 1990, p. 1567.
100. Reprinted in *Dokumente zur Deutschlandpolitik*, pp. 1478 f.
101. Hans-Jochen Vogel *et al.* to Kohl, 24 August 1990, AdsD, 9613. The letter proposed that a meeting of leaders should take place before the initialling of the treaty, and such a meeting took place on 26 August 1990.
102. Schäuble, *Vertrag*, pp. 212–14.
103. Eckert Schlemm: Notiz für Herrn Jahn. Betrifft: Einigungsvertrag mit der DDR (here, Vergleich der am 31.8.1990 unterzeichneten Fassung mit dem letzten Entwurf (Stand: 26.8.1990)), 3 September 1990, AdsD, 9634.
104. Prot. BT, 11. WP, p. 17889.
105. Telefax of Vogel to Thierse, 19 September 1990, AdsD, Bestand: SPD-Fraktion in der Volkskammer der DDR, Mappe 63. Vogel refers incorrectly to the agreement of 17, rather than 18, September 1990.
106. Statement in Prot. BT, 11. WP, pp. 17891 f.
107. Schäuble, *Vertrag*, pp. 263 f.
108. Statement by Michael von Schmude and 67 other members of the CDU/CSU parliamentary party, in Prot. BT, 11. WP, p. 17948 (appendices).
109. ibid., p. 17935 (appendices).
110. ibid., pp. 17896–8.
111. Prot. VK, 10. WP, 34. Tagung, 6 September 1990, pp. 1565–7.
112. ibid., 35. Tagung, 13 September 1990, pp. 1643–7.
113. Text of the statement in ibid., 36. Tagung, 20 September 1990, pp. 1754 f.
114. cf. the speeches by Gregor Gysi for the PDS and Konrad Weiß for Alliance 90/The Greens, Prot. VK, 10. WP, 36. Tagung, 20 September 1990, pp. 1745–7, 1749–51.
115. The CDU/DA, FDP, and DSU voted unanimously for the treaty. There were two SPD votes against, but the other SPD members voted for the treaty. One member of Alliance 90/The Greens abstained and sixteen voted against. One independent member voted for the treaty and one against. Cf. ibid., pp. 1795–8.

10 The Social Policy Actors and the Unification Process

1. In a letter of 31 May 1990 to the head of the German postal workers' union, Kurt van Haaren, Blüm countered fears that this would happen after the State Treaty had been signed: ACDP, Bestand Blüm I 504/65.
2. Interviews by the author with Blüm on 8 June 2000, Rosenberg on 5 May 2000 and Tegtmeier on 13 July 2000. Blüm also emphasized the Labour Ministry's good relations with the Chancellery, where most of the key posts with regard to questions of social policy had been filled by former Labour Ministry officials.
3. cf. *Sozialbericht 1990*, p. 12.

4. Blüm to Herr L.-B., 28 March 1990, ACDP, Bestand Blüm I 504/62.
5. Blüm to 'Dortmunder Freunde', 11 June 1990, ACDP, Bestand Blüm I 504/65. For his optimistic assessment of future prospects in east Germany, cf. also his interview, 'Zahlen für die schönste Sache', *Der Spiegel*, no. 38, 17 September 1990, pp. 24–7: 'I believe that the levels [of wages and salaries] between the former GDR and the Federal Republic will be evened out in 3 to 5 years' time.'
6. Prot. VK, 10. WP, 39. Tagung, 20 September 1990, p. 1750. The powerful role of the Finance Ministry, in contrast with that of the Economics Ministry, was also stressed by Blüm: 'I never really took the Economics Ministry seriously, because they always negotiated at a high level of ideological abstraction, in which I am a specialist. I had to take the Finance Ministry seriously, because there money was involved.' Interview of Blüm by the author, 8 June 2000.
7. Decree by Staatssekretär Dr Tegtmeier, 25 September 1990, BMA, Z b 1-00105-11.
8. Tegtmeier to Jung, 28 September 1990, BMA, Z a 1-01160-JO31.
9. cf. Ministerialdirektor Harrer, head of Zentralabteilung, BMA, to Chef des Bundeskanzleramtes, Rudolf Seiters, 7 September 1990; GDR Health Minister Kleditzsch to Minister im Amt des Ministerpräsidenten der DDR Reichenbach, 6 September 1990; BArch, B 136/20252 and BArch, DQ 3, 1890a.
10. Interview by the author with Alwin Ziel, 13 July 2000. According to Regine Hildebrandt, who thought the collapse of the coalition was 'dreadful'—in part because it meant that the social interests that were concentrated in her ministry in the final phase of the negotiations on the Unification Treaty could no longer be represented—the break-up had been provoked by de Maizière: interview by the author with Hildebrandt, 31 May 2000.
11. Interview by the author with Ziel, 13 July 2000. Ziel regarded the relationship of trust that existed between de Maizière and Schröder as crucial to collaboration within the coalition up until the break-up in August.
12. Interview by the author with Blüm, 8 June 2000.
13. In a letter of 2 May 1990 to de Maizière, Hildebrandt argued, unsuccessfully, that the responsibility for health insurance should be given to her ministry as an 'inseparable part of social insurance', in particular in order to avoid the numerous 'problems of coordination and consultation between, on the one hand, the GDR ministries and, on the other, the GDR and the Federal Republic (overlapping responsibilities)'. She cited, as further reasons, the need for social insurance to be represented externally by a single ministry, the fact that social insurance was based on the employment relationship, and the interconnection of all branches of social insurance by virtue of common basic circumstances and the role of the social law jurisdiction as a kind of roof over social insurance. Cf. BArch, DQ 3, 1889.
14. Interview by the author with Leven, 18 May 2000.
15. Interviews by the author with Ziel, 13 July 2000, and Jagoda, 5 July 2000.
16. Interview by the author with Ziel, 13 July 2000.
17. ibid., and interview by the author with Hildebrandt, 31 May 2000.
18. Interview by the author with Ziel, 13 July 2000.
19. Speech by de Maizière during the first reading of the law on the Unification Treaty in the Volkskammer, Prot. VK, 10. WP, 34. Tagung, 6 September 1990, p. 1567.
20. For the debate, cf. Prot. VK, 10. WP, 6. Tagung, 10 May 1990, pp. 177–92.
21. ibid., p. 178.
22. ibid., p. 186.
23. ibid., pp. 186 f.

24. de Maizière, Vorschlag für die Sitzung des Ministerrates am 16.7.1990 'Einigungsvertrag', BArch, DC 20/6033-1 (emphasis in original).
25. Speech by de Maizière in the Volkskammer, Prot. VK, 10. WP, 34. Tagung, 6 September 1990, p. 1567.
26. Jäger, *Überwindung*, p. 479.
27. For this warranted criticism, cf. Richard Schröder, 'Gerechtigkeit für eine Schar von Laienspielern. Auf ihre erste gewählte Volkskammer können die Ostdeutschen ein bisschen stolz sein—und die Westdeutschen sollten ihnen diesen Stolz lassen', *FAZ*, 18 March 2000.
28. Prot. VK, 10. WP, 8. Tagung, 21 May 1990, p. 230.
29. Prot. BT, 11. WP, 27 April 1990, pp. 16394–9.
30. ibid., pp. 16408–12.
31. cf. Vogel, BT, Ausschuß Deutsche Einheit, 15 June 1990, stenographic report of committee session, p. 285.
32. Prot. BT, 11. WP, 27 April 1990, pp. 16399–403. For the SPD's proposal, cf. BTDrs 11/6462, 14 February 1990 and BTDrs 11/6952, 24 April 1990. Cf. also letter of Vogel to the Presidents of the Bundestag and Bundesrat, 7 February 1990, in Die SPD im Deutschen Bundestag, BArch, B 136/26281; written question to the Federal government by the Vice-president of the Bundestag Annemarie Renger, 12 April 1990 (asking for reasons why the parliaments of the two German states were not adequately included in the process and why the draft treaty had not been supplied to the Bundestag), and Seiters' reply, 24 April 1990, BArch, B 136/21664.
33. Prot. BT, 11. WP, 27 April 1990, pp. 16422–5. Even 'benchmark' pensioners, i.e. average earners with 45 insurance years, would see a 20 per cent fall in their real incomes, as a result of the elimination of subsidies.
34. ibid., p. 16426.
35. Verfassungsrechtliche Beurteilung des Vorschlags von Vogel auf Bildung eines 'Gemeinsamen Gremiums' von Bundestag und Bundesrat durch den Leiter des Referats 332 (Verfassungsrecht), Regierungsdirektor Dr Lehnguth, Federal Chancellery, 8 February 1990: 'A committee of this sort is not provided for under constitutional law.' However, the document said, that did not preclude the formation of such a committee, and cooperation on a voluntary basis, without decision-making powers. On the other hand, if such a committee were composed of high-level individuals, its recommendations would, 'in reality, have the effect of binding decisions', so that the powers of the Bundestag and Bundesrat laid down in the Basic Law would be 'outplayed'. The formation of the committee was therefore 'undesirable' on constitutional grounds. Cf. BArch, B 136/26281. On the rejection of the SPD initiative, cf. also Vermerk von Ministerialdirigent Claus-Jürgen Duisberg [head of the 'Arbeitsstab Deutschlandpolitik' in the Bundeskanzleramt] über ein Gespräch von Seiters mit dem Chef der Staatskanzlei von NRW, Staatssekretär Clement am 9.2.1990, 12 February 1990, BArch, B 136/26281. The Prime Minister of North Rhine-Westphalia, Rau, declared himself in favour of such a committee in a government statement of 14 February 1990: cf. Ministerialrat Germelmann, head of Referat 221, 'Allgemeine Fragen der Beziehungen zur DDR', Bundeskanzleramt, to Chef des Bundeskanzleramtes Seiters, in preparation for a meeting of heads of *Bund* and *Länder* government on 15 February 1990, 15 February 1990, BArch, B 136/26281.
36. cf. BT, Ausschuß Deutsche Einheit, stenographic reports.
37. Sitzung des Fraktionsvorstandes, 5 February 1990, ACDP, Protokolle des Fraktionsvorstandes.

38. Sitzung des Fraktionsvorstandes, 12 February 1990, ACDP, Protokolle des Fraktionsvorstandes.
39. Sitzung des Fraktionsvorstandes, 26 March 1990, ACDP, Protokolle des Fraktionsvorstandes.
40. Gesammelte Arbeitsgruppen-Protokolle, Sitzung der Arbeitsgruppe 10 Arbeit und Soziales, 27 March 1990, and Sitzung der Arbeitnehmergruppe, 27 March 1990, ACDP, Ordner VIII-001 (245).
41. Sitzung des Fraktionsvorstandes, 23 April 1990, ACDP, Protokolle des Fraktionsvorstandes.
42. Fraktionssitzung, 24 April 1990, ACDP, Fraktionsprotokolle.
43. Fraktionssitzung, 8 May 1990, ACDP, Fraktionsprotokolle.
44. Fraktionssitzung, 15 May 1990, ACDP, Fraktionsprotokolle (emphasis in record).
45. Fraktionssitzung, 18 May 1990, ACDP, Fraktionsprotokolle.
46. Fraktionssitzung, 29 August 1990, ACDP, Fraktionsprotokolle.
47. Sitzung des Fraktionsvorstandes, 3 September 1990, ACDP, Protokolle des Fraktionsvorstandes.
48. For the State Treaty, cf. Tietmeyer, 'Erinnerungen', in *Tage*, pp. 64 f., 70, 84, 93–5, 111 f.
49. cf. above, p. 146.
50. Cronenberg to Jagoda, 10 May 1990, BArch, B 149/78841.
51. ibid., and cf. also Cronenberg to Tietmeyer, 10 May 1990, BArch, B 149/78841. A copy of the letter also went to Jagoda. In an interview with the author on 27 June 2000 Cronenberg emphasized that he was well informed and that the FDP was able to bring its ideas to bear, particularly through the Economics Ministry, headed by Helmut Haussmann of the FDP.
52. In his interview with the author on 8 June 2000, Blüm noted that disagreements between ministries were aired in advance of cabinet meetings and that the cabinet was merely the 'notary's office'.
53. Blüm to Kohl, 12 December 1989, ACDP, Bestand Blüm I 504/57.
54. BMA, Arbeitspapier, Sozialpolitische Aspekte der innerdeutschen Entwicklung, 9 January 1990, AdsD, 5/DGAi 002089.
55. cf. above, p. 166 f.
56. Arbeitskreis Sozialpolitik, Klaus Detlef Dietz, Dr. Manfred Hiltner, Hermann Krauthausen, Stellungnahme zu den sozialpolitisch relevanten Teilen des II. Staatsvertrages. The paper is undated, but was probably written at the end of July or the beginning of August 1990. The authors say that the paper's standpoint tallies with the basic policy position of the working group, though it has 'not yet been agreed in terms of individual policy issues, because of the holiday period'. AdsD, 9626.
57. Dreßler, too, judged that there was never any real likelihood that reforms could have been implemented in the Federal Republic by means of regulations in the GDR. However, in view of the balance of political forces they had to be on their guard to ensure that existing social policy in the Federal Republic was exported to the east without excisions. Cf. interview with Dreßler by the author, 18 May 2000.
58. Vogel in the Bundestag, 21 June 1990, in Prot. BT, 11. WP, p. 17165.
59. On the SPD's attitude, cf. also Fabian Peterson, *Oppositionsstrategie der SPD-Führung im deutschen Einigungsprozess 1989/1990. Strategische Ohnmacht durch Selbstblockade?*, Hamburg 1998.
60. cf. Besprechung des Bundeskanzlers Kohl mit den Regierungschefs der Länder, 21 December 1989, in *Dokumente zur Deutschlandpolitik*, p. 680.

61. Verständigung zwischen der Bundesregierung und den Regierungen der Länder über die Beteiligung der Länder bei Abkommen zwischen der Bundesrepublik Deutschland und der Deutschen Demokratischen Republik, 17 December 1987, BArch, B 136/20634.
62. Clement to Seiters, 25 January 1990, with enclosure, Beschlussvorlage der Länder, in *Dokumente zur Deutschlandpolitik*, pp. 721 f.
63. Besprechung des Chefs des Bundeskanzleramtes Seiters mit den Chefs der Staats- und Senatskanzleien der Länder, 30 January 1990, in ibid., pp. 735–9.
64. Dr Mahnke, Referat II A 3, BMB, to Ministerialdirigent Dr Duisberg, Bundeskanzleramt, concerning Beteiligung der Länder an Verhandlungen und Verträgen mit der DDR (here, Besprechung des Bundeskanzlers mit den Regierungschefs der Länder am 15.2.1990), 5 February 1990, BArch, B 136/20634.
65. Clement to Seiters, 6 February 1990, BArch, B 136/26281. Cf. also Gespräch des Bundesministers Seiters mit Staatssekretär Clement, 9 February 1990, in *Dokumente zur Deutschlandpolitik*, pp. 776–8.
66. Stellungnahme zu Forderungen von Clement in einer Aufzeichnung für die Kabinettssitzung am 7.2.1990, unsigned and undated, in Federal Chancellery records with title, Beteiligung der Länder an Verhandlungen und Verträgen mit der DDR (Vertragsgemeinschaft), BArch, B 136/26281.
67. Besprechung des Bundeskanzlers mit den Regierungschefs der Länder, 15 February 1990, with two attachments, Beschlussvorschlag der Länder and Beschlussvorschlag des Bundes, in *Dokumente zur Deutschlandpolitik*, pp. 834–9.
68. ibid., p. 835.
69. cf. Ministerialrat Germelmann, head of Referat 221, Bundeskanzleramt, with Vorschlag von Repliken zu Ausführungen von Ministerpräsident Rau in seiner Regierungserklärung vom 14.2.1990 und vom Regierenden Bürgermeister von Berlin, Momper, in einer Pressekonferenz vom 12.2.1990, 15 February 1990, BArch, B 136/26281.
70. cf. Besprechung des Chefs des Bundeskanzleramtes Seiters mit den Chefs der Staats- und Senatskanzleien der Länder, 2 March 1990 and 26 April 1990, in *Dokumente zur Deutschlandpolitik*, pp. 899–901, 1059–62. Cf. also letters from Clement to Seiters, 14 March, 22 March, 19 April, and 30 April 1990, BArch, B 136/26283, 26284, 26285. On these letters, cf. comment by Dr Malina, head of Referat 224, 'Kabinettsauschuss Deutsche Einheit und Bund-Länder-Verhältnis in bezug auf Deutschlandpolitik', Bundeskanzleramt, to Chef des Bundeskanzleramtes, 4 May 1990, and Seiters' reply to Clement, 8 May 1990, BArch, B 136/26285.
71. cf. comment by Thilo Sarrazin, head of interdepartmental 'Arbeitsgruppe Innerdeutsche Beziehungen', BMF, on preparation for German monetary union, in reply to a letter by Clement, 22 March 1990, BArch B 136/26284.
72. cf. Besprechung des Chefs des Bundeskanzleramtes Seiters mit den Chefs der Staats- und Senatskanzleien der Länder, 26 April 1990, in *Dokumente zur Deutschlandpolitik*, pp. 1059 f.
73. cf. Christian Dästner, 'Die Mitwirkung der Länder bei den Entscheidungen zur Wiederherstellung der Einheit Deutschlands', in *Die Rolle des Bundesrates und der Länder im Prozess der deutschen Einigung*, ed. Eckart Klein, Berlin 1998, pp. 33–60 (here, p. 35). In 1990 Dästner was head of the sectional group 'Recht und Verfassung' in the State Chancellery of North Rhine-Westphalia and a participant in the negotiations on the Unification Treaty as an adviser to Clement.

74. Besprechung des Bundeskanzlers Kohl mit den Regierungschefs der Länder, 16 May 1990, in *Dokumente zur Deutschlandpolitik*, pp. 1122–5. Cf. also Grosser, *Wagnis*, pp. 313, 319, 368–72.
75. Stahmer to Barbara Schäfer, Ministerin für Arbeit und Sozialordnung, Baden-Württemberg, 9 March 1990, with attachment, Pressemitteilung zum Thema 'Sozialpolitisches Deutschlandkonzept', 9 March 1990, BMA VIII/I a 1/15101.2.
76. Informationsgespräch zum Staatsvertrag mit der DDR mit den Ministern und Senatoren für Arbeit und Soziales am 2.5.1990 im BMA, 7 May 1990, BArch, B 149/78841.
77. Streibl to Kohl, 10 April 1990, BArch, B 136/21664. In the letter Streibl also declares the readiness of the government of Bavaria to be involved in the negotiations at governmental level on 'Währungsunion, Wirtschafts- und Sozialgemeinschaft' and strongly urges that the recommendations of the Central Bank Council concerning the currency changeover be adhered to.
78. Dästner, 'Mitwirkung', p. 36.
79. ibid., p. 37.
80. Besprechung des Chefs des Bundeskanzleramtes Seiters mit den Chefs der Staats- und Senatskanzleien der Länder, 5 July 1990, in *Dokumente zur Deutschlandpolitik*, pp. 1299–304.
81. Dästner, 'Mitwirkung', p. 44.
82. cf. especially, in addition to Schäuble, *Vertrag*, Dästner, 'Mitwirkung', pp. 37–57; 'Einleitung', *Dokumente zur Deutschlandpolitik*, esp. pp. 195–221 and the documents on the negotiations reproduced in that work; Jäger, *Überwindung*, esp. pp. 478–525.
83. Eckpunkte der Länder für die bundesstaatliche Ordnung im vereinten Deutschland, in *Dokumente zur Deutschlandpolitik*, pp. 1305–7.
84. Prot. VK, 10. WP, 36. Tagung, 20 September 1990, p. 1750.
85. cf. above, p. 200.
86. Dästner, 'Mitwirkung', p. 55.
87. Jäger, *Überwindung*, pp. 482 f.
88. Vermerk: Sitzung der Arbeitsgruppe DGB/BDA/BMA/DAG am 26.6.1990 in Köln, AdsD, 5/DGAi 000782. For the problems discussed by the working group, cf. also letter of Reinhard Dombre, Abteilung Tarifpolitik des DGB, to Franz Hantke, Abteilung Gesellschaftspolitik, 16 January 1990; note by Günther Horzetzky, DGB-Verbindungsstelle in Bonn, to SPD member of parliament Gerd Andres, 23 January 1990; note by Horzetzky on Ausführungen des BMA-Vertreters auf der Sitzung der Arbeitsgruppe, 12 March 1990; Protokoll über die Sitzung, 22 March 1990; note by Friedel Heße for the chairman of the DGB Heinz-Werner Meyer, 15 June 1990 (the latter wanted more information about the tasks of the working group prior to talks with the president of the National Union of German Employers' Associations): AdsD, 5/DGAi 002089, 002090, 000782.
89. Abteilung Wirtschaft [Metal Workers' Union headquarters], Zur Kritik des Vorstoßes für eine umgehende 'Währungsunion mit Wirtschaftsgemeinschaft' BRD-DDR und soziale Alternativen, 14 February 1990, AdsD, 5/DGAi 002089. The Metal Workers' Union's later attitude was also markedly critical: cf. Memorandum des Vorstandes der IG Metall, Die soziale Einheit gestalten—Memorandum der IG Metall zur sozialen Ausgestaltung des Prozesses der Einigung der beiden deutschen Staaten, 8 May 1990. In his letter of 23 May 1990 to Prime Minister de Maizière accompanying the memorandum, the leader of the union, Franz Steinkühler, underlined the need for

the social aspect of unity to be extended and asked that the trade unions be included in the dialogue about the development of unity. BArch, DC 20/6032.

90. Friedel Heße, Abteilung Gesellschaftspolitik, to chairman of the DGB Ernst Breit, 10 February 1990, with attachment, Deutsche Einheit—Währungsunion. Ein Problemaufriss, 8 February 1990, AdsD, 5/DGAi 002089. In the covering letter to Breit, Heße suggested that the German Trade Union Federation, in close consultation with the trade unions of the GDR, should work out how 'structural change can be shaped in a socially acceptable manner'. The Federation should also 'strongly demand to be included in decisions at government level'.
91. Dr Tyll Necker, Statement anlässlich der Besprechung im Bundeskanzleramt zum Thema deutsch-deutsche Wirtschaftsgemeinschaft und Währungsunion am 20.2.1990 in Bonn, Bundesverband der Deutschen Industrie press release, 20 February 1990, AdsD, 5/DGAi 002089. An attachment contains an 'Übersicht zu den Aktivitäten der deutschen Wirtschaft mit Blick auf die DDR', reporting *inter alia* on educational and training measures for future entrepreneurs, qualified employees, and executives, on the development of trade association structures, and on the opening of information offices and representative services of German industry.
92. Ernst Breit, Statement für das Gespräch mit Bundeskanzler Kohl am 20.2.1990 zum Thema 'Hilfen für die DDR', AdsD, 5/DGAi 002089. Cf. also Ralf Kleinfeld, 'Zwischen rundem Tisch und konzertierter Aktion. Korporatistische Formen der Interessenvermittlung in den neuen Bundesländern', in Eichener *et al.* (eds.), *Organisierte Interessen*, pp. 73–133 (here, p. 85).
93. Entschließung zur deutschen Einheit. Beschlossen vom DGB-Bundesausschuss in Bonn am 7.3.1990 bei 3 Gegenstimmen, AdsD, 5/DGAi 002090.
94. Gemeinsame Erklärung des DGB und der BDA zu einer einheitlichen Wirtschafts- und Sozialordnung in beiden deutschen Staaten, 9 March 1990, AdsD, 5/DGAi 000782.
95. The official was probably Ministerialdirektor Baldur Wagner, head of Abteilung 3, Innere Angelegenheiten, Soziales, Umwelt, in the Federal Chancellery.
96. Hans Böckler, 1875–1951: trade union leader, first chairman of the German Trade Union Federation in the British zone from 1947 to 1949, first chairman of the Federation from 1949 to 1951. Böckler worked with Federal Chancellor Adenauer on important issues in German politics and strengthened the influence of the trade unions as a result.
97. Günther Horzetzky to Werner Milert, Abteilung 'Vorsitzender des DGB', 'Persönlich/Vertraulich', 14 March 1990, AdsD, 5/DGAi 002090.
98. Note by Günther Horzetzky for Abteilungsleiter 3 des Bundeskanzleramtes, Baldur Wagner, 'Persönlich/Vertraulich', 17 March 1990, AdsD, 5/DGAi 002090.
99. cf. 'DGB läßt FDGB fallen. Im Gespräch: Ernst Breit zum gewerkschaftlichen Einigungsprozess. Vertrauen in FDGB ist unrettbar verloren', in *Frankfurter Rundschau*, 5 May 1990, AdsD, DAG-Bundesvorstand, Abt. Vors.—Anton Reuer.
100. Bundesvorstand des DGB, Grundzüge der Arbeits- und Sozialordnung in einem geeinten Deutschland, 18 April 1990, AdsD, DAG-Bundesvorstand, Abt. Vors.—Anton Reuer.
101. DGB-Vorstand, Erste Bewertung des Entwurfs der Bundesregierung für einen Staatsvertrag mit der DDR, 30 April 1990, AdsD, Bestand: SPD-Fraktion in der Volkskammer der DDR, Mappe 27.
102. DGB-Bundesvorstand/Sprecherrat der Gewerkschaften der DDR, Stellungnahme zum Entwurf der Bundesregierung für einen Staatsvertrag mit der DDR (Fassung vom 12.5.1990), 15 May 1990, AdsD, 9607.

103. cf. Gesamtdeutsche Gewerkschaftsposition zum Staatsvertrag beiden Regierungen vorgelegt, 15 May 1990, AdsD, 9607.
104. According to an analysis by the Federal Chancellery, the notice of motion on German unity drawn up by the national executive of the Trade Union Federation on 21 May 1990 at the 14th regular conference of the Federation in Hamburg on 20–6 May 1990 described the State Treaty as 'cautiously positive overall'. The analysis also noted, however, that the Federation hoped that demands which it had not been able to achieve within the Federal Republic might 'now be realized indirectly, through the GDR and the State Treaty'. Note by R. Zimmer, 23 May 1990, BArch, B 149/78843; text of the notice of motion in AdsD, 5/DGAi 002106.
105. cf. DGB-Bundesvorstand/Der Vorsitzende des Sprecherrates der Gewerkschaften und Industriegewerkschaften der DDR, Anforderungen an den angestrebten Einigungsvertrag zwischen der Bundesrepublik Deutschland und der Deutschen Demokratischen Republik, 27 July 1990; id., Stellungnahme zum 1. Entwurf eines Vertrages zwischen der Deutschen Demokratischen Republik und der Bundesrepublik Deutschland über die Herstellung der Einheit Deutschlands (Einigungsvertrag), 17 August 1990; both documents in AdsD, 9623. Cf. also 'Sozialpolitische Forderungen des DGB für den deutschen Einigungsprozess', in Informationsdienst des DGB, 20 July 1990; Ursula Engelen-Kefer, deputy chairwoman of the DGB, to Ministerin für Arbeit und Soziales der DDR, Regine Hildebrandt, 8 August 1990, with attachment, Positionen des DGB zum sozialpolitischen Teil des ersten Entwurfs des Einigungsvertrages, BArch, DQ 3, 1878a. For the Trade Union Federation's final verdict on the Unification Treaty, cf. DGB-Bundesvorstand, DGB-Informationen zum Einigungsvertrag, October 1990, AdsD, 5/DGAi 002093. This 51-page paper lists the provisions in the Unification Treaty that are of most importance for employees, discusses them, and evaluates them from the Federation's point of view.
106. Rudolf Dreßler, in his interview with the author on 18 May 2000, was critical of this fact.
107. Numerous sources in the Trade Union Federation's records attest to this. Cf., in particular, Protokoll der Besprechung mit den Vorsitzenden der DGB-Landesbezirke am 3.7.1990 in der Bundesvorstandsverwaltung, 4 July 1990, AdsD, 5/DGAi 000781; paper, Rechtsschutzleistungen des DGB in der DDR, 31 August 1990, AdsD, 5/DGAi 001092.
108. cf. Unabhängige Kommission zur Überprüfung der Vermögenswerte aller Parteien und Massenorganisationen der DDR im Amt des Ministerpräsidenten der DDR an die Vorsitzende des FDGB, Helga Mausch, 13 August 1990; note by Werner Milet, DGB-Verbindungsstelle in Berlin, on 'Aufteilung des Vermögens des FDGB', 15 August 1990; Friedel Heße to the chairman of the DGB, Heinz-Werner Meyer, 16 August 1990, concerning 'Vermögen des FDGB'; note by W. Milert, 17 August 1990, on 'Vermögen des FDGB'; letter of chairman of the Sprecherrat des Bundes der Industriegewerkschaften und Gewerkschaften, Peter Rothe, to Ministerpräsident de Maizière, 22 August 1990: all documents in AdsD, 5/DGAi 002109 and 002110. See also DGB zur Auseinandersetzung um das FDGB-Vermögen, 4 September 1990, in Nachrichtendienst des DGB, 4 September 1990 (here, AdsD, 5/DGAi 002093); letter of 1st chairman of IG Metall Franz Steinkühler to the President and parliamentary party chairmen of the Volkskammer of the GDR, the party chairmen of the GDR, the Ministerpräsident of the GDR, the Bundeskanzler, the President and parliamentary party chairmen of the Bundestag, the party chairmen, the Prime Ministers of the *Länder* of the Federal Republic, members of the federal executive

of the DGB, chairmen of DGB member trade unions, chairman of the Sprecherrat of the FDGB, chairman of IG Metall for the GDR, 24 August 1990, AdsD, Bestand: SPD-Fraktion in der Volkskammer der DDR, Mappe 116.

109. Stellungnahme der Bundesvereinigung der deutschen Arbeitgeberverbände zum Entwurf des Einigungsvertrages, with accompanying letter by Dr Himmelreich and Dr Doetsch, Hauptgeschäftsführung, sent to Bundesarbeitsminister Blüm on 15 August 1990, BArch, B 149/401174.
110. cf. above, p. 148 f.
111. cf. above, pp. 182 f.
112. cf. above, p. 194.

German Unification and Social Policy: Conclusions

1. Bundesarbeitsminister Blüm to the First Chairman of the Kassenärztliche Bundesvereinigung, Dr Ulrich Oesingmann, 15 August 1990, ACDP, Bestand Blüm I 504/67.
2. Interview by the author with Jagoda, 5 July 2000.
3. Rudolf Dreßler took this view in his interview with the author, 18 May 2000.
4. cf. above, p. 165. For the views of the Public Services and Transport Trade Union, cf. also Gesundheitspolitische und beschäftigungspolitische Perspektiven der Gewerkschaft Öffentliche Dienste, Transport und Verkehr (ÖTV) für das Zusammenwachsen beider deutscher Staaten; Ulrike Peretzki-Leid, member of the executive of the ÖTV, to the Minister für Gesundheitswesen der DDR, Jürgen Kleditzsch, 5 June 1990; Gesundheitspolitische Erklärung der ÖTV und der Gewerkschaft Gesundheits-und Sozialwesen der DDR, 11 June 1990: all documents in BArch, DQ 1, 14222.
5. Interview by the author with Jagoda, 5 July 2000.
6. Judgement of the Federal Constitutional Court, 30 May 1990, BVerfGE, 82, 1991, pp. 123–56.
7. cf. above, p. 159.
8. Judgement of the Federal Constitutional Court, 28 January 1992, BVerfGE, 85, 1993, pp. 191–214.
9. cf. *BGBl I*, 1996, pp. 1246–53.
10. *Sozialbericht 1993*, pp. 32 f.
11. *Sozialbericht 1997*, pp. 22 f.
12. cf. Frerich and Frey, *Handbuch*, vol. ii, pp. 376–8.
13. cf. above, p. 61.
14. Schwangeren- und Familienhilfegesetz, 21 August 1995, *BGBl I*, pp. 1050–7.

III CHANGES TO THE GERMAN WELFARE STATE AFTER GERMAN UNIFICATION, 1990–1994

11 The Build-up of Welfare-State Institutions and Providers in the New *Bundesländer*

1. *Allensbacher Jahrbuch 1993–1997*, p. 558.
2. ibid., p. 609.
3. cf. Sachstandsbericht der Außenstelle Berlin des BMA, 'Aufbau der Sozialverwaltung in den 5 neuen Bundesländern', sent on 14 November 1990 by the head of the Außenstelle des BMA, Ministerialdirektor Jung, to the head of the Außenstelle des Bundeskanzleramtes, Ministerialdirektor Kabel, as the basis for a meeting on 15 November 1990 of the heads of the Berlin Außenstellen of the senior Federal authorities: BArch, B 149/400150. The specific areas dealt with were the administrative system for

employment, the administration of social provision for war victims, and the development of accident insurance, pensions insurance, and health insurance.

4. cf. above, pp. 136 f.
5. von Maydell *et al.*, *Umwandlung*, p. 233.
6. Letter of the President of the BA Franke to Bundesminister Blüm, 13 August 1990, BArch, B 149/400015. Under an alternative plan, the *Land* employment office for Schleswig-Holstein-Hamburg would have been expanded by the addition of Mecklenburg-West Pomerania, with 12 regional employment offices, the creation of a *Land* office for Berlin-Brandenburg-Saxony-Anhalt, with 22 regional offices, and the establishment of a South *Land* office for Saxony and Thuringia, with 17 regional offices.
7. BMA, I a 7, Bestandsaufnahme der Aufbauhilfen zur Angleichung der Arbeits- und Sozialordnung in Deutschland, 8 February 1991, BArch, B 149/74934; *Sozialbericht 1993*, pp. 11 f.
8. BMA, Referat II b 1, to the Minister concerning 'Überprüfung von Mitarbeitern in Arbeitsämtern und Arbeitsnebenstellen im Beitrittsgebiet', 7 March 1991, BArch, B 149/400015.
9. ACDP, Fraktionsprotokolle.
10. BMA, Staatssekretär Tegtmeier to Staatssekretär Carl, BMVg, 6 November 1990, BArch, B 149/400576.
11. On this problem, cf. the Bestandsaufnahme cited in note 7 above, and Bestandsaufnahme, 30 November 1990, BArch B 149/74934.
12. cf. Matthias Knuth, 'ABS-Gesellschaften als dezentrale Akteure der Arbeitsmarkt- und Strukturpolitik: Problemlösung "vor Ort"?', in Heinelt *et* al. (eds.), *Arbeitsmarktpolitik nach der Vereinigung*, pp. 172–84. 'ABS-Gesellschaften' denotes 'Gesellschaften zur Arbeitsförderung, Beschäftigung und Strukturentwicklung', i.e. companies dealing in employment promotion, employment, and structural development. The hope that such companies would make themselves redundant, through the creation of permanent jobs, was not fulfilled.
13. cf. Blüm to Ministerin für Arbeit, Soziales, Gesundheit und Frauen des Landes Brandenburg, Hildebrandt, 26 June 1991, ACDP, Bestand Blüm I 504/81.
14. cf. BMA, *Sozialbericht 1993*, pp. 29, 34; *Sozialbericht 1997*, pp. 19, 26.
15. cf. Friedrich Buttler and Knut Emmerich, 'Kosten und Nutzen aktiver Arbeitsmarktpolitik im ostdeutschen Transformationsprozess', in *Die Wettbewerbsfähigkeit der ostdeutschen Wirtschaft. Ausgangslage, Handlungserfordnisse, Perspektiven*, ed. Gernot Gutmann, Berlin 1995, pp. 61–94, esp. p. 64.
16. cf. BMA, Abt. II b 2, to Parlamentarischer Staatssekretär Günther with copies to the Minister, Staatssekretäre and Abteilungsleiter I, 19 April 1991, BArch, B 149/400493. See also Frerich and Frey, *Handbuch*, vol. iii, pp. 611 f.
17. *Sozialbericht 1993*, p. 29; *Sozialbericht 1997*, p. 19.
18. Buttler and Emmerich, 'Kosten und Nutzen', p. 62.
19. Figures from *Sozialbericht 1993*, p. 34; *Sozialbericht 1997*, p. 25.
20. cf. interviews by the author with Cronenberg, 27 June 2000, and with Blüm, 8 June 2000. On the danger of distortion of competition resulting from employment promotion measures, and on the acknowledgement that these could not create permanent jobs, cf. also *Sozialbericht 1997*, p. 30.
21. On this, and on the resultant disputes between the new *Bundesländer*, backed by the Federal Ministry for Environmental Planning, Construction, and Urban Development, and the Labour Ministry, cf. Willibald Böck, Innenminister, Thuringia, to Bundesministerin für Raumordnung, Bauwesen und Städtebau, Irmgard Schwaetzer, 1 June

1992; Informationsvermerk über die ABM-Förderung bei der Bearbeitung von Wohngeldanträgen in den neuen Bundesländern, undated; Staatssekretär des BMBau, Herbert Schmülling, to Staatssekretär Werner Tegtmeier, BMA, 2 July 1992; Schmülling to Chef des Bundeskanzleramtes Friedrich Bohl, 18 August 1992; Schmülling to Staatssekretär Bernhard Worms, BMA, 21 August 1992; Ministerialrat Schmidt, head of Referat II b 3, 'Erhaltung und Schaffung von Arbeitsplätzen', BMA, to Bohl, 31 July 1992: all sources in BMA VIII a 1/17305, vol. i or BMA VIII a 1/17490 (5).

22. cf. Entwurf eines Antrages über die 'Ablösung des Arbeitsförderungsgesetzes durch ein Arbeits- und Strukturförderungsgesetz (ASFG)', 21 September 1992, and Ergebnisprotokoll über die Sitzung des Querschnittsgruppe 'Einheit Deutschlands' der SPD, 29 October 1992, at which meeting the motion was discussed; AdsD, 26000. Cf. also '"Eckpunkte für ein neues Arbeits- und Strukturförderungsgesetz" und für den im Bundestag 1994 eingebrachten Entwurf des Gesetzes', Heinelt and Weck, *Arbeitsmarktpolitik*, pp. 161f. For Blüm's arguments in favour of the amendment to the Employment Promotion Law, and the SPD's criticisms of it, cf. the speeches by Blüm and Ottmar Schreiner (of the SPD) in the Bundestag on 15 October 1992, Prot. BT, 12. WP, pp. 9600–4, 9604–9.
23. On the objectives of the law and the intended savings, cf. 'Arbeits- und Sozialordnung', Pressemitteilung des BMA, 1 July 1992; BMA, Ref. II b 1, Konzept des BMA zur Umsetzung des Eckwertebeschlusses des Kabinetts, 13 May 1992: both in BMA VIII a 1/17305 (2). Cf. also BMA, Ref. II b 1, Entwurf eines Gesetzes zur Änderung von Förderungsvoraussetzungen im Arbeitsförderungsgesetz und in anderen Gesetzen, 15 October 1992, BMA VIII a 1/17490 (6); on the law itself, cf. *BGBl I*, 1992, pp. 2044–57.
24. cf. Heinelt and Weck, *Arbeitsmarktpolitik*, p. 160.
25. cf. Blüm to Chef des Bundeskanzleramtes Bohl, 19 December 1992, BMA VIII a 1/17490 (6). In the Bundestag on 9 December 1992 Dreßler (of the SPD) voiced regret that the *Länder* led by the CDU—Mecklenburg-West Pomerania, Thuringia, Saxony-Anhalt and Saxony—finally voted in favour of the law, despite cabinet decisions (and, in Saxony-Anhalt's case, despite a decision by the *Land* parliament): Prot. BT, 12. WP, p. 10912. It was envisaged that there would be a lessening of the financial burden by 7,500 million DM in 1997. Cf. Blüm to the members of the CDU/CSU and FDP parliamentary parties, 12 January 1998, BMA document without designation.
26. cf. Heinelt and Weck, *Arbeitsmarktpolitik*, p. 164.
27. cf. Sven Jochen, 'Sozialpolitik in der Ära Kohl: Die Politik des Sozialversicherungsstaates', *ZeS-Arbeitspapier* no. 12/99, p. 31.
28. The account that follows is largely based on a detailed note by Referat VIII b 3 (Arbeitsrecht und Arbeitsschutz), responsible for the new *Bundesländer*, Probleme im Zusammenhang mit der Übertragung der bundesdeutschen Arbeitsrechtsordnung auf die ehemalige DDR, BArch, B 149/401615. The note itself is based on a 'wealth of individual testimonies, consultations with citizens, and discussions with judges, members of arbitration panels and works councils' and on an analysis of specialist publications and readers' letters, of legal judgements available in the branch of the Labour Ministry in Berlin, and of materials belonging to the *Treuhand.*
29. cf. below, pp. 247f.
30. Gemeinsame Erklärung des DGB und der BDA zu einer einheitlichen Wirtschafts- und Sozialordnung in beiden deutschen Staaten, 9 March 1990, AdsD, 5/DGAi 000782. Cf. also Gerhard Kleinhenz, 'Tarifpartnerschaft im vereinten Deutschland. Die

Bedeutung der Arbeitsmarktorganisation für die Einheit der Arbeits- und Lebensverhältnisse', in *APuZG*, B 12/92, pp. 14–24 (here, p. 20).

31. cf. Rudi Schmidt, 'Einleitung', in *Zwischenbilanz. Analysen zum Transformationsprozess der ostdeutschen Industrie*, ed. Rudi Schmidt, Berlin 1993, p. 22.
32. *GBl I*, p. 357.
33. Einigungsvertrag, Anlage I, Kapitel VIII, Sachgebiet A, Abschnitt III, *BGBl II*, 1990, p. 1023.
34. *Sozialbericht 1993*, p. 46. For the training sessions conducted by the trade unions the Federal government made available 57 million DM until 31 March 1993.
35. cf. Silke Röbenack, 'Betriebe und Belegschaftsvertretungen' and Renate Liebold, 'Innerbetriebliche Beziehungen in ostdeutschen Industriebezirken', both in *Industrielle Beziehungen. Institutionalisierung und Praxis unter Krisenbedingungen*, ed. Joachim Bergmann and Rudi Schmidt, Opladen 1996, pp. 161–212 and 213–35.
36. Bernd Keller, 'Arbeitspolitik in den neuen Bundesländern. Eine Zwischenbilanz des Transformationsprozesses', in *Sozialer Fortschritt*, 45 (1996), pp. 88–102, esp. pp. 95 f.
37. cf. *Gewerkschaftskongreß zur Auflösung des FDGB, Berlin 14.9.1990*, Bund der IG/Gew./Geschäftsführender Vorstand, September 1990, AdsD, 5/DGAi 002235.
38. Fax, Hantke to Wolfgang Üllenberg, 26 June 1990, with attachment, Vermerk: Betreff Termine der Vereinigung der DDR-Gewerkschaften mit den bundesrepublikanischen Gewerkschaften, 26 June 1990, AdsD, 5/DGAi 000781; paper, Überblick: Verfahrensweise und Termine bei der Aufnahme von Mitgliedern in der DDR durch die Gewerkschaften des DGB, 3 September 1990, AdsD, 5/DGAi 002092. Cf. also Schwarzer, *Arbeitsbeziehungen*, pp. 306–29; Helmut Martens, *Gewerkschaftlicher Organisationsaufbau und Mitbestimmung in Ostdeutschland. Ein eigenständiger und schwieriger Institutionalisierungsprozess und seine Folgen für die industriellen Beziehungen in der größer gewordenen Bundesrepublik*, Dortmund 1992; Michael Fichter and Hugo Reiter, 'Die Gewerkschaften', in *Intermediäre Strukturen in Ostdeutschland*, ed. Oskar Niedermayer, Opladen 1996, pp. 309–33; Oskar Niedermayer, 'Das intermediäre System', in Kaase *et al.*, *Politisches System*, pp. 155–230 (here, pp. 192–5).
39. cf. Wolfgang Schroeder, 'Industrielle Beziehungen in Ostdeutschland: Zwischen Transformation und Standortdebatte', in *APuZG*, B 40/96, pp. 25–34, esp. pp. 26f.
40. ibid.; Josef Schmid and Heinrich Tiemann, 'Gewerkschaften und Tarifverhandlungen in den fünf neuen Bundesländern. Organisationsentwicklung, politische Strategien und Probleme am Beispiel der IG Metall', in Eichener *et al.* (eds.),*Organisierte Interessen*, pp. 134–58. Cf. also Chairman of the DGB Heinz-Werner Meyer to the members of the federal executive of the DGB, Beschluß zur Finanzierung der baldmöglichen Aufnahme der Arbeit des DGB in der DDR, 9 July 1990, AdsD, 5/DGAi 002107; report by Friedel Heße, Abteilung Vorsitzender, Stand des Aufbaus der DGB-Organisation in den neuen Bundesländern, 7 May 1991; Heße, Eckpunkte. Errichtungen von DGB-Landesbezirken in den neuen Bundesländern, 26 June 1991; Heße, BV-Beratung über die Bildung von DGB-Landesbezirken in den neuen Bundesländern am 8.10.1991, 23 September 1991, with attachment on the projected staffing costs: all documents in AdsD, 5/DGAi 002271.
41. Schmid and Tiemann, 'Gewerkschaften', p. 139.
42. Heinz Knetter, Bevollmächtigter des Bundesvorstandes am Sitz des Ministerrates der DDR, to Rolf Schmachtenberg, MfAS, 9 August 1990, BArch, DQ 3, 1890.
43. Letter of Peter Seideneck, Außenstelle Berlin des DGB, to Peter Pletsch, Abteilung Organisation DGB-Zentrale, 17 September 1990, AdsD, 5/DGAi, Abt. Vorsitzender, no indication of vol.

44. Calculations based in figures in Niedermayer, 'Das intermediäre System', p. 223.
45. ibid.
46. cf. Klaus Löhrlein to Friedel Heße, 1 October 1991, with attachments, Mitglieder der Gewerkschaften in den DGB-Landesbezirken-Ost zum 30.6.1991, and Mitgliedervergleich neue/alte DGB-Landesbezirke; the latter also gives the percentage of members of the trade unions of the Federation relative to the number of people in employment: AdsD, 5/DGAi 002271.
47. Schroeder, 'Industrielle Beziehungen', p. 28. Cf. also 'Statistisches Material zur Mitgliederentwicklung der acht größten Einzelgewerkschaften und des DGB' (compiled by Martine Dorsch), in Bergmann and Schmidt (eds.), *Industrielle Beziehungen*, pp. 237–54.
48. Schroeder, 'Industrielle Beziehungen', p. 28.
49. Keller, 'Arbeitspolitik', p. 98.
50. cf. Detlef Perner, 'Entwicklung der Gewerkschaftsorganisation seit der deutschen Einigung', in *Wirtschaftliche und soziale Einheit Deutschlands. Eine Bilanz*, ed. Dirk Nolte, Ralf Sitte, and Alexandra Wagner, Cologne 1995, pp. 379–93 (here, pp. 384 f.).
51. Hans-Peter Müller, 'Gewerkschaftsvereinigung. Die Industriegewerkschaft Bergbau und Industrie im Deutschen Vereinigungsprozess', in Eckart *et al.* (eds.), *Wiedervereinigung Deutschlands*, pp. 537–59.
52. Keller, 'Arbeitspolitik', p. 98.
53. cf. Günter Hoffmann, 'Die Entstehung von Arbeitgeberverbänden im neuen Bundesgebiet am Beispiel des VME. Berlin-Brandenburg', in Walter Hantsche, Stefan Otte, Günter Hoffmann *et al.*, *Aufbau der Verbände und Arbeitsgerichte*, Opladen 1997, pp. 89–136; Fred Henneberger, 'Struktur und Organisationsdynamik der Unternehmerverbände: Probleme der Verbandsbildung und Interessenvereinheitlichung im vereinten Deutschland', in *Wirtschaft und Gesellschaft*, 19 (1993), pp. 329–57; Fred Henneberger, 'Interessenverbände in Deutschand: Aktuelle Entwicklungen unter besonderer Berücksichtigung der Situation in den neuen Bundesländern', in *SF*, vol. 42 (1993), pp. 242–51.
54. Hoffmann, 'Entstehung', esp. pp. 115–28.
55. ibid., p. 117.
56. Keller, 'Arbeitspolitik', p 97.
57. ibid..
58. Klaus Schroeder, *Preis der Einheit*, p. 128.
59. cf. above, p. 70.
60. cf. Cord Meyer, *Die Sozialplanrichtlinien der Treuhandanstalt*, Opladen 1996, pp. 34f.
61. cf. BMA, Abteilung II and Abteilung III, Vermerk: Sozialplanregelung in Treuhand-Unternehmen, 26 June 1991. Cf. also Blüm to Waigel, 1 March 1991, BMA VIII a 1/17701/1, vol. vi.
62. Richtlinie zu Sozialplänen in den neuen Bundesländern, in *Recht der Arbeit* 24 (1991), pp. 289–93.
63. Sebastian Biedenkopf, *Interessenausgleich und Sozialplan unter Berücksichtigung der besonderen Probleme bei der Privatisierung und Sanierung von Betrieben in den neuen Bundesländern*, Berlin 1994, p. 157.
64. BMA, Referat VIII b 3, Probleme im Zusammenhang mit der Übertragung der bundesdeutschen Arbeitsrechtsordnung auf die ehemalige DDR, 1 July 1992, BArch, B 149/401615.
65. ibid.; Biedenkopf, *Interessenausgleich*, pp. 160 f.
66. cf. Lothar Clasen, 'Tarifentwicklung Ost. Erste Zwischenbilanz', in *BArbBl* (1991), vol. 6, pp. 5–8; Lothar Clasen, 'Tarifverträge 1991. Schrittweise Angleichung', in

BArbBl (1992), vol. 4, pp. 5–10; Lothar Clasen, 'Tarifverträge 1992. Wieder 9000 Abschlüsse', in *BArbBl* (1993), vol. 3, pp. 14–19. These sources also contain references to other graduated pay agreements.

67. cf. Keller, 'Arbeitspolitik', p. 100.
68. cf. Reinhard Bispinck, 'Der Tarifkonflikt um den Stufenplan in der ostdeutschen Metallindustrie—Anlaß, Entwicklung, Ergebnis', in *WSI Mitteilungen*, 46 (1993), pp. 469–81 (here, p. 478); Wolfgang Schroeder, 'Westdeutsche Prägung—ostdeutsche Bewährungsproben: Industrielle Beziehungen in der Metall- und Elektroindustrie', in Bergmann and Schmidt (eds.), *Industrielle Beziehungen*, pp. 101–33.
69. cf. Keller, 'Arbeitspolitik', p. 100.
70. cf. BMA, Referat III a 1, Lohn-und Tarifwesen, to the Minister, Staatssekretäre of the BMA and Abteilungen I and VIII: Aktuelle Lohn- und Tarifsituation zur Jahresmitte 1992, 14 July 1992, BMA VIII a 1/17305, vol. i.
71. cf., for example, his *Express* interview of 4 April 1993 and his n-tv interview of 20 June 1993. Blüm favoured, in addition to a standard basic wage in the form of investment wages, a second wage component dependent on company proceeds: on this, cf. his interview in *Die Welt*, 11 October 1993. All interviews in *BPA-Dok*, Text-Bull-RFTV-AA (87–95).
72. On the discussion concerning the problems of regional collective agreements and flexibilization, cf. Hans-Herrmann Hartwich, 'Der Flächentarifvertrag. Instrument und Symbol kollektivrechtlicher Arbeitsbeziehungen in Deutschland', in *Gegenwartskunde*, 46 (1997), pp. 101–33.
73. cf. Keller, 'Arbeitspolitik', p. 98. On the withdrawal of employers from employers' associations and the growing readiness of the trade unions to see regional collective agreements made more flexible through 'opening' clauses, cf. also the fundamental study by the long-serving president of the Federal Employment Court, Otto Rudolf Kissel, *Arbeitsrecht. Ein Leitfaden*, Munich 2002 (here, pp. 60 and 95).
74. Hartwich, 'Flächentarifvertrag', p. 125.
75. cf. Joachim Fels, 'Arbeitsmärkte und Währungsunion', in *Börsen-Zeitung*, 9 January 1997, reprinted in Deutsche Bundesbank, *Auszüge aus Presseartikeln*, no. 3, 15 January 1997, pp. 16 f. On the problem generally, cf. Frank Moll, *Tarifausstieg der Arbeitgeber: Mitgliedschaft im Arbeitgeberverband 'ohne Tarifbindung'*, Berlin 2000; Wolfgang Schroeder, *Das Modell Deutschland auf dem Prüfstand. Zur Entwicklung der industriellen Beziehungen in Ostdeutschland (1990–2000)*, Wiesbaden 2000.
76. *BGBl I*, pp. 1606–708.
77. cf. Blüm to Ministerin für besondere Aufgaben, Sabine Bergmann-Pohl, 17 December 1990; Blüm to Minister für Arbeit und Soziales, Saxony-Anhalt, Werner Schreiber, with copies to the relevant Ministers of the other new *Bundesländer*, 7 January 1991, ACDP, Bestand Blüm I 504/74.
78. cf. BArch, DQ 1, 13166; also Herbert Mrotzeck and Herbert Püschel, 'Krankenversicherung und Alterssicherung', in *Beiträge zu den Berichten der Kommission für die Erforschung des sozialen and politischen Wandels in den neuen Bundesländern e.V. (KSPW)*, vol. vi.7, ed. Hans Bertram, Hildegard Maria Nickel and Oskar Niedermayer, Opladen 1997.
79. Ministerin Hildebrandt to President of the BfA, Helmut Kaltenbach, 31 May 1990, BArch, DQ 3, 1889.
80. Ministerin Hildebrandt to Rudolf Kolb, 25 July 1990, and text of the contract, 1 August 1990, BArch, DQ 3, 1889b and 1890.

81. BMA, Referat IV a 1, Ministerialdirigent Pappai to Staatssekretär Jagoda, with attachment, Aufbauhilfe der Rentenversicherungsträger, 19 November 1990, BArch, B149/74922.
82. Spree, *Sozialstaat*, pp. 73 f.
83. cf. ibid.; Jagoda to the BA, BfA, BVA, and the leading German social insurance associations, 31 August 1990, BArch, B 149/74921; BVA-Arbeitsgruppe 'Beitragseinzug beim Gemeinsamen Träger der Sozialversicherung', 19 December 1990, BMG-Bonn, 223-48123, vol. ii; VDR, *Geschäftsbericht für das Jahr 1990*, pp. 44f.
84. Ministerin Hildebrandt to 'alle Mitarbeiterinnen und Mitarbeiter der Sozialversicherung der DDR', 7 August 1990, BArch, DQ 3, 1890.
85. cf. Kleditzsch to GDR Minister of the Interior Diestel, 23 August 1990. (After Hildebrandt's resignation, Kleditzsch had also taken charge of the GDR Ministry of Labour and Social Affairs.) The note refers to the differences in start-up conditions among the various social insurance providers in the GDR and to the especially precarious position of pensions insurance: BArch, DQ 3, 1890a.
86. Franz Ruland, 'Erfolgreiche Aufbauarbeit', in *BArbBl* (1992), vol. 10, pp. 24–8 (here, pp. 24 f.).
87. Blüm to Eppelmann, 28 September 1990, with attachment, Vertrag zwischen Eppelmann und der BfA, 27 September 1990, ACDP, Bestand Blüm I 504/69.
88. Eberhard Schaub, 'Die Aufbauarbeit der Rentenversicherung in den neuen Bundesländern', in VDR, Aktuelles Presseseminar des VDR 12./13. November 1992 in Würzburg, pp. 102–18 (here, p. 105).
89. Ruland to Blüm, 24 October 1990, BArch, B 149/400576.
90. Blüm to Waigel, 30 March 1992, and Waigel's reply, 30 April 1992, BMA VIII a 1/17305 (4).
91. Ruland, 'Erfolgreiche Aufbauarbeit', p. 25.
92. ÜLA, Geschäftsführer Ammermüller, Bericht zur Tätigkeit des Gemeinsamen Trägers der Sozialversicherung im Beitrittsgebiet und dessen Rechtsnachfolger der Überleitungsanstalt Sozialversicherung zwischen 12.11.1990 und 31.12.1991. The report is contained in one of two files of documents on the work of the Social Insurance Transitional Authority. The author is grateful to Dr Ammermüller for providing access to these files.
93. Ammermüller to Blüm, 14 November 1990, Ammermüller files.
94. Ammermüller to First Director of the VDR Dr Rudolf Kolb, 12 December 1990, in Ammermüller files. The leading health insurance associations and the General Local Health Insurance Providers had already announced that they would make certain financial payments for pregnancy leave and weekly post-natal leave and for maternity support and would deal with the budget settlement of 1990 and invoicing with the benefits providers. In addition to Ammermüller's letter to Kolb of 12 December 1990, cf. also his letter of 11 December 1990 to the director of the Federal Association of the General Local Health Insurance Providers, Dr Oldiges, and his letters of 12 December 1990 to the other leading health insurance associations, in Ammermüller files.
95. Ammermüller to Kolb, 12 December 1990, Ammermüller files.
96. In addition to an organizational plan in Ammermüller files, cf. also Wolfgang Schmidt, 'Die Überleitungsanstalt Sozialversicherung', in *Die Angestelltenversicherung*, 38 (1992), pp. 65–9; Wolfgang Schmidt, 'Überleitungsanstalt Sozialversicherung zum 31.12.1991 aufgelöst', in *Die Angestelltenversicherung*, 39 (1992), pp. 142f.
97. Ammermüller, Bericht über die Tätigkeit des Gemeinsamen Trägers und der ÜLA; Ammermüller to Reuber, Labour Ministry press spokesman, with attachment, Die

Aufgaben der 'Überleitungsanstalt Sozialversicherung' im Jahre 1991, 4 February 1991, BArch, B 149/400457.

98. Gemeinsamer Träger der Sozialversicherung, Hauptverwaltung, Verfahren für die Übernahme von Vermögen, wenn einzelne Sozialversicherungsträger unmittelbare Eigentümer werden, 4 December 1990; ÜLA, Vermögensabwicklung, Aussagen zu erfassten Objekten, 28 February 1991: in Ammermüller files. Of the total of 880 properties used by the social insurance providers, 797 were assigned to the social insurance providers and 83 to other owners.
99. For the working-out of the law, cf. Winfried Schmähl, 'Sicherung bei Alter, Invalidität und für Hinterbliebene', in *Geschichte der Sozialpolitik in Deutschland seit 1945*, vol. xi, *1989–1994. Bundesrepublik Deutschland. Sozialpolitik im Zeichen der Vereinigung*, ed. Gerhard A. Ritter, Baden-Baden 2007, pp. 541–648 (here, pp. 588–601).
100. cf. VdK Deutschland, *Geschäftsbericht 1990 bis 1994*, pp. 170–3; for the preparatory work, cf. BMA, Ausarbeitung von Niem [= Ministerialdirektor Niemeyer]: Überleitung des Rentenrechts auf das beigetretene Gebiet, Stand 15.2.1991, BArch, B 149/74923.
101. cf. in particular the speech by Dreßler, 26 April 1991, in Prot. BT, 12. WP, pp. 1613–19.
102. BTDrs 12/630, 29 May 1991, attachment 2, 'Stellungnahme des Bundesrates', pp. 8–19.
103. cf. 'Stellungnahme des Sozialbeirats zum Entwurf des "Renten-Überleitungsgesetzes"', 28 May 1991, reprinted in BTDrs 12/1841, pp. 122f.
104. Dreßler in the Bundestag, 26 April 1991, Prot. BT, 12. WP, p. 1618.
105. Draft of letter by Dreßler to the Social Affairs Ministers of the SPD-led *Länder*, concerning 'Haltung der SPD im Bundesrat zum Rentenüberleitungsgesetz (RÜG), 7 May 1991, AdsD, 9662. (Dreßler wrote to each minister individually.)
106. 'Gesetzentwurf der Fraktion der SPD', BTDrs 12/724, 12 June 1991.
107. cf. the 37 motions for amendments to the draft law that had been agreed in committee, in BTDrs 12/829.
108. cf. Dreßler in the Bundestag, 21 June 1991, in Prot. BT, 12. WP, p. 2947.
109. Blüm, 18 June 1991, ACDP Fraktionsprotokolle.
110. Gisela Babel in the Bundestag, 21 June 1991, Prot. BT, 12. WP, p. 2936.
111. 'Entschließungsantrag der Fraktionen der CDU/CSU, SPD und FDP zum Entwurf des Gesetzes zur Herstellung der Rechtseinheit in der gesetzlichen Renten- und Unfallversicherung (Rentenüberleitungsgesetz—RÜG)', BTDrs 12/837, 21 June 1991.
112. cf. BMA, Abteilung IV, attachment, 23 January 1992, Sozialzuschlag, BMA VIII/LS-17320 (8).
113. Werner Niemeyer, 'Ab sofort einheitliches Recht', in *BArbBl* (1992), vol. 1, pp. 7–12 (here, p. 12); interview with Niemeyer by the author, 4 May 2000.
114. cf. above, p. 63.
115. BMA Referat IV a 2 to Staatssekretär Bernhard Worms with copies to the Minister and the other Staatssekretäre, concerning 'Regelungen über die Wiedergutmachung national-sozialistischen Unrechts auf dem Gebiet der bisherigen DDR', 14 March 1991 (here, Anordnung über Ehrenpensionen für Kämpfer gegen den Faschismus und für Verfolgte des Faschismus, with attachment, Protokolle über die Arbeitsgruppensitzungen am 25.1 und 25.2.1991), BArch, B 149/400153.
116. cf. in particular Blüm's address to the CDU/CSU parliamentary party, 10 December 1991, in ACDP, Fraktionsprotokolle.

117. Frerich and Frey, *Handbuch*, vol. iii, p. 628.
118. cf. the diagram, 'Verteilung des Auffüllbetrages am Nettorentenzahlbetrag auf Anteilsklassen am 1.7.1992.—Nur Fälle mit Auffüllbeträgen—Versichertenrenten Frauen', in Ammermüller files; Schmähl, 'Sicherung bei Alter, Invalidität und für Hinterbliebene', p. 592.
119. *Sozialbericht 1993*, pp. 57 f.
120. Blüm's term at the sitting of the Bundesrat, 14 October 1994, quoted in VDR, *Geschäftsbericht für das Jahr 1994*, p. 21.
121. Ruland, 'Erfolgreiche Aufbauarbeit', p. 26.
122. For this and other panegyrics (including one by Blüm, who described the achievement as almost one of the 'wonders of the world'), cf. VDR, *Geschäftsbericht für das Jahr 1991*, pp. 26–8.
123. cf. Winfried Hain, Hilmar Luckert, Horst-Wolf Müller, and Jürgen Nowatzki, 'Was brachte die Rentenumwertung?—Zur Übertragung des SGB VI auf den Rentenbestand in den neuen Bundesländern und im Ostteil Berlins', in *Deutsche Rentenversicherung*, 1992, pp. 521–49 (here, p. 531).
124. BMA, Abteilung IV, Wegfall von Leistungen in den neuen Bundesländern, 27 January 1992, BMA VIII/LS-17320 (8); cf. also Wienand *et al.*, *Fürsorge*, p. 30 f.
125. cf. Ralf-Peter Stephan, 'Das Zusammenwachsen der Rentenversicherungen in West und Ost. Eine Zwischenbilanz im zehnten Jahr der Deutschen Einheit', in *Die Angestelltenversicherung*, 12 (1999), pp. 546–56 (here, p. 549).
126. VDR, *Geschäftsbericht für das Jahr 1992*, p. 23.
127. cf. in particular the *Geschäftsberichte* of the VDR and of the BfA. For analysis of the data, cf. also Wilfried Klässer, 'Deutschland wächst zusammen—die Datenverarbeitung auch', in *Deutsche Rentenversicherung*, 4/92, pp. 235–52.
128. According to a letter by Blüm of 21 January 1998 to the members of the CDU/CSU and FDP parliamentary parties, in 1992 about 53,000 people took early retirement at the age of 60 as a result of unemployment, while the figures for 1994 and 1995 were 204,000 and 294,000 respectively: no file reference given.
129. For 1992–4, cf. p. 92 above. For 1995, cf. Presse- und Informationsamt der Regierung, *Aktuelle Beiträge zur Wirtschafts- und Finanzpolitik*, no. 1/1997, 16 January 1997, 'Der Aufbau in den neuen Bundesländern. Leistungsbilanz der Bundesregierung', p. 34.
130. VDR, *Geschäftsbericht für das Jahr 1994*, p. 22.
131. Winfried Schmähl, 'Rentenversicherung in der Bewährung. Von der Nachkriegszeit bis an die Schwelle zum neuen Jahrhundert. Stationen und Weichenstellungen', in *Eine lernende Demokratie. 50 Jahre Bundesrepublik Deutschland. WZB-Jahrbuch 1999*, ed. Max Kaase and Günther Schmid, Berlin 1999, pp. 397–423 (here, p. 416).
132. cf., for example, his interviews in the Munich *Abendzeitung*, 31 December 1993, in *Informationen am Morgen*, 20 May 1994, and with n-tv, 6 June 1994, *BPA-Dok*, Text-Bull-RFTV-AA (87–95).
133. ibid., interview, 6 June 1994.
134. cf. Dr Sokoll, Hauptverband der gewerblichen Berufsgenossenschaften e.V., to Ministerialdirigent Dr Friedrich Pappai, head of Unterabteilung IV a, BMA, Darstellung der Aktivitäten der gewerblichen Berufsgenossenschaften der DDR, 28 September 1990, BArch, B 149/74940. (Pappai was responsible, *inter alia*, for accident insurance.) Cf. also BMA, Referat IV a 1, Pappai to Staatssekretär Jagoda, with attachment, Aufbauhilfe der Rentenversicherungsträger, 19 November 1990, BArch, B 149/74922; BMA, Ref. I a 7, Bestandsaufnahme der Aufbauhilfen zur

Angleichung der Arbeits- und Sozialordnung in Deutschland, 8 February 1991, BArch, B 149/74934. Cf. also the special edition of the journal *Die BG*, 12 (2001), with 24 articles on the reorganization of accident insurance.

135. *Sozialbericht 1993*, p. 12.
136. Dr Sokoll to Ministerialdirigent Pappai, with attachment, 28 September 1990, BArch, B 149/74940.
137. Günther Sokoll, 'Die Unfallsicherung im Prozess der Wiedervereinigung: Zwischen Rampenlicht und "Fußnote" der Sozialgeschichte', in *Die BG*, 05 (2007), pp. 181–7 (here, p. 185).
138. ibid.
139. cf. Adrienne Windhoff-Héritier, 'Verbandspolitische Konfliktlinien in der deutschen Sozialunion. Der Kampf um das neue Territorium und Probleme der Umverteilung in der Gesetzlichen Krankenversicherung', in Eichener *et al.* (eds.), *Organisierte Interessen*, pp. 303–17 (here, p. 305).
140. BMG, Abteilung 2, Bestandsaufnahme der Entwicklung in den neuen Ländern zur Arbeitsmarkt- und Sozialpolitik. Allgemeine Entwicklungstendenzen in der gesetzlichen Krankenversicherung und in der gesundheitlichen Versorgung, BMA, I a 7/ 17700 (1).
141. *Materialien zur Deutschen Einheit und zum Aufbau in den neuen Bundesländern*, BTDrs 13/2280, 8 September 1995, p. 185.
142. Hauser *et al.*, *Ungleichheit*, p. 76. A further 0.3 per cent in the east and 1.8 per cent in the west were accounted for by the Seamen's Health Insurers and the Agricultural Health Insurers.
143. Karl Hinrichs, 'Restrukturierung der Sozialpolitik? Das Beispiel der Gesundheitspolitik', in *Grenzen des Sozialversicherungsstaates*, ed. Barbara Riedmüller and Thomas Olk, Opladen 1994, pp. 119–45 (here, p. 1124).
144. Hinrichs, 'Restrukturierung', esp. pp. 129 f. Cf. also Philipp Herder-Dornreich, *Gesundheitsökonomik. Systemsteuerung und Ordnungspolitik im Gesundheitswesen*, Stuttgart 1980; Jens Alber, 'Die Steuerung im Gesundheitswesen in vergleichender Perspektive', in *Journal für Sozialforschung*, 29 (1989), pp. 259–84; Renate Mayntz, 'Politische Steuerbarkeit und Reformblockaden: Überlegungen am Beispiel des Gesundheitswesens', in *Staatswissenschaft und Staatspraxis*, 1 (1990), pp. 283–307. Cf. also Manfred G. Schmidt, 'Warum die Gesundheitsausgaben wachsen. Befunde des Vergleichs demokratisch verfasster Länder', in *PVS*, 40 (1999), pp. 229–45.
145. Gesetz zur Strukturreform im Gesundheitswesen (Gesundheits-Reformgesetz), *BGBl I*, 1988, pp. 2477–597.
146. *Sozialbericht 1990*, pp. 57 f.; *Jahresbericht der Bundesregierung 1991*, p. 442.
147. *Sozialbericht 1993*, p. 64. Cf. also the close analysis of financial changes in statutory health insurance in the new *Bundesländer* in note, Gerhard Schulte to Gesundheitsminister Horst Seehofer via Staatssekretär Baldur Wagner and Parlamentarische Staatssekretärin Sabine Bergmann-Pohl on 'Finanzentwicklung der GKV in den neuen Bundesländern im ersten Halbjahr 1992', 14 September 1992, BMG-Bonn/ 221-48120/9, vol. ii.
148. *Sozialbericht 1993*, p. 64. Cf. also Blüm's statements on the Hessischer Rundfunk, 27 October 1991, and his discussion with leading health system figures on 'Brennpunkt', ARD, 11 December 1991: *BPA-Dok*, Text-Bull-RFTV-AA (87–95). See also Blüm's sharp comments on the 'inability of the self-administered system . . . to implement difficult projects', meeting of CDU/CSU parliamentary party, 8 October 1991, ACDP, Fraktionsprotokolle.

149. Interview of Ministerialdirektor Niemeyer by the author, 4 May 2000.
150. Seehofer, 2 June 1992, ACDP, Fraktionsprotokolle.
151. Gesetz zur Sicherung und Strukturverbesserung der gesetzlichen Krankenversicherung (Gesundheitsstrukturgesetz), *BGBl I*, 1992, pp. 2266–334.
152. cf. 'Lahnstein: Ein Jahr danach. Interviews mit den Abgeordneten Rudolf Dreßler, Dr. Dieter Thomae, Wolfgang Lohmann', in *f&w*, 10, 6/93, pp. 486–92. Dreßler was the leading social policy expert of the SPD, Thomae of the FDP was chairman of the health committee of the Bundestag, and Lohmann was the CDU/CSU spokesman on the committee.
153. Paul Hofacker, speaking for the CDU/CSU during the final reading of the bill in the Bundestag, 9 December 1992: Prot. BT, 12. WP, p. 10914.
154. ibid., p. 10980.
155. Seehofer, 6 October 1992, ACDP, Fraktionsprotokolle.
156. On the rationale for the inclusion, initially heavily criticized, of the new *Bundesländer* in the Health Service Structure Law, the special regulations drawn up for the new *Länder*, and early responses to the law in east Germany, cf. Seehofer, Gute Erfahrungen mit dem Gesundheitsstrukturgesetz in den neuen Ländern, 17 May 1993, BMG 223-48123-vol. iv.
157. Speaking in the Bundestag on 9 December 1992, Dreßler described the event as 'something of a premiere': Prot. BT, 12. WP, p. 10933.
158. Philip Manow, 'Strukturinduzierte Politikgleichgewichte: Das Gesundheitsstrukturgesetz und seine Vorgänger', MPIfG Discussion Paper, 5/94; Marian Döhler and Philip Manow, 'Formierung und Wandel eines Politikfeldes—Gesundheitspolitik von Blank zu Seehofer', MPIfG Discussion Paper, 6/95.
159. cf. the speech by Dieter Thomae (FDP) in the Bundestag, 9 December 1992: Prot. BT, 12. WP, p. 10925.
160. ibid., namentliche Abstimmung (roll-call vote), pp. 10980f.
161. *Sozialbericht 1997*, pp. 60–9, 226f. On financial developments within statutory health insurance between 1995 and 2003, cf. Deutsche Bundesbank, 'Finanzielle Entwicklung und Perspektiven der Gesetzlichen Krankenversicherung', *Monatsbericht Juli 2004*, vol. 56, pp. 15–32.
162. On this, and generally on the genesis of social care insurance, cf. Joachim Schraa, 'Soziale Pflegeversicherung. Die lange Geschichte', in *BArbBl* (1994), vols. 8–9, pp. 5–11; Karl Jung, 'Soziale Pflegeversicherung: Durchgesetzt gegen alle Widerstände', in *BArbBl* (1994), vol. 7, pp. 5–16; Karl Jung, 'Die fünfte Säule—über den langen Weg zur sozialen Pflegeversicherung', in BMA, *Sozialstaat im Wandel*, pp. 197–221. On the political arguments over the introduction of social care insurance, cf. also Ulrike Götting and Karl Hinrichs, 'Probleme der politischen Kompromissbildung bei der gesetzlichen Absicherung des Pflegefallrisikos. Eine vorläufige Bilanz', in *PVS*, 31 (1993), pp. 47–71. Ministerialdirektor (later Staatssekretär) Karl Jung was responsible, as head of Abteilung V 'Pflegeversicherung, Rehabilitation' within the Labour Ministry, for developing social care insurance. Responsibility for social care insurance was transferred to the Labour Ministry—to some extent as compensation for the splitting off of the department for health and health insurance and its incorporation in the Health Ministry—by an organizational decree of the Federal Chancellor of 23 January 1991. Cf. SPI 25, no. 9, 9 August 1991. See also Martin Sebaldt, '"Pflege" als Streitobjekt: Die parteipolitische Kontroverse um die Pflegeversicherung und die Entstehung des Pflegeversicherungsgesetzes von 1994', in

Zeitschrift für Sozialreform, 46 (2000), pp. 173–87; Jörg Alexander Meyer, *Der Weg zur Pflegeversicherung. Positionen—Akteure—Politikprozesse*, Frankfurt a. M. 1996.

163. cf. Schraa, 'Soziale Pflegeversicherung', p. 8.
164. cf. Frerich and Frey, *Handbuch*, vol. ii, pp. 376–8.
165. Norbert Blüm, 'Pflegeversicherungsgesetz. Politik der Nähe', in *BArbBl* (1993), vols. 7–8, pp. 5–9 (here, p. 5).
166. Jung, 'Soziale Pflegeversicherung', pp. 9f. On Blüm's ideas in late 1990, cf. his letter of 27 December 1990 to Jürgen Rüttgers, parliamentary whip of the CDU/CSU party in the Bundestag, in ACDP, Bestand Blüm I 504/73.
167. Discussion between Blüm, Count Lambsdorff (FDP), Renate Schmidt (SPD) and Wolfgang Ullmann (Alliance 90/The Greens) in the television broadcast 'Vor der Wahl', 15 November 1990: *BPA-Dok*, Text-Bull-RFTV-AA (87–95). The CDU election manifesto for 1990 (p. 15) gave only a general indication that 'a statutory regulation' would be created regarding protection in the event of the need of social care.
168. cf. above, p. 44.
169. cf. SPI 25, no. 9, 9 August 1991.
170. For a discussion of the different options, cf. ibid. On the financial basis for social care insurance, cf. papers by Referat I b 6 of the Labour Ministry, which was responsible, *inter alia*, for social protection statistics and econometrics: Bevölkerungsentwicklung und Beiträge zur Pflegeversicherung; Stichworte zum Umlageverfahren, with attachment, Pflegeversicherung: Umlage- oder Kapitaldeckungsverfahren?; Stichworte zum Kapitaldeckungsverfahren; all documents in BMA VIII/I a 7-17491 (1). See also Peter Rosenberg, 'Pflegeversicherung. Demographische Risiken', in *BArbBl* (1992), vol. 9, pp. 16–18; Winfried Schmähl, 'Zur Finanzierung einer Pflegeversicherung in Deutschland', *ZeS-Arbeitspapier* no. 5/92.
171. PDA, *Pressedienst der BDA*, no. 9, 30 March 1994.
172. cf. Schraa, 'Soziale Pflegeversicherung', pp. 6f. On the attitude of employers and the leading business associations towards social care insurance, cf. PDA, *Pressedienst*: no. 12, 21 February 1991; no. 32, 25 April 1991; no. 35, 3 May 1991; no. 37, 13 May 1991, where the two-component model (later elaborated) is presented for the first time; no. 39, 4 June 1991; joint declaration by BDA, BDI, DIHT, and ZDH 'zur Neuordnung der Pflegeabsicherung', no. 40, 12 July 1991; no. 43, 12 August 1991, with appendix, 'Zur Neuordnung der Pflegeabsicherung. Das Zwei-Komponenten-Modell der Arbeitgeber', BDA, Cologne, August 1991; no. 44, 22 August 1991; no. 49, 1 October 1991; no. 59, 25 November 1991; no. 7, 19 February 1992; no. 15, 24 April 1992; no. 26, 30 June 1992; no. 28, 11 September 1992; no. 14, 27 May 1993; no. 15, 2 June 1993; no. 22, 22 July 1993; no. 29, 17 September 1993; no. 32, 22 October 1993; no. 38, 19 November 1993; no. 39, 2 December 1993.
173. PDA, *Pressedienst*, no. 3, 7 February 1996.
174. cf. Jung, 'Soziale Pflegeversicherung', pp. 10f.
175. Sebaldt, '"Pflege" als Streitobjekt', p. 177.
176. Schraa, 'Soziale Pflegeversicherung', pp. 8–10; interviews by the author with Niemeyer, 4 May 2000, and Rosenberg, 5 May 2000.
177. Blüm addressing the CDU/CSU parliamentary party, 11 June 1991, ACDP, Fraktionsprotokolle.
178. ACDP, Fraktionsprotokolle.
179. cf. his interview in the *Süddeutsche Zeitung*, 15 July 1991, in which he said that as party leader, he did not 'intend . . . to intervene in this essential debate at this point'.

180. Kohl addressing the CDU/CSU parliamentary party, 27 May 1993, ACDP, Fraktionsprotokolle.
181. cf. Blüm, interview with Deutschlandfunk, 16 June 1993, in *BPA-Dok*, Text-Bull-RFTV-AA (87–95).
182. Richtigstellung, 7 July 1993, in Prot. BT, 12. WP, p. 14432; speech on behalf of FDP members opposed to the coalition's bill, 22 October 1993, in Prot. BT, 12. WP, pp. 15841–4.
183. Interview with Cronenberg by the author, 27 June 2000. Lambsdorff, 'despite huge misgivings', voted for the coalition parties' compromise on the introduction of a contributions-financed system of social care insurance, but eventually voted against the law adopted by the Bundestag on 22 April 1994, on the grounds that the conditions for compensation had not been met. Cf. his 'persönliche Erklärung' in Prot. BT, 12. WP, p. 19283.
184. Klaus Murmann, *Kontrakt für die Zukunft. Was mich bewegt. Gespräch mit Rainer Hank und Rolf Dietrich Schwartz*, Berlin 1997, p. 165. The leading German business organizations did not put forward their final model for compulsory private social care insurance until September 1993. The model envisaged quite insufficient benefits for those age groups 'approaching the age when social care might be needed'. The benefits would be topped up only in case of need, from a fund to be financed through a deduction from holiday pay. Cf. *Süddeutsche Zeitung*, 15 September 1993.
185. BTDrs 12/1156, 18 September 1991.
186. cf. Rudolf Dreßler to deputy chairman of the DAG Walter Quartier, 14 November 1990, AdsD, 9700. The German White-Collar Workers' Trade Union favoured a tax-financed benefits law. The German Trade Union Federation's scheme for social care envisaged the transfer of social care protection to the statutory health insurers, with contribution rates increased by 0.5 percentage points and the contributions ceiling raised. For a criticism of this scheme, cf. PDA, *Pressedienst*, no. 7, 19 February 1992. The SPD was opposed to the complete integration of social care insurance into statutory health insurance, as it believed that a distinction had to be maintained between ill-health and the need for social care: cf. letter from Rudolf Dreßler to Traudl Hübner, 18 June 1991, AdsD, 9680.
187. cf. SPI 25, no. 4, 27 March 1991.
188. cf. 'Beschluss der Konferenz der Arbeits- und Sozialminister der Länder auf ihrer Sondersitzung vom 23.4.1991 zur "Absicherung des Pflegerisikos"', in SPI 25, no. 9, 9 August 1991.
189. SPI 25, no. 4, 27 March 1991. Some organizations, however, would have preferred a tax-financed benefits law, though there was no prospect that such a law would be passed. For the attitude of the War Victims' Association, which put forward its own model of social care insurance, cf. VdK, *Geschäftsbericht 1990–1994*, esp. pp. 187–90, 193f.
190. BTDrs 12/5262, 7 May 1992 (Gesetzentwurf der Koalitionsfraktionen).
191. At the meeting of the CDU/CSU parliamentary party on 15 June 1993, the CDU member Walter Lieb mentioned that the 400 delegates at the last conference of the Christian Democratic Association of Employees in Chemnitz at the beginning of the month had 'implored' the party's members of parliament to abandon the plan for unpaid days of wages in the event of illness. Instead they proposed compensation through the elimination of one holiday. ACDP, Fraktionsprotokolle. Cf. also Sebaldt, '"Pflege" als Streitobjekt', pp. 180f.

192. On the process of legislation and the compromise that was finally reached, cf. Schraa, 'Soziale Pflegeversicherung', pp. 10f.; Jung, 'Soziale Pflegeversicherung', pp. 11–15. On the attitude of the coalition parties and the SPD towards the eventual compromise, cf. the short speeches by Blüm (CDU/CSU), Dreßler (SPD), and Gisela Babel (FDP) in the Bundestag, 22 April 1994. There was no roll-call vote on the law, which was passed 'with votes against from members of the FDP, the PDS/Left List and Alliance 90/The Greens and with 3 abstentions' (Prot. BT, 12. WP, pp. 1279–84). The Council of Economic Experts, in its special report published on 1 July 1995, 'Zur Kompensation in der Pflegeversicherung', said that the cancellation of one holiday in compensation for the employer's contribution at the introduction of the second stage of social care insurance was not, in fact, sufficient and that a gap of between 2,100 million and 2,600 million DM remained. It added, however, that abolition of a further holiday would constitute excessive compensation. The issue was resolved within the framework of the laws implementing the programme for greater growth and employment: cf. *Sozialbericht 1997*, p. 78.
193. Savings on income support of between 10,000 million and 11,000 million DM were expected for 1997. Cf. Norbert Blüm, 'Pflegeversicherung: Positive Zwischenbilanz', in *BArbBl* (1997), vol. 10, pp. 5–8 (here, pp. 6 f.). On the general effects of social care insurance, cf. the articles in *Die Wirkungen des Pflegeversicherungsgesetzes*, ed. Uwe Fachinger and Heinz Rothgang, Berlin 1995.
194. cf. the criticism of this regulation by the head of the department in the Labour Ministry responsible for the creation of social care insurance, Karl Jung (in collaboration with Ruth Schweitzer), *Die neue Pflegeversicherung. Sozialgesetzbuch XI. Das Recht der sozialen und der privaten Pflegeversicherung*, Bonn 1995, pp. 56f. Jung was concerned that the old *Bundesländer*, which, unlike the new *Länder*, did not receive subsidies from the Federal government, would be unable fully to meet their obligation to expand social care facilities: cf. interview with Jung by the author, 5 May 2000.
195. cf. Jung, 'Soziale Pflegeversicherung', p. 14.
196. In addition to Jung/Schweitzer, *Die neue Pflegeversicherung*, cf. also Gerhard Igl, *Das neue Pflegeversicherungsrecht. Soziale Pflegeversicherung (Sozialgesetzbuch—Elftes Buch)*, Munich 1995; *Handbuch des Sozialversicherungsrechts*, vol. iv, *Pflegeversicherungsrecht*, ed. Bertram Schulin, Munich 1997.
197. cf. Karl Hinrichs, 'Die Soziale Pflegeversicherung—eine institutionelle Innovation in der deutschen Sozialpolitik', in *Staatswissenschaften und Staatspraxis*, 6 (1995), pp. 227–59 (here, p. 252). However, Margarete Landenberger, 'Pflegeversicherung als Vorbote eines anderen Sozialstaates', in *ZSR*, 40 (1994), pp. 314–42, argues that social care insurance marks a departure from previous principles of social insurance.
198. cf. Jürgen Wasem, 'Die private Pflegepflichtversicherung—ein Modell für eine alternative Organisation der sozialen Sicherung zwischen Markt und Staat?' in *Soziale Sicherung zwischen Markt und Staat*, ed. Winfried Schmähl, Berlin 2000, pp. 79–110.
199. cf. Heinz Rothgang, 'Die Einführung der Pflegeversicherung. Ist das Sozialversicherungsprinzip am Ende?', in Riedmüller and Olk (eds.), *Grenzen*, pp. 164–87; Heinz Rothgang, 'Vom Bedarfs- zum Budgetprinzip? Die Einführung der Pflegeversicherung und ihre Folgen für die gesetzliche Krankenversicherung', in *Gesellschaften im Umbruch. Beiträge des 27. Kongreß der Deutschen Gesellschaft für Soziologie*, ed. Lars Clausen, vol. i, Frankfurt a. M. 1996, pp. 930–46.
200. 'Pflegeversicherung mit 500 Millionen im Minus', *FAZ*, 14 January 2006.
201. On the development of social care insurance and the suggested reform measures, cf. the report of the Rürup commission of 2003, BMG, *Nachhaltigkeit*, pp. 185–219. For

alternative reform proposals, cf. the report by the Herzog commission, *Bericht der Kommission 'Soziale Sicherheit'*, pp. 28–36.

202. BMA, Aufbau der Sozialverwaltung, Sachstandsbericht sent with letter by head of Außenstelle Berlin, Karl Jung, to Dr Kabel, head of Außenstelle des Bundeskanzleramtes, 14 November 1990, BArch, B 149/400150.
203. BMA, Abteilung I, Ministerialdirektor Stahl to Minister Blüm with copies to the Staatssekretäre of the BMA, with attachment, Bestandsaufnahme der Aufbauhilfen des BMA und seines Geschäftsbereichs für die Arbeits- und Sozialverwaltung in den neuen Ländern, 30 November 1990, BArch, B 149/74934.
204. cf. above, p. 194.
205. BMA, Referat VI a 1, note, signed by departmental head Abteilungsleiterin Ministerialdirigentin Ursula Voskuhl, in preparation for the third conference of the Außenstelle Berlin des Bundeskanzleramtes: Aufbau der Versorgungsverwaltung einschließlich der Hauptfürsorgestellen, 25 October 1990, BArch, B 149/74925.
206. Blüm to Hirrlinger, 3 March 1991, ACDP, Bestand Blüm I 504/74.
207. Hirrlinger to Blüm, 12 June 1991, BArch, B 149/400155.
208. BMA, Referat VI a 1, Aufbau der Versorgungsverwaltung in den neuen Bundesländern, 9 August 1991, BArch, B 149/400066. Cf. also Blüm to Senator for Health and Social Affiars of the *Land* Berlin, Ingrid Stahmer, 18 June 1991, and Blüm to the President of the VdK, 3 July 1991: ACDP, Bestand Blüm I 504/81.
209. Blüm to Kohl, 19 November 1991, with attachment prepared by Referat VI a 1 of the Labour Ministry, Aufbau der Versorgungsverwaltung sowie der Hauptfürsorge- und Fürsorgestellen, Verfahrensbeschleunigung, 15 November 1991, BMA VIII a 1/17490/1, vol. i.
210. Blüm to Kohl, 16 October 1992, BMA VIII a 1/17490 (6).
211. BMA, Referat VI a 1, Sachstandsbericht über die Kriegsopferversorgung und Kriegsopferfürsorge, 14 January 1993. The report served as preparation for talks between the Federal Chancellor and CDU members of parliament from the new *Bundesländer* on 19 January 1993: BMA VIII a 1/17305 (4).
212. ibid.
213. Presse- und Informationsamt der Bundesregierung, *Aktuelle Beiträge zur Wirtschafts- und Finanzpolitik*, no. 1, 16 January 1997, 'Der Aufbau in den neuen Bundesländern. Leistungsbilanz der Bundesregierung', p. 35.
214. *Sozialbericht 1997*, p. 243.
215. Blüm to Kohl, 19 November 1991 (cf. note 209 above).
216. Blüm to Kohl, 16 October 1992, BMA VIII 1 a/17490 (6).
217. *Materialien zur Deutschen Einheit*, BTDrs 13/2280, 8 September 1995, p. 202.
218. Blüm to Hildebrandt, 28 November 1990, ACDP, Bestand Blüm I 504/72.
219. Blüm to Hildebrandt, with attachment, Ergebnisvermerk zur Besprechung über das Netz der Berufsförderungswerke in den neuen Bundesländern am 29.10.1990 im Bundesministerium für Arbeit und Sozialordnung, 11 December 1990, ACDP, Bestand Blüm I 504/72.
220. Blüm to Hildebrandt, 28 November 1991, ACDP, Bestand Blüm I 504/72; BMA, Referat VI b 1, Koordinierung der Vorhaben des BMA und seines Geschäftsbereiches bei der Angleichung der Arbeits- und Sozialordnung in Deutschland. Bestandsaufnahme der Aufbauhilfen einschließlich Fortschreibung, Stand 16.11.1990, BArch, B 149/74922.
221. Blüm to Minister für Arbeit, Gesundheit und Soziales, *Land* Mecklenburg-Vorpommern, Klaus Gollert, 31 October 1991, BMA VIII a 1/17490/1, vol. i.

Similar letters were sent to the Social Affairs Ministers of the other new *Bundesländer*, specifying the costs of the vocational training and employment promotion facilities envisaged for the *Land* in question.

222. *Sozialbericht 1993*, pp. 78f.; *Sozialbericht 1997*, p. 81.
223. BMA, Referat VIII b 6, Überblick für die 23. Arbeitsbesprechung des Chefs des Bundeskanzleramtes mit den Chefs der Staatskanzleien der neuen Länder am 10.9.1992 über ein 'Gesamtsanierungsprogramm für die Behinderteneinrichtungen in den neuen Ländern', 7 September 1992, with attachment 1, Unterabteilung Zb, Sprechzettel zum Einzelplan 11 bei der Beratung des Bundeshaushalts 1993 im A+S-Ausschuss, 25 August 1992, BMA VIII a 1/17305 (2).
224. Presse- und Informationsamt der Bundesregierung, 'Aufbau', p. 36.
225. BMA, Referat VI b 1, Bestandsaufnahme der Aufbauhilfen, 16 November 1990, BArch, B 149/74922.
226. BMA, Referat VI a 1, Aufbau der Versorgungsverwaltung sowie der Hauptfürsorge- und Fürsorgestellen, Verfahrensbeschleunigung, 15 November 1991, BMA VIII a 1/17490/1, vol. i.
227. *Sozialbericht 1993*, p. 79.
228. cf. above, p. 180.
229. On the development of income support and the Independent Welfare Associations from the summer of 1990 onwards, cf. Wienand *et al.*, *Fürsorge*.
230. cf. Thomas Olk and Doris Rentzsch, 'Zur Transformation von Armut in den neuen Bundesländern', in Riedmüller and Olk (eds.), *Grenzen*, pp. 248–74 (here, pp. 257f.). Cf. also *Materialien zur Deutschen Einheit*, BTDrs 12/6854, 8 March 1994, p. 104.
231. Einigungsvertrag, Anlage I, Kapitel X, Sachgebiet H, *BGBl II*, 1990, p. 1095.
232. On the problems connected with the development of income support and the Independent Welfare Associations, cf. Beitrag des Bundesministeriums für Familie und Senioren zur Bestandsaufnahme in den neuen Ländern zur Arbeitsmarkt- und Sozialpolitik, undated (probably summer 1991), BMA VIII/I a 7/17711 (1).
233. ibid.; *Materialien zur Deutschen Einheit*, BTDrs 12/6854, 8 March 1994, p. 177.
234. cf. Susanne Angerhausen, *Radikaler Organisationswandel. Wie die 'Volkssolidarität' die Deutsche Vereinigung überlebte*, Opladen 2003, esp. pp. 305, 311f., 319.
235. cf. Volker Neumann and Iris Brockmann, 'Freie Wohlfahrtspflege in den neuen Bundesländern', in Wienand *et al.*, *Fürsorge*, pp. 63–133; Holger Backhaus-Maul, 'Wohlfahrtsverbände in den neuen Bundesländern. Anmerkungen zum Stand der Wohlfahrtsverbändeforschung im deutschen Einigungsprozess', in Eichener *et al.* (eds.), *Organisierte Interessen*, pp. 359–81 (here, esp. pp. 374f.).
236. Gemeinsame Presseerklärung von Bundesministerin Hannelore Rönsch und den Präsidenten der Freien Wohlfahrtspflege, undated, BArch, B 149/400149.
237. Präsident des Diakonischen Werkes der Evangelischen Kirche in Deutschland to Bundeskanzler Kohl, 6 November 1991, BArch, B 149/400081.
238. Beitrag des BMFuS zur Bestandsaufnahme in den neuen Ländern zur Arbeitsmarkt- und Sozialpolitik, BMA VIII/I a 7/17700 (1); von Maydell *et al.*, *Umwandlung*, p. 245.
239. Presse- und Informationsamt der Bundesregierung, 'Aufbau', p. 37.
240. *Sozialbericht 1997*, p. 93.
241. Klaus-Peter Schwitzer, 'Zur sozialen Lage älterer Menschen in den neuen Bundesländern', in *SF*, 42 (1993), pp. 203–10 (here, p. 207).

242. BMA, Referat VIII a 1, Betr. Gutachten des Rheinisch-Westfälischen Instituts für Wirtschaftsforschung über 'das Zusammenwirken von Steuern und Sozialtransfers in den jungen Bundesländern', 27 June 1994, BMA VIII a 1/17701/1, vol. x.
243. *Sozialbericht 1993*, p. 83; *Sozialbericht 1997*, p. 88. The figures relate to gross expenditure. Taking receipts into consideration, e.g. through reimbursements by other social insurance providers, the share of total spending accounted for by the new *Länder* was actually only 11.4 per cent in 1996.
244. cf. Thomas Liebscher and Olaf Steffen, 'Der Aufbau der Arbeitsgerichtsbarkeit und die Tätigkeit der Schiedstellen in den neuen Bundesländern', in Hantsche *et al.* (eds.), *Aufbau*, pp. 141–220 (here, p. 149).
245. Verordnung über die Bildung von Kommissionen zur Beseitigung von Arbeitsstreitfällen (Konfliktkommissionen) in den volkseigenen u. ihnen gleichgestellten Betrieben u. in den Verwaltungen, in *GBl I*, pp. 695–8.
246. cf. Einigungsvertrag, Anlage I, Kapitel III, Sachgebiet A, Abschnitt III, *BGBl II*, 1990, p. 926.
247. cf. BMA, Referat III a 5, Problempunkt: Ungesicherte Funktionsfähigkeit der Arbeitsrechtspflege im Gebiet der heutigen DDR, 21 September 1990, BArch, B 149/74942; Ministerialdirektor Wlotzke, head of Abteilung III Arbeitsrecht und Arbeitsschutz, BMA, to the Ministers and Senators for labour and social affairs of the *Länder* and the Justice Ministers of the *Länder*, and by way of information to the Federal Justice Minister and the President of the Federal Employment Court: Betr.: Arbeitsrechtlicher Rechtsschutz in den fünf neuen Bundesländern, 20 December 1990, BArch, B 149/74923. On the overall problem, cf. also Rolf Schwedes, 'Der Wiederaufbau der Arbeitsgerichtsbarkeit in den neuen Bundesländern', in *Die Arbeitsgerichtsbarkeit. Festschrift zum 100jährigen Bestehen der Deutschen Arbeitsgerichtsverbände*, Neuwied/Kriftel/Berlin 1994, pp. 147–67.
248. BMA, Sasdrich, to Ministerialdirigent Johannes Ludewig, Bundeskanzleramt: Betr.: Umsetzung des Staatsvertrages mit der DDR über die Verwirklichung der Währungs-, Wirtschafts- und Sozialunion (here, Wöchentliche Meldung über aktuelle Themen und Probleme der Umsetzung), 18 January 1990.
249. *GBl I*, 1990, p. 505. Establishment of the panels was obligatory for enterprises with more than fifty employees, optional for smaller enterprises. If agreement over the selection of the chairman could not be reached, then a chairman was appointed by the district court upon application by a member of the panel.
250. cf. head of Referat III a 5, BMA, Ministerialrat Schwedes, invitation to a meeting at the BMA on 26 August1991, undated, BMA VIII/I a 7/17701 (1); the purpose of the meeting was to discuss the question of the employment law arbitration panels and, on the basis of a report by the *Länder*, the state of legal protection through the employment courts in the new *Länder*, and also to provide orientation with regard to the new law. Cf. also BMA, Referat III a 5, Arbeitsgerichtlicher Rechtsschutz in den neuen Bundesländern. Protokoll der Besprechung im Bundesministerium für Arbeit und Sozialordnung am 26.8.1991, BArch B 149/405500; *Jahresbericht der Bundesregierung 1992*, p. 388. See also the attempt to assess the work of the arbitration panels in Liebscher and Steffen, 'Arbeitsgerichtsbarkeit', pp. 170–6.
251. Ministerialdirektor Stahl, head of Abteilung I, BMA, to Minister Blüm with copies to the Staatssekretäre, Bestandsaufnahme der Aufbauhilfen des BMA und seines Geschäftsbereichs für die Arbeits- und Sozialverwaltung in den neuen Ländern, 30 November 1990, BArch, B 149/74934.

252. BMA, Ministerialrat Schwedes to Abteilung I, BMA, giving reasons for the proposal that the 'administration of employment law in the five new *Bundesländer*' should be placed on the agenda for the talks between the Federal Chancellor and the Prime Ministers on 28 February 1991, 25 February 1992, BMA VIII/I a 7/17320 (5).
253. Blüm to the Prime Ministers of the new *Länder*, and by way of information to the Ministers and Senators for labour and social affairs of all the German *Länder* and the Justice Ministers of the new *Länder*, 21 February 1991. Cf. also the attachment, Appell von Bundesminister Blüm: Besorgniserregende Situation der arbeitsrechtlichen Rechtsprechung in den neuen Bundesländern. In this document Blüm and Kissel appealed to active and retired judges within the employment law jurisdiction to make themselves available for work in the new *Bundesländer*. The same appeal was directed to active and retired judges within the social law jurisdiction, where, according to the document, though there was no immediate threat to the administration of justice, extra judges would likewise be needed in the near future. The appeal was supported by the president of the Federal Social Court. Cf. BMA VIII/I a 7/17320 (5).
254. BMA, Referat II a 5, Arbeitsgerichtlicher Rechtsschutz, BArch, B 149/405500.
255. cf. the lengthy note, BMA, Abteilung III, Zur Arbeitsgerichtsbarkeit. Stand im Aufbau der Arbeitsgerichte in den NBL, 21 June 1991, BMA VIII a 1/17701 1, vol. vi, which discusses what kind of opposition is likely to occur 'if reinstated former heads of enterprises dismiss first those people who have taken part in demonstrations or have worked with the Round Table', and how limited the prospects are of 'dealing with the problem of the old cliques through employment law'. On the development of the employment law jurisdiction in the new *Bundesländer*, cf. also Liebscher and Steffen, 'Arbeitsgerichtsbarkeit', pp. 183–93.
256. Gesetz zur Aufhebung des Gesetzes über die Errichtung und das Verfahren der Schiedstellen für Arbeitsrecht und zur Änderung des AFG, 20 December 1991, *BGBl I*, 1991, p. 2321. The law empowered the *Länder* to abolish the panels earlier than this if they had previously decided by legislation to establish an independent employment law jurisdiction.
257. 'Arbeitsgerichtsbarkeit. Aufbau im Osten erfolgreich', in SPI 27, no. 8, 21 April 1993.
258. cf. *Materialien zur Deutschen Einheit*, BTDrs 13/2280, 8 September 1995, pp. 314–16.
259. cf. Schwedes, 'Wiederaufbau', p. 160.
260. According to BMA, Referat I a 7, Bestandsaufnahme der Aufbauhilfen zur Angleichung der Arbeits- und Sozialordnung in Deutschland, 8 February 1991, twenty-eight social court judges from the old *Bundesländer* had been sent to support the work of the social law chambers and senates of the district and regional courts in the new *Länder*. On the problems connected with the transfer of west German social law to the new *Länder*, cf. Wolfgang Heine and Jörg Eckhardt, 'Überleitungsrecht und neue Bundesländer', in *DRV* (1994), pp. 329–39.
261. *Materialien zur Deutschen Einheit*, BTDrs 13/2280, 8 September 1995, p. 319.
262. cf. letter of Blüm to Waigel, 3 September 1990, in which Blüm criticizes Waigel's view (expressed in a letter of 13 August 1990) that sending judges was a matter for the *Länder* alone and that the Federal government should accordingly shoulder no part of the costs during the budgetary years 1991 and 1992. Sending judges, Blüm argued, was 'in the interests of Germany as a whole', and '(co)-financing by the five new future *Länder*' did not seem a realistic prospect. ACDP, Bestand Blüm I 504/68.
263. BMA, Referat IV a 6, Sozialgerichtsbarkeit etc. to Referat VIII a 1, BMA, paper for 28. Arbeitsbesprechung Chef des Bundeskanzleramtes/Staatssekretäre neue

Bundesländer Top 5: Hilfe zum Aufbau der Arbeits- und Sozialgerichtsbarkeit, 10 May 1993, BMA/VIII a 1/17305, vol. vi. Of the funds, 12.1 million DM were allocated to the employment law jurisdiction and 11 million DM to the social law jurisdiction.

264. BMA, Günter Ast, head of Referat LP 3 (Öffentlichkeitsarbeit) to Abteilungen Z and I–VIII: Betr.: Gespräch des Bundeskanzlers mit den Repräsentanten der Wirtschaft und der Gewerkschaften über wirtschaftliche Fragen der neuen Bundesländer am 6. Dezember 1993 (here, Darstellung der sozialpolitischen Aufbauleistung in den neuen Ländern), 5 November 1993, BMA VIII/a 1/17491, vol. ix.
265. ibid.

12 The Debates on Germany's Economic Position and on the Problems in Financial and Social Policy Resulting from German Unity

1. OECD, *OECD Economic Outlook 51*, June 1992, Paris 1992, pp. 60 f.; Sachverständigenrat zur Begutachtung der gesamtwirtschaftlichen Entwicklung, *Für Wachstumsorientierung—Gegen lähmenden Verteilungsstreit. Jahresgutachten 1992/93*, Stuttgart 1992, p. 177.
2. cf. above, pp. 72 f.
3. cf. the excellent analysis by Roland Czada, 'Vereinigungskrise und Standortdebatte. Der Beitrag der Wiedervereinigung zur Krise des westdeutschen Modells', in *Leviathan*, 26 (1998), pp. 24–59; Roland Czada, 'Der Vereinigungsprozess—Wandel der externen und internen Konstitutionsbedingungen des westdeutschen Modells', in *Deutschland nach der Wende. Neue Politikstrukturen*, ed. Georg Simonis, Opladen 1998, pp. 55–86.
4. VdK, *Jahresbericht 96*, p. 7. According to Czada, 'Vereinigungskrise', p. 24, economic globalization served as a 'pretext for redesigning the welfare state'.
5. Sachverständigenrat zur Begutachtung der gesamtwirtschaftlichen Entwicklung, *Im Standortwettbewerb. Jahresgutachten 1995/96*, Stuttgart 1995, p. V.
6. cf. Claus F. Hoffmann and Roland Lang-Neyjahr, 'Wirtschaftsstandort Deutschland. Erfolgreicher Zehnkämpfer', in *BArbBl* (1997), vol. 9, pp. 5–15. In 1993 German direct investment abroad amounted to 25,600 million DM, while foreign direct investment in Germany stood at only 3,400 million DM (ibid., p. 6).
7. cf. Sachverständigenrat, *Jahresgutachten 1995/96*, p. 11.
8. ibid.
9. cf. Frieder Naschold, 'Ökonomische Leistungsfähigkeit und institutionelle Innovation. Das deutsche Produktions- und Politikregime im globalen Wettbewerb', in *Ökonomische Leistungsfähigkeit und institutionelle Innovation. Das deutsche Produktions- und Politikregime im globalen Wettbewerb*, ed. Frieder Naschold, David Soskice, Bob Hancké *et al.*, WBZ-Jahrbuch 1997, Berlin 1997, pp. 19–62 (here, p. 30).
10. cf. Bob Hancké, 'Vorsprung, aber nicht länger (nur) durch Technik—Die schnelle Anpassung der deutschen Automobilindustrie an internationale Wettbewerbsbedingungen', in *Ökonomische Leistungsfähigkeit*, ed. Naschold *et al.*, pp. 213–34.
11. cf. above, pp. 95 f.
12. Naschold, 'Ökonomische Leistungsfähigkeit', p. 39.
13. ACDP, Fraktionsprotokolle.
14. 'Bericht des Vorsitzenden der CDU Deutschlands', in CDU, *3. Parteitag der Christlich Demokratischen Union Deutschlands. Niederschrift. Düsseldorf, 26.–28. Oktober 1992*, pp. 16–35 (here, p. 20).

15. BMA, Ref. I a 3 (gesamtwirtschaftliche Fragen der Sozialpolitik), Erhebliche gesamtwirtschaftliche Risiken bis hin zur Rezession, 25 August 1992, BMA VIII a 1/17491, vol. ii.
16. Kohl, 'Bericht', CDU, *3. Parteitag der CDU*, p. 23.
17. cf. above, p. 86.
18. Kohl, 'Bericht', CDU, *3. Parteitag der CDU*, pp. 24 f.
19. cf. Oliver Schwinn, *Die Finanzierung der deutschen Einheit. Eine Untersuchung aus politisch-institutionalistischer Perspektive*, Opladen 1997; Sylvia Welting, *Staatsverschuldung als Finanzierungsinstrument des deutschen Vereinigungsprozesses. Bestandsaufnahme und theoretische Wirkungsanalyse*, Frankfurt a. M./Berlin/Berne etc. 1997; Reimut Zohlnhöfer, 'Der lange Schatten der schönen Illusion: Finanzpolitik nach der deutschen Einheit, 1990–1998', in *Leviathan*, 28 (2000), pp. 14–38; Uwe Andersen, 'Finanzierung der Einheit', in *Handbuch zur deutschen Einheit*, new edn., ed. Werner Weidenfeld and Karl-Rudolf Korte, Frankfurt/New York 1996, pp. 294–307; Roland Czada, 'Der Kampf um die Finanzierung der deutschen Einheit', in *Einigung und Zerfall: Deutschland und Europa nach dem Ende des Ost-West-Konflikts. 19. wissenschaftlicher Kongreß der Deutschen Vereinigung für Politische Wissenschaft*, ed. Gerhard Lehmbruch, Opladen 1995, pp. 73–102.
20. Grosser, *Wagnis*, pp. 373–9.
21. Zohlnhöfer, 'Schatten', pp. 7 f.
22. ibid., p. 8.
23. Czada, 'Kampf', pp. 85 f.
24. ibid., pp. 88–90.
25. Waigel, addressing the CDU/CSU parliamentary party, 2 March 1993, ACDP, Fraktionsprotokolle.
26. *Jahresbericht der Bundesregierung 1993*, p. 198.
27. On the compromise, cf. the record of the negotiations in *Neuordnung des Finanzausgleichs zwischen Bund und Ländern und ihre Auswirkungen auf das Land Bremen*, ed. Senator für Finanzen der Freien Hansestadt Bremen, Bremen 1993, pp. 149–58.
28. 'Solidarpakt. Zwei Milliarden mehr für ABM', in SPI 28, no. 6, 19 March 1993.
29. Figures taken from Schwinn, *Finanzierung*, p. 172.
30. On the degree of success of the campaign against abuse, cf. *Sozialbericht 1993*, pp. 38 f.
31. ACDP, Fraktionsprotokolle.
32. Prot. BT, 12. WP, pp. 12722–30 (here, p. 12722).
33. ibid., p. 12727.
34. ibid., pp. 12736–41 (here, pp. 12736 f.).
35. ibid., pp. 12741–4 (here, p. 12741).
36. ibid., pp. 12751–7; the quotations, pp. 12754, 12756.
37. ibid., pp. 12762–9, esp. pp. 12766, 12768. There are interesting indications that differences within the SPD had to be resolved as the party worked out its attitude towards the solidarity pact. On these, cf. also Querschnittsgruppe Einheit Deutschlands der SPD-Bundestagsfraktion, Protokoll der Querschnittsgruppensitzung vom 4. Februar 1993, 10 February 1993, AdsD, 26 001/SPD-BT-Frakt.
38. Schwinn, in *Finanzierung*, p. 180.
39. Czada, in 'Kampf', p. 98.
40. Zohlnhöfer, 'Schatten', p. 9.
41. cf. above, p. 91.
42. cf. Karl Feldengut, 'Hat der "Solidarpakt" noch eine Chance?', AdsD, 5/DGAi 002183.

43. cf. Blüm's interviews in various media on 12 February 1991, 6 September 1992, 22 November 1992, 26 January 1993, 11 October 1993, 26 October 1993, in *BPA-Dok*, Text-Bull-RFTV-AA (87–95). Cf. also Blüm's criticism of the unfair distribution of the financial burdens of unity in his address to the CDU/CSU parliamentary party on 2 June 1992 (ACDP, Fraktionsprotokolle), and his article 'Sozialstaatliche Kultur in der Bewährung', in *Sozialstaat im Wandel*, pp. 1–33 (here, pp. 10 f.).
44. Undated paper (probably late 1992), BMA files, Verteilungsgerechtigkeit / Finanzierung Aufschwung Ost, appendix, Verteilung der Belastung durch Solidaritätszuschlag, Anhebung von Verbrauchssteuern und geänderte Sozialversicherungsbeiträge in den Jahren 1991–1995 nach Einkommensschichten (Schätzung), BMA VIII a 1/17491, vol. iii. According to the paper, which pre-dates the decisions on the Federal Consolidation Programme, agreement was not reached between the Labour and Finance Ministries (at specialist level) regarding a 'joint assessment . . . of the table, *which was drawn up by the BMF itself*' (emphasis in original).
45. Interview of Blüm by the author, 8 June 2000.
46. Walter Riester, in a discussion contribution, in *Soziale Konflikte, Sozialstaat und Demokratie in Deutschland*, ed. Helga Grebing and Hans-Otto Hemmer, Essen 1996, p. 93.
47. Dr Heyde, BMJ to Bundesminister für Arbeit und Sozialordnung, 19 October 1992. This document from the files of the Labour Ministry on the reorganization of the financing of unemployment insurance, and the documents cited in what follows, have been made available to me in copy form by Staatssekretär Werner Tegtmeier, to whom I am grateful. They do not carry Labour Ministry file numbers.
48. BMI, Überlegungen zu einem Solidarpakt (here, Möglichkeiten der weiteren Einbeziehung von Beamten, Richtern und Soldaten), with attachment, 'Preis-und Lohnentwicklung' und die 'Kaufkraftentwicklung der tariflichen Vergütungen und Löhne' in der gewerblichen Wirtschaft und im öffentlichen Dienst, 19 October 1992, Tegtmeier files. Cf. also Dr Schnappauff, BMI to Bundeminister für Arbeit und Sozialordnung, and by way of information to Bundesminister für Justiz und für Wirtschaft, Betr.: Verfassungsrechtliche Zulässigkeit einer Arbeitsmarktabgabe, 21 October 1992, Tegtmeier files.
49. BMA, Ministerialdirektor Stahl, head of Abt. I (Grundsatz- und Planungsabteilung), to Staatssekretär Tegtmeier, with various attachments, 9 December 1992, Tegtmeier files.
50. ibid.
51. BMA, Ministerialdirektor Stahl to Minister Blüm with copies to the Staatssekretäre, paper for a discussion with Schäuble, 22 December 1992. Cf. also Ministerialrat Fendrich on instructions of Minister Blüm with copies to the Staatssekretäre, with attachment, Vorschlag zur Einführung einer Arbeitsmarktabgabe für alle Erwerbstätigen—auf der Grundlage einer Grundgesetzänderung—(BMA-Modell vom 22.12.1992), 26 January 1993. For ideas on implementation of the model, cf. Peter Rosenberg acting for Minister Blüm with copies to the Staatssekretäre, with attachment, Vorschlag zur Einführung einer Arbeitsmarktabgabe für alle Erwerbstätigen. Skizzierung der Vorstellungen zur technischen Umsetzung des BMA-Modells vom 22.12.1992, 29 January 1993. All documents in Tegtmeier files.
52. BMA, Stahl to Tegtmeier, with attachment 1, Entwurf der vorgesehenen Verfassungsänderung, 9 December 1992. Cf. also Ministerialdirigent Dr Daubenbüchel, head of Zentralabteilung, BMA, to BMA, Referat I a 5, Betr.: Verfassungsrechtliche Legitimierung einer Arbeitsmarktabgabe. Bezug: Ihre telefonische Prüfbitte vom 26.1.1993, 26 January 1993.

53. cf. Thomas Hanke and Erika Martens, 'Arbeitsmarktabgabe: Die Union ringt um einen Kompromiss zum Solidarpakt. Müssen Beamte und Selbstständige auch zahlen?', in *Die Zeit*, 5 February 1993.
54. For a description and evaluation of the model, cf. telefax, Ministerialrat Pfitzner, head of Referat I a 5 (Soziale Aspekte der Finanz- und Steuerpolitik), BMA, to Staatssekretär Tegtmeier, with attachment, Vorschläge zur Einführung einer Arbeitsmarktabgabe für alle Erwerbstätigen, 2 February 1993, Tegtmeier files.
55. ibid.
56. Ministerialdirektor Rosenmöller, head of Abteilung II (Arbeitsmarktpolitik und Arbeitslosenversicherung), BMA, to the Parlamentarischer Staatssekretär Horst Günther with copies to the Minister and the other Staatssekretäre, with a 'Bewertung des Modells von MdB Louven', 10 February 1993, Tegtmeier files.
57. Heinz-Dietrich Steinmeyer to Frau Dr Fischer, Persönliche Referentin des Staatssekretärs Tegtmeier, with attachment, Überlegungen zur Einführung einer Arbeitsmarktabgabe, 19 February 1993, Tegtmeier files (emphasis in original).
58. Ruland to Tegtmeier (personal communication), 24 February 1993, Tegtmeier files.
59. In an interview with the author on 5 May 2000, Ministerialdirektor Rosenberg stressed Waigel's firm opposition to a different form of financing of the Federal Institute of Labour. Cronenberg of the FDP, in an interview with the author on 27 June 2000, supported the financing of unification through social insurance, on the grounds that greater harm would have been done by the tax increases that would otherwise have been necessary, that empty coffers called for prudence, and that a higher level of financing through taxation would have strengthened the hand of those who favoured the introduction of a national basic pension, which his party opposed.
60. *BGBl I*, p. 544.
61. Klaus von Beyme, 'Verfehlte Vereinigung—verpaßte Reformen? Zur Problematik der Evaluation der Vereinigungspolitik in Deutschland seit 1989', in *Journal für Sozialforschung*, 1 (1994), pp. 249–69 (here, p. 265).
62. cf. BMA, Ref. II b 1 (Grundsatzfragen des Arbeitsförderungsrechts u.a.), Regierungsdirektorin Voß-Gundlach an Abt. VIII, Betr.: Gespräch des Bundeskanzlers mit CDU-Ostabgeordneten am 6.9.1993 (here, Vermerke zu den geplanten Einsparungsmaßnahmen mit einer umfangreichen Analyse vom 1.9.1993), 2 September 1993, in BMA VIII a I-17491, vol. viii.
63. cf. Heinelt and Weck, *Arbeitsmarktpolitik*, pp. 163 f.
64. Schwinn, *Finanzierung*, p. 106. The share of the budget allotted to defence expenditure fell particularly sharply, from 19 to 10 per cent.
65. cf., in addition to the documents cited in note 62 above, BMA, Abt. II b 1, Entwurf eines Gesetzes zur Umsetzung des Spar-, Konsolidierungs- und Wachstumsprogramms im Bereich des Arbeitsförderungsgesetzes und anderer Gesetze (1. SKWPG) (here, Informationsvermerk für die Kabinettssitzung am 11.8.1993 zu den den Aufgabenbereich des BMA betreffenden Gesetzesänderungen), 6 August 1993, BMA, VIII a I/17560/3, vol. i; BMA, Abt. II, Entwurf eines Gesetzes zur Umsetzung des Spar-, Konsolidierungs- und Wachstumsprogrammes im Bereich des Arbeitsförderungsgesetzes und anderer Gesetze (1. SKWPG) (here, Informationsvermerk über die Inhalte, das Einsparvolumen und die betroffenen Personen), 17 September 1993, BMA VIII a 1/17490, vol. viii.
66. Informationsvermerk, 17 September 1993 (cf. note 65 above). The savings affecting the Federal Institute of Labour alone were estimated at 9,350 million DM in 1994 and 10,100 million DM in 1995.

67. BMA, Ref. II b 1, Gespräch des Bundeskanzlers mit den Ministerpräsidenten der neuen Bundesländer am 23.9.1993 (here, Sprechvermerk für den Minister zu Top 1, Unterpunkt 6 (Kürzungen im Sozialbereich), 17 September 1993, BMA VIII a 1/17490, vol. viii.
68. cf. *Woche im Bundestag* 17/1993, p. 14.
69. Heinelt and Weck, *Arbeitsmarktpolitik*, pp. 166 f.
70. cf. *BGBl I*, 1993, pp. 2353–68; *BGBl I*, 1993, pp. 2374–7; *Sozialbericht 1993*, pp. 17–20.
71. *Sozialbericht 1993*, p. 36; *Sozialbericht 1997*, p. 25.
72. *Bericht der Bundesregierung zur Zukunftssicherung des Standortes Deutschland*, BTDrs 12/5620, 26 September 1993.
73. BMA, Ref. I a 3 (Gesamtwirtschaftliche Fragen der Sozialpolitik), Bericht zur Zukunftssicherung des Wirtschaftsstandortes Deutschland (vom Bundeskabinett am 2. Sept. 1993 verabschiedet), 3 September 1993, BMA VIII a 1/17491, vol. x.
74. Prot. BT, 12. WP, pp. 15651–60 (here, pp. 15652 f.).
75. ibid., p. 15655.
76. ibid., pp. 15660–9 (here, p. 15665).
77. ibid., pp. 15673–7 (here, p. 15676).
78. ibid., pp. 15686–91 (here, p. 15686).
79. ibid., p. 15690.
80. Entschließungsantrag der Fraktionen der CDU/CSU und FDP zu der Abgabe einer Regierungserklärung 'Aktionsprogramm für mehr Wachstum und Beschäftigung', BTDrs 12/6625, 19 January 1994.
81. Prot. BT, 12. WP, pp. 17648–51, 17651–5.
82. ibid., pp. 17656–60.
83. ibid., pp. 17656 f.
84. ibid., pp. 17672–5 (here, p. 17672).
85. ibid., p. 17673.
86. cf. Diether Restle and Matthias Rockstroh, 'Arbeitslosigkeit wirksam bekämpfen', in *BArbBl* (1994), vol. 10, pp. 15–19.
87. *BGBl I*, 1994, pp. 1786–91; *BGBl I*, 1994, pp. 1792–5.
88. 'Sozialpolitik. Hilfe für die Arbeitslosen', in SPI 26, no. 11, 14 July 1994.
89. cf. Stellungnahmen, head of Unterabteilung IV b, Dr Achenbach, with attachment, 31 March 1994; Bemerkungen, Referat I b 3, 30 March and 31 March 1994; Stellungnahme, Abt. I, für die Klausurtagung der Leitung am 9./10.4.1994, 6 April 1994; BArch, B 149/120321. Cf. also Peter Rosenberg, 'Sozialpolitik bei leeren Kassen', in *SF* 43 (February 1994), pp. 31–5.
90. cf. *Sozialbericht 1997*, esp. pp. 28–33, 43 f., 49 f.
91. cf. the interview with Blüm by editors of *Stern*, 'Eine Kompanie von Maulhelden', in which a criticism of this kind, by the president of the German Conference of Industry and Commerce, Peter Stihl, is mentioned: Presse- und Informationsdienst der Bundesregierung, *Aktuelle Presseinformation*, 9 December 1994. Blüm countered by criticizing, in particular, the use of early retirement by businesses seeking to solve their staffing problems at the expense of the social benefit funds: 'We are seeing older people put on the scrapheap, which I consider a modern form of inhumanity.'
92. Blüm addressing the members of the CDU/CSU and FDP parliamentary parties, 12 January 1998, BMA files (no file number).

13 Social Policy and its Actors, 1991–1994

1. cf. Roland Czada, 'Reformloser Wandel. Stabilität und Anpassung im politischen Akteursystem der Bundesrepublik', in *50 Jahre Bundesrepublik. Rahmenbedingungen—Entwicklungen—Perspektiven*, ed. Thomas Ellwein and Everhard Holtmann, Opladen/Wiesbaden 1999 (*PVS* Sonderheft 30/1999), pp. 397–412 (here, p. 408).
2. CDU, *3. Parteitag der Christlich Demokratischen Union Deutschlands*, quotation from Kohl's speech on p. 20.
3. The names of the organizations invited to the discussions (which were held roughly every three months), the agendas of the meetings, and the preparations for, and conclusions reached by, the discussions as these related to employment and social policy are well documented in the Labour Ministry's files. It is not possible to analyse the discussions here.
4. There is extensive documentation of these talks in the Federal Chancellery's files.
5. cf., for example, the group's Ergebnisprotokoll der 32. Arbeitsbesprechung, 6 December 1993, BMA VIII a 1/17305, vol. vii.
6. Interview of Tegtmeier by the author, 12 July 2000.
7. On the cabinet committee's work, cf., for example, the list of topics it discussed at five meetings up to 10 July 1991, BArch, B 136/26279.
8. On the committee's make-up and its tasks, cf. Manfred Malina, head of Gruppe 12, 'Aufgabenplanung der Bundesregierung; Beziehungen zwischen Bund und Ländern; Kabinettsausschuß Neue Bundesländer', Bundeskanzleramt, to Chef des Bundeskanzleramtes, 30 September 1991. The intention was that the committee should normally meet on the day preceding each plenary sitting of the Bundesrat and that it would 'address the totality of matters, affecting particularly the new *Bundesländer*, that fall within the competence of the *Bund* and that have significant consequences for the *Länder*'. Malina expected that 'the Bundesrat, on the basis of the information and understanding gained through the committee's work, [would] in future address more closely supra-ministry aspects of the completion of German unity and, in light of the current political composition of the Bundesrat, [would] engage critically with the policies of the Federal government'. A handwritten notation on the document implies that the lead role in representing the Federal government on the committee would be taken by the Federal Minister of the Interior, with other ministries participating in accordance with the particular points being discussed. Cf. BArch, B 136/26279.
9. Dienstliche Mitteilung des BMA, no. 4, 31 May 1991, pp. 27 f.
10. Dienstliche Mitteilung des BMA, no. 6, 22 August 1991, p. 51.
11. Interview of Blüm by the author, 8 June 2000; of Tegtmeier, 13 July 2000. According to Tegtmeier, preparatory work was done by the permanent Staatssekretäre responsible. Some ministers who, in contrast with the era of the Schmidt government, were not themselves required to speak to their ministries' proposals in cabinet, were often unaware exactly what points were being dealt with in their own proposals and what were being handled by other ministries.
12. Interview of Tegtmeier by the author, 13 July 2000.
13. cf. Ergebnisprotokoll der gesonderten Besprechung der beamteten Staatssekretäre am 30.1.1995 im Bundeskanzleramt, 2 February 1995, BMA a 1/17311 (1).
14. Interview of Tegtmeier by the author, 13 July 2000; of Rosenberg, 5 May 2000.
15. Interview of Blüm by the author, 8 June 2000; of Tegtmeier, 13 July 2000.
16. The importance of this supra-party social policy coalition is emphasized by leading Labour Ministry officials: cf. interviews by the author with Tegtmeier, 13 July 2000, with Niemeyer, 4 May 2000, and with Rosenberg, 5 May 2000.

17. Interview of Tegtmeier by the author, 13 July 2000.
18. For Blüm's views on specific issues of social policy, and his assessments of the strengths and weaknesses of the German welfare state, cf., in addition to his many speeches, letters, and interviews (including those already cited), his 'Prolog' to *40 Jahre Sozialstaat Bundesrepublik Deutschland*, ed. Norbert Blüm and Hans F. Zacher, Baden-Baden 1989, pp. 11–18, and his four-part series of articles, 'Sozialstaat in Deutschland—eine Bilanz', in *Welt am Sonntag*, 28 March, 4 April, 11 April, and 18 April 1993.
19. Interview of Blüm by the author, 8 June 2000; of Cronenberg, 12 June 2000.
20. cf., with particular reference to policy on the future of Germany, Karl-Rudolf Korte, 'Kommt es auf die Person des Kanzlers an? Zum Regierungsstil von Helmut Kohl in der "Kanzlerdemokratie" des deutschen Parteienstaates', in *ZParl*, 29 (1998), pp. 387–401.
21. cf. Waldemar Schreckenberger, 'Veränderungen im Parlamentarischen Regierungssystem. Zur Oligarchie der Spitzenpolitiker der Parteien', in *Staat und Parteien, Festschrift für Rudolf Morsey zum 65. Geburtstag*, ed. Karl Dietrich Bracher, Paul Mikat, Konrad Repgen *et al.*, Berlin 1992, pp. 133–57; Waldemar Schreckenberger, 'Informelle Verfahren der Entscheidungsvorbereitung zwischen der Bundesregierung und den Mehrheitsfraktionen: Koalitionsgespräche und Koalitionsrunden', in *ZParl*, 25 (1994), pp. 329–46; Philip Manow, 'Informalisierung und Parteipolitisierung—zum Wandel exekutiver Entscheidungsprozesse in der Bundesrepublik', in *ZParl*, 27 (1996), pp. 96–107. For a fierce critique of the system of coalition meetings and the 'party state', and the highly personalized style of rule, cf. Wilhelm Hennis, 'Totenrede des Perikles auf ein blühendes Land. Ursachen der politischen Blockade', in *Auf dem Weg in den Parteienstaat*, ed. Wilhelm Hennis, Leipzig 1998, pp. 155–98.
22. Interview of Tegtmeier by the author, 13 July 2000.
23. ACDP, Fraktionsprotokolle.
24. ibid.
25. Anlage zur Sitzung der Unionsfraktion von 15.10.1992: Überblick über Instrumente und Themen der Fraktionsarbeit in den letzten Monaten, ACDP, Fraktionsprotokolle.
26. Information der Fraktion der CDU/CSU über Beschlüsse der Bundesregierung durch den Bundesminister für besondere Aufgaben und Chef des Bundeskanzleramtes, Friedrich Bohl, in der Fraktionssitzung am 22.9.1992, ACDP, Fraktionsprotokolle.
27. Schäuble, addressing the meeting of the CDU/CSU parliamentary party, 15 October 1992, in ACDP, Fraktionsprotokolle.
28. Interview of Tegtmeier by the author, 13 July 2000.
29. Czada, 'Reformloser Wandel', p. 405.
30. cf. above, pp. 217, 219.
31. cf. above, p. 254.
32. cf. Blüm's appeal at the conference of *Länder* ministers of labour and social affairs in the autumn of 1990: report entitled 'Länder sollen beim Verwaltungsaufbau in der ehemaligen DDR helfen', in SPI 24, no. 11, 10 October 1990.
33. cf. above, p. 221.
34. cf. above, p. 237 f.
35. cf. Beschlussvorlage des Geschäftsführenden Vorstandes vom 28.6.1993 zur Sitzung des Bundesvorstandes des DGB vom 6.7.1993: Inhaltliche und aktionsorientierte Begleitung des Projekts 'Pflegeversicherung/Karenztage' mit dem 'Zwischenergebnis' einer Projektgruppe aus Vertretern des DGB und der Mitgliedsgewerkschaften, die u.a. längerfristige Aktionen vorschlagen und begleiten sollte, AdsD, 5/DGAi 002269.
36. cf. above, pp. 62–6.
37. cf. above, pp. 282, 285.

Concluding Reflections

1. Alber, 'Sozialstaat in der Ära Kohl', p. 255.
2. The segmentation of social policy among so many different institutions was deplored by almost all of those interviewed by the author: cf. interviews with Blüm (8 June 2000), Tegtmeier (13 July 2000), Dreßler (10 May 2000), Cronenberg (27 June 2000), Rosenberg (5 May 2000), and Leven (18 May 2000).
3. Social insurance contributions differ from taxes on income and wages in the following ways: they are proportional rather than progressive; they have no exemptions, akin to tax allowances, to relieve the burden on lower income earners; and they are increased only to a contributions ceiling, so that higher incomes are only partially drawn on.
4. cf. *Sozialbericht 1997*, p. 311.
5. cf. Wolfgang Nierhaus, 'Private Haushalte. Kaufkraftplus auf breiter Front', in Oppenländer (ed.), *Wiedervereinigung*, pp. 51–72, esp. p. 60.
6. cf. above, p. 63.
7. *Sozialbericht 1993*, p. 58.
8. *Jahresbericht der Bundesregierung 1998*, p. 53.
9. cf. above, pp. 96 f.
10. BMA, *Statistisches Taschenbuch 1997*, tables 8.5 and 8.5A. In 1992 the contribution of women to the gross joint income of married couples aged 64 and above was 21 per cent in the old *Bundesländer*, and 37 per cent in the new *Bundesländer*. Cf. Detlef Klebula and Peter Semran, 'Alterseinkommen. Meist aus mehreren Quellen', in *BArbBl* (1997), vol. 2, pp. 5–10 (here, p. 7).
11. BMA, *Arbeits- und Sozialstatistik, Hauptergebnisse 1996*, Bonn 1996, p. 127.
12. Hauser *et al.*, *Ungleichheit*, pp. 293–300.
13. cf. above, p. 273.
14. cf. Monika Kohnert, 'Pflege und Umgang mit Behinderten in der DDR', in *Materialien der Enquete-Kommission 'Überwindung der Folgen der SED-Diktatur'*, vol. iii, pp. 1726–91 (here, esp. p. 1767).
15. Klaus-Peter Schwitzer, 'Die Rentner sind die Gewinner der Einheit', in *Das Parlament*, 17/24 January 1997, p. 2.
16. Bundesanstalt für Arbeit, Institut für Arbeitsmarkt- und Berufsforschung, 'Arbeitsmarkt und Arbeitslosigkeit in den neuen Bundesländern—Ausgangsbedingungen und Einsatz aktiver Arbeitsmarktpolitik im ostdeutschen Transformationsprozeß', in *Materialien der Enquete-Kommission 'Überwindung'*, vol. iii, pp. 2806–74 (here, p. 2821).
17. BMA, *Statistische Übersichten*, West volume, p. 124.
18. Ritter, *Über Deutschland*, p. 218.
19. Martin Dielwald, Johannes Huinink, Heike Solga *et al.*, 'Umbrüche und Kontinuitäten—Lebensläufe und Veränderungen von Lebensbedingungen seit 1989', in *Kollektiv und Eigensinn. Lebensläufe in der DDR und danach*, ed. Johannes Huinink, Karl Mayer, Martin Diewald *et al.*, Berlin 1995, pp. 307–48 (here, pp. 346–8).
20. cf. Manfred G. Schmidt, 'West Germany: The Policy of the Middle Way', in *Journal of Public Policy*, 7 (1987), pp. 139–77; id., 'Learning from Catastrophes—West Germany's Public Policy', in *A Comparative History of Public Policy*, ed. Francis G. Castles, Cambridge 1989, pp. 56–99; id., 'Die Politik des mittleren Weges. Besonderheiten der Staatstätigkeit in der Bundesrepublik Deutschland', in *APuZG*, B 9–10/90, 23 February 1990, pp. 23–31; id., 'Immer noch auf dem "mittleren Weg"? Deutschlands politische Ökonomie am Ende des 20. Jahrhunderts', *ZeS-Arbeitspapier* 7/1999.
21. Typology following Gøsta Esping-Andersen, *The Three Worlds of Welfare Capitalism*, Cambridge 1990. (I have not, however, adopted Esping-Andersen's classifications of

specific countries or his explanations of their political and historical evolution and conditions of development.) For criticisms of Esping-Andersen's approach, cf. Jürgen Kohl, 'Der Wohlfahrtsstaat in vergleichender Perspektive. Anmerkungen zu Esping-Andersens "Three Worlds of Welfare Capitalism"', in *ZSR*, 39 (1993), pp. 67–82; Claus Offe, 'Zur Typologie von sozialpolitischen "Regimes"', in *ZSR*, 39 (1993), pp. 83–6; Gerhard A. Ritter, 'Probleme und Tendenzen des Sozialstaats in den 1990er Jahren', in *GuG*, 22 (1996), pp. 393–408 (here, pp. 394 f.); Manfred G. Schmidt, *Sozialpolitik in Deutschland. Historische Entwicklung und internationaler Vergleich*, 2nd edn., Opladen 1998, pp. 222–8; *Welten des Wohlfahrtskapitalismus. Der Sozialstaat in vergleichender Perspektive*, ed. Stephan Lessenich and Ilona Ostner, Frankfurt a.M. 1998.

22. For Esping-Andersen, the level of 'de-commodification' brought about by social policy—i.e. the extent to which citizens are protected from having their work treated as a commodity—is a key criterion in the typological classification of welfare state regimes.
23. cf. Paul Pierson, *Dismantling the Welfare State? Reagan, Thatcher and the Politics of Retrenchment*, Cambridge 1994, pp. 53–73.
24. Jens Alber, 'Der deutsche Sozialstaat im Licht international vergleichender Daten', in *Leviathan*, 26 (1998), pp. 199–227.
25. cf. Nico A. Siegel, 'Zwischen Konsolidierung und Umbau: Staatliche Sozialpolitik (1975–1995)—ein Vergleich. Zwischenbericht aus dem laufenden Forschungsprojekt "Politische Bestimmungsfaktoren der Umbau- und Rückbaupolitik in den sozialen Sicherungssystemen im internationalen Vergleich"', unpubl. MS, March 1999, p. 12, table 1. The level of the share of GDP allotted to social policy expenditure is considerably lower in Siegel's figures than in the data for the Federal Republic published by the German Labour Ministry, as many fewer social benefits are taken into account. Citation of the OECD data is necessary, however, for purposes of comparison with other states.
26. Alber, 'Der deutsche Sozialstaat', p. 200.
27. ibid., pp. 206, 208, 216.
28. ibid., p. 212. Apart from Germany (i.e. the old *Bundesländer*), the only other countries in which the share of GDP allotted to social policy expenditure fell between 1980 and 1994 were Luxembourg and Belgium. In the United Kingdom, Italy, Spain, and France the comparable share rose between five and six percentage points.
29. Figures based on data in Alber, 'Der deutsche Sozialstaat', pp. 200, 212.
30. Figures based on BMA, *Statistisches Taschenbuch 1998*, table 7.3. For statistics on the financing of social benefits based on 1994 sources in Germany and in other European Union states, cf. BMA, *Sozialbericht 1997*, p. 266.
31. Europäische Union, *Soziale Sicherheit in Europa 1995*, Brussels/Luxembourg 1996, p. 81.
32. BMA, *Sozialbericht 2001*, Bonn 2002, p. 469.
33. Walter Hansch, 'Soziale Sicherung im europäischen Vergleich', in *APuZG*, B 34–35/98, 14 August 1998, pp. 15–26 (here, p. 20).
34. cf. Hinrichs, 'Restrukturierung', p. 125. On the causes of the disproportionately high increase in health expenditure, cf. Manfred G. Schmidt, 'Warum die Gesundheitsausgaben wachsen. Befunde des Vergleichs demokratisch verfaßter Länder', in *PVS*, 40 (1999), pp. 229–45.
35. OECD, *The Reform of Health Care Systems: A Review of Seventeen OECD Countries*, Paris 1994, p. 37.

36. Schmidt, 'Gesundheitsausgaben', p. 232.
37. Hinrichs, 'Restrukturierung', pp. 129 f.; Alber, 'Steuerung', pp. 259–84; Mayntz, 'Politische Steuerbarkeit und Reformblockaden', pp. 283–307.
38. Jens Alber, 'Das Gesundheitswesen der Bundesrepublik im internationalen Vergleich', in *Technische Perspektiven und gesellschaftliche Entwicklungen. Trends und Schwerpunkte der Forschung in der Bundesrepublik Deutschland*, ed. Ulrich Widmaier and Thomas König, Baden-Baden 1990, pp. 67–89 (here, p. 74).
39. Alber, 'Der deutsche Sozialstaat', pp. 221 f.
40. cf. above, p. 70.
41. OECD, *OECD Economic Outlook 61*, Paris 1997, p. A24.
42. ibid., p. A23.
43. Heinz Werner, 'Beschäftigungspolitisch erfolgreiche Länder. Lehren für die Bundesrepublik Deutschland?', in *APuZG*, B 34–35/98, 14 August 1998, pp. 3–14; Paqué, *Die Bilanz*, pp. 193–203.
44. cf. Manfred G. Schmidt, 'Reform der Sozialpolitik in Deutschland: Lehren des historischen und internationalen Vergleichs', in Leibfried and Wagschal (eds.), *Der deutsche Sozialstaat*, pp. 153–70 (here, pp. 161 f.).
45. On these challenges, cf. Ralf Dahrendorf, Frank Field, Carolyn Hayman *et al.*, members of the Commission on Wealth Creation and Social Cohesion, *Report on Wealth Creation and Social Cohesion in a Free Society*, London 1995.

Sources and Bibliography

1 UNPUBLISHED (ARCHIVAL) SOURCES

Bundesarchiv Koblenz (BArch)/Federal Archive, Koblenz (BArch)

B 136 Bundeskanzleramt (Federal Chancellery)

B 149 Bundesministerium für Arbeit und Sozialordnung (Federal Ministry of Labour and Social Order)

B 189 Bundesministerium für Jugend, Familie, Frauen und Gesundheit (Federal Ministry for Young People, the Family, Women, and Health)

Bundesarchiv Berlin (BArch)/Federal Archive, Berlin (BArch)

DA 3 Arbeitsgruppe Gesundheitswesen und Soziales des 'Runden Tisches' ('Round Table' working group on health and social affairs)

DC 20 Ministerrat der DDR—Büro Krause—Arbeitsstab Deutsche Einheit (GDR Council of Ministers—Krause office—planning staff on German unity)

DQ 1 Ministerium für Gesundheitswesen/DDR/Kleditzsch (GDR Ministry of Health/Kleditzsch)

DQ 3 Ministerium für Arbeit und Soziales/DDR/Hildebrandt (GDR Ministry of Labour and Social Affairs/Hildebrandt)

DY 34 FDGB-Sozialversicherung der DDR—Direktion (FDGB social insurance, GDR—management)

Stiftung Archiv der Parteien und Massenorganisationen der DDR (SAPMO) (Foundation, Archive of the Parties and Mass Organizations of the GDR, SAPMO)

Bundesarchiv Zwischenarchiv Dahlwitz-Hoppegarten (BArch)/Federal Archive, Interim Archive, Dahlwitz-Hoppegarten (BArch)

B 126 Bundesministerium der Finanzen (Federal Ministry of Finance)

B 149 Bundesministerium für Arbeit und Sozialordnung (Federal Ministry of Labour and Social Order)

Bundesversicherungsamt Berlin/Federal Insurance Office, Berlin

Akten: Deutsch-deutsche Sozialunion (Files, social union of the two Germanys)

Bundesversicherungsanstalt für Angestellte Berlin/Federal Insurance Office for White-Collar Workers

BMA Bonn/Federal Ministry of Labour and Social Order, Bonn

BMA, Abt. VIII—Außenstelle Berlin, Jägerstraße/Federal Ministry of Labour and Social Order, department VIII — Berlin branch, Jägerstraße

BMA-Pressearchiv/Federal Ministry of Labour and Social Order, press archive

BMG Bonn/Federal Ministry of Health, Bonn

Bundespresseamt Bonn/Federal Press Office, Bonn
Dok., Text-Bell./RFTV-AA (1987–95)

Archiv der sozialen Demokratie der Friedrich-Ebert-Stiftung Bonn (AdsD)/Archive of Social Democracy of the Friedrich Ebert Foundation (AdsD)
SPD-Fraktion und Fraktionsvorstand im Deutschen Bundestag (SPD parliamentary party and parliamentary party executive, Bundestag)
SPD-Fraktion in der Volkskammer der DDR (SPD parliamentary party, Volkskammer, GDR)
SPD-Querschnittsgruppe Einheit Deutschlands, Schwanitz (SPD cross-party group on German unity, Schwanitz)
DGB-Archiv, Abt. Vorsitzender und Bundesvorstand (DGB archive, department of chairman and federal executive)
DAG-Bundesvorstand, Abt. Vorsitzender, Anton Reuer (DAG federal executive, department of chairman, Anton Reuer)

Archiv für Christlich-Demokratische Politik der Konrad-Adenauer-Stiftung St. Augustin (ACDP)/Archive of Christian Democratic Politics, Konrad Adenauer Foundation, St Augustin (ACDP)
Bestand I/504: Tageskopien BMA Dr. Norbert Blüm (Files, I/504, daily copies, Federal Ministry of Labour and Social Order, Dr Norbert Blüm)
Protokolle der Sitzungen der CDU/CSU-Fraktion des Deutschen Bundestages (Records of meetings of the CDU/CSU parliamentary party, Bundestag)
Protokolle der Sitzungen des Vorstandes der CDU/CSU-Fraktion des Deutschen Bundestages (Records of meetings of the executive of the CDU/CSU parliamentary party, Bundestag)
Arbeitsgruppe für 'Arbeit und Soziales' sowie für 'Gesundheitswesen' und Arbeitnehmergruppe der CDU/CSU-Fraktion (Kurzprotokolle der Sitzungen) (Working groups on labour and social affairs and on health, and employees' group, CDU/CSU parliamentary party, short records of meetings)

Akten von Dr. Ammermüller, Hamburg/Files of Dr Ammermüller, Hamburg

Akten von Staatssekretär Dr. Tegtmeier, Berlin/Files of Staatssekretär Dr Tegtmeier, Berlin

2 PUBLISHED SOURCES AND BIBLIOGRAPHY

Ackermann, Eduard, *Mit feinem Gehör. Vierzig Jahre in der Bonner Politik*, Bergisch-Gladbach 1994.

Alber, Jens, 'Die Steuerung im Gesundheitswesen in vergleichender Perspektive', in *Journal für Sozialforschung*, 29 (1989), pp. 259–84.

Alber, Jens, 'Das Gesundheitswesen der Bundesrepublik im internationalen Vergleich', in Widmaier and König (eds.), *Technische Perspektiven* (q.v.), pp. 67–89.

Alber, Jens, 'Der deutsche Sozialstaat im Licht international vergleichender Daten', in *Leviathan*, 26 (1998), pp. 199–227.

Alber, Jens, 'Der deutsche Sozialstaat in der Ära Kohl: Diagnosen und Daten', in Leibfried and Wagschal (eds.), *Der deutsche Sozialstaat* (q.v.), pp. 235–75.

Albrecht, Ulrich, *Die Abwicklung der DDR. Die '2+4–Verhandlungen'. Ein Insider-Bericht*, Opladen 1992.

Allensbacher Jahrbuch der Demoskopie 1984–1992, vol. ix, ed. Elisabeth Noelle-Neumann and Renate Köcher, Munich/New York/London etc. 1993.

Allensbacher Jahrbuch der Demoskopie 1993–1997, vol. x, ed. Elisabeth Noelle-Neumann and Renate Köcher, Munich 1997.

Ammermüller, Martin, and Udo Diel, 'DDR-Versicherung wird angeglichen', in *Kompaß*, 1990, vol. 7, pp. 333–42.

Ammermüller, Martin, 'Deutscher Einigungsprozess', in BMA, *Sozialstaat im Wandel* (q.v.), pp. 107–20.

Andersen, Uwe, 'Finanzierung der Einheit', in Weidenfeld and Korte (eds.), *Handbuch* (q.v.), pp. 294–307.

Angerhausen, Susanne, *Radikaler Organisationswandel. Wie die 'Volkssolidarität' die deutsche Vereinigung überlebte*, Opladen 2003.

Anzinger, Rudolf, and Rolf Wenk (eds.), *Entwicklungen im Arbeitsrecht und Arbeitsschutzrecht. Festschrift für Ottfried Wlotzke zum 70. Geburtstag*, Munich 1996.

AOK-Bundesverband, 'Die deutsch-deutsche Entwicklung und mögliche Auswirkungen auf die AOK', in *Dienst für Gesellschaftspolitik*, 10–90 (1990), pp. 5–10.

Artus, Ingrid, 'Tarifpolitik in den neuen Bundesländern. Akteure, Strategien, Problemlagen', in Bergmann and Schmidt (eds.), *Industrielle Beziehungen* (q.v.), pp. 71–100.

Arzheimer, Kai, '"Freiheit oder Sozialismus?" Gesellschaftliche Wertorientierungen, Staatszielvorstellungen und Ideologien im Ost-West-Vergleich', in Gabriel *et al.* (eds.), *Wächst zusammen, was zusammen gehört?* (q.v.), pp. 285–313.

Attali, Jacques, *Verbatim*, vol. iii, *Chronique des années 1988–1991*, Paris 1995.

Aulmann, Heinz, 'Die Verhütung und Entschädigung von Arbeitsunfällen und Berufskrankheiten in der DDR unter Berücksichtigung des Staatsvertrages', in *Kompaß*, 100 (1990), pp. 343–5.

Baar, Lothar, Rainer Karlsch, and Werner Matschke, 'Kriegsschäden, Demontagen und Reparationen', in *Materialien der Enquete-Kommission 'Aufarbeitung'*, vol. ii (q.v.), pp. 868–988.

Backhaus-Maul, Holger, 'Wohlfahrtsverbände in den neuen Bundesländern. Anmerkungen zum Stand der Wohlfahrtsverbändeforschung im deutschen Einigungsprozeß', in Eichener *et al.* (eds.), *Organisierte Interessen*, (q.v.), pp. 359–81.

Bahr, Egon, *Zu meiner Zeit*, Munich 1998.

Bähr, Johannes, 'Institutionenordnung und Wirtschaftsentwicklung. Die Wirtschaftsgeschichte der DDR aus der Sicht des zwischendeutschen Vergleichs', in *GuG*, 25 (1999), pp. 530–55.

Baker, James A., *The Politics of Diplomacy: Revolution, War and Peace, 1989–1992*, New York 1995.

Bauerkämper, Arnd, Jürgen Danyel, Peter Hübner, and Sabine Roß (eds.), *Gesellschaft ohne Eliten? Führungsgruppen in der DDR*, Berlin 1997.

BDA, *Sozialstaat vor dem Umbau. Leistungsfähigkeit und Finanzierbarkeit sichern*, October 1994.

BDA, *Die Zukunft des Sozialstaates. Wirtschafts- und sozialpolitische Perspektiven. Reden von Dr. Klaus Murmann und Dr. Wolfgang Schäuble. Jahrestagung Bonn / Bad Godesberg*, 14. Dezember 1995.

BDA, *Sozialpolitik für mehr Wettbewerb und Beschäftigung. Ordnungspolitische Grundsätze des BDA*, May 1998.

Becker-Neetz, Gerald, 'Verfassungsreform. Sozialpolitischer Spielraum gewahrt', in *BArbBl* (1995), vol. 5, pp. 5–8.

Bergmann, Joachim, and Rudi Schmidt (eds.), *Industrielle Beziehungen. Institutionalisierung und Praxis unter Krisenbedingungen*, Opladen 1996.

Bergmann, Joachim, 'Industrielle Beziehungen in Ostdeutschland: Transferierte Institutionen im Deindustrialisierungsprozeß', in Lutz *et al.* (eds.), *Arbeit* (q.v.), pp. 257–94.

Bericht der Bundesregierung zur Zukunftssicherung des Standortes Deutschland, BTDrs 12/5620.

Bericht der Gemeinsamen Verfassungskommission, BTDrs 12/6000, 5 November 1993.

Bericht der Kommission 'Soziale Sicherheit' zur Reform der sozialen Sicherungssysteme, Berlin, 29 September 2003.

Berichte der Forschungsgruppe Wahlen e.V., 'Bundestagswahl 1994. Eine Analyse der Wahl zum 13. Deutschen Bundestag am 16.10.1994', no. 76, 21 October 1994, Mannheim.

Beyme, Klaus von, 'Verfehlte Vereinigung—verpaßte Reformen? Zur Problematik der Evaluation der Vereinigungspolitik in Deutschland seit 1989', in *Journal für Sozialforschung*, 1 (1994), pp. 249–69.

Biedenkopf, Kurt, *1989–1990. Ein deutsches Tagebuch*, Berlin 2000.

Biedenkopf, Sebastian, *Interessenausgleich und Sozialplan unter Berücksichtigung der besonderen Probleme bei der Privatisierung und Sanierung von Betrieben in den neuen Bundesländern*, Berlin 1994.

Biermann, Rafael, *Zwischen Kreml und Kanzleramt. Wie Moskau mit der deutschen Einheit rang*, Paderborn/Munich/Stuttgart 1997.

Billing, Werner, 'Die rheinland-pfälzische Landtagswahl vom 21. April 1991: Machtwechsel in Mainz nach 44 Jahren', in *ZParl*, 22 (1991), pp. 584–601.

Birg, Herwig, '188 Millionen Einwanderer zum Ausgleich? Demographische Alterung und Bevölkerungsschrumpfung bei uns—Konsequenzen für das soziale Sicherungssystem', in *FAZ*, 12 April 2000.

Birg, Herwig, *Die demographische Zeitenwende. Der Bevölkerungsrückgang in Deutschland und Europa*, 2nd edn., Munich 2002.

Birg, Herwig, 'Deutschlands Weltrekorde', in *FAZ*, 22 February 2005.

Birsl, Ursula, and Peter Lösche, 'Parteien in West- und Ostdeutschland: Der gar nicht so feine Unterschied', in *ZParl*, 29 (1998), pp. 7–24.

Bispinck, Reinhard, 'Der Tarifkonflikt um den Stufenplan in der ostdeutschen Metallindustrie—Anlaß, Entwicklung, Ergebnis', in *WSI Mitteilungen*, 46 (1993), pp. 469–81.

'Blühende Landschaften?', in *Süddeutsche Zeitung*, 30 May 2000.

Blüm, Norbert, and Hans F. Zacher (eds.), *40 Jahre Sozialstaat Bundesrepublik Deutschland*, Baden-Baden 1989.

Blüm, Norbert, 'Schritt für Schritt—die Netze müssen langsam verknüpft werden', in *Die Welt*, 2 March 1990.

Blüm, Norbert, 'Rücksicht auf Tradition nehmen', in SPI 18/1992, 19 December 1992.

Blüm, Norbert, 'Sozialstaat in Deutschland—eine Bilanz', in *Welt am Sonntag*, 28 March, 4 April, 11 April, and 18 April 1993.

Blüm, Norbert, 'Pflegeversicherungsgesetz. Politik der Nähe', in *BArbBl* (1993), vols. 7–8, pp. 5–9.

Blüm, Norbert, 'Sozialstaatliche Kultur in der Bewährung', in BMA, *Sozialstaat im Wandel* (q.v.), pp. 1–33.

Blüm, Norbert, 'Pflegeversicherung: Positive Zwischenbilanz', in *BArbBl* (1997), vol. 10, pp. 5–8.

BMA, *Sozialpolitische Informationen*, 1989–95.

BMA, Dienstliche Mitteilungen des BMA, 1990–4.

BMA, *Sozialbericht 1990*, Bonn 1990.

BMA, *Sozialbericht 1993*, Bonn 1994.

BMA, *Sozialstaat im Wandel*, Bonn 1994.

BMA, *Arbeits- und Sozialstatistik. Hauptergebnisse 1996*, Bonn 1996.

BMA, *Sozialbericht 1997*, Bonn 1998.

BMA, *Statistisches Taschenbuch 1997 und 1998. Arbeits- und Sozialstatistik*, Bonn 1998.

BMA, *Statistische Übersichten zur Sozialpolitik in Deutschland seit 1945*, West vol. ed. Hermann Berié, East vol. ed. André Steiner with Thomas Reichl, Bonn 1999.

BMA, *Sozialbericht 2001*, Bonn 2002.

BMFuS, *Familien und Familienpolitik im geeinten Deutschland.—Zukunft des Humanvermögens. Fünfter Familienbericht*, Bonn 1994.

BMG, *Nachhaltigkeit in der Finanzierung der sozialen Sicherungssysteme. Bericht der Kommission*, Berlin 2003.

BMG, *Sozialbericht 2005*, Bonn 2005.

Böhm, Stefan, and Arno Pott, 'Verteilungspolitische Aspekte der Rentenüberleitung. Eine Analyse ausgewählter Verteilungswirkungen der Übertragung des bundesdeutschen Rentenrechts auf die neuen Bundesländer', in Schmähl (ed.), *Sozialpolitik im Prozeß der deutschen Vereinigung* (q.v.), pp. 166–227.

Boldorf, Marcel, *Sozialfürsorge in der SBZ/DDR 1945–1953. Ursachen, Ausmaß und Bewältigung der Nachkriegsarmut*, Stuttgart 1998.

Bouvier, Beatrix, *Die DDR—ein Sozialstaat? Sozialpolitik in der Ära Honecker*, Bonn 2002.

Boyer, Robert, and Daniel Drache (eds.), *States Against Markets: The Limits of Globalisation*, London/New York 1996.

Bozo, Frédéric, *Mitterrand, la fin de la guerre froide et l'unification allemande. De Yalta à Maastricht*, Paris 2005.

Bracher, Karl Dietrich, Paul Mikat, Konrad Repgen *et al.* (eds.), *Staat und Parteien. Festschrift für Rudolf Morsey zum 65. Geburtstag*, Berlin 1992.

Brand, Christoph-Matthias, *Souveränität für Deutschland. Grundlagen, Entstehungsgeschichte und Bedeutung des zwei-plus-vier Vertrages vom 12. September 1990*, Cologne 1993.

Breuel, Birgit, and Michael C. Burda, *Ohne historisches Vorbild. Die Treuhandanstalt 1990–2004*, Berlin 2005.

Bruck, Elke, and Peter M. Wagner (eds.), *Wege zum '2+4'-Vertrag. Die äußeren Aspekte der deutschen Einheit*, Munich 1996.

Buchheim, Christoph, 'Kriegsschäden, Demontagen und Reparationen. Deutschland nach dem Zweiten Weltkrieg', in *Materialien der Enquete-Kommission 'Aufarbeitung'*, vol. ii (q.v.), pp. 1030–69.

Bulletin des Presse- und Informationsamtes der Bundesregierung, Bonn.

Bulletin of the European Communities, supplement 1/90, Luxembourg 1990.

Bulmahn, Thomas, 'Das vereinte Deutschland—eine lebenswerte Gesellschaft? Zur Bewertung von Freiheit, Sicherheit und Gerechtigkeit in Ost und West', in *Kölner Zeitschrift für Soziologie und Sozialpsychologie*, 52 (2000), pp. 405–27.

Bundesanstalt für Arbeit, Institut für Arbeitsmarkt- und Berufsforschung, 'Arbeitsmarkt und Arbeitslosigkeit in den neuen Bundesländern—Ausgangsbedingungen und Einsatz aktiver Arbeitsmarktpolitik im ostdeutschen Transformationsprozess', in *Materialien der Enquete-Kommission 'Überwindung'*, vol. iii (q.v.), pp. 2806–74.

Bundesarbeitsblatt (*BArbBl*), 1989–97.

Bundesgesetzblatt (*BGBl*), 1949 ff.

Bundesinstitut für Bevölkerungsforschung, *Bevölkerung. Fakten—Trends—Ursachen—Erwartungen*, Wiesbaden 2000.

Bürklin, Thomas, and Dieter Roth (eds.), *Das Superwahljahr. Deutschland vor unkalkulierbaren Regierungsmehrheiten?*, Cologne 1994.

Bürklin, Wilhelm, Hilke Rebenstorf *et al.* (eds.), *Eliten in Deutschland. Rekrutierung und Integration*, Opladen 1997.

Burmeister, Joachim (ed.), *Verfassungsstaatlichkeit. Festschrift für Klaus Stern zum 65. Geburtstag*, Munich 1997.

Bush, George, and Brent Scowcroft, *A World Transformed*, New York 1998.

Buttler, Friedrich, Heinrich Reiter, and Horst Günther (eds.), *Europa und Deutschland—Zusammenwachsende Arbeitsmärkte und Sozialräume. Festschrift für Heinrich Franke zum 65. Geburtstag, 26. Januar 1993*, Stuttgart/Berlin/Cologne 1993.

Buttler, Friedrich, and Knut Emmerich, 'Kosten und Nutzen aktiver Arbeitsmarktpolitik im ostdeutschen Transformationsprozeß', in Gutmann (ed.), *Wettbewerbsfähigkeit* (q.v.), pp. 61–94.

Castles, Francis G. (ed.), *A Comparative History of Public Policy*, Cambridge 1989.

CDU, *Ja zu Deutschland—Ja zur Zukunft. Wahlprogramm der Christlich Demokratischen Union Deutschlands zur gesamtdeutschen Bundestagswahl am 2. Dezember 1990*, publ. CDU-Bundesgeschäftsstelle.

CDU, *3. Parteitag der Christlich Demokratischen Union Deutschlands. Niederschrift. Düsseldorf, 26.–28. Oktober 1992.*

CDU/CSU, *Wir sichern Deutschlands Zukunft: Regierungsprogramm von CDU und CSU*, Bonn 1994.

Clasen, Lothar, 'Tarifentwicklung Ost. Erste Zwischenbilanz', in *BArbBl* (1991), vol. 6, pp. 5–8.

Clasen, Lothar, 'Tarifverträge 1991. Schrittweise Angleichung', in *BArbBl* (1992), vol. 4, pp. 5–10.

Clasen, Lothar, 'Tarifverträge 1992. Wieder 9000 Abschlüsse', in *BArbBl* (1993), vol. 3, pp. 14–19.

Clausen, Lars (ed.), *Gesellschaften im Umbruch. Beiträge des 27. Kongreß der Deutschen Gesellschaft für Soziologie*, vol. i, Frankfurt a.M. 1996.

Conrad, Christopher, Michael Lechner, and Welf Werner, 'East German Fertility after Unification: Crisis or Adaptation?', in *Population and Development Review*, 22 (1996), pp. 331–58.

CSU, *Heimat Bayern. Zukunft Deutschland. Mit uns. CSU. Programm der Christlich-Sozialen Union zur Bundestagswahl am 2. Dezember 1990*, passed by party executive of CSU 29 October 1990.

Czada, Roland, 'Der Kampf um die Finanzierung der deutschen Einheit', in Lehmbruch (ed.), *Einigung und Zerfall* (q.v.), pp. 73–102.

Czada, Roland, 'Der Vereinigungsprozeß—Wandel der externen und internen Konstitutionsbedingungen des westdeutschen Modells', in Simonis (ed.), *Deutschland nach der Wende* (q.v.), pp. 55–86.

Czada, Roland, 'Vereinigungskrise und Standortdebatte. Der Beitrag der Wiedervereinigung zur Krise des westdeutschen Modells', in *Leviathan*, 26 (1998), pp. 24–59.

Czada, Roland, 'Reformloser Wandel. Stabilität und Anpassung im politischen Akteursystem der Bundesrepublik', in Ellwein and Holtmann (eds.), *50 Jahre Bundesrepublik* (q.v.), pp. 397–412.

Dahrendorf, Ralf, *Fragmente eines neuen Liberalismus*, Stuttgart 1987.

Dahrendorf, Ralf, Frank Field, Carolyn Hayman, *et al.*, *Report on Wealth Creation and Social Cohesion in a Free Society* (Commission on Wealth Creation and Social Cohesion), London 1995.

Dästner, Christian, 'Die Mitwirkung der Länder bei den Entscheidungen zur Wiederherstellung der Einheit Deutschlands', in Klein (ed.), *Die Rolle des Bundesrates* (q.v.), pp. 33–60.

Däubler, Wolfgang, *Rechtsexport. Einführung des bundesdeutschen Arbeitsrechts im Gebiet der früheren DDR*, Frankfurt a.M. 1996.

de Maizière, Lothar, *Die deutsche Einheit—eine kritische Betrachtung*, Fürstenfeldbruck 1994.

de Maizière, Lothar, *Anwalt der Einheit. Ein Gespräch mit Christine de Maizière*, Berlin 1996.

Der Tagesspiegel, 2002–6.

Der Vertrag über die Schaffung einer Währungs-, Wirtschafts- und Sozialunion zwischen der Bundesrepublik Deutschland und der Deutschen Demokratischen Republik. Erklärungen und Dokumente, publ. Presse- und Informationsamt der Bundesregierung, Bonn June 1990.

Derlien, Hans-Ulrich, 'Kommunalverfassungen zwischen Reform und Revolution', in Gabriel and Voigt (eds.), *Kommunalwissenschaftliche Analysen* (q.v.), pp. 47–78.

Deutsche Bundesbank, *Monatsberichte*, 1989–2006.

Deutsche Bundesbank, *Auszüge aus Presseartikeln*, 1989–2006.

Deutsche Bundesbank, 'Zur Finanzentwicklung der gesetzlichen Rentenversicherung seit Beginn der neunziger Jahre', in *Monatsbericht*, 47, March 1997, pp. 17–31.

Die Arbeitsgerichtsbarkeit. Festschrift zum 100jährigen Bestehen der Deutschen Arbeitsgerichtsverbände, Neuwied/Kriftel/Berlin 1994.

Die BG, 'Nach einem Jahrzehnt: "Wie hat die Unfallversicherung die Wiedervereinigung erlebt und gestaltet?"', special edn., 12 (2001).

Die neue Verfassung der DDR mit einem einleitenden Kommentar von Dietrich Müller-Römer, Cologne 1974.

Die SPD im Deutschen Bundestag, 1989–1995.

Die Zeit, 1989–2000.

Diewald, Martin, Johannes Huinink, Heike Solga *et al.*, 'Umbrüche und Kontinuitäten—Lebensläufe und Veränderungen von Lebensbedingungen seit 1989', in Huinink *et al.* (eds.), *Kollektiv und Eigensinn* (q.v.), pp. 307–48.

Diewald, Martin, Anne Goedecke, and Karl Ulrich Mayer (eds.), *After the Fall of the Wall: Life Courses and the Transformation of East Germany*, Stanford 2006.

Döhler, Marian, and Philip Manow, 'Formierung und Wandel eines Politikfeldes—Gesundheitspolitik von Blank zu Seehofer', MPIfG Discussion Paper, 6/95.

Dokumente zur Deutschlandpolitik. Deutsche Einheit. Sonderedition aus den Akten des Bundeskanzleramtes 1989/90, ed. Hanns Jürgen Küsters and Daniel Hofmann, Munich 1998.

Dombois, Rainer, 'Der schwierige Abschied vom Normalarbeitsverhältnis', in *APuZG*, B 37/99, pp. 13–20.

Drauschke, Petra, and Margit Stolzenburg, 'Familie', in Winkler (ed.), *Sozialreport 1995* (q.v.), pp. 276–328.

Dreher, Klaus, *Helmut Kohl. Leben mit Macht*, Stuttgart 1998.

Dreßler, Rudolf, Ingrid Matthäus-Maier, Wolfgang Roth *et al.* (eds.), *Fortschritt 90. Fortschritt für Deutschland*, Munich 1990.

Dreßler, Rudolf, 'Soziale Gerechtigkeit in Deutschland', in Dreßler *et al.* (eds.), *Fortschritt 90* (q.v.), pp. 93–103.

Dreßler, Rudolf, 'Erste Schritte zur Sozialunion. Bundesrepublik Deutschland—DDR Diskussionspapier', in *Dienst für Gesellschaftspolitik*, 11–90 (1990), pp. 5–10.

Drucksachen Deutscher Bundestag (BTDrs), Deutscher Bundestag, Bonn 1989–2006.

Duisberg, Claus J., *Das deutsche Jahr. Einblicke in die Wiedervereinigung 1989/90*, Berlin 2005.

Eckart, Karl, Jens Hacker, and Siegfried Mampel (eds.), *Wiedervereinigung Deutschlands. Festschrift zum 20jährigen Bestehen der Gesellschaft für Deutschlandforschung*, Berlin 1998.

Ehlers, Bernd, *Arbeitsmarktpolitik im Transformationsprozeß. Einsatz und Neuorientierung des aktiven arbeitsmarktpolitischen Instrumentariums des Arbeitsförderungsgesetzes in den neuen Bundesländern*, Edewecht 1996.

Eichener, Volker, Ralf Kleinfeld, Detlef Pollack, *et al.* (eds.), *Organisierte Interessen in Ostdeutschland*, 2 half-vols., Marburg 1992.

Eichenhofer, Eberhard, 'Das Sozialrecht in der Rechtsprechung des Europäischen Gerichtshofes. Zur Genealogie der Thematisierung des Sozialrechts durch den EuGH', in *ZeS-Arbeitspapiere*, no. 9/96.

Ellwein, Thomas, and Everhard Holtmann (eds.), *50 Jahre Bundesrepublik. Rahmenbedingungen—Entwicklungen—Perspektiven*, Opladen/Wiesbaden 1999 (*PVS* Sonderheft 30/1999).

Emmert, Thomas, and Andrea Stögbauer, 'Volksparteien in der Krise. Die Wahlen in Baden-Württemberg, Schleswig-Holstein und Hamburg', in Bürklin and Roth (eds.), *Das Superwahljahr* (q.v.), pp. 86–110.

Emmert, Thomas, 'Politische Ausgangslage vor der Bundestagswahl 1994. Entwicklung der Parteien, Themen und Kandidaten in Ost und West', in Bürklin and Roth (eds.), *Das Superwahljahr* (q.v.)., pp. 54–85.

Entscheidungen des Bundessozialgerichts (BSGE), 1989 ff.

Entscheidungen des Bundesverfassungsgerichts (BVerfGE), 1973 ff.

Esping-Andersen, Gøsta, *The Three Worlds of Welfare Capitalism*, Cambridge 1990.

Europäische Union, *Soziale Sicherheit in Europa 1995*, Brussels/Luxembourg 1996.

Fachinger, Uwe, and Heinz Rothgang (eds.), *Die Wirkungen des Pflegeversicherungsgesetzes*, Berlin 1995.

Falter, Jürgen W., 'Wahlen 1990. Die demokratische Legitimation für die deutsche Einheit mit großen Überraschungen', in Jesse and Mitter (eds.), *Die Gestaltung der deutschen Einheit* (q.v.), pp. 163–88.

Falter, Jürgen W., and Markus Klein, 'Die Wähler der PDS bei der Bundestagswahl 1994. Zwischen Ideologie, Nostalgie und Protest', in *APuZG*, B 51–52/94, pp. 22–34.

Falter, Jürgen W., with Markus Klein, *Wer wählte rechts? Die Wähler und Angehörigen rechtsextremischer Parteien im vereinigten Deutschland*, Munich 1994.

Farny, Dieter, Peter Lütke-Bornefeld, and Gertrud Zellenberg (eds.), *Lebenssituation älterer Menschen. Beschreibung und Prognose aus interdisziplinärer Sicht*, Berlin 1996.

FDP, *Das liberale Deutschland. Programm der F.D.P. zu den Bundestagswahlen am 2. Dezember 1990.*

FDP, *Liberal denken. Leistung wählen. Das Programm der F.D.P. zur Bundestagswahl 1994.*

Feist, Ursula, and Hanns-Jürgen Hoffmann, 'Landtagswahlen in der ehemaligen DDR am 14. Oktober 1990: Föderalismus im wiedervereinigten Deutschland—Tradition und neue Konturen', in *ZParl*, 22 (1991), pp. 5–34.

Feist, Ursula, and Hanns-Jürgen Hoffmann, 'Die Hamburger Bürgerschaftswahl vom 19. September 1993: Rundumangriff auf die Etablierten', in *ZParl*, 25 (1994), pp. 217–34.

Fels, Joachim, 'Arbeitsmärkte und Währungsunion', in *Börsen-Zeitung*, 9 January 1997; reprinted in Deutsche Bundesbank, *Auszüge aus Presseartikeln*, no. 3, 15 January 1997, pp. 16 f.

Fichter, Michael, and Hugo Reister, 'Die Gewerkschaften', in Niedermayer (ed.), *Intermediäre Strukturen* (q.v.), pp. 309–33.

Fisch, Stefan, and Ulrike Haerendel (eds.), *Geschichte und Gegenwart der Rentenversicherung in Deutschland. Beiträge zur Entstehung, Entwicklung und vergleichenden Einordnung der Alterssicherung im Sozialstaat*, Berlin 2000.

Fischer, Ilse (ed.), *Die Einheit sozial gestalten. Dokumente aus den Akten der SPD-Führung 1989/90*, Bonn 2009.

Flora, Peter, Jens Alber, and Jürgen Kohl, 'Zur Entwicklung der westeuropäischen Wohlfahrtsstaaten', in *PVS*, 18 (1977), pp. 707–72.

Flora, Peter, *State, Economy and Society in Western Europe, 1815–1975: A Data Handbook in Two Volumes*, vol. i, *The Growth of Mass Democracies and Welfare States*, Frankfurt a.M./London 1983; vol. ii (with Franz Kraus and Werner Pfennig), *The Growth of Industrial Societies and Capitalist Economies*, Frankfurt a.M./Chicago 1987.

Flora, Peter (ed.), *Growth to Limits: The Western European Welfare States since World War II*, vols. i, ii, and iv, Berlin/New York 1986/7.

Franke, Heinrich, 'Aufbau in den neuen Ländern', in *BArbBl*, 5 (1993), pp. 5–9.

Frankfurter Allgemeine Zeitung (*FAZ*), 1989–2005.

Frankfurter Rundschau, 1989–95.

Frerich, Johannes, and Martin Frey, *Handbuch der Geschichte der Sozialpolitik in Deutschland*, vol. ii, *Sozialpolitik in der Deutschen Demokratischen Republik*, 2nd edn., Munich/Vienna 1996; vol. iii, *Sozialpolitik in der Bundesrepublik Deutschland bis zur Herstellung der Deutschen Einheit*, 2nd edn., Munich/Vienna 1996.

Fuchs, Dieter, 'Zum Wandel politischer Konfliktlinien; Ideologische Gruppierungen und Wahlverhalten', in Süß (ed.), *Die Bundesrepublik in den achtziger Jahren* (q.v.), pp. 69–86.

Gabriel, Oscar W., and Rüdiger Voigt (eds.), *Kommunalwissenschaftliche Analysen*, Bochum 1994.

Gabriel, Oscar W., 'Politische Orientierungen und Verhaltensweisen', in Kaase *et al.* (eds.), *Politisches System* (q.v.), pp. 231–312.

Gabriel, Oscar W. (ed.), *Politische Orientierungen und Verhaltensweisen im vereinigten Deutschland*, Opladen 1997.

Gabriel, Oscar W., 'Einleitung: Politische Orientierungen und Verhaltensweisen im Transitionsprozeß', in Gabriel (ed.), *Politische Orientierungen* (q.v.), pp. 9–33.

Gabriel, Oscar W., Jürgen W. Falter, and Hans Rattinger (eds.), *Wächst zusammen, was zusammen gehört? Stabilität und Wandel politischer Einstellungen im wiedervereinigten Deutschland*, Baden-Baden 2005.

Gabriel, Oscar W., 'Wächst zusammen, was zusammen gehört?', in Gabriel *et al.* (eds.), *Wächst zusammen, was zusammen gehört?* (q.v.), pp. 385–423.

Gawel, Erik, in collaboration with Markus Grünewald and Michael Thöne, *Die deutsch-deutsche Währungsunion. Verlauf und geldpolitische Konsequenzen*, Baden-Baden 1994.

Geißler, Heiner, *Die Neue Soziale Frage*, Freiburg 1976.

Geißler, Rainer, *Die Sozialstruktur Deutschlands. Zur gesellschaftlichen Entwicklung mit einer Zwischenbilanz zur Vereinigung*, 2nd edn., Opladen 1996.

Gemeinsam für Deutschland—Mit Mut und Menschlichkeit, coalition agreement between the CDU, CSU, and SPD, 11 November 2005.

Genscher, Hans-Dietrich, *Erinnerungen*, Berlin 1995.

Gerstenberger, Wolfgang, *Grenzen fallen—Märkte öffnen sich. Die Chancen der deutschen Wirtschaft am Beginn einer neuen Ära*, Berlin/Munich 1990.

Geschichte der Sozialpolitik in Deutschland seit 1945, publ. Bundesministerium für Arbeit und Sozialordnung/Bundesministerium für Arbeit und Soziales and Bundesarchiv. Vol. i, *Grundlagen der Sozialpolitik*, Baden-Baden 2001; vol. ii, *1945–1949. Die Zeit der Besatzungszonen. Sozialpolitik zwischen Kriegsende und der Gründung zweier deutscher Staaten*, ed. Udo Wengst, Baden-Baden 2001; vol. iii, *1949–1957. Bundesrepublik Deutschland. Bewältigung der Kriegsfolgen, Rückkehr zur sozialpolitischen Normalität*, ed. Günther Schulz, Baden-Baden 2005; vol. iv, *1957–1966. Bundesrepublik Deutschland. Sozialpolitik im Zeichen des erreichten Wohlstands*, ed. Michael Ruck and Marcel Boldorf, Baden-Baden 2007; vol. v, *1966–1974. Bundesrepublik Deutschland. Eine Zeit vielfältigen Aufbruchs*, ed. Hans Günter Hockerts, Baden-Baden 2006; vol. vi, *1974–1982. Bundesrepublik Deutschland. Neue Herausforderungen, wachsende Unsicherheiten*, ed. Martin H. Geyer, Baden-Baden 2008; vol. vii, *1982–1989. Bundserepublik Deutschland. Finanzielle Konsolidierung und institutionelle Reform*, ed. Manfred G. Schmidt, Baden-Baden 2005; vol. viii, *1949–1961. Deutsche Demokratische Republik. Im Zeichen des Aufbaus des Sozialismus*, ed. Dierk Hoffmann and Michael Schwartz, Baden-Baden 2004; vol. ix, *1961–1971. Deutsche Demokratische Republik. Politische Stabilisierung und wirtschaftliche Mobilisierug*, ed. Christoph Klessmann, Baden-Baden 2006; vol. x, *1971–1989. Deutsche Demokratische Republik. Bewegung in der Sozialpolitik, Erstarrung und Niedergang*, ed. Christoph Boyer, Klaus-Dietmar Henke, and Peter Skyba, Baden-Baden 2008; vol. xi, *1989–1994. Bundesrepublik Deutschland. Sozialpolitik im Zeichen der Vereinigung*, ed. Gerhard A. Ritter, Baden-Baden 2007.

Gesetzblatt der DDR (*GBl*), 1957–90.

Gewerkschaftskongreß zur Auflösung des FDGB, Berlin 14.9.1990, Bund der IG/Gew./ Geschäftsführender Vorstand, September 1990.

Glaeßner, Gert-Joachim (ed.), *Der schwierige Weg zur Demokratie. Vom Ende der DDR zur Deutschen Einheit*, 2nd edn., Opladen 1992.

Glatzer, Wolfgang, and Gerhard Kleinhenz (eds.), *Wohlstand für alle?*, Opladen 1997.

Gorbatschow, Michail S., *Gipfelgespräche. Geheime Protokolle aus meiner Amtszeit*, Berlin 1993.

Gorbatschow, Michail, *Erinnerungen*, Berlin 1995.

Gorbatschow, Michail, *Wie es war. Die deutsche Wiedervereinigung*, Berlin 1999.

Götting, Ulrike, and Karl Hinrichs, 'Probleme der politischen Kompromissbildung bei der gesetzlichen Absicherung des Pflegefallrisikos. Eine vorläufige Bilanz', in *PVS*, 31 (1993), pp. 47–71.

Götting, Ulrike (ed.), *Transformation der Wohlfahrtsstaaten in Mittel- und Osteuropa. Eine Zwischenbilanz*, Opladen 1998.

Grebing, Helga, and Hans-Otto Hemmer (eds.), *Soziale Konflikte, Sozialstaat und Demokratie in Deutschland*, Essen 1996.

Grigoleit, Klaus Joachim, *Bundesverfassungsgericht und deutsche Frage. Eine dogmatische und historische Untersuchung zum judikativen Anteil an der Staatsleitung*, Tübingen 2004.

Grönebaum, Stefan, 'Wird der Osten rot? Das ostdeutsche Parteiensystem in der Vereinigungskrise und vor den Wahlen 1998', in *ZParl*, 28 (1997), pp. 407–25.

Grosser, Dieter, *Das Wagnis der Währungs-, Wirtschafts- und Sozialunion. Politische Zwänge im Konflikt mit ökonomischen Regeln*, Stuttgart 1998.

Grünen, Die, *Das Programm zur 1. gesamtdeutschen Wahl*, 1990.

Grundsätze der Koalitionsvereinbarungen zwischen den Fraktionen der CDU, der DSU, der DA, der Liberalen (DFD, BFD, FDP) und der SPD, in *Informationen*, 24 April 1990, no. 8 (Beilage), publ. by BMB.

Grundsatzprogramm der Sozialdemokratischen Partei Deutschlands, Beschlossen vom Programm-Parteitag der Sozialdemokratischen Partei Deutschlands am 20. Dezember 1989 in Berlin, in Nacke *et al.* (eds.), *Eine neue christliche Sozialverkündigung* (q.v.), pp. 234–320.

Grünert, Holle, 'Das Beschäftigungssystem der DDR', in Lutz *et al.* (eds.), *Arbeit* (q.v.), pp. 17–68.

Gutmann, Gernot (ed.), *Die Wettbewerbsfähigkeit der ostdeutschen Wirtschaft. Ausgangslage, Handlungserfordernisse, Perspektiven*, Berlin 1995.

Hain, Winfried, Hilmer Luckert, Horst-Wolf Müller, and Jürgen Nowatzki, 'Was brachte die Rentenumwertung?—Zur Übertragung des SGB VI auf den Rentenbestand in den neuen Bundesländern und im Ostteil Berlins', in *Deutsche Rentenversicherung*, 1992, pp. 521–49.

Hampele, Anne, and Stefan Naevecke, 'Erwerbslosigkeit von Frauen in den neuen Bundesländern—Lebensmuster unter Druck', in Glaeßner (ed.), *Der schwierige Weg* (q.v.), pp. 107–41.

Hancké, Bob, 'Vorsprung, aber nicht länger (nur) durch Technik—Die schnelle Anpassung der deutschen Automobilindustrie an internationale Wettbewerbsbedingungen', in Naschold *et al.* (eds.), *Ökonomische Leistungsfähigkeit* (q.v.), pp. 213–34.

Handelsblatt, 1989–95.

Hanesch, Walter, 'Soziale Versicherung im europäischen Vergleich', in *APuZG*, B 34–35/98, 14 August 1998, pp. 15–26.

Hanke, Thomas, and Erika Martens, 'Arbeitsmarktabgabe: Die Union ringt um einen Kompromiß zum Solidarpakt. Müssen Beamte und Selbständige auch zahlen?', in *Die Zeit*, 5 February 1993.

Hantsche, Walter, Stefan Otte, Günter Hoffmann, *et al.* (eds.), *Aufbau der Verbände und Arbeitsgerichte*, Opladen 1997.

Hantsche, Walter, and Stefan Otte, 'Die Situation der Gewerkschaften der DDR nach der Wende und der Einfluß der gewerkschaftlichen Tätigkeit aud die Arbeits- und Sozialordnung', in Hantsche *et al.* (eds.), *Aufbau* (q.v.), pp. 9–87.

Hartwich, Hans-Herrmann, 'Die Flächentarifvertrag. Instrument und Symbol kollektivrechtlicher Arbeitsbeziehungen in Deutschland', in *Gegenwartskunde*, 46 (1997), pp. 101–33.

Haschke, Ingrid, and Udo Ludwig, 'Produktion und Nachfrage', in Pohl (ed.), *Herausforderung Ostdeutschland* (q.v.), pp. 93–106.

Hauser, Richard, Wolfgang Glatzer, Stefan Hradil *et al.*, *Ungleichheit und Sozialpolitik*, Opladen 1996.

Hauser, Richard, and Gerd Wagner, 'Die Einkommensverteilung in Ostdeutschland: Darstellung und Determinanten im Vergleich zu Westdeutschland für die Jahre 1990 bis 1994', in Glatzner and Kleinhenz (eds.), *Wohlstand für alle?* (q.v.), pp. 11–61.

Heering, Walter, and Klaus Schröder, 'Die DDR war kein Bollwerk der Emanzipation. Legenden und Wirklichkeit im ostdeutschen Emanzipationsprozeß: Das Beispiel Frauenbeschäftigung', in *FAZ*, 21 December 1995.

Heidemeyer, Helge, *Flucht und Zuwanderung aus der SBZ/DDR 1945/1949–1961. Die Flüchtlingspolitik der Bundesrepublik Deutschland bis zum Bau der Berliner Mauer*, Düsseldorf 1994.

Heine, Wolfgang, and Jörge Eckhardt, 'Überleitungsrecht und neue Bundesländer', in *DRV* (1994), pp. 329–39.

Heinelt, Hubert, Gerhard Bosch, and Bernd Reissert (eds.), *Arbeitsmarktpolitik nach der Vereinigung*, Berlin 1994.

Heinelt, Hubert, and Michael Weck, *Arbeitsmarktpolitik vom Vereinigungskonsens zur Standortdebatte*, Opladen 1998.

Heinz, Walter R., and Stefan E. Hormuth (eds.), *Arbeit und Gerechtigkeit im ostdeutschen Transformationsprozeß*, Opladen 1997.

Heinze, Rolf G., Josef Schmidt, and Christoph Strünck, *Vom Wohlfahrtsstaat zum Wettbewerbsstaat. Arbeitsmarkt- und Sozialpolitik in den 90er Jahren*, Opladen 1999.

Henneberger, Fred, 'Interessenverbände der Unternehmer in Deutschland: Aktuelle Entwicklungen unter besonderer Berücksichtigung der Situation in den neuen Bundesländern', in *SF*, 42 (1993), pp. 242–51.

Henneberger, Fred, 'Struktur und Organisationsdynamik der Unternehmerverbände: Probleme der Verbandsbildung und Interessenvereinheitlichung im vereinten Deutschland', in *Wirtschaft und Gesellschaft*, 19 (1993), pp. 329–57.

Hennis, Wilhelm, 'Totenrede des Perikles auf ein blühendes Land. Ursachen der politischen Blockade', in id. (ed.), *Auf dem Weg in den Parteienstaat*, Leipzig 1998, pp. 155–98.

Herbst, Andreas, Winfried Ranke, and Jürgen Winkler, *So funktionierte die DDR*, Hamburg 1994.

Herder-Dorneich, Philipp, *Gesundheitsökonomik. Systemsteuerung und Ordnungspolitik im Gesundheitswesen*, Stuttgart 1980.

Hertfelder, Thomas, and Andreas Rödder (eds.), *Modell Deutschland. Erfolgsgeschichte oder Illusion?*, Göttingen 2007.

Hertle, Hans-Hermann, *Der Fall der Mauer. Die unbeabsichtigte Selbstauflösung des SED-Staates*, 2nd edn., Opladen 1999.

Heydemann, Günther, 'Die britisch-deutschen Beziehungen und das Deutschlandbild Großbritanniens. Zwischen Margaret Thatcher und Tony Blair.—Eine kritische Rückblende', in Eckart *et al.* (eds.), *Wiedervereinigung Deutschlands* (q.v.), pp. 627–47.

Heydemann, Günther, Gunther Mai, and Werner Müller (eds.), *Revolution und Transformation in der DDR 1989/90*, Berlin 1999.

Hinrichs, Karl, 'Restrukturierung der Sozialpolitik? Das Beispiel der Gesundheitspolitik', in Riedmüller and Olk (eds.), *Grenzen des Sozialversicherungsstaates* (q.v.), pp. 119–45.

Hinrichs, Karl, 'Die Soziale Pflegeversicherung—eine institutionelle Innovation in der deutschen Sozialpolitik', in *Staatswissenschaften und Staatspraxis*, 6 (1995), pp. 227–59.

Hockerts, Hans Günter, 'Grundlinien und soziale Folgen der Sozialpolitik in der DDR', in Kaelble *et al.* (eds.), *Sozialgeschichte* (q.v.), pp. 519–44.

Hockerts, Hans Günter, 'Soziale Errungenschaften? Zum sozialpolitischen Legitimitätsanspruch der zweiten deutschen Diktatur', in Kocka *et al.* (eds.), *Von der Arbeiterbewegung zum modernen Sozialstaat* (q.v.), pp. 790–804.

Hockerts, Hans Günter (ed.), *Drei Wege deutscher Sozialstaatlichkeit. NS-Diktatur, Bundesrepublik und DDR im Vergleich*, Munich 1998.

Hoffmann, Dierk, *Sozialpolitische Neuordnung in der SBZ/DDR. Der Umbau der Sozialversicherung 1945–1956*, Munich 1996.

Hoffmann, Dierk, 'Rentenversicherung und SED-Rentenpolitik in den achtziger Jahren', in Kuhrt *et al.* (eds.), *Am Ende des realen Sozialismus*, vol. iv (q.v.), pp. 375–419.

Hoffmann, Dierk, and Michael Schwartz (eds.), *Sozialstaatlichkeit in der DDR. Sozialpolitische Entwicklungen im Spannungsfeld von Diktatur und Gesellschaft 1945/49–1989*, Munich 2005.

Hoffmann, Edeltraut, and Ulrich Walwei, *Beschäftigung: Formenvielfalt als Perspektive?*, part 1, 'Längerfristige Entwicklung von Erwerbsformen in Westdeutschland', IAB Kurzbericht, no. 2, 27 January 1998.

Hoffmann, Günter, 'Die Entstehung von Arbeitgeberverbänden im neuen Bundesgebiet am Beispiel der VME. Berlin-Brandenburg', in Hantsche *et al.* (eds.), *Aufbau der Verbände* (q.v.), pp. 89–136.

Hofmann, Claus F., and Roland Lang-Neyjahr, 'Wirtschaftsstandort Deutschland. Erfolgreicher Zehnkämpfer', in *BArbBl*, 9 (1997), pp. 5–15.

Hölder, Egon (ed.), *Im Trabi durch die Zeit—40 Jahre Leben in der DDR*, Wiesbaden 1992.

Hübner, Peter, *Konsens, Konflikt und Kompromiß. Soziale Arbeiterinteressen und Sozialpolitik in der SBZ/DDR 1945–1970*, Berlin 1995.

Hünig, Hasko, and Gero Neugebauer, 'Die PDS', in Niedermayer (ed.), *Intermediäre Strukturen* (q.v.), pp. 67–85.

Hünig, Hasko, and Hildegard Maria Nickel, 'Großbetriebliche Dienstleistungen. Rascher Aufbau und harte Konsolidierung', in Lutz *et al.* (eds.), *Arbeit* (q.v.), pp. 297–346.

Huinink, Johannes, Karl Ulrich Mayer, Martin Diewald *et al.* (eds.), *Kollektiv und Eigensinn. Lebensläufe in der DDR und danach*, Berlin 1995.

Huinink, Johannes, 'Sozialpolitik und individuelles Handeln. Zu unbeabsichtigten Folgen politischer Intervention am Beispiel der DDR', in *ZSR*, 42 (1996), pp. 1–16.

Hurd, Douglas, *Memoirs*, London 2003.

Hutchings, Robert J., *American Diplomacy and the End of the Cold War: An Insider's Account of U.S. Policy in Europe, 1989–1992*, Washington, DC, 1997.

Igl, Gerhard, *Das neue Pflegeversicherungsrecht. Soziale Pflegeversicherung* (*Sozialgesetzbuch—Elftes Buch*), Munich 1995.

Informationsdienst der Bundespressestelle des DGB, 1989–1994.

Inglehart, Ronald, *The Silent Revolution: Changing Values and Political Styles*, Princeton 1977.

Inglehart, Ronald, *Culture Shift in Advanced Industrial Society*, Princeton 1990.

Inglehart, Ronald, *Modernization and Postmodernization: Cultural, Economic and Political Change in 43 Societies*, Princeton 1997.

Ipsen, Jörn, Hans Werner Rengeling, Jörg Manfred Mössner, and Albrecht Weber (eds.), *Verfassungsrecht im Wandel. Wiedervereinigung Deutschlands. Deutschland in der Europäischen Union. Verfassungsstaat und Föderalismus. Zum 180–jährigen der Carl Heymanns Verlag KG*, Cologne/Berlin/Bonn etc. 1995.

Isensee, Josef, and Paul Kirchhof (eds.), *Handbuch des Staatsrechts*, vol. viii, *Die Einheit Deutschlands: Entwicklung und Grundlagen*, Heidelberg 1995; vol. ix, *Die Einheit Deutschlands. Festigung und Übergang*, Heidelberg 1997.

Jackisch, Klaus-Rainer, *Eisern gegen die Einheit. Margaret Thatcher und die deutsche Wiedervereinigung*, Frankfurt a.M. 2004.

Jäger, Wolfgang, in collaboration with Michael Walter, *Die Überwindung der Teilung. Der innerdeutsche Prozeß der Vereinigung 1989/90*, Stuttgart 1998.

Jahresberichte der Bundesregierung, 1990–1994, publ. Presse- und Informationsamt der Bundesregierung.

Janke, Barbara, and Manfred Ebert, 'Von "jeder zweiten" Frau zu "neun von zehn" Frauen—Der Arbeitsmarkt gekennzeichnet durch viele berufstätige Frauen', in Hölder (ed.), *Im Trabi durch die Zeit* (q.v.), pp. 77–95.

Jarausch, Konrad H., *Die unverhoffte Einheit 1989–1990*, Frankfurt a.M. 1995.

Jesse, Eckhard, and Arnim Mitter (eds.), *Die Gestaltung der deutschen Einheit. Geschichte—Politik—Gesellschaft*, Bonn/Berlin 1992.

Jochem, Sven, 'Sozialpolitik in der Ära Kohl: Die Politik des Sozialversicherungsstaates', *ZeS-Arbeitspapier* no. 12/99.

Jochem, Sven, and Nico A. Siegel, 'Wohlfahrtskapitalismus und Beschäftigungsperformanz—Das "Modell Deutschland" im Vergleich', in *ZSR*, 46 (2000), pp. 38–64.

Jung, Karl, 'Soziale Pflegeversicherung: Durchgesetzt gegen alle Widerstände', in *BArbBl*, 7 (1994), pp. 5–16.

Jung, Karl, 'Die fünfte Säule—Über den langen Weg zur sozialen Pflegeversicherung', in BMA, *Sozialstaat im Wandel* (q.v.), pp. 197–221.

Jung, Karl, in collaboration with Ruth Schweitzer, *Die neue Pflegeversicherung. Sozialgesetzbuch XI. Das Recht der sozialen und der privaten Pflegeversicherung*, Bonn 1995.

Jung, Matthias, 'Parteiensystem und Wahlen in der DDR. Eine Analyse der Volkskammerwahl vom 18. März 1990 und der Kommunalwahlen vom 6. Mai 1990', in *APuZG*, B 27/90, pp. 3–15.

Kaase, Max, Andreas Eisen, Oskar W. Gabriel *et al.* (eds.), *Politisches System*, Opladen 1996.

Kaase, Max, and Günther Schmid (eds.), *Eine lernende Demokratie. 50 Jahre Bundesrepublik Deutschland*, WZB-Jahrbuch 1999, Berlin 1999.

Kaelble, Hartmut, *Auf dem Weg zu einer europäischen Gesellschaft. Eine Sozialgeschichte Westeuropas 1880–1980*, Munich 1987.

Kaelble, Hartmut, Jürgen Kocka, and Hartmut Zwahr (eds.), *Sozialgeschichte der DDR*, Stuttgart 1994.

Kaina, Viktoria, 'Wertorientierung im Eliten-Bevölkerungsvergleich: Vertikale Distanzen, geteilte Loyalitäten und das Erbe der Trennung', in Bürklin *et al.* (eds.), *Eliten* (q.v.), pp. 351–89.

Kaps, Carola, 'Welches Rezept steckt hinter dem Job-Wunder in Amerika?', in *FAZ*, 3 January 2000.

Kaufmann, Franz-Xaver, 'Sozialstaatlichkeit unter den Bedingungen moderner Wirtschaft', in Korff (ed.), *Handbuch der Wissenschaftsethik*, vol. i (q.v.), pp. 800–30.

Keller, Bernd, 'Arbeitspolitik in den neuen Bundesländern. Eine Zwischenbilanz des Transformationsprozesses', in *SF*, 45 (1996), pp. 88–102.

Keller, Bernd, *Einführung in die Arbeitspolitik. Arbeitsbeziehungen und Arbeitsmarkt in sozialwissenschaftlicher Perspektive*, 5th edn., Munich/Vienna 1997.

Kettenacker, Lothar, 'Britain and German Unification, 1989/90', in Larres and Meehan (eds.), *Uneasy Allies* (q.v.), pp. 99–123.

Kinitz, Horst, *Aufbau der Arbeitsverwaltung in den neuen Bundesländern und die Entwicklung des Arbeitsförderungsrechts seit 1989*, Opladen 1997.

Kirchhof, Paul, '§221. Der demokratische Rechtsstaat—die Staatsform der Zugehörigen', in Isensee and Kirchhof (eds.), *Handbuch des Staatsrechts*, vol. ix (q.v.), pp. 957–1064.

Kissel, Otto Rudolf, *Arbeitskampfrecht. Ein Leitfaden*, Munich 2002.

Klässer, Wilfried, 'Deutschland wächst zusammen—die Datenverarbeitung auch', in *Deutsche Rentenversicherung*, 4/92, pp. 235–52.

Klebula, Detlef, and Peter Semran, 'Alterseinkommen. Meist aus anderen Quellen', in *BArbBl*, 2 (1997), pp. 5–10.

Klein, Eckart, 'Deutsche Einigung und Rechtsprechung des Bundesverfassungsgerichts. Vorläufiger Überblick mit Anmerkungen', in Ipsen *et al.* (eds.), *Verfassungsrecht im Wandel* (q.v.), pp. 91–107.

Klein, Eckart (ed.), *Die Rolle des Bundesrates und der Länder im Prozeß der Einheit Deutschlands*, Berlin 1998.

Klein, Eckart, 'Die verfassungsrechtliche Bewältigung der Wiedervereinigung', in Eckart *et al.* (eds.), *Wiedervereinigung Deutschlands* (q.v.), pp. 417–28.

Klein, Hans H., 'Kontinuität des Grundgesetzes und seiner Änderungen im Zuge der Wiedervereinigung', in Isensee and Kirchhof (eds.), *Handbuch des Staatsrechts*, vol. viii (q.v.), pp. 557–602.

Klein, Yvonne, 'Obstructive or Promoting? British Views on German Unification, 1989/90', in *German Politics*, 5 (1996), pp. 403–31.

Kleinhenz, Gerhard (ed.), *Sozialpolitik im vereinten Deutschland I*, Berlin 1991.

Kleinhenz, Gerhard, 'Tarifpartnerschaft im vereinten Deutschland. Die Bedeutung der Arbeitsmarktorganisation für die Einheit der Arbeits- und Lebensverhältnisse', in *APuZG*, B 12/92, pp. 14–24.

Kloten, Norbert, 'Deutsche Einheit: Die wirtschaftliche Last der Folgen für Ost und West', in Deutsche Bundesbank, *Auszüge aus Presseartikeln*, no. 8, 5 February 1996, pp. 11–17.

Kloth, Hans Michael, *Vom 'Zettelfalten' zum freien Wählen. Die Demokratisierung der DDR 1989/90 und die 'Wahlfrage'*, Berlin 2000.

Knuth, Matthias, 'ABS-Gesellschaften als dezentrale Akteure der Arbeitsmarkt- und Strukturpolitik: Problemlösung "vor Ort"?', in Heinelt *et al.* (eds.), *Arbeitsmarktpolitik nach der Vereinigung* (q.v.), pp. 172–84.

'Koalitionsvereinbarung für die 12. Legislaturperiode des Deutschen Bundestages', in *Union in Deutschland*, Informationsdienst der CDU, no. 2, 17 January 1991.

Köcher, Renate, 'Auf einer Woge der Euphorie. Veränderungen der Stimmungslage und des Meinungsklimas im Wahljahr 1994', in *APuZG*, B 51–52/94, pp. 16–21.

Kocka, Jürgen, Hans-Jürgen Puhle, and Klaus Tenfelde (eds.), *Von der Arbeiterbewegung zum modernen Sozialstaat. Festschrift für Gerhard A. Ritter zum 65. Geburtstag*, Munich/New Providence/London etc. 1994.

Kohl, Helmut, *'Ich wollte Deutschlands Einheit'*, presented by Kai Diekmann and Ralf Georg Reuth, Berlin 1996.

Kohl, Helmut, *Erinnerungen 1982–1990, Erinnerungen 1990–1994*, Munich 2005, 2007.

Kohl, Jürgen, 'Die Wohlfahrtsstaat in vergleichender Perspektive. Anmerkungen zu Esping-Andersens "Three Worlds of Welfare Capitalism"', in *ZSR*, 39 (1993), pp. 67–82.

Köhler, Horst, 'Alle zogen mit', in Waigel and Schell (eds.), *Tage* (q.v.), pp. 118–34.

Kohnert, Monika, 'Pflege und Umgang mit Behinderten in der DDR', in *Materialien der Enquete-Kommission 'Überwindung'*, vol. iii (q.v.), pp. 1726–91.

Kolb, Rudolf, and Franz Ruland, 'Die Rentenversicherung in einem sich einigenden Deutschland', in *DRV*, 3 (March 1990), pp. 141–53.

Kommission für Zukunftsfragen der Freistaaten Bayern und Sachsen, *Erwerbstätigkeit und Arbeitslosigkeit in Deutschland. Entwicklung, Ursachen und Maßnahmen*, part I, *Entwicklung in Erwerbstätigkeit und Arbeitslosigkeit in Deutschland und anderen frühindustrialisierten Ländern*, Bonn 1996.

König, Thomas, and Thomas Bräuninger, 'Wie wichtig sind die Länder für die Politik der Bundesregierung bei Einspruchs- und Zustimmungsgesetzen?', in *ZParl*, 28 (1997), pp. 605–28.

Korff, Wilhelm (ed. for Görresgesellschaft), *Handbuch der Wissenschaftsethik*, vol. i, *Verhältnisbestimmung von Wirtschaft und Ethik*, Gütersloh 1999.

Korte, Karl-Rudolf, 'Kommt es auf die Person des Kanzlers an? Zum Regierungsstil von Helmut Kohl in der "Kanzlerdemokratie" des deutschen Parteienstaates', in *ZParl*, 29 (1998), pp. 387–401.

Kowalczuk, Ilko-Sascha, *Endspiel. Die Revolution von 1989 in der DDR*, Munich 2009.

Kreikenbom, Henry, 'Nachwirkungen der SED-Ära. Die PDS als Katalysator der Partei- und Wahlpräferenzen in den neuen Bundesländern', in *ZParl*, 29 (1998), pp. 24–46.

Kuhn, Ekkehard, *Gorbatschow und die deutsche Einheit. Aussagen der wichtigsten russischen und deutschen Beteiligten*, Bonn 1993.

Kuhrt, Eberhard, Gunter Holzweißig, and Hannsjörg F. Buck (eds.), *Am Ende des realen Sozialismus. Beiträge zu einer Bestandsaufnahme der DDR-Wirklichkeit in den 80er Jahren*, vol. ii, *Die wirtschaftliche und ökologische Situation der DDR in den 80er Jahren*, Opladen 1996.

Kuhrt, Eberhard, in collaboration with Hannsjörg F. Buck and Gunter Holzweißig for Bundesministerium des Innern, *Am Ende des realen Sozialismus. Beiträge zu einer Bestandsaufnahme der DDR-Wirklichkeit in den 80er Jahren*, vol. iv, *Die Endzeit der DDR-Wirtschaft—Analysen zur Wirtschafts-, Sozial- und Umweltpolitik*, Opladen 1999.

Lafontaine, Oskar, 'Nicht das Weggehen prämieren, sondern das Dableiben', in *Süddeutsche Zeitung*, 25/26 November 1989.

Lafontaine, Oskar, *Deutsche Wahrheiten. Die nationale und die soziale Frage*, Hamburg 1990.

Lafontaine, Oskar, *Das Herz schlägt links*, Munich 1999.

Lambert, Martin (ed.), *Umbau der Sozialsysteme*, publ. Ludwig-Erhard-Stiftung, Krefeld 1994.

Landenberger, Margarete, 'Pflegeversicherung als Vorbote eines anderen Sozialstaates', in *ZSR*, 40 (1994), pp. 314–42.

Lang, Jürgen P., and Patrick Moreau, 'Das Erbe der Diktatur', special edn. of *Politische Studien*, 45 (September 1994).

Larres, K., and E. Meehan (eds.), *Uneasy Allies: British-German Relations and European Integration since 1945*, Oxford 2000.

Lehmann, Ines, *Die deutsche Vereinigung von außen gesehen. Angst, Bedenken und Erwartungen*, vol. i, *Die Presse der Vereinigten Staaten, Großbritannien und Frankreichs*, Frankfurt a.M./Vienna/New York etc. 1996.

Lehmbruch, Gerd, 'Die improvisierte Vereinigung: Die Dritte deutsche Republik. Unentwegter Versuch, einem japanischen Publikum die Geheimnisse der deutschen Transformation zu erklären', in *Leviathan*, 18 (1990), pp. 462–86.

Lehmbruch, Gerhard (ed.), *Einigung und Zerfall: Deutschland und Europa nach dem Ende des Ost-West-Konflikts. 19. wissenschaftlicher Kongreß der Deutschen Vereinigung für Politische Wissenschaft*, Opladen 1995.

Leibfried, Stephan, 'Grenzen deutscher Sozialstaatlichkeit. Vom gemeinsamen Arbeitsmarkt zu erzwungener europäischer Sozialreform', in Riedmüller and Olk (eds.), *Grenzen des Sozialversicherungsstaates* (q.v.), pp. 313–23.

Leibfried, Stephan, and Uwe Wagschal (eds.), *Der deutsche Sozialstaat. Bilanzen—Reformen—Perspektiven*, Frankfurt a.M. 2000.

Leithäuser, Johannes, '"Wir sind einfach müde geworden"', in *FAZ*, 22 August 2000.

Lemke, Christiane, 'Neue soziale Bewegungen', in Ellwein and Holtmann (eds.), *50 Jahre Bundesrepublik* (q.v.), pp. 440–53.

Lepsius, M. Rainer, 'Die Rolle der Sozialpolitik in der Bonner Republik und in der DDR', in Grebing and Hemmer (eds.), *Soziale Konflikte* (q.v.), pp. 41–50.

Lerche, Peter, '§194. Der Beitritt der DDR—Voraussetzungen, Realisierung, Wirkungen', in Isensee and Kirchhof (eds.), *Handbuch des Staatsrechts*, vol. viii (q.v.), pp. 403–46.

Lessenich, Stephan, and Ilona Ostner (eds.), *Welten des Wohlfahrtskapitalismus. Der Sozialstaat in vergleichender Perspektive*, Frankfurt a.M. 1998.

Leven, Klaus, 'Nach der Revolution im Osten Deutschlands—Arbeitsämter zwischen Norm und Wirklichkeit', in Buttler *et al.* (eds.), *Europa und Deutschland* (q.v.), pp. 235–42.

Liebold, Renate, 'Innerbetriebliche Beziehungen in ostdeutschen Industriebezirken: Die (ost)deutsche Einheit zwischen Management und Betriebsrat', in Bergmann and Schmidt (eds.), *Industrielle Beziehungen* (q.v.), pp. 213–35.

Liebscher, Thomas, and Olaf Steffen, 'Der Aufbau der Arbeitsgerichtsbarkeit und die Tätigkeit der Schiedsstellen in den neuen Bundesländern', in Hantsche *et al.* (eds.), *Aufbau* (q.v.), pp. 141–220.

Linhart, Helmut, and Olgierd Adolph, 'Einstieg in die Sozialhilfewanderung in der Europäischen Union?', in NDV, August 2004, pp. 282–5.

Linnemann, Rainer, *Die Parteien in den neuen Bundesländern. Konstituierung, Mitgliederentwicklung, Organisationsstrukturen*, Münster 1994.

Lutz, Burkart, Hildegard M. Nickel, Rudi Schmidt *et al.* (eds.), *Arbeit, Arbeitsmarkt und Betriebe*, Opladen 1996.

Lutz, Burkart, and Holle Grünert, 'Der Zerfall der Beschäftigungsstruktur der DDR 1989–1993', in Lutz *et al.* (eds.), *Arbeit* (q.v.), pp. 69–120.

Maier, Charles S., *Dissolution: The Crisis of Communism and the End of East Germany*, Princeton 1997.

Mampel, Siegfried, 'Das Ende der sozialistischen Verfassung der DDR', in *DA*, 23 (1990), pp. 1377–96.

Mangoldt, Hans von, *Die Verfassungen der neuen Bundesländer. Einführung und synoptische Darstellung. Sachsen, Brandenburg, Sachsen-Anhalt, Mecklenburg-Vorpommern, Thüringen*, 2nd edn., Berlin 1997.

Manow, Philip, *Gesundheitspolitik im Einigungsprozeß*, Frankfurt a.M./New York 1994.

Manow, Philip, 'Strukturinduzierte Politikgleichgewichte. Das Gesundheitsstrukturgesetz und seine Vorgänger', MPIfG Discussion Paper, 5/94.

Manow, Philip, 'Informalisierung und Parteipolitisierung—zum Wandel exekutiver Entscheidungsprozesse in der Bundesrepublik', in *ZParl*, 27 (1996), pp. 96–107.

Manow, Philip, 'Entwicklungslinien ost- und westdeutscher Gesundheitspolitik zwischen doppelter Staatsgründung, deutscher Einigung und europäischer Integration', in *ZSR*, 43 (1997), pp. 101–31.

Manow-Borgwardt, Philip, 'Die Sozialversicherung in der DDR und BRD, 1945–1990: Über die Fortschrittlichkeit rückschrittlicher Institutionen', in *PVS*, 35 (1994), pp. 40–61.

Manz, Günter, *Armut in der 'DDR'-Bevölkerung. Lebensstandard und Konsumptionsniveau vor und nach der Wende*, Augsburg 1992.

Martens, Helmut, *Gewerkschaftlicher Organisationsaufbau und Mitbestimmung in Ostdeutschland. Ein eigenständiger und schwieriger Institutionalisierungsprozess und seine Folgen für die industriellen Beziehungen in der größer gewordenen Bundesrepublik*, Dortmund 1992.

Maschatzke, Jörg, 'Einstellungen zum Umfang staatlicher Verantwortung.—Zum Staatsverständnis der Eliten im vereinten Deutschland', in Bürklin *et al.* (eds.), *Eliten* (q.v.), pp. 321–50.

Materialien der Enquete-Kommission 'Aufarbeitung von Geschichte und Folgen der SED-Diktatur in Deutschland', publ. Deutscher Bundestag, vol. ii, *Machtstrukturen und Entscheidungsmechanismen im SED-Staat und die Frage der Verantwortung*, Baden-Baden 1995.

Materialien der Enquete-Kommission 'Überwindung der Folgen der SED-Diktatur im Prozeß der deutschen Einheit', publ. Deutscher Bundestag, vol. iii, *Wirtschafts- Sozial- und Umweltpolitik*, Baden-Baden 1999; vol. viii, 3, *Das geteilte Deutschland im geteilten Europa*, Baden-Baden 1999.

Materialien zur Deutschen Einheit und zum Aufbau in den neuen Bundesländern, BTDrs 13/2280, 8 September 1995.

Materialien zur Deutschen Einheit, BTDrs 12/6854.

Maydell, Bernd von, and E.-M. Hohnerlein (eds.), *Die Umgestaltung der Systeme sozialer Sicherheit in den Staaten Mittel- und Osteuropas. Fragen und Lösungsansätze. Kolloquium des Max-Planck-Instituts für Ausländisches und Internationales Sozialrecht in Tutzing vom 9.–12. Februar 1993*, Berlin 1993.

Maydell, Bernd Baron von, and Bernd Schulte (eds.), *Zukunftsperspektiven des Europäischen Sozialrechts*, Berlin 1995.

Maydell, Bernd Baron von, and Franz Ruland (eds.), *Sozialrechtshandbuch*, 2nd edn., Neuwied/Kriftel/Berlin 1996.

Maydell, Bernd Baron von, Winfried Boecken, Wolfgang Heine *et al.*, *Die Umwandlung der Arbeits- und Sozialordnung*, Opladen 1996.

Mayntz, Renate, 'Politische Steuerbarkeit und Reformblockaden: Überlegungen am Beispiel des Gesundheitswesens', in *Staatswissenschaft und Staatspraxis*, 1 (1990), pp. 283–307.

Meck, Sabine, Hannelore Belitz-Demiriz, and Peter Brentzke, 'Sozialdemographische Struktur und Einstellungen von DDR-Flüchtlingen/Übersiedlern. Eine empirische Analyse der innerdeutschen Migration im Zeitraum Oktober 1989 bis März 1990', in Voigt and Mertens (eds.), *Minderheiten* (q.v.), pp. 9–38.

Meimberg, Rüdiger, 'Landwirtschaft: Großbetriebe prägen den ländlichen Raum', in Oppenländer (ed.), *Wiedervereinigung* (q.v.), pp. 383–400.

Merten, Detlef, *Grundfragen des Einigungsvertrages unter Berücksichtigung beamtenrechtlicher Probleme. Zur Verfassungsmäßigkeit des Art.6 EinigungsV.*, Berlin 1991.

Merten, Detlef, 'Rentenversicherung und deutsche Wiedervereinigung', in Fisch and Haerendel (eds.), *Geschichte* (q.v.), pp. 317–32.

Meyer, Cord, *Die Sozialplanrichtlinien der Treuhandanstalt*, Opladen 1996.

Midgley, James, *Social Welfare in Global Context*, Thousand Oaks, Calif., 1997.

Mitterrand, François, *De l'Allemagne, de la France*, Paris 1996.

Modrow, Hans, *Aufbruch und Ende*, Hamburg 1991.

Modrow, Hans, *Die Perestroika. Wie ich sie sehe. Persönliche Erinnerungen und Analysen eines Jahrzehntes, das die Welt veränderte*, 2nd edn., Berlin 1998.

Mohn, Jörg, 'Die Rechtsentwicklung der Überführung der Ansprüche und Anwartschaften aus Zusatz- und Sonderversorgungssystemen der ehemaligen DDR in die Rentenversicherung', in *DAngVers*, 12 (1993), pp. 438–47.

Moll, Frank, *Tarifausstieg der Arbeitgeber: Mitgliedschaft im Arbeitgeberverband 'ohne Tarifbindung'*, Berlin 2000.

Montada, Leo, 'Gerechtigkeitsansprüche und Ungerechtigkeitserleben in den neuen Bundesländern', in Heinz and Hormuth (eds.), *Arbeit und Gerechtigkeit* (q.v.), pp. 231–74.

Moreau, Patrick (in collaboration with Marcus Overmann), Walter Süß, Annette Weinke *et al.*, 'Die Politik der letzten DDR-Regierung und ihre Folgen', in *Materialien der Enquete-Kommission 'Überwindung'*, vol. viii/3 (q.v.), pp. 2008–173.

Mrotzeck, Herbert, and Herbert Püschel, *Krankenversicherung und Alterssicherung*, Opladen 1997.

Müller, Hans-Peter, 'Gewerkschaftsvereinigung. Die Industriegewerkschaft Bergbau und Energie im deutschen Vereinigungsprozess', in Eckart *et al.* (eds.), *Wiedervereinigung Deutschlands* (q.v.), pp. 537–59.

Murmann, Klaus, *Kontakt für die Zukunft. Was mich bewegt. Gespräch mit Rainer Hank und Rolf Dietrich Schwartz*, Berlin 1997.

Mutz, Michael, 'Renten der Zusatzversorgung der Intelligenz in der DDR—Chronik der Überführung in die gesetzliche Rentenversicherung', in *DAngVers*, 12 (1995), pp. 426–32.

Mutz, Michael, 'Aufstieg und Fall eines Konzepts. Die Zusatz- und Sonderversorgungssysteme der DDR und ihre Überführung', in *DAngVers*, 11 (1999), pp. 509–19.

Nacke, B., M. Köster, and S. Nacke (eds.), *Eine neue christliche Sozialverkündigung. Das Sozialwort der Kirchen und die Grundsatzprogramme von Parteien und DGB. Ein Quellenband*, Würzburg 1998.

Naschold, Frieder, David Soskice, Bob Hancké, *et al.* (eds.), *Ökonomische Leistungsfähigkeit und institutionelle Innovation. Das deutsche Produktions- und Politikregime im globalen Wettbewerb*, WZB-Jahrbuch 1997, Berlin 1997.

Neller, Katja, '"Auferstanden aus Ruinen?" Das Phänomen "DDR-Nostalgie"', in Gabriel *et al.* (eds.), *Wächst zusammen, was zusammen gehört?* (q.v.), pp. 339–81.

Neubert, Ehrhart, *Unsere Revolution. Die Geschichte des Jahres 1989/90*, Munich 2008.

Neugebauer, Gero, 'Die SDP/SPD in der Einigung; Zur Geschichte und Entwicklung einer unvollendeten Partei', in Niedermayer and Stöss (eds.), *Parteien* (q.v.), pp. 75–104.

Neugebauer, Gero, and Richard Stöss, *Die PDS. Geschichte. Organisation. Wähler. Konkurrenten*, Opladen 1996.

Neumann, Volker, and Iris Brockmann, 'Freie Wohlfahrtspflege in den neuen Bundesländern', in Wienand *et al.*, *Fürsorge* (q.v.), pp. 63–133.

'1994—Das Jahr der 19 Wahlen. Vier Jahre nach der Vereinigung sind die großen Volksparteien in Bedrängnis', in *FAZ*, 20 December 1993.

Neuordnung des Finanzausgleichs zwischen Bund und Ländern und ihre Auswirkungen auf das Land Bremen, publ. Senator für Finanzen der Freien Hansestadt Bremen, Bremen 1993, pp. 149–58.

Niedermayer, Oskar, and Richard Stöss (eds.), *Parteien und Wähler im Umbruch. Parteiensystem und Wählerverhalten in der ehemaligen DDR und den neuen Bundesländern*, Opladen 1994.

Niedermayer, Oskar (ed.), *Intermediäre Strukturen in Ostdeutschland*, Opladen 1996.

Niedermayer, Oskar, 'Das intermediäre System', in Kaase *et al.* (eds.), *Politisches System* (q.v.), pp. 155–230.

Niemann, Heinz, *Meinungsforschung in der DDR. Die geheimen Berichte an das Politbüro der SED*, Cologne 1993.

Niemeyer, Werner, 'Ab sofort einheitliches Recht', in *BArbBl*, 1 (1992), pp. 7–12.

Nierhaus, Wolfgang, 'Private Haushalte. Kaufkraftplus auf breiter Front', in Oppenländer (ed.), *Wiedervereinigung* (q.v.), pp. 51–72.

Noelle-Neumann, Elisabeth, 'Die PDS als Kristallisationspunkt der Unterschiede', in *FAZ*, 16 December 1997.

Nolte, Dirk, Ralf Sitte and Alexandra Wagner (eds.), *Wirtschaftliche und soziale Einheit Deutschlands. Eine Bilanz*, Cologne 1995.

OECD, *OECD Economic Surveys: Germany 1989/1990*, appendix, 'Basic Statistics—International Comparisons', Paris 1990.

OECD, *Economic Outlook 51*, June 1992, Paris 1992.

OECD, *The Reform of Health Care Systems: A Review of Seventeen OECD Countries*, Paris 1994.

OECD, *OECD Economic Outlook 61*, Paris 1997.

Offe, Claus, 'Zur Typologie von sozialpolitischen "Regimen"', in *ZSR*, 39 (1993), pp. 83–6.

Oldenburg, Fred, 'Gorbatschows Deutschlandpolitik und die Implosion der DDR', in Eckart *et al.* (eds.), *Wiedervereinigung Deutschlands* (q.v.), pp. 259–82.

Olk, Thomas, and Doris Rentzsch, 'Zur Transformation von Armut in den neuen Bundesländern', in Riedmüller and Olk (eds.), *Grenzen des Sozialversicherungsstaates* (q.v.), pp. 248–74.

Olk, Thomas, and Heinz Rothgang, 'Demographie und Sozialpolitik', in Ellwein and Holtmann (eds.), *50 Jahre Bundesrepublik* (q.v.), pp. 258–78.

Oppenländer, Karl Heinrich (ed.), *Wiedervereinigung nach sechs Jahren: Erfolge, Defizite, Zukunftsperspektiven im Transformationsprozeß*, Berlin/Munich 1997.

Otting, Albrecht, 'Von Maastricht nach Amsterdam', in *BArbBl*, 11 (1997), pp. 10–13.

Paffrath, Constanze, *Macht und Eigentum. Die Enteignungen 1945–1949 im Prozess der deutschen Wiedervereinigung*, Cologne/Weimar/Vienna 2004.

Papier, Hans-Jürgen, 'Der Einfluß des Verfassungsrechts auf das Sozialrecht', in Maydell and Ruland (eds.), *Sozialrechtshandbuch* (q.v.), pp. 73–124.

Papier, Hans-Jürgen, 'Das Rentenversicherungsrecht vor dem Grundgesetz. Eigentum, Gleichheit und Schutz der Familie', in *FAZ*, 11 June 2001.

Paqué, Karl-Heinz, *Die Bilanz. Eine wissenschaftliche Analyse der Deutschen Einheit*, Munich 2009.

PDA (Pressedienst der Bundesvereinigung Deutscher Arbeitgeberverbände), 1990–5.

PDS, *Programm der Partei des Demokratischen Sozialismus. Angenommen auf dem Wahlparteitag der PDS am 25. Februar 1990.*

Perner, Detlef, 'Entwicklung der Gewerkschaftsorganisation seit der deutschen Einigung', in Nolte *et al.* (eds.), *Wirtschaftliche und soziale Einheit* (q.v.), pp. 379–93.

Peterson, Fabian, *Oppositionsstrategie der SPD-Führung im deutschen Einigungsprozess 1989/90. Strategische Ohnmacht durch Selbstblockade?*, Hamburg 1998.

Pieper, Bernhard, 'Industrie. Rasche Angleichung an die westdeutsche Beschäftigtenstruktur', in Oppenländer (ed.), *Wiedervereinigung* (q.v.), pp. 401–18.

Pierson, Paul, *Dismantling the Welfare State? Reagan, Thatcher and the Politics of Retrenchment*, Cambridge 1994.

Pirker, Theo, M. Rainer Lepsius, Rainer Weinert *et al.*, *Der Plan als Befehl und Fiktion. Wirtschaftsführung in der DDR. Gespräche und Analysen*, Opladen 1995.

Plato, Alexander von, *Die Vereinigung Deutschlands—ein weltpolitisches Machtspiel. Bush, Kohl, Gorbatschow und die geheimen Moskauer Protokolle*, Berlin 2002.

Pöhl, Otto, 'Wir sind im Jahre 1990 überrumpelt worden', in *Süddeutsche Zeitung*, 29 June 2000.

Pohl, Rüdiger (ed.), *Herausforderung Ostdeutschland*, Berlin 1995.

Pohlmann, Markus, and Rudi Schmidt, 'Management in Ostdeutschland und die Gestaltung des wirtschaftlichen und sozialen Wandels', in Lutz *et al.* (eds.), *Arbeit* (q.v.), pp. 191–226.

Pollack, Detlef, 'Zwischen alten Verhaltensdispositionen und neuen Anforderungsprofilen. Bemerkungen zu den mentalitätsspezifischen Voraussetzungen des Operierens von Interessenverbänden und Organisationen in den neuen Bundesländern', in Eichener *et al.* (eds.), *Organisierte Interessen* (q.v.), pp. 489–508.

Pollack, Detlef, and Gert Pickel, 'Die ostdeutsche Identität—Erbe des DDR-Sozialismus oder Produkt der Wiedervereinigung? Die Einstellung der Ostdeutschen zu sozialer Ungleichheit und Demokratie', in *APuZG*, B41–42/98, pp. 9–23.

Powaski, Ronald E., *The United States and the Soviet Union, 1917–1991*, New York/Oxford 1998.

Presse- und Informationsamt der Bundesregierung, *Aktuelle Beiträge zur Wirtschafts- und Finanzpolitik*, 1990–5.

Presse- und Informationsamt der Bundesregierung, *Aktuelle Presseinformationen*, 1990–5.

Presse- und Informationsamt der Bundesregierung, press communications 1990–5.

Protokolle der Volkskammer der Deutschen Demokratischen Republik (Prot. VK), 1989–90.

Protokolle des Deutschen Bundestages, Ausschuß Deutsche Einheit.

Protokolle des Deutschen Bundestages (Prot. BT), 1989–95.

Rechtsgrundlagen für die Wahl zum 12. Deutschen Bundestag, 2nd edn., publ. Bundeswahlleiter, October 1990.

Reich, Jens, 'Bescheidenheit war politisches Programm', in *Die Zeit*, 18 October 1996.

Rentenversicherungsbericht 1996 ('Bericht der Bundesregierung über die gesetzliche Rentenversicherung, insbesondere über die Entwicklung der Einnahmen und Ausgaben, der Schwankungsreserve sowie des jeweiligen erforderlichen Beitragssatzes in den künftigen 15 Kalendarjahren gemäß §154 SGB VI'), BTDrs 13/5370, 29 July 1996.

Restle, Diether, and Matthias Rockstroh, 'Arbeitslosigkeit wirksam bekämpfen', in *BArbBl*, 10 (1994), pp. 15–19.

Richter, Michael, *Die Bildung des Freistaates Sachsen. Friedliche Revolution, Föderalisierung, deutsche Einheit 1989/90*, Göttingen 2004.

Riedmüller, Barbara, and Thomas Olk (eds.), *Grenzen des Sozialversicherungsstaates*, Opladen 1994.

Rieger, Elmar, and Stephan Leibfried, 'Globalisation and the Western Welfare State: An Annotated Bibliography', *ZeS-Arbeitspapier* no. 1/95, Bremen 1995.

Rieger, Elmar, and Stephan Leibfried, 'Welfare State Limits to Globalization', in *Politics and Society*, 26 (1998), pp. 363–90.

Ringler, Jochen C. K., *Die Europäische Sozialunion*, Berlin 1997.

Ritter, Gerhard A., and Merith Niehuss, *Wahlen in Deutschland 1946–1991. Ein Handbuch*, Munich 1991.

Ritter, Gerhard A., and Merith Niehuss, *Wahlen in Deutschland 1990–1994*, Munich 1995.

Ritter, Gerhard A., 'Probleme und Tendenzen des Sozialstaats in den 1990er Jahren', in *GuG*, 22 (1996), pp. 393–408.

Ritter, Gerhard A., *Über Deutschland. Die Bundesrepublik in der deutschen Geschichte*, 2nd edn., Munich 2000.

Ritter, Gerhard A., 'Thesen zur Sozialpolitik der DDR', in Hoffmann and Schwartz (eds.), *Sozialstaatlichkeit* (q.v.), pp. 11–29.

Ritter, Gerhard A., *Wir sind das Volk! Wir sind ein Volk! Geschichte der deutschen Einigung*, Munich 2009.

Ritter, Gerhard A., *Der Sozialstaat. Entstehung und Entwicklung im internationalen Vergleich*, 3rd edn., Munich 2010.

Röbenack, Silke, 'Betriebe und Belegschaftsvertretungen', in Bergmann and Schmidt (eds.), *Industrielle Beziehungen* (q.v.), pp. 161–212.

Rödder, Andreas, 'Staatskunst statt Kriegshandwerk. Probleme der deutschen Vereinigung von 1990 in internationaler Perspektive', in *Historisches Jahrbuch*, 118 (1998), pp. 223–60.

Rödder, Andreas, '"Durchbruch im Kaukasus"? Die deutsche Wiedervereinigung und die Zeitgeschichtsschreibung', in *Jahrbuch des Historischen Kollegs*, 2002, pp. 113–40.

Rödder, Andreas, *Deutschland einig Vaterland. Die Geschichte der Wiedervereinigung*, Munich 2009.

Roesler, Jörg, 'Die Produktionsbrigaden in der Industrie der DDR. Zentrum der Arbeitswelt?', in Kaelble *et al.* (eds.), *Sozialgeschichte* (q.v.), pp. 144–70.

Rogner, Klaus Michael, *Der Verfassungsentwurf des Zentralen Runden Tisches der DDR*, Berlin 1993.

Roller, Edeltraud, *Einstellungen der Bürger zum Wohlfahrtsstaat der Bundesrepublik Deutschland*, Opladen 1992.

Roller, Edeltraud, 'Kürzungen von Sozialleistungen aus der Sicht der Bundesbürger', in *ZSR*, 42 (1996), pp. 777–88.

Roller, Edeltraud, 'Sozialpolitische Orientierungen nach der deutschen Vereinigung', in Gabriel (ed.), *Politische Orientierungen* (q.v.), pp. 115–46.

Roller, Edeltraud, 'Staatsbezug und Individualismus: Dimensionen des sozialkulturellen Wertwandels', in Ellwein and Holtmann (eds.), *50 Jahre Bundesrepublik* (q.v.), pp. 229–46.

Rosenberg, Peter, 'Pflegeversicherung. Demographische Risiken', in *BArbBl*, 9 (1992), pp. 16–18.

Rosenberg, Peter, 'Sozialpolitik bei leeren Kassen', in *SF*, 43 (February 1994), pp. 31–5.

Rosenow, Joachim, 'Die Altersgrenzenpolitik in den neuen Bundesländern: Trends und Regulationsmechanismen im Transformationsprozeß—Differenzen zur Entwicklung in den alten Bundesländern', in *ZSR*, 38 (1992), pp. 682–97.

Ross, Sabine, '"Karrieren auf der Lochkarte". Der Zentrale Kaderdatenspeicher des Ministerrates der DDR', in Bauerkämper *et al.* (eds.), *Gesellschaft ohne Eliten?* (q.v.), pp. 109–30.

Roth, Dieter, 'Die Wahlen zur Volkskammer in der DDR. Der Versuch einer Erklärung', in *PVS*, 31 (1990), pp. 369–92.

Roth, Reinhold, 'Die niedersächsische Landtagswahl vom 13. Mai 1990', in *ZParl*, 21 (1990), pp. 449–60.

Rothgang, Heinz, 'Vom Bedarfs- zum Budgetprinzip? Die Einführung der Pflegeversicherung und ihre Folgen für die gesetzliche Krankenversicherung', in Clausen (ed.), *Gesellschaften im Umbruch*, vol. i (q.v.), pp. 930–46.

Rüfner, Wolfgang, 'Das Sozialrecht in der Rechtsprechung des Bundesverfassungsgerichts', in *JBSozRG*, 12–21 (1990–9).

Ruland, Franz, 'Erfolgreiche Aufbauarbeit', in *BArbBl*, 10 (1992), pp. 24–8.

Rürup, Bert, 'Alterndes Deutschland. Herausforderung des demographischen Wandels', in *Deutsche Rentenversicherung*, 1–2 (2000), pp. 72–81.

Rürup, Bert, and Werner Sesselmeier, 'Die demographische Entwicklung Deutschlands: Risiken, Chancen, politische Optionen', in *APuZG*, B 44/93, pp. 3–15.

Sachverständigenrat für die Konzertierte Aktion im Gesundheitswesen, *Jahresgutachten 1991: Das Gesundheitswesen im vereinten Deutschland*, Baden-Baden 1991.

Sachverständigenrat zur Begutachtung der gesamtwirtschaftlichen Entwicklung, *Jahresgutachten 1989/90–1997/98*, Stuttgart 1989–97.

Salmon, P., K. A. Hamilton, and S. R. Twigge (eds.), *German Unification, 1989–1990, Documents on British Policy Overseas*, series 3, vol. vii, London 2010.

Sander, Peter, *Interessenvertretung der Arbeitnehmer im Betrieb*, Opladen 1997.

Sarrazin, Thilo, 'Die Entstehung und Umsetzung des Konzepts der deutschen Wirtschafts- und Währungsunion', in Waigel and Schell (eds.), *Tage* (q.v.), pp. 160–225.

Schabert, Tilo, *Wie Weltgeschichte gemacht wird. Frankreich und die deutsche Einheit*, Stuttgart 2002.

Schabowski, Günter, *Der Absturz*, Berlin 1991.

Schaefer-Kehnert, Walter, 'Die LPG-Nachfolger sind für den Staat ein Faß ohne Boden', in *FAZ*, 3 January 2000.

Scharpf, Fritz W., 'Wege zu mehr Beschäftigung', in *Gewerkschaftliche Monatshefte*, 48 (1997), pp. 203–16.

Scharpf, Fritz W., 'The Viability of Advanced Welfare States in the International Economy: Vulnerabilities and Options', MPIfG Working Paper 99/9, September 1999.

Schaub, Eberhard, 'Die Aufbauarbeit der Rentenversicherung in den neuen Bundesländern', in VDR, Aktuelles Presseseminar des VDR 12./13. November 1992 in Würzburg, pp. 102–18.

Schäuble, Wolfgang, *Der Vertrag. Wie ich über die deutsche Einheit verhandelte*, ed. Dirk Koch and Klaus Wirtgen, paperback edn., Munich 1993.

Schäuble, Wolfgang, 'Ich habe einen Traum', account by Mark Kayser, in *Die Zeit*, 30 September 1999.

Schenk, Petra, and Bianca M. van der Weiden, *Die deutsche Sozialdemokratie 1989/90. SDP und SPD im Einigungsprozeß*, Munich 1997.

Schiller, Theo, and Kerstin Weinbach, 'Die FDP: Wahlen und Wähler', in Niedermayer (ed.), *Intermediäre Strukturen* (q.v.), pp. 135–50.

Schindler, Peter, *Datenhandbuch zur Geschichte des Deutschen Bundestages 1983 bis 1991*, with appendix, *Volkskammer der Deutschen Demokratischen Republik*, Baden-Baden 1994.

Schindler, Peter, *Datenhandbuch zur Geschichte des Deutschen Bundestages 1949 bis 1999*, 3 vols., Baden-Baden 1999.

Schlecht, Otto, 'Soziale Sicherung als Aufgabe der Sozialen Marktwirtschaft', in Lambert (ed.), *Umbau der Sozialsysteme* (q.v.), pp. 7–14.

Schmähl, Winfried, 'Alterssicherung in der DDR und ihre Umgestaltung im Zuge des deutschen Einigungsprozesses', in Kleinhenz (ed.), *Sozialpolitik* (q.v.), pp. 49–95.

Schmähl, Winfried (ed.), *Sozialpolitik im Prozeß der deutschen Vereinigung*, Frankfurt a.M. 1992.

Schmähl, Winfried, 'Zur Finanzierung einer Pflegeversicherung in Deutschland', *ZeS-Arbeitspapier* no. 5/92.

Schmähl, Winfried, and Herbert Rische (eds.), *Internationalisierung von Wirtschaft und Politik—Handlungsspielräume der nationalen Sozialpolitik*, Baden-Baden 1995.

Schmähl, Winfried, 'Migration und soziale Sicherheit. Über die Notwendigkeit einer differenzierten Betrachtung: das Beispiel der gesetzlichen Kranken- und Rentenversicherung', in *Hamburger Jahrbuch für Wirtschafts- und Gesellschaftspolitik*, 14 (1995), pp. 247–71.

Schmähl, Winfried, and Uwe Fachinger, 'Einkommen und Vermögen älterer Haushalte. Anmerkungen zur heutigen Situation und zur künftigen Entwicklung', in Farny *et al.* (eds.), *Lebenssituation älterer Menschen* (q.v.), pp. 93–124.

Schmähl, Winfried, and Herbert Rische (eds.), *Europäische Sozialpolitik*, Baden-Baden 1997.

Schmähl, Winfried, 'Europäische Sozialpolitik und die sozialpolitische Bedeutung der europäischen Integration', in Schmähl and Rische (eds.), *Europäische Sozialpolitik* (q.v.), pp. 9–37.

Schmähl, Winfried, 'Rentenversicherung in der Bewährung: Von der Nachkriegszeit bis an die Schwelle zum neuen Jahrhundert. Stationen und Weichenstellungen', in Kaase and Schmid (eds.), *Eine lernende Demokratie* (q.v.), pp. 397–423.

Schmähl, Winfried (ed.), *Soziale Sicherung zwischen Markt und Staat*, Berlin 2000.

Schmähl, Winfried, 'Alterssicherung in Deutschland an der Jahrtausendwende—Konzeptionen, Maßnahmen und Wirkungen', in *Deutsche Rentenversicherung*, 1–2/2000, pp. 50–71.

Schmähl, Winfried, 'Einkommenslage und Einkommensverwendungspotential Älterer in Deutschland', in *Wirtschaftsdienst*, 85 (March 2005), pp. 156–65.

Schmähl, Winfried, 'Sicherung bei Alter, Invalidität und für Hinterbliebene', in *Geschichte der Sozialpolitik in Deutschland seit 1945*, vol. xi, *1989–1994* (q.v.), pp. 541–648.

Schmid, Josef, and Heinrich Tiemann, 'Gewerkschaften und Tarifverhandlungen in den fünf neuen Bundesländern. Organisationsentwicklung, politische Strategien und Probleme am Beispiel der IG-Metall', in Eichener *et al.* (eds.), *Organisierte Interessen*, 1st half-vol. (q.v.), pp. 134–58.

Schmidt, Manfred G., 'West Germany: The Policy of the Middle Way', in *Journal of Public Policy*, 7 (1987), pp. 139–77.

Schmidt, Manfred G., 'Learning from Catastrophes—West Germany's Public Policy', in Castles (ed.), *A Comparative History* (q.v.), pp. 56–99.

Schmidt, Manfred G., 'Die Politik des mittleren Weges. Besonderheiten der Staatstätigkeit in der Bundesrepublik Deutschland', in *APuZG*, B 9–10/90 (23 February 1990), pp. 23–31.

Schmidt, Manfred G., *Sozialpolitik in Deutschland. Historische Entwicklung und internationaler Vergleich*, 2nd edn., Opladen 1998.

Schmidt, Manfred G., 'Grundzüge der Sozialpolitik in der DDR', in Kuhrt *et al.* (eds.), *Am Ende des realen Sozialismus*, vol. iv (q.v.), pp. 273–319.

Schmidt, Manfred G., 'Warum die Gesundheitsausgaben wachsen. Befunde des Vergleichs demokratisch verfaßter Länder', in *PVS*, 40 (1999), pp. 229–45.

Schmidt, Manfred G., 'Immer noch auf dem "mittleren Weg"? Deutschlands politische Ökonomie am Ende des 20. Jahrhunderts', *ZeS-Arbeitspapier* no. 7/1999.

Schmidt, Manfred G., 'Die Europäisierung der öffentlichen Aufgaben', in Ellwein and Holtmann (eds.), *50 Jahre Bundesrepublik* (q.v.), pp. 385–94.

Schmidt, Manfred G., 'Reform der Sozialpolitik in Deutschland: Lehren des historischen und internationalen Vergleichs', in Leibfried and Wagschal (eds.), *Der deutsche Sozialstaat* (q.v.), pp. 153–70.

Schmidt, Rudi (ed.), *Zwischenbilanz. Analysen zum Transformationsprozeß der ostdeutschen Industrie*, Berlin 1993.

Schmidt, Rudi, 'Restrukturierung und Modernisierung der industriellen Produktion', in Lutz *et al.* (eds.), *Arbeit* (q.v.), pp. 227–56.

Schmidt, Ute, 'Transformation einer Volkspartei.—Die CDU im Prozeß der deutschen Vereinigung', in Niedermayer and Stöss (eds.), *Parteien* (q.v.), pp. 37–74.

Schmidt, Ute, 'Die CDU', in Niedermayer (ed.), *Intermediäre Strukturen* (q.v.), pp. 13–39.

Schmidt, Wolfgang, 'Die Überleitungsanstalt Sozialversicherung', in *DAngVers*, 38 (1992), pp. 65–9.

Schmidt, Wolfgang, 'Überleitungsanstalt Sozialversicherung zum 31.12.1991 aufgelöst', in *DAngVers*, 39 (1992), pp. 142 f.

Schmidt-Bleibtreu, Bruno, 'Zur rechtlichen Gestaltung des Staatsvertrags vom 18. Mai 1990', in Waigel and Schell (eds.), *Tage* (q.v.), pp. 226–42.

Schmitt, Manfred, and Leo Montada (eds.), *Gerechtigkeitserleben im wiedervereinigten Deutschland*, Opladen 1999.

Schmitt, Manfred, and Leo Montada, 'Psychologische, soziologische und arbeitswissenschaftliche Analysen der Transformation nach der deutschen Wiedervereinigung', in Schmitt and Montada (eds.), *Gerechtigkeitserleben* (q.v.), pp. 7–18.

Schraa, Joachim, 'Pflegeversicherung. Die lange Geschichte', in *BArbBl*, 8–9 (1994), pp. 5–11.

Schreckenberger, Waldemar, 'Veränderungen im Parlamentarischen Regierungssystem. Zur Oligarchie der Spitzenpolitiker der Parteien', in Bracher *et al.* (eds.), *Staat und Parteien* (q.v.), pp. 133–57.

Schreckenberger, Waldemar, 'Informelle Verfahren der Entscheidungsvorbereitung zwischen der Bundesregierung und den Mehrheitsfraktionen: Koalitionsgespräche und Koalitionsrunden', in *ZParl*, 25 (1994), pp. 329–46.

Schröder, Richard, 'Zum Bruch der Großen Koalition der letzten DDR-Regierung', in *ZParl*, 22 (1991), pp. 473–80.

Schröder, Richard, 'Gerechtigkeit für eine Schar von Laienspielern. Auf ihre erste gewählte Volkskammer können die Ostdeutschen ein bißchen stolz sein—und die Westdeutschen sollten ihnen diesen Stolz lassen', in *FAZ*, 18 March 2000.

Schröder, Richard, 'Zeitverschobene Vernunft. Schritt für Schritt zum 3. Oktober', in *FAZ*, 5 October 2000.

Schröder, Richard, *Die wichtigsten Irrtümer über die deutsche Einheit*, Freiburg im Breisgau 2007.

Schroeder, Klaus, *Der Preis der Einheit. Eine Bilanz*, Munich/Vienna 2000.

Schroeder, Wolfgang, 'Industrielle Beziehungen in Ostdeutschland: Zwischen Transformation und Standortdebatte', in *APuZG*, B 40/96, pp. 25–34.

Schroeder, Wolfgang, 'Westdeutsche Prägung—ostdeutsche Bewährungsproben: Industrielle Beziehungen in der Metall- und Elektroindustrie', in Bergmann and Schmidt (eds.), *Industrielle Beziehungen* (q.v.), pp. 101–33.

Schroeder, Wolfgang, *Das Modell Deutschland auf dem Prüfstand. Zur Entwicklung der industriellen Beziehungen in Ostdeutschland (1990–2000)*, Wiesbaden 2000.

Schulin, Bertram (ed.), *Handbuch des Sozialversicherungsrechts*, vol. 4, *Pflegeversicherungsrecht*, Munich 1997.

Schulte, Bernd, 'Das Sozialrecht in der Rechtsprechung des Europäischen Gerichtshofs', in *JBSozRG*, vols. 10 (1988)–20 (1998).

Schulte, Bernd, and Hans F. Zacher (eds.), *Wechselwirkungen zwischen dem Europäischen Sozialrecht und dem Sozialrecht der Bundesrepublik Deutschland*, Berlin 1991.

Schulte, Bernd, 'Die Entwicklung der Europäischen Sozialpolitik', in Winkler and Kaelble (eds.), *Nationalismus* (q.v.), pp. 261–87.

Schürer, Gerhard, *Gewagt und verloren. Eine deutsche Biographie*, Frankfurt a.d. Oder 1996.

Schürer, Gerhard, 'Planung und Lenkung der Volkswirtschaft der DDR—ein Zeitzeuge berichtet aus dem Zentrum der DDR-Wirtschaftslenkung', in Kuhrt *et al.* (eds.), *Am Ende des realen Sozialismus*, vol. iv (q.v.), pp. 61–98.

'Schürers Krisen-Analyse', in *DA*, 25 (1992), pp. 1112–20.

Schwarzer, Doris, *Arbeitsbeziehungen im Umbruch gesellschaftlicher Strukturen. Bundesrepublik Deutschland, DDR und neue Bundesländer im Vergleich*, Stuttgart 1995.

Schwedes, Rolf, 'Der Wiederaufbau der Arbeitsgerichtsbarkeit in den neuen Bundesländern', in *Die Arbeitsgerichtsbarkeit* (q.v.), pp. 147–67.

Schwedes, Rolf, 'Arbeitsgesetzbuch der DDR und seine Neufassung', in Anzinger and Wenk (eds.), *Entwicklungen im Arbeitsrecht und Arbeitsschutzrecht* (q.v.), pp. 145–72.

Schwinn, Oliver, *Die Finanzierung der deutschen Einheit. Eine Untersuchung aus politisch-institutionalistischer Perspektive*, Opladen 1997.

Schwitzer, Klaus-Peter, 'Die Rentner sind die Gewinner der Einheit', in *Das Parlament*, 17/24 January 1997.

SDP, *Protokoll der Delegiertenkonferenz der Sozialdemokratischen Partei in der DDR 12.1.–14.1.1990*, publ. executive of Sozialdemokratische Partei in der DDR, Berlin 1990.

Sebaldt, Martin, '"Pflege" als Streitobjekt: Die parteipolitische Kontroverse um die Pflegeversicherung und die Entstehung des Pflegeversicherungsgesetzes von 1994', in *ZSR*, 46 (2000), pp. 173–87.

Seehofer, Horst, 'Das faule Ei vom Runden Tisch. Sozialisten lernen nichts dazu', in *Bayernkurier*, 17 March 1990.

Seibel, Wolfgang, Arthur Benz, and Heinrich Mäding (eds.), *Verwaltungsreform und Verwaltungspolitik im Prozeß der deutschen Einigung*, Baden-Baden 1993.

Seibel, Wolfgang, in collaboration with Hartmut Maaßen, Jörg Raab, and Arndt Oschmann, *Verwaltete Illusionen. Die Privatisierung der DDR-Wirtschaft durch die Treuhandanstalt und ihre Nachfolger 1990–2000*, Frankfurt a.M./New York 2005.

Siebert, Horst, 'Drei deutsche Schwächen', in *FAZ*, 11 March 2002.

Siegel, Nico A., 'Zwischen Konsolidierung und Umbau: Staatliche Sozialpolitik (1975–1995)—ein Vergleich. Zwischenbericht aus dem laufenden Forschungsprojekt "Politische Bestimmungsfaktoren der Umbau- und Rückbaupolitik in den sozialen Sicherungssystemen im internationalen Vergleich"', unpubl. MS, March 1999.

Siegel, Nico, and Sven Jochem, 'Zwischen Sozialstaats-Status quo und Beschäftigungswachstum. Das Dilemma des Bündnisses für Arbeit im Trilemma der Dienstleistungsgesellschaft', *ZeS-Arbeitspapier* no. 17/99, Bremen 1999.

Simonis, Georg (ed.), *Deutschland nach der Wende. Neue Politikstrukturen*, Opladen 1998.

Sinn, Gerlinde, and Hans-Werner Sinn, *Kaltstart. Volkswirtschaftliche Aspekte der deutschen Vereinigung*, 3rd edn., Munich 1993.

Sinn, Gerlinde, 'Lohnentwicklung und Lohnpolitik in den neuen Bundesländern', in Oppenländer (ed.), *Wiedervereinigung* (q.v.), pp. 253–80.

Sinn, Hans-Werner, *Volkswirtschaftliche Probleme der deutschen Vereinigung*, Opladen 1996.

Sokoll, Günther, 'Die Unfallversicherung im Prozess der Wiedervereinigung: Zwischen Rampenlicht und "Fußnote" der Sozialgeschichte', in *Die BG*, 05 (2007), pp. 181–7.

Sozialverband VdK Deutschland, *Jahresbericht 95*, Bonn-Bad Godesberg.

Sozialwissenschaftliches Forschungszentrum Berlin-Brandenburg e.V., *Sozialreport 50+ 1996. Daten und Fakten zur sozialen Lage von Bürgern ab dem 50. Lebensjahr in den neuen Bundesländern*, 1966

SPD, Presseservice der SPD, 1990–5.

SPD, *Parteitag in Leipzig 22. bis 25. Februar 1990. Ja zur deutschen Einheit—eine Chance für Europa. Wahlprogramm der SPD zum ersten frei gewählten Parlament der DDR*, publ. executive of SPD, February 1990.

SPD, *Regierungsprogramm 1990–1994. Der neue Weg, ökologisch, sozial, wirtschaftlich stark. Beschlossen vom SPD-Parteitag in Berlin am 28. September 1990.*

Spree, Hans-Ulrich, *Der Sozialstaat eint. Zur sozialen Einheit Deutschlands—Entwicklungen und Eindrücke. Eine Aufzeichnung*, publ. BMA, Baden-Baden 1994.

Starck, Christian, 'Die Verfassungen der neuen Länder', in Isensee and Kirchhof (eds.), *Handbuch des Staatsrechts*, vol. ix (q.v.), pp. 353–402.

Stark, Isolde, 'Wirtschafts- und sozialpolitische Vorstellungen der neuen Parteien und Bewegungen in der Zeit vom Sommer 1989 bis zum Oktober 1990', in *Materialien der Enquete-Kommission 'Überwindung'*, vol. iii (q.v.), pp. 2530–715.

Statistisches Bundesamt, *Datenreport 1992. Zahlen und Fakten über die Bundesrepublik Deutschland*, Bonn 1992.

Statistisches Bundesamt, *Datenreport 1994. Zahlen und Fakten über die Bundesrepublik Deutschland*, Bonn 1994.

Statistisches Bundesamt, *Tabellensammlung zur wirtschaftlichen und sozialen Lage in den neuen Bundesländern. Arbeitsunterlage 3/97*, Wiesbaden 1997.

Statistisches Bundesamt, *Bevölkerung Deutschlands bis 2050. 1. koordinierte Bevölkerungsvorausberechnung*, Wiesbaden 2003.

Statistisches Bundesamt, in collaboration with Wissenschaftszentrum Berlin für Sozialforschung (WZB) and Zentrum für Umfragen, Methoden und Analysen, Mannheim (ZUMA), *Datenreport 2006. Zahlen und Fakten über die Bundesrepublik Deutschland*, Bonn 2006.

Statistisches Jahrbuch der DDR 1990, Freiburg/Berlin 1990.

Steiner, André, *Von Plan zu Plan. Eine Wirtschaftsgeschichte der DDR*, Munich 2004.

Steinmeyer, Heinz Dietrich, 'Akteure, Instrumente und Maßnahmen europäischer Sozialpolitik.—Ein Überblick', in Schmähl and Rische (eds.), *Europäische Sozialpolitik* (q.v.), pp. 39–57.

Stephan, Ralf-Peter, 'Das Zusammenwachsen der Rentenversicherungen in West und Ost.—Eine Zwischenbilanz im zehnten Jahre der Deutschen Einheit', in *DAngVers*, 12 (1999), pp. 546–56.

Sturm, Daniel Friedrich, *Uneinig in die Einheit. Die Sozialdemokratie und die Vereinigung Deutschlands 1989/90*, Bonn 2006.

Suckut, Siegfried, and Dietrich Staritz, 'Alte Heimat oder neue Linke? Das SED-Erbe und die PDS-Erben', in Niedermayer and Stöss (eds.), *Parteien* (q.v.), pp. 169–94.

Süddeutsche Zeitung, 1989–95.

Süß, Werner (ed.), *Die Bundesrepublik in den achtziger Jahren. Innenpolitik, politische Kultur, Außenpolitik*, Opladen 1991.

Süß, Winfried, 'Gesundheitspolitik', in Hockerts (ed.), *Drei Wege* (q.v.), pp. 55–97.

Tegtmeier, Werner, 'Wechselwirkungen zwischen dem Europäischen Sozialrecht und dem Sozialrecht der Bundesrepublik Deutschland', in Schulte and Zacher (eds.), *Wechselwirkungen* (q.v.), pp. 27–43.

Tegtmeier, Werner, 'Beschäftigung, Arbeitsmarkt und Sicherung bei Arbeitslosigkeit', in BMA, *Sozialstaat im Wandel* (q.v.), pp. 85–105.

Tegtmeier, Werner, 'Die Zusammenführung der beiden deutschen Sozialsysteme—Probleme und mögliche Folgerungen für den Umwandlungsprozeß in Mittel- und Osteuropa', in Gesellschaft für Versicherungswissenschaft und -gestaltung e.V. (ed.), *Probleme der Umwandlung der Sozialordnungen der Staaten Mittel- und Osteuropas*, Cologne/Bergisch-Gladbach 1994, pp. 10–46.

Teltschik, Horst, *329 Tage. Innenansichten der Einigung*, Berlin 1991.

Thatcher, Margaret, *The Downing Street Years*, London 1993.

Thaysen, Uwe, *Der Runde Tisch. Oder: Wo blieb das Volk? Der Weg der DDR in die Demokratie*, Opladen 1990.

Thaysen, Uwe, 'Wirtschafts- und sozialpolitische Vorstellungen der neuen Parteien und Bewegungen in der DDR zur Zeit des Zentralen Runden Tisches (1989/90)', in *Materialien der Enquete-Kommission 'Überwindung'*, vol. iii (q.v.), pp. 2716–805.

Thaysen, Uwe (ed.), *Der Zentrale Runde Tisch der DDR. Wortprotokolle und Dokumente*, 5 vols., Wiesbaden 2000.

Thierse, Wolfgang, 'Fünf Jahre deutsche Vereinigung: Wirtschaft—Gesellschaft—Mentalität', in *APuZG*, B 40–41/95, pp. 3–7.

Tietmeyer, Hans, 'Erinnerungen an die Vertragsverhandlungen', in Waigel and Schell (eds.), *Tage* (q.v.), pp. 57–117.

Toman-Banke, Monika, 'Die Wahlslogans von 1949 bis 1994', in *APuZG*, B 51–52/94, pp. 47–55.

Trappe, Heike, *Emanzipation unter Zwang? Frauen in der DDR zwischen Beruf, Familie und Sozialpolitik*, Berlin 1995.

Treaty Establishing the European Economic Community, The, 25 March 1957.

Tschernajew, Anatoli, *Die letzten Jahre einer Weltmacht. Der Kreml von innen*, Stuttgart 1993.

Ullrich, Carsten G., Ingrid Wemken, and Heike Walter, 'Leistungen und Beiträge als Determinanten der Zufriedenheit mit der gesetzlichen Krankenversicherung. Ergebnis einer empirischen Untersuchung zur Akzeptanz des Krankenversicherungssystems bei den gesetzlich Versicherten', *ZeS-Arbeitspapier* no. 3/94.

VdK Deutschland, *12. Bundesverbandstag, 18. bis 20. Mai 1994, Bonn: Geschäftsbericht 1990–1994. Aufgabe und Leistung*, Bonn-Bad Godesberg 1994.

VdK, *Jahresberichte*, 1990–6.

Verfassungsentwurf für die DDR, publ. Arbeitsgruppe 'Neue Verfassung der DDR' des Runden Tisches, Berlin 1990.

Verhandlungen des Deutschen Bundesrates, 12. und 13. Wahlperiode, stenographic reports.

Vertrag zwischen der Bundesrepublik Deutschland und der Deutschen Demokratischen Republik über die Herstellung der Einheit Deutschlands, BGBl, no. 35, 29 September 1990.

Vogel, Hans-Jochen, 'Die SPD vor der Bundestagswahl', preface to Dreßler *et al.* (eds.), *Fortschritt 90* (q.v.).

Vogel, Hans-Jochen, *Nachsichten. Meine Bonner und Berliner Jahre*, paperback edn., Munich/Zurich 1997.

Vogler-Ludwig, Kurt, 'Arbeitsmarkt Ost: ist die Beschäftigungspolitik am Ende?', in Oppenländer (ed.), *Wiedervereinigung* (q.v.), pp. 233–248.

Voigt, Dieter, and Lothar Mertens (eds.), *Minderheiten in und Übersiedler aus der DDR*, Berlin 1992.

Volkens, Andrea, and Hans-Dieter Klingemann, 'Die Entwicklung der deutschen Parteien im Prozeß der Vereinigung', in Jesse and Mitter (eds.), *Die Gestaltung der deutschen Einheit* (q.v.), pp. 189–214.

Volze, Arnim, 'Zur Devisenverschuldung der DDR—Entstehung, Bewältigung und Folgen', in Kuhrt *et al.* (eds.), *Am Ende des realen Sozialismus*, vol. iv (q.v.), pp. 151–87.

Vorbeck, Antje, 'Regierungsbildung 1990/1991: Koalitions- und Personalentscheidungen im Spiegel der Presse', in *ZParl*, 22 (1991), pp. 377–89.

Vorländer, Hans, 'Die FDP. Entstehung und Entwicklung', in Niedermayer (ed.), *Intermediäre Strukturen* (q.v.), pp. 113–33.

Wagner, Matthias, 'Gerüst der Macht. Das Kadernomenklatursystem als Ausdruck der führenden Rolle der SED', in Bauerkämper *et al.* (eds.), *Gesellschaft ohne Eliten?* (q.v.), pp. 87–108.

Waigel, Theo, and Manfred Schell (eds.), *Tage, die Deutschland und die Welt veränderten. Vom Mauerfall zum Kaukasus. Die deutsche Währungsunion*, Munich 1994.

Walter, Franz, 'Die SPD nach der deutschen Vereinigung—Partei in der Krise oder bereit zur Regierungsübernahme?', in *ZParl*, 26 (1995), pp. 85–112.

Walter, Jens, 'Von der Gründung der SDP in der DDR zum SPD-Vereinigungsparteitag—356 Tage ostdeutsche Sozialdemokratie im Spannungsfeld der deutschen Einheit', in Heydemann *et al.* (eds.), *Revolution und Transformation* (q.v.), pp. 407–28.

Walwei, Ulrich, 'Bestimmungsfaktoren für den Wandel der Erwerbsformen', part 2, Hoffmann and Walwei, *Beschäftigung* (q.v.), IAB Kurzbericht, no. 3, 28 January 1998.

Wasem, Jürgen, *Vom staatlichen zum kassenärztlichen System. Eine Untersuchung des Transformationsprozesses der ambulanten ärztlichen Versorgung in Deutschland*, Frankfurt a.M./New York 1997.

Wasem, Jürgen, 'Die private Pflegeversicherung—ein Modell für eine alternative Organisation der sozialen Sicherung zwischen Markt und Staat?', in Schmähl (ed.), *Soziale Sicherung zwischen Markt und Staat* (q.v.), pp. 79–110.

Weidenfeld, Werner, and Wolfgang Wessels (eds.), *Jahrbuch der europäischen Integration 1990/91*, Bonn 1991.

Weidenfeld, Werner, and Karl-Rudolf Korte (eds.), *Handbuch zur deutschen Einheit*, new edn. 1996, Frankfurt/New York 1996.

Weidenfeld, Werner (with Peter M. Wagner and Elke Bruck), *Außenpolitik für die deutsche Einheit. Die Entscheidungsjahre 1989/90*, Stuttgart 1998.

Weinert, Rainer, and Franz-Otto Gilles, *Der Zusammenbruch des Freien Deutschen Gewerkschaftsbundes (FDGB). Zunehmender Entscheidungsdruck, institutionalisierte Handlungsschwäche und Zerfall der hierarchischen Organisationsstruktur*, Wiesbaden 1999.

Welt am Sonntag, 1989–95.

Welting, Sylvia, *Staatsverschuldung als Finanzierungsinstrument des deutschen Vereinigungsprozesses. Bestandsaufnahme und theoretische Wirkungsanalyse*, Frankfurt a.M./Berlin/Berne etc. 1997.

Werner, Heinz, 'Beschäftigungspolitisch erfolgreiche Länder. Lehren für die Bundesrepublik Deutschland?', in *APuZG*, B 34–35/98 (14 August 1998), pp. 3–14.

Widmaier, Ulrich, and Thomas König (eds.), *Technische Perspektiven und gesellschaftliche Entwicklungen. Trends und Schwerpunkte der Forschung in der Bundesrepublik*, Baden-Baden 1990.

Wienand, Manfred, Volker Neumann, and Iris Brockmann, *Fürsorge*, Opladen 1997.

Wiesendahl, Elmar, 'Volksparteien im Abstieg. Nachruf auf eine zwiespältige Erfolgsgeschichte', in *APuZG*, B 34–35/92, pp. 3–14.

Wilke, Manfred, and Hans-Peter Müller, *Zwischen Solidarität und Eigennutz. Die Gewerkschaften des DGB im deutschen Vereinigungsprozess*, Melle 1991.

Windhoff-Héritier, Adrienne, 'Verbandspolitische Konfliktlinien in der deutschen Sozialunion. Der Kampf um das neue Territorium und Probleme der Umverteilung in der Gesetzlichen Krankenversicherung', in Eichener *et al.* (eds.), *Organisierte Interessen*, (q.v.), pp. 303–17.

Winkel, Olaf, 'Die deutsche Einheit als verfassungspolitischer Konflikt', in *ZParl*, 28 (1997), pp. 474–501.

Winkler, Gunnar (ed.), *Sozialreport 1995. Daten und Fakten in den neuen Bundesländern*, Berlin 1995.

Winkler, Heinrich August, and Hartmut Kaelble (eds.), *Nationalismus—Nationalitäten—Supranationalität*, Stuttgart 1993.

Winkler, Heinrich August, *Der lange Weg nach Westen*, vol. ii, *Deutsche Geschichte vom 'Dritten Reich' bis zur Wiedervereinigung*, Munich 2000.

Wollmann, Hellmut, and Wolfgang Jaedicke, 'Neubau der Kommunalverwaltung in Ostdeutschland—zwischen Kontinuität und Umbruch', in Seibel *et al.* (eds.), *Verwaltungsreform* (q.v.), pp. 98–116.

Wollmann, Hellmut, 'Institutionenbildung in Ostdeutschland: Neubau, Umbau und "schöpferische Zerstörung"', in Kaase *et al.* (eds.), *Politisches System* (q.v.), pp. 47–153.

Würtenberger, Thomas, 'Die Verfassung der DDR zwischen Revolution und Beitritt', in Isensee and Kirchhof (eds.), *Handbuch des Staatsrechts*, vol. viii (q.v.), pp. 101–30.

WZB-Mitteilungen, 97, September 2002.

Zacher, Hans F. (ed.), *Materialien zum Sozialgesetzbuch*, loose-leaf edn., April 1979, Percha am Starnberger See.

Zacher, Hans F., 'Grundfragen des internationalen Sozialrechts', in *Mitteilungen der Landesversicherungsanstalten Oberfranken und Mittelfranken*, 12 (1983), pp. 481–92.

Zacher, Hans F., *Abhandlungen zum Sozialrecht*, ed. Bernd Baron von Maydell and Eberhard Eichenhofer, Heidelberg 1993.

Zacher, Hans F., 'Grundtypen des Sozialrechts', in Zacher, *Abhandlungen* (q.v.), pp. 257–8.

Zacher, Hans F., 'Was kann der Rechtsstaat leisten?', in Burmeister (ed.), *Verfassungsstaatlichkeit* (q.v.), pp. 394–406.

Zacher, Hans F., 'Der Wandel der Arbeit und der sozialen Sicherheit im internationalen Vergleich', in *ZIAS*, 13 (1999), pp. 1–47.

Zacher, Hans F., 'Grundlagen der Sozialpolitik in der Bundesrepublik Deutschland', in *Geschichte der Sozialpolitik in Deutschland*, vol. i (q.v.), pp. 333–684.

Zank, Wolfgang, *Wirtschaft und Arbeit in Ostdeutschland 1945–1949. Probleme des Wiederaufbaus in der Sowjetischen Besatzungszone Deutschlands*, Munich 1987.

Zelikow, Philip, and Condoleeza Rice, *Germany Unified and Europe Transformed: A Study in Statecraft*, Cambridge, Mass., 1995.

Zeng, Matthias, *'Asoziale' in der DDR. Transformation einer moralischen Kategorie*, Münster 2000.

Zimmermann, Hartmann, 'Überlegung zur Geschichte der Kader und der Kaderpolitik in der SBZ/DDR', in Kaelble *et al.* (eds.), *Sozialgeschichte* (q.v.), pp. 322–56.

Zohlnhöfer, Reimut, 'Der lange Schatten der schönen Illusion: Finanzpolitik nach der deutschen Einheit', in *Leviathan*, 28 (2000), pp. 14–38.

Zweiter Zwischenbericht der Enquete-Kommission Demographischer Wandel—Herausforderungen unserer älter werdenden Gesellschaft an den einzelnen und die Politik, BTDrs 13/11460, 5 October 1998.

Zwischenbericht der Enquete-Kommission Demographischer Wandel—Herausforderungen unserer älter werdenden Gesellschaft an den einzelnen und die Politik, BTDrs 12/7876, 14 June 1994.

3 INTERVIEWS

Martin Ammermüller, 21 April 1997
Norbert Blüm, 8 June 2000
Dieter-Julius Cronenberg, 27 June 2000
Rudolf Dreßler, 18 May 2000
Regine Hildebrandt, 31 May 2000
Bernhard Jagoda, 5 July 2000
Karl Jung, 5 May 2000
Klaus Leven, 18 May 2000
Werner Niemeyer, 4 May 2000
Peter Rosenberg, 5 May 2000
Werner Tegtmeier, 13 July 2000
Heinz Weiße, 8 April 1997
Alwin Ziel, 13 July 2000
Josef F. Zolk, 22 September 2000

Glossary of Terms and Abbreviations

1 MINISTERIAL DEPARTMENTS AND OFFICIALS

In Germany a *Bundesministerium* (Federal ministry) is headed, politically, by a *Bundesminister* (Federal minister), supported by 1 or 2 *Parlamentarische Staatsekretäre* (parliamentary state secretaries, analogous to British junior ministers), and, on the official side, by 1 or 2 *Staatssekretäre* (analogous to British permanent secretaries). A Ministry is divided into between 5 and 10 *Abteilungen* (departments), each headed by a *Ministerialdirektor* (analogous to a deputy secretary). Departments are in turn usually subdivided into 2 *Unterabteilungen* (sub-departments), each usually headed by a *Ministerialdirigent* (analogous to an under-secretary). Sub-departments are generally divided into roughly 8 *Referate* (sections), usually headed by a *Ministerialrat* (analogous to an assistant secretary) or by a lower-ranking *Regierungsdirektor* (analogous to a principal).

2 GERMAN TERMS AND ABBREVIATIONS

ABM	*Arbeitsbeschaffungsmaßnahme(n)*—job creation scheme(s)
Absatz	paragraph
Abt.	*Abteilung* (q.v.)
Abteilung	department (of ministry); cf. '1 Ministerial departments and officials', above
ACDP	Archiv für Christliche Demokratische Politik der Konrad-Adenauer-Stiftung
AdsD	Archiv der sozialen Demokratie der Friedrich-Ebert-Stiftung
AFG	Arbeitsförderungsgesetz—Employment Promotion Law (both Federal Republic and GDR)
AG	*Aktiengesellschaft*—public limited company
AGB	Arbeitsgesetzbuch—Labour Statute Book (GDR, 1977)
amtierender Vorsitzender	acting chairman
AOK	Allgemeine Ortskrankenkasse(n)—General Local Health Insurance Provider(s)
AOK-Bundesverband	Federal Association of AOK (q.v.)
APuZG	*Aus Politik und Zeitgeschichte* (journal)
Arbeitslosengeld	unemployment benefit (a legal entitlement for a limited period)
Arbeitslosenhilfe	unemployment assistance (means-tested, subsequent to and lower than *Arbeitslosengeld*)
Arbeitspapier	working paper

ARD	Arbeitsgemeinschaft der öffentlich-rechtlichen Rundfunkanstalten der Bundesrepublik Deutschland—association of public service broadcasting corporations of the Federal Republic of Germany
Artikel	article
AVL	Aktionsbündnis Vereinigte Linke (Die Nelken)—Action Alliance United Left (The Carnations)
B90	Bündnis 90—Alliance 90
BA	Bundesanstalt für Arbeit—Federal Institute of Labour
BArbBl	*Bundesarbeitsblatt*
BArch	Bundesarchiv (q.v.)
BDA	Bundesvereinigung Deutscher Arbeitgeberverbände—National Union of German Employers' Associations
BDI	Bundesverband der Deutschen Industrie—Federal Association of German Industry
Bestand	holdings, papers
BfA	Bundesversicherungsanstalt für Angestellte—Federal Insurance Office for White-Collar Workers
BFD	Bund Freier Demokraten—Association of Free Democrats
BGBl	*Bundesgesetzblatt*
BK	Bundeskanzleramt (q.v.)
BMA	Bundesministerium für Arbeit und Sozialordnung—Federal Ministry of Labour and Social Order
BMB	Bundesministerium für innerdeutsche Beziehungen—Federal Ministry for Internal German Relations
BMBau	Bundesministerium für Raumordnung, Bauwesen und Städtebau—Federal Ministry for Environmental Planning, Construction and Urban Development
BMF	Bundesministerium der Finanzen—Federal Ministry of Finance
BMFuS	Bundesministerium für Familie und Senioren—Federal Ministry for the Family and Senior Citizens
BMG	Bundesministerium für Gesundheit—Federal Ministry of Health
BMI	Bundesministerium des Innern—Federal Ministry of the Interior
BMJ	Bundesministerium der Justiz—Federal Ministry of Justice
BMJFFG	Bundesministerium für Jugend, Familie, Frauen und Gesundheit—Federal Ministry for Young People, the Family, Women, and Health

BMVg	Bundesministerium der Verteidigung—Federal Ministry of Defence
BMWi	Bundesministerium für Wirtschaft—Federal Ministry of Economics
BPA-Dok	*Dokument des Presse- und Informationsamtes der Bundesregierung*—document of the Federal Government press and information office
BSGE	Entscheidungen des Bundessozialgerichtes—Decisions of the Federal Social Court
BT	Deutscher Bundestag—first chamber of German parliament
BTDrs	Drucksachen Deutscher Bundestag—printed papers of Deutsches Bundestag
Bund	federation, Federal government
Bundesarchiv	Federal Archive
Bundesbank	Federal Bank
Bundeskanzleramt	Federal Chancellery
Bundesknappschaft	Federal Miners' Insurance Institute
Bundesland/Bundesländer	Land/Lands of the Federal Republic of Germany
Bundesrat	Federal Council, second chamber of German parliament
Bundestag	first chamber of German parliament
Bundesverfassungsgericht	Federal Constitutional Court
Bundeswehr	Federal Armed Forces
BVA	Bundesversicherungsamt—Federal Insurance Office
BVerfGE	Entscheidungen des Bundesverfassungsgerichts—Decisions of the Federal Constitutional Court
CDA	Christlich-Demokratische Arbeitnehmerschaft—Christian Democratic Association of Employees
CDU	Christlich Demokratische Union Deutschlands—Christian Democratic Union of Germany
CPSU	Communist Party of the Soviet Union
CSCE	Commission on Security and Cooperation in Europe
CSU	Christlich-Soziale Union—Christian Social Union (Bavaria)
DA	Demokratischer Aufbruch—Democratic Awakening
DA	*Deutschland-Archiv* (journal)
DAG	Deutsche Angestelltengewerkschaft—German White-Collar Workers' Trade Union
DAngVers	*Die Angestellten-Versicherung* (journal)
DBD	Demokratische Bauernpartei Deutschlands—Democratic Farmers' Party of Germany

DDR	Deutsche Demokratische Republik—German Democratic Republic (GDR)
Deutsche Forumspartei	German Forum Party
DFD	Demokratischer Frauenbund Deutschlands—Democratic Women's Federation of Germany
DGB	Deutscher Gewerkschaftsbund—German Trade Union Federation
DIHT	Deutscher Industrie- und Handelstag—German Industry and Commerce Conference
DJ	Demokratie jetzt—Democracy Now
DM	Deutsche Mark
DRV	*Deutsche Rentenversicherung* (journal)
DSU	Deutsche Soziale Union—German Social Union
DVU	Deutsche Volksunion—German People's Union
Einigungsvertrag	Unification Treaty
Ersatzkassen	Substitute Sickness Funds
e.V.	eingetragener Verein—registered association
FAZ	*Frankfurter Allgemeine Zeitung*
FDGB	Freier Deutscher Gewerkschaftsbund—Free German Trade Union Federation (GDR)
FDP	Freie Demokratische Partei—Free Democratic Party
FKP	Föderales Konsolidierungsprogramm—Federal Consolidation Programme
Forum	Deutsche Forumspartei
Fraktionsprotokolle	parliamentary party records
GBl	*Gesetzblatt* (GDR)
GDR	German Democratic Republic
GKV	Gesetzliche Krankenversicherung—statutory health insurance
GmbH	Gesellschaft mit beschränkter Haftung—limited liability company
Graue/Die Grauen	The Greys
Grüne/Die Grünen	The Greens
GuG	*Geschichte und Gesellschaft* (journal)
IAB	Institut für Arbeitsmarkt- und Berufsforschung—Institute for Labour Market and Employment Research
IG Chemie	Industriegewerkschaft Chemie—Chemical Workers' Industrial Trade Union
IG Metall	Metal Workers' Industrial Trade Union
IG Wismut	Bismuth Workers' Industrial Trade Union

Initiative für Frieden und Menschenrechte	Peace and Human Rights Initiative
JBSozRG	*Jahrbuch des Sozialrechts der Gegenwart* (journal)
KOF	Kriegsopferfürsorge—welfare for war victims
KOV	Kriegsopferversorgung—social provision for war victims
Land/Länder	Land/Lands of the Federal Republic of Germany
LDP	Liberal-Demokratische Partei—Liberal Democratic Party
LDPD	Liberal-Demokratische Partei Deutschlands—Liberal Democratic Party of Germany (GDR)
Leiter	head (of ministry department)
Linke, Die	The Left (formed in 2007 through merger of PDS and WASG, q.v.)
LL	Linke Liste—Left List
LS	Leitungsstab neue Bundesländer—management staff, new *Bundesländer* (in BMA)
MdB	Mitglied des Deutschen Bundestages—member of the German Bundestag
MfAS	Ministerium für Arbeit und Soziales—Ministry of Labour and Social Affairs (GDR)
MfG	Ministerium für Gesundheitswesen—Ministry of Health (GDR)
Ministerialdirektor	cf. '1 Ministerial departments and officials', above
Ministerialdirigent	cf. '1 Ministerial departments and officials', above
Ministerialrat	cf. '1 Ministerial departments and officials', above
Ministerium	Ministry
MPIfG	Max-Planck-Institut für Gesellschaftsforschung—Max Planck Institute of Social Research
NATO	North Atlantic Treaty Organization
NBL	*Neue Bundesländer*—new *Bundesländer*
NDPD	National-Demokratische Partei Deutschlands—National Democratic Party of Germany
NDV	Nachrichtendienst des Deutschen Vereins für öffentliche und private Fürsorge—news service of the German Association for Public and Private Welfare
Nelken, Die	AVL (q.v.)
NF	Neues Forum—New Forum
NPD	Nationaldemokratische Partei Deutschlands—National Democratic Party of Germany (right-wing party)
NRW	Nordrhein-Westfalen—North Rhine-Westphalia
NSDAP	Nationalsozialistische Deutsche Arbeiterpartei—National Socialist German Workers' Party (Nazi party)

NVA	Nationale Volksarmee—National People's Army (GDR)
ÖDP	Ökologisich-Demokratische Partei—Ecological Democratic Party
OECD	Organization for Economic Cooperation and Development
ÖTV	Gewerkschaft Öffentliche Dienste, Transport und Verkehr—Public Services and Transport Trade Union
Parlamentarischer Staatssekretär	cf. '1 Ministerial departments and officials', above
PDA	Pressedienst der deutschen Arbeitgeberverbände—press service of the German Employers' Associations
PDS	Partei des Demokratischen Sozialismus—Party of Democratic Socialism
Prot. BT	Protokolle des Deutschen Bundestages—Records of the German Bundestag
Prot. VK	Protokolle der Volkskammer der Deutschen Demokratischen Republik—Records of the Volkskammer of the German Democratic Republic
PVS	*Politische Vierteljahresschrift* (journal)
RD	*Regierungsdirektor* (q.v.)
Ref.	*Referat* (q.v.)
Referat	section (of ministry); cf. '1 Ministerial departments and officials', above
Regierungsdirektor	cf. '1 Ministerial departments and officials', above
Rentenüberleitungsgesetz	Pensions Transition Law
Rep	Die Republikaner—The Republicans
SBZ	Sowjetische Besatzungszone—Soviet Zone of Occupation
SDAP	Sozialdemokratische Arbeiterpartei—Social Democratic Workers' Party
SDP	Sozialdemokratische Partei—Social Democratic Party (GDR)
SED	Sozialistische Einheitspartei Deutschlands—Socialist Unity Party of Germany (GDR)
SF	*Sozialer Fortschritt* (journal)
SGB	Sozialgesetzbuch—Social Statute Book
SKWPG	Spar-, Konsoldierungs- und Wachstumsprogramm—savings, consolidation and growth programme
Sozialhilfe	income support
Sozialstaat	welfare state
SPD	Sozialdemokratische Partei Deutschlands—Social Democratic Party of Germany

SPI	Sozialpolitische Informationen (Federal Ministry of Labour and Social Order)
Sprecherrat	Representative Council (FDGB, q.v.)
Staatssekretär	cf. '1 Ministerial departments and officials', above
Staatsvertrag	State Treaty
Stasi	State security service (GDR)
STATT	STATT-Partei (Die Unabhängigen)—The Independents
SVG	Gesetz über die Sozialversicherung—Social Insurance Law (GDR)
Tagung	session
TASS	Soviet news agency
taz	*tageszeitung*
Treuhand(*anstalt*)	Trusteeship (Agency)
UFV	Unabhängiger Frauenverband—Independent Association of Women
ÜLA	Überleitungsanstalt Sozialversicherung—Social Insurance Transitional Authority
Unterabteilung	sub-department (of ministry); cf. '1 Ministerial departments and officials', above
USA	United States of America
USSR	Union of Soviet Socialist Republics
VdK	Verein der Kriegs- und Wehrdienstopfer, Behinderter und Sozialrentner Deutschlands e.V.—Association of War Victims, the Disabled and Social Pensioners of Germany
VDR	Verband Deutscher Rentenversicherungsträger—Association of German Pensions Insurance Providers
Vereinigte Linke	United Left
Verfassungsgrundsätzegesetz	Law on Constitutional Principles
VfZ	*Vierteljahreshefte für Zeitgeschichte* (journal)
VK	Volkskammer (q.v.)
VME	Verband der Metall- und Elektroindustrie in Berlin and Brandenburg e.V.—Registered Association of the Berlin and Brandenburg Metal-Working and Electrical Industries
Volkskammer	People's Chamber (GDR)
Volkssolidarität	'People's Solidarity' (GDR), primarily involved in care for the elderly
Vorsitzende	chairwoman, chairmen
Vorsitzender	chairman

WASG	Wahlalternative Arbeit und Soziale Gerechtigkeit—Electoral Alternative for Labour and Social Justice
WP	*Wahlperiode*—parliamentary term
WSI	Wirtschafts- und Sozialwissenschaftliches Institut des Deutschen Gewerkschaftsbundes—Economics and Social Science Institute of the German Trade Union Federation
WZB	Wissenschaftszentrum Berlin für Sozialforschung—Centre for Social Research, Berlin
ZDH	Zentralverband des Deutschen Handwerks—Central Association of German Craft Trades
ZeS	Zentrum für Sozialpolitik—Centre for Social Policy, University of Bremen
ZfSGB	*Zeitschrift für Sozialhilfe und Sozialgesetzbuch* (journal)
ZIAS	*Zeitschrift für ausländisches und internationales Arbeits- und Sozialrecht* (journal)
ZK	Zentralkomitee—Central Committee
ZParl	*Zeitschrift für Parlamentsfragen* (journal)
ZSR	*Zeitschrift für Sozialreform* (journal)
Zulage	supplement
Zuschlag	allowance

3 ENGLISH TRANSLATIONS OF PRINCIPAL GERMAN SOCIAL POLICY TERMS, INSTITUTIONAL NAMES, AND ITEMS OF LEGISLATION

added pensionable years *Zurechnungszeit*
administrative system for employment *Arbeitsverwaltung*
administrative system for social security/social affairs *Sozialverwaltung*
agreements on protection measures against rationalization *Rationalisierungsschutzabkommen*
allowance *Zuschlag*
arbitration panel *Schiedstelle*
Association of German Pensions Insurance Providers *Verband Deutscher Rentenversicherungsträger*
Basic Law *Grundgesetz*
basic right *Grundrecht*
'benchmark pension' *Eckrente*
child benefit *Kindergeld*
child-raising allowance *Erziehungsgeld*
Christian Democratic Association of Employees *Christlich-Demokratische Arbeitnehmerschaft*
co-determination *Mitbestimmung*
continued payment of wages in the event of illness *Lohnfortzahlung*
contributions ceiling *Beitragsbemessungsgrenze*

early retirement regulation *Vorruhestandsregelung*
economic law *Wirtschaftsrecht*
employment court *Arbeitsgericht*
employment law *Arbeitsrecht*
Employment Promotion Law *Arbeitsförderungsgesetz* (both Federal Republic and GDR)
employment relationship *Arbeitsverhältnis*
Federal Association of German Industry *Bundesverband der Deutschen Industrie*
Federal Consolidation Programme *Föderales Konsolidierungsprogramm*
Federal Constitutional Court *Bundesverfassungsgericht*
Federal Employment Court *Bundesarbeitsgericht*
Federal Institute of Labour *Bundesanstalt für Arbeit*
Federal Insurance Office *Bundesversicherungsamt*
Federal Insurance Office for White-Collar Workers *Bundesversicherungsanstalt für Angestellte*
Federal Social Court *Bundessozialgericht*
Federal Social Provision Law *Bundesversorgungsgesetz*
Federal Union of Health Insurance Physicians *Kassenärztliche Bundesvereinigung*
Free German Trade Union Federation *Freier Deutscher Gewerkschaftsbund* (GDR)
General Local Health Insurance Provider *Allgemeine Ortskrankenkasse* (AOK)
'General Outline Law' *Mantelgesetz* (GDR)
German Trade Union Federation *Deutscher Gewerkschaftsbund*
German White-Collar Workers' Trade Union *Deutsche Angestelltengewerkschaft* (DAG)
health and safety regulation *Arbeitsschutz*
Health Insurance Companies Contracts Law *Krankenkassen-Vertragsgesetz*
Health Insurance Companies Establishment Law *Krankenkassen-Errichtungsgesetz*
Health Reform Law *Gesundheitsreformgesetz*
Health Service Structure law *Gesundheitsstrukturgesetz*
housing benefit *Wohngeld*
income replacement principle/benefits *Lohnersatzprinzip/-leistungen*
income support *Sozialhilfe*
Independent Welfare Association *Freier Wohlfahrtsverband*
indexed *dynamisiert*
job centre *Arbeitsamt* (Federal Republic)
job creation schemes *Arbeitsbeschaffungsmaßnahmen, AB-Maßnahmen*
Joint Social Insurance Provider *Gemeinsamer Träger der Sozialversicherung*
labour and wages office *Amt für Arbeit und Löhne* (GDR)
labour market policy schemes *arbeitsmarktpolitische Maßnahmen*
labour office *Amt für Arbeit* (GDR, *Kreis* level)
Labour Statute Book *Arbeitsgesetzbuch* (GDR)
***Land* employment office** *Landesarbeitsamt* (Federal Republic)
***Land* insurance authority** *Landesversicherungsanstalt*
Law on Constitutional Principles *Verfassungsgrundsätzegesetz*
Maintenance Advance Law *Unterhaltsvorschussgesetz* (alimony)
maintenance benefit/payments *Unterhaltsgeld*
maternity leave *Schutzfrist bei Mutterschaft*
Mediation Committee *Vermittlungsausschuss* (Bundesrat and Bundestag)
Miners' guild *Knappschaft*
multipartite *gegliedert*

National Union of German Employers' Associations *Bundesvereinigung Deutscher Arbeitgeberverbände* (BDA)
Pensions Alignment Law *Rentenangleichungsgesetz*
Pensions Transition Law *Rentenüberleitungsgesetz*
pre-pension transitional benefit *Altersübergangsgeld*
redundancy schemes *Sozialpläne*
regional collective pay agreement *Flächentarifvertrag*
social allowance *Sozialzuschlag* (GDR Pensions Alignment Law)
social care insurance *Pflegevesicherung*
social court *Sozialgericht*
Social Insurance Law *Sozialversicherungsgesetz* (Federal Republic and GDR)
Social Insurance Transitional Authority *Überleitungsanstalt Sozialversicherung*
social law *Sozialrecht*
social provision for war victims *Kriegsopferversorgung*
Social Statute Book *Sozialgesetzbuch* (Federal Republic)
solidarity contribution *Solidarbeitrag*
solidarity supplement *Solidaritätszuschlag*
State Treaty *Staatsvertrag*
Statute Book of Labour *Gesetzbuch der Arbeit* (GDR, 1961)
statutory health insurance *gesetzliche Krankenversicherung*
Substitute Sickness Funds *Ersatzkassen*
supplement *Zulage*
supplementary pension *Zusatzrente* (GDR)
system of special provision for particular groups *Sonderversorgungssystem* (GDR)
system of supplementary provision for particular groups *Zusatzversorgungssystem* (GDR)
trade guild insurers *Innungskrankenkassen*
unemployment assistance *Arbeitslosenhilfe* (cf. '2 German terms and abbreviations', above)
unemployment benefit *Arbeitslosengeld* (cf. '2 German terms and abbreviations', above)
Unification Treaty *Einigungsvertrag*
Voluntary Supplementary Pensions Insurance *Freiwillige Zusatzrentenversicherung* (GDR)
Works Constitution Law *Betriebsverfassungsgesetz*
works council *Betriebsrat*

The Principal Actors in the Process of German Unification

Achenbach, Klaus (1941–), Federal Ministry of Labour and Social Order, Ministerialdirigent 1979, Ministerialdirektor 1996, head of sub-department 1978–1995, head of department V Pflegeversicherung, Prävention, Arbeitsschutz (social care insurance, prevention, health and safety regulation) 1995 and of department III Arbeitsrecht, Arbeitsschutz (employment law, health and safety regulation) 1996–1998, Staatssekretär 1998–2002.

Albrecht, Ulrich, Professor of Political Science at Freie Universität Berlin, head of planning staff in GDR Ministry of Foreign Affairs April 1990 to October 1990, member of GDR 'Two-Plus-Four' delegation.

Ammermüller, Martin (1943–), Federal Ministry of Labour and Social Order, Ministerialrat and head of section for basic principles and benefits law in statutory pensions insurance and for pensions/earnings link, adviser to GDR Ministry of Labour and Social Affairs 1990, chief executive of Joint Social Insurance Provider and of Social Insurance Transitional Authority in accession region 1990–1992, president of Federal Insurance Office 1992–1993, Ministerialdirektor and head of BMA department II Arbeitsmarktpolitik, Arbeitslosenversicherung (labour market policy, unemployment insurance) 1993–1997.

Baker, James A. (1930–), Secretary of State, United States of America, 1989–1992.

Bangemann, Martin (1934–), FDP, member of Bundestag 1972–1984 and 1987–1988, member of European Parliament 1973–1984, Federal Minister of Economics 1984–1988, European Community Commissioner and Vice-President, European Community, 1989–1999.

Biedenkopf, Kurt (1930–), jurist, CDU, General Secretary of CDU 1973–1977, member of Bundestag 1976–1980 and 1987–1990, Prime Minister of Saxony 1990–2002.

Blüm, Norbert (1935–), CDU, Federal Minister of Labour and Social Order 1982–1998, *Land* chairman of CDU in North Rhine-Westphalia 1977–1998, member of Bundestag 1972–1981 and 1983–2002.

Bohley, Bärbel (1945–2010), co-founder of New Forum 1989, member of Berlin City Council 1990, official representative for refugees from German-speaking territories in the department of the High Representative for Bosnia and Hercegovina Carl Bildt from 1996.

Böhme, Ibrahim (1944–1999), co-founder of eastern SPD and its representative on the Central Round Table 1989, chairman of eastern SPD 1990, exposed as unofficial collaborator of Stasi and expelled from SPD 1992.

Brandt, Willy (1913–1992), SPD, Federal Foreign Minister 1966–1969, Federal Chancellor 1969–1974, federal chairman of SPD 1964–1987, chairman of Socialist International 1976–1992.

Braunmühl, Carlchristian von, adviser (political director) in GDR Foreign Ministry April 1990 to October 1990, member of GDR 'Two-Plus-Four' delegation.

Breit, Ernst (1924–), chairman of German Trade Union Federation 1982–1990.

Bush, George H.W. (1924–), Vice-President of United States of America 1981–1989, President 1989–1993.

Chory, Werner (1932–1991), Staatssekretär, Federal Ministry for Young People, the Family, Women, and Health 1982–1990, Staatssekretär, Federal Ministry for Women and Young People January 1991 to August 1991.

Clement, Wolfgang (1940–), SPD, Chief of North Rhine-Westphalia State Chancellery 1989–1995, Minister with Special Responsibilities 1990–1995, North Rhine-Westphalia Minister for Economics, Small and Middle-Sized Firms, Technology and Transport 1995–1998, Prime Minister of North Rhine-Westphalia 1998–2002, Federal Minister of Economics and Labour 2002–2005.

Conradi, Peter (1932–), SPD, member of Bundestag 1972–1998, member of SPD control commission 1984–1993.

Cronenberg, Dieter-Julius (1930–), FDP, Vice-president of Bundestag 1984–1994, member of Bundestag 1976–1994.

Czaja, Herbert (1914–1997), CDU, member of Bundestag 1953–1990, president of Expellees' Association 1970–1994.

Däubler-Gmelin, Herta (1943–), SPD, member of Bundestag 1972–2009, Federal Minister of Justice 1998–2002.

Delors, Jacques (1925–), French Socialist Party, elected to European Parliament 1979, French Economics and Finance Minister 1981–1985 (additionally Budget Minister 1983–1985), President of Commission of European Community 1985–1995.

Dregger, Alfred (1920–2002), jurist, CDU, member of Hesse Landtag 1962–1972, member of Bundestag 1972–1998, chairman of CDU/CSU parliamentary party in Bundestag 1982–1991.

Dreßler, Rudolf (1940–), Parlamentarischer Staatssekretär in Federal Ministry of Labour and Social Order April 1982 to October 1982, deputy chairman of SPD and spokesman on social policy for SPD parliamentary party in Bundestag 1987–2000, member of Bundestag 1980–2000, German ambassador to Israel 2000–2005.

Dumas, Roland (1922–), French Socialist Party, French Europe Minister 1983–1984, Foreign Minister 1984 and 1988–1993.

Ehrenberg, Herbert (1926–), SPD, Federal Minister of Labour 1976–1982, adviser to GDR government 1990, member of Bundestag 1972–1990.

Engholm, Björn (1939–), Prime Minister of Schleswig-Holstein 1988–1993, chairman of SPD 1991–1993.

Eppelmann, Rainer (1943–), bricklayer, clergyman. Founder member of chairman of Demokratischer Aufbruch (Democratic Awakening) 1990. CDU, member of Volkskammer 1990 and of Bundestag 1990–2002, Minister without Portfolio in second Modrow cabinet and Minister of Disarmament and Defence in de Maizière cabinet 1990.

Fink, Ulf (1942–), CDU, deputy federal chairman of German Trade Union Federation 1990–1994, federal chairman of Christian Democratic Association of Employees 1987–1993, member of Bundestag 1994–2002.

Franke, Heinrich (1928–2004), CDU, member of Lower Saxony Landtag 1955–1965, member of Bundestag 1965–1984, Parlamentarischer Staatssekretär in Federal Ministry of Labour and Social Order 1982–1984, president of Federal Institute of Labour 1984–1993.

Geisler, Hans (1940–), Demokratischer Aufbruch (Democratic Awakening), CDU, Parlamentarischer Staatssekretär, GDR Ministry for the Family and Women, and member of Volkskammer 1990, member of Bundestag 1990–1991, Saxony Minister for Social Affairs, Health, Young People and the Family 1990–2002, Deputy Prime Minister of Saxony 1995–2002.

Geißler, Heinrich (Heiner) (1927–), CDU, General Secretary of CDU 1977–1989, Federal Minister for Young People, the Family and Health 1982–1985, member of Bundestag 1965–1967 and 1980–2002, a deputy chairman of the CDU/CSU parliamentary party in Bundestag 1991–1998.

Genscher, Hans-Dietrich (1927–), FDP, member of Bundestag 1965–1998, Federal Minister of Interior 1969–1974, party chairman of FDP 1974–1985, Federal Foreign Minister and Vice-Chancellor 1974–1992.

Gorbachev, Mikhail (1931–), General Secretary of Central Committee, Communist Party of the Soviet Union 1985–1991, Chairman of Supreme Soviet 1988–1991, State President May 1990 to 1991.

Günther, Horst (1939–), CDU, member of Bundestag 1980–1998, Parlamentarischer Staatssekretär in Federal Ministry of Labour and Social Order 1991–1998.

Gutzeit, Martin (1952–), clergyman, co-founder of SDP/eastern SPD 1989–1990 and of Central Round Table 1990.

Gysi, Gregor (1948–), chairman of SED/PDS 1989–1993, PDS representative on Central Round Table and member of Volkskammer 1990, member of Bundestag 1990–2002, parliamentary chairman (until 2009, with Lafontaine) of Die Linke (The Left) from 2005.

Hasselfeldt, Gerda (1950–), CSU member of Bundestag from 1987, Federal Minister for Environmental Planning, Construction and Urban Development 1989–1991, Federal Minister of Health 1991–1992.

Haussmann, Helmut (1943–), FDP, member of Bundestag 1976–2002, Federal Minister of Economics 1988–1991.

Hildebrandt, Regine (1941–2001), biologist, member of Demokratie Jetzt (Democracy Now) September 1989, SDP and then SPD from October 1989, member of Volkskammer from March 1990, GDR Minister of Labour and Social Affairs April 1990 to August 1990, member of Brandenburg Landtag from October 1990, Brandenburg Minister for Labour, Social Affairs, Health and Women November 1990 to 1999.

Hirrlinger, Walter (1926–), SPD, Baden-Württemberg Minister of Labour and Social Affairs 1968–1972, president of VdK from 1990.

Honecker, Erich (1912–1994), First Secretary of Central Committee of SED 1971–1976, General Secretary 1976–1989, Chairman of GDR Council of State 1976–1989.

Hurd, Douglas (1930–), British Minister for Northern Ireland 1984–1985, Home Secretary 1985–1989, Foreign Secretary 1989–1995.

Jagoda, Bernhard (1940–), CDU, member of Hesse Landtag 1970–1980, member of Bundestag 1980–1987 and 1990–1993, permanent Staatssekretär in Federal Ministry of Labour and Social Order 1987–1990, president of Federal Institute of Labour 1993–2002.

Jahn, Gerhard (1927–1998), SPD, Federal Minister of Justice 1969–1974, SPD parliamentary party whip in Bundestag 1974–1990, member of Bundestag 1957–1990.

Jung, Karl (1930–2005), Federal Ministry of Labour and Social Order, Ministerialdirektor and head of department V Gesundheit, Versicherung (health, insurance) 1983–1991, head of new department V Pflegeversicherung, Prävention und Rehabilitation (social care insurance, prevention and rehabilitation) 1991–1995, head of Berlin branch of Ministry of Labour and Social Order 1990–1991, Staatssekretär 1995–1996.

Kaltenbach, Helmut (1926–), president of Federal Insurance Office for White-Collar Workers 1989–1991.

Kleditzsch, Jürgen (1944–), CDU, member of Volkskammer March 1990 to October 1990, GDR Minister of Health April 1990 to October 1990, GDR Minister of Labour and Social Affairs August 1990 to October 1990.

Kohl, Helmut (1930–), CDU, Prime Minister of Rhineland-Palatinate 1969–1976, Federal Chancellor 1982–1998, party chairman of CDU 1973–1998, member of Bundestag 1976–2002.

Köhler, Horst (1943–), economist, department of basic principles in Federal Economics Ministry 1976–1980, Schleswig-Holstein State Chancellery 1981–1982. On transfer to Federal Ministry of Finance 1982, successively head of ministerial private office, head of department of basic principles of financial policy, head of money and credit department, Staatssekretär January 1990 to July 1993. Chief German negotiator of Maastricht treaty on European monetary union, president of German Savings Banks and Giro Association 1993–1998, president of European Bank for Reconstruction and Development in London 1998–2002, managing director of International Monetary Fund in Washington 2000–2004. President of German Federal Republic 2004–2010.

Kolb, Rudolf (1927–), chief executive of Association of German Pensions Insurance Providers 1973–1992.

Kopp, Reinhold (1949–), SPD, Chief of Saarland State Chancellery 1985–1991.

Krause, Günther (1953–), CDU, Professor of Informatics and Architecture. Member of Volkskammer, chairman of CDU parliamentary party in Volkskammer and Parlamentarischer Staatssekretär in office of GDR Prime Minister March–October 1990; in latter role central participant on GDR side in negotiations on State and Unification Treaties between Federal Republic and GDR. Member of Bundestag 1990–1994, Federal Minister with Special Responsibilities 1990–1991, Federal Minister of Transport 1991–1993.

Krenz, Egon (1937–), Deputy Chairman of GDR Council of State 1984–1989, General Secretary of Central Committee of SED and Chairman of Council of State 1989.

Lafontaine, Oskar (1943–), SPD, Prime Minister of Saarland 1985–1998, candidate for Federal Chancellor 1990, *Land* chairman of SPD in Saarland 1977–1996, federal chairman of SPD 1995–1999, Federal Minister of Finance October 1998 to March 1999, parliamentary chairman (with Gysi) of Die Linke (the Left) 2005–2009, member of Bundestag for SPD 1994–1999 and for Die Linke from 2005, party chairman (with Lothar Bisky) of Die Linke 2007–2010.

Lambsdorff, Count Otto (1926–), FDP, Federal Minister of Economics 1977–1982 and 1982–1984, federal chairman of FDP 1988–1993, president of Liberal International 1991–1994, member of Bundestag 1972–1998.

Lehr, Ursula (1930–), CDU, member of Bundestag 1991–1994, Federal Minister for Young People, the Family, Women, and Health 1988–1991.

Leven, Klaus (1936–), Federal Ministry of Labour and Social Order, head of sub-department VI Kriegsopferversorgung, Versorgungsmedizin (social provision for war victims, care medicine) 1986–1990, adviser to GDR Ministry of Labour and Social Affairs 1990, vice-president of Federal Institute of Labour 1990–1998.

Louven, Julius (1933–), CDU, member of Bundestag 1980–2002, member of Bundestag committee on economic cooperation 1990–1994 and Bundestag committee on labour and social order 1998–2002.

Maizière, Lothar de (1940–), musician, lawyer and politician, member of eastern CDU from 1956, elected chairman 10 November 1989, deputy chairman of GDR Council of Ministers and Minister for Church Affairs in Modrow government November 1989 to March 1990, GDR Prime Minister 12 April 1990 to 3 October 1990, subsequently deputy chairman of CDU until September 1991, Federal Minister with Special Responsibilities October 1990 to December 1990, member of Bundestag October 1990 to October 1991, returned to legal practice from 1991.

Meckel, Markus (1952–), clergyman, co-founder of SDP/eastern SPD 1989–1990, chairman of eastern SPD, member of Volkskammer 1990, member of business committee 1990, GDR Foreign Minister April 1990 to August 1990, member of Bundestag from 1990, SPD representative on Enquete-Kommission 'Aufarbeitung von Geschichte und Folgen der SED-Diktatur in Deutschland' (appraisal of the history and effects of SED dictatorship in Germany).

Merkel, Angela (1954–), member of Demokratischer Aufbruch (Democratic Awakening) 1989, deputy spokeswoman for de Maizière government, member of CDU and member of Bundestag from 1990, Federal Minister for Women and Young People 1991–1994, Federal Minister for Environment, Conservation and Reactor Safety 1994–1998, CDU General Secretary 1998–2000, CDU federal chairwoman from 2000, chairwoman of CDU/CSU parliamentary party in Bundestag 2002–2005, Federal Chancellor from 2005.

Meyer, Heinz-Werner (1932–1994), SPD, member of Bundestag 1987–1990, chairman of German Trade Union Federation 1990–1994.

Misselwitz, Hans-Jürgen (1950–), clergyman, co-founder of GDR SDP, peace researcher, Parlamentarischer Staatssekretär in GDR Foreign Ministry and leader of GDR delegation to 'Two-Plus-Four' negotiations April 1990 to July 1990, later head of Brandenburgische Zentrale für politische Bildung in Potsdam.

Mitterrand, François (1916–1996), President of France 1981–1995.

Modrow, Hans (1928–), member of Volkskammer 1958–1990, member of Central Committee of SED 1967–1989, chairman of Council of Ministers 1989–1990, member of Bundestag October 1990 to 1994.

Möllemann, Jürgen (1945–2003), FDP, Federal Minister of Education and Science 1987–1991, Federal Economics Minister 1991–1993, Deputy Federal Chancellor 1992–1993, member of Bundestag 1972–2003.

Murmann, Klaus (1932–), president of Federal Union of German Employers' Associations 1986–1996, honorary president from 1997.

Necker, Tyll (1930–2001), economist, entrepreneur, president of Federal Association of German Industry 1987–1991 and 1992–1994, vice-president 1991–1992.

Niemeyer, Werner, lawyer, official of Federal Ministry of Labour and Social Order from 1967, Ministerialdirektor and head of department Sozialversicherung und Sozialgesetzbuch (social insurance and Social Statute Book) from December 1985 until temporary retirement in November 1998.

Pappai, Friedrich (1927–), Ministerialdirigent and head of sub-department IVa of Federal Ministry of Labour and Social Order 1977–1992, responsible *inter alia* for Social Statute Book and accident insurance.

Pöhl, Karl-Otto (1929–), economist, head of department in Federal Chancellery 1971–1972, Staatssekretär in Federal Finance Ministry 1972–1977, vice-president of German Bundesbank 1977–1979, president 1980–1991, chairman of Central Bank Council 1980–1991.

Pollack, Peter (1930–), political independent, GDR Minister of Food, Agriculture and Forestry April 1990 to August 1990.

Poppe, Gerd (1941–), signatory of Charter 77, founder of opposition group Initiative Frieden und Menschenrechte (Peace and Human Rights Initiative) 1985 and its representative on Central Round Table 1989–1990, Minister without Portfolio in Modrow government, Bündnis 90 (Alliance 90) member of Volkskammer, co-founder of Kuratorium für einen demokratisch verfassten Bund deutscher Länder (Committee for a democratically constituted federation of German states), Greens member of Bundestag 1990–1998, representative of Greens on Enquete-Kommission 'Aufarbeitung von Geschichte und Folgen der SED-Diktatur in Deutschland' (appraisal of the history and effects of SED dictatorship in Germany)

Rau, Johannes (1931–2006), SPD, Prime Minister of North Rhine-Westphalia 1978–1998, President of Federal Republic 1999–2004.

Romberg, Walter (1928–), GDR Finance Minister 1990.

Rönsch, Hannelore (1942–), CDU, Federal Minister for the Family and Senior Citizens 1991–1994, CDU member of Bundestag 1983–1998, deputy chairwoman of CDU/CSU parliamentary party in Bundestag from 1994.

Rosenberg, Peter (1938–), Federal Ministry of Labour and Social Order, Ministerialdirigent 1979, Ministerialdirektor 1993, head of sub-department 1b Mathematische und finanzielle Fragen der Sozialpolitik; Sozialbudget (mathematical and financial issues in social policy; social budget) 1978–1993, head of department I Grundsatz- und Planungsabteilung (basic principles and planning department) 1993–2001.

Rühe, Volker (1942–), CDU, Federal Minister of Defence 1992–1998, deputy chairman of CDU/CSU parliamentary party in Bundestag 1982–1989, general secretary of CDU 1989–1992, member of Bundestag 1976–2005.

Ruland, Franz (1942–), Professor of Public Law at Hanover University from 1980, deputy chief executive of Association of German Pensions Insurance Providers 1983, chief executive 1992–2005.

Sarrazin, Thilo (1945–), economist, SPD, Federal Ministry of Finance 1975–1978, Federal Ministry of Labour and Social Order 1978–1981, Federal Ministry of Finance 1981–1991. Central participant in preparations for monetary union between Federal Republic and GDR as head of section Nationale Währungsfragen (national monetary questions) from 1989 and head of cross-departmental working group Innerdeutsche Beziehungen (internal German relations) from 1990. Head of sub-department Treuhandanstalt-Rechts- und Fachaufsicht (supervision of *Treuhand* legal and technical questions) in Federal Finance Ministry from October 1990 to May 1991, Staatssekretär in Rhineland-Palatinate Finance Ministry 1991–1997, Senator for Finance in Berlin 2002–2009, a director of German Bundesbank from 2009.

Sasdrich, Werner (1946–), Federal Ministry of Labour and Social Order, Referent 1990–1991, head of section management group 1 Unterstützung der Leitung im Bereich Arbeitsmarkt- und Sozialpolitik in den neuen Bundesländern (support for senior management in the area of labour market and social policy in the new *Bundesländer*).

Scharping, Rudolf (1947–), SPD, chairman of SPD in Rhineland-Palatinate 1985–1993, Prime Minister of Rhineland-Palatinate 1991–1994, SPD chairman 1993–1994, chairman of SPD parliamentary party in Bundestag 1994–1998, Federal Minister of Defence 1998–2002, member of Bundestag 1994–2005.

Schaub, Eberhard (1934–), head of principal department, rehabilitation and social medicine, Association of German Pensions Insurance Providers 1980–1992, deputy chief executive 1992–1999.

Schäuble, Wolfgang (1942–), CDU, member of Bundestag from 1972, CDU/CSU parliamentary party whip in Bundestag 1981–1984, Chancellery Minister 1984–1989, Federal Minister of Interior 1989–1991, chairman of CDU/CSU parliamentary party in Bundestag 1991–2000, CDU party chairman 1998–2000, Federal Minister of Interior from November 2005 to 2009, Federal Finance Minister from 2009.

Schmidt, Christa (1941–), CDU, member of Volkskammer and GDR Minister for the Family and Women April 1990 to October 1990, member of Bundestag 1990–1998.

Schönfelder, Horst (1932–), CDU, member of Volkskammer 1979–1990, Staatssekretär and GDR deputy Minister of Health May 1990 to October 1990.

Schreiner, Ottmar (1946–), jurist, SPD, federal executive director of SPD 1998 to September 1999, chairman of SPD study group on employee questions from March 2000, member of Bundestag from 1980, a deputy chairman of SPD parliamentary party in Bundestag from March 1997 to November 1998.

Schröder, Gerhard (1944–), SPD, Prime Minister of Lower Saxony 1990–1998, Federal Chancellor 1998–2005, SPD party chairman 1999–2004, member of Bundestag 1980–1986 and 1998–2005.

Schröder, Richard (1943–), theologian and clergyman, Lecturer in Philosophy at Humboldt University 1977–1990, chairman of SPD parliamentary party in Volkskammer 1990, subsequently member of Bundestag for a few weeks, Professor of Philosophy at Humboldt University from 1990.

Schürer, Gerhard (1921–), GDR specialist in economic policy, chairman of GDR State Planning Commission 1965–1989.

Schwedes, Rolf (1934–), Federal Ministry of Labour and Social Order, head of section IIIa5 Arbeitsgerichtsbarkeit, Seearbeitsrecht, Ausbildungsvertragsrecht (employment law jurisdiction, maritime employment law, apprenticeship law) 1972–1990, adviser to GDR Ministry of Labour and Social Affairs May 1990 to August 1990, head of section IIIa1 Grundsatz- und Sonderfragen des Arbeitsrechts, Beendigung des Arbeitsverhältnisses, Arbeitsgerichtsbarkeit (questions of basic principle and special questions in employment law, termination of the employment relationship, employment law jurisdiction) 1990–1999.

Seehofer, Horst (1949–), CSU, CSU *Land* group spokesman on social policy 1983–1989, Parlamentarischer Staatssekretär in Federal Ministry of Labour and Social Order 1989–1992, Federal Minister of Health 1992–1998, Federal Minister of Food, Agriculture and Consumer Protection from November 2005, member of Bundestag 1980–2008, Bavarian Prime Minister and party chairman of CSU from 2008.

Seiters, Rudolf (1937–), CDU, Federal Minister with Special Responsibilities, Chief of Federal Chancellery 1989–1991, Federal Minister of Interior 1991–1993, member of Bundestag 1969–2002.

Shevardnadze, Eduard (1928–), Soviet Union Foreign Minister 1985–2000, member of Politburo of Central Committee of Communist Party of the Soviet Union and member of Supreme Soviet.

Sokoll, Günther (1937–), chief executive of Central Association of Commercial Professional Co-operative Associations 1990–2002.

Solms, Hermann Otto (1940–), member of Bundestag from 1980, chairman of FDP parliamentary party in Bundestag 1991–1998, vice-president of Bundestag from 1998.

Stahmer, Ingrid (1942–), Mayor of Berlin and Senator for Health and Social Affairs 1989–1991.

Steinkühler, Franz (1937–), SPD, first chairman of IG Metall (Metal Workers' Industrial Trade Union) 1986–1993.

Stobbe, Dietrich (1938–), SPD, Governing Mayor of Berlin 1977–1981, member of Bundestag 1983–1990.

Stolpe, Manfred (1936–), member of SPD 1990, Prime Minister of Brandenburg 1990–2002, Federal Minister of Transport 2002–2005.

Stoltenberg, Gerhard (1928–2001), CDU, Prime Minister of Schleswig-Holstein 1971–1982, Federal Minister of Finance 1982–1989, Federal Minister of Defence 1989–1992, member of Bundestag 1953–1971, 1982–1998.

Streibl, Max (1932–1998), CSU, Prime Minister of Bavaria 1988–1993.

Süssmuth, Rita (1937–), CDU, member of Bundestag 1987–2002, Federal Minister for Young People, the Family and Health 1985–1986, Federal Minister for Young People, the Family, Women, and Health 1986–1988, president of Bundestag 1988–1998.

Tegtmeier, Werner (1940–), commercial training, studies in economics and social sciences, head of basic principles and planning department in Federal Ministry of Labour and Social Order 1976, permanent Staatssekretär 1988–2002, representative of Federal government on supervisory organs of Federal Institute of Labour and board chairman 1977–2002.

Teltschik, Horst, Ministerialdirektor, head of department 2 Auswärtige und innerdeutsche Beziehungen, Entwicklungspolitik, äußere Sicherheit (foreign and internal German relations, development policy, external security) in Federal Chancellery 1982–1991, close adviser to Federal Chancellor Kohl.

Thatcher, Margaret (1925–), Conservative British Prime Minister 1979–1990.

Thielmann, Klaus (1933–), SED, professor of medicine, GDR Minister of Health (and Social Affairs) February 1989 to October 1989, Minister of Health and Social Affairs November 1989 to April 1990.

Thierse, Wolfgang (1943–), member of New Forum 1989, member of eastern SPD 1990, deputy chairman of SPD parliamentary party in Volkskammer 1990, chairman from August 1990, chairman of eastern SPD, subsequently deputy chairman, member of Bundestag from 1990, president of Bundestag 1998–2005, vice-president from 2005.

Tietmeyer, Hans (1931–), economist, Staatssekretär in Federal Finance Ministry 1982–1990, head of west German delegation to negotiations on economic, monetary and social union, member of board of directors of German Bundesbank 1990–1993, board president 1993–1999.

Vogel, Hans-Jochen (1926–), SPD chairman 1987–1991, member of Bundestag 1972–1994.

Vogt, Wolfgang (1929–), CDU, Parlamentarischer Staatssekretär in Federal Ministry of Labour and Social Order 1982–1991, member of Bundestag 1969–1998.

Waigel, Theodor (1939–), CSU, Federal Minister of Finance 1989–1998, chairman of CSU *Land* group 1982–1989, deputy chairman of CDU/CSU parliamentary party in Bundestag 1989–1998, member of Bundestag 1972–2002.

Weiß, Konrad (1942–), member of Demokratie Jetzt (Democracy Now) on Central Round Table 1989–1990, member of Volkskammer for Bündnis 90 (Alliance 90) 1990, member of Bundestag for Alliance 90/Greens 1990–1994.

Weißgerber, Gunter (1955–), engineer, member of New Forum, co-founder of Leipzig SPD November 1989, member of SPD parliamentary party in Volkskammer 1990, member of Bundestag from 1990.

Wieczorek-Zeul, Heidemarie (1942–), SPD, member of Bundestag and SPD spokeswoman on European policy from 1987, Federal Minister for Economic Co-operation 1998–2009.

Wulff-Mathies, Monika (1942–), chairwoman of ÖTV 1982–1994, EU Commissioner for European regional policy 1994–1999.

Wünsche, Kurt (1929–), GDR Justice Minister 1965–1972 and 1990.

Ziel, Alwin (1941–), SDP/SPD from 1989, member of Volkskammer 1990, Parlamentarischer Staatssekretär in Brandenburg Ministry of Labour and Social Affairs and member of Brandenburg Landtag from 1990, Brandenburg Minister of Interior 1991–1999, Brandenburg Minister of Labour and Social Affairs, of Health and for Women 1999–2002.

Index